Irene C. Fountas
Gay Su Pinnell

Teaching for
Comprehending
and Fluency

Thinking, Talking, and Writing
About Reading, K–8

HEINEMANN, Portsmouth, NH

Heinemann
A division of Reed Elsevier Inc.
361 Hanover Street
Portsmouth, NH 03801-3912
www.heinemann.com

Offices and agents throughout the world

Cover Photography: Robert Mirani
Interior Photography: Robert Mirani (unless otherwise indicated)

0-325-00308-4

Library of Congress Cataloging-in-Publication Data

Fountas, Irene C.
    Teaching for comprehending and fluency, K-8 : thinking, talking, and writing
about reading / Irene C. Fountas and Gay Su Pinnell.
        p. cm.
    Includes bibliographical references and index.
    ISBN 0-325-00308-4 (alk. paper)
    1. Reading (Elementary) 2. Language arts (Elementary) I. Pinnell, Gay Su. II. Title.
    LB1573.F645 2006
    372.47—dc22
                                2006005953

Printed in the United States of America on acid-free paper

10 11 12 13 14   PAH   24 23 22 21 20 19

The authors and publisher would like to thank those who have generously given permission to reprint borrowed material.

From CAM JANSEN AND THE MYSTERY OF THE CIRCUS CLOWN by David A. Adler, illustrated by Susanna Natti, copyright © 1983 by Susanna Natti, illustrations. Used by permission of Viking Penguin, A Division of Penguin Young Readers Group, A Member of Penguin Group (USA) Inc., 345 Hudson Street, New York, NY 10014. All rights reserved.

IS THIS A MOOSE? By Jenny Armstrong, published by Scholastic Canada Ltd. © 2006 as a part of the *Literacy Place for the Early Years* program.

From ALL ABOUT FROGS by Jim Arnosky. Copyright © 2002 by Jim Arnosky. 2000 by Ann Warren Turner. Reprinted by permission of Scholastic Inc.

From SO FAR FROM THE SEA by Eve Bunting, Illustrated by Chris K. Soentpiet. Text copyright © 1998 by Eve Bunting. Illustrations copyright © 1998 by Chris K. Soentpiet. Reprinted by permission of Houghton Mifflin Company.

From THE DOG THAT PITCHED A NO-HITTER by Matt Christopher. Copyright © 1988 by Matthew F. Christopher (Text); Copyright © 1988 by Daniel Vasconcellos (Illustrations). By permission of Little, Brown and Co., Inc.

From BAT LOVES THE NIGHT. Text © 2001 by Nicola Davies. Illustrations © 2001 by Sarah Fox-Davies. Reproduced by permission of the publisher Candlewick Press, Inc., Cambridge, MA., on behalf of Walker Brooks Ltd., London.

Reprinted with the permission of Simon & Schuster Books for Young Readers, an imprint of Simon & Schuster Children's Publishing Division from GOOD DOG, CARL by Alexandra Day. Copyright © 1985 Alexandra Day.

From BECAUSE OF WINN-DIXIE. Copyright © 2000 Kate DiCamillo. Cover Illustration Copyright © 2000 Chris Sheban. Reproduced by permission of the publisher Candlewick Press, Inc., Cambridge, MA.

From THE EYE, THE EAR AND THE ARM by Nancy Farmer. Copyright © 1994 by Nancy Farmer. Reprinted by permission of Orchard Books, an imprint of Scholastic Inc.

From THE BONE DETECTIVES by Donna M. Jackson. Photographs by Charlie Fellenbaum. Text copyright © 1996 by Donna M. Jackson. Photographs copyright © 1996 by Charlie Fellenbaum. Reprinted by permission of Little, Brown & Company.

From SEEDFOLKS by Paul Fleischman, illustrated by Judy Pedersen. Text copyright © 1997 by Paul Fleischman. Used by permission of HarperCollins Publishers.

From MEET YO-YO MA by Meish Goldish. Copyright © 2004 by Houghton Mifflin Company. All rights reserved. Reprinted by permission of Houghton Mifflin Company.

From TALKIN' ABOUT BESSIE by Nikki Grimes, illustrated by E.B. Lewis. Illustrations copyright © 2002 by E.B. Lewis. Reprinted by permission of Orchard Books, an imprint of Scholastic Inc.

From MAKING ICE CREAM by Natalie Lunis. Copyright © 2002 Benchmark Education Company, LLC. Reprinted by permission.

From FOX AND HIS FRIENDS by Edward Marshall, pictures by James Marshall, copyright © 1982 by Edward Marshall, text; 1982 by James Marshall, pictures. Used by permission of Dial Books for Young Readers, A Division of Penguin Young Readers Group, a Member of Penguin Group (USA) Inc., 345 Hudson Street, New York, NY 10014. All rights reserved.

From MAKING SOUP by Lea Martin. Illustrated by R.W. Alley. Copyright © 2006 by Houghton Mifflin Company. All rights reserved. Reprinted by permission of Houghton Mifflin Company.

From MY CAT by Will McGovern, illustrated by Doreen Gay-Kassel. Copyright © 2004 by Houghton Mifflin Company. All rights reserved. Reprinted by permission of Houghton Mifflin Company.

From A DEEP BLUE LAKE by Lisa Moore. Copyright © 2004 by Houghton Mifflin Company. All rights reserved. Reprinted by permission of Houghton Mifflin Company.

From WILLY THE HELPER by Catherine Peters, illustrated by Ashley Wolff. Copyright © 1995 by D.C. Heath and Company, a Division of Houghton Mifflin Company. All rights reserved. Reprinted by permission of Houghton Mifflin Company.

From BABY BEAR GOES FISHING by Beverley Randell. Text © Beverley Randell 1994. Illustrations © Nelson Price Mulburn Ltd. 1994. Reprinted by permission of Nelson ITP.

From BABY BEAR'S PRESENT by Beverley Randell. Text © 1994 Beverley Randell. Illustrations © 1994 Nelson Price Milburn. Reprinted by permission of Nelson ITP.

From THE LAZY PIG by Beverley Randell. Text © 1994 Beverley Randell. Illustrations © 1994 Nelson Price Milburn. Reprinted by permission of Nelson ITP.

From LOOK AT ME! By Willa Reid, illustrated by Amy Vangsgard. Copyright © 2006 by Houghton Mifflin Company. All rights reserved. Reprinted by permission of Houghton Mifflin Company.

From PEACHES THE PIG by Kana Riley, illustrated by Ellen Childers. Copyright © 1995 by D.C. Heath and Company, a Division of Houghton Mifflin Company. All rights reserved. Reprinted by permission of Houghton Mifflin Company.

From ROSIE'S POOL by Kana Riley, illustrated by Kevin Hawkes. Copyright © 1995 by D.C. Heath and Company, a Division of Houghton Mifflin Company. All rights reserved. Reprinted by permission of Houghton Mifflin Company.

From POPPLETON by Cynthia Rylant, illustrated by Mark Teague. Text copyright © 1997 by Cynthia Rylant. Illustrations copyright © 1997 by Mark Teague. Reprinted by permission of Scholastic Inc.

From THE BROCCOLI TAPES by Jan Slepian, copyright © 1988 by Jan Slepian. Used by permission of G.P. Putnam's Sons, a Division of Penguin Young Readers Group, A Member of Penguin Group (USA) Inc., 345 Hudson Street, New York, NY 10014. All rights reserved.

From BUTTERFLIES! By Josie Strummer. Copyright © 2004 by Houghton Mifflin Company. All rights reserved.

TABLE OF CONTENTS (BOOK)

KEY TO **DVD ICONS** IN TEXT

Throughout this book, these icons will indicate places where you can find video segments on the DVD to support your learning. The letters that accompany the icon indicate the specific section of the DVD containing relevant video segments.

In addition, you'll see indicated throughout the text places where there are forms or other teaching resources that can be found on the DVD. These are all housed in the **Teaching Resources** section of the DVD.

 This icon indicates that the relevant video is in the **Whole Group Teaching** section of the DVD.

 This icon indicates that the relevant video is in the **Small Group Teaching** section of the DVD.

 This icon indicates that the relevant video is in the **Individual Teaching** section of the DVD.

 TABLE OF CONTENTS (DVD–ROM)

To Lois Bridges,

*with deep appreciation for her enduring passion and
dedication to the life's work of
literacy teachers and its impact on the lives of our children*

Acknowledgments

It has been a deep learning experience to work with teachers across grade levels K-8 as we wrote this book. Indeed, this volume is the product of over two decades of study during which we have been informed by conversations about children's literacy learning over time. We wish to acknowledge the work of these teachers. They represent a wide variety of learning communities—separated by geography, culture, and economics, but all dedicated to the goal of helping children lead lives that are enriched by literacy. Teachers who have contributed to this volume are excellent in that they provide for high student achievement and also strive toward the higher goals of literacy education. Through the learning communities they create in classrooms, they support children not only in proficient reading and writing but in ways that permit them, from the very first days of schooling to young adulthood, to live literate lives.

We acknowledge the many study groups of teachers who have worked with us over the years, as well as literacy coordinators in schools connected to the Literacy Collaborative, a comprehensive approach to creating literate communities in schools, K–8. We are especially grateful to the teachers who shared their teaching with us in the transcripts and on the DVD included with this book as well as the many teachers who generously contributed examples of students' writing. We thank the many teachers who have shared their students' reading and writing work with us. Our long list of colleagues includes Carly Bannish, Erik Berg, Christine Brennan, Laurie Burrage, Jodi Burroughs, Christopher Buttimer, Rosemary Campbell, Shannon Campbell, Chris Deleo, Katy Deysher, Jill Duffield, Christine Gallo, Rebecca Goodman, Chuck Hatt, Kris Haveles-Pelletier, Rhonda Hayes, Loretta Hopper, Craig Hyland, Jacy Ippolito, Crystal Jefferson, Christine Kennedy, Alice Marullo, Caitlin McArdle, Randy Methven, Toni Newsom, Nikki Randle, Connie Redden, Christine Reina and her many colleagues at P.S. 142 in Brooklyn, Catherine Richardson, Christina Royster, Kristina Seeley, Amy Staley, Susan Sullivan, and Linda Towlen. We also thank Pat Gordon and Jennifer Jarvis for a great example of a child using language syntax.

We continue to be grateful to Carol Kim for her gracious assistance as well as her many examples of artful teaching and to Jennifer Winkler who has provided expert assistance in helping this volume reflect the authentic work of teachers and students in classrooms.

This book is filled with the work of children, and we acknowledge all of those who have graciously contributed. We are especially grateful to Sara Greenberg Bryk, Natalie Marie Cole, and Thomas Ruiz, who have generously shared their thinking about their literacy and their writing with us. We thank all the wonderful children we have learned from and who have shared their literacy with us throughout this publication.

The time for writing and production of *Teaching for Comprehending and Fluency, K–8* has certainly been the longest in our own record of publications! It has truly been a team effort. We especially acknowledge the advice and contributions of our dear friend and colleague Mike Gibbons, whose creative input, vision, and hard work have enriched our professional publications for many years. We also thank John Gayle for his valuable contributions to the preparation of the DVD for this book.

Lesa Scott, whose support for our work on this volume has been extraordinary, and her Heinemann team, as always, have put their professional touch on this work, and we acknowledge this strong partnership that has disseminated our thinking to our colleagues in the field. We thank our dear editor Lois Bridges, not only for working on the text and giving feedback, but for creative and visionary thinking through the process.

We also want to thank Leigh Peake and Kevin Carlson for their wonderful work on the DVD, Alan Huisman for his highly professional editing, and Lisa Fowler, who has contributed in so many ways to elements of the production. Thanks, also, to Tina Miller for her generous and thought-ful support throughout this effort. And a special note of thanks to Gloria Pipkin for her eagle-eyed proofing.

We deeply appreciate the meticulous work of Michael Cirone, our exceptional production manager. We thank him for maintaining a standard of excellence in every detail of this publication. Without his patience, guidance, and countless hours of work, this book would not have been possible. He is truly our partner in his care for the quality and presentation of our thinking in all its forms.

Our colleagues at Lesley University and The Ohio State University continue to astound and inspire us with the high quality and integrity of the work they do with teachers. We thank them for encouragement, inspiration, and feedback. We wish to express appreciation to Mechelle Abney, Margaret Crosby, Toni Czekanski, Jill Eurich, Helen Sisk, Eva Konstantellou, Diane Powell, Leslie Ryan, and Meredith Teany at Lesley University and to Laurie DeSai, Justina Henry, Kecia Hicks, Marsha Levering, Andrea McCarrier, Lynda Mudre, and Joan Wiley at Ohio State. We especially value the help of Pat Scharer, Emily Rodgers, and Sonny Whitehead in coordinating the work at OSU.

We are always appreciative of the entire Lesley administrative and support staff, including the very capable efforts of Kate Mealer. We are very grateful for the efforts of Carol Woodworth, who gives of her expertise in so many ways to our work, and to Patty Federow for her capable assistance. We want to acknowledge the invaluable assistance of Sharon Freeman, who has contributed in so many ways we could not list them here.

As always, our families are a wonderful source of support and encouragement. We thank Ron Heath and Ron Melhado for endless patience, and for their love, support, and humor throughout this very long project. They show their understanding of how important it is for us to share our voices in supporting the literacy learning of children.

INTRODUCTION

While writing this volume we were reminded over and over again how our lives have been shaped by reading. Books have provided adventures to thrill us, information to surprise and satisfy us, places and times to explore, and friends that we can return to again and again. Over the past several years, we have investigated how readers are built over a period of time. Starting in early kindergarten and moving through the teenage years, we have gotten a picture of reading not as a skill to be acquired and used but as an integral part of the way we learn to understand our world. Comprehension begins with learning language in connection with experiences with text—hearing written language read aloud and engaging with and talking about books. We continue developing these processes throughout our lives as we experience written language through a wide range of genres. Even listening to the news or watching a movie involves engagement with written language! We are always encountering text, learning from it, and changing in response to it.

The title of this book emphasizes *comprehending* and *fluency.* These two words convey the *active* nature of reading as well as the *ease* that is essential for understanding and enjoyment. Readers are always actively working to construct meaning, so comprehending is an ongoing *process* rather than simply the outcome or *product* of reading. Readers apply many complex and interrelated systems of *strategic actions* in order to comprehend written language—not as single, disparate cognitive actions but simultaneously, as thinking. Readers work fluently, the processing occurring in a largely unconscious way as they concentrate on the information in the text. The few problems they experience in processing are solved quickly and efficiently, requiring very little attention. The book may be in the hand and the eyes moving across the page, but the reader's thinking is somewhere else—climbing Mt. Everest or exploring New York in the 1800s.

Individuals who love reading do it voluntarily and often. They recommend texts to friends, love talking about them, and usually try to read the book before seeing the movie.

They have their own tastes and preferences, as well as their own techniques for selecting books. They have no trouble finding books to read; in fact, they usually have a few "in reserve" at any given time. They look forward to the expansion of their thinking that comes from reading both fiction and nonfiction, a process that is made even better if they have a chance to talk about a book with others. We have seen these attitudes toward reading at all grade levels; it's what we want for our students. If active, easy, fluent reading is not experienced from the beginning, it is difficult (although not impossible) to develop as a reader later in life.

Throughout this volume, we emphasize how we can support our students' active processing as we work with them before, during, and after reading as well as in other instructional contexts. As noted in the second part of the title, we can support students by engaging them in *thinking, talking,* and *writing* about reading. Thinking, talking, and writing (or drawing) bring new dimensions to the reading process and help students of all ages continue to grow. In achieving our goals, we are always thinking about readers, texts, and teaching.

We begin with readers. Two introductory chapters offer three short portraits of readers—Sara, a kindergarten student; Luis, in grade four, and Natalie, an eighth grader who describes her literate life in her own voice—followed by an overview of how you can create a literate community in your own classroom.

Section I explores the dynamics of the reading process and the systems of strategic actions that readers develop over time. Two chapters focus on fluent processing and how it develops. The final chapter of this section discusses evidence of effective processing as revealed through dynamic assessment of your students.

In Section II, we investigate the next logical element in reading instruction—texts. During the last twenty years we have spent many enjoyable and productive hours analyzing the texts that we read to students and that they read for themselves. What supports does the text offer the reader?

What challenges will there be? What must a reader know and be able to do to read this text with understanding and fluency? As teachers, we have found that the more analytically we can think about texts ourselves, the more powerful the instruction that we can offer our students. In five chapters, we explore the text variety and quality needed to support readers across the elementary and middle grades. We discuss ten factors related to text difficulty, as well as a gradient from A to Z that can be used as a teacher's tool to support and document students' reading progress through the grades. The last two chapters explore the demands of nonfiction and fiction texts and poetry.

With knowledge of the reading process and an analytic view of text features as a foundation, we are ready to design effective instruction. Section III, Teaching, makes up the largest portion of this book. Teaching reading cannot be confined to one instructional setting. In the chapters that make up this section, we describe effective teaching for comprehending and fluency in whole-group, small-group, and individual settings. The first three chapters focus on building a literate culture in the classroom while at the same time providing a foundation for comprehending. Always, encounters with texts are surrounded by talk. Discussing books with others supports effective processing in many ways and makes the experience of reading richer for individuals, but it is *learned behavior* and for most students requires explicit instruction. In highly productive classrooms, students learn to talk about books during interactive read-aloud, literature study (which we also call book club), reading minilessons and shares, guided and independent reading. The fourth chapter of this section describes moving from interactive read-aloud to literature study; the fifth presents many practical tips for getting started with book clubs, including guidelines for the first thirty-five days.

In Section III we also describe shared and performed reading as a way to expand comprehending powers and build fluency. Two additional chapters provide information on elements of a reading workshop, including minilessons that will support thinking about texts. Three chapters are then devoted to an in-depth look at guided reading—small-group instruction explicitly focused on teaching for comprehending and fluency. Through guided reading, you can help students expand their reading powers by applying

strategic actions to increasingly difficult texts. Teaching support makes this learning progress possible.

We also include two chapters on *writing about reading,* a powerful tool that can be used in all instructional contexts. As students experience more texts, they can move from talking to writing (and often drawing) about the texts they've read. These two chapters do not present a writing program or guidelines for writing workshop, an essential instructional component that we have described elsewhere. The writing described in this volume has a very particular purpose: to expand students' thinking about reading. In these chapters we describe many genres and forms for writing about reading that can be used in connection with interactive read-aloud, literature discussion, and guided and independent reading.

The final three chapters also deal with teaching within these instructional contexts. One chapter is devoted to meeting the needs of English language learners. Another, based on the information presented in Section I, focuses on the many ways to teach for fluency. Finally, we describe a variety of instructional approaches to help students increase vocabulary.

The book concludes with some final thoughts related to teaching through the lens of comprehension. Reading, from the beginning, must be filled with meaning. We cannot assure comprehending and fluency through a few lessons; it must be fostered all of the time, at least throughout the nine years leading to high school. Children need year after year of effective instruction if they are to become highly effective readers. Primary teachers will benefit from looking forward through the years, understanding that what they provide in those early years forms the foundation for very complex learning. Upper elementary and middle school teachers will find there is much to learn by examining early learning. Our own learning as we worked on this book has been profound; it has led us to the production of a very detailed continuum of learning that will be published as a companion volume (Pinnell and Fountas, *A Continuum of Reading Progress: A Guide to Teaching,* Portsmouth, NH: Heinemann, 2006). We hope that volume and the one you hold in your hand will provide invaluable support as you work with your colleagues to prepare literate world citizens.

LIVING A LITERATE LIFE:
THE RIGHT OF CHILDHOOD

"Learning to read and write ought to be one of the most joyful and successful of human undertakings."
— DON HOLDAWAY, *THE FOUNDATIONS OF LITERACY*, (NEW YORK: SCHOLASTIC, 1979, P. 11)

Sara, a first grader, page xi

Thomas, a fifth grader, page xv

Natalie, an eighth grader, page xx

What does it mean to lead a literate life?

*In this introductory chapter, we visit three children, each of whom lives a life rich with the gifts of literacy. They are **Sara**, a first grader; **Thomas**, a fifth grader; and **Natalie**, an eighth grader. You may want to read the portrait of the student closest to the age of the students you teach, or you may read all three, noticing the parallels in their lives as well as the expanding resources available to them as learners.*

A portrait of a grade one student, Sara

First grader Sara is an avid reader and writer. Typically, she begins her day by eating a quick breakfast as her parents get ready to go to work. She sees them reading the newspaper and making lists of things to do or buy. Her mother writes notes to the babysitter and places

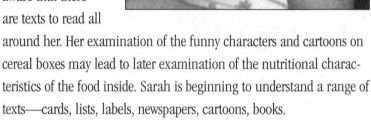

Sara's library books and other school materials by the door so that she will not forget them. By observing these daily activities, Sara has learned that writing is a way of communicating with someone who is not present and that it also can serve as a tool to aid memory. She is aware that there are texts to read all around her. Her examination of the funny characters and cartoons on cereal boxes may lead to later examination of the nutritional characteristics of the food inside. Sarah is beginning to understand a range of texts—cards, lists, labels, newspapers, cartoons, books.

Sara regularly commemorates important occasions through writing. She plans Valentine and special-occasion cards that she wants to send to her godmother ("big Sara") or her brother, who is away at college. She sees her parents reading and writing every day—material for work and books for enjoyment, certainly, but also texts related to simple daily activities. She sees them making lists, writing notes, doing email on the computer and wireless devices, consulting directions and recipes, finding and reading information on the Internet, and generally commemorating family events. Sara is learning that writing is a way of communicating with others, whether they are close or far, and can be a tool to mark significant events and express deep feelings. For example, when her goldfish died, one of Sara's first actions was to write a simple tribute (Figure 1).

In a corner of the family room there is a small table and chairs where Sara does a great deal of her writing. She has paper, crayons, markers, and scissors. This inexpensive set-up teaches her to value these supplies and keep them in order. It is always there, which leads her to read and write often. (Sometimes

Figure 1
Sara's
"Memorial for
a Goldfish"

she makes place cards for guests when they come for dinner and distributes questionnaires for them to fill out.)

Books are a part of Sara's world. She brings books home from school, and there is a designated place to keep them so they do not get lost. She also goes to the local library every other weekend, where she hears stories and is learning to pick out new books. She already has some favorite authors: she wants to hear Kevin Henkes's classic *Lilly's Purple Plastic Purse* read aloud again and again, and the book has prompted Sara to take her own purse to school!

Things We Like to Do with Friends
- Play games
- Sing songs
- Read books and poems
- Draw pictures and paint together
- Ride the bus
- Share food with each other
- Share our writing
- Help each other
- Have fun together

We like our friends at school!

Figure 2   "Things We Like To Do With Friends"

Sara's first-grade classroom provides many opportunities to read and write. Her teacher, Ms. Peters, finds time to read aloud to the children several times each day, and she engages children in oral discussion before, during, and after reading. For example, in a discussion of *My Best Friend Moved Away*, by Nancy Carlson, the children talked about their own experiences with moving or having a friend leave, the feelings that the main character was probably having, what might happen next in the story, how the girl's feelings changed during the story—and why! Ms. Peters has taught these young children routines such as brief "turn and talk" interactions with a partner so they have more opportunity for conversation and also learn they are expected to talk about their thinking in response to reading. These powerful conversations enrich Sara's understanding. She is learning that reading can be a social activity.

Sara is learning that writing is a way of communicating with others, whether they are close or far, and can be a tool to mark significant events and express deep feelings.

Often, Sara and her classmates participate in interactive or shared writing, in which they compose a message or story together and Ms. Peters writes it. At times, children "share the pen" to help them develop greater ownership of the writing and also focus on letters, words, and sounds. In composing "Things We Like to Do With Friends" (Figure 2), the children twice turned back to the book *My Best Friend Moved Away* for more ideas. After completing each item in the list, they reread the piece so far together. When they had finished their list, they made a few comparisons between it and the events in the book. This list will be a good resource for them if they want to write stories about friends in a writing workshop.

i hav a BLaceT
taT has BEN iN Mi
FAMLE for a vare LoNG
TiM AND Mi MoMY
GaV MY ThE BLAC-T
WEN i Was a BaB6
i CEPiT oN MY BauD
i LiK ThE CuLR oN ThE NDS
iT is a Vare
sPashL BLaeeT
iaM GO WiNG TO
GiVET TO Mi BaBE
WENihav wuaN.

Figure 3   "Sara's Blanket"

Literary experiences like those related to *My Best Friend Moved Away* involve Sara in thinking, talking, and writing about reading. In every way except decoding the words she has processed a text—making predictions, noticing details, empathizing with characters, noticing character changes, and reflecting on the meaning of friendship and loss. With group support, she has helped to compose and write a text that she and her classmates can read first in a shared way and ultimately independently.

Phonics is an important part of Sara's classroom. She takes part in a daily minilesson on some aspect of sounds, letters, and words, and applies her knowledge in a word study center or an individual assignment. More important, however, she has the chance to apply her knowledge of letters and sounds in writing and reading for real purposes. At the beginning of each day she has an opportunity for independent work: listening to stories and responding by drawing or writing; independently reading from "browsing boxes" (books she has read before or new books within her reading range); sorting words by first letter or pictures by first sound; putting together poems in the pocket chart and reading them to check for accuracy. In fact, Sara learns to read a new poem almost every day. She first encounters the poems in shared reading. After they become familiar, Ms. Peters hands out a photocopied version so that children can glue it in their personal poetry notebooks and illustrate it. When Sara finishes the year, she will take home a wonderful book of over two hundred illustrated poems that she can read.

As children work independently, Ms. Peters provides small-group instruction called guided reading. Each year, she closely observes children in the class and systematically assesses their reading strengths and needs. She uses this information to form groups so that she can do some explicit teaching. In guided reading, Sara is introduced to a new book that is just a little more difficult that she can read independently. With teacher support, however, she stretches her reading powers. Working in her small group allows Sara to use everything she knows about reading to solve words, follow and understand a text, and apply different strategic actions. The process is supported by conversation with Ms. Peters and the other group members.

Working in her small group allows Sara to use everything she knows about reading to solve words, follow and understand a text, and apply different strategic actions.

One of Sara's favorite parts of the day is writing workshop. It begins with a minilesson from Ms. Peters on aspects of the writing process; then students work independently on self-selected topics, such as this piece about Sara's blanket (Figure 3). Notice that there are some conventionally spelled high-frequency words, that every syllable has a vowel, and that the sounds of most consonants are represented. She has produced complex sentences with embedded clauses and is developing her own voice as a writer. Sara connects her life with school and expresses her unique meanings through writing every day. She is beginning to use conventions in the service of meaning and is growing as a writer. In Section III you will see a letter to an author that Sara wrote in second grade.

As part of her school day, Sara hears several texts read aloud, reads several texts herself, responds to texts in writing, writes about topics of importance to her, and talks about her reading and her thinking with others. She examines the details of written language through phonics and spelling lessons and learns to apply her knowledge while writing and reading continuous text. She takes books, poems, and her own writing home with her and brings her home experiences to school. During each day, at home and at school, Sara has the opportunity to live a literate life. Her everyday experiences incorporate some aspect of literacy at almost every moment. She uses language in the form of talking, reading, and writing to expand her understanding of the world.

During each day, at home and at school, Sara has the opportunity to live a literate life.

A portrait of a grade five student, **Thomas**

Through books, Thomas and his classmates expand their knowledge of times, events, and people beyond their own experiences.

Thomas, a fifth grader, lives with his mother and two younger brothers in a small suburb within a large city. He walks to the neighborhood school, a very large K–8 complex. Thomas's mother has designated the kitchen table as the "homework center." His grandmother, who stays with the boys until their mom gets home from work, is firm about the activity. Thomas usually works on spelling, math, and writing assignments. Each evening, he spends thirty minutes reading a book that he has selected for reading workshop; he may also work on the weekly

letter he writes to his teacher about his thinking regarding the book. He also writes for fifteen minutes each night in a writer's notebook, a writer's tool introduced to him by his teacher, Mr. Ruiz. At first, Thomas didn't know what to do with the notebook, but after classroom demonstrations and instruction, he now uses the notebook fluidly, recording his thoughts and experiences, noting observations, making lists of interesting topics he wants to write about, sketching interesting objects he sees. In fact, just about anything goes into this notebook. While Thomas does his homework, the two younger boys read, draw, and write. Plenty of TV is watched in this house, but this short time reserved for homework really pays off!

Even though Thomas can read proficiently for himself, Mr. Ruiz regularly reads to the class. Often, he chooses sophisticated picture books, like *The Cats in Kracinski Square,* by Karen Hesse; *Rose Blanche,* by Roberto Innocenti, and *Faithful Elephants: A True Story of Animals, People, and War*, by Yukio Tsuchiya. Mr. Ruiz also reads chapter books in a variety of genres, like Jerry Spinelli's *Milkweed*, which gives students a chance to hear a new book on a sophisticated theme by a favorite author, and *Firewing*, a volume in the animal fantasy trilogy about silverwing bats, by Kenneth Oppel. For literature discussion, Thomas has read and talked with others about *Max the Mighty*, a sequel to *Freak the Mighty*, by Rodman Philbrick. This story about a kid who is large for his age deals with some serious issues, like child abuse.

Through books like these, Thomas and his classmates expand their knowledge of times, events, and people beyond their own experiences. Mr. Ruiz refers to the times he reads aloud as "interactive" because he intentionally guides his students in conversations that will expand their understanding of themselves and the world. Interactive read-alouds have helped the students in this class develop favorite authors and illustrators, notice writing styles, compare themes, and analyze aspects of the writer's craft. Always, literature discussion surrounds the interactive read-aloud session.

Thomas experiences direct lessons on spelling and engages in a five-day sequence of word study. He has direct instruction on vocabulary, with the opportunity to notice the connections between word parts and meaning. He also learns a great deal about spelling and vocabulary from participation in reading and writing workshop.

Reading workshop is Thomas's favorite part of the school day. It begins with a couple of "book talks," very short descriptions of books students might want to read. Often, Thomas jots down a title in his Books to Read list in his reader's notebook

Reader's Notebook

Reading List — Books to Read — Letters — Guided Reading/Book Club

Books to Read

Title	Author
Firewing	Kenneth Oppel
Max the Mighty	Rod Philbrick

Figure 4   Thomas's reader's notebook

(Figure 4). This reader's notebook is the repository of his records and
responses to reading. In it, he also keeps a list of books he *has* read, with
appropriate dates and comments. The major part of the notebook is devoted
to the letters that Thomas exchanges with Mr. Ruiz. Each week, he is
expected to write a thoughtful letter that shows what he is thinking in
response to what he is reading. He can comment on any text (for example,
one that he has listened to on tape or heard in interactive read-aloud), but
he is particularly expected to address the book he has selected for independent reading. The notebook has space for "short writes" and other directed
and open responses in a variety of genres that may occur in any reading
context—guided reading, literature discussion, or interactive read-aloud.

Early in the year, Mr. Ruiz spent some instructional time explicitly
teaching students how to select books for themselves, and that has paid off.
Thomas has favorite topics, genres, and authors, but he also regularly
explores new genres. He chooses books that are just about right for his current strategies and skills; all it takes is reading a few pages as a test. He
also is well aware of his own interests in both nonfiction and fiction.

At the beginning of reading workshop, Mr. Ruiz provides a minilesson that demonstrates some aspect of reading to the students. He tries to
express the principle in a clear statement that students can understand
and act on, like "readers think about what the author is really trying to
say." Often he uses texts that he has read aloud and students have discussed as examples. About *An Angel for Solomon Singer*, by Cynthia
Rylant, he says: "I'm thinking that Solomon was a very lonely man
who missed his home in the country. When they made him so welcome in the cafe, he still missed the country but he was not so lonely
anymore because he had connected with other people." Each day,
Mr. Ruiz encourages students to think about the deeper meaning in
the texts that they are currently reading, and then, after the minilesson, students settle down to read individually and silently.

Look at Thomas's letters to Mr. Ruiz shown in Figure 5. About
Firewing, he says he has recommended it to his friend MacKenzie. He
also comments on *Max the Mighty*, which he had discussed with
peers; *Mariel of Redwall*, which he has selected for independent reading; and *The Journal of Douglas Allen Deeds: The Donner Party*

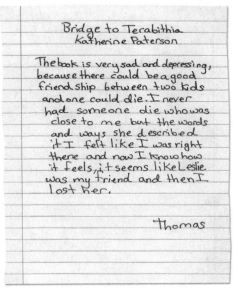

Figure 6   Thomas's response to
Bridge to Terabithia

Using his writer's notebook as a resource, Thomas regularly constructs "discovery drafts" to get his thinking down and then works through the revising and editing processes.

Expedition, 1846, which was introduced to him in guided reading. In these letters, Thomas's goal is not to summarize the text, except perhaps as background evidence; his real purpose is to explain his own responses and thinking. He writes freely about his own preferences and hunches; he raises questions and makes predictions. He feels free to ask questions of his teacher.

Mr. Ruiz's response is also shown in Figure 7. He responds to Thomas's question and prompts him to make connections between two works by the same writer. He comments on Thomas's reading of the genre of fantasy during the year.

Thomas's next letter shows that he is truly enjoying the book about the Donner party and has noticed some of the graphic language used by the writer. He seems to be a devoted reader of fantasy, since he is finishing *Mariel of Redwall* and simultaneously beginning *Dragonflight*, by Anne McCaffrey. He provides some summary information about Redwall and makes a prediction.

While students are reading silently or writing in their notebooks, Mr. Ruiz has the opportunity to work with small groups. He alternates guided reading instruction with literature discussion groups. In guided reading, he selects and introduces texts that will give his fifth graders an opportunity to learn more about reading; he carefully varies genre and type of text. In literature discussion, which he calls "book clubs," students usually have a limited choice. They sign up for a small-group discussion and prepare by reading and making notes. In both guided reading and book club, students often write in response to what they've read. For example, after a discussion of *Bridge to Terabithia*, which Mr. Ruiz read aloud, Thomas wrote the short comment shown in Figure 6.

At the end of reading workshop, students engage in a brief discussion that effectively sums up the minilesson and promotes further conversation. Students often "turn and talk" about their reading, focusing on the minilesson principle. About the series *Among the Betrayed*, Thomas says, "In these books a group of people are in charge and they keep everything for themselves. The rest of the people have no power and live a very poor life. They even have laws that say a family can have only two children. These books really show you how when one group gets too much power they can oppress the other groups."

Thomas has been involved in writing workshop since kindergarten. In fact, he has learned to write in both Spanish and English. Using his writer's notebook as a resource, he regularly constructs "discovery drafts" to get his thinking down and

Figure 7   Thomas's report on whale sharks

then works through the revising and editing processes. His portfolio has many "final drafts" and a few published pieces. One piece he has published is his report on sharks (Figure 7). The report provides evidence that Thomas has had some experience in reading informational texts. He has created an interesting lead page and an ending. He has organized his information into three categories: appearance, food, and behavior. Notice that he receives interesting feedback from his classmates (see Figure 8)! As directed by Mr. Ruiz, he saves his drafts and regularly reflects on his progress as a writer. For each piece, he is expected to write what he has learned from it. For this piece, Thomas wrote: "I learned to organize my information and use headings to help readers know what kind of information I am writing about."

Writing workshop sometimes begins with a couple of "author talks," short sharings of information about writers that students can learn from. Thomas always partic-ipates in a minilesson about some aspect of writing—procedures for the workshop, strategies and skills, or the writer's craft. These short lessons often involve the use of "mentor texts" that students have heard read aloud. Through studying the craft and technique of other writers, Thomas is trying on new roles and techniques.

Throughout his day, Thomas does a great deal of reading and writing. At the end of the day, Thomas takes his independ-

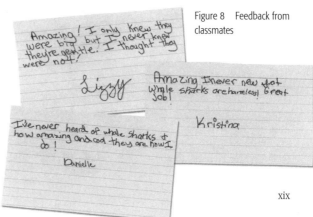

Figure 8   Feedback from classmates

ent reading book home. All in all, he spends about five hours reading every week (this does not include hearing texts read aloud or reading textbooks in the content areas). He reads about a chapter book a week of his own choosing and many other texts as directed by Mr. Ruiz. Daily instruction and focused support in reading and writing are just as important to this fifth grader as they are to students in younger grades.

A portrait of an grade eight student, Natalie

Natalie is an eighth grader who lives in a large city and is excited about moving on to high school. Below she describes her own literate life.

A Portrait in Literacy by Natalie Marie Cole

My name is Natalie Marie Cole, and I am happy to describe how reading and writing fit into my life. I will start with my school. I think of my classroom as a real community, and it is nice to be part of it. We have all known each other for at least three years and most of us for five years. None of us really wants to leave our school and be split up. In a farewell to the school this year, I wrote:

To all the teachers, I leave the memory of a class so tight knit that no matter how much you put into a seating chart, everyone can just turn around and spark a conversation with anyone.

Some of the books I have read this year have really made me think. I like reading history. I'm particularly fascinated with information about early America so I can see the roots of American ideals. I also like reading about wars and how political strategies are used. Alexander the Great is probably my favorite figure in history because he started his legacy by being the only person observant enough to figure out why a horse was being rebellious. I first learned about him in sixth grade when we studied ancient history. That shows that you don't have to wait until you are an adult to actually accomplish something important. I liked how Alexander did not see himself as being greater than his men. He looked at soldiers as peers.

We all read To Kill a Mockingbird and then had student-led discussions. At the end, we all wrote essays about it. I found it interesting that it was the only book that Harper Lee ever wrote. Even though I had read a lot about the author and the setting, I still had no idea what to expect from the book. To me, Boo Radley was very important. It may seem like he was only in part of the book, but he was actually there all the time. When Scout was standing on Boo's porch looking out on the road, seeing what Boo would have seen throughout the timeframe of the book—that really explained his character (that is, if you didn't get it from the first!). Boo was just all about protecting Scout and Jim.

Some of the books I have read this year have really made me think.

I also read The Giver. When we read that book, we were supposed to write about a memory that we wanted to keep, just like in the story. I wrote about a day at sailing camp with six of my friends. This memory was special to me. The wind was good, so we stayed on the heel the whole time. We were on the high side and sailing was fast. At one point the cleat on the mainsheet was twisted so that it would stick and wouldn't let the mainsheet go through. We tied a knot on the mainsheet and we were on a heel and this supposedly uncapsizable boat capsized! We ended up capsizing that boat a third time! We were all in the water—just hanging out. It was just a fun day. We thought we would get in trouble but we didn't. I wanted to pass on this good memory of just being a kid and having fun and doing crazy things—the simple pleasures of life.

Over the last few years I've been reading the Ender series, which includes eight books by Orson Scott Card. I started reading this series when somebody gave the book to my mom to give to me. (This was Christmas of fourth or fifth grade.) I didn't read it then, but one day over the summer, I picked it up and started reading it. The books in the series are classified as science fiction, but they are really political and philosophical in many ways. In the end, all the countries join the Free People of Earth except for the United States, which was holding out and deciding to do things on its own, still thinking that it was the superior country. Even though the series is set many years in the future, I can see that America has this kind of attitude today

At first I didn't think I would like Animal Farm. It seemed kind of weird. George Orwell did make a lot of statements about Trotsky and Stalin— but it wasn't just that. It was all about how people can be so easily controlled if you just send them the right message. I took the position that in the way the book was portrayed in the film, they lost the message that George Orwell was trying to send.

About December, we started to get ready for our trip to Spain. We studied the Spanish culture and learned what to expect. We made sure that everybody had a good foundation in Spanish so we could talk to people who do not speak English. We had many meetings and fund raisers. Working together in our last year and getting ready for this trip made us close, which is why we actually talk to each other now even though we are spread out to other schools. It also tied us to the school and our teachers. I want to go back to Spain someday and see more. One of the best things about the trip to Spain was that my mom went, too. We liked having that experience together. After the trip, I wrote thank you notes to both my dad and my mom. Here's the one for Mom (Figure 9). Notice my Spanish signature!

How do I use reading and writing in my daily life? For one thing, I am happy that I read and write Spanish, especially because my mother

Figure 9   Natalie's thank you note to her Mom

Dear Mom,

Thank-you!

Very much for coming on the trip with me. It made me feel a lot safer to have you there. I've had a lot of people, both kid and grown-up alike tell me that they wouldn't have been able to do the trip without you. I wouldn't have gone if you weren't there. I'm glad that I could spend this once in a lifetime experience with you.

Te amo much o,
Maria Natalie

↑
The signature I put on tons of receipts!

Figure 10 Natalie's letter to her grandmother

> Querida Grandmamí y Bito,
>
> Estoy escribiendo porque no les e llamado. Primero, quiero decir que te amo mucho. Estoy en España con Mamí y mis amigos. Fuí a muchas iglesias y acueductos. Todo era Romano en España y fuí a todas las minas. Me gusta mucho España pero ahora tengo que ir a la cama. Voy a escribir mas luego.
>
> Cariñosamente,
> Maria Natalia

and grandparents are Puerto Rican. I write to my grandparents in Spanish. Here is a sample from one of those letters [Figure 10].

I'm in sports right now, and that requires a lot of study. Before games and practices, I check the labels of what I am eating to make sure I have enough potassium and carbohydrates so that I have enough energy for the game. I also write about sports. Right now I am working on a piece called "Soccer Is Like Life." It may be an essay or a poem. Here is a bit of it [Figure 11].

Figure 11 "Soccer is Like Life"

Soccer is like Life
by
Natalie Cole

Soccer is like life
Every scenario that pops up hits you like a blow to the head
You never know when someone could just suddenly get smart and do something right
When you do something beneficial it makes you feel energized and ready for more
When you mess up, you come down really hard on yourself, but it makes you hungry for vengeance
When you score a goal, you say in your head
YEAH! TAKE THAT!
And a maliciousness creeps from your inner evil and curls your lips into a forewarning smile
The first player to meet your gaze feels all the fear that was in you float over and well up inside of them
They back off, but someone else will come to break you
Your fight now becomes one of survival rather than victory
You can never let your spirit be broken
When you overcome that obstacle, another comes up
Your team is losing and you have to help set up the attack
You do your part right but somebody isn't paying attention
You have to clean up the mess
It's too late
Game's done
Game's lost
You walk away devastated
You blame yourself for the entire thing even though it's not your fault, it's your burden

But it's not over
There will be other games
And you'll be ready
There's another battle yet to come
The war still goes on
Life still goes on

Our family likes to play cards and games together. I remember that when I was younger, I read all of the instructions for Texas Hold'em and taught the family. Before we have company, I study the Cranium cards to make sure I know all of the answers. I'd say I'm a little competitive.

When I'm home in the summer, I usually make dinner for the family. My mom will write recipes for me and notes for what she wants me to do, but I do a lot of experimenting on my own. One night I wanted to make dessert, but we did not have a lot of ingredients. So I searched through the cookbook to find something that I could make with what we had. Peanut streusel pie—3 layers! It was delicious.

Reading and writing also come into my music. I can play the trumpet, and I study the lyrics of CDs until I learn them. I am self-taught. I listen to the song, look up the notes, play the song and then change things around. Somehow, working at the keyboard helps me play the trumpet. I can play it on the keyboard and see how it is supposed to sound.

I do instant messaging just about every day. My friends and I come home from school and talk to each other about what's going on. In a way, it is a different language and kids like it. I find talking on the computer more expressive than talking on the *phone. And also, it's a lot easier to multitask while on line. I can be doing my homework, listening to music, AND talking to several people all at the same time! You can also just go into a chat room, and everyone can communicate—coordinate events and get things done.*

Speaking of events, my thirteenth birthday was a night to remember. Here is the invitation I created [Figure 12]. On the front you'll notice my logo, which I designed myself—NA.7! This invitation had to be persuasive. The party was late at night so I had to appeal to the parents and convince them that the kids would not be with big crowds of strangers. I needed to maximize the number of guests so that we could have the Family Fun Center all to ourselves. Notice that I put the minimum number needed. It was a fun party!

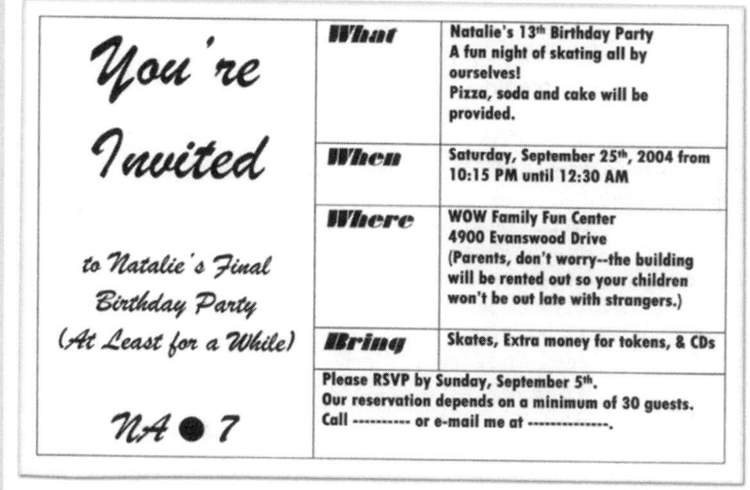

You're Invited

to Natalie's Final Birthday Party (At Least for a While)

NA ● 7

What	**Natalie's 13th Birthday Party A fun night of skating all by ourselves! Pizza, soda and cake will be provided.**
When	**Saturday, September 25th, 2004 from 10:15 PM until 12:30 AM**
Where	**WOW Family Fun Center 4900 Evanswood Drive (Parents, don't worry--the building will be rented out so your children won't be out late with strangers.)**
Bring	**Skates, Extra money for tokens, & CDs**

Please RSVP by Sunday, September 5th.
Our reservation depends on a minimum of 30 guests.
Call ---------- or e-mail me at --------------.

Figure 12 Natalie's party invitation

I read for pleasure all the time and sometimes I read books over and over. I also like to write about my thinking and to write poetry. I like science fiction because to follow the story you have to think logically. I loved The Hitchhiker's Guide to the Galaxy *and* The Restaurant at the End of the Universe *by Douglas Adams. Science fiction makes you explore a lot of ideas that you don't think about every day, and it's easy to just get lost in the story, especially the Adams books. You think it's really crazy, but then you think about it again, and then you think it could happen.*

What started me reading? As a child I had Dr. Seuss books and I read them over and over. (That's what started me reading books more than once!) After a short time, those were easy. In fifth grade, I read the book Hatchet, *and in sixth grade I discovered there was another book called* Brian's Winter. *That may have started me reading books in a series. I remember* Maniac Magee. *That book took my reading to a higher level and it started my thinking about people's mindsets. I used to collect rocks and find books to read about them—how they were formed and how they got their names, and that would start me reading.*

I read for pleasure all the time and sometimes I read books over and over.

The only magazine I still read is Nickelodeon. *It has a little bit of everything that pertains to kids—sports, comics, puzzles, stories. Each book has its own theme, which makes it really easy to read straight through instead of skipping around.*

I would like to become a lawyer and after I get into a pretty good position, then become a politician to work against corruption. I see politics as controlling people and using things to your advantage. If you want to get elected, you say and do things that you think people are going to like or that they think are good qualities to have. Take Animal Farm, *for example. The pigs, to have all the animals follow them, showed that the pigs were more qualified. They only told them all of the bad things about the humans and none of the good things. When Stalin took over, he manip-*

Figure 13 Natalie's poem "A Moral Decision"

ulated the people and told them it would be a Utopia. If everyone worked as hard as they could, they would all be prosperous and live happy lives. The idea seemed without flaws, but his execution was corrupted because of the power. Once someone gets control over a group of people or even one person, the power they have can corrupt them. Even if they start out with good intentions, it doesn't end very well. You can learn a lot from history. I'll end with a poem I wrote about Alexander, my favorite political figure [Figure 13].

A Moral Decision Made by Rote

A horse thrashes about
Men try to calm the beast
A vigilant boy comprehends its actions
Fearlessly, he approaches the steed,
Turns him toward the sun,
It calms
The men stand in awe
"He is more fearful than we; it's his own shadow that causes his distress"
A legend is born.
Alexander of Macedonia with his now fearless Bucephalus

Young Alexander sets out to conquer the world
He moves across the map,
Fighting alongside his men
Building the Greek empire
Yet he does not know that his fate is sealed,
That his end is near

Surging on,
Alexander of Macedonia has left his mark for generations to come
Yet Alexander the Great needs to rest
He ignores his council
His men must suffer,
Therefore he shall suffer as well

A moral decision made by rote

The great conqueror,
The beloved leader,
A great man of morality
Dies at the age of thirty-three
Of old war wounds,
Not properly healed
Received by fighting alongside his men
With no regard to himself

A moral decision made by rote

-Natalie Cole

Learning Across Contexts

Children are learning how to comprehend their world during every moment of every aspect of their lives. Given our increasingly busy schedules, weekdays include very little time for families to interact around literacy or structured learning; yet, as the stories of Sara, Thomas, and Natalie make clear, they manage a good deal of it. All three students carry out their search for meaning before, during, and after school

The kinds of things that families do on weekends also contribute to the comprehending process: fishing, helping or watching adults fix a car, taking care of babies, listening to family stories, participating in family cooking, riding bikes, and helping or watching someone sew, paint, or build. Many children have the opportunity to go to the aquarium or the zoo, go shopping at the mall or supermarket, go to movies. Activities such as church attendance offer opportunities to sing, read, listen, discuss. Going to club meetings or summer day-camp helps children develop independence and social skills and enables students to participate in dance or music.

Ideally, teachers and families work together as partners to support students' developing literacy. School personnel need to be aware of their students' community and culture so that they can enrich their conversations with students with meaningful examples. The more teachers know about children's home languages, for example, the better they can help them build bridges to English proficiency.

Teachers can encourage children to talk and write about their own lives, and can demonstrate daily that they value the children's experiences and the community in which they live. If you are teaching children who live in constrained economic circumstances, it's very important to remember that most of them do not think of themselves as "poor." They are interested in the exciting things that are happening around them and usually appreciate what they have. Of course many children do experience hardship and tragedy, and our job as teachers is to support our students in any way we can. The central goal of literacy teaching, though, is to create a literate life for children in classrooms and to enrich their home literacy as much as possible and appropriate.

Sara, Thomas, and Natalie provide evidence that lives are shaped by opportunities. These three children are in different places in their lives. They have different backgrounds, interests, and aspirations. All three children bring many strengths to their education, but all three *need school* to experience the high-quality literate life that is their right. They remind us that school is more than passing tests or becoming proficient as a reader and writer. The greater goal of school, and particularly of literacy teaching, is helping children grow into adults whose lives are enriched by the reading and writing they do every day and whose futures offer every opportunity.

CREATING A CLASSROOM COMMUNITY OF READERS AND WRITERS

"Children, just like adults, learn better in a supportive environment in which they can risk trying out new strategies and concepts and stretching themselves intellectually.

—Peter Johnston. *Choice Words: How Our Language Affects Children's Learning.* Portsmouth, ME: Stenhouse, 2004. p. 65

Key Principles in Effective Reading Instruction

Children learn not only from your instruction but from the environment in which they live and work every day. They spend about six hours a day, 180 days a year, in a classroom— approximately 1,080 hours a year. During the nine years it takes children to progress from kindergarten through eighth grade, our children spend 9,720 hours in school—or, combining elementary and secondary schooling, 14,040 hours! That's a lot of time to be in a room with twenty or thirty other people. Students learn best in a variety of social settings that take full advantage of the community learning power of collaboration and shared ideas. As they approach the challenge of reading, they benefit from the many social contexts that are possible within a classroom community—whole-group, small-group, and individual instruction.

Let's think about some underlying principles of good reading instruction:

1. *Students learn to read by reading continuous text.*

    There are many times during the school day when your students will focus on how to spell a word, the relationship between letters and sounds, or the meaning of a word, but it is essential that they spend the bulk of their time processing continuous text. Their reading power grows only when they can orchestrate the systems of strategic actions needed to process a text efficiently. They need a massive amount of practice solving words "on the run" while reading for meaning.

2. *Students need to read high-quality texts to build a reading process.*

    If they are going to become readers, students must have high-quality experiences with text. You will have a range of materials, including some very simple "readers" for beginners, but the whole collection should reflect literary quality. No one will voluntarily continue to read something that is inherently nonsensical or boring. Engaging texts are their own reward. Also, high-quality texts can greatly expand a child's language and thinking abilities. Angelillo (2003) has written about the landmark book, "a book that remains in someone's mind long after the last page is read" (p. 33) and changes his or her life. Thinking back, you may remember books that have remained with you and in some way changed your thinking as a person or your sense of yourself as a reader. In the sense Angelillo uses the term, landmark books are few, but we uncover them as we read and reflect on a great many texts. During the elementary and middle school years, we must offer children enough captivating and well-written texts that their own "landmark books" emerge.

3. *Students need to read a variety of texts to build a reading process.*

    As they encounter texts that make different demands, readers become more flexible. Section 2 of this book describes the wide range of fiction, nonfiction, and poetry that an effective reader should be able to process. A steady diet of any one kind of text may make the reader familiar with that genre or subgenre but will not help her or him learn to adjust reading to accommodate different kinds of texts—an essential strategy that is characteristic of effective processing. An effective processing system means reading many different kinds of texts well—long, short, humorous, mysterious, factual. This kind of flexibility is not created without a great deal of variety.

4. *Students need to read a large quantity of texts to build a reading process.*

    Just as it is important to read a variety of high-quality texts, quantity also matters. Reading is thinking grounded in text. From kindergarten through eighth grade, students must do a lot of reading every day. The more texts you have read, the more information you have to bring to your reading.

5. *Students need to read different texts for different purposes.*

All reading involves strategic actions like decoding words and processing language, but effective readers vary what they do. They may become engrossed in a thriller, reading rapidly to follow the action to the last page. They may scan an informational text looking for the specific facts they need or skim a text to get the gist. They may read and reread slowly to puzzle out subtle meanings of a complex poem. You read differently if you know you are going to talk with your book club about a text or if you are following directions to hook up your new DVD player so it will work. You may enjoy the sounds of language in a rhyming book or dip in and out of nonfiction, not reading sections in order. Your purpose for reading might even be to notice how the writer has used language, presented information, or in any other way crafted a text; that is, you might "read like a writer." This ability to vary according to purpose typifies effective reading and should be present in all classroom reading contexts.

6. *Students need to hear many texts read aloud.*

Reading to children plays an essential role at all grade levels. When you listen to someone read a text aloud, you are free from some aspects of processing (decoding and pronouncing words, for example) and can give your complete attention to meaning. You may have listened to books on your car's cassette or CD player. Chances are your memory of the text is influenced by that experience. Hearing a text read aloud expressively and being invited to talk about it afterward may lead a reader to one of those important landmark texts.

7. *Students need different levels of support at different times.*

Whether you teach kindergarten or eighth grade, the students in your classroom are learning how to read—just at different levels of sophistication as demanded by increasingly difficult texts. Upper elementary students, for example, are introduced to new and more sophisticated genres. They learn to follow multiple plots and complex characters. They read about threatening social issues or engage in research. All of those activities involve learning new reading skills or expanding existing ones. All students need varying levels of teacher support as they take on this new learning. To effectively process a more difficult text, for example, your students will require the support of small-group instruction. For books they read independently, they may need to talk about them with other students or with you in order to extend their thinking.

8. *"Level" means different things in different instructional contexts.*

In Chapter 8, we discuss how a gradient of text, levels A–Z, supports readers. This precise definition of "level" is important in some contexts—guided reading, for example—but not in others. The challenges in a text mean something different in each instructional context. In interactive read-aloud, for example, you are thinking more globally about appropriate ideas, vocabulary, and issues, which are different for first graders than they are for fifth graders. In shared reading, some general features such as length of sentences and number of lines will differ for kindergarten and first graders. As a teacher, you think in different ways about texts according to your purpose and use in supporting the development of readers.

9. *The more students read for authentic purposes, the more likely they are to make a place for reading in their lives.*

A classroom is intentionally structured to help students learn a specified body of knowledge, so some learning experiences of necessity are contrived. But, as much as possible, reading and writing in the classroom need to mirror the real purposes and types of texts used by readers and writers in the outside world. For example, students can choose books according to their interests. They can read to find information. They can develop and pursue favorite authors or genres. All of those functions are part of our daily lives as readers.

10. *Students need to see themselves as readers who have tastes and preferences.*

Because you have intentional instruction in mind, and because you know your students, you will choose books for them to hear you read aloud or to read with your support in small-group instruction. Often you will guide their choices so that they learn how to select the right books for themselves. But ultimately readers make their own choices. It is important for choice to be part of every student's day; selection is an important factor in becoming a reader. Choice breeds engagement. As they come to know themselves through the reading material they select, your students will become aware of their own tastes and preferences and will see themselves as readers.

Ideally, teachers and families work together as partners to support students' developing literacy. School personnel must be aware of their students' community and culture so that they can enrich their conversations with students with meaningful examples. The more teachers know about children's home languages, for example, the better they can help them build bridges to English. Teachers can encourage children to talk and write about their own lives, can demonstrate daily that they value the children's experiences and the community in which they live. If you are teaching children who live in constrained economic circumstances, it's very important to remember that most of them do not think of themselves as "poor." They are interested in the exciting things that are happening around them and usually appreciate what they have. Of course many children do experience hardship and tragedy, and our job as teachers is to support our students in any way we can. The central goal of literacy teaching, though, is to create a literate life for children in classrooms and to enrich their home literacy as much as possible and appropriate.

What Makes a Community?

Think about communities you have learned from and enjoyed being a part of. What were those communities like? Your answer might include some of the following characteristics.

Community members:

- Are interested in one another—they talk and listen and share their thinking.
- Trust one another and are willing to take risks.
- Value contributing and sharing more than winning.
- Share memories of all kinds, both funny and sad. They have common experiences they can build on.
- Create a specialized language to talk with one another.
- Feel valued and included.
- Are respected as having different and complementary strengths.
- Aren't afraid to ask for help.
- Take responsibility for themselves while helping others do their best.
- Care for the environment, the materials, and other physical aspects of the communal space.
- Create established routines, so that all the work gets done.
- Understand how people should work together in cooperative and productive ways.
- Share a sense of accomplishment.

The work of the classroom community is learning. The more you and your students become a community, working together for a year, the more successful everyone will be. Let's examine some characteristics of a classroom learning community.

SHARED LITERARY EXPERIENCES

Throughout the year, you and your students build many shared experiences to which you can refer. Specific to literacy, potentially every text you read aloud to your class—and hold an interesting discussion about—becomes a shared language and literary experience. Students learn about one another's opinions, likes and dislikes, cultural backgrounds, even their personal lives. New texts can be connected to those they have already experienced, creating a rich source for further conversation and thinking.

SHARED LANGUAGE

Any group of people who work together over time creates a shared language that they can use to communicate with one another. The shared language refers to their routines and artifacts but also to the concepts and ideas they are learning. Your students, for example, will know the meaning of routines like *turn and talk* (Calkins 2002), *book club*, *share around*, and *partner share*. They will have names for artifacts, like *reader's notebook*, *writer's notebook*, *stick-on notes*, and *thinkmark*. They will learn to talk about tools such as *character webs*, *story maps*, *pronunciation guides*, or the *table of contents*. They will learn technical terminology like *author*, *illustrator, folktale, characters, setting, fiction, nonfiction, poetry, strong verbs, leads, rhyme, patterns, punctuation.*

You cannot assume that members of the group, especially those who are new or who are just learning English, will immediately learn the shared language. A shared language must be explicitly developed over time, with strong demonstrations and frequent use. The more students have a chance to use this language (instead of just listening to the teacher, for example), the more they will make it their own.

A shared language makes classroom communication more efficient. Everyone understands what others mean right away. Fewer words are needed so that ideas can be more quickly expanded. When teachers in an elementary or middle school work together over time, the entire school community develops a shared language. Just imagine fifth graders who have been talking about the characters in stories or about different genres for the last five years!

MUTUAL RESPECT

In a community of learners, a core value is respect for others. Individuals are seen as having different strengths and contributing in a variety of ways to the learning of the classroom. Children need to see that helping others learn is part of their responsibility as members of the group. That might mean being quiet during independent reading and writing, listening courteously to others' ideas, understanding that everyone makes mistakes, encouraging others to share, or sharing their own ideas generously as a contribution to the group.

SHARED RESPONSIBILITY

The work of the classroom does not belong to the teacher; it belongs to all its members. Creating a neat, relaxing, and organized environment will take effort from everyone. The classroom should contain only the supplies, books, and materials students use (instead of stacks of clutter that have no real purpose), and they should be visibly well organized. That accomplished, it must be every student's responsibility to keep materials in good order. Students will not come into your classroom knowing how to organize their learning materials, so explicit teaching is necessary; once they are knowledgeable, they can instigate appropriate actions and help one another.

A SAFE ENVIRONMENT

If a community has shared responsibility and mutual respect, it will be "safe." That means individuals do not have to be afraid to share their ideas or their work. They know that others will listen and carefully consider the suggestions they make. In this kind of atmosphere, members of a community can seek honest and helpful feedback, knowing that it is given in the spirit of mutual respect.

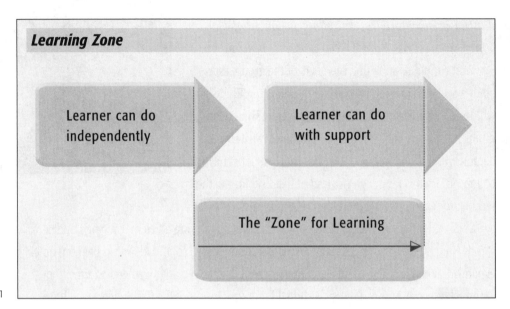

Figure 1

Teaching and Learning

Within the learning community, instruction has to pay off. Every student needs the social support of the community but must also be continuously stretched beyond his or her present level of skill and understanding. There are opportunities for children to learn from each other, but the teacher plays the central role in assuring that instruction leads each child forward.

We learn best when we are successful, and we can be competent even at doing something hard when we have the support of a person who knows and can do more than we can. Every time we are successful, with support, we take on more of the task for ourselves. What was difficult is performed efficiently, and what was performed efficiently becomes easy and automatic, allowing the learner to take on new, even more difficult tasks.

The Russian psychologist Lev Vygotsky (1978) postulated a powerful framework for understanding how a "more expert other" can help a learner. Instead of waiting for the learner to develop and grow into the new behavior, the more expert other supports the learner in successful performance of tasks that are just a little bit harder than he could accomplish independently. In this way, the learner can experience the success and learn from it. In a sense, then, teaching leads development and makes it happen faster.

Some researchers describe this help as a "scaffold," not meaning a rigid structure but rather a flexible support system (Wood, Bruner, and Ross 1976). When a learner is working on the edge of her current ability and reaching out to develop a more complex level of understanding, Russian psychologist Vygotsky postulated that the learner is in the "zone of proximal development" (Figure 1). This powerful idea is important for all learners, infant to adult. No matter what the task, the more expert other acts as the "wind beneath the wings" of the learner. As adults, we use more expert others to help us learn to use new technology or grow in our writing skills, and we may also learn much from books and guides. For elementary and mid-

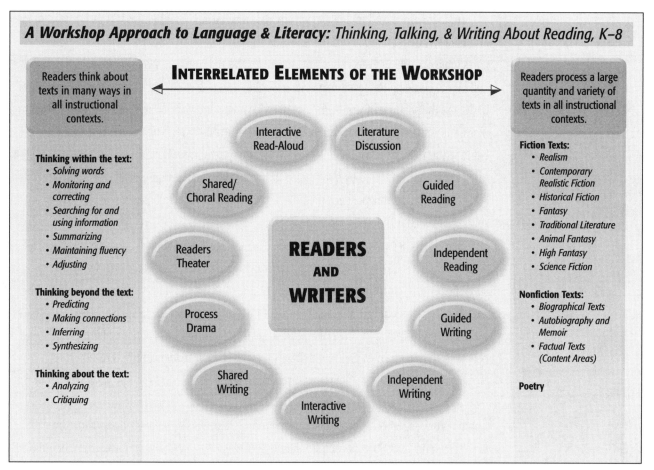

A Workshop Approach to Language & Literacy: *Thinking, Talking, & Writing About Reading, K–8*

INTERRELATED ELEMENTS OF THE WORKSHOP

Readers think about texts in many ways in all instructional contexts.

Thinking within the text:
• Solving words
• Monitoring and correcting
• Searching for and using information
• Summarizing
• Maintaining fluency
• Adjusting

Thinking beyond the text:
• Predicting
• Making connections
• Inferring
• Synthesizing

Thinking about the text:
• Analyzing
• Critiquing

Interactive Read-Aloud
Literature Discussion
Shared/Choral Reading
Guided Reading
Readers Theater
Independent Reading
Process Drama
Guided Writing
Shared Writing
Independent Writing
Interactive Writing

READERS AND WRITERS

Readers process a large quantity and variety of texts in all instructional contexts.

Fiction Texts:
• Realism
• Contemporary Realistic Fiction
• Historical Fiction
• Fantasy
• Traditional Literature
• Animal Fantasy
• High Fantasy
• Science Fiction

Nonfiction Texts:
• Biographical Texts
• Autobiography and Memoir
• Factual Texts (Content Areas)

Poetry

Figure 2

dle school students, teaching is essential in all instructional contexts. Your role as a teacher will vary, but each time you interact with students as a whole group, in a small group, or individually, you have the chance to boost their learning. That's why children go to school.

Interrelated Elements of a Workshop Approach

As the term *workshop* implies, students must be actively engaged in exploring texts in many different ways. The various components of the workshop together provide flexibility and allow you to plan your instruction. But it is important to remember that the kinds of thinking your students do and the *genres of text* they explore (as described in Sections 1 and 2 of this book) flow across instructional contexts. Figure 2, above, shows the "big picture" of language and literacy instruction.

We include writing instruction because text exploration in classrooms is interrelated. For example, kindergarten students might hear their teacher read *Mary Wore Her Red Dress* and *Henry Wore His Green Sneakers* (Peek 1985) aloud several times. After one or two readings, children would begin to join in on refrains. Then, using the book as a model, the teacher might use shared writing or interactive writing to create a chart about children in the class (see Figure 3).

Figure 3

What are you wearing today?

Talizah wore a blue dress all day long.

John wore black shoes all day long.

Candi wore a red necklace all day long.

Josi wore a green sweatshirt all day long.

In both shared and interactive writing, the teacher and children work together to compose and then write an enlarged text on an easel. In shared writing, you act as scribe but children participate actively in every other way. In interactive writing, you sometimes ask individual children to come up to the easel to write a word or part of a word. There are many opportunities to discuss the spelling of words, the use of space and punctuation, and so on within the writing of an authentic text. There is much shared reading (unison reading) of the text while it is being written, and it is available afterward for group reading. The text may even be placed in a large book and illustrated by children so that it becomes a classroom artifact available for buddy reading and independent reading. Children may also take home a reproduced version so they can read it independently.

Here's another example. A third-grade teacher might read several memoirs and then use Tomie DePaola's *Nana Upstairs and Nana Downstairs* as a mentor text in writing workshop, presenting a minilesson on the kinds of information DePaola selected to tell about his grandmothers—details that made them seem real to readers, such as the way they wore their hair. After the minilesson, students spend some time writing in a notebook about events or people in their own lives, giving the details they want their readers to understand.

The point is that texts flow between reading and writing contexts. Rather than the old "get your books out now, it's time for reading" feeling, which placed barriers between instructional periods, the workshop builds understanding about texts, reading, and writing over the day, week, and year. Students acquire a large number of shared texts that they have heard or read and discussed with one another.

Instructional Contexts for Teaching Reading

Students need different levels of support as they engage with a variety of texts. You can provide these levels of support through a variety of instructional contexts, some that include social interaction with peers and some that focus on individual learning (Figure 4). In the primary and intermediate grades, and in the middle school, students receive whole-group, small-group, and individual instruction.

WHOLE-GROUP INSTRUCTION

Whole-group instruction usually involves students sitting together on a rug or other meeting area so that they can be close to the teacher and see and hear easily. Some contexts for whole-group instruction are defined below (variations between primary and higher grades are noted).

INTERACTIVE READ-ALOUD Interactive read-aloud provides a rich foundation of texts on which you can build much teaching and learning. You select and read a variety of fiction and nonfiction texts throughout the year in an intentional sequence that allows concepts to be built one upon the other. The experience provides unequaled opportunities for expanding background knowledge, vocabulary, literary knowledge, and shared language.

Contents for Learning to Read

	K–2	3–8
Whole-Group Teaching	• Interactive Read-Aloud • Shared/Choral Reading • Poetry Share • Readers' Theater • Storytelling • Phonics/Word Study Minilessons	• Interactive Read-Aloud • Poetry Minilesson • Poetry Share • Choral Reading • Readers' Theater • Process Drama • Interactive Vocabulary • Word Study Lessons • Reading Minilessons
Small-Group Teaching	• Guided Reading • Literature Study (Book Club)	• Guided Reading • Literature Study (Book Club)
Individual Teaching	• Independent Reading • Buddy Reading • Reading Conference	• Independent Reading • Reading Conference

Figure 4

These texts then serve as resources for discussion and writing. In primary, intermediate, and middle school grades, you'll "embed teaching" (intentional teaching of the specific understanding you want to be sure children develop) to demonstrate and involve children in thinking about important aspects related to reading or to engage them in discussion that lays a foundation for literary analysis. These embedded lessons are characterized by developmentally friendly language, but the concepts are complex.

For example, you might help the children think about the "problem" in the story and discuss the ways in which the characters solved it. In this discussion, they are building the concept of "plot" without being expected to understand and use high-ly technical language. As they discuss how the little red hen is a responsible hard worker and the most important character in the story, they are building the concept of a "main character" or "protagonist." If children are given the intentional teaching they need to implicitly understand literary concepts, it's easier for them to attach the labels later.

In the intermediate grades or middle school, texts used for interactive read-aloud are a rich resource for learning in many instructional contexts. Teachers can read texts aloud that include complex ideas and focus on issues that will spark discussion. These texts can be brought up again as "mentor texts" in specific minilessons in reading or writing workshop. For example, children can look at examples of strong leads, interesting vocabulary, and text organization.

They can learn how to write from writers of high-quality fiction and nonfiction texts. Literature selections that are read to students can also be the focus of literature study groups or book clubs. We discuss interactive read-aloud in more detail in Chapters 12, 13, and 14.

SHARED/CHORAL READING When children read in unison they engage in *shared* or *choral reading*. There are some differences between the two, but both involve reading the same text as a group. In shared reading, you read an enlarged version of an engaging text (a chart or book) as the children follow along and join in. (When working with emergent readers, you may point to the text to help them.) The text becomes more familiar with each rereading. There are opportunities to examine any aspect of print or engage in various strategic actions of the reading process. For choral reading, you may also use an enlarged text, or each student may have an individual copy. Here, readers concentrate on making the voice reflect the meaning of the story. Children may be assigned roles or particular sections. The intent is to make the text interesting to an audience.

Shared or choral reading is frequently used in the primary grades. Some texts, especially poems, are also appropriate for choral reading by upper elementary or middle school students. Teachers sometimes use the overhead projector to provide an enlarged version, or students may have individual copies. To interpret a text with your voice, you have to think about the language of the piece, the underlying meaning, and the message or "slant" you want the audience to understand.

POETRY You will want to read a variety of poetic texts to your students. You may want to write some poems on chart paper or project them on an overhead transparency. Some may be performed with sound effects or by alternating voices. Children may respond to poetry with a painting or a drawing. Be sure the students talk about the poems and notice how the poet has mapped out meaning in unusual and effective ways.

In the primary grades, children enjoy creating and illustrating poetry notebooks. They glue reproduced versions of poems they have read during shared reading into their notebooks, make illustrations, and read them many more times. This collection becomes a rich resource for enjoyable, fluent reading.

In the intermediate grades and middle school, students enjoy creating and illustrating personal anthologies of poems that are meaningful and enjoyable to them. They can write comments about poems, copy poems, and write original poetry. Often students share their own poetry or particular poems they like during workshop time. In upper grades, some teachers implement a poetry workshop that includes reading, writing, and performing poetry on a regular basis (see Fountas and Pinnell 2001).

The goal is to build a sense of poetic language and to help children notice and appreciate some of the elements of poetry, such as rhythm, word choice, and visual images. Also, students develop knowledge of poetry as a type of text that does not follow the same rules as prose. They learn that poems are laid out differently, are usually briefer, and contain rich meaning in a compact form.

READERS' THEATER Even younger readers can participate in readers theater, which involves readers taking parts: a narrator and several characters who read a scene or a whole text. Children may perform a simple text that they have read together in guided reading, or they may create a piece of readers' theater after hearing a favorite story like "The Three Little Pigs" read aloud. We discuss readers' theater in greater detail in Chapter 17.

PROCESS DRAMA Many teachers set up contexts in which students assume the roles of characters in the story in order to get inside the text and build greater meaning. This "process drama" is not the same as memorizing or reading a part. The participants have the context and parameters in mind, and the process may be fueled by the stories they have read or heard. With that background, the participants behave as they think their characters would behave. Often, this involves solving problems, taking perspectives, and working out relationships with others.

Primary-grade children love pretending to take care of animals or assuming the role of the three bears. Taking on roles is a natural kind of childhood play. Process drama brings this kind of play into the classroom and shapes it to promote learning.

One goal of process drama is that participants learn to take the perspective of another. Also, they are able to use language in widely varying ways according to their roles. For older children, the drama may involve research or writing.

STORYTELLING Storytelling is the oldest form of literature, and children find it fascinating. In storytelling, we often use voice and gestures to engage interest and emotions. When we tell stories, our students create visual images and are less dependent on written text, yet the language they are processing is complex. We are not suggesting that you teach young children the art of storytelling as formal performance but that they create oral texts. They can practice composing their ideas as they retell stories orally from books they have heard or read or tell stories from their own lives. Oral storytelling is important preparation for reading, since it gives children opportunities to use story structures and form texts. This ability helps them anticipate what to expect in texts they read for themselves. Storytelling is also a powerful opportunity to develop oral language. Children can use language for a real purpose and have a real audience. Finally, storytelling provides the opportunity for children to think through and practice what they want to say in writing.

INTERACTIVE VOCABULARY Students in grades 3 through 8 are generally ready to formally consider the meaning of words and to intentionally add to their speaking, reading, and writing vocabularies. Interactive vocabulary is a brief but very active experience designed to build students' understanding of the meaning of words. They may look at a word and talk about how it is used in a sentence. They may change a word in a sentence to make it more interesting. They can create word webs or work with analogies or add prefixes or suffixes to words in order to change their meaning. The intent is to create curiosity about words and develop ways of thinking and talking about them.

PHONICS/WORD STUDY MINILESSONS These are regular, brief, explicit minilessons on an aspect of phonics or spelling. The goal is to help children learn principles that they can use to solve words in reading and writing. Being able to solve words efficiently lets you direct your attention to the meaning of texts and aspects of the writer's craft. Word study minilessons are usually a whole-group activity throughout the grades, becoming quite sophisticated at the upper levels. The study of words can be interesting and inquiry-oriented.

READING MINILESSONS Reading workshop is implemented throughout elementary and middle school. In kindergarten and grade 1, we suggest between sixty and ninety minutes a day, to include whole-group experiences (such as interactive read-aloud), and small-group teaching while the other children engage in meaningful literacy work (Fountas and Pinnell 1996). Specific teaching is embedded in read-aloud and shared reading. In grades 2 through 8, we suggest a sixty-minute workshop consisting of (1) a minilesson; (2) independent reading and conferring, guided reading, and literature study; and (3) sharing (Fountas and Pinnell 2001). The reading minilesson is a brief, concise lesson on any aspect of reading. We have identified three kinds of minilessons: (1) procedural, which help students learn and practice the routines of the reading workshop; (2) strategies and skills, which focus on any aspect of the reading process; and (3) literary analysis, which focus on literary aspects of texts. The reading minilesson is designed to help the entire group learn something about reading; then, students apply the principle immediately to their own independent reading of books they have chosen or to the books they read in small-group lessons. At the end of the period, the minilesson principle is usually revisited.

SMALL-GROUP INSTRUCTION

There are two contexts for small-group instruction, with some important differences. Neither takes the place of the other. Both are essential experiences for children.

GUIDED READING Guided reading involves teaching a small group of children that you have brought together because your assessment shows that they have similar needs and can benefit from the same text. In other words, guided reading involves *homogeneous* groups to the extent that any individuals are alike. You use "leveled" texts as defined by the gradient in Chapter 8. You consider the students' abilities and needs and the texts available, select a text, and introduce it. The students read the text individually, either softly or silently. Then you invite them to discuss the meaning of the text, perhaps making a few teaching points that will help them
process text more effectively. You may conclude by spending a minute or two helping students develop flexibility in recognizing and analyzing words and/or helping them extend their thinking through talk, writing, or art.

Guided reading is a way to help readers work on the "cutting edge" of their learning. You select a text that is just a little harder than students can read independently but that provides enough support so they can process this challenging text successfully with your support.

LITERATURE STUDY (BOOK CLUB) Beginning late in grade 2, you may want to work with small groups of children in literature discussion groups, often called *literature circles* or *book clubs*. The discussions students have had as kindergartners and first graders during interactive read-aloud are extremely important in preparing them to take this step. They have learned to talk about books with one or two partners and can now move to small-group discussions involving between four and eight students. (Discussion during interactive read-aloud can still be used to help students learn to talk about new types of texts or talk in new ways.)

Literature discussion groups are small *heterogeneous* groups of students. They are mixed by ability because a goal of literature study is to enable students to talk with others about their ideas and to experience age-appropriate texts. You select a text or, better, a group of texts from which your students can choose one. All texts are available to all students in the group, even though some may need to hear the book on tape or have an adult read it aloud. Students

who cannot read the text independently can engage in the same kinds of thinking about the text as those who read it for themselves.

Literature study groups take place during the reading workshop. You work with a small group while others are reading silently. You will want to begin literature study by using texts that you have read aloud to the whole group during interactive read-aloud.

Literature study includes (1) choosing books, (2) reading and preparing for discussion, (3) discussing the text, (4) and evaluating the discussion, occasionally writing a response or doing a group project. The goals of literature study are to help children learn to talk with others about texts, to benefit from the thinking of others, to build a deeper understanding of the text, and to stretch their thinking. We describe literature study in more detail in Chapter 16.

INDIVIDUAL INSTRUCTION

Individual instruction take place as you move about the room, talking with specific children; alternatively, you may call a student up to a special table for a one-on-one conference about some aspect of his or her reading.

INDEPENDENT READING Throughout the grades, students read independently during the reading workshop. In primary grades, younger children may read from "browsing boxes" that contain books they have previously read or that you know will be easy for them. During any one session a child might reread several selections. As part of your teaching and assessment, you find opportunities to listen to individuals read, taking notes as you do so. As a primary teacher you will want to take "running records" (described in Chapter I-8) using a book that the child has read only once before. Examining accuracy, error behavior, and other indications of the development of a processing system gives you information about the appropriateness of the text and student groupings as well as needed teaching. During these individual interactions you can also do some targeted individual teaching.

CHAPTER ONE

UNDERSTANDING READERS, TEXTS, AND TEACHING

Reading has always been
my sustenance,
my great joy.
—ANNA QUINDLEN

Readers love books. They buy them, enjoy them, and treasure them. Books help readers understand their world and themselves. Our ultimate goal as teachers is to help each student in our schools become a reader who loves books and all they have to offer. Reading is more than basic decoding competency. It has the potential to nourish the intellect, the emotions, and the spirit. It feeds and replenishes the art and skill of writing. A child who lives a literate life in school and has pleasurable experiences with written language will make a place for reading and writing throughout life.

WHAT DOES IT MEAN TO BE A READER?

Think of yourself as a reader. You carry books with you all the time, and you are constantly buying more. During a pause in your day, you are likely to pick up a newspaper, a magazine, even a piece of advertising. You refer frequently to books, borrowing the language you find there. You notice words in texts and sometimes search for printed words that fit, express, or extend your feelings.

Reading sustains you on long and tedious airline flights, bus rides, or train trips. You gobble up some books, tearing through them as quickly as you can. Others, you savor, reading a few pages at a time and then thinking and even talking to someone about the ideas you find there. Still others, you dip into for particular purposes, to get information or to learn a skill. When you share a whole text or a brief section of it with someone else by reading the words aloud, you modulate your phrasing to help your listener fully understand not only the text but also your own interpretation of it.

You visit bookstores frequently, not so much as a busy, task-oriented shopper but as a dedicated browser. You always leave a bookstore with a few more purchases than you intended. Often you read a book simply because it is connected to something you have previously found interesting—the topic, author, or style of writing.

You are always on the lookout for a new book to love; you write down titles and authors generated by Internet searches. Sometimes you see a book and buy it instantly, without even looking through it, because you know and love the writer or a good friend found it wonderful. You know how to get information from books. You give books as gifts and like to receive books yourself. You have a library card (or at least you have fond memories of childhood days spent in libraries); you probably have a frequent-customer card from a bookstore. You always have unread books in your house that you are saving up for vacations. While driving, you listen to books on tape. There are books by your bed, by your favorite chair, in the kitchen, in your car. You converse with others about particular authors, titles, and genres. You see films based on books, but you always try to read the book first and usually like it better! You create visual images of characters in books; some, you feel you know. You have some favorite books; you reread them over the years.

You seldom think about your own reading process. To you, the print, the words, even the language, are almost transparent. You may appreciate language or notice interesting words, but the way you read allows you to connect directly with the ideas being conveyed. Books and other forms of written language are simply a part of your life. Above all, reading means using your mind: asking questions, challenging the status quo, absorbing information with a critical eye. You see that being a reader is a critical challenge and an essential responsibility in a democratic way of life.

What Does It Mean to Be Literate?

No doubt many of the above characteristics resonate with you: they are about reading ability but also about reading habits, attitudes, and interests. No one can be deeply connected to written language unless the experience of reading, over time, has been meaningful and often intensely gratifying. A highly literate person is constructing meaning all the time while anticipating reading, during reading, during pauses from reading, and after reading—sometimes long after. A real reader tends to recall books read many years before and sometimes brings new understanding to those texts in the context of the present. Thus, we cannot speak of comprehension as simply the "product" or even the "goal" of reading. Comprehension is the vital, central core of the broader and more complex ability to reason.

Literacy comprises a network of in-the-head processes that enable the reader to pick up all kinds of information from the text and construct the author's intended meaning. *Comprehending* is actively making meaning using this kind of in-the-head problem solving. All the complex operations of the brain before, during, and after reading a text—cognitive, linguistic, sensory-motor, emotional, artistic, and creative—are operating as readers process texts.

In *Thank You, Mr. Falker*, Patricia Polacco describes a lonely little girl who cannot read until a very kind and effective teacher notices her strengths and teaches her. From the moment that Mr. Peters showed his third graders the cover of this book (which shows a frustrated little girl frowning at a book and a teacher looking thoughtfully at her), students had something to think about. For example, some concluded that the teacher was making the student do hard schoolwork. Yet, questioned another, "Why would the title say 'thank you'?" Literacy, in all its complexity, was underway.

An interchange between Mr. Peters and his third graders later in the reading is shown in Figure 1-1. Stopping to invite student interaction, Mr. Peters prompted a "comprehension conversation" instead of administering a "comprehension check." Nevertheless, he found out how at least some students were thinking about the text, and everyone was able to benefit from one another's thinking.

Discussion of *Thank You, Mr. Falker*, by Patricia Polacco

Mr. Peters: (reading) *"One evening they lay on the grass together and counted the lights from heaven. 'You know,' her grandma said, 'all of us will go there someday. Hang on to the grass, or you'll lift right off the ground, and there you'll be!'*

They laughed, and both hung on to the grass.

But it was not long after that night that her grandma must have let go of the grass, because she went to where the lights were, on the other side. And not long after that, Trisha's grandpa let go of the grass, too.

School seemed harder and harder now." [p. 9]

Patricia Polacco is telling something about Trisha's grandmother and grandfather, but she's not saying it directly. Do you know what she means, though, by "letting go of the grass"?

Julia: Did they die?

Mr. Peters: What does everyone think of that? What makes you think so?

Josh: It said "heaven" before, and that would be the other side.

Julia: Why didn't she say they died?

Mr. Peters: Maybe the writer thought that would be an interesting way to say it.

Kara: Or maybe it really happened and she knew somebody who really did that and said that.

Mr. Peters: Maybe she was trying to help us know how she really felt about her grandparents.

Julia: And that she was sad when they let go and everything seemed sad.

Mr. Peters: It does have a sad sound to it, doesn't it? And then, listen (reads), "School seemed harder and harder now." I wonder why.

Josh: Trish was getting older, so they had harder work, and she didn't have anyone to help her.

Kara: It might not really be harder, but she didn't have her grandmother and grandfather to make her feel good, and all the kids were teasing her.

Julia: Because she couldn't read. I think letting go of the grass sounds better than dying—not as sad.

Josh: Maybe everything just seemed harder after they died.

Figure 1-1. *Discussion of* Thank You, Mr. Falker, *by Patricia Polacco*

Still later the text tells about Trisha's move to California, where she meets Mr. Falker, a teacher who helps her learn to read. Mr. Peters chose another place to pause and invite conversation. The students' discussion covered not only the idea that Mr. Falker is kind to the girl and makes the other students stop teasing her but also that he thinks she is smart and brave to be able to compensate so cleverly. The idea that someone can be really smart but not good at something like reading is an important concept.

For these third graders, comprehending *Thank You, Mr. Falker* involved thinking deeply about the events, as demanded by the text. Literal understanding would not have been enough. Polacco's book is more than a story about a child who cannot read and then learns how—although that, in itself, is a great story. Mr. Falker is a hero, not just because he teaches Trisha to read but because through him, Patricia Polacco, Trisha's alter ego, has been able to write and illustrate so many beautiful books for children. Think of the discussion that might follow this last sentence of the book:

> He hugged me and asked me what I did for a living. "Why, Mr. Falker," I answered. "I make books for children. . . . Thank you, Mr. Falker. Thank you." (p. 35)

We would expect children to appreciate the significance of Polacco's going on to write so many good books for children, which would not have been possible without Mr. Falker. Although the writer did not say so, as readers we know that the "thank you" is not just from Patricia Polacco but from all the readers who have loved her books.

Mr. Peters' third graders supported each other in building more complex understandings while thinking about a text they heard read aloud. Their purpose was not to practice applying a strategy but to understand the girl's problem and its solution. There were no scheduled times to use an assigned strategy; Mr. Peters did not use a list of questions to test their knowledge afterward or ask them to retell the story, but important learning occurred.

The act of comprehending a text occurs before, during, and after reading. And not only is the reader thinking about everything that the writer includes in the message but is going well beyond it. A struggling reader (or a former struggling reader), for example, might experience *Thank You, Mr. Falker* in ways that a proficient reader could not

even imagine because he brings a unique set of experiences to the text.

The critical elements of comprehension—the readers, the text, and the teaching (see Figure 1-2)—are evident in Mr. Peters' interchange with his students:

- The *readers* are the listeners, who process the meaning and language of the text in their heads, as well as their teacher, Mr. Peters, who processes the print and reads aloud with fluency. Through the medium of his voice, Mr. Peters uses pauses and emphasis to convey the meaning of the text.

- The *text* consists of Polacco's story as well as the accompanying illustrations, the dedication to Mr. Falker, and the afterword. Processing the text makes demands on the readers/listeners. Readers respond to the text in different ways, of course, because their individual backgrounds are part of the processing system.

- The *teaching* consists of the way Mr. Peters presents the text orally, the places at which he chooses to stop and invite discussion, the demonstration of his own responses, the probing questions he uses to find out what students are thinking, even the way he no doubt refers back to the text or links it to other texts across the year—all the moment-to-moment decisions teachers employ to mediate (intervene) in the reading in a way that does not disrupt but instead enhances students' understanding and enjoyment.

Processing means that readers are engaging in complex systems of strategic, in-the-head actions in response to the demands of text. We cannot see strategic actions, but we can look for evidence that they are occurring in the reader's head. We can look at reading behaviors and hypothesize what the readers are able to do as they think their way through a text. Instruction supports processing, but strategic actions only happen in the heads of individual readers. Here's an itemized breakdown:

1 Processing demands are inherent within each written text. For a reader to meet the textual demands means engaging in a complex range of in-the-head actions, including

- Using visual information from print and graphics.

- Putting together all the kinds of information in the text to gain its literal meaning.

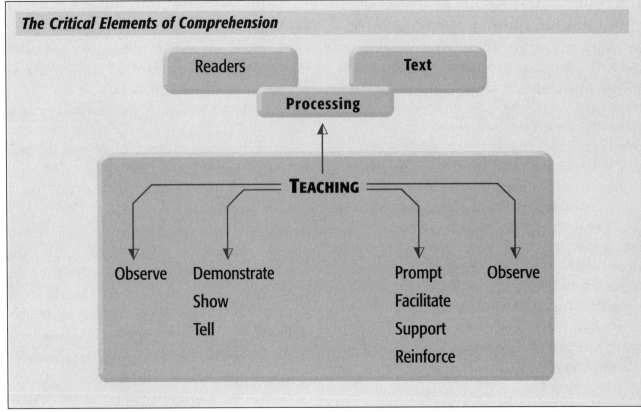

Figure 1-2. *The Critical Elements of Comprehension*

- Remembering the important information while reading and also while thinking beyond the text.
- Sometimes thinking about the quality, structure, or similar aspects of the text (is the language familiar, recognizable, well constructed?).

2 Readers respond to these demands in different ways because their own background knowledge is an important part of the processing.

3 The teacher supports the processing of the text in a variety of ways, including,

- Reading aloud with fluency and phrasing.
- Talking about reading in many different ways.
- Showing students how texts "work" and giving them information they will need to process or problem-solve the text.
- Prompting and helping readers to engage in strategic actions.
- Reinforcing behaviors that evidence students are processing the text in effective ways.

READERS

When we say that the reader is a critical element of the comprehending process, we are not talking about the student's "level" or "ability." Instead, we mean the whole of the reader's prior experience, knowledge of language, and knowledge of the world—the reader brings all this to the processing of every single text: the transaction between reader and text results in the ongoing construction of understanding (Rosenblatt 1938/1983, 1978). As Louise Rosenblatt has said,

> Terms such as *the reader* are somewhat misleading, though convenient, fictions. There is no such thing as a generic reader or a generic literary work; there are in reality only the potential millions of individual readers or individual literary works. . . . The reading of any work of literature is, of necessity, an individual and unique occurrence involving the mind and emotions of some particular reader and a particular text at a particular time under particular circumstances. (1938/1983, p. 34)

We know that reading is both a cognitive and an emotional experience. Interest and motivation play strong roles in constructing the meaning that readers take from text, and the outcome is somewhat different for every reader.

The act of comprehending a text is also affected by contextual factors, which, again, are different for individuals and even different for the same reader over time. For example, it matters whether you are reading "on the run" for a short time in a crowded place or at home on a long Sunday afternoon, whether the text you are reading helps you connect with your own cultural past or not, whether you have heard people talking about the text or read a review before you read it, whether you have seen the movie first, whether you are expected to take a test on your reading, whether you plan to discuss the text with friends, whether the text discusses a place you have lived or previously visited, and so on. Reading, as a thinking process, is part of everything that happens to you as a person, and comprehending a text is intimately related to your life.

TEXTS

As comprehenders, we seek to meet the demands of whatever texts we decide to read. It is helpful for us as teachers to ask: What does the reader need to know or know how to do to be able to read this text with understanding and fluency? To answer that question, we would need to think about:

- What is the overall meaning of this text?
- What layers of meaning will the reader need to understand?
- Will the reader need to gather information from a variety of places—for example, graphics, illustrations, text body, and glossaries?
- What new or unusual language structures will the reader need to understand?
- What kinds of structural elements both help and represent a challenge to the reader—for example, narrative, flashbacks, "stories within stories," insets, graphics, categorized lists?
- Are there sophisticated uses of words such as metaphors, similes, and idioms?
- Is there a large number of multisyllable or technical words?
- To what degree is inference required to understand the text?
- Does the text demand that the reader understand below-the-surface uses of language, such as irony?

- What background knowledge or experience is required to understand the text?
- What prior experience with this kind of text (genre, structure, style) is needed to help the reader process it with rich comprehension?
- How many unfamiliar words or words beyond the reader's present decoding ability are present?

Clearly, assessing the demands of a text is a complex task. As teachers, we are not thinking of the text in isolation but in relation first to readers in general and then to the particular readers we are teaching. Processing involves meeting the emotional as well as the cognitive demands of a text. To richly understand a text like *Thank You, Mr. Falker,* the reader must have empathy for Trisha and a feeling of joy at the final outcome.

Let's think about how a reader's response to a text reveals her understandings and how her teacher interacts to "lift" her further thinking. Each week, Haylea and her teacher, Ms. Winkler, exchange letters about books that the students have either read themselves or heard read aloud to the class. This week's letter includes Haylea's response to *Because of Winn-Dixie* (DiCamilillo) which Ms. Winkler is reading aloud. *Because of Winn-Dixie* is the story of a young girl who moves to a new town. Her loneliness is relieved when she acquires a large friendly dog in the supermarket. Haylea apparently tried to read this book the previous year but abandoned it. As an independent reading choice, she is enjoying *The Secret Garden* (Burnett). Her letter to her teacher (see Figure 1-3) is an opportunity for her to share her thinking about the texts she is reading during the week. What can we learn about Haylea as a reader from the written conversation between Haylea and her teacher Ms. Winkler?

Notice that Ms. Winkler begins her letter to Haylea by responding to a comment Haylea made in last week's letter that *Because of Winn-Dixie* seems different this year: she asks her to be more specific. She also focuses Haylea's attention on the writing style of *The Secret Garden*.

Haylea's response indicates that this interchange is not a "test" but a conversation. She agrees that the way a person reads a book affects comprehension and gives examples to show that she is different this year from last in her understanding of *Because of Winn-Dixie.* She provides some

Dear Haylea,
    I am glad you enjoy writing letters in your reader's notebook — I enjoy writing back to you! Sometimes it's good to take a break from the things you love. Then you can be refreshed and do your best when you get going again!
    I have read Because of Winn-Dixie several times and it's always different. Sometimes it's how a person reads a book to you that makes it different. Other times it's the point in your life that you're at when you read the story. Do you think you're different now than you were when you last heard Because of Winn-Dixie? In what ways?
    I vaguely remember reading The Secret Garden when I was a kid. One of the reasons you might find the language of the book confusing is because it was written a long time ago. Do you see differences between the style of writing in The Secret Garden and contemporary books? Think about Sharon Creech's books — how is her writing different?
                  Love,
                  Ms. Winkler

Dear Ms. Winkler,
    I do agree that the way a person reads a book, does effect the story. I think I am different from last year because I am more mature, and I see things in a different way. Last year, it seemed to me that Because of Winn-Dixie was just some crazy story, but now it's starting to make sense.
    I do see different language in books — very different from The Secret Garden! Sharon Creech's books are very diffrent. None of the books I've read so far by her have "thee," "thou," "thy," or "tha" in them. In Absolutely Normal Chaos there's a little of "an's" and that kind of thing, but no old language. I do agree that The Secret Garden is a very old book!
    I am still reading The Secret Garden and like it very much so far. What I predicted was right! She found the garden. Two new characters are introduced, and, sort of told about the garden. Dickon is now helping her, and I've realized that the

garden has changed her impact on life, and now I understand more about when you said to write about something that has shaped you, because the garden definitely shaped Mary!
    Colin is yet another character, disabled and may die. I can connect to him because when I think about dying I get scared. I wonder how he can speak about so often, even though he's scared. Mary has yet seen another thing that has changed her life. Colin is spoiled, like her, and she has seen another version of herself, right before her eyes. I think she doesn't really realize yet, though.
    I think that Because of Winn-Dixie is a good book. I think maybe something might happen at the party later on to make Opal friends with Amanda, and, possibly, a closer relationship with her father. Maybe they might even find her mother!
    I used to think that the author named the book, Because of Winn-Dixie, after the dog. But now I sort of

think that she named it after the store, Winn-Dixie. I think so because if Opal hadn't gone to the store, she wouldn't have the dog, and if she didn't have him, then all of the friends she has probably wouldn't be her friends now. I look forward to finding out more!
            Sincerely,
               Haylea Erickson

Figure 1-3. *Haylea's letters to Ms. Winkler*

examples of how a contemporary author, Sharon Creech, writes differently from the way Frances Burnett does in *The Secret Garden* and goes on to discuss how the garden has "shaped" Mary's character. Interestingly, Haylea shows that she is aware of her own growth as a reader—that is, she recognizes an example in the book that helps her understand her teacher's advice to write about something that has stimulated her thinking.

TEACHING

There is much debate over whether complex, unseen, unconscious processing can be directly taught. Earlier in this chapter we commented that ultimately it is the individual who must process and interpret the text. But teaching can make a difference by providing support that will help readers simultaneously:

- Process the text with understanding and accuracy.

- Create reasonable interpretations of the ideas in the text.

- Help readers expand their processing powers in a way that transfers to other texts.

As we engage readers with texts, we are always teaching because we are encouraging active thinking; however, we need to recognize that most comprehending occurs implicitly and is highly related to the individual's own current understandings. We may have to let go of the traditional instruction, which in the past has consisted of a series of questions that emphasize right answers and single interpretations. At the same time, it's not true that "anything goes." After all, students are reading a particular text written by an author who has particular meanings in mind. Tierney and Pearson (1994) have addressed this tension:

> Consider the notion that accuracy of a reader's understanding should be regarded as relative. The key point here is that what is considered an appropriate understanding is likely to vary from reader to reader and from context to context. That is, accuracy of understanding is relative and should be considered a function of an individual reader and individual text characteristics, as well as a function of purposes for reading. In constructing an interpretation, a reader selects, inserts, substitutes, deletes, and connects ideas in conjunction with what he or she perceives as "making sense." And what "makes sense" depends upon the text as well as the reader's purposes and background knowledge. . . . It would seem that teachers need to respect both authorship and readership. (pp. 509–510)

Tierney and Pearson go on to say that one of the goals of teaching reading comprehension is to help readers recognize students' interpretations while at the same time instilling in them the responsibility to address the writer's intentions. Readers must come up with plausible interpretations and be able to justify them with important evidence from the text or from personal experience. The emphasis here is not on "right answers," but on the reasoning process, which is transferable to their reading of other texts. This focus increases the likelihood that important, rather than trivial, aspects of a text will be noticed.

This kind of reasoning can be promoted by engaging readers in processing and discussing written texts that they hear read aloud or read for themselves. Listening, reading, thinking, talking, drawing, and writing flow across many instructional contexts. In well-designed programs, opportunities for engaging with many texts occur throughout the day.

Figure 1-4 summarizes the ways in which readers process and respond to texts and lists a variety of instructional contexts in which teachers can help children do so.

LISTENING TO TEXTS

Even though listeners are not processing the visual information within the text themselves, in every other way they are actively constructing understanding. They are thinking within, beyond, and about the text. They encounter the text through the oral rendition of written language. When you watch the evening news, for example, most of the time you are processing a text that the announcer is reading aloud to you. Even some of the more conversational segments are scripted. The same is true when you watch films or plays. Making it possible for students to comprehend material without having to process the print and other visual information allows them to direct a huge amount of attention to thinking and feeling. As they listen to a text read aloud, students can think in complex ways about texts that are harder than those they can read independently. Comprehension is even more powerful when students have the opportunity to discuss their reading or to use writing or drawing as a tool to reflect on it.

Interactive Read-Aloud

We call reading aloud to students *interactive* read aloud because the teacher assures the students actively engage in

Engaging with Texts: Listening, Reading, Responding

	DEFINITION	PURPOSE	INSTRUCTIONAL CONTEXTS
Processing Written Texts by Listening Individuals listen to and think about texts that are read aloud to them and discuss the text before, during, and/or after reading.	Listeners pick up information through oral language (written language read aloud) and put it together with what they know. They actively construct meaning and also notice aspects of the text being read (such as language, new ideas, story lines, characters). They select interesting ideas and talk about them with others.	▫ Make possible thinking and talking about texts without requiring independent processing of print. ▫ Expand linguistic, vocabulary, factual, and experiential knowledge. ▫ Provide a model of fluent, phrased reading. ▫ Improve listening comprehension.	▫ Interactive read-aloud ▫ Literature discussion (before, during, and after hearing texts read aloud) ▫ Listening to texts (via tapes, CDs, DVDs, computers, etc.) for various purposes
Processing Written Texts Orally or Silently Individuals read texts for themselves either independently or with teacher support and discuss them after reading.	Readers pick up information from the written text and put it together with what they know. They problem-solve the text using knowledge of any kind (visual, phonological, vocabulary, syntactic, linguistic, factual, experiential). They use multiple sources of information in an integrated way.	▫ Enable readers to build their processing systems as they use a variety of strategic actions. ▫ Expand readers' ability to process more challenging texts. ▫ Enable readers to work independently on the information in texts.	▫ Guided reading ▫ Shared reading ▫ Choral reading ▫ Readers' theater ▫ Literature discussion (book clubs) ▫ Independent reading
Acting on the Meaning of Written Texts After Reading Individuals extend their understanding of texts through a variety of ways of expressing meaning—writing, talking, creating visual products, performing.	Readers or listeners reconsider the text and sometimes revisit parts of it to extend their thinking about the text and express their ideas to others.	▫ Develop a deeper understanding of a text. ▫ Enable shared perspectives to enrich understanding. ▫ Enable close analysis of textual features. ▫ Support synthesis of ideas and information. ▫ Provide tools to understand text organization and structure.	▫ Interactive and shared writing (group story, charts) ▫ Independent writing (letters about reading, notes, double-entry diary entries, charts, graphic organizers, book reviews, informational articles, etc.). ▫ Extension through visual representation (interactive read-aloud, guided reading, or literature discussion in book clubs). ▫ Extension through performance (oral reading, readers' theater, choral reading, drama, etc.). ▫ Extension through discussion related to the text or responses to the art.

Figure 1-4 *Engaging with Texts*

thinking and talking about a text. Brief discussion takes place *before* and *after* reading as well as at a few planned times *during* the reading. Interaction between the teacher and students extends understanding of a text. All participants benefit from the thinking of each other.

Technological Access to Written Language

Technological access to written texts is provided through CDs, DVDs, and audio- and videotapes. Many teachers provide these resources in the classroom and allow students to take them home. In addition, students can access a variety of oral and written texts on the Internet.

Literature Discussion

Even if students cannot read a text independently (or even with teacher support), they can think about and respond to the ideas in it and extend their understanding through discussion with others. Literature discussion can take place in pairs, trios, quartets, or book clubs of various sizes and may focus on material that students have read for themselves, that the teacher has read to them, or that they have heard via technology. (See Chapter 19.)

PROCESSING WRITTEN TEXTS INDEPENDENTLY

As they read texts for themselves, readers process the print, simultaneously thinking about the meaning of the text and generating their own ideas that go well beyond the literal meaning. The reading can be oral or silent. They use multiple sources of knowledge in an integrated way to process texts. Ultimately, the goal is for them to engage in this process in a highly independent way. Several instructional contexts support readers' independent processing of texts.

Independent Reading

Each day, students read self-selected books (at school or at home) that are easy enough for them to read independently. Independent reading should not be considered an exercise. This is the time to get lost in a book. Independent reading gives students the opportunity to practice reading in a smoothly orchestrated way; it is a context in which comprehension is largely unconscious but may be subtly mediated by a teacher's minilesson or reading conference or by sharing with others after reading. It is important for young children to have a time when they reread easy texts independently. (See Chapter 22.)

Guided Reading

Guided reading is small-group instruction that builds each student's ability to process increasingly challenging texts with fluency and understanding. The teacher brings together students who are alike enough in their abilities that they can learn how to read better with the same level of text. The teacher selects a book and, by introducing it and providing support, helps children take on a more difficult text than they could read alone. Through guided reading, teachers can shore up students' use of their background knowledge as they process a new text and help them think in new ways about a text. (See Chapter 24.)

Literature Discussion

When readers know that they are going to be discussing books with others, their independent reading inevitably changes; processing is subtly different. Students may read independently or listen to the text prior to the discussion, but participating in a book club provides a way for students to reflect, reprocess a text, and build a deeper meaning as they benefit from the interpretations of other readers. (See Chapter 20.) They revisit parts of a text to read orally or silently to support their thinking in a discussion.

Shared Reading

When the teacher and children read together in unison from a shared text, readers' processing of print is highly supported. The shared text can be enlarged (in large print on a chart, or projected on a screen), or each person can have a copy. The shared text may be a story, poem, or a text students have produced together through interactive writing, which involves teacher and children "sharing the pen." (See Chapter 21.)

Readers' Theater

Students may perform a text, such as a story, a chapter, or a scene, orally. They reread the text with the goal of using their voices to interpret the meaning of the text. (See Chapter 21.)

Choral Reading

Here, children read in unison, using their voices to reflect the meaning in the text and/or make it rhythmic and artistic. The activity requires fast, automatic processing. Often, alternating passages read by all the voices, small groups of voices, and solo voices contribute to the interpretation and effect of the text. (See Chapter 21.)

ACTING ON THE MEANING OF TEXTS

We can act on the meaning in a text in different ways. Of course, we are always responding to texts, before, during, and after reading them. When we read something sad and have an emotional reaction, we are responding "on the spot." But teachers help readers extend their understanding through talking, writing, and sometimes drawing about reading. They may also engage students in drama to explore the deeper meaning of a text.

Talking About Reading

Book discussions—in pairs, trios, quartets, or larger groups like the whole class—take place all the time. Students share what they are thinking about their independent reading during literature discussion groups, in guided reading groups, and before, during, and after interactive read-aloud. Talk surrounds reading. Through "text" talk, students share their interpretations with others, but they also change those interpretations by hearing other perspectives and developing a richer understanding. (See Chapter 16.)

Writing About Reading

Many different kinds of writing can help readers expand their thinking about texts. We discuss a range of authentic ways to use writing to explore the meaning of texts in Chapter 28. The letters between Haylea and Ms. Winkler earlier in this chapter (undertaken during the reading workshop) are an example. As another example, while reading aloud, teachers and children can make group charts about almost anything—time lines, story maps, comparisons. The important thing about making charts together is that they are a visual representation of all the talk and thinking that is going on. Readers can make notes, double-entry diary entries, and individual charts. They can use graphic organizers to help them think about texts in different ways. Ideally, these organizers are not used as worksheets to be filled out, but as a tool for talking and thinking about ideas and information and their organization. (See Chapters 27 and 28.)

Extending Understanding Through Drawing

Drawing or sketching can be used effectively to represent one's thinking about a text in almost any reading context—independent reading, guided reading, literature study, or interactive read-aloud. (See Chapters 27 and 28.)

Extending Understanding Through Performance

Above we discussed how the support provided by shared reading, choral reading, and readers' theater and drama can lead children to reread a text and process it more deeply. Performance also gives students an opportunity to interpret a text vocally.

All of the above instructional contexts help children develop a broad foundation for processing texts effectively. Comprehending the fullest meaning of a text is the goal every time we read anything. We do not teach comprehension by applying one strategy to one book during one lesson: we help students learn how to focus on the meaning and interpretation of texts all the time, in every instructional context, each instance contributing in different ways to the same complex processing system.

SUGGESTIONS FOR PROFESSIONAL DEVELOPMENT

OPPORTUNITIES FOR PROCESSING TEXTS

1 Bring together a cross-grade-level group of colleagues to think about text experiences. You may want to have them work in small grade-level groups and then share as a whole group.

2 Use large chart paper divided into columns. As a group, consider (1) processing orally presented written texts; (2) processing written texts; and (3) acting on the meaning of texts after reading. These three actions occur across instructional contexts.

3 Have each group use their weekly schedules to discuss a week of instruction in their classroom. Make a list of all the processing opportunities students have in each of the three areas in the three columns on the chart paper.

4 Review the charts. Have the whole group participate in a larger discussion of how these opportunities can be expanded. Emphasize that there are specific ways of teaching for comprehending in each of these settings.

CHAPTER TWO

HELPING STUDENTS BUILD A SYSTEM FOR PROCESSING A VARIETY OF TEXTS

Effective processing should not be labored, even when the reader is highly focused on problem-solving; it must become faster and more efficient and for the most part covert, and not observable.

—MARIE M. CLAY

What we think reading is influences the way we teach students to read, so it is important to understand the nature of literacy. And that is no easy assignment. Processing written texts with understanding and fluency is a complex undertaking. According to Marie Clay (2001):

> Complex theories of literacy processing are usually applied only to older children for whom the process of learning to read is already well under way. There is a need to choose a complex theory to guide and to understand beginning reading as well. (p. 105)

A PROCESSING SYSTEM

A literacy processing system is an integrated set of strategic actions by which readers extract and construct meaning from written language.

As readers we engage in complex thinking that is largely transparent to us as a process. That is, we concentrate on ideas without being aware of what is happening in the brain, which is simultaneously controlling every part of the body. But inside the human brain, processing, or problem solving, is taking place. According to Clay, "Processing refers to getting access to and working with several different types of information to arrive at a decision" (2001).

Over time, educators have tried to measure and teach comprehension, which is a key aspect of the larger literacy processing system. Following textbooks or curriculum guides, many of us have unconsciously thought of "doing comprehension" as asking children questions during or after reading. We may have required proof of comprehension in the form of answers to questions or detailed retellings. Our interactions with children around texts may even have sounded like interrogations! The teacher asked question after question, and the students learned that their role was to try and give the teacher the answers he wanted.

Some questioning often occurred before, during, and after reading. In that case, we were testing comprehension rather than teaching it and not doing a very good job of that. In fact, heavy-handed prompting can actually interfere with the development of smooth, largely unconscious processing of text.

Suppose, for example, in reading *Thank You, Mr. Falker* aloud to his students, Mr. Peters paused frequently, asking a barrage of questions:

- Who did Trisha live with?
- Who was Mr. Falker?
- How do you think the stars look?
- Why didn't Trisha like school?
- What are you predicting about Trisha's new school?
- Do any of you have grandparents? Are they like Trisha's grandma?
- Why did Trisha say thank you to Mr. Falker?

Some of these questions call for literal understanding of the story; others require readers to think beyond the text. They may elicit some interesting comments from students, and no one question would be wrong to ask, but it would be a mistake to think that we are teaching processing strategies merely by asking questions. At best, getting answers to these questions would reassure the teacher that at least some students were able to answer them.

A productive and dynamic interchange will show students ways of thinking about texts before, during, and after reading. Engaging students in brief conversation prior to reading helps them become active listeners: they can share their expectations, and we can draw their attention to information or ways of thinking about the text that will be important. Before reading *Thank You, Mr. Falker*, for example, Mr. Peters pointed out the author's name. The students had heard other Patricia Polacco books read aloud before and had some expectations of the author. The front-cover illustration evoked comments such as: "It might be about the teacher." Mr. Peters planned a few (but not too many) pauses during the reading, but he did not always ask questions. Sometimes he "wondered aloud" or shared his own thinking. Sometimes he asked probing questions because he was interested in the personal responses students were making. But he worked to make the interchange more like a conversation than questioning, and he took many opportunities to demonstrate to children how readers think. Mr. Peters interacted with his students as a reader, expressing his own thoughts and conclusions. Students might agree, disagree, or expand on what he said, but their attention was on the text and what it meant to them, not on labeling their thinking or trying to figure out what Mr. Peters wanted them to say.

In an attempt to make students more aware of processing, we may have sometimes required students to *name* the

strategies they are using. We do not see this practice as helpful. "Practicing" simple reading strategies such as "making inferences" or "calling visual images to mind" one skill at a time and labeling them can become an exercise that takes away from effective processing. In any reading lesson, even though our ultimate goal is to teach for effective processing strategies, we want to keep students actively thinking about the full meaning of the text rather than "practicing" a skill. A reader needs to engage a variety of complex strategic actions simultaneously to process a text well.

Let's look at two scenarios for complex strategic actions. Both teachers are using the book *Deborah Sampson: Soldier of the Revolution* (Justice) (Figure 2-1 and 2-2). This story is about a young girl in 1776 who lives as a servant but longs for liberty and dresses as a man to fight in the Massachusetts revolutionary army. Understanding this text demands that the reader make some hypotheses about Deborah's adventurous character and understand that she has the confidence, sense of adventure, and physical strength to pull it off! The reader also must think about why this

When she turned eighteen, Deborah began working in people's homes as a weaver. She also taught children for two summers. But by the time she was twenty-one, she was eager for a change.

Deborah had an active mind. She was quiet, but in a strong, confident way. Deborah looked strong, too. And she had grown taller than other women of the time. In fact, she was taller than many men.

But while men her age had a chance to see the world and taste freedom, women didn't. Deborah decided she wanted adventure, too.

12

13

Figure 2-1. Deborah Sampson: Soldier of the Revolution

CONTRASTING APPROACHES TO SCAFFOLDING READING:
Deborah Sampson: Soldier of the Revolution

SCENARIO 1	SCENARIO 2
T: Remember how we talked about how readers visualize or get mind pictures when they read? Read page 12 and then close your eyes. Visualize how Deborah looked.	**T:** There's Deborah on page 12. When she was eighteen, she worked as a weaver and a teacher, but when she got a little older she wanted to do something else. She was the type of person who wanted adventure. She was very confident. Do you know what that means?
[Silence while reading and visualizing.]	**S1:** She thought she could do anything.
T: What did you visualize?	**T:** She even looks confident, doesn't she? And you are going to read how she looks. Read the second paragraph of page 13 to yourself.
S1: I visualized she was tall.	
S2: She's sitting down.	*[Silence while reading.]*
S3: She had long hair in a braid.	**S1:** She was strong, almost like she does exercises or something.
S4: She's doing something at a desk.	**S2:** She was taller than a lot of men and maybe she wanted to do things that men could do.
S1: She has brown hair and a skirt.	**S3:** She always liked to do stuff like learning to read and she really believed in the revolution, so maybe she's going to try to be a soldier like in the title.
T: Read page 13 and then close your eyes. Visualize what is happening.	**T:** What might help her if she wants to try to be a soldier? Remember, only men could go.
S2: I visualized there's a girl carrying a bucket.	**S1:** She's so tall, they might think she is an older boy.
S3: There's a boy and a man at the desk.	**S3:** I don't know why she would want to do that.
S1: I visualized a girl dressed up like a boy.	**S4:** I do—because she wants to be free and to win the war.
S2: She's tall.	**T:** In the next section you're going to find out how Deborah becomes a soldier. Remember that in those days, women were not allowed to be soldiers with the men and could be punished for trying to be.
S3: She has long hair and a pony tail.	**S4:** I bet they don't even know she's a girl.
S2: You can't even tell she's a girl.	**T:** Well, you will find out all the details as you read. Enjoy your reading.
T: So when you are reading today, stop and think about places where you are visualizing. Put a stick-on note each time you visualize so we can talk about those places together.	

Figure 2-2. *Contrasting Approaches to Scaffolding Reading:* Deborah Sampson: Soldier of the Revolution

young girl wants to be a soldier. (There are several viable theories.)

Column 1 of Figure 2-2 shows students being prompted to "practice" a strategy. They do come up with what they can remember about how Deborah looks, but their discussion is focused on the task and misses major points of interest as the students attend to the single goal of "visualizing," using language that may be unnatural to readers. In contrast, column 2 is a piece of conversation during the introduction to the story. Here, the teacher provides a little information and checks on students' understanding of the word *confident.* Students offer some descriptions of Deborah and also express some theories about why Deborah might want to be a soldier. They are asking questions of the text and foreshadowing further reading, using natural language to share their thinking about the text.

These students are not consciously naming strategies, but they are using them. The proficient processing system is always operating—accessing visual information from print, using word meaning, making connections to prior knowledge and personal experiences outside the text, following the writer's reasoning, making predictions. A whole range of cognitive and linguistic actions are taking place simultaneously. When a reader focuses on only one aspect at a time, the processing system cannot function in the same way. Our goal is to help readers build and strengthen an integrated system of strategic actions that operate effectively across many kinds of texts.

COMPREHENDING IS THINKING

Comprehending refers to the thinking readers do before, during, and after reading. *Processing* refers to the reader's complex set of strategic actions, including the use of the visible information in the text print and art and the thinking that readers do before, during, and after reading. Before even beginning to read *Deborah Sampson: Soldier of the Revolution,* students will immediately try to recall what they know about the American Revolution. They may be cued by the flag with thirteen stars and the old-fashioned dress. They may start to question how the girl pictured on

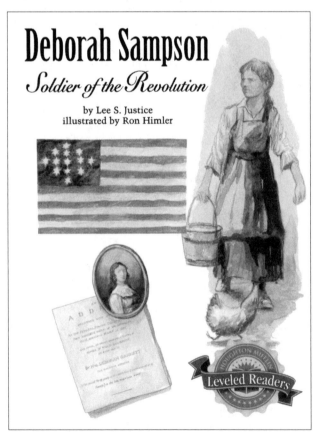

Figure 2-3. Deborah Sampson: Soldier of the Revolution

the front cover (see Figure 2-3) could be a soldier and may contrast today's opportunities for women in the military with those in earlier times.

While they are reading the book, we expect students to pick up vital facts, including:

- The hard life that led Deborah to want freedom.
- Her determination and confidence.
- Her physical strength.
- Her ability to read, write, and think.
- The circumstances under which she might escape notice as a recruit.
- Her willingness to endure pain to avoid discovery.
- Her courage to take on new ventures even at the end of the book.

This basic information should lead students to continue to make predictions and form theories about the development of Deborah's character. All of this happens automatically: the events of the story carry readers along, and they are absorbed in the meaning.

After reading, students may reflect on some of the information from the text, finding evidence to support their opinions. They may even move on to a more abstract discussion of women's rights in the military without losing sight of the character of the heroine.

We cannot separate thinking into compartments. Before, during, and after reading, individuals constantly:

- Notice the important information and details within the text, putting them together in a coherent way.
- Make their own connections beyond the text, bringing their prior knowledge to bear and making hypotheses.
- Notice and evaluate important aspects about the text, such as language, organization, and the writer's craft.

All of these complex operations occur simultaneously as readers meet the demands of texts. When we say that a text places demands on a reader, we are really asking, "What must the reader be able to do in order to read this text with understanding?" The answer to that question helps us realize what readers are required to do as they engage with the text. No matter how simple the text is, the answer is always more than decoding the words. Readers must draw on a wide range of information to process a text successfully.

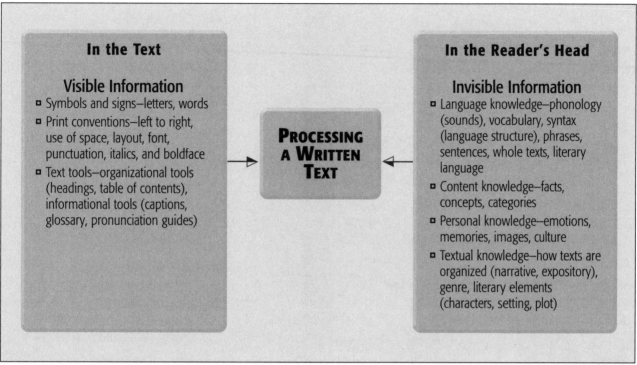

In the Text

Visible Information
- Symbols and signs—letters, words
- Print conventions—left to right, use of space, layout, font, punctuation, italics, and boldface
- Text tools—organizational tools (headings, table of contents), informational tools (captions, glossary, pronunciation guides)

PROCESSING A WRITTEN TEXT

In the Reader's Head

Invisible Information
- Language knowledge—phonology (sounds), vocabulary, syntax (language structure), phrases, sentences, whole texts, literary language
- Content knowledge—facts, concepts, categories
- Personal knowledge—emotions, memories, images, culture
- Textual knowledge—how texts are organized (narrative, expository), genre, literary elements (characters, setting, plot)

Figure 2-4. *Processing Visible and Invisible Information*

TWO KINDS OF INFORMATION

When readers process a text, they integrate invisible information with visible information to construct meaning.

Readers use many different kinds of information in an integrated way as they process texts (see Figure 2-4; Clay 2001). According to Clay, some information is *visible;* that is, you can see it in the text (the symbols and the art). Some information is *invisible;* it exists in the reader's brain. It includes knowledge of the world, texts, and language as well as all the experience the reader brings to reading the text. Texts demand that readers "mix" visible and invisible information to construct the author's intended meaning. The reader is constantly processing both kinds of information.

The different kinds of information that readers use are complex and wide-reaching. Within a processing system, visible and invisible information work together. Readers see the print and other text features (such as graphics), and these visual forms cue a wide range of knowledge that is "invisible" to the eye. This process exists even when the reader cannot see: blind readers access signs through their fingertips. Any time we listen to someone read, we are accessing the visible information through the eyes and voice of the other per-

son. Visible and invisible information are always used in a seamlessly interactive way. Figure 2-5 contains a detailed summary of *visible* and *invisible* information.

VISIBLE INFORMATION

Visible information is presented *in the text.* It is what you can see as your eyes move across continual text and also as you access information from the ways print is presented and from the graphics or other text features.

KNOWLEDGE OF VISUAL SIGNS

Readers look at the letters and automatically recognize clusters, parts of words, and words. They attach meaning to all these signs. The larger the visual units that the reader automatically recognizes and instantly attaches to meaningful words, the more efficient the reading will be. Beginners who are just learning to distinguish letters may find the visual information tricky at first; they will overtly solve words at the letter or letter-cluster level. Proficient readers hardly realize that they are processing visual information because they are so focused on the meaning of the text and their access to it is automatic. All of us, however, no matter how proficient, might hesitate for an instant and might need to look hard-

Figure 2-5. *A Summary of Visible and Invisible Information*

READER PROCESSING A TEXT

Visible Information

Knowledge of Print
- Directional conventions
- Use of space
- Layout–font, white space, placement of sentences and paragraphs
- Punctuation
- Special uses of print–italics, boldface

Knowledge of Text Tools
- Organizational tools–preface, table of contents, index, headings, subheadings
- Informational tools–captions, glossary, pronunciation guide, appendix

Knowledge of Visual Signs
- Letters
- Letter clusters
- Words
- Word parts

Knowledge of Artistic Information
- Artistic appreciation of illustrations
- Recognition of information in graphics–maps, charts, diagrams, time lines, overlays, cutaways, tables, graphs, sketches
- Artistic appreciation of the text as a whole

Invisible Information

Knowledge of Language
- Phonology
- Morphology
- Syntax or structure
- Vocabulary
- Meaning–phrases, sentences, whole texts
- Literary language

Knowledge of Texts
- Text structure of fiction
- Text structure of nonfiction biographical texts
- Text structure of nonfiction factual texts (underlying structures)
- Knowledge of how to integrate information from illustrations and text
- Knowledge of genre characteristics

Knowledge of Content
- Facts
- Concepts
- Categories of information
- Images

Knowledge from Personal Experience
- Emotions
- Memories–events, people and animals, sensory images
- Culture

18

er at visual information to process a text like this, from the wonderful book *A Wizard of Earthsea* (LeGuin):

> The world's wind was cold and gusty from the northeast, but Ged had raised the magewind: the first act of magery he had done since he left the Isle of the Hands. They sailed very fast due eastward. The boat shuddered with the great, smoking, sunlit waves that hit her as she ran, but she went gallantly as her builder had promised, answering the magewind as true as any spell-enwoven ship of Roke. (p. 173)

KNOWLEDGE OF PRINT

Beginning readers are just learning how print works; proficient readers know where and how to look at print automatically. Nevertheless, all readers use print conventions—everything about the print—including:

- The direction of print on the page, left to right.
- The return sweep to the left margin.
- The direction print is presented, top to bottom and left page to right page (in English and many other languages).
- The ways white space is used to differentiate words, lines, paragraphs, graphics, or insets.
- The presentation of print—size, font, italics, boldface—and its placement.
- Punctuation, which signals units of meaningful language such as phrases as well as provides critical information about the writer's message.

These kinds of visual information become so automatic that we are not even aware of using them, but readers in elementary or middle school may still need to be directed to the craft of arranging print in space to convey meaning or the precise meaning that may be attached to words in italics or bold. For example, in fiction, italics or boldface emphasizes a word's meaning; in nonfiction, words in italics or boldface may be key concepts or vocabulary words that are defined in a glossary. Most readers need instruction in order to develop this knowledge of print.

Even experienced readers are still learning things about punctuation. Readers encounter periods, commas, question marks, and exclamation marks in the earliest levels of text then go on to learn the meaning of dashes, semicolons, colons, and ellipses. When reading aloud, for example, your voice automatically conveys the difference between the pause at a comma and the longer pause at a dash or elongates the word before an ellipsis to suggest suspense.

KNOWLEDGE OF TEXT TOOLS

More advanced readers are still learning about tools such as tables of contents, indexes, glossaries, and pronunciation guides. These organizational and semantic features have particular conventions. Diacritical markings that signal the way words are to be pronounced may be indicated in parentheses following a specific word or in a special section at the end of a text. Tables of contents appear at the beginning of a text and are in list form. Indexes and glossaries are presented as alphabetized lists at the end of a text. Informational tools such as captions, headings, subheadings, and sub-subheadings appear in particular places and signal particular kinds of information. Throughout elementary and middle school, readers are still learning how to use these sophisticated tools to gain information from the text.

KNOWLEDGE OF ARTISTIC INFORMATION

Readers also increase their understanding by responding to the information in illustrations—paintings and drawings, photographs, graphs, maps, charts, overlays, tables, cutaways, diagrams. Many picture books are works of art in which the illustrations are an integral part of the text. They impart mood, emotion, and symbolic meaning. We want beginning and more advanced readers to continue to grow in their ability to notice and use visible information.[1] Even as adults, we sometimes have to work to understand the visual information in complex graphics.

INVISIBLE INFORMATION

Invisible information is *in the reader's head* and includes all the thinking readers do in response to the visual information. There would be no reading without the visible information that cues thinking, but the greatest sources of information available to the reader—one's knowledge of and experience with language, facts, and the world—cannot be seen. Some of these forms of knowledge are so vast and complicated that it is hard even to describe them. Readers' knowledge of language, in particular, is an enormously important source of information, because other kinds of knowledge are represented by language.

A FOUNDATION OF LANGUAGE LEARNING

It is quite amazing, in fact, that before the age of about five, almost all children develop full knowledge of their native language—phonology; specific words (the *lexicon*);

"grammar," or underlying rules for the way words are put together in sentences; and a range of socially influenced meanings. Clay (2001) refers to oral language acquisition as the first example of a "self-extending" system, one that continues to expand as it is used because the user is developing a deep knowledge of how it works. In the acquisition of literacy, children "lean on" their knowledge of the language they speak. Although oral language is acquired first, connections to written language are close behind. If we harness the established power of children's oral language to literacy from the beginning, *so that literacy knowledge and oral language processing power move forward together, linked and patterned from the start,* that will surely be more effective (2001, p. 95).

Language is multifaceted. Linguists have described interrelated systems that work together to create the meanings that speakers of a language understand (see Figure 2-6).

Phonology

A *phoneme* is the smallest unit of sound in a language. The phonological system of a language is implicitly known to those who speak it; they respond to the very particular sounds that, put together in words, have meaning to fellow speakers. Children come to reading with this implicit knowledge, but as they grapple with written language, they give more attention to specific sounds that are associated with a letter or group of letters. They learn to hear and identify the sounds in words, which they then relate to the visible information in letters.

Morphology

A *morpheme* is the smallest unit of sound (or combination of sounds) that carries meaning in a language. For example /h/ all by itself means nothing, but combined with /ä/ has meaning: "Ha!" Some morphemes (for example, *mom, a, drink, some*) stand alone; these are "free" morphemes. Others, called "bound morphemes," like the *s* in *drinks* or the *ful* in *thankful* or the *re* in *reinvent,* cannot stand alone because they do not communicate meaning in isolation. Nevertheless, they do add meaning to free morphemes. This may sound like linguistic jargon, but it is actually pretty important for us to understand as teachers. Free and bound morphemes are the building blocks of language. The concept helps us understand how words can be

Language Knowledge	
Phonology	The sound system of a language, the *phoneme* is a single sound. There are 44 phonemes in English, but the relationship between letters and sounds is not one-to-one.
Morphology	A *morpheme* is the smallest unit of sound that carries meaning. A *free* morpheme stands alone. A *bound* morpheme adds meaning to a free morpheme. Morphemes are the building blocks of words. Words are made up of free and bound morphemes.
Syntax	Syntax is sometimes called the structure of language. The *syntax* of a language is the way words are arranged in phrases and sentences. There are underlying "rules" that form the grammar or description of a language. Syntax does not mean "correct grammar."
Lexicon	The *lexicon* refers to the words in a language. An individual's *vocabulary* consists of the words that are known and have meaning. *Signal words* point to underlying structures such as sequence *(after, before, finally);* compare/contrast *(although, but, yet);* or cause/effect *(if . . . then, so that, as a result);* and question/answer *(who, what, when, where, why, how).*
Semantics	*Semantics* refers to the meaning of language. Meaning is communicated through all aspects of language—phonology, morphology, words, syntax.
Figurative Language	Words in a language take on unique meanings related to the culture. *Similes* and *metaphors* help us make comparisons for richer meaning. *Idioms* are unique constructions that have cultural roots.

Figure 2-6. *Language Knowledge*

deconstructed. It is easy to see how word parts help us understand plurals, inflectional endings, prefixes, and suffixes. (We are still talking about oral language here—the invisible information that speakers of a language can bring to their learning about reading and spelling—but this information can be connected to the visible information, that is, word parts.)

Syntax, or Language Structure

Every speaker of every language implicitly adheres to a set of underlying rules (grammar).

Language is highly systematic and rule-governed. This knowledge, remarkably, is largely acquired before age five or six (children learn these rules as they use language to get their needs met), although children continue to learn more-complex structures over the next several years. This underlying knowledge of rules is separate from the idea of "good grammar." It forms our understanding of the order of nouns, verbs, adjectives, and other types of words in sentences. There are many possible alternatives for phrasing groups of English words, for example, but "You go will me with" is not one of them. Speakers of English would agree unanimously that the previous sentence is not acceptable. It must be phrased in one of the following ways:

1 Will you go with me?

2 You will go with me.

3 With me, you will go.

Speakers of English would also agree that sentence three would not be commonly used, although the meaning would be understood. The speaker might not be a native speaker of English. With another possible alternative, "Me will go with you," speakers would assume the utterance came from a child. Finally, speakers would also agree that the meaning of the first two sentences is subtly different. The first is a question, signaling a request. The second is a statement that carries command and possibly threat.

Knowing a language's syntax is a powerful source of invisible information that helps readers check on whether their reading "sounds right." They use this implicit knowledge to monitor and self-correct their reading. However, for *all* speakers of a language, the written form has important syntactical differences. For example:

"Would you go with me?" Joan inquired.
"No," replied Carl. "It is not convenient at the moment."

Were Joan and Carl to say the direct speech attributed to them above, they would omit the identifying tags. For young children, these differences pose some challenges. Some authors of books for beginning readers take great care to make the syntax sound more natural. Also, reading aloud to children can build an internalized sense of how written language sounds, making written language syntax more accessible to them in their own reading.

Vocabulary

Every language has a collection of words, a *lexicon,* that has particular meanings. Speakers of a language share the lexicon. A single word can have multiple meanings or connotations based on context. Take, for example, the simple word *ring* and consider its meaning in the following sentences:

1 She is wearing a new *ring* on her hand.

2 Give me a *ring* when you are ready to go.

3 The bell began to *ring.*

4 He was a dead *ringer* for my brother.

5 The boxer was ready to enter the *ring.*

6 The spy *ring* plotted to overthrow the government.

7 That name certainly *rings* a bell for me.

8 The candidate threw his hat into the *ring.*

9 The bells are *ringing* for me and my gal.

By reasoning, you can connect sentences 1, 5, and 6 to the shape of the concrete ring, although it is highly abstract in number 6. All three of these words are nouns. In sentences 3 and 7, *ring* as a verb indicates a sound; *ring,* with a similar meaning, is used as a noun in sentence 2. In sentences 7, 8 and 9, *ring* is used metaphorically, with sentence 7 related to the meaning in 2 and 3. Sentence 8 is related to 1, 5, and 6. And look at the added meaning achieved by attaching the bound morpheme *er* to the free morpheme *ring.* Many of these figurative uses are probably related to how the word was used in prior historical periods.

Words are truly fascinating, especially when you look at their origins. Helping students expand their listening and speaking vocabularies is essential, as Carver (2000) has noted. For a text to be comprehensible to a reader, he or she must know or be able to quickly solve (and understand the meaning) of about ninety percent of the words. Of course, knowing the words is only part of comprehension, so you cannot base text selection solely on accurate decoding.

A panel assembled by the National Institute of Child Health and Development examined research on vocabulary development and found important links to comprehension.

> Vocabulary occupies an important position in learning to read. As a learner begins to read, reading vocabulary encountered in texts is mapped onto the oral vocabulary the learner brings to the task. That is, the reader is taught to translate the relatively unfamiliar words in print into speech, with the expectation that the speech forms will be easier to comprehend. A benefit in understanding text by applying letter-sound correspondences to printed material only comes about if the resultant oral representation is a known word in the learner's oral vocabulary. If the resultant oral vocabulary item is not in the learner's vocabulary, it will not be better understood than it was in print. Thus, vocabulary seems to occupy an important middle ground in learning to read. Oral vocabulary is a key to learning to make the transition from oral to written forms, whereas reading vocabulary is crucial to the comprehension processes of a skilled reader. (pp. 4–15)

Of course, knowing the words is only part of comprehending, so you cannot base text selection solely on accurate decoding or even understanding the words.

Speakers and writers use *signal words* to help listeners and readers access underlying structures (see Figure 2-7). These words are part of our vocabulary, but we need to be aware of syntax in order to use them.

Semantics

Semantics has to do with meaning. All aspects of language work together in the creation and communication of meaning, which includes words but is considerably more than the sum of the words. Meaning is derived from words and word parts like morphemes and also from whole texts. The meaning of words (often in very subtle shades) depends on the context within which they are placed. Take the following sentences:

1 He *paid* the bill.

2 He *paid* his debt to society.

3 He *paid* the ultimate price for our freedom.

As a speaker of English you implicitly know that sentence 1 refers to using money, sentence 2 probably refers to serving time in jail, and sentence 3 refers to dying. All texts demand that the reader do this kind of reasoning rapidly and unconsciously.

Figurative Language

In addition to using words to convey their straightforward meaning (or meanings—many words have several), speakers of language use them in symbolic ways, creating new meanings. Figurative language represents a concept with something that is not exact or literal but rather an analogy. Idioms—forms of speech peculiar to themselves, such as "all thumbs" and "keep your eye on the ball"—appear in oral language all the time and represent a challenge for new speakers of English. Readers also encounter figurative and idiomatic words and phrases in written language, used by writers to make comparisons that evoke sensory images. Figurative language may include:

- Simile—a figure of speech in which one thing is compared to another using the words *like* or *as* (for example, "fast as lightning").

Signal Words

Signal words help the reader anticipate the organization of the ideas presented in a fiction or nonfiction text. Signal words are especially important in comprehending nonfiction texts because they are related to the underlying structures through which writers provide information.

Sequence	*after; before; first, second; finally; not long after; then; next*
Compare/Contrast	*although; but; same as; similar to; yet; on the other hand; like; unlike; in contrast to; compared to*
Problem/Solution and Cause/Effect	*If … then; so that; due to; because; because of; as a result; since; therefore; for this reason; so that; that's why*
Question/Answer	*who; what; when; where; why; how; how many*

Figure 2-7. *Signal Words*

- Metaphor—an implied comparison (for example, "silence was a wall between them").

- Idiom—a phrase or expression used by a particular groups of speakers and recognized as a unit. It may differ from the usual or expected syntactic pattern or depart from the literal meaning. An idiom may also be a simile or metaphor (for example, "If it were a snake, it would have bitten me," meaning that the object you were looking for was right there and you didn't see it, or, "fast as a New York minute," referring to the busy tempo of life in New York City).

Figurative language has little or no literal meaning, so learning about this additional layer of meaning is essential, especially for children who are English language learners. A text with a great deal of figurative language demands that readers understand these sophisticated uses of English.

CONTENT KNOWLEDGE

Content knowledge includes the networks of understanding that we form in our brains and represent with language. Content knowledge is built through experience with the world and language:

- *Facts* are items of information that are true (or that we believe are true). We all have massive collections of facts that are connected to words as well as to visual and other sensory images and to emotions.

- Facts are connected and generalized into ideas or *concepts,* which are more abstract notions but are still connected to language, sensory images, and emotions.

- Concepts are networked to large *categories* of information, logical entities into which all knowledge can be classified. We are always reorganizing categorical information as we acquire new facts and concepts.

Texts demand a certain amount of content knowledge. The more background the text requires, generally the harder it is. Both fiction and nonfiction texts make content demands. For example, some works of historical fiction can be understood only if the reader knows something about the period in which it is set. Nonfiction texts are especially challenging because they focus on content knowledge. Some texts are very "friendly" to readers in that they explain and demonstrate key concepts within the text. Others simply assume that the reader already knows a great deal about the topic.

Textual content can be very challenging for children who have limited experiences and have not built up the range of concepts and ideas they need to read the texts required at their grade level. Teachers often lament, "They can read it, but they don't understand it." But if that is true, children are not truly reading. They need to do a large amount of reading at a level they can understand so that they can synthesize new knowledge. Content knowledge is related to and highly affected by personal knowledge. There is no such thing as truly objective knowledge. It is always constrained by cultural and personal perspectives.

PERSONAL KNOWLEDGE

As Tennyson said, "I am a part of all that I have met" (1973, p. 416). We are products of our own particular environment. By way of our home, family, neighborhood, region, and country, we develop the concepts, ideas, and emotional attachments that form our perspectives on the world. We learn not only the values of our own family and community but also a culture (see Figure 2-8):

- Our *memories* of past experiences influence these connections, so that while there are shared meanings, at some level they are always unique to each individual.

- We remember *emotions* that are connected with past experiences, and these feelings influence the connections we make to content knowledge and language.

- We grow up within a *culture,* which is invisible (although artifacts such as food or music may be seen or heard) but influences our every act as well as our use of language.

Our experience is always culturally bound. As we encounter and learn about cultures different from our own, we expand our ability to think from multiple perspectives. Many texts demand this kind of expanded thinking. Understanding Tree-ear's reverence for the master potter in Linda Sue Park's *A Single Shard* requires thinking about the artistry and technology of the times in twelfth-century Korea. In Kate DiCamillo's *Because of Winn-Dixie,* understanding Opal's loneliness brought on by the loss of her mother and her father's unwillingness to talk is essential to grasping the significance of her love for the dog Winn-Dixie. Readers are required to reach outside their own lives.

Personal knowledge is intimately connected to oral language, which is learned so early in life that we cannot remember doing so. Pronunciation, sentence structure,

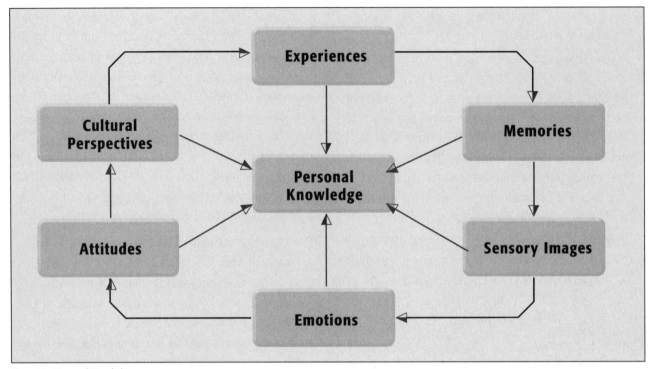

Figure 2.8. *Personal Knowledge*

vocabulary, experiences—all reflect our early learning. Children soak it up; if family structures change, children adapt and learn new ways of talking. But in the teenage years and adulthood, it becomes much harder to be flexible. Culture is essential to the human condition: it is expressed in and communicated through language. Culture is both a support and a limitation. As Peter Johnston claims:

> We are immersed in language from birth. Just as we do not normally feel the air that surrounds us, we are normally unaware of the language we use to render the world sensible. It is transparent. This language that we did not choose gives us the power to name the world and to know ourselves. At the same time, though, it imprisons us in its own borders. We become trapped within the words and stories of our culture, with all of its stereotypes and prejudices. (1997)

Children are attracted to books that reflect their own lives, but as readers become more advanced, they need to learn about other cultures and see different perspectives. A wide variety of texts can offer them not only many opportunities to make connections to themselves but also gradually to expand their knowledge.

TEXT KNOWLEDGE

Text knowledge refers to our repertoire of information about a wide range of different kinds of texts. When we turn on the television, we know instantly whether we are listen-ing to a newscast or a soap opera. 'Infomercials'' cleverly take the form of news talk shows to sell their products. A learned and implicitly held body of understanding allows for recognition, the expectations that arise from it, and the interpretation of the text in the light of this lens. At first glance, one might wonder why "text knowledge" is invisi-ble information. After all, when we say *text*, we are usually talking about written language. But texts can be oral or written, even visual, and we learn about both. In this book, *text knowledge* refers to an individual's understanding of the characteristics of texts and how they are organized.

Genre

In English education, teachers usually use the word *genre* to refer to different types of written texts. We could use the term much more broadly. *Genre* simply means type, and it could be applied to a reality show, a coach's pep talk to the team, a series of toasts at a wedding, an adult talking to a two-month-old child, and so on. Realizing that there are texts with common characteristics that may be recognized is helpful to readers. True understanding of a text does not necessarily mean a reader must name the genre—biogra-phy, fantasy, and realism, for example—but the reader is required to use the organizational structure to gather and understand the information.

Even young children listening to picture books read aloud will begin to identify "real" or "pretend" stories, a basis for categorizing realistic fiction and fantasy or nonfiction. As they listen to more texts read aloud and also read them themselves, these categories expand and become more differentiated. Proficient readers have deeply held knowledge of the characteristics of genre. Our previous knowledge of these categories is available for us to draw on as we approach and process each text. Probably, we are completely unaware that when we read a mystery, we are searching for the details that make up clues. Our intuitive knowledge of how that kind of text works is guiding our actions. When we read historical fiction, we unconsciously access our present knowledge of the particular period in history to provide perspective and extra meaning. (Genre is discussed in some detail in Chapter 11.)

Text Structure

Text structure refers to the overall way the writer has organized the content; this factor is related to genre. For example, a nonfiction text may present information in categories. A biography may present a time line, or sequence of events in a person's life. A thriller (realistic fiction or fantasy) includes a fast-moving series of events, "cliff-hangers," a culminating event, and a quick wrap-up. A fantasy will begin by describing the unreal setting. Readers draw on their knowledge of how texts are organized to anticipate these structures and therefore unconsciously attend to the critical information.

Literary Elements and Underlying Structures

Fiction texts typically have literary elements such as characters, plot, and setting. Hearing stories told and read aloud helps children internalize the elements of fiction. When they begin to read, they expect that there will be characters and that some will be more important than others. They also expect a resolution, a satisfying ending. In nonfiction texts, readers expect to search for and use underlying structures like compare and contrast that provide information. The more readers build up knowledge about these elements and underlying structures, the better they can use them as sources of information.

ACCESSING VISIBLE AND INVISIBLE INFORMATION

Every text demands that the reader access both visible and invisible information in a highly coordinated way.

It seems simplistic to say that visible information is accessed with the eyes, but young readers do need to learn "how to look" at print. Searching for and using visual information requires practice and instruction. The text demands that the reader search for information in the print, which includes layout and special features as well as letters and words, and graphics where appropriate. While accessing visible information, the reader must also use invisible information from various domains; this combination allows him to make a series of decisions while reading. Marie Clay (2001) uses the term *working systems* to describe the in-the-head strategic actions that readers assemble and mobilize to solve problems at any moment in time.

A working system, as defined by Holmes, "may be described as a dynamic set of sub-abilities which have been mobilized for the purpose of solving a particular problem" (1970, p. 189). Sub-abilities, or *substrata,* are elements that lie below the surface and form the foundation for a larger element or ability. These substrata simultaneously allow us to:

- Scan features of letters and recognize them.
- Look for letter sequences that form words or parts of words.
- Access knowledge of syntax, recognizing language that is meaningful.
- Access knowledge of text structure to support the search for information.
- Access background knowledge and combine it with information from the text.
- Bring out emotions and responses that make characters, events, or information meaningful.

These are only a few of the strategic actions that are going on in a second of reading.

Invisible knowledge is constructed through the sum total of an individual's life experiences. It includes everything in the complex and highly organized body of knowledge related to the language we speak, as well as the concepts and ideas we have acquired from real and vicarious experiences (reading, TV, films). It includes the most personal experiences held in our memory, both conscious and unconscious emotional responses, and sensory images, as well as all the implicit and explicit knowledge related to being a member of a culture or even several cultures.

Invisible information is related to previous experiences with all kinds of texts, resulting in our knowing how different kinds of texts are organized. It is easy to see how reading can be considered a kind of thinking and also how people who have a large store of experience are more able to meet the demands of texts. In meeting these demands, two kinds of texts are helpful to readers:

1 Those they can process independently with only a few problems to solve. Texts in this category allow the reader to practice using an orchestrated system. The demands of the text can be met with only a little effort, yet learning takes place, because the reader is developing his sources of knowledge.

2 Those that they can successfully process with instructional support. Texts in this category make more demands on the reader, but teaching provides the critical "edge" that allows for new strategic actions. Over time, the reader can meet higher demands.

Neither type of text will have the desired effect if children do not read much. They need the opportunity to process a great deal of continuous text. If the act of reading is important, then every day students must read texts that are matched to their abilities.

PROFICIENT READERS

Proficient readers build complex reading processes from the beginning.

Using all this information makes reading seem an overwhelming task. Yet young children begin to use all kinds of visible and invisible information simultaneously, even if at first they may do it slowly and somewhat primitively. The proficient reader, on the other hand, uses this wide range of information in a smoothly integrated way, without conscious awareness. As teachers, our task is to help children move from the beginnings of processing to fully functioning systems that expand in strength over time and across texts.

During the reading of a text, proficient processors make hundreds, perhaps thousands, of decisions. At each moment, proficient readers have "working systems" that allow them to access the kinds of information they need. These working systems change from moment to moment as readers encounter different challenges and problems. Moreover, the very act of processing changes and expands the system, especially if the text is making greater demands that "stretch" the reader.

Let's look at Henry's reading of *Peaches the Pig* (Riley), a

"Yes," said the kittens.
"You can climb with us."

But pigs can't climb.
So Peaches went on.

Figure 2-9. Peaches the Pig

level G text (Figure 2-9). (See Chapter 12, gradient.) The running record (Figure 2-10) shows how Henry is putting working systems together. The check marks show accurate word reading. The incorrect responses are indicated above the line, and what the text says is below the line. The letter *A* means the reader appealed for help and *T* means the teacher told the word. His accurate reading is evidence that his current systems are adequate for this level of text. His errors provide further information about what he controls—the richness of the systems he is able to assemble for using information. Henry consistently notices and processes the first letters of words and connects them to sounds. At times, he ignores this information in favor of his strong feeling for the syntax of language, especially as it fits with what makes sense to him. At points of error, the text poses greater demands on his processing system; we can see evidence of self-monitoring

and of searching for more information. Dissonance creates the need for strategic action. In this process, with the teacher's support, Henry appears to acquire and use a wider variety of information sources as he moves through the text. Where systems fail (for example, when he appeals to the teacher), instruction provides the necessary information for Henry to move forward and keep on processing the text.

Henry's errors on pages 2, 5, and 8, all of which involve repeating language patterns, exhibit a changing pattern of behavior:

1 From substituting *said* for *asked* and moving along, accessing meaning and language syntax but apparently neglecting visual information . . .

2 To substituting *said* for *asked* but accessing some kind of additional information that results in an appeal to the teacher . . .

Henry's Running Record on Peaches the Pig

PAGE THINKING ABOUT HENRY'S READING:

1 The substitution of *went* for *wanted* is evidence that Henry has established a working system integrating recognition of the letter *w* and connecting it to his knowledge of sounds and his knowledge of syntax. While his attempt falls short of the precise meaning of the text, he has produced what to him is a meaningful sentence. He is not fully incorporating knowledge of letter clusters or word parts.

2 When Henry substitutes *seen* for *saw,* he is accessing the knowledge of syntax learned in his home but has not yet expanded this information source to include the grammar found in books. The substitution of *said* for *asked* is evidence that Henry is relying on his knowledge of language structure and meaning. Later in the sentence, he again substitutes *said* for *asked.* Most likely, he scanned letter features and connected them with his knowledge of probable language structure and meaning. Although he probably knows the letters *a* and *s,* this visual information is neglected.

3 Henry encounters dissonance when he attempts to start the word *climb.* He accesses his knowledge of the letter *c* and the associated sound (voiced aloud) and then appeals to the teacher, who tells him the word.

4 Henry again encounters a problem with the word *went* and makes no attempt; the teacher tells him the word.

Figure 2-10. *Henry's Running Record on* Peaches the Pig

Henry's Running Record on Peaches the Pig (CONTINUED)

PAGE **THINKING ABOUT HENRY'S READING:**

5 On the word *saw*, Henry notices the *s* and connects it with the sound, voicing it aloud, then appeals to the teacher. This sentence has the same pattern as the one on page 2, but Henry's behavior is a little different. He recognizes and voices the *s*, but then stops and appeals to the teacher. Later, on that page, he again substitutes *said* for *asked*, but this time he stops and appeals to the teacher. He has probably noticed the mismatch between the first letter (and the connected sound) and his own substitution.

6 We see similar behavior on other pages. Henry notices the *g* and connects it to the sound he knows, voicing it aloud before appealing to the teacher.

7 This page, read accurately, provides evidence that Henry is using the language pattern more easily and also that he has the word *gallop* at least in his short-term memory and is accessing it in connection with visual information.

8 In this line, we find the same error as on pages 2 and 5, but this time Henry corrects it. We can only hypothesize what led to this correction, but it may have been that when the teacher told Henry the word *saw* on page 5, he reprocessed the syntax and implicitly recognized that it fit the "rules" of the kinds of phrases and sentences he had heard and read before.

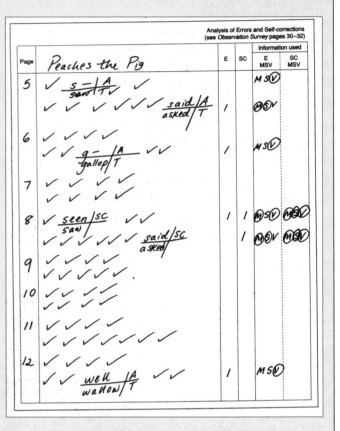

9 Accurate reading provides evidence that Henry is putting together adequate systems for processing the text. He is picking up momentum.

10 Again, Henry's adequate reading is evidence of searching for and using information. He may be depending on the pattern, which by now he has internalized, but his systems are working together.

11 Henry is producing accurate reading. By this time, he is moving smoothly through the text. Notice the almost automatic solving of the words *saw* and *asked*.

12 On this page we see a good attempt at word solving, one in which Henry is using more visual information. His substitute of *well* for *wallow* indicates that he is looking beyond the first letter and attempting to connect word parts to syllables, but the word probably is not in his spoken vocabulary and so is inaccessible.

Figure 2-10. *Henry's Running Record on* Peaches the Pig *(continued)*

3 To substituting *said* for *asked* but noticing additional information (possibly the first letter, connected to the sound and then reconnected to his knowledge of meaning and language structure) to produce a self-correction, resulting in accurate reading.

We have only to observe even beginning readers closely to realize that they are using many different sources of infor-mation while reading. The system becomes more complex and integrated as readers grow in experience and the ability to think about complex ideas.

Throughout this book we will refer to a continuum of learning that describes processing texts at various levels of difficulty (see Chapter 12 and Pinnell and Fountas, *The Continuum of Literacy Learning, PreK–8: A Guide to*

Writing letters left to right helps them understand directional movement and the way print "works." As readers mature, they become better able to use writing and drawing as ways to extend their thinking about reading. Through instruction, we can take advantage of this reciprocity, achieving higher-quality processing in both reading and writing.

FLUENCY

Proficient readers process a text with fluency and phrasing.

Everything about the processing system contributes to fluency. By fluency, we do not mean speed alone, although reading should move along with good momentum. Fluency involves:

▫ Accessing visible and invisible information rapidly and integrating it smoothly.

▫ Reconstructing written signs into language in a largely unconscious process.

▫ Performing all operations rapidly and smoothly.

▫ Reading with ease so that the greatest amount of attention is freed to think about the text.

▫ Reading phrase units or groups of words with the voice in a way that shows recognition of the deeper meanings of the text.

▫ Reading punctuation to assist in understanding the text.

Only the last bulleted points refer to oral reading; the rest apply to both silent and oral reading. Reading the above list, you may think that fluency is almost indistinguishable from comprehending, and you are right. To read fluently, the reader must engage in the same operations needed to comprehend (see Chapters 7 and 8). Fluency is a key characteristic of proficient literacy, as is a wide range of *ways of thinking* about texts. We explore ways of thinking about texts in the next chapter as we shift our attention from thinking about readers and the reading process to the demands of texts on readers.

SUGGESTIONS FOR PROFESSIONAL DEVELOPMENT

LOOKING AT TEXTS

1 Invite a group of colleagues to come to a meeting with several texts that are appropriate for their grade level and that they would use for small-group reading instruction.

2 In mixed groups, examine one text at a time. It's helpful to look at the texts that are appropriate for grades below and above the specific grades you teach.

3 Take a global view. Make a two-column list of the visible information that readers will need to access to read the text successfully, that is, to process it with fluency and comprehension. Then make a list of the invisible information that will be required.

4 Compare the information generated with the chart at the beginning of this chapter:

▫ What are the major differences between visible and invisible information?

▫ How are these two concepts helpful in gauging the demands of a text?

▫ What would be important to help readers understand before reading a text?

▫ What would be important to discuss with readers after reading a text?

SUGGESTIONS FOR PROFESSIONAL DEVELOPMENT (ALTERNATIVE)

LOOKING AT READERS

1 Listen to two readers: James M. and Nyazia on the DVD accompanying this book. Look at the records of their processing of texts with your colleagues.

2 With your colleagues, discuss the following:

▫ What evidence is there that the reader is drawing on invisible sources of information?

▫ What evidence is there that the reader is using visible information?

▫ What evidence is there that the reader is connecting visible and invisible information?

▫ What evidence is there that the text requires the reader to expand the processing system?

▫ What are the implications for teaching each reader to process texts more successfully?

---

[1] This general discussion should not be confused with coding running records (Clay 1991). The *running record* is a tool that teachers use to observe closely the reading behavior of beginners. In coding error behavior, a *V* indicates that the reader is using the *print*. Processing print effectively is a key to building an effective reading system. Attending to the meaning in pictures is coded with an *M*, for *meaning*, to clearly distinguish the extent to which young readers are using picture information instead of print.

CHAPTER THREE

READING IS THINKING: WITHIN, BEYOND, AND ABOUT THE TEXT

Reading cannot be separated from thinking. Reading might be defined as thought stimulated and directed by written language.

—FRANK SMITH

Processing a text involves a wide range of actions—physical, emotional, cognitive, and linguistic. All are involved in the in-the-head activity we call *thinking*. When you think, all you have to do is respond from within, but when you read, you have to connect your thinking to an author's thinking. Students need to engage in three kinds of thinking in order to process a text with understanding: thinking within the text, thinking beyond the text, and thinking about the text (see Figure 3-1). We cannot see these mental acts of processing, but we can infer them by closely observing our students' reading behaviors and the talking, writing, and drawing they do as they act on the meaning they derive from their reading. All three kinds of thinking are occurring simultaneously before, during, and after reading (see Figure 3-2).

THINKING WITHIN THE TEXT

Readers process print to gather the basic information. They decode the words, use word meaning, notice aspects of print, use language knowledge, monitor for accuracy and understanding, search for information, sort important details from minor details, adjust reading, and sustain fluency across the text. Literal understanding (sometimes dismissed as "lower level") represents a challenge for many readers and is essential in processing a text. Although all kinds of thinking occur simultaneously, readers must understand the basic message of a text as a foundation for thinking beyond and about it. Inferences, for example, must be grounded in the text; otherwise, they are just loosely associated thoughts. Grasping the literal meaning of the text is, in itself, a complex process. It requires that the reader decode the words and, even more important, understand the meaning of the words as they exist within the context of sentences, paragraphs, and sections of the text.

THINKING BEYOND THE TEXT

When we say that readers are "thinking beyond the text," we do not mean that they have connected with some piece of information in the text and then gone off on a tangent. Rather, they have well understood the literal information and gone more deeply into its meaning.

A group of students was listening to *A Chair for My Mother* (Williams) in an interactive read-aloud lesson. This text focuses on a little girl and her mother who are saving to buy a new chair. As the story flashes back in time, we learn that most of their belongings were destroyed in a fire. The illustrations show how terrified they were to return and see their home burning. So, the beautiful new chair means a great deal to the family. In the discussion during and after reading, some students' comments were:

- "We got a new chair for my room."

- "I've been in the back of a truck like that one, but my mom wouldn't let me stay when it was going."

- "My grandmother gave us a chair sort of like that one."

These comments are not evidence that students are thinking beyond the text. Contrast them with these comments that are grounded in the text:

- "This story goes back in time to the fire."

- "They were so scared about the fire, but it's good that they weren't home so that they didn't get burned or nothing."

- "The girl wanted the chair to make her mother feel happy because she was working so hard to get over the fire and get new furniture and stuff for the kitchen."

In thinking beyond the text, readers actually use the information *within* the text as evidence for their thinking. They go deeper into the motivations of characters, the influence

Thinking Within, Beyond, and About a Text

THINKING	DESCRIPTION	VALUE TO THE READER
Within the Text	The reader processes the information in the text in order to gain the basic or literal meaning. Strategic actions include: □ Solving words by decoding and recognizing the meaning. □ Monitoring and self-correcting as needed for accurate reading. □ Searching for and using all kinds of information in the text. □ Remembering information in summary form during and after reading. □ Maintaining rate and phrasing to produce fluent reading. □ Adjusting speed and technique according to purpose and type of text.	Thinking within the text enables the reader to gather essential information from the text. Thinking within the text allows the reader to: □ Derive the basic information from the text. □ Process the literal meaning of the text. □ Reconstruct the text in summary form if needed in order to remember the gist. □ Have basic information available as a foundation for thinking beyond and about the text.
Beyond the Text	The reader brings information to the text that is not explicitly there. Strategic actions include: □ Predicting what comes next. □ Bringing content knowledge to the understanding of a text. □ Making connections to one's personal experiences. □ Integrating existing content knowledge with new knowledge. □ Relating and comparing the text to others one has heard or read. □ Inferring what is implied in the text but not told directly. □ Synthesizing the information to realize the greater meaning of text.	Thinking beyond the text enables the reader to understand the text more fully, because the real meaning may be different qualitatively from the literal meaning. Almost all texts require thinking beyond the text for true understanding. Thinking beyond the text allows the reader to: □ Understand the motivations of characters in fiction and biography. □ Derive universal human truths from the reading. □ Learn about life vicariously by seeing through the eyes of another. □ Enjoy the connections between one's own life and the texts one reads. □ Learn from text through identifying new information and incorporating it into one's existing understanding.
About the Text	Thinking about the text is analytical. The reader considers the text as an object, noticing: □ Aspects of the writer's craft. □ Organization and structure. □ Use of language. □ Use of literary devices. □ Aspects of the text that indicate high-quality writing. □ Underlying organizational structures that represent the ways the writer provides information, for example, temporal sequence, compare/contrast, cause/effect, description. □ Characteristics of the genre. □ Features that can be used to evaluate quality or authenticity.	Thinking about the text enables the reader to learn more about how texts work and, as a result, apply that information to achieve a high level of understanding and enjoyment. Thinking about the text allows the reader to: □ Follow and appreciate the complexities of plot design. □ Notice how the writer produces texts and apply this knowledge to appreciating other texts or to one's own writing. □ Identify underlying structures that the writer uses to provide information . □ Understand a variety of genres and use that knowledge as a tool for selecting, evaluating, and understanding texts. □ Evaluate texts for quality and authenticity. □ Think critically about reading.

Figure 3-1. *Thinking Within, Beyond and About a Text*

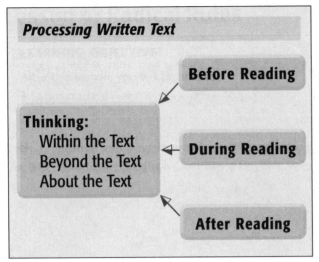

Processing Written Text

Before Reading

Thinking:
Within the Text
Beyond the Text
About the Text

During Reading

After Reading

Figure 3-2. *Processing Written Text*

of setting, the nuances of the plot. They have vicarious experiences as they follow plot lines and make connections to their own lives. This ability to think beyond the text stretches thinking in general. Thinking beyond the text provides the reader with sensory images and greatly increases enjoyment.

THINKING ABOUT A TEXT

Thinking about a text means becoming analytical, in a way "standing back" to consider the text as an object. Students may become somewhat analytical in their thinking even before reading a text. For example, children who have read or listened to other texts written by author Gary Paulsen will expect certain text features even before reading another of his books. They might be thinking:

- This might be a survival story about a boy alone in the wilderness.

- The boy will have a lot of problems to solve.

- The boy will overcome obstacles by using his wits and knowledge of nature.

- There will be many exciting moments, but the story will end happily.

- The boy will learn a lot about nature and about himself from his experiences.

- This book might be pretty exciting.

This kind of analytical thinking provides supports for processing, because the reader already has structures on which to rely. Of course, there are often surprises, and that makes for a good time reading.

While reading, readers may notice aspects of the writer's craft (for example, language they enjoy, literary devices such as flashbacks) and other features of the text. As they move through a text, they can identify and use various underlying structures such as temporal sequence or compare and contrast. Noticing and understanding these patterns will help the reader comprehend.

After reading, readers may become even more analytical as they revisit parts of the text. Having the big picture enables them to see and understand how texts work. They can notice features of the text that allow them to evaluate quality or authenticity, a process that goes far beyond simple likes and dislikes.

THINKING MADE EVIDENT

To illustrate thinking before, during, and after reading, we will explore two texts and what they require of readers. By readers, we also mean listeners, because these texts are appropriate to read aloud, allowing students to process the text in every way except solving the individual words for themselves.

SUMMARY OF *THE OTHER SIDE*

The Other Side, by Jacqueline Woodson, is a story told from the point of view of Clover, a young African American girl who lives next to the fence that divides the white and black sides of town. One day a white girl about her age gets on the fence from the other side and sits there. All alone, the white girl watches the central character and her friends and then asks to play. She is immediately told "no" by one of the girls, but Clover continues to wonder about the newcomer as she watches her playing in the rain (something her own mother will not let her do).

One day, when the rain is over, the girl telling the story feels brave enough to approach the fence, and the white girl asks her name. "Clover," she replies, and then learns that the new girl's name is Annie. Both of their mothers have told their daughters not to go to the other side, so the new friends sit on the fence together all summer, even though Clover's friends stare at them. Clover's mother watches them too, but does nothing to prevent or encourage the growing friendship.

By the end of the story, Clover's friends say "yes" when she and Annie ask to jump rope, and then all the girls sit on the fence together in a line. As the summer ends, Annie predicts that someday someone will knock down the fence and Clover agrees.

SUMMARY OF *TELL ME, TREE: ALL ABOUT TREES FOR KIDS*

Tell Me, Tree: All About Trees for Kids, by Gail Gibbons, provides a great deal of well-organized information about trees, including their parts (roots, bark, branches, leaves), how they grow, the different types of trees and how you distinguish them, what trees are used for, and how readers can record their understandings. Some complicated concepts (photosynthesis, for example) are explained clearly and simply. Some technical vocabulary is included, but in general it is not necessary to read or remember these technical words to understand the text.

The body of the text is a straightforward presentation of information in different categories: (1) Trees; (2) Different Kinds of Trees; (3) Seeds; (4) Bark; (5) Inside a Tree; (6) Roots; (7) Leaves; (8) Evergreens; (9) Broadleaf Trees; (10) Identifying Trees; (11) an untitled section on uses of trees; and (12) Make Your Own Tree Identification Book. Text and illustrations provide information by:

- Comparing and contrasting different kinds of trees.
- Describing trees and their parts.
- Describing temporal sequences related to the growth of trees, photosynthesis, and other natural processes.
- Describing causes of growth (photosynthesis).
- Providing step-by-step directions for procedures such as making leaf rubbings.

Every section has the words "Tell me, tree" or "Tell me more, tree" at the top. These words are connected to a picture of children involved in investigation. A subtext of the book is that children can find out more about trees by examining them—looking closely at the bark, leaves, or fruit. In every section, you see pictures of a group of children doing something to learn about trees—examining an acorn, looking closely at the bark of a tree, using a book to learn about the roots of trees, looking at leaves, enjoying a picnic under a tree, and recording facts about trees (accompanied by drawings, pressed leaves, and bark rubbings) in a notebook.

The illustrations include drawings of trees (many labeled), cutaways showing roots, close-ups showing bark

patterns and leaf patterns. The text communicates the process of inquiry. The illustrations are so simple and clear that by the end of the book, readers can imagine making their own illustrated book about trees.

The book ends with a section called "Tell Me Lots More About Trees . . . ," which presents thirteen bulleted facts about trees. Each of these interesting "sound bites" is accompanied by a small picture.

THE DEMANDS OF TEXT

Even though both are picture books and designed to be read aloud to students, *Tell Me, Tree* and *The Other Side* are two very different texts. In general, both texts require readers to use all aspects of processing, including:

- Reading with divided attention, focusing on meaning while solving words. (If they are hearing the text read aloud, little word solving is needed, but readers will still have to think about the meaning of some words.)
- Using language units (phrases or sentences) to derive meaning.
- Monitoring to check understanding.
- Searching for information.
- Making predictions about what will follow.
- Sustaining fluency and phrasing.
- Adjusting reading for different purposes.
- Making connections to their own lives.
- Interpreting and extending the text in light of what they know about the world.
- Connecting the information in the text to other information that they already have.
- Acquiring new information and reorganizing existing understanding.
- Making connections to other texts they have read or heard read.
- Identifying information that is implied but not directly stated.
- Remembering important details from the text in summary form.
- Noticing aspects of the writing that are well crafted.
- Deriving the overall organization of the text and using it to gain meaning.

- Taking a critical stance toward the text, and using background knowledge, personal knowledge, or textual knowledge to evaluate it.

Looking more specifically at what readers or listeners need to do when processing the two texts, we see that these general strategies are applied in unique combinations that differ for each text at particular points.

THE THINKING DEMANDED BY *THE OTHER SIDE*

The earlier summary of *The Other Side* is only a superficial indicator of the kind of thinking required to deeply understand this text. From the moment you hear the title, you are thinking about its meaning. It implies something separated, distant, even hostile. The illustration on the cover shows the two girls, the African American child, Clover, in a tire swing, and Annie, the white child, looking over the fence. Immediately, you notice that the girls are of different races, are on different sides of the fence, and are staring at each other with curiosity but not smiling or waving as friends might. As a reader you might predict that the text will be about the separation of racial groups. There is no indication of the time, but you get a sense from the cover that the story takes place in a rural setting.

The text begins: "That summer the fence that stretched through our town seemed bigger." The words *that summer* signal that the story is being told in retrospect; you might be thinking that this is a memory of the author. You immediately shift the setting back in time. Then you get more information about the fence and realize it's going to be important in the story: Clover's mother has warned her never to climb over the fence because it "wasn't safe." Right away, the fence takes on symbolic value.

As you read on, you notice supportive details, such as Annie's pink sweater, that help create a feeling of reality. It becomes evident that Annie is lonely, and you may feel sorry for her when the other girls refuse to let her play. You may also simultaneously remember segregation, with its Jim Crow laws separating races, and understand why the girls couldn't socialize. This thinking is confirmed when you read:

> That summer everyone and everything
> on the other side of that fence
> seemed far away.
> When I asked my mama why, she said,
> "Because that's the way things have always been."

While reading *The Other Side,* you rapidly consider a wide range of ideas—some presented in the text, others based on your own experience—and these ideas will probably differ in some ways from the ideas of other readers. For example, contrasting the description of Annie dancing around in puddles, not caring if she gets wet, with Clover's mother's admonition to stay dry might generate a number of different responses:

- Annie can entertain herself; she's very independent.
- Annie is a "free spirit" who doesn't care what other people think.
- This is a story about two innocent girls who haven't taken on all of the baggage racism brings.
- I remember when I used to love to wade in puddles.
- I used to have a yellow raincoat and boots like that.
- These two girls are being raised differently; Annie has more freedom.
- Clover's mom has good reason to make her stay inside; she doesn't want to fix her hair again.
- Both girls seem a little lonely, but they're afraid to be friends.

Probably no one person would have all these thoughts, but you might have several such fleeting thoughts almost in the same instant.

While reading *The Other Side,* you might also be thinking about what the writer is implying but not saying directly. If you see the fence as a symbol of separation, then the ending, when the two girls agree that someday the fence might be torn down, becomes more profound. You may see a deeper meaning in the rain stopping and the sunshine making Clover feel brave and free. You might find it significant that the illustrations shift from girls with somber faces to girls who smile as they face each other.

As the story continues and even after it's over, you may reflect on your own experiences (or those that have been reported to you by family members) with either segregation or discrimination or speculate whether this story reflects a real memory of the author. You may recall what you have read about that time period and wonder precisely when the story takes place. You may even recall other books or stories you have read, heard, or seen on film, such as *To Kill a Mockingbird* (Lee)*, Sister Anne's Hands* (Lorbiecki),

Under the Quilt of the Night (Hopkinson), or *A Circle Unbroken* (Hotze).

You may develop respect for the two girls, who are able to create a friendship in spite of adverse circumstances. You may wonder or draw some conclusions about the feelings of Clover's mother, who even though she appears to be very protective of her daughter, seems to realize that she needs to give Clover the freedom to get to know Annie. Maybe she is thinking of her own childhood.

There is much to notice about the way the writer has used language and symbolism to communicate her message. She does not describe racism in a didactic way, but through the story of the two girls, she weaves a picture of separated groups and the pain that it causes. The writing is crafted to create the feeling that a child is telling the story (Clover is always saying, "Me and Annie," for example). Instead of using complex sentences full of figurative speech, the author uses plain, simple language in short sentences: "She smiled then. She had a pretty smile."

The simplicity of the story carries the deeper meanings. The repeated phrase "that summer" gives the feeling of nostalgia. The book is full of contrasts—the two girls and their lives, the simple story and the complex message, the plain language and the sophisticated meanings, the quiet sleepy summer town and the imminence of the civil rights movement. The text is laid out in a poetic way (see the quotation that follows) to suggest how it might be read aloud. Illustrations create the feeling of quiet, slow movement of time and unchanging traditions, yet the message in the text foreshadows the idea that great changes are ahead:

> "Someday somebody's going to come along
> and knock this old fence down," Annie said.
> And I nodded. "Yeah," I said. "Someday."

Literally, the girls are talking about the fence. But as a reader you may be thinking: "These girls don't realize it, but soon there will be peaceful demonstrations and violent protests for civil rights. I wonder if they will remember this summer and join in knocking the fence down. Maybe that's why the author or the author's mother remembers the summer so vividly. In the innocence of their childhood, these girls were ignoring some of the barriers that separated adults; but already, they were beginning to grow up."

This is only a fraction of the thinking a reader might do in processing this text, and each reader's thinking would in some sense be unique. As Louise Rosenblatt has said, "A text is merely ink on a page until a reader breathes life into it" (Rosenblatt 1938).

THE THINKING DEMANDED BY *TELL ME, TREE: ALL ABOUT TREES FOR KIDS*

Tell Me, Tree is a text you can read from front to back, but you can also choose to roam around in it. In contrast to *The Other Side,* in which meaning builds throughout the text, the information in *Tell Me, Tree* is presented in categories. As a reader, you can see that the writer has created a logical sequence, but some of her decisions are arbitrary.

Much of your processing of *Tell Me, Tree* depends on what you already know and/or are interested in knowing. For example, you might pay closer attention to trees that grow in your own region of the country or that you are familiar with for other reasons. Looking for new information involves:

- Remembering what you already know.
- Comparing what you know to the information in the text.
- Realizing what is new information.
- Revising your own knowledge to accommodate the new information, either changing it or adding to it.
- Getting ideas on how to explore a topic.

For example, you may know that plants take in carbon dioxide and give off oxygen through photosynthesis but not know that the tree's food is called sugar. You may not have realized that trees are the main source of oxygen in the air. That may lead you to reflect that it is important to preserve forests.

On some pages of *Tell Me, Tree,* you will likely peruse the illustrations before reading the text. You may even search through the illustrations before reading the book, stopping at pages that catch your attention. You could get "hooked" by the interesting facts on the last page:

- Trees cover about a third of the earth's land surface.
- In the spring, when the days get warm but the nights are still cold, some people make maple syrup from sugar maple trees. They boil the sap they gather from the trees until it becomes sweet maple syrup.

You may study some leaves closely, comparing the shapes to the leaves of trees you know; you may be struck with the great variety in trees as you read the text and look at the illustrations showing height relationships, leaf types, and bark textures. At almost the same instant you may remember a tree associated with special times, like a big tree in a park that you used to climb up or one that your family used to picnic under.

The illustrations in the book are clear and accessible, but you do need to search for information in different places. Bits of information are included in labels, pictures that "zoom in," and cutaways that reveal unseen elements such as roots. If you are familiar with botany, you might recognize words like *deciduous* but need a second to process them because you haven't seen them recently. If you haven't paid much attention to the natural world, words like *conifers* might be new. You may see known words used in new ways: "The leafy top of a tree is called a crown." (This phrase is located at the top of an illustration of a tree, so the very placement of print conveys meaning.)

Trees is an expository text, but it is obvious that your thinking will go far beyond the information provided. You may reflect on how valuable trees are and renew your commitment to sustaining the quality of the environment. You may remember Arbor Day, think about how Chinese people in Beijing are expected to plant one tree every year, or see the results of a reforestation project in your mind's eye. You may recall the old but classic picture book *A Tree Is Nice* (Udry), with its tall shape; Shel Silverstein's poem "Tree House"; or the story or film *A Tree Grows in Brooklyn* (Smith). You might think about a time when you observed sugaring off in late fall, or just recall the taste of maple sugar.

With its simple drawings and watercolor illustrations and its juxtaposition of far and close-up views, this book is reminiscent of a botanist's notebook. The pages may even create enough interest that you begin to collect leaves and press them, sketch and label representations, make bark rubbings, and record information in a notebook, dating your entries. These activities may spread beyond trees to include all kinds of plants.

THINKING PROMPTED BY TEXT

Any time we immerse ourselves in the reading of text, a mass of thinking arises that is almost too complicated to understand. Some of it comes at our bidding as we try to grasp the author's specific messages, but most of it embroiders those messages with our own particular responses—both intellectual and emotional. As we search for and use visible and invisible information, we actively:

- Construct the literal meaning of the text—exactly what is there.
- Notice how the text is organized.
- Read "between the lines" to infer meaning that is not explicitly stated.
- Add to and revise our own ideas and funds of knowledge in response to the new information or insights (including inferences) provided in the text.
- Appreciate and/or analyze the craft or skill of the writer.
- Respond emotionally to ideas, events, and characters.

All the above happen with lightning speed, and we are almost always unconscious that these complex thinking processes are taking place.[1]

THINKING WITHIN *THE OTHER SIDE* AND *TELL ME, TREE*

The title *The Other Side* definitely requires word solving. The word *Other* demands that the reader notice two syllables: an *o* with the *schwa* sound, the consonant digraph *th* with an *er* ending (an *r*-controlled vowel). Of course, most readers at this level will recognize the word at once rather than needing to take it apart. The skilled reader who has not read the word before will automatically recognize these word parts. Meaning is added because the word is followed by the word *Side*.

Reading the book, the reader must search for and use information, all the while monitoring accuracy. Furthermore, the pertinent information (not every detail) must be remembered and carried through the text. Readers summarize the vital information in order to be able to access it afterward. All of these strategic actions are involved in processing the text and deriving the literal meaning, but much more is demanded.

Literal meaning should not be overlooked: without it, the "higher" levels of processing are not possible. You will want to be sure that your students' thinking is grounded in a substantive understanding of the text. In a recent discussion, some of our colleagues remarked that their students seemed to be capable of divergent thinking but had difficulty remembering exactly what happened in a story. They felt that many of their students were so intent on making different kinds of connections and reporting them that they were missing vital details in the story.

To understand the deeper meanings of *The Other Side*, a reader has to know that two girls who do not know each other live on either side of a fence. The reader must then follow the story line, learning step-by-step what happens in the story. It is very important to get the facts straight—that there is a fence, the girls are from different races and parts of town, and some danger and disapproval are involved in their meeting. A long, rambling discussion in which children talk about the fences in their own yards or things they like to do in the summer is not evidence that they are comprehending this specific text.

Your goal in reading *Tell Me, Tree* is not to come away from the book remembering every bit of the information presented. Such an assumption would "bog down" the reading and make it tedious. Even a short children's book would take hours to process. Instead, you sift through the information, unconsciously setting aside what you already know. You mentally highlight and remember interesting information that is new to you.

THINKING BEYOND *THE OTHER SIDE* AND *TELL ME, TREE*

Each time you encounter a text, you sort information in a very systematic (although unconscious) way. Information, concepts, ideas, and attitudes are stored in an organized way—often by category. The brain is tuned to recognize information that is already known, to notice new information, and to constantly revise existing ideas and attitudes.

For example, in reading *The Other Side*, you might access background knowledge about the history of segregation, using this information to fix an approximate time for the memoir and to understand the context. But as you process the text, especially if it is far from your experience, you may take on a new perspective by wondering what it must have been like for children in those times. Thinking in new ways about what you already know is one of the gifts of reading.

Reading *Tell Me, Tree,* you might notice ways the writer has presented ideas that make you think in new ways. By reading the book, you store up a few important concepts and ideas, along with a memory of the content of the text, which will be useful if you need to revisit it for more details. If it has made an impact on your thinking, this text may become a reference and resource the next time you want to check some facts about trees.

Predicting is involved in comprehension at the sentence level because of the redundancy of language. For example, in the phrase "that's the way things have always been," the word *been* is highly predictable both because of the past perfect tense and also because the saying is so familiar. The reader uses this predictability automatically both to solve words "on the run" and to check on reading accuracy. Readers also make predictions related to the meaning of the text. Every time you read, you go beyond the literal meaning of the text to generate ideas that:

- Are implied but not stated.

- Spark memories or emotions.

- Give rise to sensory images.

- Raise questions in your mind.

- Provide a basis for predictions.

All of these ways of thinking are possible because you are bringing meaning to the process.

Of course, there is an overlap between your own thinking and the writer's intended meaning (see Figure 3-3); that is the whole point of reading a text. Writers select and use language to express their own emotions, ideas, and themes. Fiction writers who create characters and tell their stories are also exploring and expressing some dimensions of human problems. Writers of nonfiction juxtapose facts in certain ways, again to express meaning. Readers who are effectively processing a text derive much of the writer's intended meaning.

For example, effectively comprehending *The Other Side* would require the reader to understand the historical significance of the setting and the deep societal divisions symbolized by the fence. The reader and writer would share a sense of the two girls' curiosity about each other and an awareness of peer pressure. In addition, the reader would probably create meaning that the writer could

Shared Meaning Between Writer and Reader

WRITER	SHARED MEANING	READER
▫ Life experiences	▫ Progression of events	▫ Personal connections
▫ Literary experiences	▫ Characters	▫ Interpretation of themes
▫ Symbols of meaning	▫ Descriptions of setting	▫ Sensory images
▫ Themes—intended meaning	▫ Facts	▫ Particular connotations for words, ideas
▫ Language resources	▫ Language	

Figure 3-3. *Shared Meaning Between Writer and Reader*

never anticipate, such as evoking childhood memories or connections to other texts like *Through My Eyes* (Bridges) or Robert Frost's poem "The Wall." As a reader, you might well miss some of the author's intentions, for example, the symbolic meaning of Annie's dancing in the rain, but that omission would not necessarily mean that you did not comprehend the text. Your selection and construction of meaning overlap the author's intentions but are not identical with them.

THINKING ABOUT *THE OTHER SIDE* AND *TELL ME, TREE*

For those who have lots of reading experience, *The Other Side* is a powerful scaffold for reading with understanding. Getting into the story, you realize that a contrast is being presented—Clover's side and Annie's side. This underlying structure flows through the book, helping you as a reader hold the deeper meanings in your mind. You anticipate that the plot demands that something be done to bring the two sides together, and you look for a resolution.

Another way of thinking involves stepping back from a personal involvement in the text to take an analytical stance. Analytical thinking allows you to consider the text as an object, noticing aspects of the writer's craft. In *The Other Side,* you may notice how the writer has signaled a feeling of nostalgia by using language like "that summer" or how the writer focuses on the fence not so much as a literal object but as a symbol of barriers as well as a bridge that makes it possible for the girls to become friends, each by moving into and staying in a neutral zone between their backyards. In *Tell Me, Tree* you might notice how the writer has skillfully inserted suggestions to help readers find out about trees for themselves, communicating aspects of the scientific process along with information about trees. This technique adds interest to the text.

An analytical stance enables readers to think critically, evaluating the content and quality of a text. Questions like these may come into your mind while reading *The Other Side:*

▫ Could this have really happened?

▫ Would girls have behaved that way in a small town at that time in history?

▫ Do the illustrations accurately reflect the times?

▫ Is the moral too obvious?

▫ Why doesn't the writer tell us more about Annie's family?

▫ Would Clover's mother really allow the friendship without warning her daughter to be careful?

▫ Why is the writer telling this story?

▫ What does the writer want to persuade me to think or do?

Processing *Tell Me, Tree* might raise these questions:

▫ Is this accurate information?

▫ What qualifications does the writer have?

▫ What evidence is there that the information is accurate?

▫ Are these good suggestions for finding out about trees?

▫ Is there enough information to make the text interesting?

▫ Is the information presented in an interesting way?

▫ What are the writer's perspectives, values, or attitudes?

▫ What is the writer trying to persuade me to do or think?

Questions like those above are not always answered, but effective, strategic readers, always raise them. In interpreting historical, biographical, current events, and similar texts, a reader's ability to think critically is an important aspect of deep comprehension.

On a first reading, aspects of craft are "transparent,"

because you are responding to the deeper meanings. Revisiting a text, however, leaves more attention free for analysis and can add to the enjoyment and interpretation of a text. Indeed, most of the time, we are unaware of our thinking processes. Too much analysis, especially during a first reading, can get in the way of deep engagement in and response to a text. No doubt you remember a novel or poem that you now dislike because it was overly dissected in a literature course.

IMPLICIT VERSUS EXPLICIT THINKING

This chapter examines thinking and describes the complex processes involved in broad strokes. The resulting understandings form a foundation for students' strategic actions. In drawing implications for instruction, though, we must exercise caution, because it is quite difficult to teach or even to demonstrate these complex internal operations.

Any time processes are made too explicit, there is a risk of interrupting comprehension. For example, just suppose while listening to a reading of *The Other Side*, you were instructed to take notes on all of the actions indicating that the girls liked each other. As sophisticated readers, you could perform that task, but there might be a drawback: you might not engage in the kind of deep reflection that allows you to understand the tone of the memoir or the symbolism of the fence. Or suppose you were instructed to read *Tell Me, Tree* in order to find out why trees are important. You would likely scan the text, finding the answer to the question but missing other interesting information that would have led you to revise your background knowledge. Of course, if finding the answer to one question is the only goal, scanning for that purpose may be appropriate. And this may be appropriate in a subsequent reading. But if the goal is to understand the text, a single purpose is not enough.

Whenever we instruct readers, we mediate (or change) the meaning they derive from their reading. Yet we must offer instruction that helps readers expand their abilities. There is value in drawing readers' attention to important aspects of the text that will enrich their understanding, but we need to understand that using effective reading strategies is not like exercising one muscle. The system must always work together as an integrated whole. Conversation before reading, at points during reading, and after reading

can stimulate questions and ideas in a reader's mind. By expressing your own ideas, you can demonstrate the kinds of thinking that readers do. All of this amounts to instruction, but it must be "light" enough to allow room for readers to expand and express their own thinking, not as an exercise but as a response to events or ideas in the text.

SYSTEMS OF STRATEGIC ACTIONS

The twelve strategic actions shown in Figure 3-4 will be explained in greater detail in the next two chapters. These twelve actions:

- Take place in the reader's head.
- Are not observable but can be inferred from the reader's behavior.
- Are related to thinking within, beyond, and about a text.
- Are used simultaneously by readers in highly integrated ways.
- Are activated constantly—before, during, and after reading.

These twelve actions, which are briefly categorized and defined below, help us realize the complexity of thinking that allows readers to gain the literal meaning of a text and simultaneously think beyond and about it. True, a great deal of the analytical thinking readers do happens as they reflect after the first or even subsequent readings, but this action is grounded in connections they have made or aspects of the text they have noticed while reading. And during reflection, readers often return to the text to reread the words (process them again) and gather more information.

STRATEGIC ACTIONS FOR SUSTAINING PROCESSING

Readers sustain processing by coordinating a variety of means to pick up and use information. This kind of information is, as Raphael (1986) says, "right there." The readers are thinking about information within the text, which is the basic foundation for other kinds of thinking.

Readers Solve Words

An efficient processor reads with high accuracy and knows the meaning of most of the words in a text. Readers use a range of word-solving strategies that involve:

- Relationships between the letters, letter clusters, and word parts (visible information) and the sounds of language (invisible information).

Systems of Strategic Actions for Thinking Within, Beyond, and About the Text

WAYS OF THINKING ABOUT THE TEXT	STRATEGIC ACTIONS FOR PROCESSING WRITTEN TEXTS	
Thinking Within the Text	Solving Words	Using a range of strategies to take words apart and understand what words mean while reading continuous text.
	Monitoring and Correcting	Checking on whether reading sounds right, looks right, and makes sense.
	Searching for and Using Information	Searching for and using all kinds of information in a text.
	Summarizing	Putting together important information while reading and disregarding irrelevant information.
	Maintaining Fluency	Integrating sources of information in a smoothly operating process that results in expressive, phrased reading.
	Adjusting	Reading in different ways as appropriate to purpose for reading and type of text.
Thinking Beyond the Text	Predicting	Thinking about what will follow while reading continuous text.
	Making Connections ▫ Personal ▫ World ▫ Text	Searching for and using connections to knowledge that readers have gained through their personal experiences, learning about the world, and reading other texts.
	Inferring	Going beyond the literal meaning of a text to think about what is not there but is implied by the writer.
	Synthesizing	Putting together information from the text and from the reader's own background knowledge in order to create new understanding.
Thinking About the Text	Analyzing	Examining elements of a text to know more about how it is constructed.
	Critiquing	Evaluating a text based on the readers' personal, environmental, or textual knowledge.

Figure 3-4. *Systems of Strategic Actions for Thinking Within, Beyond, and About the Text*

▫ Anticipation based on language knowledge (invisible information checked against visible information) at the word, phrase, and sentence level.

Word solving must take place within the context of continuous texts. In other words, readers must take words apart without losing meaning. They must also attend to the meaning of words.

Readers Monitor Their Reading and Correct Themselves When Needed

Efficient readers are always checking whether their reading sounds right, looks right, and makes sense. When all the information does not fit together, the reader notices and works on solving the problem until it does.

Readers Search for and Use Information

Literal understanding depends on accessing the important information in the text. Readers search all visible information in the text (print and illustrations) and derive what they need.

Readers Summarize as They Read

While processing a text, readers need to hold the important information in memory, which we can think of as continually reorganizing an ongoing summary. They put together important information and disregard what they think is irrelevant.

Readers Maintain Fluency

Proficient readers integrate information (visible and invisible) in a smoothly operating process that results in expressive, phrased reading. They read in phrases, use punctuation, and place stress on words to indicate awareness of meaning. Their voices rise and fall in an expressive way.

Readers Adjust their Reading

Individuals unconsciously change their reading behaviors as they encounter different texts for different purposes. They may scan for particular information then slow down to study that section. They may skim a text to get the gist. They may become so engrossed in a text that they "gobble it up." They may revisit texts to appreciate the writer's language.

STRATEGIC ACTIONS FOR EXPANDING THINKING

Thinking within the text is a complicated process, but doing so effectively frees one's attention for thinking beyond and about the text.

Readers Predict

Readers are constantly anticipating words, phrases, and sentences, but in a more global sense, we are always using information we already have and thinking about what will follow. Predictions in fiction are based on our understanding of characters, on the progression of the plot, on the influence of the setting, and many other kinds of information. Predictions in nonfiction arise from putting together what you already know with new ideas and information.

Readers Make Connections

Readers are always actively searching for connections to many different kinds of knowledge:

- Their personal experiences through which they have learned about people and life. Memories, emotions, atti-

tudes, perspectives, and sensory images arise in response to the processing of a text.

- Their content knowledge, gained through practical experience and other reading. Texts require that readers use background knowledge.

- Their textual knowledge, gained through reading experiences. By encountering many different kinds of texts, readers learn how they "work." (The genre discussion in Chapter 11 elaborates on this information.)

Readers Infer

Proficient readers use the literal meaning of a text to think beyond it. They hypothesize about what is not said explicitly but is implied by the writer. This "reading between the lines" is necessary on just about all texts but becomes more demanding at higher levels and is part of a reader's enjoyment of well-crafted texts.

Readers Synthesize

One of the primary purposes of reading is to learn. Readers:

- Acquire new information to add to what is previously known, reorganizing existing information in the process.

- Encounter new ideas, weigh them against their current attitudes, and decide whether to change.

- Grow in their understanding of people, settings, and events beyond their personal experience.

They put together information from either fiction or nonfiction texts with their own background knowledge in order to create new understanding.

Readers Analyze

Predicting, making connections, synthesizing, and inferring involve thinking beyond the text. Ultimately, though, proficient readers must be able to hold up texts as objects to think about them. Readers often reflect on a text after reading, but this thinking is based on what they notice while reading. Readers who are highly attuned to this kind of thinking find themselves thinking analytically even during processing.

Readers Critique

Readers also think critically about their reading, which is an important life skill. They evaluate a text based on their personal, environmental, or textual knowledge. They can speak to its quality, accuracy, or authenticity.

EFFECTIVE SYSTEMS FOR PROCESSING TEXTS

Readers build their network of strategic actions across time as they engage with increasingly challenging texts. In the next chapters, we will help you think about how you can help readers build these systems.

SUGGESTIONS FOR PROFESSIONAL DEVELOPMENT

ANALYZING OPPORTUNITIES FOR THINKING ABOUT TEXTS

Explore the comprehending process by observing readers discussing a common text.

1 Convene a group of colleagues who teach children about the same age—for example, grades three and four.

2 Select a fiction or nonfiction text that is appropriate for your students.

3 As a group, talk about the text, noting different kinds of thinking that are required by readers. Talk about opportunities for readers to attend to each aspect of the processing system.

4 Read and discuss this same text with your students in an interactive read-aloud, a guided reading lesson, or a literature discussion group. If possible, observe each other's classes and take notes.

5 Soon after, meet again to discuss the variety of student responses each of you observed. Discuss the evidence of:

□ Shared understandings that most readers/listeners derived.

□ Individually held meanings that may go beyond the writer's intentions.

□ Inferential thinking or examples when the readers were discussing what was implied but not stated.

□ Analytical thinking or examples when the readers reflected on the writer's craft.

6 Revisit the chart, "Strategic Actions for Thinking Within, Beyond, and About the Text" (Figure 3-4) to discuss how the students were using a variety of systems in the reading experience.

---

[1] These broad categories will be broken down into more detail in the next chapter.

CHAPTER FOUR

HELPING STUDENTS DEVELOP SYSTEMS OF STRATEGIC ACTIONS TO SUSTAIN PROCESSING

All readers, from the beginning reader to the fluent adult reader, have to use and integrate various kinds of information to create meaning from text.

—NEW ZEALAND MINISTRY OF EDUCATION

A written text prompts several kinds of thinking. In fact, systems of strategic actions are being used and expanded through the very act of thinking while reading. We want to support processing while at the same time realizing that heavy-handed teaching can actually interfere with text processing. Our goal as teachers is to enable readers to assimilate, apply, and coordinate *systems of strategic actions* without being fully aware that they are doing so. Readers' attention must be on the meaning of the text rather than on how to make their brains perform a particular operation.

Readers sustain the processing of a text by coordinating a variety of strategic actions for perceiving, internalizing, and using the information. While getting information by reading words, they must also sustain momentum and check on accuracy and literal understanding. Sum-

marizing the important information and adjusting the speed and style of reading make the process more efficient. The broad range of strategic actions related to reading introduced in Chapter 3 includes six systems for sustaining processing—for thinking within the text (see Figure 4-1).

WORD SOLVING

An efficient processor of text is one who reads the words with high accuracy, knows or can easily solve their meaning, and derives meaning from the larger units of language—phrases, sentences, paragraphs. It is obvious from the long list of operations in Figure 4-2 that readers use a wide range of strategic actions to solve words, but employ them in flexible ways.

Reading a text proficiently requires being able to recognize most of the words instantly and unconsciously, so that

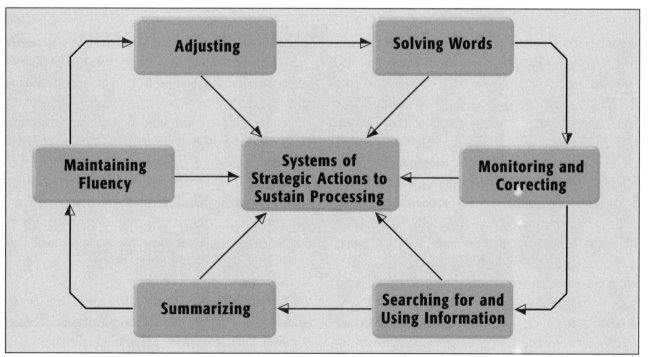

Figure 4-1. *Systems of Strategic Actions to Sustain Processing*

STRATEGIC ACTIONS FOR
Solving Words

Readers:
- Solve words using a wide range of efficient, flexible actions.
- Engage in sound analysis of words left to right.
- Recognize known words quickly.
- Partially sound words and complete the solving using language and meaning.
- Analyze words quickly by attending to critical features.
- Analyze words from left to right, using letters, letter clusters, syllables, or other word parts.
- Use text meaning, language, and visual information to support word solving.
- Use what is known about other words to solve unfamiliar words.
- Take words apart efficiently while reading continuous text.
- Use base or root words, prefixes, and suffixes to take apart longer, unfamiliar words.
- Use letter/sound relationships and visual information in connection with meaning and language.
- Use language and meaning to understand individual words.
- Use meaningful parts of words (e.g., roots, inflectional endings) to understand individual words.
- Perform all word-solving actions efficiently while understanding the meaning of the text.

Figure 4-2. *Strategic Actions for Solving Words*

one is free to think about the meaning. Developing readers stretch themselves by reading texts that contain some new and challenging words. They need to learn how to take these words apart while still focusing on meaning. If they know a large number of words on sight and are familiar with appropriate strategic actions for word-solving, readers are all set to do some good thinking; but comprehension is much more than just reading the words accurately.

Adults must recognize several hundred thousand words without effort in order to read proficiently. Word-solving strategies are built over time. It's important that young readers acquire a core of high frequency words that they know in every detail and can recognize instantly. It's also important for them to learn quick ways of relating word similarities by noticing word parts and using letter-sound relationships in strategic ways. If too much word solving

is required or if it is very slow, the process breaks down. Thinking becomes more limited.

Vocabulary generally refers to words for which we know the meaning. We all have *speaking, listening, writing,* and *reading* vocabularies, and while these sets of words overlap in large part, they are not precisely the same. Our speaking and writing vocabularies include those words we choose to express our meaning. We vary our oral vocabulary to suit the occasion. For example, we might use *acquire* in a formal presentation, *get* in a more casual conversation.

Reading and listening vocabularies are *receptive* and include words we know the meaning of when others (speakers and writers) use them. We read and understand many words we do not usually think to use in speaking or writing. For example, suppose you are reading *Resistance,* a novel by Anita Shreve, and encounter the word *triage:*

> Thérèse Dinant had not slept since the previous night, but, unlike Henri, she showed no signs of fatigue. She walked noisily into the house, as if all rooms in Belgium were open to her.
> "We treat the aviator first," Dinant announced, as though there had never been any question. Claire knew the aviator would be a priority: Save the airmen at all costs. But it was also triage. Tend to those who had the best chance of life. (p. 72)

Hmmm. You pronounce the word correctly by implicitly recognizing its French origin and connecting it with *trio* and *collage*. You also rapidly recall that you have read the word *triage* in connection with the practice of providing extra educational programs to only those children who *nearly* passed the test and thus show the best potential for improving a district's scoring profile. All of this happens in the blink of an eye, and you may be only peripherally aware of the process by which you determined the meaning of the word.

If you as an adult are reading *Tell Me, Tree* (a book described in Chapter 3), the words will not be difficult, but you may give a little more attention to the ones that are new to you, are highly technical, or are used in new ways. For example, the author introduces the word *crown* as meaning the top of a tree, and you may make a lightning-quick connection to the top of a person's head or something worn by royalty.

Employing these rapid actions in an almost unconscious way is a characteristic of effective readers. They use a range of problem-solving strategies to take words apart and understand word meanings while reading continuous text. These strategies include *anticipating* words, phrases, and sentences. For example, in the sentence "I see three little kittens" you know the noun *kitten* will end in *s* and do not need to give it a great deal of attention. The ability to anticipate comes from our knowledge of language. It is separate from the broader strategic action of *predicting*, which refers to putting together ideas to predict what might come next in a text or even after the conclusion, requiring the reader to think beyond the literal information provided. Prediction involves thinking beyond the text.

MONITORING AND CORRECTING

Proficient readers have strategies that operate in largely unconscious ways to check whether reading sounds right, looks right, and makes sense. They make sure there is a good fit among all sources of information (see Figure 4-3). The dissonance created by a mismatch alerts readers to search for more information, reconsider an idea, think about the meaning of a word, etc. If they read a word wrong, they may not even notice until a gap in meaning is detected, but then they will make repairs. Beginning readers often self-correct by returning to the beginning of the sentence, but as they become more proficient, they reread a phrase, or self-correct at the point of the word. Eventually this self-correction behavior is no longer overt as readers self-correct "in the head." (Clay 1991)

Reading *Tell Me, Tree,* you may make quick little mistakes in processing that you spend fractions of seconds repairing. For example, realizing that the book is about trees and having previously read about "white pine cones," you read the heading *Pin Oak Bark* as *Pine Oak Bark.* Dissonance is created as you wonder how a tree could be called a pine oak, then notice that *pin* has no *e*. You correct the mismatch, perhaps making a mental note to find out what distinguishes a pin oak tree.

After reading a few pages of *The Other Side*, you may realize that the story is told in the first person and you do not know the names of the two girls; thinking you simply missed the names, you search back quickly. Finding that there has been no mention of them, you become alert for when the names are revealed. Or, since *The Other Side* is written in childlike language, you may occasionally think you are misreading; using your own knowledge of syntax,

> ### STRATEGIC ACTIONS FOR
> ## *Monitoring and Correcting Reading*
>
> ***Readers:***
> - Check on themselves consistently while reading.
> - Know when reading makes sense and when they don't understand.
> - Use prior knowledge to notice whether reading makes sense, sounds right, and looks right.
> - Notice errors and work at correcting them while reading.
> - Work at fixing attempts that don't fit with the language, meaning, or print.
> - Notice whether reading makes sense in the context of the text or whether their own understandings fit with what is being read.
> - Stop, think, and search back or forward in the text to ensure correct understanding.
> - Notice when words make sense or sound right but don't look right.
> - Notice and use a range of punctuation or other textual features to check on or correct reading.
> - Self-correct when essential for understanding or reading out loud.
> - Use multiple sources of information to check on and correct reading.

Figure 4-3. *Strategic Actions for Monitoring and Correcting Reading*

you may even unconsciously rework the syntax, which in the case of this text would be inaccurate since the author has used a particular voice.

SEARCHING FOR AND USING INFORMATION

Understanding the literal meaning of the text requires searching for and using visible and invisible information. The strategic actions for acquiring and using information (see Figure 4-4) require the reader to be selective and to juxtapose many different sources. Information is used to monitor and check on reading accuracy, but it is also used to interpret, predict, infer, and otherwise construct meaning.

For example, reading *The Other Side,* you may wonder just what year the author is flashing back to (maybe the 1950s?) then search in the text for clues. By looking at the style of dresses worn by the girls and their mothers in the illustrations, you would have more information.

Reading *Tell Me, Tree,* you may encounter the unfamiliar words *phylum* and *cambium*, but you are unlikely to stop reading to look up the definitions. Simply by reading the

STRATEGIC ACTIONS FOR
Searching for and Using Information

Readers:

- Recognize and locate important information.
- Actively search for important information.
- Grasp the literal meaning of the text.
- Follow important events and characters.
- Select important facts and weave them together.
- Ask questions for which they want answers.
- Select information from narrative and expository texts.
- Use text structure to gain important information.
- Notice a variety of ways writers present information.
- Read the precise visual information to gain the exact meaning of the text.
- Recognize and use print features (punctuation, italics, headings), graphic features (diagrams, photographs, illustrations), and text tools (index, glossary, table of contents) to identify information.

Figure 4-4. *Strategic Actions for Searching for and Using Information*

STRATEGIC ACTIONS FOR
Summarizing

Readers:

- Accumulate and organize information extracted from a text.
- Select important information after reading and bring it together in a concise report.
- Remember and discuss important ideas, events, details, or other information related to comprehending the whole text.
- Distinguish between remembering/retelling all the details of a text and constructing a more selective account that serves as a brief report of important information.
- Put together text information in order to engage in ongoing interpretation.
- Put together what has been read while continuing to process the text.

Figure 4-5. *Strategic Actions for Summarizing*

words and mentally pronouncing them, you have already searched for and used the visual information in the words themselves. You then examine the context of the sentence and the paragraph and the graphic information in a labeled cutaway of a tree for information to help you understand what the words mean. In fact, your eyes would probably move to the illustration even before you read more of the text, because that is the most efficient way to get quick information.

SUMMARIZING

A summary is a reconstruction of the important information in a text. The reader remembers the text by selecting and sometimes organizing ideas and information (see Figure 4-5).

It is neither possible nor desirable for readers to remember every detail of what they read. Preparing for a test, we may try to remember pieces of information as we encounter them, but we quickly discover how helpful it is to select the important information and place it into categories. It's almost impossible to remember a string of unrelated facts.

All texts demand that the reader put together and hold in memory what has already been read while at the same time continue to process new information. As we process a text, we gain momentum. We carry information forward, using it to help us interpret the rest of the text. We store this information as a continually revised summary. You have probably had the experience of raising a sudden question about a character or event in a novel and searching back in the text for some important information you've left out of your ongoing summary. This is especially true with mysteries, because seemingly unimportant details may turn out to be essential in solving the crime.

The Cam Jansen mystery series makes the process of remembering details very easy for second-grade readers. Cam (short for Camera) is a young detective with a photographic memory. When she says "click," she stores the details she sees; at certain points in solving a mystery, she explicitly recalls these visual images. For example:

> Cam stood at the corner. She faced the park. "This is where I first saw the UFOs." Cam said. "Sometimes, if I stand where I first saw something, it helps me to remember."
> Cam closed her eyes. She said, "Click."
> Then she said, "I see it! It's a small tree between two evergreens. Come on, Eric. Let's go there and take a look. Maybe the UFOs left something behind."
> "Something," Eric said, "or someone." (Adler, p. 25)

This simple device scaffolds the reader's thinking as Cam remembers the important information.

The textual information that you access when you make connections among texts depends in part on your ability to remember them in summary form. In a sense, you carry a great deal of information around with you—probably thousands of text summaries on which you can draw to expand your thinking while reading. It is no wonder that good readers have the possibility of becoming better readers—the more you read, the more you have to bring to the comprehending process.

MAINTAINING FLUENCY

With all of these operations going on at the same time, the reader must sustain good momentum through the text. Reading is a fast-moving process related to the way language operates—all systems working smoothly together. Slowed down too much, it becomes unintelligible. Readers need to use language, meaning, and print in an integrated process that results in phrased, expressive reading. Figure 4-6 lists the evidence of fluent processing that good readers exhibit.

Reading fluency is a complicated business: every kind of strategy needed to achieve comprehension—rapid word solving, anticipating, monitoring, accessing and using information—works together to propel the reader through the text. In addition, fluency is related to the reader's purposes and the kind of text being read. You might skim over the print, looking for some specific piece of information. You might read slowly to savor beautiful language patterns or help you remember vital information.

Fluency is often described as speed or "expression," but it is much more. It is true that readers must maintain a good momentum simply to process the language with meaning, and it is obvious that expression is not identifiable in silent reading. Here, the reader is simply thinking about the ideas in the text, although some particularly poetic language might lead the reader to appreciate the sound of the words or the voice of a character. In oral reading, speed and expression become tangible. Of necessity, oral reading is much slower than silent reading and the voice reflects the meaning of the piece.

Fluency incorporates both phrasing and speed. Efficient processing means that readers group their words to reflect meaning and also move along at around 200 words per minute. Speed varies according to the reader's purpose, the type of text, the context for reading, and the level of difficulty. You might quickly read *The Other Side* to yourself to get ready for reading it aloud. When you read it aloud, you

> ### STRATEGIC ACTIONS FOR
> ## *Maintaining Fluency*
>
> **Readers:**
> - Recognize words rapidly and take apart unfamiliar words efficiently, automatically, and quickly.
> - Engage processing actions at a good rate (in *oral* reading, not too slow and not too fast).
> - Anticipate meaning and syntax.
> - Notice and use phrases as meaning units.
> - Use a rising and falling voice (intonation) to interpret the text.
> - Use appropriate stress on words to convey meaning.
> - Notice punctuation and use it (pausing appropriately) to produce accurate phrasing.
> - Slow down to problem-solve when needed but speed up for smooth, expressive processing.
> - Process all sources of information in a smooth, orchestrated way.

Figure 4-6. *Strategic Actions for Maintaining Fluency*

would read much more slowly, to communicate meaning to your listeners. You might also reread parts of the text slowly with emphasis to enjoy the language or reflect on the concepts. Consider how your reading rate would vary if you read *Tell Me, Tree* for these different reasons:

- Skimming to find out about a particular tree.
- Looking at the details in the pictures.
- Figuring out a lot of new words.
- Preparing for a test.
- Finding the answers to particular questions.
- Making a close comparison between bark textures.
- Taking notes for a report.

But fluency and phrasing also figure in silent reading. Certainly, your eyes are gathering the information from print rapidly, moving through the text with good momentum. But you are probably also processing the language by parsing the sentences into meaningful units. A great many factors work together to achieve fluent, phrased reading, including:

- Recognizing and analyzing words rapidly.
- Monitoring accuracy and understanding.
- Using prediction to make reading efficient.
- Recognizing meaningful phrases.

- Thinking about the meaning while reading.

It is essential to help readers maintain fluency as they read continuous texts every day, and matching books to their current abilities is a critical factor in providing support.

ADJUSTING READING

Efficient processors of text vary their reading in many different ways, depending on the demands of particular texts, the context for reading, and their purposes for reading (see Figure 4-7). They skim over ideas that don't interest them and slow down to examine a particular section closely. They slow down to problem-solve a word or resolve a question and then speed up again. They turn back in the text to check a hypothesis or search for information.

In addition, readers read different types of texts in different ways. You must read *The Other Side* from beginning to end, spending enough time on each page to appreciate the mood and feelings the pictures evoke. And this is definitely a book for rereading several times, not because you don't know how it turns out but because you need to think more about the layers of meaning. You read humorous stories in a different way than you read newspaper articles; you read mysteries by searching for and noticing clues that fill in pieces of the puzzle. Reading *Tell Me, Tree,* you might start at the beginning but turn pages rapidly, looking for sections of interest. Once you've read this book, you probably won't reread it unless you are searching for a particular piece of information or studying for a test.

Readers also read for different purposes. If you know you are going to discuss a text with others, you read it with a different lens than if you are just browsing. If you think you will be tested on the book, you may get very involved in trying to remember details. All of these adjustments are important for readers and are a rationale for having students read a great variety of texts: they need to become flexible as readers who can adjust.

STRATEGIC ACTIONS FOR
Adjusting Reading

Readers:
- Adapt reading for different genres and purposes.
- Vary rate and intonation as appropriate to text, audience, and purpose.
- Vary speed to accommodate problem solving.
- Skim or scan a text to search for particular information and slow down to examine some sections of a text in detail.
- Read some texts slowly, searching for and remembering important information.
- Scan for particular information as appropriate.
- Reread texts or parts of a text to confirm understanding.
- Read sections of a text as appropriate.

Figure 4-7. *Strategic Actions for Adjusting Reading*

SUGGESTIONS FOR PROFESSIONAL DEVELOPMENT

ANALYZING READING BEHAVIORS: SUSTAINING PROCESSING

1 Listen to Sheila and Francesca reading on the DVD included with this book. We have provided typed copy of the text for your reference.

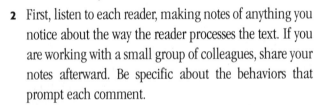

2 First, listen to each reader, making notes of anything you notice about the way the reader processes the text. If you are working with a small group of colleagues, share your notes afterward. Be specific about the behaviors that prompt each comment.

3 Then, examine the summary chart *Systems of Strategic Actions to Sustain Processing*, in Figure 4-1. Use the following form (Figure 4-8) to categorize your comments. Provide examples from your observations. You can also print this form from the DVD accompanying the book.

4 Share your findings with your colleagues. What particularly productive reading behaviors do you want to help each reader to use more often? Is anything getting in the way?

5 Don't worry if some of your observations seem to fit more than one category. Remember that all of these systems of strategic actions are happening simultaneously and the lines between them are not exact.

You may have some observations that simply do not fit into the framework of sustaining processing. Consider whether this evidence indicates that the reader is thinking beyond the text or about the text.

Analyzing Reading Behaviors Related to Sustaining Processing

QUESTIONS	COMMENTS	EXAMPLE(S)
1 Is there evidence that the reader is solving words (for example, using the first letter, taking words apart, recognizing words rapidly, using sentence context)?		
2 Is there evidence that the reader is monitoring and checking (for example, making several attempts, self-correcting, or asking for help)?		
3 Is there evidence that the reader is searching for and using different kinds of information (for example, rereading or turning back to search, searching for information in pictures, examining the text closely by repeating)?		
4 Is there evidence that the reader is remembering information in summary form (for example, recalling something previously read, self-correcting by using previous information, gaining momentum and ease toward the end of the reading)?		
5 Is there evidence that the reader is using fluent, phrased reading (for example, parsing language into phrases, reading the punctuation, reading at a good rate, making the voice reflect the meaning)?		
6 Is there evidence that the reader is adjusting reading pace or focus across the reading of the text (for example, slowing down to problem-solve and then speeding up)?		
General comments:		

Figure 4-8. *Analyzing Reading Behaviors Related to Sustaining Processing*

CHAPTER FIVE

HELPING STUDENTS DEVELOP SYSTEMS OF STRATEGIC ACTIONS FOR EXPANDING THINKING

I am always reading or
thinking about reading.

—JOYCE CAROL OATES

Knowledge of what texts demand in terms of strategic actions is the foundation for *teaching with a lens of comprehension*. Taking this stance, you keep strategic actions in mind during every form of reading instruction—interactive read-aloud, shared reading, literature circles or book clubs, guided reading, and independent reading.

Teaching decisions during reading instruction are made on the spot. You have an overall lesson plan, and this planning is very important, but moment-to-moment interactions during lessons focus readers' attention and show them how to engage or prompt them to engage in effective strategic actions. It is impossible to preplan all of those interactions, but you will be ready for them if you base your teaching on an integrated foundation of information. As shown in Figure 5-1, you have three sources of information to inform your teaching, each of which is important:

- Your students' present reading abilities as revealed by ongoing systematic observations of their oral reading, their talk about texts, their writing, plus your hypotheses about what they need to know and learn how to do as readers.

- The strategic actions that comprise proficient processing systems and that generate the kind of thinking that readers must do. You always teach with this processing system in mind. At whatever level students are currently reading, you want them to engage these strategic actions in a proficient way.

- The demands of the particular text you have selected to read aloud and use as a basis for a whole-group minilesson or have chosen to introduce in a shared or guided reading lesson.

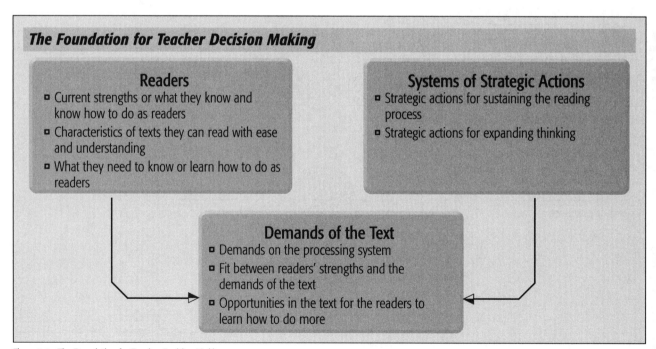

The Foundation for Teacher Decision Making

Readers
- Current strengths or what they know and know how to do as readers
- Characteristics of texts they can read with ease and understanding
- What they need to know or learn how to do as readers

Systems of Strategic Actions
- Strategic actions for sustaining the reading process
- Strategic actions for expanding thinking

Demands of the Text
- Demands on the processing system
- Fit between readers' strengths and the demands of the text
- Opportunities in the text for the readers to learn how to do more

Figure 5-1. *The Foundation for Teacher Decision Making*

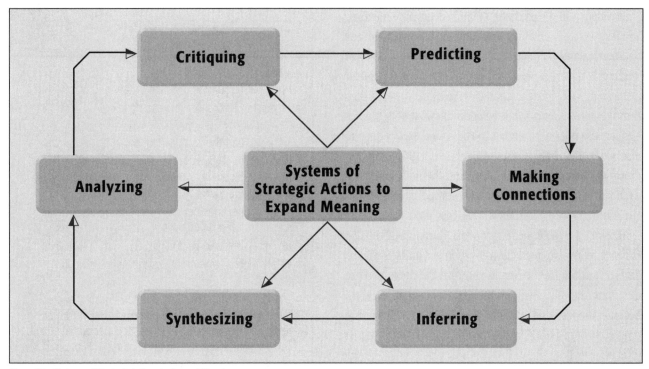

Figure 5-2. *Systems of Strategic Actions to Expand Meaning*

A wide range of strategic actions allows readers to expand their thinking about texts (see Figure 5-2).

PREDICTING

Prediction is a human trait, one that is essential for survival. Based on what we already know, we predict and prepare for what is coming next. Prediction makes reading more efficient and "safe," just as it does in connection with driving, cooking, or other activities. Efficient readers make predictions all the time (see Figure 5-3).

Language redundancy is a key factor in predicting. Readers use their implicit knowledge of the structure of language to narrow possibilities when decoding words. For example, reading the sentence "She walked noisily into the room," your knowledge of grammar predicts the *-ily* on the end of *noisily*, so less attention is needed to solve the word. The phrase "into the room" is also quite predictable for the reader with an implicit knowledge of English. We are not suggesting that the reader does not see or use the *-ily* ending; indeed, the proficient reader can always use it (for example, to check on the reading) if needed. But prediction provides a forward motion, which enables the reader to spend much less attention on letters and word parts.

STRATEGIC ACTIONS FOR
Predicting

Readers:

- Generate expectations based on genre, author, illustrator, or topic.

- Use knowledge of language syntax to narrow possibilities when decoding words.

- Parse the text into meaningful syntactic units that reduce the attention needed to decode words and allow the reader to determine meaning.

- Use knowledge of language syntax and meaning to propel reading forward.

- Use language redundancy to read words efficiently.

- Use meaning and syntax to anticipate and predict, making processing more efficient.

- Use knowledge of characters, plot, setting, or theme to anticipate what will happen next.

- Given the topic or organization, anticipate kinds of information in the text.

- Use prior knowledge to anticipate text content before reading, attend to content while reading, and reflect on content after reading.

Figure 5-3. *Strategic Actions for Predicting*

Readers also use prediction to help determine meaning. You may occasionally find it difficult to sort out the setting, characters, and conflict of a novel when you first begin reading it. Then, as you read on, you become completely immersed, following the characters and feeling with them through event after event. Prediction allows that to happen. Readers use not only their own background experiences but also what they have come to know about this particular group of characters, plot, setting, and theme to anticipate what will happen next. Using and holding this information (in summary form) in their minds, they gain momentum.

Earlier, we described how your thinking about *The Other Side* involves predictions as soon as you hear the title and look at the front cover. As you read the book, you predict that the girls will eventually meet, that they will become friends, that barriers may be broken down. You may even be a little disappointed that the integration the girls achieve is so slight. But you may also predict, beyond the story, that these girls will grow up and their memories of that summer will make them better people.

It is humanly impossible to encounter phenomena without making predictions. Even when reading an informational text like *Tell Me, Tree,* you do not sit passively waiting to be fed more information. Here are just a few of the kinds of predictions you make:

- You use the structure to anticipate the kind of information that will be presented in the book.
- You know to look for information in the labels.
- You know that when you see a section title you will find certain kinds of information.
- You know that a list means you will be following a series of events in sequence.

MAKING CONNECTIONS

Readers also make connections between the text and a wide variety of other kinds of knowledge. These connections create a rich fabric for expanding one's thinking, as shown in Figure 5-4. The kinds of connections readers make can be categorized as those based on personal knowledge, knowledge of the world, and knowledge of text.

PERSONAL KNOWLEDGE

Personal knowledge is made up of our everyday life experiences and our memories of those experiences. These expe-

---

STRATEGIC ACTIONS FOR
Making Connections

Readers:

- Bring background knowledge to the reading of a text.
- Understand purposes for reading texts.
- Interpret texts using personal experiences and knowledge of the world.
- Connect the topic, characters, plot, and setting to personal experience, knowledge of the world, and knowledge of other texts.
- Make connections between and among texts, noticing similarities and differences.
- Relate words to visual images.
- Relate feelings and emotions to the meaning in the text.
- Search for relationships among texts using a wide range of criteria—the same genre, author, illustrator, topic, theme, issue, setting, historical period, character (or a similar character), culture, ethnic group, or age group.

Figure 5-4. *Strategic Actions for Making Connections*

---

riences and memories are often tied to emotions, which we feel again as we interpret texts. Personal knowledge may include memories of people, events, and places. Memories can evoke sensory images. In reading *The Other Side,* for example, you may look at the illustration of Clover's mother hanging clothes on the line and remember the smell of fresh laundry that has been dried outdoors. You may look at the picture of the girls in town and remember wearing black patent-leather shoes with anklets. Reading *Tell Me, Tree,* you might remember the smell of leaves when you walk in the woods in the fall. Texts that evoke a great deal of personal knowledge are very interesting—even gripping—for readers. And even when we read about things far outside our personal experience, we can still use our personal knowledge to enhance our understanding.

KNOWLEDGE OF THE WORLD

We develop our knowledge about the world we live in—facts and the deeper implications of those facts—in many ways, including direct observation (most effective but not always possible), reading, being told by others, and watching films. When you approach an informational text like *Tell Me, Tree,* you automatically summon up what you already know about trees and recognize it in the text. Your attention is then directed to the information you don't know.

The Other Side is fiction, but your knowledge about the world is very helpful here too. Knowing something about interracial relationships in the U.S. is essential to truly understand this book. At its most basic level, the book is about two children who become friends. A reader who understands only that an African American and a white child got to know each other over one summer still misses the point. Only a reader who knows what segregation meant in those times (and is aware of the separations that still exist today) can richly understand the text.

KNOWLEDGE OF TEXT

Previous reading experiences have everything to do with processing a text successfully. The more you have read, the more information you carry with you the next time you read. An adult who has read *To Kill a Mockingbird* will have a richer understanding of *The Other Side*. Younger readers of *The Other Side* can make rich connections to books like *White Socks Only* (Coleman). Connecting texts is something readers do automatically; our individual reading histories figure strongly in our interpretations of texts. It does not matter which texts; the point is that we remember the texts that have strongly influenced us or raised our emotions. What you are reading provides the prompt, and you find yourself thinking of some book you read or a film you saw many years ago and haven't thought about since! But it is there in your repertoire. These connections may take any form—the setting, the time in history, the theme or problem, a character, the style of writing, the genre, and so on. Throughout Section III we discuss how teachers can deliberately foster students' ability to make connections to texts.

Connecting texts is the source of much of the pleasure of reading. We are drawn to texts that help us remember and better understand our own experiences and emotions, creating links between our own lives and those of other human beings who may be far distant in terms of culture, geography, or time. These personal connections arise from both fiction and nonfiction, and connections among texts enrich understanding in every genre. You might read a historical account of the Vietnam War, for example, and remember your own or your parents' or grandparents' experiences during that time. You might read *The*

Tapestries (Nguyen 2002), a fictional account of Vietnam before the war, and be struck by how starkly the war changed things. These personal and textual elaborations add interest and understanding, perhaps raise feelings and emotions, and create visual images.

INFERRING

As shown in Figure 5-5, true understanding means going well beyond what the author has explicitly stated. Proficient readers construct subtle meanings that the writer has implied through text or illustrations. They develop theories to explain characters and their actions. They often build elaborate visual images that they can recall even years later. You may have had the experience of first reading a book and picturing a character or setting and then being quite disappointed by the screen images shown in a film based on the book. That is why casting and screenplay were so important in *Harry Potter* films. Young fans were alert to detect any discrepancy. Impressed by a riveting performance, we can sometimes be persuaded to change our mental images, but the influence of the text is strong.

Sometimes we build whole worlds based on an author's sketchy descriptions. In one scene in *The Other Side*, Clover's mother watches the two girls on the fence. She says nothing, but as readers, we imagine the thoughts that may be going through her mind:

STRATEGIC ACTIONS FOR
Inferring

Readers:
- Understand what is not stated but is implied in the text (both print and illustrations).
- Make conclusions that are not stated but are based on information found in the text or illustrations.
- Make judgments about characters, events, theme, and plot that have not been explicitly stated.
- Think about the deeper meanings of text.
- Recognize symbolism and use it to interpret the text.
- Develop theories that explain characters' motives or events.
- Develop empathy for characters.
- Use background knowledge and information from the text to form theories about the significance of events.

Figure 5-5. *Strategic Actions for Inferring*

- "I hope this doesn't get Clover in trouble."
- "Annie seems like a nice girl, but I can't trust her."
- "Clover may be losing her other friends."
- "I'd better watch to be sure they don't go any further."
- "I wonder when things will change."

We don't know precisely what the author intended, but one purpose for including this scene may have been to raise such ideas in our minds.

Inferences spring from the language a writer uses. It is often more powerful to *show* than to tell. For example, instead of saying someone felt offended, a writer may say, "Her shoulders stiffened." It is left to the reader to seek the meaning through inference. We learn about characters in fiction by reading what they say or think, what they do, and what others say about them, and we draw conclusions and create theories based on that information.

When reading a biography, we search for insights into the thoughts, feelings, influences, and underlying motivations of the subject. Even if the author is not able to tell us what his subject said or thought, the information can be presented in such a way that the subject comes alive through inference.

Almost every text we read requires some understanding of its implications. Even a simple story such as *Baby Bear's Present* (Cowley) demands that readers make inferences. In this story (two pages are shown in Figure 5-6), Mother and Father Bear take Baby Bear to the store to buy a present. Baby Bear wants a car, but Father Bear tries to persuade him to get a train. It is not hard to figure out from the illustrations and text that Father Bear wants to play with the train himself, but this is not explicitly stated until Mother Bear intervenes on the next-to-last page. Working with children on a text like *Baby Bear's Present,* you would want to be sure that the discussion of the text involves talk about what Father Bear might have been thinking or why he was looking at the train.

This simple example makes very clear that literacy requires complex understanding that must be part of the reading process from the very beginning. The ability to make inferences is required in order to comprehend ever more challenging texts. It is not possible suddenly to begin to read between the lines in third or fourth grade. There is some demand for inference in every level of text, and we can intentionally foster the growth of this kind of strategic action in our teaching.

SYNTHESIZING

Learning is an integral part of reading. Whether we are reading fiction or nonfiction, we expect to gain something—enjoyment, ideas, amusement, escape, new information, different perspectives and insights, and so on. We expect reading to change us in some way. We take these new insights and information, and reorganize our previous thinking and knowledge. Most of the time, new information only adds to or slightly changes our existing knowledge, but there is always the chance that we will receive startling new insights or information that will force a major change in our own knowledge. Figure 5-7 lists some aspects of synthesizing.

"I like this toy train,"
said Father Bear.
"This little key makes it go."

"I can help Baby Bear
play with it at home.
Let's get the toy train," he said.

8   9

Figure 5-6. Baby Bear's Present

STRATEGIC ACTIONS FOR
Synthesizing

Readers:
- Develop new understandings from reading a text.
- Add new information to existing personal, environmental, and literary knowledge.
- Integrate new information into existing personal, environmental, and literary knowledge.
- Reorganize personal, environmental, and literary knowledge based on new information.
- Think about what the text really means.
- Think about how the text fits or doesn't fit with what is known.
- Deepen understanding of topics, concepts, or ideas by integrating new knowledge with prior knowledge.
- Expand personal understandings by incorporating experiences lived vicariously through texts.

Figure 5-7. *Strategic Actions for Synthesizing*

Students with little understanding of segregation may listen to *The Other Side* and not understand why the fence was such a "big deal." If that's the case, it would be important to provide some background information and help students develop new insights about the text. Chances are, they will then have a revised set of understandings to bring to the reading of texts like *Dear Willie Rudd* (Gray), a memoir in which a middle-aged lady in the South remembers the societal restrictions surrounding her dealings with an African American servant when she was a girl, or *Chicken Sunday* (Polacco), in which a little girl has a close relationship with a family of another race.

We find an informational text like *Tell Me, Tree* uninteresting unless it provides either new information or new ways of looking at what we already know. While reading, we quickly recognize, and perhaps confirm, the information we already know, but we especially notice new ideas that stand out as important. Synthesizing information gained by reading simply means learning, which makes reading worthwhile and pleasurable. As we synthesize, we deepen our understanding of topics, concepts, or ideas and expand our personal understanding of our own lives and those of others.

ANALYZING

As we experience many texts, we come to recognize the scaffolds that underlie understanding (see Figure 5-8). Most of

STRATEGIC ACTIONS FOR
Analyzing

Readers:
- Examine a fictional or informational text closely to better understand its elements and how it is constructed.
- Discover how writers craft meaning for readers.
- Understand how a text "works."
- Understand how texts are organized to provide important information.
- Understand how language is used in a text to convey meaning and emotions.
- Recognize various genres and their characteristics.
- Support thinking with textual evidence or evidence from personal experiences.
- Notice how word choice conveys particular meanings.
- Examine illustrations or other graphic features and how they evoke aesthetic responses and convey meaning.
- Recognize and use graphic features of texts (such as maps and charts) to increase understanding.
- Recognize and use literary features to expand understanding.
- Examine the whole text to determine how illustrations, text, and format communicate meaning in an integrated way.

Figure 5-8. *Strategic Actions for Analyzing*

us are so familiar with narrative structure we don't even think about it as we read, but this implicit knowledge helps us follow a story:

- Presentation of central and supporting characters and the setting.
- Presentation of a problem.
- Episodes or events.
- High point or climax of the story.
- A resolution of the problem or conclusion.
- Brief closing or denouement.

Of course, narrative texts can be much more difficult than the simple outline above. Some ways of introducing complexity into a narrative include:

- Multiple or parallel stories involving different characters.
- Changes of setting, each having a different impact on characters.
- Presentation of episodes in some order other than chronological.

- Surprise endings that present additional high points after the story seems to be finished.

- Devices such as flashbacks or "stories within stories," in which the narrative switches to a character's own memories.

- Changes of perspective to reflect different characters' stories or points of view.

The more complex the structure, the more demands are placed on the reader. In *The Kitchen God's Wife* (Tan), for example, the central character, Pearl, begins the narrative, and the book is told from her point of view. At a point, however, the story becomes that of Pearl's mother, also told in the first person. The reader is required to construct the larger meaning by weaving together the stories of both women.

The structure an author chooses is related to genre. For example, fantasy is usually narrative, but the writer first spends a lot of time creating the imaginary world, so that the reader can suspend reality and accept the parameters of the new world. Once this world is established, the writer may not violate it by suddenly introducing elements that clash with it. In fantasy, dealing with the characteristics of the setting often increases the demands on the reader.

Nonfiction texts are organized in quite different ways from fiction. Even a quick examination of *Tell Me, Tree* reveals that the information is not presented in narrative form. Instead, the reader explores information that is organized into categories: types of trees, how trees grow, descriptions of trees, as well as descriptions of the processes of growth and photosynthesis. Writers of nonfiction employ underlying structures in ways that help them present information. For example, by contrasting the different kinds of trees and where they grow, the reader can build concepts about trees in general. The idea that the sun is a causal agent, triggering photosynthesis, which, in turn, helps trees grow, is a fundamental understanding. Readers of nonfiction learn to look for underlying structures, including:

- Enumeration (presenting information in sequence).

- Description (providing language that helps to build visual images).

- Chronological sequence (telling something in the order it appears).

- Cause and effect (presenting something that has happened and telling one or more reasons or causes).

- Comparison and contrast (presenting two objects, characters, issues, situations, settings, etc., and telling how they are alike and different).

- Problem/solution (presenting a problem and posing a solution or solutions.)

To process description, readers gather and integrate important details that may raise visual images. Illustrations are often present in informational texts because it is so important for readers to be able to see as well as read about what is being described. Temporal sequence, on the other hand, requires not only noticing order but also understanding that the order of events, steps, procedures, or processes is extremely important. Compare/contrast entails still other demands. Readers must accurately derive descriptions or details of two different phenomena or events and identify what is similar or different between them. Cause and effect requires readers to relate an effect to its cause. Problem/solution provides a related demand. Here, readers need to recognize aspects of a problem and then search the text for solutions. They also need to see relationships between problems and ways to solve them in order to understand why solutions are workable.

All About Frogs, by Jim Arnosky, begins by presenting a comparison between frogs and toads (see the sample pages in Figure 5-9). By helping the reader see how these two "look alike" animals are similar, as well as how they are different, the writer not only imparts useful information and perhaps clears up common misunderstandings but also helps the reader understand frogs better—their size, their habitat, their color, and so on. He also describes the life span of frogs from egg to adult, a temporal sequence. Finally, at the end of the book, Arnosky points out how environmental pollution may pose problems for frogs—a problem with an implied solution.

All About Frogs uses all the underlying structures mentioned above. In fact, almost no text will be "pure" in that it includes only one kind of structure; writers typically use them in combination. Readers recognize and use these structures in combination and in sequence, largely unaware of how they are processing the information.

Figure 5-9. All About Frogs

Novices, however, may not know how to look for and use text structure to assist their understanding. Chapters 13 and 14 provide more information about text structure, and you will find instructional approaches.

Analyzing a text involves stepping back and considering it as an object, a highly sophisticated set of strategic actions. Another aspect of analysis is to recognize aspects of the writer's craft:

- How has the writer used language to create mood or help us understand the significance of an event?

- What details and events has the writer chosen to help readers understand how a character feels?

- What language helps us understand what motivates characters in the book?

- How is the writer showing us rather than telling us?

- How does the writer engage us from the very first sentence?

- How does the writer signal that time has passed (or employ other signals)?

- What language lets you know what the character is really like?

- How does the writer help us feel that the character is real—through what he says or thinks, what he does, and what others say or think about him?

By closely examining texts, readers not only better understand the meaning but also gain insights into the writer's craft, which contributes to their own writing ability. They notice word choice and figurative language such as metaphor, understand the importance of symbolism, and examine how writers use illustrations or other graphic features to evoke aesthetic responses. Viewing a text as an object usually requires revisiting and discussing it.

CRITIQUING

The ultimate requirement of the reader is to take a critical stance (see Figure 5-10). Reading critically is a necessity in a free society. Not everything you read is accurate; often persuasive material must be judged on its merit and connected to its source. One perspective may be presented, but the reader must seek other perspectives. Moreover, readers are required to judge the quality of a text. Questions to ask of fiction texts include:

- Do characters and their actions seem real? Are plot, characters, and events consistent with life experience?

- Do characters develop in a plausible way? Are their motivations believable? Would people really act this way, given the motivations stated or implied?

- Is the writer's use of language skillful?

- Is the plot believable? Is it engrossing?

- Does this story come from the writer's own experience? If not, how could this writer have learned about this kind of story?

- Am I enjoying this reading?

Questions to ask of nonfiction texts include:

- What are the qualifications of the writer to produce this text?

- What references are offered to support the information in the text?

- Has the writer organized the information in a coherent way?

- How well has the writer selected the information presented? Are there any gaps?

- What is the writer's perspective? Are there other perspectives?

- What is the writer trying to persuade the reader to think or do? Is it warranted?

- Are there underlying messages that the writer is trying to convey? Are they justified?

- Does the writer have biases? What are they? How are they justified? What are the competing points of view?

It is obvious from this array of questions that critical reading demands highly sophisticated strategic actions. Yet, even young children can talk about which version of *The Three Little Pigs* they like best and why. As students become more sophisticated, they delve more deeply into texts. Upper ele-

---

STRATEGIC ACTIONS FOR
Critiquing

Readers:
- Make judgments about a text.
- Reflect on and evaluate a text.
- Consider thoughtfully the strengths and weaknesses of every aspect of a text.
- Use information from a text to think about social issues, world issues, human problems.
- Assess whether a text is consistent with what is known through life experiences.
- Judge whether a text is authentic in terms of plot, setting, or characters.
- Judge whether a text provides accurate information.
- Judge the qualifications of a writer to produce an authentic fiction or nonfiction text.
- Examine and discover gender, racial, cultural, religious, or age bias in a text.
- Appreciate the aesthetic qualities of a text.
- Evaluate the completeness of a text.
- Judge the writer's perspective.
- Evaluate the effectiveness of a text.

Figure 5-10. *Strategic Actions for Critiquing*

---

mentary students, for example, may explore a text like Lowry's *The Giver* not just as a good story but as a warning against an oppressive governmental or religious presence in society.

A FINAL CAVEAT

It is always hazardous to try to describe what is going on in a reader's mind, and any discussion of strategic actions risks simplifying the complex process of proficient reading. There are hundreds of ways to describe mental processing, and we have not dissected all the thinking we do while reading. But we must be explicit about some of the important systems of strategic actions that are part of the complex processing network that goes on in our heads so that we can use this knowledge as a lens for teaching. Paying attention to and understanding these systems of strategic actions is a foundation for planning explicit lessons, helping students during individual conferences, introducing texts in guided reading, and guiding discussion after reading.

SUGGESTIONS FOR PROFESSIONAL DEVELOPMENT

ANALYZING READING BEHAVIORS: EXPANDING THINKING

1 Gather a group of colleagues. Make a plan to audiotape reading conferences with two readers at two points in time. Select two readers who are reading at two very different levels.

2 Sit next to each reader and invite him to share what he is thinking about a text he is reading as you take notes. You may want to ask probing questions related to the six systems of strategic actions for expanding thinking as outlined in the chart below. You can also print this form from the DVD that accompanies this book.

3 Gather together and discuss each of the six areas using examples from your conference notes.

4 Finally, talk about key understandings about the systems that you gained from the activity with your students and your collegial discussion. List the key understandings on a chart.

5 Share your findings with your colleagues. In what areas is the reader's thinking particularly productive? How do you want to expand this reader's thinking?

6 Don't worry if some of your observations seem to fit more than one category. Remember that all of these systems of strategic actions are happening simultaneously and the lines between them are not exact.

Analyzing Reading Behaviors Related to Expanding Thinking		
QUESTIONS	COMMENTS	EXAMPLE(S)
1 Is there evidence that the reader is making predictions (for example, making comments while reading, acting surprised or validated, responding to invitations to predict, making predictions about what will happen next after the story ends)?		
2 Is there evidence that the reader is making connections (for example, connecting any ideas in the text to his own life, to his background knowledge of the world, or to other texts)?		
3 Is there evidence that the reader is making inferences (for example, interpreting characters' motivations, expressing what the author might have meant)?		
4 Is there evidence that the reader is synthesizing new information (for example, identifying new learning, expressing curiosity about learning more)?		
5 Is there evidence that the reader is analyzing the text (for example, commenting on the author's writing style, noticing how the text is organized, noticing particular techniques the writer uses to provide information or make the text believable)?		
6 Is there evidence that the reader is thinking critically (for example, going beyond opinion to agree or disagree with something in the text, providing evidence for comments)?		

General comments:

Figure 5-11. *Analyzing Reading Behaviors Related to Expanding Thinking*

CHAPTER SIX

UNDERSTANDING THE FLUENT READER: EFFECTIVE PROCESSING

The most compelling reason to focus instruction on fluency is the strong correlation between reading fluency and reading comprehension.

—RICHARD ALLINGTON

Think of something you can do fluently: ride a bike, drive a car, surf, play the piano, bake bread. Words like *fluid, easy, coordinated, unconscious, effortless, trouble-free, flowing, adaptable, flexible, fast* probably come to mind. All these activities involve smoothly coordinated movements and rapid adjustments. Any one of them performed dysfluently can lead to disaster.

Proficient computer keyboarders are only subliminally aware of the automatic fingering patterns they are using. Alerted to a mistake by undecipherable letter patterns on the screen or a feeling in the fingers, they instantaneously decide whether to correct the error immediately, go on to the end of the line or paragraph before doing so, or run the spell-checker software later. Their main stream of thought, however, remains focused on constructing the text. In fact, while emailing or text messaging, keyboarders often ignore errors and print conventions. Fluent keyboarders have a real advantage: the less attention we have to pay to our typing, the freer we are to think about what we are saying on email.

Learning any task begins slowly and involves approximations, but the goal is to achieve enough fluency within a short time to be able to feel comfortable with the whole activity and how it is supposed to go. Everything we do proficiently has this quality of fluent action. It may take years to become really good at something, and we may slow down from time to time for study and practice, but in general, building expertise means engaging in as fluent a rendition of the activity as we can manage each time we try it.

Fluent reading is usually described as being fast and expressive. Rapid word recognition is a necessary factor, but that alone does not explain reading fluency, which is as complex as comprehension itself. We define fluent reading as *using smoothly integrated operations to process the meaning, language, and print*. We do not necessarily include the word *fast,* although certainly momentum is important. We may read prose or poetry aloud slowly in order to covey the meaning. We may skim an article looking for the section we want, processing basic information quickly but without much attention to language structure or writing style. Fluent readers adjust their speed according to purpose and context.

FLUENT AND DYSFLUENT READERS

Fluency is a critical element of reading instruction, even though some curriculum guides and benchmark assessments encourage teachers to focus solely on accuracy. But accurate reading, especially if it is slow or sounds robotic, is no guarantee of comprehension. While fluent, phrased reading and comprehension are not identical, they are highly interrelated. In 1998, a national report (Snow, Burns, and Griffin 1998) emphasized the important role of fluency in a proficient reading process. In 1995, a large-scale descriptive study found high correlations between scores on a rubric measuring phrased and fluent oral reading and scores on tests of comprehension (Pinnell, et al.). In 2002, a national panel convened to synthesize the body of research on reading instruction pointed out the important connections between fluency and comprehension (NICHD 2002). Yet, as Allington said in 1983, fluency is often neglected in today's reading instruction.

As teachers, our ears are tuned to judge the accuracy of our students' comments on the content of a text. Sometimes "passing" a benchmark or criterion involves those judgments alone. But we also need to tune our ears to phrasing and intonation. No one characteristic describes the complexity of what fluent readers do. In fact, it is sometimes easier to describe reading that is *not* fluent. Figure 6-1 compares fluent and nonfluent readers in terms of both observable behaviors and hypotheses about the underlying cognitive/linguistic processes.

When we observe fluent readers or listen to them on tape, we notice how they group words together into phrases, stress words in a meaningful way, use rising and falling tones to reflect punctuation and meaning, and vary their speed. Fluent readers may deliberately slow down for emphasis and then speed up again. If fluent readers make an error or need

Observable Behaviors of Fluent and Nonfluent Readers

NONFLUENT READER	FLUENT READER
Observable behavior:	**Observable behavior:**
▫ Fails to reflect punctuation with variation in the voice.	▫ Reflects punctuation with variation in the voice—pausing, intonation, pitch, stress.
▫ Pauses randomly, not reflecting logical phrase units.	▫ Pauses appropriately to reflect meaningful phrase units (although not always) in response to punctuation.
▫ Reads in a choppy or word-by-word way.	
▫ Uses few rising and falling tones or monotonously applies rising and falling tones to produce "droning."	▫ Groups words into phrases that reflect meaning.
	▫ Uses rising and falling tones in a way that is related to text meaning and punctuation (is not monotonous).
▫ Stresses few words, or places inappropriate stress on words.	▫ Places stress on words in a way that reflects meaning.
▫ Uses little or no expression; sometimes uses inappropriate expression.	▫ Uses expression to reflect his interpretation of the meaning of the text.
▫ Reads slowly.	▫ Reads with good momentum, although not so fast that phrasing is lost.
▫ Fails to vary speed or varies it in an inconsistent and unpredictable way.	▫ Varies speed, slowing down and speeding up for various purposes.
▫ Fails to differentiate dialogue from other forms of text.	
▫ Reads slowly or stops in an attempt to pick up and remember all the details.	▫ Reads dialogue in a way that reflects aspects of characters, their ways of expressing themselves, and oral language.
▫ Reads in a way that does not reflect awareness of language syntax.	▫ Focuses on meaning; doesn't get bogged down in details.
	▫ Reads in a way that reflects awareness of language syntax, with error behavior indicating such awareness.
Underlying strategic actions:	**Underlying strategic actions:**
▫ Processes visual information slowly with many attempts at words and many overt self-corrections.	▫ Processes visual information rapidly and efficiently.
▫ Has inefficient word-solving strategies; tends to "sound out" words using the smallest units (individual letters).	▫ Understands how pauses, pitch, and stress communicate the author's intended meaning.
	▫ Recognizes features of known words and uses these features to get to words that are unknown.
▫ Reads one word at a time instead of word groups.	▫ Reads word groups instead of single words.
▫ Reads as if not aware of oral language, with errors that do not indicate knowledge of structure.	▫ Uses oral language to anticipate what may happen next in the text.
▫ Tends to ignore punctuation as a tool for constructing meaning.	▫ Uses punctuation to construct meaning.
▫ Does not differentiate dialogue from other text.	▫ Notices dialogue and processes it as the character's voice, including hypotheses of intonation patterns and quality.
▫ Tends to stop often or to read very slowly even when accurate.	▫ Easily solves problems "on the run," slowing down but speeding up again in a smooth process.
▫ Reads slowly or stops in an attempt to pick up and remember all the details.	▫ Doesn't get bogged down in details.
▫ Misses much of the meaning and has to slow down to consider meaning.	▫ Rapidly accesses meaning.
▫ Gives so much attention to word solving that there is little left to give to prior knowledge; doesn't anticipate meaning.	▫ Uses prior knowledge and understanding of the world to anticipate what will happen in the story.

Figure 6-1. *Observable Behaviors of Fluent and Nonfluent Readers*

to solve a word, they will often repeat the sentence, gathering momentum by first producing a meaningful phrase. Fluent readers sometimes correct misread ending punctuation (for example, using a falling tone when there is a question mark). Fluent readers avoid a monotonous, singsong "reading voice." Their tones rise and fall; pauses are strategic, adding to the interpretation. They sound as if they are speaking, not reading individual words.

All these observable behaviors are evidence that language is being processed in a meaningful way. The phrasing is logical and conveys meaning—both the readers' idea of the writer's intended meaning as well as their own interpretation. Readers use punctuation as well as their own knowledge of syntax or structure to guide phrasing. Fluent readers use their anticipation of what will come next in a text as a way to move forward. As they read, they notice dialogue and differentiate it from other parts of the text. Their attention is on the meaning of the text.

Most readers in your classroom are still expanding their ability to process written texts and are probably somewhere in between the two extremes described in Figure 6-1. It also makes a difference what they are reading! Most readers cannot be labeled simply as *fluent* or *nonfluent,* because their performance depends on:

- The familiarity of the concepts in the text.
- Their familiarity with the genre or text type.
- The accessibility of language structures.
- Their vocabulary.
- The number of known words in the text.
- The number of words that are easy to solve.

Almost any reader in your class will be able to read certain texts fluently; other texts will be so difficult that the reading process breaks down. Even proficient adult readers may become dysfluent when processing a challenging text, such as a legal document, an archaic text, or a highly technical scientific report. Think how difficult "The Twa Corbies" (see Figure 6-2) would be to read aloud fluently even after several practices. (We'll visit this poem again in Chapter 31).

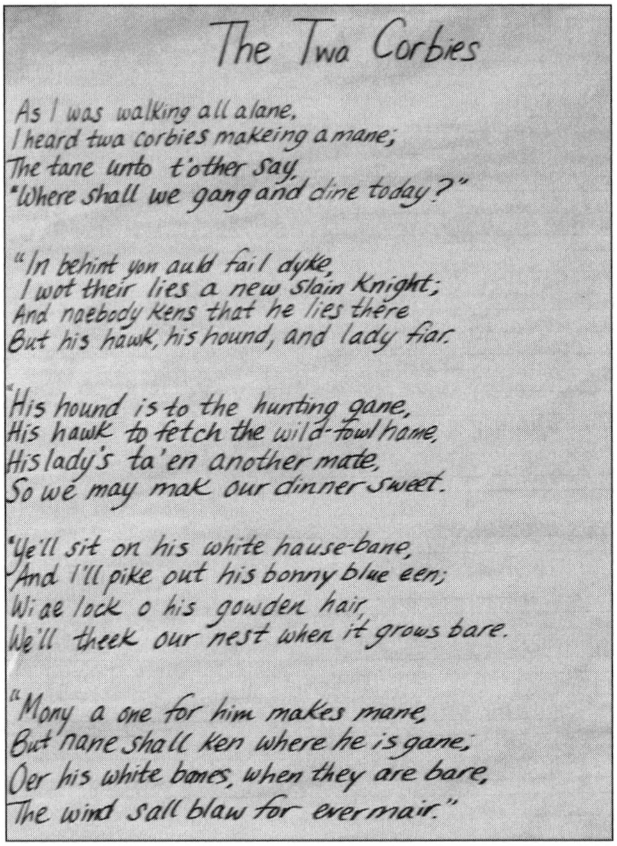

The Twa Corbies

As I was walking all alane,
I heard twa corbies makeing a mane;
The tane unto t'other say,
"Where shall we gang and dine today?"

"In behint yon auld fail dyke,
I wot their lies a new slain Knight;
And naebody kens that he lies there
But his hawk, his hound, and lady fiar.

"His hound is to the hunting gane,
His hawk to fetch the wild-fowl hame,
His lady's ta'en another mate,
So we may mak our dinner sweet.

"We'll sit on his white hause-bane,
And I'll pike out his bonny blue een;
Wi ae lock o his gowden hair,
We'll theek our nest when it grows bare.

"Mony a one for him makes mane,
But nane shall ken where he is gane;
Oer his white bones, when they are bare,
The wind sall blaw for evermair."

Figure 6-2. The Twa Corbies

DIMENSIONS OF FLUENCY

Fluency in itself is not the goal of reading; our concern is its integral connection with comprehension (and all aspects of the processing system). We know that when fluency is disrupted, so is understanding:

> Nothing destroys the meaning more rapidly than droning through the phrases and punctuation marks, pausing at points which break up the syntactic group and the sense. (Clay 1991)

We can look at fluency from many different angles:

- Fluency is not one-dimensional; it has many aspects.
- Fluency is needed at many levels of processing.
- Fluency is integral to language processing.
- Rapid, accurate word recognition and word analysis play important roles in fluent reading.
- Readers have resources that contribute to fluency.

We will examine key contributors to fluency. Think about how each involves different aspects of the print, language, and meaning in texts.

ORAL VERSUS SILENT READING

Up to now, our discussion of fluency has centered on oral reading. This focus may seem paradoxical, since most of the reading we do as adults is silent, and the current emphasis in both instruction and testing, at least after about late grade one, is on silent reading. At one time, oral reading received great attention in society and school. In a review of the history of reading fluency, Rasinski (2005) points out that oral reading was the "end" goal or outcome of instruction in colonial times. Books were scarce and many people could not read. Literate individuals performed a valuable role in reading aloud to others.

As literacy became more commonplace, the need for oral reading declined. Silent reading became dominant—and was tested via standardized measures—in schools from the early part of the 1900s to today. Attention to fluency in instruction and assessment consequently declined (Rasinski 2005). "Round-robin" reading still took place, but teachers generally listened mainly for accuracy.

More recently, however, researchers' explanations of processing have brought fluency to the fore as an important contributor to proficient reading. Upper elementary or middle school students who are struggling have real problems with fluency, perhaps even more than with decoding.

What we can observe to measure fluency are superficial characteristics of reading, but there is a link to deeper processing (Rasinski 2005). Even when we read silently, essential elements of fluency are probably present. Processing takes little or no attention; we are absorbed in the information or the story.

When individuals are reading with fluency, they process the text smoothly; solve words easily, efficiently, and rapidly; discern syntax; and focus on the meaning. So what evidence is there that your students' silent reading is fluent? If they move through the text in a reasonable period of time, if they can talk coherently about the text in a way that shows they understand it, and if they can remember and return to specific evidence in the text that supports their opinions, then they are probably reading with fluency. Sampling oral reading performance, always assuming the text is one they can read with accuracy, provides the final behavioral evidence you need to judge the quality of their reading.

LEVELS OF FLUENT PROCESSING

It is helpful to conceptualize fluent processing at a number of levels: letter, word, phrase/sentence, and text (see Figure 6-3). Fluency at each of these levels is needed to ensure that the reader is processing effectively. Some of your students may be fluent at one or two of these levels but not all four, in which case they will need the benefit of specific instruction.

Fluency at the Letter Level

Fluent readers pick up the visual information in print quickly. The differences between the letters of the alphabet are extremely small but very important. It is necessary, for example, to slide the eyes along print, picking up the information needed to distinguish letter features. Fluent readers know these distinguishing features so well they detect them rapidly, unconsciously, and precisely. Readers seldom think about letters; they simply use them. They have learned how to look at print.

Young children who are just learning to read may find letters a challenge, but when they have had a great deal of practice noticing and using letters, the process becomes automatic. At the early text levels (A through about C text levels are explained in Chapter 12), young readers are just beginning to use visual information along with language and meaning in texts. They may not read fluently because they are learning how to look at print and understand how it works. They must learn, for example, to:

- Make the eyes move left to right and return to the left margin for each new line.
- Match one spoken word with one written word, noticing and using space.
- Notice mismatches based on the letters in words.
- Solve words using letter/sound relationships.
- Check on their reading using visual information and meaning.

Beginners give more attention to letters because they are just establishing a reading process.

Fluency at the letter level is essential but not sufficient for effective processing. Readers must move beyond this level and use letter information smoothly and automatically. Their eyes will still pick up all visual information, but they do not need to give conscious attention to it. They do not see letters as isolated units but as connected to the other letters that make up word parts. Only when some dissonance arises do they give closer attention to letters.

Fluency at the Word Level

Fluent readers recognize whole words quickly and auto-

Fluency at Four Levels of Processing

LEVEL	KEY TO PROCESSING WITH FLUENCY
Letter	□ Distinguish the features of letters. □ Access the visual information rapidly and automatically. □ See letters not as isolated items but in connection with other letters within words. □ Process the visual information without need for conscious attention.
Word	□ Recognize whole words quickly, both short and more complex ones; be free to concentrate on meaning. □ Recognize familiar words easily. □ Use word parts automatically in a largely unconscious process. □ Solve words rapidly while reading continuous text. □ Treat words as connected rather than isolated items.
Phrase/ Sentence	□ Parse language into phrases that make sense. □ Notice and use punctuation to assist in identifying phrase units and sentence structure. □ Notice and use sentence structure as key to meaning. □ Notice and use sentence structure to support reading momentum. □ Stress words in ways that reflect the author's meaning. □ Understand how one sentence flows into another in the creation of meaningful text.
Text	□ Anticipate what will logically come next. □ Use previous information, syntax, vocabulary, and writer's tone to provide momentum while reading. □ Understand and use the structure, or organization, of the text to process it effectively. □ Use personal background knowledge to support momentum.

Figure 6-3. *Fluency at Four Levels of Processing*

matically, both short and complex, without engaging in conscious problem solving. With both longer known words and new words, they automatically use larger word parts to solve words, cue phrasing, and arrive at meaning. Fluent readers do not treat words as isolated items, solving one at a time. Instead, they see words as related to one another in highly systematic ways. They are not processing words, but recognizing strings of language. These processes are largely unconscious.

Fluency at the Phrase/Sentence Level

Although it is more evident in oral reading, effective processors always parse language (group words) into phrases that make sense. They understand they are reading language, not words. Sometimes punctuation assists in this process, but the reader must go beyond these signals to use knowledge of meaningful syntax. For example, to process the text in Figure 6-4, a reader would put words together into phrases, like this:

["Yes,"] [said the ducks.]
["You can fly] [with us."]
[But] [pigs can't fly.]
[So] [Peaches went on.]

Or

["Yes,"][said the ducks.]
["You can] [fly with us."]
[But pigs can't fly.]
[So Peaches] [went on.]

There are a limited number of additional ways to parse the text above. Speakers of a language have ways of parsing, or dividing language into phrases, that are shared. That is why we notice the "accent" of a non-native speaker of English not only in the way the words are pronounced but also in the unfamiliar intonations and phrase groupings.

Readers must also group these phrase units into sentences, again assisted by punctuation. When reading aloud to your students, you may sometimes read right over a period or question mark then correct yourself by repeating the

"Yes," said the ducks.
"You can fly with us."

But pigs can't fly.
So Peaches went on.

Figure 6-4. Peaches the Pig

sentence or last phrase using a falling tone for the period or a rising tone for a question mark. Whether and how the sentence ends is an essential part of conveying the meaning to the listener. Sometimes deliberate misuse of stress and pitch is funny. For example, turn the question "What are you doing?" into "What are you? Doing." The second expression sounds quite strange, even humorous.

Today's new technology demands a written language with more of the characteristics of oral language; expression must be there to convey meaning. Text messaging by cell phone requires instant, expressive, highly communicative language, so new abbreviations, punctuation marks, and symbols have been added. For example, Tessie sent a text message to her Aunt Irene from Greece:

Hey ANT I!
gone 2 a kool island zabynthos. ive nvr seen n e thing as butiful as their port! awsum, met soccer team—cute boyz, haha, ill brb. Have smthing 4 u. nm. ttyl. lol! Tessie

(Note: *brb* = be right back; *nm* = never mind; *ttyl* = talk to you later; *lol* = lots of love.)

These new forms of communication emphasize and require fluency.

Fluency at the Text Level

Ultimately, the reader must use comprehension itself to support fluency. The National Reading Panel examined empirical research on reading fluency and described it as "a bridge between comprehension and phonics." While this description is heuristic (that is, it stimulates our thinking), we cannot look at fluency solely in terms of this concrete image. Comprehension and fluency are intricately and intercausally connected. Each benefits from and influences the other. They are, in fact, parts of the whole act of reading—the complex processing that readers do—and they are extremely hard to separate. Readers use the structure, or organization, of the text, as well as their background knowledge, to support both comprehension and fluency.

For example, a person reading *Poppleton* (Rylant) understands it is a narrative text—one that has a beginning in which the characters and setting are revealed and the problem described (see Figure 6-5). The reader knows that Poppleton is a foolish but nice pig who is always grappling with some domestic problem. The reader will expect several of these episodes and a satisfactory conclusion. This structure carries the reader along, supporting both compre-

Some mornings Poppleton did not
want oatmeal.
He wanted to sleep.

Some afternoons Poppleton did not
want toasted cheese.
He wanted TV.
Some nights Poppleton did not
want spaghetti.
He wanted to practice
playing his harmonica.
But Cherry Sue kept calling,
"Yoo-hoo! Poppleton!"

15

Figure 6-5. Poppleton

hension and fluency. The reader can anticipate what will logically come next and use previous information to fuel forward momentum. The reader will also use understanding of the character Poppleton and the whimsical nature of the text to guide fluent reading of dialogue.

Alison, a kindergarten student, listening to her teacher read *A Very Quiet Cricket* (Carle) soon understands that the text is composed of recurring episodes in which a little cricket meets insect after insect. Each insect gives a greeting, like "good afternoon," and the little cricket wants to answer. Time after time, although he rubs his wings together, not a sound comes out. The teacher nears the final page: "And then the cricket saw another cricket. She was also a very quiet cricket. So the little cricket rubbed his wings together one more time, and this time . . . " During this small pause, Alison says, "It made a sound!"

No doubt Alison has based her comment on a number of signals:

- The reader is nearing the end of the story, so the problem needs resolution.

- The cricket is for the first time meeting another cricket, so a change in response is possible.

- The words within the sentence—*one more time, and this time*—indicate something different is going to happen.

Readers who understand text structure can better understand how one sentence flows into another in the creation of a meaningful text. Someone reading *All About Frogs* (Arnosky) realizes that different kinds of information about frogs will be presented in different parts of the book. This reader also knows that he can go immediately to the section of most interest. In the section shown in Figure 5-9, the reader understands right away that the author is contrasting frogs with toads. Detecting the underlying structure, comparison/contrast, the reader uses it to anticipate what the text will say. (This may also happen at the word level— the antonyms *smooth* and *bumpy,* for example.)

Fluency at the text level can be achieved only when readers are working in a smooth and orchestrated way that helps them remember and actively think about the organization of information in the text. We don't mean that readers actually say to themselves, *This is comparison and contrast, so I need to think about that.* The process is much more fluid, and in proficient readers, at least, largely unconscious. By experiencing many texts, readers internalize these powerful notions of structure and use them without giving them a great deal of conscious attention. We may design various activities to help readers notice and understand elements of text structure, but our ultimate goal is to have them use this powerful source of information in an automatic and unconscious way.

SIX DIMENSIONS OF READING FLUENCY (FIGURE 6-6)

Pausing

When reading aloud, proficient readers pause to reflect meaning in several different ways. They have an unconscious sense of when and how long these pauses should be, built on their knowledge of talking (how language sounds), and also on what they have learned about the use of punctuation. They know that one pauses at the end of a sentence (after a falling or rising tone) and also, more briefly, after a comma, moving on quickly to the next phrase. One barely pauses between words, pauses slightly longer between phrases, and pauses distinctly at commas. There is a longer pause at a dash (but not a falling tone). Pausing adds to the interpretation of a text.

Six Dimensions of Fluency

Pausing refers to the way the reader's voice is guided by punctuation (short breath at a comma; full stop with voice going down at periods and up at question marks; full stop at dashes).

Phrasing refers to the way readers put words together in groups to represent the meaningful units of language. Phrased reading should sound like oral language, although more formal. Phrasing involves pausing at punctuation as well as at places in the text that do not have punctuation.

Stress refers to the emphasis readers place on particular words (louder tone) to reflect the meaning as speakers would do in oral language.

Intonation refers to the way the reader varies the voice in tone, pitch, and volume to reflect the meaning of the text—sometimes called "expression."

Rate refers to the pace at which the reader moves through the text. An appropriate rate moves along rapidly with a few slowdowns or stops and long pauses to solve words. If a reader has only a few short pauses for word solving and picks up the pace again, look at the overall rate. The pace is also appropriate to the text and purpose of the reading—not too fast and not too slow.

Integration involves the way the reader consistently and evenly orchestrates pausing, phrasing, stress, intonation, and rate. The reader moves smoothly from one word to another, from one phrase to another, and from one sentence to another, incorporating pauses that are just long enough to perform their function. There is no space between words except as part of meaningful interpretation. When all dimensions of fluency—pausing, phrasing, stress, intonation, and rate—are working together, the reader will be using expressions in a way that clearly demonstrates that he understands the text and is even thinking beyond the text.

Figure 6-6. *Six Dimensions of Fluency*

Oral Reading with Pauses

READER #1	READER #2
But then / he felt Rex's fingers tickling him. / He tickled her back. / Soon / he forgot all about Amanda, / who was busy in the front seat / counting the number of bug spots / on the windshield.	But / then he felt Rex's fingers / tickling him. / He tickled her back. / Soon he forgot / all about Amanda, / who was busy in the front seat / counting the number of bug spots / on the windshield.
"I'm glad / I have twenty-seven dinosaurs / and you have twenty-seven animals,"/ Rex told Pinky / when they stopped their tickling. / "That way / we have everything / the same!" /	"I'm glad I have / twenty-seven dinosaurs and you have / twenty-seven animals," / Rex told Pinky / when they stopped their tickling. / "That way we have / everything the same!" /
Pinky nodded his head. / "We have to have / everything the same," / he said. / "We're best friends." /	Pinky nodded / his head. / "We have to have everything / the same,"/ he said. / "We're best / friends." /

Figure 6-7. *Oral Reading with Pauses*

Figure 6-7 shows the pauses two different people made while reading the same section of text. If you do this with several readers, there will always be a few differences, which have to do with the individual reader's interpretation. But there are some "givens," such as the pause after a period or pauses to indicate dialogue.

Phrasing

We have mentioned phrasing many times in this chapter, because it is such a critical dimension of fluency. The skillful reader does not pause randomly but strategically, in ways that reflect his knowledge of the language patterns and meaning. There are no spaces between words when a proficient reader processes text. Of course, you will hear the spaces in the staccato reading that beginners use when they are working out word-by-word matching, but after about level C or D, you should hear long stretches of reading with no pauses between individual words. Instead, pauses reflect phrases, or groups of words, those indicated by meaning as well as required by punctuation. And, the pauses vary in length, with short pauses at commas and phrases within sentences, longer pauses for dashes and at the end of sentences.

Stress

Monotone reading is not truly fluent, even when it is fast. Lack of variation in stress or volume makes reading sound as if it was being generated by a computer or a robot. Strategic readers use stress and volume in connection with pauses to reflect the writer's intended meaning and communicate their interpretation of a text. In every sentence, the reader will stress one or more words by reading them slightly louder or more distinctly than others. Try reading this sentence with the stress on several different words:

Why are you eating that? [I want to know your reason.]

Why *are* you eating that? [I didn't ask before, but I've just now realized I want to know your reason.]

Why are *you* eating that? [That wasn't meant for you, so I'm wondering why you are eating it.]

Why are you *eating* that? [That's really just for attractive presentation—not for eating.]

Why are you eating *that?* [There are some other things you would like better or should eat instead.]

The changes are subtle but real. By stressing different words, the reader indicates variations in the underlying connotations. (This is true for all languages.) Fluent readers automatically build stress variations related to meaning into the way they process print. When producing written language, we may make our meaning clear by using boldface, all caps, underlining, or italics.

Stress as a factor in silent reading is more difficult to conceptualize: we're seldom even aware of how the language sounds. Yet, even when reading silently, individuals probably are subconsciously aware of word stress in sentences. And you may remember reading some books so compelling that you can just "hear the people talking" in your head. You may become especially aware of this when you see a film based on a book and a particular piece of dialogue isn't there or is said differently from the way you remember from your reading.

Intonation

Good reading expresses itself in intonation, which is signaled both by the pitch, or "tone," of the voice and by stress. A falling tone signals that a sentence is ending; a rising tone at the end of a sentence indicates a question.

When we listen to books on tape, which have become very popular, one of the pleasures we experience is the way the reader's voice strokes the language, revealing interesting, enjoyable patterns—almost like listening to melodies. These readers are professionals. They use higher and lower tones to reflect meaning, perhaps lower the voice at points of suspense or expressing supporting ideas more quietly than the main or summary ideas.

Really skillful oral reading takes practice, but we should see in all proficient readers a consideration for the audience, for how the reading sounds. The ability to reflect language through rhythm and tone increases appreciation for a text and may figure into the reader's ability to engage in analysis.

Rate

Pace is usually a very important focus of attention in reading. Many adults invest money in "speed reading" courses because they think rate is the key factor in consuming text: people who can read a book in a day will be able to gain more information; studying will be easier. In one sense those things are true, but reading skill is far more complex than speed. A reader who processes print strategically will slow down and speed up depending on purpose and genre.

Some texts we deliberately read slowly because we want to understand complex problems or enjoy the craft of the writer. We may reread specific portions of a text or skim it looking for the information we want.

The experts have specified optimum reading pace, but we need to use these guidelines cautiously: a reader's behavior depends on many factors and will vary. Reading rate is affected by the text difficulty, content, format, and sentence complexity. Also, some studies report average words per minute while others report average correct words per minute. Some address oral reading rate while others address silent reading rate. The recommended optimum reading rate varies by grade level, rising consistently from kindergarten to grade eight.

You can calculate WPM (words per minute) by having a student read a grade level passage for exactly one minute and point to the last word he has read. You count the number of words read. You can also use a formula:

$$\text{WPM} = \frac{\text{\# of words x 60 seconds}}{\text{\# of seconds student read}}$$

After reviewing a variety of studies on oral and silent reading rates, we suggest the guide shown in Figure 6-8 for a range of average reading rates that should serve as end-of-year goals. If the reader is more than twenty percent below the norm, fluency should be a concern.

One thing is obvious: reading rates vary, but they are very important. Some generalizations we can make are:

- After the emergent-to-early-reader transition, during which children take on word-by-word matching, reading rate is an important aspect of reading fluency.

- The reading rate gradually rises each year throughout elementary school.

- After the transition to silent reading, students can generally read faster silently than orally.

- A student's reading rate is not more important than comprehension.

- Faster rates of reading correlate to higher comprehension (Allington 2001).

- An adequate reading rate allows the reader to attend to the meaning of a text.

The actual reading rate of a student is not as important as its increase over time. As you assess your students' fluency, look

Oral and Silent Reading Rates

END OF GRADE	ORAL READING RATES (WPM)
1	75–100
2	90–120
3	100–140
4	120–160
5	140–180
6	160–200
7–8	180–220

END OF GRADE	SILENT READING RATES (WPM)
1	55–80
2	80–110
3	110–135
4	135–165
5	165–190
6	190–210
7–8	210–230

Figure 6-8. *Oral and Silent Reading Rates*

at the increase in their reading rate. They will be taking on harder texts, and the rate on instructional material may be lower than on easy texts, but if they are building strength as readers, you should see increases across the board.

Integration

Oral reading should flow smoothly to the listeners' ears, word after word, sentence after sentence except for deliberate pauses. This smoothness allows the listeners to follow what is happening—the characters and plot or the information being shared—as it unfolds without thinking about the words and sentences. Language read aloud must be transparent. In silent reading, too, we want this effortless movement through text. Expression (the technical term is *prosody*) includes pausing, phrasing, rhythm, pitch, smoothness, and stress, all working together in an integrated way to reflect the reader's interpretation of the text. The expressive oral reader adds meaning using all of those means as he orchestrates pausing, phrasing, stress, and intonation to produce oral reading that sounds like meaningful language, not simply a string of words. (Chapter 8 includes a rubric for assessing fluency based on these dimensions.)

We sometimes forget this idea of the integrated whole,

because as teachers we are almost always focusing directly on how the reader processes the text. But occasionally, you need to be able to sit back and enjoy (without evaluation) a story that one of your students is reading aloud. If that is possible, you have supported the development of a fluent reader.

THE ROLE OF ACCURACY

Fluency is not only about "reading the words," but a high level of accuracy is important and must be recognized as essential to understanding texts. Think of accuracy as a kind of basic, or minimal, requirement. Certainly, readers can be accurate without being fluent or comprehending what they read. But readers who are not reading with high accuracy (below about 90 percent) have little chance of fluency or understanding. Fluent readers are able to read words quickly and accurately. When readers expend little effort in word analysis, they can have more attention for the meaning of texts.

We're not talking about very young children who have heard a text read before or participated in a shared reading of it and then "read" it for themselves, sometimes inventing text. These youngsters do sound fluent, and they are— in oral renditions of the language they have heard and internalized. Reading and rereading a favorite text and then "reenacting" it is an important part of a child's development. However, it is not, strictly speaking, processing print, because the children are not using visual information as a check on their knowledge of language and their understanding of what is being read.

For readers who know the details of print and the constraints of written language, high accuracy is a must. Unless a text is accessible, the reader will not achieve fluency. It is possible for a child to read a text three, four, five, or more times and eventually achieve some kind of fluency, but that is not what we are after. An effective reader of an accessible text will exhibit phrasing and fluency even on a first reading. Accuracy does not tell the whole story, so you will need to look beyond the numbers. A reader may process a text with a high accuracy rate and poor processing (e.g., numerous attempts at the same word or long pauses). A reader may process a text at an accuracy rate below 90 percent and demonstrate good processing (e.g., there was an error that was repeated many times).

Accuracy at 95–100 Percent

When you are reading at about 95 to 100 percent accuracy, you have the optimum opportunity to orchestrate many different kinds of information, read with phrasing and fluency, and engage in a minimum amount of on-the-run problem solving while reading for meaning. Little attention needs to be devoted to solving words, so you can concentrate on the meaning (and, if reading aloud, on the way the voice reflects the meaning). An accuracy rate of 95 to 100 percent provides a rich base for fluency.

An older reader can sometimes be 95 percent accurate and yet read so slowly as to be dysfluent, but if you look closely at such a person's reading behavior, you will probably find word mispronunciations (suggesting he doesn't truly understand the word), awkward phrasing, and low comprehension. For most readers, high accuracy forms a base for fluency and must be present if you are to teach it effectively.

Accuracy at 90–95 Percent

When you are reading at 90 to 95 percent accuracy, a small, but somewhat significant, amount of problem solving will be required; however, these operations will take place against a strong backdrop of accurate reading. The reader may give more attention to word solving, but not much more; you should not be hearing a struggle going on throughout the text.

When you provide texts that children can read with a maximum error rate of ten percent, the load is light enough for readers to sustain meaning and monitor language structure. They can work to integrate all sources of information—what they know and are learning, how the language "sounds" based on their knowledge of oral and written language syntax, and their processing of visual information (letters, sounds, words). You will observe readers slowing down and sometimes repeating to solve problems, but you will also observe meaningful phrasing and good momentum throughout the reading.

At progressively more challenging levels, it is important for there to be long stretches of accurate, phrased reading even in the processing of a new text. We recommend being conservative: It is better for a student to read with high accuracy, thinking actively about the meaning of a text, acquiring and using vocabulary, and demonstrating phrasing, than to move to higher levels of text where struggle is evident. Even a ten percent error rate can mean that the reader is having to give too much attention to word solving, leaving less for meaning.

Accuracy Below 90 Percent

When readers are processing texts at below a 90 percent accuracy rate, fluency and comprehension are severely undermined. It is true that a highly motivated reader, perhaps because she is so interested in a particular subject, may occasionally pick up a harder text and work to make sense of it. In the course of research, we all take up challenges driven by a "need to know." But very difficult reading as a steady diet interferes with the opportunity for readers to build systems of strategic actions that are needed for proficient, independent processing.

When readers are struggling with text that is too hard, oral reading sounds like this:

- The reading is word by word, with frequent stops and starts.

- Phrasing is awkward, interrupted so much that it is difficult for a listener to follow.

- Words may be mispronounced or stressed on the wrong syllable.

- Reading sounds monotonous and/or choppy.

In both oral and silent reading of texts that are too difficult:

- The reading slows down for word solving and may remain slow even during stretches of accurate reading.

- Reading is often so slow that readers find it hard to sustain their attention.

- Readers find it hard to finish texts and may lose interest, wanting only to get to the end.

- Readers do not effectively use phrase and sentence units to access meaning.

- There are not enough stretches of accurate reading for the reader to sustain the meaning.

- Readers have difficulty searching for and using the range of information they need.

- Readers find it hard to remember the important details of a text and understand the literal meaning.

- Readers make conceptual errors that mislead them in comprehending the text.

- Readers find it difficult to go beyond the text, to engage in inferential, synthetic, or analytical thinking.

As teachers we have the serious responsibility of matching texts to readers, and the level of difficulty is not the only consideration. We have to be sure that readers are able to direct all of their strengths toward smooth and fluent processing.

CONTRIBUTORS TO FLUENCY

Readers bring all their resources to the fluent processing of texts, and these are the same resources that contribute to effective comprehension. Bringing background knowledge of the world to reading reduces its difficulty. Vocabulary is more accessible. Experience with other texts that have similar characteristics contributes to fluency. Excellent, flexible word-recognition and word-solving strategies help reading go smoothly, with large stretches of accurate reading in which one concentrates on meaning. The more readers bring to texts or can connect texts with their own personal and literary experiences, the better they will be able to use prosody in their oral reading.

SUGGESTIONS FOR PROFESSIONAL DEVELOPMENT

ANALYZING FLUENT READING

1   Listen to Francesca, Forest, Nyazia, and James P. on the DVD that accompanies this book.

2   Discuss what you notice about each reader. Is there evidence of:

- Strategic pausing to create phrasing?

- Using punctuation to cue the reading?

- Varying pitch and stress to reflect meaning?

- Using rhythm and tone to reflect meaning?

- Good pacing?

- Orchestration of strategic actions?

3   Audiotape (rather than videotape; it will help you focus on how the reading *sounds*) some of your own students with the goal of capturing fluent reading.

4   Bring the tapes to a grade-level meeting to share and discuss each aspect of fluency with colleagues.

5   Think about reading when the text is easy. Compare the reading when the text is difficult.

CHAPTER SEVEN

RECOGNIZING CHANGE OVER TIME IN FLUENT READING

Fluent reading will arise from teacher attention to the role of oral language and thinking and meaning, and increasing experience with the visual information in print, and practice in orchestrating complex processing on just-difficult-enough texts.

—MARIE CLAY

As teachers, we certainly do not expect fluency at all times and on all materials read. Developing readers are encountering the very textual challenges that help them build a processing system; they need to do "reading work"—word solving, making sources of information fit, puzzling out new vocabulary, noticing punctuation, repeating to confirm, stopping to think and reflect. We expect our students to read fluently easy texts (those that they understand), exhibit dimensions of fluency most of the time when reading new texts, and become more fluent over time.

Fluency is an attribute of reading, not a "stage" or a label for readers. It is a characteristic of effective reading at every level. As noted by the National Reading Panel:

> Fluency is not a stage of development at which readers can read all words quickly and easily. Fluency changes, depending on what readers are reading, their familiarity with the words, and the amount of their practice with reading text. (*Put Reading First*, 23)

As shown in Figure 7-1, reading fluency can be established after readers have control of word-by-word matching and their eyes have taken over the process—when they can read one word after another smoothly without the need to point. This should be firmly accomplished by about level C or D in text levels (see Chapter 24). In this chapter we will exam-

---

Change in Fluency over Time

"Pretend Reading" (After Listening to a Text) Shared Reading (Without Leveled Texts)	Levels A – C	Levels D – I	Levels J – Z+
READING REENACTMENT "TALKING LIKE A BOOK"	**EARLY READING BEHAVIORS**	**FLUENT AND PHRASED ORAL READING**	**FLUENT AND PHRASED ORAL READING, RAPID SILENT READING**
□ Responding to meaning and language □ Imitating adults □ Remembering stretches of familiar text, cued by the pictures □ Sounding fluent, but not tied to print □ Stretches of fluent reading in shared reading when teacher is supporting	□ Checking language with print □ Using word-by-word matching □ Reading slowly and carefully with crisp pointing under words □ Sounding dysfluent but sometimes indicating an awareness of phrases	□ Tracking print with eyes □ Fast, smooth word recognition and word solving □ Reading faster and in phrased units that show an awareness of meaning and syntax □ Sounding fluent on easy texts □ Sounding fluent on stretches of challenging novel texts	□ Tracking print with eyes □ Quick word recognition and word solving □ Reading faster □ Processing longer texts □ Implicitly aware of language syntax and phrase units □ Sounding fluent in oral reading of easy texts and stretches of reading in challenging texts

Figure 7-1. *Change in Fluency over Time*

ine fluent reading and how it changes as texts become more demanding on readers.

EMERGENT READING: "TALKING LIKE A BOOK"

We know that even very young children have a concept of fluent reading, because they will often pretend to read texts they have heard over and over, using smooth, expressive language. Turning pages and looking at the pictures, they reproduce their own version of the story, much of it accurate.

In her reenactment of *Where the Wild Things Are* (Sendak), a much-loved bedtime story, five-year-old Jenny does a good job of sticking to the story (see Figure 7-2 and the DVD that accompanies this book). She adds details from the pictures. Her version coincides word-for-word with Sendak's on the last part: "and into the light of his very own room where his supper was waiting for him and it was still hot." She "reads" fluently, with expression, her voice

falling at periods and loudly emphasizing Max's shout, "Be still!" Jenny is not yet tracking print, but she (and many other children like her) has the advantage of a deeply held knowledge of what oral reading is supposed to sound like. This knowledge does not guarantee she will become a proficient, fluent reader, but it is an important resource.

All literacy learning, including the development of fluent reading, is grounded in oral language. Children develop language—incredibly rapidly—as they interact with adults in their environment. While adults may simplify their speech somewhat when they address children, they use highly sophisticated language compared to that of two-, three-, and four-year-olds. Children absorb these sophisticated patterns and try them out in speech:

> The child's everyday speech is linked to the fluency with which he will read. Certainly he has to learn to work on new words and to predict what sounds are produced by which letter

---

Reading Reenactment of Where the Wild Things Are

SUMMARY OF *WHERE THE WILD THINGS ARE* (SENDAK)	JENNY'S "READING," AGE 5
Where the Wild Things Are This story concerns a little boy named Max whose mother sent him to bed without supper. In the angry Max's imagination, a forest grows in his room. He steps into a small boat and ". . . sailed off through a night and day and in and out of weeks and almost over a year to where the wild things are." Max reaches the land of the wild things, who ". . . roared their terrible roars and gnashed their terrible teeth and rolled their terrible eyes and showed their terrible claws 'til Max said, 'BE STILL!'" Max tames the wild things by staring into their big yellow eyes without blinking once. He is made king of the land and immediately proclaims a "wild rumpus." The wild things jump up and down, hang from trees, and give Max rides on their backs. Then Max stops the rumpus and sends the wild things to bed without their supper (just like himself). Suddenly, Max feels lonely and wants ". . . to be where someone loved him best of all." Smelling good things to eat, Max gives up being king. Although the wild things beg him not to go, and they roar and gnash their teeth and show their claws, Max sails back ". . . over a year and in and out of weeks and through a day and into the night of his own room where he found his supper waiting for him and it was still hot."	Where the Wild Things are. Once upon a time there was a little boy named Max. He was hanging on a rope, tied. His room was a mess. max made a picture. it was a picture of a monster. it says By Max, and there was steps and there was a dog. His mother called him wild thing even though . . . But, the moon was out. his windows were open. he had his door closed. he looks angry. And then there were trees in his bedroom, and then there was lots and lots of trees and vines, too. And now there were so many vines he couldn't believe it. And then Max said, "Well, I think I'll take my boa." The wild thing said . . . and in out of weeks and over, over a year to where the wild things are. And then Max said to the wild things, "I hate you." They roared their terrible roars. They stomped their terrible feet. They blinked their eyes at them eighty times. And the wild things cry back, "let a rumble start." It looks like that they are going up in the air. One's climbing in the tree. Max is too. they're all being nice. And then he said, "Well, I think I'll crunch my terrible teeth. I'm gonna eat you up!" And sailed back over a year without of weeks and throughout the day. Into the night of his very own room where he found his supper waiting for him and he was happy and it was still hot.

Figure 7-2. *Reading Reenactment of* Where the Wild Things Are

combinations. But such details can be discovered within larger chunks of meaningful language. The child who already uses a wide range of language features in a flexible manner will find it easier to work with the sentence structures in his reading book. He simply has to select the appropriate structures from his speech repertoire. The child with rich experience of books will have greater understanding of bookish forms of language and more motivation to master the art of reading. (Clay 1991, p. 81)

Kindergartners who enter school having heard very few books read aloud or having had few conversations with adults need a great many literature and language experiences, but it is possible to build this foundation quickly.

Reading aloud to children is an important model of fluency in all its dimensions. Kindergartners and first graders ask for favorite stories to be read over and over, join in on refrains, and demonstrate the kind of reading reenactments shown in Figure 7-2. Although they are not processing the print, in every other way, they are thinking like readers as they process the meaning and language of the text they hear.

A read-aloud is a very carefully orchestrated ritual— one that teachers of younger children will recognize. One custom is that children join in at certain points in a story. This does not mean they "mumble along" throughout but join in after they can anticipate what the text is going to say. Sometimes, watching an interactive read-aloud with young children, we almost feel as though we are watching a dance where everyone "knows his moves." The children are taking on the grammar and vocabulary of written language, which will contribute to fluency in the future.

EARLY READING BEHAVIOR—LEVELS A–C

SHARED READING

Shared reading has an important role in helping children learn about fluent oral reading. By reading an enlarged text in unison with the teacher's support, children have a chance to internalize the structures of written language while giving some attention to print. When teachers begin working with shared texts, they read them aloud to the children to familiarize them with the language. The texts are very simple. They are often characterized by repetition and rhyme which make it easy to remember. Quickly, children are invited to join in on the reading. Since one of the purposes of shared reading is to help children learn word-by-word matching and left-to-right directionality, teachers usually make the demonstration explicit by using a point-er under each word. On well-known texts, however, it is possible to glide the pointer under a group of words to show children how to make the reading sound better.

In shared reading, level of the text is important. The concept of increasing complexity is viable, because the goal is to demonstrate to children how they can track print with their eyes. If the text is too long and complex, many children will simply treat it as a read-aloud, without bothering to notice the print. Therefore, we do think about easier to harder texts, as indicated by our literacy continuum (see Pinnell and Fountas, in press). But we do not use the precise text gradient we use in guided reading; that kind of precision in matching texts to readers is unnecessary, because there is so much group support. In shared reading, children may read along with others, remembering long stretches of text while supported by the group. In that way, they can experience a variety of texts as teachers offer a high level of support for harder texts and less support for easier ones.

GUIDED/INDEPENDENT READING

For a brief time, as they learn to track print, children have to let go of the fluency they achieve in a reenactment. The children are reading texts at about levels A to C or D in instructional contexts. Some children are reluctant to point and match word-by-word, and it's easy to see why. It means moving from a fluent and interesting rendition of a known text to the kind of staccato reading that results from moving left to right and looking at each word. Your goal is to get them to become dysfluent for a time as they slow down their language to match each spoken word with each written word, pointing crisply under each word as they read.

Some children take on these early word-matching behaviors very quickly, but others need much more teaching to achieve coordinated eye-hand-voice movement. For a brief period they need to take it slow, tediously matching word-by-word as they read from left to right. They will pause between each word as they attend to the white spaces on the page.

During this time, reading will not sound fluent, but watch for spontaneous reflection of phrases and for momentum to pick up on familiar texts. If they are connecting the text to their knowledge of language structure, children learn to "put some words together" even while they are still pointing. Texts with some repetition will help children put words together more confidently.

If children get stuck in word-by-word processing, explicitly demonstrate how to put known words together (for example, "at the zoo") in phrased units and prompt them to do so as well. After a brief period, usually only a few weeks, children will spontaneously drop the finger or slide it under the print, because they will be reading faster than they can point. (They may still use the finger at difficult spots.)

Level of text becomes important in reading instruction when children need to learn how to track print for themselves. Children who are just beginning to develop concepts about how print works need extremely easy texts so that they can concentrate on orchestrating motor behaviors and language. An A-level text, with one line of print, natural, repetitive language, and a clear, somewhat oversized font, can be read by a child who has very few visual signposts (known letters, words, etc.).

As soon as they learn to match word-by-word, children can move on to level B and then C, extending their repertoire to longer lines of text, longer sentences, more lines of text on a page, and less repetition. By this time, we should see some important transitions, though there will be variations in the speed at which they happen:

> Developmentally there is usually a gradual transition in good readers from finger pointing, to staccato reading, to light stress of word breaks, and finally to phrasing. The fast learners make this transition so rapidly that it may hardly be noticed. Slow learners may take several weeks to coordinate reading and a slow gradual change to dependence on the eyes alone. (Clay, p. 166)

Figure 7-3 is a more detailed look at the important transitions between being "carefully glued to the print" and letting the eyes take over the process as readers gain control of one-to-one matching from level A to about level C or D.

Important Transitions

FROM:	→	TO:
□ Slow, careful, and precise pointing.	□ Pointing but moving along the line quickly.	□ Occasional pointing and sometimes sliding the finger or removing it altogether on easy parts of the text.
□ Space between each word, coordinated with pointing.	□ Less space between words, with some following one another smoothly.	□ Putting many words together in groups with little space between.
□ Frequent repeating to correct when pointing is "off" (for example, running out of words).	□ Making pointing match most of the time without needing to self-correct.	□ Automatic pointing with more attention to checking visual information within words than with matching.
□ "Sing-song" quality to reading, monotonous most of the time.	□ Evidence of putting words together on easy-to-say phrases like "said David" or "to the zoo."	□ Phrasing within most sentences, reflecting the meaning of the text.
□ Little stress on words or change of pitch.	□ Stress on important words and change of pitch.	□ Using stress and variation in pitch to convey the meaning of the story.
□ Some voice reflection of basic punctuation such as periods and question marks.	□ Consistent voice reflection of basic punctuation such as periods and question marks.	□ Automatic voice reflection of a range of punctuation.
□ Emphasis on "reading" for its own sake.	□ More attention to and emphasis on the story.	□ Overt signs of enjoyment or interest in the story.
□ Stopping frequently to check on reading, solve words slowly, and assure matching.	□ Forward movement, stopping less frequently.	□ Few stops for problem solving; matching is automatic and does not need correction even when slightly "off."
Likely to happen on new texts that are challenging.	*Likely to happen on texts that are easy or when rereading familiar texts.*	

Figure 7-3. *Important Transitions*

The "pointing" phase is not static: it is always changing. Children who are taking on their first easy texts have very limited understanding or control of matching. But they quickly gain more control. For example, they start to slide the pointing finger under easy phrases, perhaps even removing the finger entirely on stretches of easy text, bringing it back when needed for closer problem solving. Spaces between words become shorter, with many words following each other smoothly. The voice is more likely to reflect meaning by variations in stress and pitch; punctuation is also noticed and reflected in the voice.

These transitions do not follow in strict sequence, although they do represent continuous progress over time. They depend on the degree to which the text matches the reader's current strengths and on the amount of support provided by the teacher. On subsequent rereadings of the same text, the familiarity of the text supports the reading. The teacher's text introduction can also support transitions. Each time the reader moves up a level, there are new challenges. The point is to provide many opportunities for readers to gain control over time through reading easy texts, rereading texts, and encountering challenging texts with teacher support. By about level C or D, however, we would expect the eyes to have taken over the process.

It may seem paradoxical to demonstrate word-by-word matching, encourage children to read one word at a time, show them how to use a finger to point, and prompt them to do so; then, after a relatively short period of learning, prompt them to "read with their eyes" and put their words together; and very soon ask them to read silently, "in their heads." These transitions could be confusing to some children and they must be explained carefully as you go along.

In the interest of accuracy, sometimes teachers encourage finger pointing far too long, to the detriment of fluent reading. Some upper elementary students who point with a finger or pencil while reading aloud say they are doing it so that the teacher can follow their reading. A misconception like this can greatly inhibit oral reading fluency. It encourages readers to focus on one word at a time instead of reading groups of words.

At about levels C and D, it is time to encourage children to drop the finger, assuring them they can use it again if they need to. They are most likely to drop the finger when rereading familiar texts, so it may be wise to stay on levels where their eyes can easily take over the process. Moving to higher levels too quickly will make the process break down and children can become dependent on pointing.

ESTABLISHED FLUENCY AND PHRASING IN ORAL READING: LEVELS D–I

Once the eyes are able to track print unaided, it is reasonable to expect phrasing and fluency on every level with no finger pointing. Pace will gradually increase to a point of clear, expressive oral reading. Children are putting together all sources of information in a smoothly operating process as they apply their current operating systems to increasingly difficult levels of text. As Clay has said, "Reading is a message-gaining, problem-solving activity that gains in power and flexibility the more it is practised" (sic) (1991, p. 6) These young readers do not need the complex skills of proficient readers, because the texts are carefully selected so they can process them with their current understandings and the teacher's support.

As before, the level of fluency will vary according to the number of challenges in the text as well as the teacher's support. Readers do need challenge. Successfully processing more difficult texts will enable them to cope with:

- Longer stretches of print with fewer pictures.
- More complex sentences.
- Harder and more varied words.
- More difficult concepts.
- The full range of punctuation.

Teachers use the text gradient (see Chapter 12) to help them select a text that is just a little more challenging. Then they introduce the text, prompt as necessary while students read it, and talk about the text afterward in order to help students process it effectively.

What should the oral reading of a new text sound like from about level C or D and up? In general, you will hear many stretches of fluent reading on a new text but should not expect fluency throughout. There will and must be points at which the reader will work on words; repeat to check accuracy, language, or meaning; or stop to figure out what is happening. This is natural. But you also should observe:

- Stretches of fluent reading throughout.
- Self-correcting or rereading for better phrasing.

- Rereading to reflect punctuation.
- Improved momentum and fluency as the reader learns the writer's concepts and becomes familiar with the content language and style.

Here as at previous levels, it is important for readers to occasionally read new but easier texts and re-read texts to build fluency. Nothing increases a reader's fluency more than reading a great many easy texts. You should be able to observe oral reading fluency in all dimensions at all levels.

ESTABLISHED FLUENCY IN BOTH ORAL AND SILENT READING: LEVELS J–Z+

THE ROLE OF SILENT READING

When readers are processing texts at about level J or K, they should begin switching to more silent reading of texts. Most readers do so spontaneously, gradually reading more softly and with less articulation. Many children begin to read silently even before these levels as they gain control and reading becomes easier. There are several reasons for this spontaneous change:

- Less attention is needed to process visual information, and the eyes slide along the print ahead of the voice.
- Readers find that articulating the words slows them down.
- They learn that unvoiced reading is faster and more efficient.
- "Thinking the words" rather than saying them out loud frees one to pay more attention to the text meaning.
- Reading becomes more enjoyable when processed silently.

Think back to a time when you were reading aloud to your students and simultaneously thinking about something else. It is possible for most proficient adult readers to separate these two processes, a sort of "multitasking." Nevertheless, it is a little harder to concentrate when reading aloud, and it certainly is slower.

For efficiency, almost all of our reading is silent. We usually read aloud only to provide pleasure or information to others, but there are some exceptions. We may read poetry aloud to ourselves to enjoy the sound of the language. Writers sometimes read their own work aloud to test it against their intentions and evaluate the sound of it.

Speakers read aloud to practice their speeches. Some proofreaders read aloud to a companion who follows closely along in the text and marks discrepancies. All of us are listeners, by the way. We are read aloud to every evening as we watch the news! But our independent reading is for the most part silent.

As students move from one level of text to another, you will want to sample oral reading to check fluency. Fiction texts at level J or K are considerably longer than previous levels: beginning "chapter books" are introduced, and plot and character development are more complex. Informational texts may cover topics that require more background knowledge, including some technical vocabulary, and have many features such as simple graphics that students must learn to read. All kinds of texts require greater and more efficient word solving while sustaining attention, sometimes over a number of days.

Many students do not automatically begin reading silently: it seems not to occur to them. Others think they are expected to read orally even when working independently. Still others continue to articulate words with their lips though not voicing them.

When you know from their oral reading that students can track print with their eyes and can read texts at about levels J, K, or L with high accuracy, fluency, and good understanding, begin to encourage them to read silently. It is impossible to demonstrate the act of silent reading, but you can prompt students about what to do:

- "Read it with your eyes."
- "Think about what the words say."
- "Follow the line with your eyes."
- "You can look back if you need to."
- "Read it in your head."

What are the characteristics of fluency when students are reading silently most of the time? We can only hypothesize what is happening, because we cannot observe it directly, but here are some possibilities:

- The eyes are tracking print, giving attention to the least amount of visual information necessary.
- The eyes slide smoothly along the print, hesitating only when absolutely necessary.
- The eyes may slide back and forth in search of information when needed and/or may reread to check.

- Readers are storing important information and using it as they read the next sentences, paragraphs, and sections of the text.

- Readers are noticing and consuming phrases.

- Readers unconsciously attend to word stress.

- Aspects of speech, particularly the emphasis of an idea or dialogue spoken by the characters, call to mind known speech patterns.

- Readers appreciate vivid language and call up sensory images.

- Readers use punctuation and print characteristics such as **bold** and *italic* to bring expressive meaning to the text.

It is difficult but not impossible to find evidence of fluency in silent reading. You might, for example:

- Notice how long it takes readers to process a text and compare it with the amount of information they were able to take from it.

- Ask students if they remember any memorable language from the text.

- Ask about what characters say. Does their dialogue reveal anything about them?

- Ask students to find something quickly in the text, a task that depends partly on memory and partly on the ability to scan previously read text.

- In a discussion of a text, notice how quickly readers can find textual evidence to support their observations and opinions.

As in oral reading, it is very important for readers to have many opportunities to read easy texts silently. Think of a text you "devoured" or "couldn't put down" while you became unaware of everything around you. Chances are that text was easy for you, and you could concentrate on the compelling plot or interesting characters. The language was fully transparent, so you didn't have to work hard. That's not to say that you didn't acquire some new vocabulary; every worthwhile text has its challenges. But by and large, the reading was smoothly executed. That's the kind of experience you want your students to have every day if possible. Through independent reading, they build up stamina, as well as experience again and again the pleasure of fluent silent reading.

THE CHANGING ROLE OF ORAL READING

What about oral reading? Is it important for individuals to continue practicing how to read aloud? Obviously, teachers have a direct, job-related need to be competent in oral reading, but what about the rest of the population?

Oral reading has a significant role in students' success, although it is not a "deal breaker." People can be very fluent silent readers but be unable to give polished oral reading performances. Nevertheless, competent oral reading has some distinct advantages:

- We may be asked to read aloud at a moment's notice, in a community or business meeting. Inability to do so articulately can be embarrassing, create lack of confidence, and make one reluctant to take on any leadership role.

- At some point, most people are asked to make some kind of public presentation, to small or large groups. A few lucky people are comfortable speaking extemporaneously, but for most of us, being able to read orally from notes, a script, PowerPoint slides, or a teleprompter saves the day.

- Oral reading is an important parenting skill: parents greatly benefit their children by reading aloud to them in an interesting way.

Oral reading does not have to be, and probably should *not* be, excessively dramatic—simple, competent, and expressive oral reading does the trick.

Throughout schooling, you can develop your students' oral reading skills by asking them to read aloud for authentic purposes. We're not talking about a boring "round-robin" exercise in which individual students take turns reading while the rest "follow along." This kind of activity has never been shown to foster fluency; instead, the attendant embarrassment causes many students to develop a lifelong fear of reading aloud. Chapter 21 on shared and performance reading describes many ways you can engage your students in authentic oral reading. The next chapter focuses on teaching for fluency in many instructional contexts.

Fluency in oral reading is a life skill worthy of instruction because of its strong connection to comprehending, its contribution to reading efficiency, and its role in many work and social contexts.

THE RELATIONSHIP BETWEEN THE DEMANDS OF TEXTS AND READING FLUENCY

Reading fluency is intricately related to the demands that texts place on readers. Elsewhere in this book, we explore the analysis of texts and their demands. See *The Continuum of Literacy Learning, PreK–8: A Guide to Teaching* (Heinemann, 2008, 2011) for detailed descriptions of the way demands increase with the levels on the text gradient. Here, we explore the particular text factors that impact fluency, which include genre, text structure, content, themes and ideas, language and literary features, sentence complexity, vocabulary, words, and book and print features (see Figure 7-4).

Any prior information the reader has supports fluency. It makes the text easier to predict and provides a "feed forward" mechanism (Clay 1991, p. 326). The reader is always thinking ahead, anticipating the next word, sentence, paragraph. This forward motion propels the reading in ways that support fluency. For example, most of the time you recognize a question by the structure of the sentence and unconsciously prepare yourself to use a rising tone at the end. The eyes work ahead of the reading, but the thinking works ahead of the eyes.

GENRE

If readers are familiar with a particular genre, it will be easier for them to anticipate how a text in that genre will be organized and what kinds of characters, actions, and plots they will meet. They know when reading fables, for example, that turtles are slow and foxes are sly. They get to know types of characters and anticipate dialogue. You may recall trying a new genre yourself or introducing one to your students. The reading is not as fluent, because searching for information is more difficult.

Readers' knowledge of fiction and nonfiction influences the stance they take toward a text. Recognizing characteristics of the genre, they immediately access different kinds of background information, search for information in ways most efficient for the genre, and even learn to expect specific vocabulary. The reader already has a mind-set that makes the process go smoothly. In informational text, for example, readers know to search for information in headings and subheadings or to use graphic illustrations. All of these kinds of knowledge propel the reading in ways that support fluency.

TEXT STRUCTURE

Writers organize texts in ways related to the genre. If readers understand the organizational structure of narrative texts, they understand that events will follow one another to a high point in the story and that the end will come quickly after that. Expository or informational texts are organized very differently. Here, readers anticipate related categories of information. Knowing that one kind of information is contained under a main heading and that subheadings signal a subcategory of that information not only supports reading fluency but also allows the reader to move around easily in a text, searching for information.

CONTENT

Prior knowledge is a key factor in the fluent reading of a text. If too much new information is included, the reader is overloaded and fluency diminishes. Ideally, the text should include enough new information to interest readers and increase their knowledge but not so much that the process breaks down. When readers are able to bring a large amount of content knowledge to the reading of a text, particularly nonfiction, then less attention will be needed for word recognition or determining the meaning of the vocabulary the writer is using. Of course, there must be tension for the text to be interesting. Readers always want to learn something new; if they already know almost everything in a text, there isn't much point in reading it. The goal is for understanding to be within reach.

THEMES AND IDEAS

The closer the themes and ideas are to readers' own level of understanding, the easier it will be for them to read with understanding, which contributes to the momentum that underlies fluency. Of course, we want readers to grasp ideas and concepts that are beyond their present understanding, and, increasingly, reading is a real tool toward that end. But to support fluency, the ideas must be easily within reach.

LANGUAGE AND LITERARY FEATURES

The writer's use of language and the literary merit of a text greatly add to our enjoyment of it, but these qualities also place complex demands on readers. In her book *Momma, Where Are You From?* Marie Bradby frames a memoir of a rural childhood with a mother's poetic responses to her daughter's questions. Answers like "I am from where the

Text Factors and Reading Fluency

FACTOR	HOW KNOWLEDGE OF THE FACTOR BENEFITS FLUENCY
Genre	□ Understanding characteristics supports the reader's ability to anticipate and predict. □ Knowing the genre helps the reader form expectations for the organization of the text and sometimes the use of words or the style.
Text Structure	□ Knowing how the text is organized makes it easy to find and use information, freeing one to concentrate on understanding. □ Knowing text structure allows the reader to form expectations and access prior knowledge. □ Understanding the structure of narrative texts helps readers know what to expect while moving through the text easily. □ Readers detect patterns and signal words in expository texts that make the text more accessible. □ Understanding the organization of the text helps readers more easily relate ideas within categories of information.
Content	□ Prior knowledge of content means less work is needed to understand a text. □ Difficult content unfamiliar to the reader can undermine fluency. The more the reader brings to the text, the more fluently he can process it.
Themes and Ideas	□ The closer themes and ideas are to those that are familiar to readers, the easier it will be for them to understand the text. □ If readers meet only a few new concepts in the text, it will be possible to read with greater fluency.
Language and Literary Features	□ Descriptive language, perhaps including figurative language such as metaphor and simile, increases the demands on the reader. □ Literary devices such as flashback and foreshadowing enable readers to follow a sequence of events and increase anticipation and enjoyment. □ The use of dialogue lets readers approximate oral language. □ If readers have heard literary language before (through read-aloud), it will be easier for them to read it when they encounter it in text.
Sentence Complexity	□ Long, complex sentences increase the difficulty of the text. □ Simple sentences, without a large number of phrases or embedded clauses, make a text easier. □ The more familiar the syntax, the easier the text is to read.
Vocabulary	□ Texts that include many word choices that are within the reader's speaking, listening and reading vocabularies increase the chances of fluent reading.
Words	□ Texts that include many easy high-frequency words (that the reader knows or can get to easily) increase the chances of fluent reading. □ Texts that have words that are easily recognized or taken apart support fluency.
Illustrations	□ The illustrations, photos, and other art give the reader information that supports more fluent processing of the print.
Book and Print Features	□ Text layout can facilitate fluent reading (phrase layout, new line for new sentence). □ Illustrations support meaning construction and fluent reading. □ Graphics add information and can be a challenge; the more the reader knows how to integrate different kinds of information, the more easily he can move around in the text.

Figure 7-4. *Text Factors and Reading Fluency*

sidewalk ends . . ." conjure up not a specific place (although obviously there is one) but the experiences that made up her young life—what she remembers about people, visual images, sounds, and smells. These images make up who she is. The text is told descriptively from the point of view of the young child the mother once was, but the reader must also infer an underlying theme, one that wonders why racist and Jim Crow policies existed. This seemingly simple story is quite complex. Understanding literary allusions, recognizing that things are not always literal, and realizing that the writer uses imagery to evoke emotional responses help the reader move forward confidently.

VOCABULARY

Having good word-solving skills as well as large speaking, listening, and reading vocabularies make it possible to read fluently. Readers can apply flexible word-solving strategies more rapidly, easily, and successfully when they already know the word from their speaking or listening vocabularies. Less checking is required.

WORDS

If a reader has heard a word or used it, he can read it more fluently. If readers also understand the multiple meanings and connotations of words, they can use context to solve them. All readers derive new words from their reading. The more they read, the easier it is for them to learn new words; they make hypotheses as to the meaning from information in the context. Sometimes words are explicitly defined within a text. But a reader needs many encounters with a word to truly know it. If a text has too many words readers cannot solve easily or do not already have in their vocabularies, fluency is undermined.

SENTENCE COMPLEXITY

The more familiar the syntax of a text, the more the reader can anticipate the words that will follow and read words as a group. Longer, more complex texts make more demands on readers in terms of phrasing and fluency. Even a proficient reader may have to work at reading a text that has many compound sentences with many embedded clauses, uses unusual sentence structure, and perhaps violates the "rules" in creating a unique voice. Try the paragraph below:

"All right. Here I go." I took off running, my sneakers splashing rainwater from puddles, the hand clutching the kite end of the string held high above my head. It had been

so long, so many years since I'd done this, and I wondered if I'd make a spectacle of myself. I let the spool roll in my left hand as I ran, felt the string cut my right hand again as it fed through. The kite was lifting behind my shoulder now, lifting, wheeling, and I ran harder. The spool spun faster and the glass string tore another gash in my right palm. I stopped and turned. Looked up. Smiled. High above, my kite was tilting side to side like a pendulum, making that old paper-bird-flapping-its-wings sound I always associated with winter mornings in Kabul. I hadn't flown a kite in a quarter of a century, but suddenly I was twelve again and all the old instincts came rushing back. (Hosseini 2003, p. 368)

It helps young children to read texts—sometimes called "natural language texts"—that are very close to the way they really talk. Of course, no texts are exactly like oral language, so adjustments must always be made. But keeping the language simple and familiar is truly helpful at the easier levels.

On the mistaken notion that limiting the words or sound units will make a text easier, some companies publish books consisting of very contrived language. Most teachers will be familiar with the kinds of texts shown in Figure 7-5. The words may be easier to read, but do we want children to think of reading as calling one word after another? Fluent readers see written language as *language,* and they use everything they know about language in the processing. While you may sometimes want to use a slightly controlled text for a specific reason, most of the time you

---

Contrived Texts

CONTROLLED BY WORD SELECTION	CONTROLLED BY PHONOGRAMS
Look, look.	Nan can run.
Look, Jan, look.	Dan can run.
Look at the cat.	Nan and Dan can run.
Look at the mouse.	Nan can fan.
Look at the cat look at	Dan can fan.
the mouse.	Nan can fan Dan.
Look at the mouse.	Dan can fan Nan.
Look, look.	Nan and Dan can fan.
Run, mouse, run.	
Illustrations show a child pointing to a cat that is looking threateningly at a mouse and then starts to chase it.	*Illustrations show Nan and Dan having a race and getting hot. Then they fan each other to cool off.*

Figure 7-5. *Contrived Texts*

will want even your youngest readers to process texts with normal syntax. This doesn't mean that words are unimportant—far from it—but they must be understood in relation to one another. The more a text is "contrived," the harder it will be for young readers to achieve fluency.

ILLUSTRATIONS

The art in a text provides support for the meaning of a text and helps readers bring more knowledge to the act of processing. It feeds the reader's body of knowledge and makes the reading easier. Illustrations provide information that helps readers understand the meaning and the words; they can also extend meaning or even present a conflicting meaning. For example, look at the conflict between the illustration and the text in Figure 7-6. A quick glance at the picture helps the reader understand that Willy doesn't really help and that knowledge would fuel fluency and an expressive rendition of "What a mess!"

Illustrations help early readers understand specific words—what the text actually says. That kind of support is not necessary for older readers, but the illustrations can still extend the meaning, adding to understanding and even providing motivation to make the voice express emotion or irony.

BOOK AND PRINT FEATURES

Length

The length of a text can support fluency. The more background the reader has, the more momentum he can pick up. Did you ever notice a reader become more fluent after processing the first few paragraphs of a text?

Print and Layout

Text layout can support fluency. A "friendly" layout and font, with generous space between words and lines, make the reader's work easier and contribute to fluency. You may know what it's like to read a long book with very packed and tiny print and narrow margins. You tire more easily, and it is harder to read with ease.

Some texts for younger readers are laid out in ways that promote phrasing. In the pages from *The Lazy Pig* (Randell) shown in Figure 7-7, notice how the reader can use the layout of the lines to know how to group words into phrases. Some texts have a layout that is very complex causing the reader to adjust reading in many ways.

Punctuation

Punctuation is a key feature in assisting fluent reading, one that we all use. Think about the pauses cued by the punc-

Figure 7-6. Willy the Helper

tuation in the two-page spread from *Fox and His Friends* (Marshall) shown in Figure 7-8.

Tools

Tools support readers by providing more information. They help organize the reader's thinking. For example, headings or chapter titles support the reader to think about what is ahead. These tools support the forward processing that makes a reader more fluent.

All of these text features—genre, text structure, content, themes and ideas, language and literary features, sentence complexity, vocabulary, words, illustrations, and book and print features—affect the individual's ability to read with fluency and phrasing. Punctuation in particular is an

"I am asleep," said the pig.

The **lazy** pig!

Figure 7-7. The Lazy Pig

"What have you two been up to?"
asked Mom.
Fox held his breath.
"We went to the park," said Louise.
"And?" said Mom.
"And Fox bought me
an ice cream cone," said Louise.
"And?" said Mom.
"And then we came home,"
said Louise.
"How sweet, Fox," said Mom.

Figure 7-8. Fox and His Friends

important source of information for helping a person read with fluency and phrasing, but it does not provide all of the information needed to assist fluent, expressive reading. The fluent reader connects all his knowledge of oral language and its functioning in helping human beings make meaning out of the information offered in print to create and re-create oral renditions of written text that sound like the human language experience.

SUGGESTIONS FOR PROFESSIONAL DEVELOPMENT
ANALYZING TEXT FACTORS AND FLUENCY

1 Gather texts at three different difficulty levels that are of interest to you and your colleagues. Stretch yourself a bit to include lower and higher levels than you usually use in your classroom.

2 Spend some time examining the three texts in relation to the characteristics discussed in Figure 7-4. Use the chart that is included on the DVD that accompanies this book.

3 Think about each of the text features and how they support fluent, phrased reading. Then discuss the challenges to the reader in relation to each characteristic.

4 Share and discuss your findings, and add any new insights to Figure 7-4.

5 Discuss how an introduction to each of the texts can support fluent, phrased reading. For example, if readers hear some of the unusual language, look at two or three difficult words, or are given more background information, how will the reading be more fluent?

CHAPTER EIGHT

ASSESSING COMPREHENSION AND FLUENCY TO DOCUMENT PROGRESS AND INFORM TEACHING

Assessment of individual students' progress is essentially diagnostic. Such assessment is integral to the teaching and learning program. Its purpose is to improve teaching and learning.

—NEW ZEALAND MINISTRY OF EDUCATION

Making teaching decisions to help learners move forward is no simple task. As teachers, we need a great deal of information about the learners to do our best work day-to-day in the classroom. Many formal testing programs are not designed to give us the specific information that informs our daily teaching, but are intended to show trends in group performance. We can occasionally be wonderfully surprised by the way students reveal their thinking in response to standardized assessments. For example, as seen in Figure 8-1, a first grader took it upon himself to correct the grammar of the writer of the test directions on the state test!

This young child's insertion reveals that he knows reading and writing are language; he expects what he reads to

Figure 8-1. *A First-Grader Corrects the Grammar on a Standardized Test*

sound like meaningful language, and he is ready to engage his own powers of writing to correct it if necessary. (He has not yet learned the features of the genre of testing directions, of course, or he would simply follow them.)

We want our ongoing reading assessments to provide us with evidence that students are using systems of strategic actions across instructional texts. In this chapter, we examine informal and formal systematic assessments of reading comprehension and fluency. We will not present a comprehensive guide to all aspects of assessment, but refer you to other sources for more information (Johnston 1997; Fountas and Pinnell 2001, Chapter 28). Our goal here is to present observations of specific student behaviors, both formal and informal, that provide useful information to inform teaching and help us document student progress. Our goal is to develop readers who have a deep understanding of texts as well as a sense of the kind of phrasing, stress, and tone that will best reflect the meaning the writer intended and even some interpretation that the reader adds. We begin with key questions that will inform your use of specific assessments.

WHY DO YOU NEED TO ASSESS?

You cannot teach effectively without gathering information about each learner. You will want to collect data on your students for many purposes. The most important one is to inform in a way that will improve student performance.

WHAT DO YOU WANT TO ASSESS?

Some important issues related to assessment include *what* kinds of knowledge and skills you want to assess, *how* you can assess them, *what you think* about the information you gather from your observations of each student, *how you can use* the information, and how the information provides evidence of progress. The following are important questions that you will want to ask to guide your plan for assessing comprehension and fluency:

- What do you want to assess?
- How can you assess it?
- How can you interpret and use the information to teach readers?
- How can you use the information to document change in readers across time?

The answers to these questions reveal what you value in your classroom. What you as a teacher notice and attend to, your students will also notice, attend to, and learn (Clay 2001). So, the assessment plan that you implement in your classroom has great power. Not only does it guide your teaching decisions, but it also contributes to the culture of the classroom. What you value, your students will value, and you will develop unconscious ways of constantly rewarding by showing your appreciation of what students say and do.

If you value readers' development of a complex literacy processing system, then you will want to assess all aspects of the processing system. Weakness in any one aspect can diminish the reader's full understanding of a text. Your goal is not comprehension and fluency alone but the reader's ability to engage all the systems of effective processing. So, you will want to include in your assessment plan and show students that you value all of the following systems of strategic actions:

- Recognizing words quickly and automatically.
- Solving words "on the run" while reading continuous text.
- Self-monitoring of not only word accuracy but also of the syntax and meaning of texts.
- Searching for and using all kinds of information in the text.
- Noticing when the information doesn't make sense and searching further.
- Remembering important information from a text, which requires an organized summary.
- Sustaining momentum in reading as well as appreciation for the phrasing, stress, and pausing that are related to the meaning of the text based on what is known.

- Adjusting reading according to purpose and genre and also according to the difficulty spots in the text (slowing down to problem-solve and speeding up again).
- Predicting what will come next in a text based on what is known.
- Connecting texts to readers' own lives and personal experiences, to content knowledge, and to other texts.
- Identifying and appreciating new information and reorganizing their own knowledge to accommodate it.
- Thinking beyond the text to consider what the writer is implying but not telling directly.
- Considering the text analytically by noticing its organization or structure or aspects of the writer's craft such as language.
- Thinking critically about a text in terms of evaluating its accuracy, the writer's point of view, the writer's qualifications or credentials, the documentation of information, or any underlying prejudices the writer may have.

You might be asking: Can I really assess such complex cognitive actions? The answer is "yes" and "no." Although you cannot directly observe students' thinking, you can infer a great deal from their reading behaviors about what aspects of processing they control, almost control, and do not yet control with particular texts; and that is the foundation for your teaching and for the culture of the classroom you want to build.

Assessment is based on behaviorial evidence. When you are looking at readers in your classroom, you have what the reader says and does to inform your teaching and evaluation. You form hypotheses about the reader's thinking from these two categories: (1) the *act,* or the process, of reading (what the reader does); and (2) the reader's *response* to reading through talk, writing, or the other venues (what the reader says).

The challenge of assessment is to put ourselves in a good position to observe and analyze the *process* and *product* of reading. Too often, when you ask students to answer questions about texts, you end up assessing what they already knew. Consider these questions about *Bat Loves the Night* (Davies).

1 How do bats sleep?
2 How do bats know where they are going?

3 How is the bat's voice like a flashlight?

4 What do bats eat?

5 What is a batling?

6 Is a bat a bird?

7 What does *nocturnal* mean?

Possibly you have never read *Bat Loves the Night,* but you can probably answer all of the above questions and receive 100 percent, or A+, on your test! Questions #1, #2, #3, #4, and #6 may come from your background knowledge. For question #5, you might depend on linguistic knowledge. A *duckling* is a baby duck, so a *batling* must be a baby bat. The meaning of *nocturnal* would depend on vocabulary knowledge, but even if you didn't know the meaning of the precise word, you might connect it to *Blue Nocturne,* a dreamy musical composition, appropriate for the night.

Nocturnal means "of the night." Giving a test or posing oral questions such as #1 through #7 will not give you enough knowledge about the ability of readers to process the text. In fact, many good test takers look at the questions first to see what they can answer without even reading the selection, thus saving time.

Writing provides evidence of a student's thinking about a text. Compare the above list of comprehension questions to the following analysis of a letter from Jackie's reader's notebook (see Figure 8-2) in which she shares her thinking about *A Year Down Yonder* by Richard Peck in a written conversation with her teachers.

Jackie's letter provides a rich source of evidence regarding her level of understanding. Without using any specific "labels" for her understanding, she notices the language of the text, analyzing and critiquing the writer's craft. She sees

Evidence of Understanding—Jackie's Letter

JACKIE'S LETTER

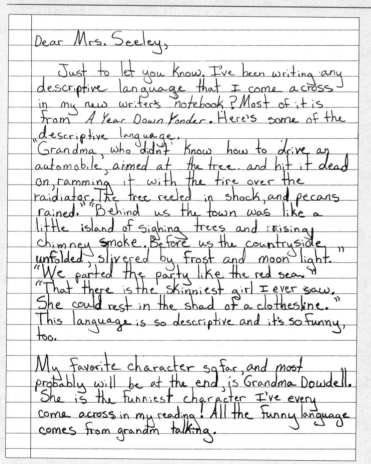

Dear Mrs. Seeley,

Just to let you know. I've been writing any descriptive language that I come across in my new writer's notebook? Most of it is from *A Year Down Yonder.* Here's some of the descriptive language.
"Grandma, who didn't know how to drive an automobile, aimed at the tree, and hit it dead on, ramming it with the tire over the raidiator. The tree reeled in shock, and pecans rained." "Behind us the town was like a little island of sighing trees and rising chimney smoke. Before us the countryside unfolded, slivered by frost and moon light." "We parted the party like the red sea." "That there is the skinniest girl I ever saw. She could rest in the shad of a clothesline." This language is so descriptive and it's so funny, too.

My favorite character so far, and most probably will be at the end, is Grandma Dowdell. She is the funniest character I've every come across in my reading! All the funny language comes from grandm talking.

WHAT COUNTS AS EVIDENCE?

Jackie can consider the text as an object and as a writer (*analyzing*). In her selection of language from the text, there is an implicit evaluation, meaning that she has considered the quality of the writing (*critiquing*).

Her ability to collect language from the text and her ability to critique require that she has used many different systems of strategic actions. She has read the words, self-monitored her reading, used information, remembered details, and made predictions.

Jackie takes a critical eye to the text (*critiquing*). She picks out a favorite character and tells why she likes her, which involves analyzing the text (*analyzing*).

Figure 8-2. *Evidence of Understanding—Jackie's Letter*

Evidence of Understanding—Jackie's Letter (CONTINUED)

JACKIE'S LETTER	WHAT COUNTS AS EVIDENCE?
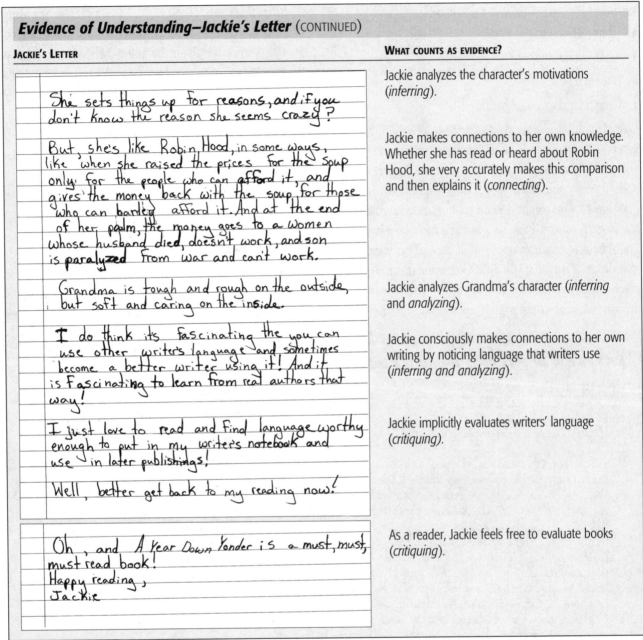 She sets things up for reasons, and if you don't know the reason she seems crazy?	Jackie analyzes the character's motivations (*inferring*).
But, she's like Robin Hood, in some ways, like when she raised the prices for the soup only for the people who can afford it, and gives the money back with the soup, for those who can barely afford it. And at the end of her palm, the money goes to a women whose husband died, doesn't work, and son is paralyzed from war and can't work.	Jackie makes connections to her own knowledge. Whether she has read or heard about Robin Hood, she very accurately makes this comparison and then explains it (*connecting*).
Grandma is tough and rough on the outside, but soft and caring on the inside.	Jackie analyzes Grandma's character (*inferring* and *analyzing*).
I do think it's fascinating the you can use other writer's language and sometimes become a better writer using it! And it is fascinating to learn from real authors that way!	Jackie consciously makes connections to her own writing by noticing language that writers use (*inferring and analyzing*).
I just love to read and find language worthy enough to put in my writer's notebook and use in later publishings!	Jackie implicitly evaluates writers' language (*critiquing*).
Well, better get back to my reading now!	
Oh, and *A Year Down Yonder* is a must, must, must read book! Happy reading, Jackie	As a reader, Jackie feels free to evaluate books (*critiquing*).

Figure 8-2. *Evidence of Understanding—Jackie's Letter (continued)*

deep into a favorite character, inferring motives, and she engages in that pervasive characteristic of good readers, recommending books to others. This letter provides ample and authentic evidence to the teacher that Jackie has read every word and understands the deeper meaning of *A Year Down Yonder*. Jackie has connected the text to her background knowledge of a cultural icon (Robin Hood) and has also made her own selection of valuable language examples.

This letter tells us a great deal about Jackie as a reader. Her reflection on reading counts as valuable evidence. Of course her writing is just a piece of the puzzle. The teacher will gather much more evidence of her ability to process a text successfully each day across the year to build her picture of Jackie as a reader and writer. But already, as assessors, we have some important evidence to answer this question: "What is Jackie able to do as a reader?" But another even more important question is: "How did Jackie learn how to think like a reader?" This question adds to our working theories about instruction in general. We learn from what our students show us what they are able to do as readers. And a still more important question is: "What does she need to learn how to do next as a reader?" If we can answer all three of those questions, then we can plan for instruction that brings our readers forward in their abilities to process texts.

Within any plan to assess reading abilities and needs, you will want to gather many different kinds of evidence across time. Much of the evidence will come from your observation of students' behaviors. It involves noticing oral reading behaviors such as errors, substitutions, and fluency. It also involves noticing how students talk and write in response to reading. Some of the assessment evidence will be systematically gathered at particular points in time; other evidence will emerge as a natural result of your everyday teaching. The key to good assessment is to get evidence from authentic contexts. You do not want to "clutter" your assessment plan with too much data or with meaningless information. Also, you want to spend your time on assessments that give you good information for teaching. That is why it is so important to use assessment techniques for analyzing the processes that students engage in on a daily basis as part of their ongoing learning rather than taking the time for too many tests.

WHAT ARE VALUABLE SOURCES OF ASSESSMENT INFORMATION?

Since you cannot directly measure what is going on in students' heads, our best information comes from two sources:

1 Observation of the act or process of reading, which may be oral or silent processing.

2 Analysis of response to reading, which will include thinking as revealed in talking or writing.

Each aspect yields products for analysis, and each can be assessed in a formal or informal way (see Figure 8-3).

As this figure indicates, students demonstrate their competence in comprehending and fluency in multiple ways. Students' oral reading has often been assessed traditionally, with a set of questions to test comprehension. When you ask questions, you are testing a student's comprehension, or the product of reading. You are evaluating their ability to understand what the questions require and provide a response that matches the teacher's expectations.

Though we can collect data about comprehension after reading, we need to pay more attention to children's fluency and problem-solving behaviors during reading and also to use talking, writing, and drawing as important evidence of comprehending. Written products have often been the

Assessment of Reading Performance

CONTEXT	INFORMAL ASSESSMENTS	FORMAL/SYSTEMATIC ASSESSMENT TOOLS
Talk About Texts		
▫ Interactive read-aloud and literature discussion	Observational notes	Interviews
▫ Book clubs	Conference notes	
▫ Guided reading (discussion after reading)		
▫ Independent reading conference		
Observable Reading Behaviors in Oral Reading		
▫ Shared/performance reading	Observational Notes	Running records
▫ Guided reading (reading the text)	Conference Notes	Records of reading behavior
▫ Independent reading	Audiotapes (or computer recordings)	Benchmark assessments
Writing About Texts (in response to reading)		
▫ Interactive read-aloud (written in response)	Written Products	Writing to a prompt
▫ Guided reading (extending the meaning of the text)	—Analysis in relation to strategic actions	Formally administered teacher tests
▫ Book clubs (preparing, note taking, writing in response)	—Quality of products	Standardized tests
▫ Independent reading (readers' notebook)	—Expression of personal thinking	

Figure 8-3. *Assessment of Reading Performance*

focus of comprehension assessment, but now teachers are finding that observation of students' talk and of oral reading behaviors are equally important in understanding readers' strengths and needs.

In a dynamic literacy program, you have many opportunities to observe students as they talk about reading. One of the advantages of teaching children to talk with each other about texts is that you can observe their thinking as they build deeper understanding of texts. In the process, you gather concrete information about what they are taking from texts. In Figure 8-4, you see notes on Amber's reading behaviors during one week in guided reading, independent reading, and literature discussion contexts. *LD* indicates literature discussion, *GR* is guided reading, *SR* is shared/performance reading, and *IR* is independent reading. Notice the wealth of assessment information the teacher has gathered about Amber's processing across instructional contexts.

The notes that the teacher has taken are very brief, but looking across contexts, you see evidence that Amber works at taking apart words; in guided and independent reading, she reads with a high level of accuracy. She can pick up important details from a text, as evidenced by her noticing information in pictures. In guided reading, the teacher asked for a summary of a chapter for the chart, and Amber successfully reported information in an organized way. In literature discussion she reported changing her knowledge base when she said she didn't know that boys could go to a war. The teacher noticed more problem solving on the text that she read in a guided reading lesson than the one she read independently.

This chart, with only brief notes taken over one week, provides a great deal of information on how Amber is building systems of strategic actions. You may want to use a form like this periodically or on a regular basis to gather evidence of comprehension and fluency. You can find a copy

Systems of Strategic Actions for Processing Written Texts: Observational Notes

Student Name: Amber Woods **Dates Recorded:** 1/7–1/11 **Context:** LD ✓ SR ___ GR ✓ IR ✓

OBSERVATIONAL NOTES	SYSTEMS OF STRATEGIC ACTIONS FOR PROCESSING WRITTEN TEXTS: Strategic Actions for Sustaining Reading		Strategic Actions for Expanding Thinking		OBSERVATIONAL NOTES
GR – The Stories Julian Tells took apart measures, noted sound of S. Difficulty (m) of pliers IR – The Littles accurate reading noticed silent b/plumbing	Solving Words	Using a range of strategies to take words apart and understand what words mean.	Predicting	Using what is known to think about what will follow while reading continuous text.	GR – Julian and Gloria will be friends IR – The Newcombs will have a cat
IR – Littles accurate reading GR – asked for (m) of pliers	Monitoring and Correcting	Checking on whether reading sounds right, looks right, and makes sense and. working to solve problems.	Making Connections ▫ Personal ▫ World ▫ Text	Searching for and using connections to knowledge gained through their personal experiences, learning about the world, and reading other texts.	IR – It's funny their names – little and big IR – "Little's afraid of mice b/c mice like bears or lions or something"
LD – Ank + Say – noticed same pattern of cloth in dresses / Mo Mo. Bay and little girl	Searching for and Using Information	Searching for and using all kinds of information in a text.	Inferring	Going beyond the literal meaning of a text to think about what is not stated but is implied by the writer.	IR – they really like to listen to the stories GR – Julian talked about cats to tease people and be important.
GR – summarized chapter succinctly	Summarizing	Putting together and remembering important information and disregarding irrelevant information while reading.	Synthesizing	Putting together information from the text and from the reader's own background knowledge in order to create new understandings.	LD – "Didn't know boys could be in war!"
GR – mostly accurate; slows at points of difficulty	Maintaining Fluency	Integrating sources of information in a smoothly operating process that results in expressive, phrased reading.	Analyzing	Examining elements of a text to know more about how it is constructed and noticing aspects of the writer's craft.	GR – found figurative language difficult
IR – reads more fluently	Adjusting	Reading in different ways as appropriate to purpose for reading and type of text.	Critiquing	Evaluating a text based on the readers' personal, world, or text knowledge and thinking critically about the ideas in it.	LD – Good book – he really touched Abraham Lincoln

Figure 8-4. *Systems of Strategic Actions for Processing Written Texts: Observational Notes*

of this form on the DVD included with this book. You can use it to gather observational notes on one student's behaviors in one or more of several contexts: literature discussion (during interactive read aloud or book clubs), guided reading, shared/performance reading, or independent reading). You will also find three other blank forms that can be used for observational assessment.

Collecting data on your students over several weeks of time will be productive in another way—it will sharpen the "lens of comprehending" that you apply to teaching. Once you have looked with these eyes you will look at readers differently. You will internalize the twelve systems of strategic actions and attend to them across the day.

Comprehending strategies develop across instructional contexts. As teachers you need to learn to look for behavioral evidence across these contexts. It is not always necessary to write notes on behaviors, but it is essential to notice them. Whether assessment is informal, "on the run" observation or something much more systematic, such as this note taking, simply engaging in the act sharpens our observational powers and makes teaching more powerful.

FORMAL AND INFORMAL READING ASSESSMENTS

In a way, you collect assessment data all the time, "on the run," as you move through your busy life. You assess whether you have enough food or need to run by the market on the way home. You may even write a quick list. You assess whether the dishwasher has been run to see if you can add more dishes or must first empty it. You may sample several dishes to test it out. This kind of assessment is second nature to us. It helps us live our lives. In the classroom, you are always noticing whether students are engaged, whether their comments show you that they have read and understood texts, whether their writing is evidence of interesting thinking about their reading. You may make some notes to record this evidence, and you may reflect on it later. This kind of assessment is *informal*. It does not take much time away from teaching because it becomes a habitual, integral part of teaching.

You can easily think of a time when you made a more formal approach to the everyday tasks mentioned above. If you are giving a dinner party, planning for a week of menus, or looking toward a large family gathering, you might seriously inventory your food supply and make

extensive lists before going to the market. You might even do some reading of new recipes (or watch the Food Channel) to further refine your lists. Realizing that you sometimes do such a good job rinsing dishes that they *look* clean but might not be sanitized, you might select particular dishes to examine or even interview family members to see if anyone washed them. You would be taking a more formal approach to assessment. In the classroom, you will find that you cannot depend solely on your "on the run" observations. You need systematic and regularly applied observations that help you look at change over time.

Formal tests of reading, with multiple-choice questions and essay questions (short and long), are usually administered only once a year and measure the product, not the process, of reading. They are designed to provide information to policy makers about how well the schools are doing. They help educators look at trends. These tests rarely inform teaching in specific ways. For one thing, they are almost always administered toward the end of the year, so they deal with outcomes only. These formal tests do present a particular *genre* of reading and writing that you want to help students become sophisticated in using so that they can show their competencies on a high-stakes test.

In Fountas and Pinnell (2001), you will find an entire chapter devoted to helping students understand and use the testing genre. You understand the need for students to become more sophisticated test takers. But what proponents of test practice sometimes fail to recognize is one unavoidable fact: if students cannot read the texts that are expected, then no amount of test practice will help them. Sometimes students spend hours of time in laborious practice without results. Meanwhile, they miss valuable instructional time and fall further behind. If we have rigorous literacy programs and only brief instructional sessions to help students grow in text sophistication, literacy scores will improve.

So our primary goal as teachers must be to support students to the highest levels of literacy possible in the one short year that you usually have with them. That means finding ways to assess "on the run" while teaching.

INFORMAL ASSESSMENT: OBSERVATIONAL ANALYSIS OF READING PROCESS AND PRODUCT

Your classroom assessment can vary along a continuum from informal to more systematic. For example, Sue was working with a guided reading group who was reading *The Stories Julian Tells,* a Level N book of realistic fiction. After the introduction, students began to read silently. Sue took the opportunity to sample oral reading by sitting beside each student, one at a time, and asking them to raise their voices to audible level for a few paragraphs. She listened and took notes, sometimes interacting with the student to make a teaching point (see Figure 8-5). She added to these notes as students discussed the story after reading.

Sue placed stick-on notes on a Guided Reading Observation form (included on the DVD with this book). She can later duplicate the group records and remove individual stick-on notes to place in students' folders. It takes very little time to keep these kinds of records because you can do it simultaneously with teaching; nevertheless, you build up a great deal of information. Notice that Sue has included notes on about three days of reading on her form. From these brief records, Sue can remember that:

- Nora is reading accurately but rather slowly, although she did increase phrasing over the three days. She can remember details from the story, and she is inexperienced in dealing with words that are hyphenated at the end of the line.

- Amber slowed down in spots and her reading was mostly accurate. She was able to hypothesize why Julian "spun the yarn" about the catalogue cats, fooling his little brother Huey. Although she did not know the concept of *pliers,* she made good word-solving attempts using visual information. She found some of the figurative language in the text difficult.

- Jocelyn read the story with ease. Her accuracy was high, and she had good phrasing, especially on dialogue; often her reading was expressive. She found figurative language challenging.

- Brittany read fast but had some difficulty with the double meaning of words such as *whipped,* and had trouble remembering details. She needs to increase her phrasing.

- Jeremy was highly accurate but read slowly and with little phrasing or stress. He worked to break down *prehistoric.* He responded to the story in a very personal way.

- Jazmyne made connections to her own experiences and described characters' traits and motives. She noticed and used italics while reading. Her reading was phrased and fluent.

Across the group, Sue could see that noticing and using figurative language was something that the children in general were beginning to understand but could learn more about. Also, the group in general needs some work on phrasing. Sue might consider creating some readers' theater scripts from texts they read or having them read poetry. She can keep this information in mind when planning introductions to texts in guided reading lessons, teaching points while working with individuals, and teaching points

Guided Reading Observations

The Stories Julian Tells	Level N
Nora 3/13 - accurate reading throughout, but slow rate 3/14 - remembered details from story, some phrasing 3/15 - highly accurate with increase in phrasing - solved hyphenated words with difficulty	**Amber** 3/13 - reading mostly accurate - slowed down in some spots 3/14 - inferred why Julian talked about cats 3/15 - Didn't know concept of *pliers* but good attempt pillars/pliers - figurative language was hard
Jocelyn 3/13 - accurate reading - good phrasing on dialogue 3/15 - easy text - made predictions - remembered details, but missed play on words- figurative language 3/16 - expressive and fast	**Brittany** 3/13 - fast reading. She finished first. - difficulty with figurative language - double meaning of "whipped" 3/14 - had trouble remembering details 3/15 - needs to increase phrasing went wait
Jeremy 3/13 - Highly accurate but slow reading. Asked "Is Julian real?" 3/14 - increased in fluency but little expression 3/15 - worked to break down *prehistoric* - contributed personal experiences	**Jazmyne** 3/13 - connections to own experience cooking - phrased, fluent reading 3/14 - described character traits - "argues" "gets in trouble" - inferred Julian's motive to tell fib 3/15 - noticed and used italics

Appendix 48

Figure 8-5. *Guided Reading Observations*

for the group after reading. Over time, even this anecdotal kind of information provides an excellent foundation for teaching.

FORMAL, SYSTEMATIC ASSESSMENT OF PROCESS AND PRODUCT: RECORDS OF READING BEHAVIOR

As we can see from Sue's notes about readers in one group, we cannot see what readers are thinking as they process texts, but we can observe reading behaviors as evidence for our hypotheses about these "in-the-head" processes. Some important actions to notice are:

▫ Noticing and correcting errors.

▫ Working at difficulty.

▫ Initiating problem solving.

▫ Searching for and using information.

▫ Solving words in a variety of ways.

▫ Using language structure as a support for and a check on word solving.

How can we tell when students are engaging in active problem solving? We have not found it very helpful to ask students to tell us what they are doing as readers. Many of these in-the-head operations are unconsciously applied. Some good readers are highly strategic but cannot fully describe what they are doing. (It should be a warning to us that many researchers have spent their entire professional lives trying to figure out, describe, and argue with other scholars about what is happening in the head of the reader.) Some poor readers are able to parrot "strategies" but not apply them, for example:

"I sounded it out."
"I thought about it."
"I made a connection."

In fact, when there is too much emphasis on talking about strategies and trying to consciously use them, the act of reading is itself modified (see Chapter 3).

We can learn a great deal from observing reading behaviors and looking at how students talk and write about their reading. Young children are easy to observe. Because they are just learning, their behaviors are more overt and they read orally most of the time. For older students who are reading silently most of the time, we can still sample oral reading behaviors for assessment purposes. We will mention two ways of documenting reading behaviors: (1)

the running record and reading record; and (2) using benchmark assessments.

EARLY READERS: USING RUNNING RECORDS TO ASSESS PROCESS AND PRODUCT

The running record was designed by Clay (2002) to help teachers observe reading behaviors systematically. We have been using this powerful tool for over twenty years, and we have found that it gives us a great deal of information about students' use of strategic actions. For one thing, it gives us information about whether a text is easy, instructional level, or too hard for the reader. That information is key from the start, since there is no point in assessing a reader's comprehension when the text is too hard. A reader who has to struggle to read more than about ten percent of the words has too little attention to give to the meaning. Keep in mind that readers might be able to comprehend and think very well on a text that is accessible. When you assess on texts that are too difficult, you are evaluating only accuracy.

We prefer using a running record to capture reading behaviors to asking "comprehension questions" after reading, especially for younger children whose answers are often more related to understanding the question than to their own thinking processes. We do find it helpful to have a brief comprehension conversation with the child after reading. As Clay (2002, p. 61) has said, "Conversation with a child about the story after taking running records adds to the teacher's understanding of the reader in useful ways." This conversation can take any form and often involves questions, but these may be very open-ended, such as:

▫ "Were you surprised by anything in that story?"

▫ "What were you thinking about the book?"

▫ "I was wondering about _____. What do you think?"

If you are concerned that the reader might have missed something important, you can choose to direct questions to that element, but you will not need to ask many such questions.

We would not usually ask the child to "retell" the story after taking a running record. For one thing, you have just heard the reading! You may sometimes want to have children practice retelling a story or to create a summary (two different things), but you will not want to have them perform the same kind of assessment all of the time. Retelling and summarizing are skills that generally address literal knowledge.

Particularly with retelling, the child may get the idea that "more is better." Trying to remember all the details of what you are reading may actually get in the way of comprehending. In all of the assessments in which you sample students' talk after reading, you want to get as close as you can to their thinking about the text, not simply giving back the information. Consider not only what the reader understands but what the reader thinks about what he understands.

Coding and Scoring a Running Record

To take a running record, you sit beside the child so that you can hear and closely observe reading behaviors, as well as see the text. You use a form, such as the one for Tony's record of reading *Peaches the Pig* (see Figure 8-6). (This form was designed by Marie Clay and can be found in *An Observation Survey of Early Literacy Achievement,* 2002.) The checks (✔) indicate accurate reading. When the reader makes an error, what the child said is recorded above the line, with the word from the text below it. The *T* means the teacher told the word, and the *R* indicates rereading or repetition in reading. When you see *SC* it means the reader self-corrected the error. The analysis in the right column shows what information sources the reader used in the attempts—meaning, structure, or visual information. The circles in the far right column show the kinds of information the reader used to self-correct the error.

A running record is usually taken on a text that a child has read once before (seen text). Sometimes it is taken on a "cold" text with just a few words of introduction (unseen text).

It is obvious that these two approaches will give you different information. If you are using running records as a part of a schoolwide assessment system, you will want to make an agreement as to which approach to use. For example, you may use first-time readings for benchmark assessment two or three times a year and record that information on children's records. You will need to consider it is a first reading in making conclusions. On a daily basis, you may want to take running records on texts that children read once before so the child has had one opportunity to process through the meaning.

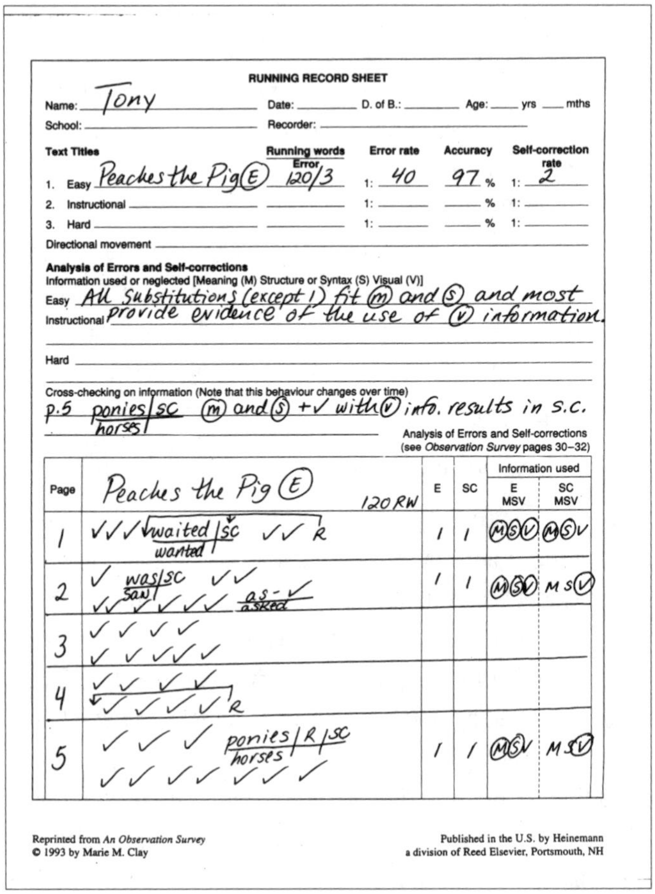

RUNNING RECORD SHEET

Name: Tony   Date: ____ D. of B.: ____ Age: ___ yrs ___ mths
School: ____   Recorder: ____

Text Titles	Running words Error	Error rate	Accuracy	Self-correction rate
1. Easy Peaches the Pig (E)	120/3	1: 40	97 %	1: 2
2. Instructional		1:	%	1:
3. Hard		1:	%	1:

Directional movement

Analysis of Errors and Self-corrections
Information used or neglected [Meaning (M) Structure or Syntax (S) Visual (V)]
Easy All substitutions (except 1) fit (m) and (S) and most
Instructional provide evidence of the use of (V) information.
Hard

Cross-checking on information (Note that this behaviour changes over time)
p.5 ponies/SC horses (m) and (S) + ✓ with (V) info. results in s.c.

Analysis of Errors and Self-corrections (see *Observation Survey* pages 30–32)

Page	Peaches the Pig (E) 120 RW	E	SC	Information used E MSV	Information used SC MSV
1	✓✓✓ waited/SC (wanted) ✓✓ R	1	1	(M)(S)(V)	(M)(S)V
2	✓ was/SC (saw) ✓✓ / ✓✓✓✓✓ as-/asked ✓	1	1	(M)(S)(V)	M S (V)
3	✓✓✓✓ / ✓✓✓✓✓				
4	✓✓✓✓ / ✓✓✓✓✓ R				
5	✓✓✓ ponies/R/SC (horses) / ✓✓✓✓✓✓✓	1	1	(M)(S)V	M S (V)

Reprinted from *An Observation Survey* © 1993 by Marie M. Clay
Published in the U.S. by Heinemann a division of Reed Elsevier, Portsmouth, NH

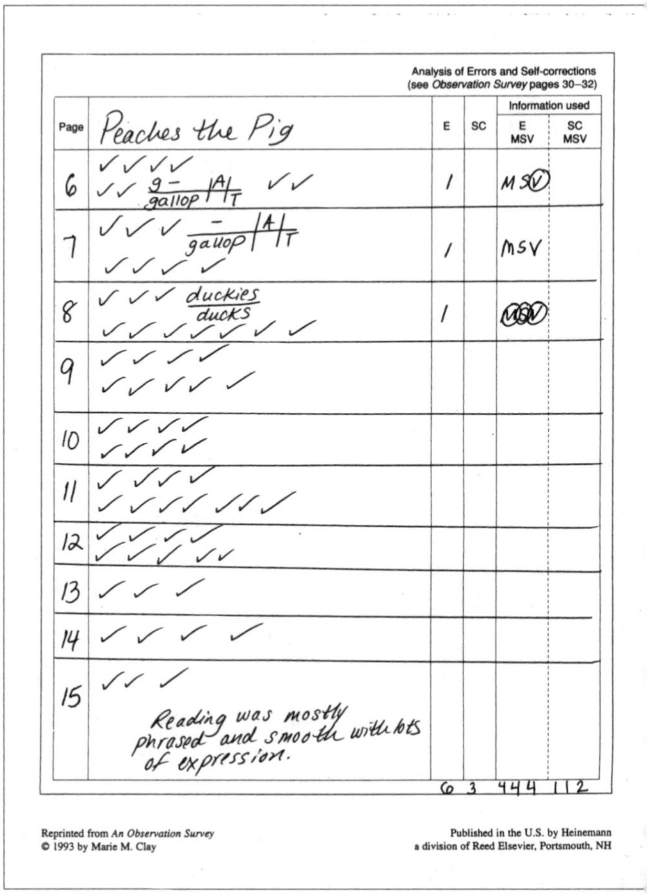

Analysis of Errors and Self-corrections (see *Observation Survey* pages 30–32)

Page	Peaches the Pig	E	SC	Information used E MSV	Information used SC MSV
6	✓✓✓✓ / ✓✓ g- (gallop) /A/T ✓✓	1		M S (V)	
7	✓✓✓ - (gallop) /A/T / ✓✓✓✓	1		M S V	
8	✓✓✓ duckies (ducks) / ✓✓✓✓✓✓✓	1		(M)(S)(V)	
9	✓✓✓✓ / ✓✓✓✓✓				
10	✓✓✓✓ / ✓✓✓✓				
11	✓✓✓✓ / ✓✓✓✓✓✓✓				
12	✓✓✓✓ / ✓✓✓✓✓				
13	✓✓✓				
14	✓✓✓✓				
15	✓✓✓ Reading was mostly phrased and smooth with lots of expression.				
		6	3	4 4 4	1 1 2

Reprinted from *An Observation Survey* © 1993 by Marie M. Clay
Published in the U.S. by Heinemann a division of Reed Elsevier, Portsmouth, NH

Figure 8-6. *Tony's Running Record for* Peaches the Pig

Making Time to Take Running Records

A frequently asked question is: "How often do you need to take a running record on a child?" Our best answer is: avoid prescribing a certain number of records for every child. For some high progress children, you may need only a minimal number of records to document progress, for example, every four to six weeks. For others, you may need to assess reading much more frequently. Many teachers take a running record daily first thing in the morning when students are coming in and getting settled. Others bring a student to the guided reading table for a few minutes before the rest of the group to take a running record. Another plan that works is to have students do a bit of familiar rereading or easy reading before the lesson while you take a record on another student. For primary students, running records do not take very long. The texts are short or you use only about 150–200 words of a text to capture the child's processing.

Analysis of a Running Record

The running record involves six levels of analysis that provide a wealth of information about the process and product of reading. You have a rich collection of data related to the reader's comprehension and fluency as well as the reader's use of the print. Let's examine Tony's record for the type of information that it reveals.

1 *Accuracy.* The accuracy rate gives you information about the efficiency of the reader's word solving and the text's accessibility to the reader. Accuracy does not guarantee comprehension; and, certainly, readers do not have to read every word accurately to understand a text. But it is a good first check. Accuracy is determined by the following formula:

$$\frac{100-E}{RW} \times \frac{100}{1} = \text{Accuracy Ratio}$$

E indicates errors, and *RW* is running words or words read.

Tony read *Peaches the Pig*, a level E text at ninety-seven percent accuracy, making only three errors in the 120 words of the text. This is a high level of accuracy, indicating that Tony is monitoring his reading.

2 *Self-Correction.* Self-correction is important because it indicates that the reader is monitoring his own reading using different sources of information, for example, visual and letter/sound analysis of words, language syntax, and meaning. For younger children, self-correction is extremely important because it indicates *monitoring*. You can have very high accuracy and a poor processing system. For example, if a reader makes meaningless substitutions (with no effort to self-correct them), if there is no rereading to confirm, or if there is constant appeal to the teacher, then systems of strategic actions are not being built adequately. You will notice that self-correction changes over time. Readers may reread a whole sentence to self-correct a word, or later maybe a phrase, or just the word. Eventually, self-correction goes underground. You don't observe it even though the reader may be doing the problem solving in the head. Later, you will likely see readers who only reread the phrase to correct the word. Then you will notice they self-correct at the point of the error. The self-correction ratio is determined by the following formula:

$$\frac{SC}{E} = SC$$

The closer the ratio is to one, the better the processing.

Overall, Tony made six errors while reading *Peaches the Pig,* and he self-corrected three of them, for a ratio of one out of two. On his first attempt, he substituted *waited* for *wanted. Waited* was correct syntactically (verb/past tense), was very similar visually to *wanted,* and made sense in the story, so the teacher circled Meaning (M), Structure (S), and Visual Information (V) in the Error (E) analysis column. It is important to note that Tony has substituted a word close to the meaning but not close enough. It is also the same part of speech, which is related to the phrasing and fluency as well as to the meaning. At the end of the line, Tony went back to *wanted* and this time read it correctly. The teacher's hypothesis was that the reader thought *wanted* fit the overall meaning of the story better (that the little pig really wanted to play with friends) so she circled M in the SC (Self-Corrected) analysis column. (Keep in mind that the correct word always fits meaning, structure, and visual information. The analyzer's job is to hypothesize the source of information the reader probably used to self-correct.)

On page 2, Tony read *was* for *saw,* which up to that point made sense, sounded right, and was visually similar. He quickly self-corrected to say *saw,* however, and the teacher hypothesized that he attended more closely to the visual features of the word. On page 5, Tony said *ponies* for *horses* then stopped, repeated the word, and self-corrected the error. *Ponies* would have made sense, but was obviously not correct visually. The repetition indicates that Tony knew right away *ponies* was wrong and needed to study the word a little more carefully, thinking what else it would be (that would *look right* and *make sense*). The running record provides evidence that readers are making sources of information fit.

3 *Sources of Information Used and Neglected.* After analyzing a running record, the teacher takes note of the sources of information that readers are using and those that they are not using as effectively as they should. You can notice whether the reader is using each type of information—meaning (m), structure (s), or visual information (v). You will want to think about whether the reader is consistently using meaning as an information source as you think about the reader's attention to understanding the text. This analysis helps in the individual teaching that may follow and can guide group teaching. On this easy text, all of Tony's substitutions except one (*ponies*) indicated that he was using meaning, language structure, and visual information. His self-correction provides evidence that he was able to use visual information. The teacher will be working to help him continue to use all sources of information together on more difficult texts.

4 *Strategic Actions.* You can now look at the left side of the record to analyze the processing actions in which the reader engages. How does the reader use the sources of information? Does the reader self-monitor? How does the reader engage in self-correction or problem solving? What are the ways the reader engages in processing?

Think about Tony's actions. He makes substitutions that are meaningful. He tries unfamiliar words. He tries parts of words, rereads to self-correct. These problem-solving actions are critical to the building of a processing system.

5 *Fluency and Phrasing.* Sampling oral reading behavior through using running records provides ample evidence of the student's ability to read fluently and with phrasing, provided you are using a text that is within the control of the reader. None of us can read a text fluently if it is too hard, so accuracy is also important here. Think about all of the fluency dimensions discussed in Chapters 6 and 7 and make notes at the end of the record. Notice that at the end of Tony's record, the teacher wrote, "Reading was mostly phrased and smooth with lots of expression." The fact that Tony was able to understand the meaning of the story is evident not only in the conversation afterwards but also in the way he interpreted the story with his voice.

6 *Comprehension.* As you observe students while taking running records, you can find evidence that reveals the extent to which they are working to make meaning. This record provided evidence that Tony was attending to meaning as he used different sources to predict and self-correct his reading. By searching to make sources of information fit, Tony was engaging in strategic actions. He monitored his reading, making sure that it made sense at all times. In addition, if you look at the brief conversation Tony had with his teacher after the running record, you will see that it provides evidence of understanding (see Figure 8-7).

CONVERSATION WITH TONY AFTER READING
Peaches the Pig, LEVEL E

TEACHER: So what did you think about Peaches?

TONY: She was sad 'cause she wanted to play and nobody like her.

TEACHER: She couldn't play with some of those animals, though.

TONY: No, 'cause she could do stuff like go up trees and...what horses did.

TEACHER: Gallop?

TONY: Yeah, gallop.

TEACHER: Do you know want gallop means?

TONY: Run fast?

TEACHER: That's about right, and gallop is the way they do it. (ACTS IT OUT.) Well, was the problem solved?

TONY: Yeah, she saw pigs and she could do what other pigs did. She was happy to be in the mud with the pigs.

TEACHER: I'm glad she found the pigs!

TONY: Me too.

Figure 8-7. *Conversation with Tony After Reading* Peaches the Pig. *Level E*

Tony accurately identified Peaches' problem and also understood her solution and inferred her feelings at the beginning and ending of the story. This conversation makes it evident that even simple stories like this one require thinking beyond the text.

ASSESSING MORE PROFICIENT READERS: USING RECORDS OF READING BEHAVIOR TO ASSESS PROCESS AND PRODUCT

As students begin to read much longer texts, you will want to continue to sample oral reading behavior on a regular basis. In brief interactions with students using a book they are reading in a guided reading lesson or independently, you can gather a great deal of assessment information to inform teaching. You will want to note errors, observe phrasing and fluency as they read, and notice what they say about the text.

We have found that when students are reading long texts, accuracy is not as reliable as a guide to the appropriateness of the text. Certainly, readers must have a high level of accuracy, but they must also know the meaning of almost all of the words that they encounter and be able to parse complex sentences. They must be able to remember information over time, from the beginning of their reading of a text to the end, which sometimes may be days later. To capture the complexity of this act and make assessment systematic and also practical, you may want to use a photocopy or typed copy of a text to record reading behavior periodically. You will want to code the reading by marking the actions and errors using the following coding system developed by Clay (2000) (Figure 8-8).

After coding the behavior, you can analyze it to help you think about the sources of information the reader used and the actions taken as noted earlier in this chapter. Calculate the accuracy rate and think about what the student's substitutions and other errors indicate about solving words and using sources of information. Also, notice and make notes about the extent to which the student read with fluency, phrasing, and appropriate expression and pace. You will want to have a conversation with the reader so you can gather more behavioral evidence of text understanding. You may want to ask the reader to do some writing about the reading as well. In Figure 8-9, you see an example of

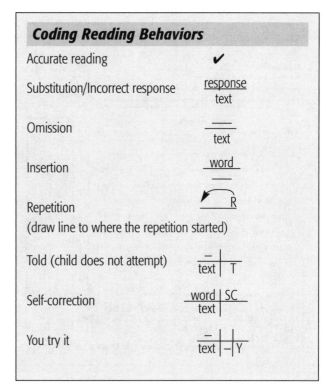

Figure 8-8. *Coding Reading Behaviors*

Jocelyn's reading of *The Big Snow,* a level N fiction selection, as coded and analyzed by her teacher.

As you can see from the record, Jocelyn read the text easily. She read with high accuracy and good phrasing. She paused and appropriately used punctuation. Several times, she slowed down to problem-solve words but speeded up again. She was using meaning information, language structure, and visual information. We can notice self-correction, indicating that she was monitoring her reading, but on a couple of errors, she did not self-correct, probably because they did not change the meaning. She may have noticed these errors but did not take the time to correct them. On two occasions, she read the words accurately but repeated to correct her intonation. All in all, the record indicates that Jocelyn was processing this text with high competence. You can calculate her accuracy and self-correction rate, but more important are the strategic actions you observe.

Following the reading of the story, Jocelyn's teacher engaged her in a brief oral conversation about the text. Jocelyn's responses to the teacher's probes are presented in Figure 8-10.

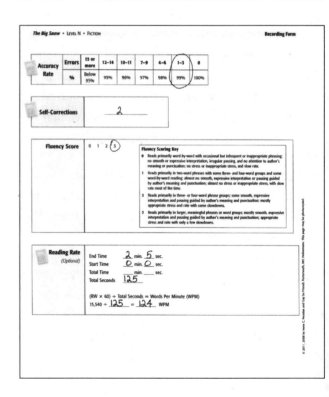

Figure 8-9. *Jocelyn's Recording Form,* The Big Snow

Notice that the teacher began the conversation in an open-ended way so that it felt more like a conversation than a list of questions. For example, Jocelyn volunteered information about the snowstorm and how Patrick, although nervous, does things to keep himself and his brothers safe until Mom and Dad get home.

Recording Form   *The Big Snow* • LEVEL N • FICTION

Part Two: Comprehension Conversation

Have a conversation with the student, noting the key understandings the student expresses. Use prompts as needed to stimulate discussion of understandings the student does not express. It is not necessary to use every prompt for each book. Score for evidence of all understandings expressed—with or without a prompt. Circle the number in the score column that reflects the level of understanding demonstrated.

Teacher: Talk about what happened in this story.

Comprehension Scoring Key

0   Reflects **unsatisfactory** understanding of the text. Either does not respond or talks off the topic.

1   Reflects **limited** understanding of the text. Mentions a few facts or ideas but does not express the important information or ideas.

2   Reflects **satisfactory** understanding of the text. Includes important information and ideas but neglects other key understandings.

3   Reflects **excellent** understanding of the text. Includes almost all important information and main ideas.

Key Understandings	Prompts	Score
Within the Text There was a huge snowstorm in Chicago and it was causing a lot of problems. *Before school out it starts snowing* Recounts important episodes in the sequence of events, such as: Snow is falling; Patrick struggles home and finds no one there; the lights go off; Patrick and his family solve a lot of problems; Dad is still not home; everyone finally gets home. In the end, they were okay. They were at home (or his dad was home). *Note any additional understandings:*	What was the big problem at the beginning of the story? What were some of the problems that Patrick had? How did Patrick solve the problems? How did the story end?	0 1 2 **(3)**
Beyond the Text *Sorta – we had a big snowstorm and it took a long time to get home on the bus.* This reminds me of when our lights went out (or provides a similar example). Patrick started to get scared when he got home and was alone. *He was nervous 'cause no one was home when he got there.* His dad was a really nice person because he was always helping people. *Nice person – he helped a stuck car.* Patrick did a good job of (gives a plausible answer). He didn't complain but just did what he needed to do. *Kinda brave and scared at the same time* *Note any additional understandings:*	Have you ever had an experience like this? How did Patrick feel when he got home alone? What kind of person do you think Patrick's dad was? *Why?* What kind of person do you think Patrick was?	0 1 2 **(3)**
About the Text The author told what Patrick was thinking to show how *worried* he was about the dangerous snowstorm. *everything that was happening.* The author showed what kind of person Patrick was by telling everything he did. *(no further responses than already provided)*	How did the author help you know this was a kind of dangerous situation? How did the author show you what kind of person Patrick was?	0 1 **(2)** 3

Guide to Total Score
9–10 Excellent Comprehension
7–8 Satisfactory Comprehension
5–6 Limited Comprehension
0–4 Unsatisfactory Comprehension

Subtotal Score: **8**/9
Add 1 for any additional understandings: **/1**
Total Score: **8**/10

Fountas & Pinnell Benchmark Assessment System 1

Figure 8-10. *Comprehension Conversation of* The Big Snow

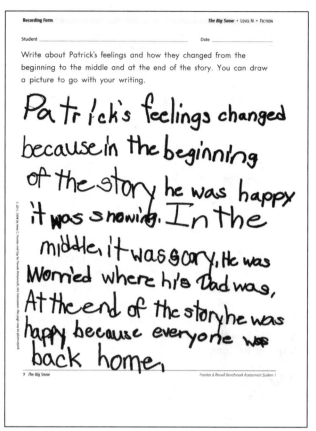

Recording Form   *The Big Snow* • LEVEL N • FICTION

Student _____ Date _____

Write about Patrick's feelings and how they changed from the beginning to the middle and at the end of the story. You can draw a picture to go with your writing.

Patrick's feelings changed because in the beginning of the story he was happy it was snowing. In the middle, it was scary, He was worried where his Dad was, At the end of the story he was happy because everyone was back home.

7   *The Big Snow*   *Fountas & Pinnell Benchmark Assessment System 1*

Figure 8-11. *Jocelyn's Writing in Response to* The Big Snow

Jocelyn's writing in response to the text is presented in Figure 8-11.

This brief piece of writing indicates that Jocelyn can think beyond the text to infer characters' motives and reasons for acting.

To conclude this section on the systematic observation of reading behaviors using running records or reading records, we present Figure 8-12, a summary of the variety of types of information related to comprehension and fluency that you gain from a running record or a record of reading behavior.

Earlier in the year, Sue took the opportunity to get some general information about Jocelyn's perspectives on her own reading (see Figure 8-13) to add to her literacy folder and to use to support her literacy learning.

You don't need to ask questions like these very often because you will have plenty of information about students' perspectives from observing their reading behaviors, but you may want to gather information about individual readers early in the year. Notice that Jocelyn can name some favorite books and series and can articulate how she chooses books and what she likes about books. Over the next few years, she will grow in her ability to describe the characteristics of genres along with her own tastes and preferences. She may develop more self-awareness of her own strengths as a reader and be able to talk about how she helps herself; but in fact, it is not really necessary for her to be able to describe her cognitive processing—only to do it. Her idea that she reads a lot and reads and discusses books with others has a great deal of validity for her.

All of the assessment procedures Sue used with her guided reading group were observational. You will always want to use ongoing note taking to capture information about your readers. You will also want to use some systematic coding of reading behaviors periodically to look at the student's precise processing.

TYPES OF INFORMATION FROM READING RECORDS:
Evidence of Comprehension and Fluency

INFORMATION	DEFINITION	WHAT IT TELLS ABOUT READING
Accuracy Rate	A reader's ability to read words correctly.	The reader's ability to use information and check on reading using all sources of information in the text. An indicator of the reader's ability to pay attention to the meaning of the text and notice when all information fits.
Self-Correction Rate	The rate at which a reader notices errors and is able to work them out independently.	The reader's ability to notice mismatches and to work at problem solving by searching for and checking different kinds of information (meaning, print, and language) against each other.
Sources of Information Used/Neglected	The reader's use of the print, language, and meaning from a text.	The reader's ability to search for and use each type of information while reading and the type of information the reader is not using.
Reading Behaviors: Use of Problem-Solving Actions	How the reader engages in actions to problem solve or think his way through a text.	The reader's ability to initiate actions that assure the meaning of the text is intact along with the other kinds of information provided in the text.
Fluency and Phrasing	The reader's ability to orchestrate the author's intended meaning with his voice.	The reader's ability to attend to meaningful units of language, pause at points to convey meaning, stress words that contribute to meaning, use punctuation to guide meaning, and use expression to interpret meaning.
Comprehension	The reader's understanding of the author's meaning as evidenced by facial expressions, comments, talk, or writing after reading.	The reader's ability to think about, understand, and talk or respond nonverbally to the content and ideas in a text.

Figure 8-12. *Types of Information from Reading Records: Evidence of Comprehension and Fluency*

ASSESSING READING FLUENCY

As you listen to oral reading, you will always want to collect data that provides information about the reader's understanding of a text. The reader's ability to interpret the text with his voice is highly related to the reader's understanding of a text.

When listening to children read aloud, you will want to assess the degree to which they can process a text with fluency. Each time you sample your students' oral reading individually on a running record, reading record, or observational form, make notes about the student's reading fluency. In Chapter 7, we outlined six dimensions of fluency that are important to keep in mind. At times, you may want to conduct a systematic assessment of your students' reading fluency.

A SIX-DIMENSION SCALE FOR ASSESSING FLUENCY

Here we present a rubric that will help in providing more detail about your students' oral reading (see Figure 8-14). (You can find a copy of "A Scale for Assessing Fluency" on the DVD that accompanies this book.)

Looking below the surface to determine factors related to fluency will provide more specific guidance for teaching decisions. For example, a student might be reading fast enough but not pausing appropriately. A student may be pausing and reading at a good rate, but inappropriately stressing words. This scale allows you to analyze students' reading fluency in some detail along the dimensions described in Chapter 7, including:

◻ Pausing (using the punctuation).

◻ Phrasing (reflecting meaningful units of language).

Figure 8-13. *Jocelyn's Reading Interview*

- Stress (placing emphasis appropriately on words).

- Intonation (varying the voice in tone, pitch, and volume to reflect the meaning).

- Rate (using an appropriate pace—not too slow or too fast).

- Integration (consistently and evenly orchestrating pausing, phrasing, stress, intonation, and rate).

To use this scale, you will want to find a readable text for the student, one that he can read with ninety to ninety-four percent accuracy for levels A–K and ninety-five to one hundred percent accuracy for levels L–Z. You can decide whether to use a first or second reading. You will not be able to accurately assess fluency if the text is not within reach. Surprisingly, you may find that some students read with a high accuracy rate but do not exhibit some of the dimensions of fluency, all of which are important. If you are assessing fluency on a first reading, provide a brief, standardized introduction to the text.

Ask the student to read a significant portion of the text aloud. You may decide to have the student read it silently (or softly) first and then read it orally. Or you can ask the student to read it aloud as a "cold" reading. In general, fluency is best assessed on a second reading.

Follow along as the student reads, using your own copy of the text. You may or may not decide to mark errors, but be sure to note whether the text is too hard. Then use the scale, with definitions, to rate the reading along with the first five dimensions. Remember that you are rating this reading rather than the reader. Any individual might read fluently on one text and dysfluently on another. You are taking a snapshot at one place in time on one text. Often when assessing fluency, teachers search for texts that students read with varying degrees of fluency. This process helps in determining the appropriate level for instruction. There are students who have developed a habit of slow, word-by-word reading at every level; these students need intensive instruction.

Then, make an overall assessment of the student's fluency using "integration," which refers to the way the reader has used all of the dimensions. If you can avoid it, don't simply average your ratings. Think about the reading holistically. To what extent does this reading sound like fluent, phrased, expressive reading to your ear? If you repeat the assessment for a group of students, you can analyze students' needs as to the dimensions that require instruction. Then, you can plan small- and large-group instruction to address areas of need.

This assessment must always be interpreted in relation to the difficulty of the text. For any reader at any level, there is an inverse relationship between the text difficulty and fluency; the chance for fluency increases as the difficulty of the text decreases.

In this chapter we have described a range of formal and informal tools for gathering data to show student strengths and needs, inform teaching, and to document reading progress over time. In the next chapter, we will show how conversational and writing provide concrete evidence of student learning. We will also help you link oral and silent reading, talk, and writing in a benchmark assessment to determine a student's instructional level.

SUGGESTIONS FOR PROFESSIONAL DEVELOPMENT

Using the six-dimension scale, listen to Francesca, Forest, Nyazia, and James P. read the text on the DVD that accompanies this book. We suggest you listen for one dimension at a time and rate the reading. This exercise will help you tune into the many dimensions of fluency. We will address the teaching of fluency in Chapter 30.

Name _____ Level _____

A Six Dimensions Fluency Scale

		0	**1**	**2**	**3**
1	**Rate** — Rate refers to the pace at which the reader moves through the text. An appropriate rate moves along rapidly with few slow-downs, stops, or long pauses to solve words. If a reader has only a few short pauses for word solving and picks up the pace again, look at the overall rate. The pace is also appropriate to the text—not too fast and not too slow.	Almost no evidence of appropriate rate during the reading.	Very little evidence of appropriate rate during the reading.	Some evidence of appropriate rate during the reading.	Almost all the reading evidences appropriate rate.
2	**Phrasing** — Phrasing refers to the way readers put words together in groups to represent the meaningful units of language. Phrased reading should sound like oral language, although more formal.	Almost no evidence of appropriate phrasing during the reading.	Very little evidence of appropriate phrasing during the reading.	Some evidence of appropriate phrasing during the reading.	Almost all the reading is appropriately phrased.
3	**Intonation** — Intonation refers to the way the reader varies the voice in tone, pitch, and volume to reflect the meaning of the text—sometimes called "expression."	Almost no variation in voice or tone (pitch) to reflect the meaning of the text.	Very little evidence of variation in voice or tone (pitch) to reflect the meaning of the text.	Some evidence of variation in voice or tone (pitch) to reflect the text.	Almost all the reading is characterized by variation in voice or tone (pitch) to reflect the meaning.
4	**Pausing** — Pausing refers to the way the reader is guided by punctuation (short breaths at commas; full stop at ending punctuation or dashes). Pausing also refers to how the reader uses the way print is organized on the page (line layouts, paragraphs, etc.)	Almost no pausing to reflect the punctuation and meaning of the text.	Very little pausing to reflect the punctuation and meaning of the text.	Some pausing to reflect the punctuation and meaning of the text.	Almost all the reading is characterized by pausing to reflect the punctuation and meaning of the text.
5	**Stress** — Stress refers to the emphasis readers place on particular words (louder tone) to reflect the meaning as speakers would do in oral language.	Almost no stress on appropriate words to reflect the meaning of the text.	Very little stress on appropriate words to reflect the meaning of the text.	Some stress on appropriate words to reflect the meaning of the text.	Almost all the reading is characterized by stress on appropriate words to reflect the meaning of the text.
	Provide an overall assessment of fluency below:				
6	**Integration** — Integration involves the way the reader consistently and evenly orchestrates rate, phrasing, pausing, intonation, and stress.	Almost none of the reading is fluent.	Very little of the reading is fluent.	Some of the reading is fluent.	Almost all of the reading is fluent.

Using the Scale to Assess Fluency

1	Find a readable text for the student, one that he or she can read with over 95% accuracy.
2	Decide whether you want to assess the first or second reading.
3	Provide a brief, standardized introduction to the text.
4	Ask the student to read a significant portion of the text aloud; or have the student read the text once in full and then read it aloud for the second time.
5	Follow along as the student reads, using your own copy of the text, and marking errors.
6	Check the reading for accuracy—noting whether it is above 95%.
7	Use the rubric to rate the reading along the first five dimensions.
8	Make an overall assessment of the student's fluency—dimension 6 which refers to integrating the first five factors.
9	Repeat the assessment for a group of students.
10	Analyze reading fluency to determine what students are doing and not doing.
	Plan small and large group instruction to address areas of need.

Figure 8-14. *A Scale for Assessing Fluency*

CHAPTER NINE

THE ROLE OF TALK, WRITING, AND BENCHMARK BOOKS IN ASSESSING COMPREHENSION

Because classroom-based assessment grows out of classroom work, focuses on individual students, and feeds back directly to teachers and students, it is most likely to improve teaching and learning.

—SHEILA VALENCIA

If you observe students' discussion and written responses to reading with a "lens of comprehending," you will always be noticing evidence of different kinds of thinking as students discuss and write about texts in different instructional contexts.

ASSESSING TALK ABOUT TEXTS

One of the side benefits of including assessment of talk in your plan for following student progress is that you will get an ongoing profile of the class, including:

- The balance of teacher and student talk.
- Whether the amount of student talk increases over time.
- The quality of student talk.
- Evidence of different kinds of thinking across the group.
- Changes in the kind of thinking expressed across the group.

ASSESSING COMPREHENSION THROUGH TALK ABOUT TEXT

We have put together the chart in Figure 9-1 as a guide for observing talk across several contexts during interactive read-aloud, literature discussion, guided reading, and any other setting in which students discuss texts.

There are three blank versions of this form for recording observations from talk about texts on the DVD that accompanies this book: (1) form for observing ten students; (2) form for observing five students; and (3) an open-ended form (see Forms—Talking About Reading: Observing for Evidence of Thinking).

The questions in each category can serve as a guide for noticing students' comments. You can make quick notes in the boxes or make checks on the form.

Categories on this form parallel the twelve systems of strategic actions for thinking within, beyond, and about the text. For this observation form, we have broken down the

categories to make it easier to notice specific ways of recording your observations of talk. For example, "making connections" is broken down into the following categories:

- Connects the text to personal experiences. ["This story reminds me of when my family went on vacation and the car broke down and nobody would stop and help us."] Here, we are not talking about just any personal experience that the student decides to share. The personal experience should be connected logically to the text in question, and the student should be able to articulate why he made the connection.

- Brings background knowledge to the text. ["Some butterflies can travel for hundreds of miles."] Students can talk about what they already know about content. In the process, they will be helping other students use content knowledge, and it will help them to identify new information.

- Connects the text to other texts. ["*Roberto Clemente* reminds me of the book *Dad, Jackie, and Me* because both of them were baseball players and they had to overcome lots of things. Jackie was the first African American player, and Roberto didn't have any money and couldn't speak English."] You do not want students to make connections simply to "perform" or be able to say, "I made a connection." You want connections to be deep and eventually spontaneous. A connection that a student brings up should be worth mentioning rather than just another text that is related in some way.

In the chart, "critiquing" is broken down into the following categories:

- Evaluates the accuracy or authenticity of the text. ["I think *Coolies* is a true story because they really did bring Chinese workers over to build railroads, and some of

TALKING ABOUT READING:
Observing for Evidence of Thinking

CONTEXT: _____ **INTERACTIVE READ-ALOUD** _____ **LITERATURE DISCUSSION** _____ **GUIDED READING** _____ **READING CONFERENCE**

Thinking Within the Text

Notices and discusses interesting vocabulary.	▫ How do students respond to vocabulary words that you bring to their attention?
	▫ Do students independently notice new vocabulary and bring it into the discussion?
	▫ Are students able to define new vocabulary in their own words?
	▫ Do students notice new vocabulary as it comes up again in a new text?
Recalls important information from the text.	▫ Can students recall details from the text?
	▫ Are students able to locate information in a text that they have just read or heard?
	▫ Do students offer evidence from the text to support their points and conclusions?
Summarizes parts of a text or the entire text.	▫ Can students produce an organized summary of a section or chapter of a text?
	▫ Can students produce a brief, organized summary of a text they have just read or heard?

Thinking Beyond the Text

Makes predictions about what will happen.	▫ Can students use characteristics of the text (author, genre, title, content) to make predictions before reading or hearing it?
	▫ Can students use information they have gained from reading/hearing the text to make predictions about what will come next?
	▫ Can students make predictions after reading as to what might happen?
Connects the text to personal experiences.	▫ Do students offer personal experiences that are logically connected to the events, characters, information, or ideas in the text?
	▫ Do students identify with characters or events and provide specific information to say why? (Provide evidence.)
Brings background knowledge to the text.	▫ Do students talk about what they already know about the content of the text?
	▫ Do students apply their own background of knowledge to understand the content of the text, the setting, the plot, or any other aspect of the text?
Connects the text to other texts.	▫ How do students respond when you bring connections to other texts to their attention?
	▫ Do students independently make connections and talk about other texts that the one they are reading/hearing reminds them of?
Identifies new information and incorporates it into present understandings.	▫ Do students identify information or ideas in texts they are reading/hearing that is new to them?
	▫ Can students locate new information in a text they have just read or heard?
Infers characters' motives and feelings; infers what the writer has implied.	▫ Do students talk about how characters feel?
	▫ Do students talk about the underlying reasons for characters' actions?
	▫ Can students discuss what the writer was really saying or showing?
Infers cause and effect.	▫ Can students identify the underlying causes for events or characters' actions?
	▫ Can students identify underlying causes for phenomena described in informational texts?

Figure 9-1. *Talking About Reading: Observing for Evidence of Thinking*

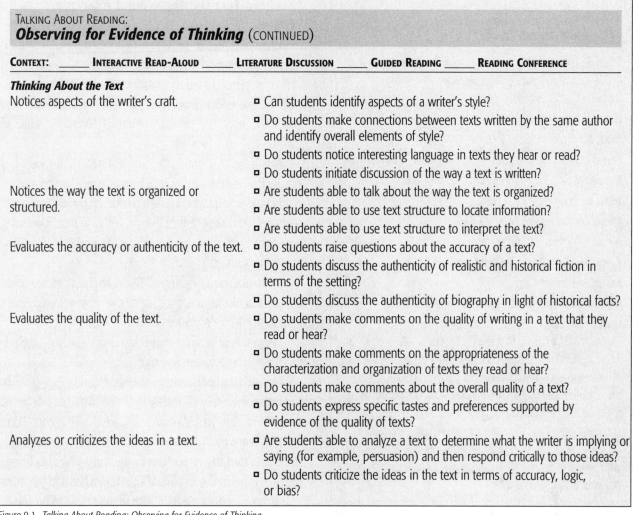

TALKING ABOUT READING:
Observing for Evidence of Thinking (CONTINUED)

CONTEXT: _____ INTERACTIVE READ-ALOUD _____ LITERATURE DISCUSSION _____ GUIDED READING _____ READING CONFERENCE

Thinking About the Text

Notices aspects of the writer's craft.	□ Can students identify aspects of a writer's style?
	□ Do students make connections between texts written by the same author and identify overall elements of style?
	□ Do students notice interesting language in texts they hear or read?
	□ Do students initiate discussion of the way a text is written?
Notices the way the text is organized or structured.	□ Are students able to talk about the way the text is organized?
	□ Are students able to use text structure to locate information?
	□ Are students able to use text structure to interpret the text?
Evaluates the accuracy or authenticity of the text.	□ Do students raise questions about the accuracy of a text?
	□ Do students discuss the authenticity of realistic and historical fiction in terms of the setting?
	□ Do students discuss the authenticity of biography in light of historical facts?
Evaluates the quality of the text.	□ Do students make comments on the quality of writing in a text that they read or hear?
	□ Do students make comments on the appropriateness of the characterization and organization of texts they read or hear?
	□ Do students make comments about the overall quality of a text?
	□ Do students express specific tastes and preferences supported by evidence of the quality of texts?
Analyzes or criticizes the ideas in a text.	□ Are students able to analyze a text to determine what the writer is implying or saying (for example, persuasion) and then respond critically to those ideas?
	□ Do students criticize the ideas in the text in terms of accuracy, logic, or bias?

Figure 9-1. _Talking About Reading: Observing for Evidence of Thinking_

them were children. The pictures look like real railroad bridges. The pictures really make it seem real—how hard their life was. Also, the letters make it seem real."] You want students to carefully consider their opinions about the text and be able to cite evidence to support them.

□ Evaluates the quality of the text. ["In _Sadako,_ I thought the way the writer kept counting the cranes helped me want her to live and to hope the cranes would work, but I thought she might die. It was so sad when her friends finished the cranes. It was a really good story."] Comments in this category must go beyond, "I liked it," or "I didn't like it." You want your students to provide examples to support their opinions.

□ Analyzes or criticizes the ideas in a text. ["In _The Day Eddie Met the Author,_ I think the writer was really trying to tell us how to write better, not just telling a story.

It could have been a book about how to write." In a "safe" conversational atmosphere, students will learn to think critically about what they read. You want them to be able to cite reasons for their opinions from sources within and outside texts.

Through conversation, even young children can express a complex range of thinking. For example, in Figure 9-2, you will see an excerpt from the conversation of some kindergarten children who were listening to _The Very Quiet Cricket_ (Carle).

As Mrs. S., the teacher, read the text aloud, she occasionally paused to invite students' comments. Kyla's question, "What's wrong?" is one that the teacher is hoping is in everyone's heads. Notice that they have several theories and that the teacher encourages multiple opinions. This brief discussion "sets them up" for confirming or disconfirming

---

The Very Quiet Cricket

MRS. S. (THE TEACHER): (READING) *The little cricket wanted to answer, so he rubbed his wings together. But nothing happened. Not a sound!*

KYLA: What's wrong?

MRS. S.: I'm wondering too,

JOHN: Maybe he's just a baby and can't do it 'til he's grown.

SHADA: Maybe he can do it later with his dad.

MRS. S.: Maybe he's too little.

MIKE: Maybe he lost his voice.

KYLA: My mom lost her voice once.

CARA: Maybe it has to be nighttime.

JACEY: Maybe he's shy.

MRS. S.: Let's see what's going to happen.

Later in the reading, night fell, and Mrs. S. reminded students of the theory that the cricket could talk only at night. Children hypothesized that it must be one of the other reasons or that it needed to get even darker. When the cricket finally met another cricket and rubbed his wings together, Alison blurted out: "And it made a sound!" All children agreed that this situation might have the desired outcome, and they were right. In addition, the page ended with "and this time . . .," a phrase that signals something different is going to happen.

Figure 9-2. *Excerpt from Conversation During the Reading of* The Very Quiet Cricket

predictions. After this reading, Mrs. S. could reflect that she had noticed the children talking about cause and effect and also had made and confirmed predictions.

Students achieve the sophistication exhibited in the discussion of *Seedfolks* (Fleischman) (see Chapter 25 and the DVD that accompanies this book), not because they have a few lessons on comprehending strategies or learn to name strategies, but because they are actively engaged in processing and discussing texts every day over the years of elementary and middle school. Deep thinking cannot be generated through exercises, but it can be supported through authentic conversation surrounding texts. Additionally, these conversations are highly enjoyable for students and teachers.

In Chapters 4 and 5, we discussed the value of conversation around texts. Your attention to the content of the conversations will be a valuable data-gathering context in your assessment plan.

ASSESSING TEXT UNDERSTANDING: ANALYZING WRITING

Students' writing can provide a rich source of information about their comprehending. Just about any of the genres of written response noted in Chapters 27 and 28 can be analyzed to find evidence about thinking within, between, and about the text. For example, look at Nicholas' letter to Cynthia Rylant (see Figure 9-3).

This letter was not written for assessment purposes but was instead an integral part of instruction. The very nature of the task prompts the student to discuss the writer's craft. Nicholas speaks to Cynthia Rylant, writer to writer, noticing aspects of craft, providing examples, and talking about the writing process.

In the following example, Tasha responds in her reader's notebook to a quote that she has selected from *Charlotte's Web* (White) (see Figure 9-4).

Tasha was able to interpret characters' feelings, including the reason Fern got so angry.

For an example from a younger child, let's look at Natanya's letter to a character in a story that she has heard read aloud, *Tops and Bottoms* (Stevens) (see Figure 9-5).

This letter provides evidence that Natanya understands the events and the characters in the story. She also brings her own thinking to the whole situation when she theorizes that it was good for Bear to actually get up and do something but that he did not do enough. She captured the main idea—that Bear needed to learn to pay attention!

Students who experience many years of writing about reading, along with strong teaching, will internalize many genres for expressing their thinking about texts, creating a number of possibilities in their repertoires. For assessment purposes, you may assign a genre in order to zoom in on students' ability to produce a particular kind of response, or you may allow them to choose the form of response. Just look at the evidence of thinking that Natalie provides in this character sketch of Boo Radley (*To Kill a Mockingbird*), presented in Figure 9-6.

In this highly sophisticated piece of written response, Natalie weaves together her assessment of the character, referencing pages in the text as evidence. She exhibits thinking within the text by her reference to specific details, such as Boo's appearance and actions; she exhibits thinking beyond and about the text with her analysis of Boo's inter-

Nicholas' Letter to Cynthia Rylant

EVIDENCE OF THINKING

Identifies genre.

Notices aspects of the writer's craft—interesting language and provides example.

Questions process of writing.

Recalls information from the text.

Expresses a personal connection.

Expresses opinion about the construction of the text.

Judges the experience.

Dear Cynthia Rylant,

I've read many of your books, and lots of people read your books to me. I loved them. My teacher reads a lot of your books to us. and your autobiography too. I loved learning about you. Sometimes when I'm doing a piece of writing I get ideas from you. I like when you put your words together with and just like you did in The Relatives Came. I wrote "The Roller Coaster was long and windy and scary!" I just finished that piece not to long ago.

Before I start a piece of writing I go back to my "Writer's Notebook" and see if I want to use any of my stories. I wonder if you do that too, do you? I do most of my writing at school in class, but I like to write in my Writers Notebook at home in my bedroom. I get ideas from you. When I'm stuck I think of stories you wrote.

I said lots of stuff about me. Let's talk more about you.

I read the book Dog Heaven. I felt real sad that your friend dog died. I think it was nice to write a book for your friend.

It reminded me of when my cat died. I felt the same way. I think it was cool that you did your own pictures in Dog Heaven. (I always do a sketch to go with my writing too.)

We had fun with your book Night in the Country. We read it a lot and then we turned it into a poem and acted it out. We all had favorite lines.

I hope you keep writing because I like reading your books.

Sincerely,
Nicholas

Figure 9-3. *Nicholas' Letter to Cynthia Rylant*

nal motivations. Unless she becomes a university professor of literature, Natalie will probably not continue to write about her reading in ways like this the rest of her life, but she will have acquired the ability to think and talk about characters in a way that will contribute to her enjoyment and appreciation of literature.

No one piece of writing will give you all of the evidence that you are seeking in order to assess your students' ability to comprehend. If they talk and write about reading on a regular basis and in a variety of ways, you will build evi-

dence over time. For an example of a more formal and systematic assessment of the letters that students write in their reader's notebooks, you can find a sample rubric on page 183 of *Guiding Readers and Writers* (Fountas and Pinnell 2001). This rubric covers areas such as:

- Demonstration of text understanding (including providing evidence and making connections).
- Voice or personality.
- Clarity of expression.
- Use of conventions (spelling, grammar, punctuation).

Quote	My Thinking
"Control Myself?" yelled Fern."This is a matter of life and death and you talk about controlling myself." Charlottes Web E.B. White	When you read this quote you could almost cry because it sounds like youre there with Fern and you can hear her yelling at her papa. When you read this text it sounds like Fern is standing up for the little runt runt pig and trying to keep it alive. When she said she was to take care of the pig I thought she changed because first she was sad, and then she got mad that papa was going to kill the runt pig just because it was small.

Figure 9-4. *Tasha's Response to a Quote from* Charlotte's Web

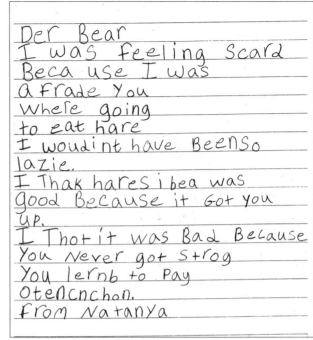

Der Bear
I was feeling scard
Beca use I was
a frade You
where going
to eat hare
I woudint have Beenso
lazie.
I Thak haresibea was
good Because it Got you
up.
I Thot it was Bad BeCause
You Never got strog
You lernb to Pay
otencnchon.
from Natanya

Figure 9-5. *Natanya's Letter to a Character in the Story,* Tops and Bottoms

□ Awareness of self as a reader and writer.

Rating several of a student's letters along these five dimensions will help you make decisions about what you do in individual interactions. Assessing letters from the entire class will give you ideas for the minilessons you need to teach.

If you need to turn letter writing or other genres of writing into a grading system, you can "weight" aspects of letter writing, such as in this example from one teacher (see Figure 9-7). You can find the form, Assessing Letters in the Reader's Notebook, for your use with individual students on the DVD that accompanies this book.

You can adjust the weight you give to any factor according to your priorities for the group. Notice that conventions are only a part of the rating. It is important for students to use what they know in terms of conventions, and they should present you with their best handwriting, spelling, and punctuation. They should know and use the form for a friendly letter. Your real goal in assessing letters is to see students grow in their ability to express their thinking about reading.

USING BENCHMARK BOOKS: SYSTEMATIC ASSESSMENT TO DETERMINE READING LEVELS

Finally, we will discuss using an assessment system that allows you to gather data about comprehension and fluency by combining text reading, talk, and writing. A bench-

mark is a standard against which to measure something. Benchmark books are an established set of text examples or "exemplars," that can be used to assess individual readers and their progress across time. Benchmark books have numerous uses. You can correlate them to your school or district expectations, at least informally, by using the books on the same group of students and comparing the results. You will get a good idea of how well performance on the benchmark books predicts scores on your district assessments. You can also create a class profile to judge results over a year's work and can use them to group students at the beginning of the school year for guided reading, or to make an assessment of a student who is new to the class. This information will be helpful for parent conferences.

FOUNTAS & PINNELL BENCHMARK ASSESSMENT SYSTEM

If possible, we recommend you use the *Fountas & Pinnell Benchmark Assessment System,* (Heinemann 2008, 2011) to gather data about your students because the levels will correlate directly to the A–Z text gradient. There are two systems: *System 1* for Levels A–N (grades K–2) and *System 2* for levels L–Z (grades 3–8). The books contained within this system have been written, edited, and extensively field-tested to ensure that they reflect the characteristics of texts and the demands on the reader at each level, A–Z. There are two

NATALIE'S *Character Sketch of Boo Radley* (TO KILL A MOCKINGBIRD)	
▫ Noticing and remembering important details. ▫ Noticing the writer's craft.	Boo Radley, being a recluse, has barely seen the sun. His skin is extremely pale, and his eyes are so light he looks blind. He has a thin frame and in his face he looks almost gaunt. He is definitely not the giant monster people make him out to be. "His face was as white as his hands, but for a shadow on his jutting chin." "His cheeks were thin to hollowness." (p. 270)
▫ Noticing and remembering important details. ▫ Noticing the writer's craft.	His movements are not swift and secure. Boo moves as if very unsure of himself, and his cough makes him shaky. "Every move he made was uncertain, as if he were not sure his hands and feet could make proper contact with the things he touched." (p. 277)
▫ Noticing and remembering important information. ▫ Inferring character's motivations.	Boo Radley does not need to communicate with people very often, and only interacts with people when he has to. He uses body language that Scout has to catch on to to express what he's thinking. Scout said that he was sort of like a child.
▫ Analyzing the text to learn how it "works." ▫ Inferring a character's feelings.	Boo Radley has three main relationships in this book. One is with his father who originally put him into seclusion and took care of him. When he died Nathan Radley took over and was stricter with Boo. The only thing people seemed to notice was that he talked to the neighbors more. The last and most important was indirect and sometimes hidden. Through the kind and constant observation, Boo Radley developed a relationship with Scout and Jim. He cared deeply about them and it wasn't known until they needed him.
▫ Analyzing the text to learn how it "works." ▫ Noticing text structure. ▫ Noticing the writer's craft. ▫ Thinking critically about the text.	Boo Radley had two functions in society even though he preferred not to be a part of it. He was the notorious legend among children. Kids were scared to go near it and always sprinted past the house. With the grownups he was a scapegoat to blame things on. He was often forgotten as well. He had two separate functions in the novel, though. He was another example of prejudice, but it was not in the form of racism. He was one of the harmless mockingbirds. He was a major part in the children learning things about life. In a way, you could use the way they acted around the house as a gauge on how much they mastered.
▫ Noticing the writer's craft. ▫ Thinking critically about the text.	Boo is not exactly a constant character. He doesn't really need to be since he's static, and the author only uses him when he's needed. For example, when Scout says Maycomb had forgotten about Boo Radley, he was not mentioned until he saved the children. If Boo had been constantly around too much, the ending would not have been the same and the realization Scout had wouldn't be as big.
▫ Inferring the impact of a character. ▫ Noticing plot structure.	Even though Boo Radley only left the house long enough to be seen once, he influenced people throughout the book. Jim learned a lot after pondering subjects as a result from an experience with Boo. Dill was fascinated by the Boo Radley story (however untrue) and his fascination started the entire series of events. Scout learned about it from Jim through experiences with the Radley house, and he had one major influence on events when he killed Bob Ewell and saved Jim and Scout.

Figure 9-6. *Natalie's Character Sketch of Boo Radley* (To Kill a Mockingbird)

Assessment of Letters in Reader's Notebooks

ELEMENT	EXPECTATION	POINTS
Response to Teacher's Questions/Comments	Provides a clear response to teacher or peer's comments/questions.	25
Quantity and Quality of Thinking	Provides about one written page of thinking. Shares interesting content about the week's reading. Shares thinking within, beyond, and about the text.	25
Support for Thinking	Uses evidence from the text or personal experience to provide evidence or support. Uses examples to support thinking.	25
Use of Conventions	Title spelled correctly, capitalized, and underlined. Author spelled correctly. Complete sentences. Use of capitals. Use of punctuation. Best spelling. Legible handwriting.	20
Format of Friendly Letter	Date. Greeting. Body (one or more pages). Closing. Signature.	5
TOTAL		**100**

Figure 9-7. *Assessment of Letters in Reader's Notebooks*

equivalent books provided at each level—one fiction and one nonfiction. Following a standardized procedure, you use the leveled books to identify each student's independent, instructional, and hard levels. The assessment is administered during a one-on-one student-teacher conference. For about twenty to thirty minutes, a student reads aloud, and talks about a series of books while you observe and note his behavior on standardized Recording Forms. Using established scoring conventions and procedures for analysis, you not only establish optimal learning levels but also gather valuable information about each individual's processing strategies, fluency, and comprehension—all of which give you insights about how to target your teaching. (For more information about the *Fountas & Pinnell Benchmark Assessment System,* go to *www.fountasandpinnell.com.*)

OTHER BENCHMARK ASSESSMENT SYSTEMS

If you do not have access to the *Fountas & Pinnell Benchmark Assessment System,* you can use any other benchmark assessments you have in your school or district. Many publishers provide correlation charts to connect their assessment with the Fountas and Pinnell A–Z levels, although they are less reliable. You can also create our own system by selecting two books at each level of our gradient and establishing an assessment conference protocol that each teacher uses to collect information about readers.

Benchmark assessments are critical for determining a student's instructional and independent level. You will want to conduct a benchmark assessment at the start of the school year to identify your students' reading level strengths and needs in processing, comprehension, and fluency. You will use this information to form instructional groups. You can re-administer benchmark assessments near year end.

You can decide, or work with colleagues in the school, to make a uniform decision as to when to use more systematic assessments, such as benchmark books at different levels. Here are some variations:

- At the beginning of the year to form instructional reading groups and guide teaching.
- At the beginning, middle, and end of the year to document progress.
- At the entry point for a student new to the school during the year.
- At reporting time or in preparation for parent conferences.

Figures 9-8 and 9-9 are examples of information gathered from Kulsum, an early reader and Figures 9-10 and 9-11 show information from Gabriel, a more-proficient reader. You will notice that the teacher will be able to use the information to place each child in a guided reading group and will also have a rich collection of information to inform teaching.

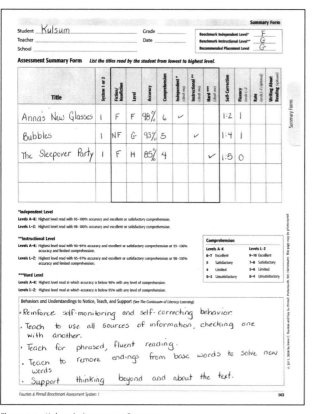

Student: **Kulsum**
Teacher:
School:
Grade:
Date:

Summary Form

Benchmark Independent Level* **F**
Benchmark Instructional Level** **G**
Recommended Placement Level **G**

Assessment Summary Form   *List the titles read by the student from lowest to highest level.*

Title	System 1 or 2	Fiction/Nonfiction	Level	Accuracy	Comprehension	Independent* (check one)	Instructional** (check one)	Hard*** (check one)	Self-Correction	Rate Levels J-Z (optional)	Writing About Reading (optional)
Anna's New Glasses	1	F	F	98%	6	✓			1:2	1	
Bubbles	1	NF	G	93%	5		✓		1:4	1	
The Sleepover Party	1	F	H	85%	4			✓	1:5	0	

*Independent Level
Levels A–K: Highest level read with 95–100% accuracy and excellent or satisfactory comprehension.
Levels L–Z: Highest level read with 98–100% accuracy and excellent or satisfactory comprehension.

**Instructional Level
Levels A–K: Highest level read with 90–94% accuracy and excellent or satisfactory comprehension or 95–100% accuracy and limited comprehension.
Levels L–Z: Highest level read with 95–97% accuracy and excellent or satisfactory comprehension or 98–100% accuracy and limited comprehension.

***Hard Level
Levels A–K: Highest level read at which accuracy is below 90% with any level of comprehension.
Levels L–Z: Highest level read at which accuracy is below 95% with any level of comprehension.

Comprehension		
Levels A–K		Levels L–Z
6–7 Excellent		9–10 Excellent
5 Satisfactory		7–8 Satisfactory
4 Limited		5–6 Limited
0–3 Unsatisfactory		0–4 Unsatisfactory

Behaviors and Understandings to Notice, Teach, and Support (See *The Continuum of Literacy Learning*)
• Reinforce self-monitoring and self-correcting behavior.
• Teach to use all sources of information, checking one with another.
• Teach for phrased, fluent reading.
• Teach to remove endings from base words to solve new words.
• Support thinking beyond and about the text.

Fountas & Pinnell Benchmark Assessment System 1
143

Figure 9-8. *Kulsum's Assessment Summary*

Anna's New Glasses • LEVEL F • FICTION   **Recording Form**

Student: **Kulsum**   Grade: Date:
Teacher: School:

Recording Form
Part One: Oral Reading

Place the book in front of the student. Read the title and introduction.

Introduction: Anna was getting ready for school. Her mom said she might need to get glasses to see better. But Anna didn't want glasses. Read to find out what happened when she got her new glasses.

Summary of Scores:
Accuracy
Self-correction
Fluency
Comprehension
Writing

Page	Text	E	SC	E M S V	SC M S V
2	"I am ready for school," said Anna. She had a new red backpack and new shoes. "We have one more thing to do," said her mom. "You may need to get some glasses."				
4	"I **don't** need glasses!" said Anna. "You may need glasses to help you read," said her mom. "Do you want to read at school?"				
	Subtotal	0	1	1 1 0	0 1

Figure 9-9a. *Kulsum's Recording Form*

Recording Form   *Anna's New Glasses* • LEVEL F • FICTION

Part One: Oral Reading *continued*

Page	Text	E	SC	E M S V	SC M S V
5	"I want to read," said Anna. "I love books! But I don't want glasses."	1			
6	Anna went to the doctor. "You **do** need glasses," said the doctor.				
7	Anna looked at the glasses.				
8	"I don't like these glasses," she said.				
9	"Look at the purple glasses," said Mom. Anna put on the purple glasses.				
	Subtotal	1	0	0 0 0	0 0 0

Figure 9-9b. *Kulsum's Recording Form (cont.)*

Anna's New Glasses • LEVEL F • FICTION   **Recording Form**

Part One: Oral Reading *continued*

Page	Text	E	SC	E M S V	SC M S V
11	Anna put on some red glasses. "I like red and I like these red glasses," she said. "You look great in those glasses," said Mom.	1		M S V	M S V
12	It was the first day of school. Anna put her new red glasses in her new red backpack.	1		M S V	M S V
13	"Don't forget your glasses," said Mom. "I put them in my backpack," said Anna.	1		M S V	M S V
	Subtotal	2	2	2 1 3	1 1 1

Figure 9-9c. *Kulsum's Recording Form (cont.)*

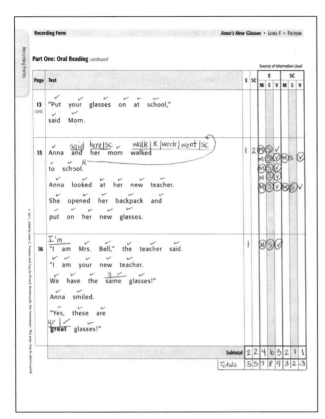

Figure 9-9d. *Kulsum's Recording Form (cont.)*

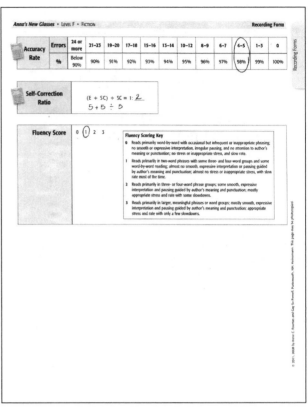

Figure 9-9e. *Kulsum's Recording Form (cont.)*

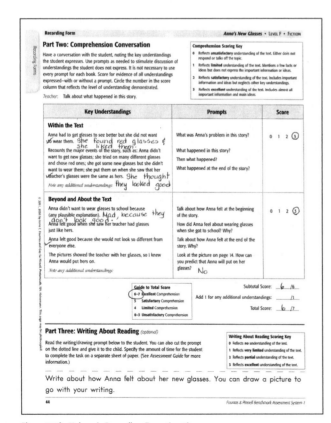

Figure 9-9f. *Kulsum's Recording Form (cont.)*

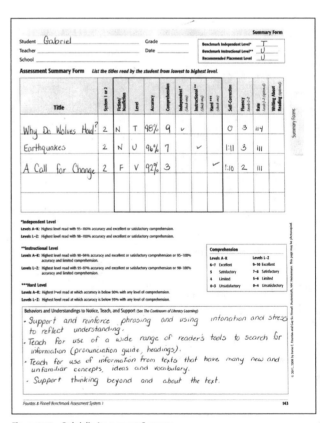

Figure 9-10. *Gabriel's Assessment Summary*

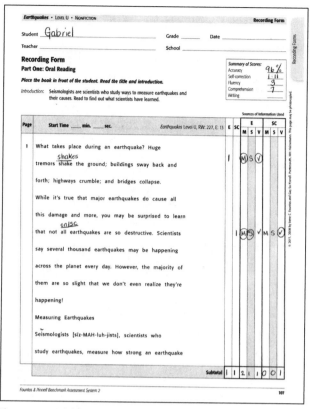

Figure 9-11a. *Gabriel's Recording Form*

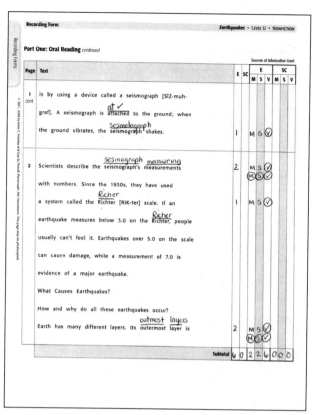

Figure 9-11b. *Gabriel's Recording Form (cont.)*

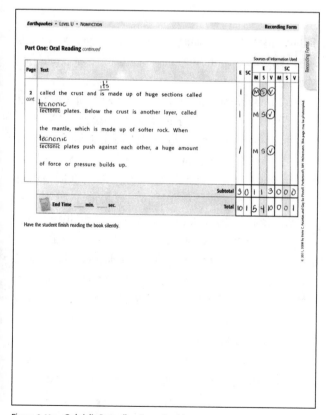

Figure 9-11c. *Gabriel's Recording Form (cont.)*

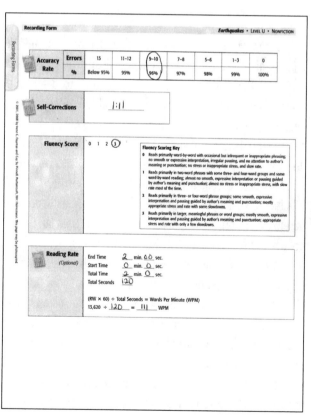

Figure 9-11d. *Gabriel's Recording Form (cont.)*

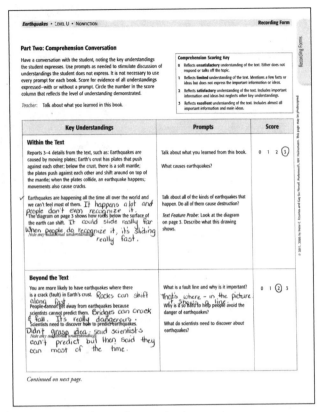

Figure 9-11e. *Gabriel's Recording Form (cont.)*

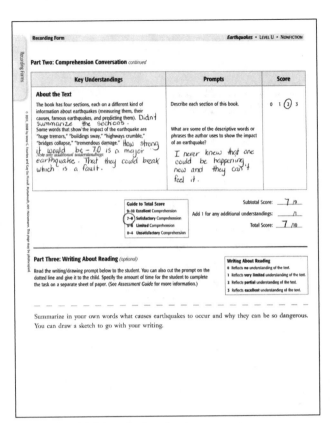

Figure 9-11f. *Gabriel's Recording Form (cont.)*

A short Benchmark Assessment conference revealed a great deal of information to guide Kulsum's instructional program. Her teacher used the information to determine Kulsum's independent, instructional, and hard levels at the beginning of grade one (see Figure 9–8 on page 113).

Kulsum demonstrated that she could read the level F text, *Anna's New Glasses*, at an independent level, with very high accuracy and excellent understanding, though her fluency was not good. This is a simple narrative fiction text with plot development and resolution, divided dialogue, and line breaks that suggest phrasing. Kulsum went on to read a level G text, *Bubbles*, at an instructional level with high accuracy and satisfactory comprehension, but again with poor fluency. This is a nonfiction text that asks readers to take a closer look at something familiar. Features include a large font, sequential presentation of information, and varying lines of print on each page. It placed more demand on Kulsum's reading process as she was required to use more complex language structures and vocabulary. Kulsum's final reading of a level H text, *The Sleepover Party*, proved to be too hard for her to read

and understand. Her fluency score of zero suggested she was not reading with phrasing, intonation, or appropriate rate which may have interfered as well with her understanding.

Kulsum's error behavior on the instructional level G text was very informative (see Figure 9–9 on pages 113–114). She used meaning, structure, and visual information in some of her attempts at unknown words *(those/these, color/colors)*. Other times she used only visual information *(sin/shiny, pray/pretty)*. Kulsum problem-solved as she worked through the text. She attempted all familiar words except one. Some of her pronunciations indicated dialect differences. Her self-monitoring was also evident as she noticed and corrected several of her errors without teacher support *(sop/soap, stray/straw, bubble/gum)*. She asked for help for only one word, *enormous*, which she probably had not heard before. The comprehension conversation after the reading showed satisfactory understanding. She had a better grasp of thinking within the text than beyond the text.

Kulsum's teacher identified several goals for her. The first was to support her in reading with phrasing and fluency.

Another goal was to help her with self-monitoring and using meaning, structure, and visual information to problem-solve words. Finally, thinking beyond the text was an important goal for Kulsum to apply to texts she read.

Now let's look at the Benchmark Assessment results for Gabriel, an older reader (see Figure 9–10 on page 114). Gabriel read a level T book, *Why Do Wolves Howl?,* with very high accuracy and excellent comprehension and fluency, making this his independent level. This informational text includes sections with headings, and a variety of sentence lengths and nonfiction text features such as charts, photos with captions, and a glossary. Next Gabriel read a level U book, *Earthquakes,* at an instructional level with high accuracy, satisfactory comprehension, and excellent fluency. This nonfiction book requires the reader to make inferences about the subject matter and to have some understanding of historical information about earthquakes. It also contains some technical vocabulary, diagrams, photos with captions, and a glossary. Gabriel reached his hard level with the level V fiction book, *A Call for Change,* with a lower accuracy rate and unsatisfactory comprehension.

A closer look at Gabriel's instructional level reading record shows that most of his errors were related to his not knowing the vocabulary or how to pronounce the words (see Figure 9–11). His use of visual information was not precise so he made approximations that were incorrect. He seemed unaware of how to use the pronunciation guide for words like *Richter* and *seismologoists.* His analysis of syllable parts was also imprecise. His self-monitoring of errors was an issue as he did not make further attempts or ask for help. His oral reading however was fluent and he read at a good rate, using punctuation consistently. In the comprehension conversation, Gabriel was able to share understandings within the text but provided only partial evidence of understanding beyond and about the text.

Following the conference, Gabriel's teacher set some specific goals for him including teaching him how to use a pronunciation guide, helping him with taking apart multisyllabic words, and insisting on monitoring when words don't fit the visual information. She also planned to focus on expanding his thinking beyond the text so when he read he engaged in higher-level thinking.

ASSESSING READING PROGRESS OVER TIME

The kind of interval assessment illustrated by the *Benchmark Assessment System* can be used at any grade level. We recommend conducting an assessment at the beginning of the school year to determine reading levels and to provide data against which to measure progress and guide the emphasis of teaching. We also recommend giving the assessment again towards the end of the year to document progress. Some teachers prefer to administer the final assessment a couple of months before the end of the year so they have an objective marker of progress. In between interval benchmark assessments, it is important to use other systematic assessments such as reading records to monitor student progress.

While the *Benchmark Assessment System* provides a tool for documenting changes in levels and processing, you will also want to refer to *The Continuum of Literacy Learning PreK–8* (Pinnell and Fountas, Heinemann 2008, 2011) contained within the system for specific teaching goals. This comprehensive continuum will help guide your teaching at each level of the gradient around seven continua of literacy learning.

To help you document student progress over time you may want to use the *Longitudinal Record of Reading Progress* (see Figure 9–12) or if you prefer an electronic record, the CD-ROM and online versions of the *Data Management System*. All of these options are included as part of the *Benchmark Assessment System*.

SUGGESTIONS FOR PROFESSIONAL DEVELOPMENT
Using Assessment Data to Plan for Teaching

1. Gather a group of colleagues. Bring copies of reading records and an audio tape of student reading along with copies of books he read.

2. Discuss the six areas of reading behavior analysis (accuracy, self-correction, sources of information used and neglected, strategic actions, comprehension, fluency and phrasing).

3. Make recommendations for specific teaching to support student's development as a reader.

4. Use the fluency rubric from Chapter 8 to rate each of the dimensions of fluency. Score it independently then discuss your ratings as a group.

WHY DO WE ASSESS COMPREHENDING AND FLUENCY?

Throughout this chapter we have argued that assessment is an important component of a literacy program. We want to be quite conservative, however, about assessing comprehension; that is, we do not want to assume students understand texts when they do not. At the same time we need to carefully consider what they show us in terms of their thinking so we can build on their ideas and encourage them to "dig deeper." Above all, assessment must result in informed teaching. Assessment is *not* teaching; it is gathering information for teaching.

Students at all levels need demonstrations and opportunities, clear expectations, and the support of their peers to extend their thinking over time. When you assess a student's ability to comprehend texts, you're working in a complex area requiring a great deal of inference. At any point in time at best you have hypotheses in a number of areas. Comprehension and fluency assessment has multiple purposes, for example, to:

- Capture all of the behaviors that help us know and teach readers.

- Note readers' strengths and needs in processing.

- Assess text difficulty for reading (at instructional and independent levels).

- Inform teaching of comprehension and fluency.

- Note how readers are changing over time.

- Group and regroup readers for instruction.

- Serve as a foundation for sharing evidence with parents to help them understand how their children are developing as readers and writers.

- Serve as a basis for grading to indicate progress to stakeholders.

You'll notice we placed grading at the end of the list. Grading is not the most important reason for assessment but it is sometimes the first thing we are concerned about. If you are charged with providing this public evaluation of a student's work, then you will want to have a clearly defined evaluation plan that is visible to students and parents. You will want to establish criteria for the processes and products of reading and goals for change across time. Assessment may include your evaluation plan but must go beyond it to inform your teaching. If it does not result in improved student performance, it will be a waste of time.

We summarize the numerous contexts for gathering data to inform teaching and document change over time in a variety of instructional contexts in Figure 9–13.

Summary Form

Longitudinal Record of Reading Progress

Student **Ronald T.**   School **Washington Elem.**

Record the date and draw a circle in the box to indicate student's level. Check one: _____ Benchmark Independent Level   ✔ Benchmark Instructional Level

Level	Benchmark Title
Z	Train at the Top
	Surviving the Blitz
Y	Int'l Space Station
	Saying Goodbye
X	The Internet
	A Weighty Decision
W	Coretta Scott King
	Summer Vacation
V	Tsunamis
	A Call for Change
U	Earthquakes
	Canyon Mystery
T	Wolves Howl
	"Get a Horse!"
S	Animal Adaptations
	Could Be Worse
R	Fishing Smarts
	The Election
Q	Polar Bear
	A Secret Home
P	Animal Instincts
	Plenty of Pets
O	Snake Myths
	The New Girl
N	Dogs at Work
	Vanessa's Butterfly
M	City Hawks
	Saving Up
L	Baby Monkey
	Ernie Learns

(System 2)

Level	Benchmark Title
N	Exploring Caves
	The Big Snow
M	Monarch Butterfly
	Thing About Nathan
L	Giants of the Sea
	Dog Stories
K	Animal Senses
	Edwin's Haircut
J	More Than a Pet
	Our New Neighbors
I	All About Koalas
	The Best Cat
H	Trucks
	The Sleepover Party
G	Bubbles
	Bedtime for Nick
F	From Nest to Bird
	Anna's New Glasses
E	The Zoo
	The Loose Tooth
D	Mr. Brown
	Nice Little House
C	Shopping
	Socks
B	Playing
	My Little Dog
A	At the Park
	Best Friends

(System 1)

Date: 10/5, 1/9, 3/20, 6/2, 10/4, 1/7, 3/19, 6/8, 10/3, 1/11, 3/21, 6/7, 10/6, 1/20, 3/17, 6/8, 10/4, 1/5, 3/13, 6/7, 10/6, 1/5, 3/5, 9/1

Grade: K, 1, 2, 3, 4, 5, 6, 7, 8

© 2011, 2008 by Irene C. Fountas and Gay Su Pinnell. Portsmouth, NH: Heinemann. This page may be photocopied.

Fountas & Pinnell Benchmark Assessment System 1

Figure 9-12. *Longitudinal Record of Reading Progress*

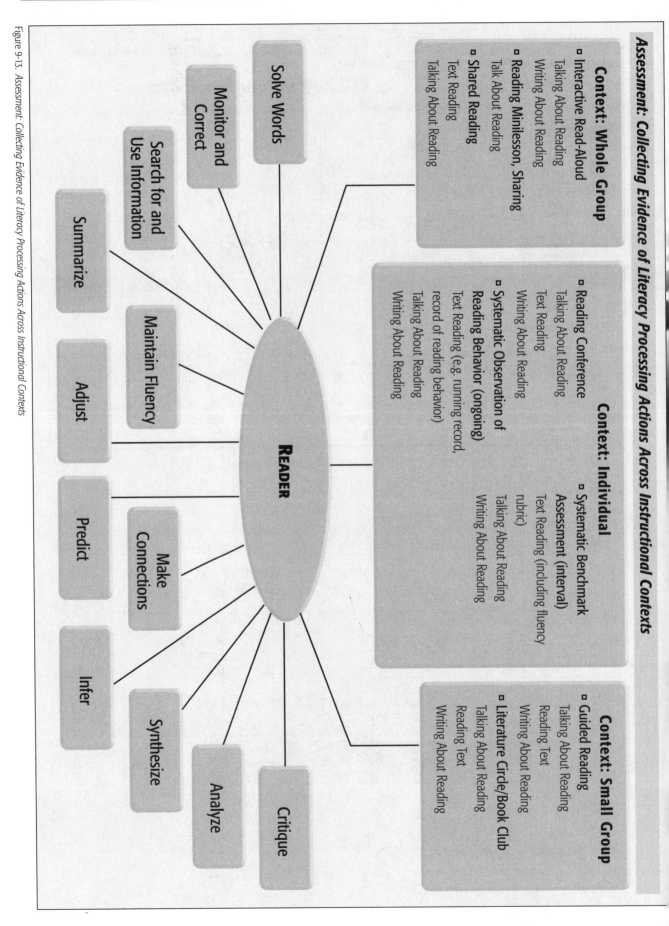

Assessment: Collecting Evidence of Literacy Processing Actions Across Instructional Contexts

Context: Whole Group
- Interactive Read-Aloud
  Talking About Reading
  Writing About Reading
- Reading Minilesson, Sharing
  Talk About Reading
- Shared Reading
  Text Reading
  Talking About Reading

Context: Individual
- Reading Conference
  Talking About Reading
  Text Reading
  Writing About Reading
- Systematic Observation of Reading Behavior (ongoing)
  Text Reading (e.g. running record, record of reading behavior)
  Talking About Reading
  Writing About Reading
- Systematic Benchmark Assessment (interval)
  Text Reading (including fluency rubric)
  Talking About Reading
  Writing About Reading

Context: Small Group
- Guided Reading
  Talking About Reading
  Reading Text
  Writing About Reading
- Literature Circle/Book Club
  Talking About Reading
  Reading Text
  Writing About Reading

READER

Solve Words

Monitor and Correct

Search for and Use Information

Summarize

Maintain Fluency

Adjust

Predict

Make Connections

Infer

Synthesize

Analyze

Critique

Figure 9-13. Assessment: Collecting Evidence of Literacy Processing Actions Across Instructional Contexts

SECTION II
TEXTS

TEXTS

As teachers of reading, we need to think deeply and analytically about the texts we offer our students. Our time with them is limited; they can read only so many books, so the ones they do must be carefully chosen. Chapter 10 describes the use of a variety of high-quality texts to support learning; it is followed by a chapter focusing on supporting thinking across a variety of genres. The texts we use for interactive read-aloud, independent reading, and literature discussion are organized by genre, author, topic, and other categories so that we can ensure that students have a variety of experiences. Only in guided reading do we turn our attention to precise "levels" of text complexity, because we are helping students progress through a series of gradated challenges. In Chapter 12, we discuss using a gradient of text to match books to readers. Whether we are talking about whole-class minilessons, independent reading, interactive read-aloud, small-group literature discussion, or guided reading, we are always considering the demands of texts. Chapters 13 and 14 discuss the very specific demands of different genres as categorized under the major headings of nonfiction, fiction, and poetry. Knowing how to think about texts is the foundation for effective teaching.

CHAPTER TEN

USING A VARIETY OF HIGH-QUALITY TEXTS TO SUPPORT LITERACY LEARNING

It is not enough to simply teach children to read; we have to give them something worth reading.

—KATHERINE PATERSON

For readers to build effective and flexible literacy processing systems, the texts they encounter in their literacy education must be varied, well written, accessible, and plentiful. Moreover, texts must be engaging. As we know from our own reading lives, there is simply no substitute for a good book. Is our reading purposeful? Is it interesting? Is it satisfying in some way? Has it changed us or influenced the way we think? With regard to most of the material we read as adults, the answer to these questions is yes, because we are volunteers. No one has assigned the reading.

A goal in introducing a book to students is to make them want to read it. If the book is inherently uninteresting, the goal will be difficult to achieve. Some teachers offer incentives such as stickers worth points redeemable for a pizza, competition with peers to earn points, or a similar extrinsic reward to motivate reading, but this practice runs against the value of promoting the intrinsic rewards of reading that will last a lifetime. And even with such inducements, poor-quality books or texts that are ill matched to readers are a very hard sell and unlikely to increase motivation long term. Selecting engaging texts in enough variety to tempt the wide range of readers in your class is the first step in creating motivated readers. You want to appeal to children from a variety of backgrounds—various regions, different language groups, boys and girls. All readers must see themselves (and what they can be) in books.

Introducing books to students is a great responsibility, because we must engage and interest them in ways that make them want to make reading a part of their lives. For elementary and middle school students, texts must:

- Be age, content, and gender appropriate.
- Be interesting and engaging.
- Be informative in a compelling way.
- Be suitable for their developing processing systems or accessible to them in some other way.
- Be available in quantity.
- Be available in great variety.
- Reflect our multicultural and diverse world.

The classroom must include a richness of texts, a many-faceted collection of books. As a teacher you create this text base and provide your students access to it. These texts not only contribute to students' developing capabilities as readers and writers but also demand growth in a variety of ways. The collection will vary by grade level but will:

- Comprise works of high quality.
- Encompass a variety of genres, including fiction, informational texts, and poetry.
- Include authors and illustrators that are sure to become favorites.
- Comprise enough copies to meet students' needs and the demands of the curriculum.
- Include enough variety to meet a range of interests, including those of male and female readers.
- Include enough variety to address a range of reading levels.

WAYS IN WHICH TEXTS VARY

Think of the variety of texts one student encounters from the time he enters kindergarten to his first weeks of high school! Then think of the experiences students need in order to process these texts with understanding and maximum enjoyment, and you have the essence of the text base. There are many ways to talk about the variety of texts children need to experience during the nine grades of elementary and middle school (see Figure 10-1). It is not enough simply to provide an assortment.

The kind of variety we envision is deliberately planned so that students encounter good examples within many genres and have the opportunity to compare and connect texts across genres. Variety does not have to be experienced every few moments or even every day. Students need a "run" of similar texts—short studies of texts that are quite similar—in order to learn about them and become familiar with their characteristics; the variety might be in the format, author,

Variety in the Classroom Text Base

ELEMENT	DEFINITION	EXAMPLES
Format	Format refers to size, layout, placement of print, binding, provision of art, as well as the way elements interact to form a coherent whole.	□ Picture storybooks □ Picture biographies, autobiographies, and memoirs □ Illustrated informational books □ "Readers" or Leveled Readers □ Short stories □ Easy chapter books □ Chapter books □ Poems □ Short informational texts
Genre	The type of fiction or informational text. Texts in a particular genre have particular characteristics that are recognizable and help the reader form expectations.	Fiction □ Contemporary realistic fiction □ Historical fiction □ Fantasy □ Science fiction Nonfiction □ Informational text □ Biography, autobiography, memoir
Special Types	Across genres, special types of texts are written that have similar characteristics. Readers soon learn how to recognize them and often form favorites.	□ Mystery stories □ Sports stories □ Survival stories □ Series books □ Adventure stories
Content	A wide range of content is necessary to appeal to as many students as possible. It may be important to have a large number of high-quality texts related to required curriculum for the grade level, but it is also necessary to have varied content to meet individual interests.	□ Social studies topics □ Science topics □ Literary content (traditional, classic, contemporary) □ "How-to" books
Diversity	The text base for a collection should represent the highly diverse population of the country and world in which students live.	□ Cultural diversity □ Regional diversity □ Racial diversity □ Religious diversity □ Linguistic diversity □ Diverse views and perspectives
Accessibility	Texts can be provided in different media so that all students have access to a wide variety.	□ Texts to read aloud to students □ Texts on tape or CD □ Texts on the computer □ Movies on videotape or DVD

Figure 10-1. *Variety in the Classroom Text Base*

genre, illustrator, version, or kind of experience they have. For example, kindergartners might hear a folk tale read aloud, participate in shared reading of a simplified "big book" version of the same tale, and then act out their own adaptation orally using puppets. A group of fifth graders might listen to their teacher read aloud a biography of Eleanor Roosevelt, after which some students might read (or listen to) and then discuss Eleanor's own childhood journal.

FORMATS

Texts are presented in different *formats*—sizes, shapes, designs, layouts, illustrations, bindings, fonts, styles of print (see Figure 10-2). In a high-quality text, the elements that make up the format work together to form an artistic and coherent whole.

There is usually an important relationship between the format and the content and purpose of the text. For example, popular *magazines* are of a size convenient to slip into a pocket or briefcase, are printed on thin paper so that they are both lightweight and inexpensive, are flimsily constructed to reflect their disposable nature, present the gist "up front" in headlines, leads, and under pictures, are illustrated to provide extra meaning and capture interest, and so on.

A *short story* condenses meaning to form a "whole" in just a few pages; the writer may provide intense details over a short period of time or skip or imply details, but the reader comes away with the significance of the story. Some short stories in a collection stand alone. Others contribute to a greater meaning (e.g., *A View from Saturday*, Konigsburg). A *novel* has many chapters, often with few pictures, so that a story can be elaborated over time, with full character development; it may be a hardback or paperback (a cheaper binding that will not last as long). A *poem* offers meaning, sensory images, abstract ideas, and feelings sometimes in very few words; the placement of every word in a poem is important to the meaning and the "voice." A poem often has a lyrical quality. It is no wonder poems are read over and over and analyzed line by line.

The purpose of a *picture book* is to communicate meaning within a larger artistic form that includes illustrations that communicate information and mood as well as appeal to the senses. The text of a picture book is integrated with the pictures in a highly coherent way. Placement of print and illustrations, size and style of print,

division of text across pages—all of these factors are used to convey the author's and illustrator's ideas.

Of course, formats are sometimes combined within texts. A magazine may include a short story or a longer narrative article. A short story collection may include individual stories that stand alone but that when read in relation to one another also communicate a greater meaning. An informational text may contain a brief biography or narrative. A picture book may include labels and legends.

Children need to experience texts in a wide range of formats, each of which makes its own contribution to the development of processing systems. Readers develop the ability to process texts in this range of formats, to include both the language and the visual information. The formats described below are the ones most frequently used in elementary classrooms.

Picture Storybooks

In a picture book, art and print work together to convey meaning. Usually, there are carefully designed illustrations on every page that extend the meaning of the print on that page—a selected line, sentence, or paragraph of the whole text.

Most picture storybooks combine text and art, but a few have illustrations only, like *Good Dog, Carl,* by Alexandra Day, or *Pancakes for Breakfast,* by Tomie de Paola. The story is there, but it is inferred from the art. In *Good Dog, Carl,* for example, the illustrator shows a warm, protective dog whose character and importance to the family are evident (see Figure 10-3).

The illustrations in good picture storybooks are truly art rather than just "pictures." They include a wide variety of media—photographs, line drawings, etchings, charcoal, watercolor, acrylics, oils, scratchboard, collage, photographic representations of quilting, sewing, soft sculpture, or clay, and many more. Just about every art medium has appeared in picture storybooks for children.

An example of a picture storybook is *So Far from the Sea* (see Figure 10-4), written by Eve Bunting and illustrated by Chris K. Soentpiet. A young narrator recounts a 1972 visit to Manzanar. In the book, the Iwasakis family makes a visit to Manzanar, a relocation camp in which the father of the family had been interned for three and a half years as a child. While the story is fiction, it rests on historical truth. The story is told from the point of view of Laura, now

Text Formats

FORMAT (GRADE-LEVEL RECOMMENDATION)	DESCRIPTION	MAJOR INSTRUCTIONAL USES	VALUE
Picture Storybooks (K–8)	A cohesive text in which narrative and art work together to convey meaning and mood.	Interactive read-aloud Literature study Minilessons in reading and writing workshop Genre study	▫ Offer all class members access to high-quality literature. ▫ Provide shared literary experiences for the group. ▫ Provide mentor texts for writing workshop. ▫ Expand content knowledge, text knowledge, and literary knowledge.
Picture Biographies, Autobiographies, and Memoirs (1–8)	A short biographical or autobiographical work that is illustrated on most pages; the illustrations provide insight into the subject's life.	Interactive read-aloud Literature study Reading and writing Minilessons Genre study	▫ Offer all class members access to well-written and -designed biographies and autobiographies. ▫ Help students understand the characteristics of biographical and autobiographical writing. ▫ Provide mentor texts for writing workshop. ▫ Expand students' knowledge of the subjects of biographies and autobiographies and help them learn why people write them.
Illustrated Informational Books (K–8)	A well-designed informational text with large, clear, and informative illustrations and graphics.	Interactive read-aloud Literature study Reading and writing Minilessons Independent reading	▫ Offer high-quality examples of informational texts and the features that assist readers. ▫ Expand content knowledge, text knowledge, and literary knowledge. ▫ Serve as a basis for minilessons. ▫ Provide mentor texts for writing workshop.
Easy Chapter Books (1–3)	Texts that take the form of chapter books but have special characteristics that make them an easy transition to the reading of longer texts.	Guided reading Independent reading	▫ Provide a shorter text that illustrates the form of a chapter book. ▫ Usually include many easy high frequency words. ▫ Have easy-to-follow plots. ▫ Have engaging but easy-to-understand characters. ▫ Often are presented in a series of books (e.g., same characters, same setting).

Figure 10-2. *Text Formats*

Text Formats (CONTINUED)

FORMAT (GRADE-LEVEL RECOMMENDATION)	DESCRIPTION	MAJOR INSTRUCTIONAL USES	VALUE
Chapter Books (2–8)	Longer works of fiction or nonfiction organized into chapters (or sections in the case of informational texts).	Guided reading Independent reading Interactive read-aloud	▫ Provide opportunities for readers to become engrossed in longer texts. ▫ Present examples of characters that develop and change over time. ▫ Present examples of books with prequels and sequels. ▫ Present examples of several books with the same setting. ▫ Present examples of complex plots. ▫ Provide opportunities for readers to develop stamina by reading a text over several days. ▫ Sometimes are part of a series or have sequels.
Series Books (2–8)	Books about the same characters in different situations. They are usually chapter books and are usually fiction (but may be nonfiction).	Guided reading Independent reading Interactive read-aloud	▫ Build knowledge of text that can be used in processing more volumes in the series. ▫ Support readers in bringing knowledge of characters, events, settings, plots, and general writing style to the reading of a new text. ▫ Often engage readers' interest so they read many books in a series. ▫ Provide a great deal of reading practice.
Short Stories (K–8)	Brief works of fiction that present a complete plot.	Interactive read-aloud Guided reading Independent reading	▫ Offer the whole meaning of a story in a text that can be read in one setting. ▫ Provoke discussion. ▫ Present examples of texts in which all the language is heavy with meaning because there is not much of it. ▫ Engage readers' attention.
Short Informational Texts (1–8)	Articles and other short pieces that can usually be finished in one session. Texts may include short biographies, news accounts, "how to" pieces, movie and book reviews, historical accounts, commentaries, and editorials.	Guided reading Independent reading Research	▫ Provide concise information, organized in a way that makes it available to the reader. ▫ May be assembled in enough variety to meet students' interests and research needs. ▫ Provide illustrations of the craft of nonfiction writing.

Figure 10-2. Text Formats (cont.)

Text Formats (CONTINUED)

FORMAT (GRADE-LEVEL RECOMMENDATION)	DESCRIPTION	MAJOR INSTRUCTIONAL USES	VALUE
"Readers"—Texts Designed Specifically for Reading Instruction (K–8)	Books especially designed for reading instruction and arranged along a gradient of difficulty.	Guided reading Independent reading	▪ Support the development of reading strategies over time. ▪ Offer opportunities for students to build independent reading strategies. ▪ Support reading instruction by helping teachers select texts that are appropriate for individual readers and offer opportunities to learn more about reading. ▪ Offer examples of new genres and writing styles to stretch students' reading abilities. ▪ Provide a basis for guided reading instruction. ▪ Help teachers guide students' choices for independent reading.
Poems (K–8)	Individual poems or anthologies. Many poetry anthologies are organized along a theme. Some poets publish books of their poetry. Poetry offers condensed meaning through language.	Poetry minilessons Interactive read-aloud Independent reading	▪ Provide examples of language that evokes sensory images. ▪ Provide a high level of meaning within a very short and highly structured text. ▪ Expand students' knowledge of poetic language. ▪ Provide material for choral reading or other forms of oral performance.

Figure 10-2. *Text Formats (cont.)*

Figure 10-3. Good Dog, Carl

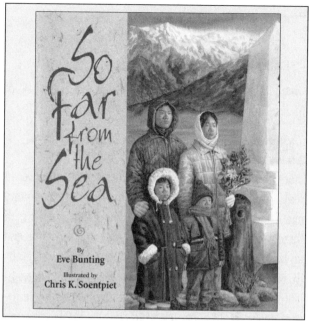

Figure 10-4. So Far from the Sea

about the same age her father was then. They visit the grave of Laura's grandfather, who died in the camp. This story, full of symbolism, is one of sorrow and regret for situations that cannot be changed. Soentpiet's watercolor illustrations, alternating between color and black-and-white as the story moves from present to past and back again, perfectly complement the story.

Not all picture storybooks treat such haunting subjects. Just about every kindergarten or first-grade teacher and many parents will be familiar with the joyous *Brown Bear, Brown Bear, What Do You See?* (Martin), whose repetitive language accompanied by appropriate illustrations offers readers the opportunity to predict the answers to questions. In *We're Going on a Bear Hunt* (Rosen), the illustrations depict the traditional game as it grows in the protagonists' imaginations.

Picture storybooks can also introduce students to historical fiction. In *Mailing May,* Michael O. Tunnell tells the heartwarming story of a young girl whose parents, unable to afford train fare, "mailed" her to her grandmother's home in the mountains. In *Who Was the Woman Who Wore the Hat?* (Patz), the writer presents thoughts about a woman who once wore a hat now on display in the Jewish Historical Museum, in Amsterdam. The illustrations combine pencil drawings, watercolors, and old photographs to depict the Holocaust. The text, which is spare but

arresting, is appropriate to read aloud to upper elementary or middle school students.

In elementary and middle school classrooms, picture storybooks range from beautifully illustrated hardbacks (often printed in paperback editions as well) to the massive numbers of small paperbacks produced solely to help students learn to read and not usually read aloud. In middle school, exquisite picture books may include short literary stories and informational articles related to social studies or science. Since picture storybooks include everything from simple stories and ideas to highly complex and sophisticated characters, issues, and topics, elementary teachers from kindergarten through middle school can and should make a practice of reading picture books aloud to students and showing them the illustrations. Doing so, they can:

- Demonstrate fluent, phrased reading.
- Involve children in a shared literary experience of high quality.
- Foster a literary community within the classroom.
- Encourage children to share their thinking.
- Use texts as a basis for helping readers think in new ways about the meaning of texts.
- Build background and literary knowledge.
- Expose children to new language.
- Extend vocabulary.

- Build interest in books.

- Introduce excellent authors and illustrators.

- Expand students' knowledge of genre.

Chapter 15 provides an extensive discussion of the use of picture storybooks in interactive read-aloud.

Illustrated Memoirs, Picture Biographies, and Picture Autobiographies

Many beautiful picture books tell stories about the lives of real people. These texts are ideal for helping elementary age readers understand the structure and characteristics of these genres. A *biography* is the story of a person's life, and an *autobiography* is the story of a person's life written by that person him- or herself. A *memoir* is an autobiographical account of personal experiences over a specific period of time especially meaningful to the writer. These genres are particularly important for elementary and middle school students to experience, because they will be writing about their own lives and learning to write about the lives of others.

Illustrated memoirs and picture biographies and autobiographies are excellent short mentor texts that can usually be read in one interactive read-aloud session. Even students who are not able to read these texts independently can be exposed to these genres and learn how they "work" through these shared literary experiences. Some memoirs and picture biographies and autobiographies are simple enough for first or second graders to enjoy, but more of these texts are appropriate for grades three and above. Some are quite sophisticated.

An example of a straightforward picture biography is *Thomas Jefferson: A Picture Book Biography*, by James Cross Giblin. High-quality oil paintings by Michael Dooling draw the reader into the major events of Jefferson's life. The writer includes many interesting details, such as the mockingbird that kept Jefferson company in his study, which should intrigue upper elementary students. This book could spark a good discussion of temporal sequence as well as why the writer selected certain events and details.

An unusual picture book memoir based on some early recollections by Margaret Wise Brown (Blos) is appropriate for older students; most of them will remember reading Brown's book *Good Night, Moon* in their early childhood

and will find it interesting to hear the author's own reminiscences. They may even want to talk about connections they see between the writer's childhood experiences and her writing. The crayon drawings add a nostalgic quality.

A Letter from Phoenix Farm is a book in the form of a long letter by Jane Yolen—the author of *Owl Moon*, the Commander Toad books, and *The Devil's Arithmetic*—in which she describes her current life and talks about the place she lives, her work, and her family. The text is accompanied by photographs of Jane and her family. The book is part of a series called Meet the Author; these glimpses of what writers' lives are like are a wonderful way for students to learn that the creators of some of their favorite books are just people like themselves.

Joanna Cole, author of the popular Magic School Bus series, has also written an autobiography, entitled *On the Bus with Joanna Cole: A Creative Autobiography*. Sections like "I Knew I Should Have Stayed Home Today!" are sure to pique students' interest and lend themselves to being read aloud. In addition, students will enjoy pouring over artifacts such as dummy pages and pencil sketches that take them "behind the scenes" of book production.

A very unusual and highly literary text is *Talkin' About Bessie: The Story of Aviator Elizabeth Coleman*, by Nikki Grimes. The writer presents imagined poetic monologues by a group of characters, all of whom knew Bessie at a different time in her life. The voice and perspective change with each monologue. This text is ideal for reading aloud to middle school students and lends itself to readers' theater; however, readers would need to have quite a bit of prior knowledge about Bessie Coleman and her life in order to fully appreciate the text. This text could be used as a mentor text showing alternative formats for writing biographies (see Figure 10-5).

Illustrated Informational Books

Recent years have seen an explosion of informational books that are equal to picture storybooks in literary quality. Some of these informational books are simple enough for kindergartners. For example, Donald Crews's *Trucks* is a very simple "label" book that young children will go back to again and again. Also appropriate to read to younger primary children is *My Car*, by Byron Barton. This book has very clear collage-type drawings with few details. Each page

Figure 10-5. Talkin' About Bessie

tells a simple fact about a car. Another simple informational text to read to kindergartners or first graders is *How a Seed Grows,* by Helene Jordan, in which the writer talks directly to the reader and gives simple illustrated directions for growing seeds and noticing details about how the seeds change. The book has some inset pictures and cutaways. An experiment is described on the last page.

Bugs, by Nancy Winslow Parker and Joan Richards Wright, consists of more complex informational text introduced by simple question-and-answer riddles, such as "What ran over Grandma's brooch? A roach." Scientific information is provided about the insect in question, and there are labeled drawings on the right-hand page. Sections of this text can be read aloud to students, and they can "borrow" the format for books of their own. Jim Arnosky has written many informational picture books that are ideal for reading aloud in second through about fourth grade. One entitled *All About Deer* includes beautiful labeled drawings. Arnosky's texts provide a huge amount of information and illustrate just about every way writers of informational texts organize information. Barbara Brenner's *Thinking About Ants* offers drawings and text that direct readers to think from an ant's perspective.

There are many informational books that are appropriate for upper elementary readers. *Bat Loves the Night,* by Nicola Davies, can be enjoyed by children in grades two

through five (see Figure 10-6). This book offers facts about bats but also employs very sophisticated language that evokes sensory images. Another useful format is question-and-answer. An example, *Why Don't Haircuts Hurt? Questions and Answers About the Human Body,* by Melvin and Gilda Berger, includes a wide variety of interesting information about different parts of the body. A very sophisticated informational text is *Cave,* by Diane Siebert, which is beautifully illustrated and poetic and can be used with intermediate or middle school students. Technically, this book is not simply informational, since the cave is "talking," but the personification brings the information to life. It can be considered "literary nonfiction." It will be most appreciated by students who already know something about caves.

Easy Chapter Books

Chapter books range from simple books suitable for first graders to young-adult novels. They are also appropriate for use as leveled books for guided reading instruction. "Easy" chapter books, often called transition chapter books, are a special category: they are easy to read and have many illustrations, but they introduce children to longer texts divided into chapters. The Henry and Mudge series, for example, has two- to four-page chapters with a very limited amount of print on each page and many easy words.

Figure 10-6. Bat Loves the Night

Nevertheless, each chapter features an engaging series of events, ends with a plot resolution, and builds toward the book's conclusion.

Chapter Books

From about third grade on, students read an increasingly challenging array of chapter books encompassing a variety of genres—contemporary realistic fiction, historical fiction, fantasy, biography and autobiography, and informational texts as well as numerous short stories. (Many informational books for children are presented in sections rather than chapters.)

These longer texts are satisfying because they provide in-depth reading experiences over an hour or several hours. Reading chapter books, children:

- Get to know characters (both fictional and real) as they develop and function over time.

- Usually attend to the attributes and development of a larger number of characters, sometimes switching focus from one to another.

- Develop knowledge of places, times, and events that are distant from their personal experiences (the writer has the space in which to create a context).

- Experience meaning that they think about and come back to over time.

- Understand a topic or theme more deeply (the author has the space in which to explain and describe it fully).

Chapter books are challenging to the reader because they require:

- Sustaining energy and attention over time.

- Remembering information from earlier reading and using it to understand subsequent sections of the text.

- Following more complex plots or presentations of information.

- Envisioning story characters and events without the help of illustrations (or with only a few).

- Understanding complex relationships between characters and among characters and events as they change over time.

Longer chapter books sometimes have many sequels; popular current examples are the Henry and Mudge or Anastasia books. Usually, sequels have more sophisticated plots and literary language. Characters are complex and develop over time, and some continue from book to book. The range is great. The Magic Tree House, Time Warp Trio, or Horrible Harry books are written to be entertaining and feature easy concepts. Gary Paulsen's Brian stories (*Hatchet, The River, Brian's Winter, Brian's Return, Brian's Hunt*) deal with surviving in the natural world. The writer follows the character's development over time, but each book is a self-contained literary work.

Series Books

Many easy chapter books are parts of series, such as Mr. Putter and Tabby or Pinky and Rex. Series books usually center on the same group of characters who encounter similar problems. Sometimes the characters remain the same age and stay in the same setting (the Commander Toad or Horrible Harry series, for example). Often the characters grow older over time (Beverly Cleary's Ramona books follow a family over several years; Amber Brown moves through third and fourth grade over a series of eight books). Series books support readers in that:

- They meet characters over and over and can't help applying prior knowledge.

- They usually encounter familiar settings, so, again, they can bring this knowledge to the text.

- They get used to the language and writing style typically employed by the writer; even vocabulary can be built over time.

Series books may have the same characters, setting, plot, topic, or theme (some have all four). Sometimes series books are not even written by the same author.

Short Stories

High-quality picture storybooks are short stories, with the difference being that much of the meaning and mood is conveyed in the art. Short stories:

- Can usually be read in ten to twenty minutes.

- Present and develop characters with a limited amount of text.

- Communicate setting and background quickly.

- Communicate the whole meaning of the story using a limited amount of words.

- Communicate meaning using fewer events and less dialogue compared to chapter books.

- Sometimes offer a "slice of life" that makes the reader understand herself or humanity better.
- Sometimes provide a lesson or moral.
- Often appear in collections along with stories by other authors; sometimes a collection of stories by one author, although each can stand alone, is so connected that, cumulatively, they all contribute to a larger story or theme (for example, they may take place in the same setting, have the same characters, or exemplify similar moral positions).

The short story has particular advantages for reading aloud to elementary and middle school students. For example:

- Listeners get a cohesive piece of text within one five- to fifteen-minutes session.
- It is easier to engage readers because all story elements—characters, setting, plot, resolution—are encountered during a single reading.
- Usually, enough happens to generate a good discussion.

Short stories may be any type of fiction and may include short biographies and myths, legends, fairy tales, and folktales from various cultures.

Short Informational Texts

Another kind of short text that is becoming increasingly important in the elementary/middle school classroom is the shorter informational text. A wider variety of research tools is available to younger students than ever before. There are numerous journals for children geared to the interests and reading abilities of students from first grade through middle school. While it can be difficult to find usable informational books for students in kindergarten and first and second grade, an exploding number of websites for children include timely information in a wide range of forms:

- Short biographies of individuals.
- Current news accounts.
- News of scientific discoveries in many fields.
- "How to do it" pieces.
- Background pieces for headline news.
- Historical accounts.
- Informational articles in all content areas.
- Character sketches.
- Movie and book reviews.

Related fictional pieces or poetry can also be juxtaposed with expository pieces.

Students can experience these shorter informational pieces in many ways:

- As summaries of information on authors or topics prepared from material drawn from the Internet.
- In a magazine to which the class subscribes.
- In a class newsletter.
- By researching a topic and preparing a presentation or report.
- By exploring (beyond the textbook) a topic of interest in a content area.
- By learning how to read short informational pieces in guided reading.

Shorter informational pieces have the advantage of providing a focused, well-structured text that students can use not only to expand their knowledge but also to gradually internalize the various ways writers use to present information:

- Comparison and contrast.
- Cause and effect.
- Description.
- Temporal sequence.
- Problem and solution.

"Readers" (Leveled Texts Specifically Designed for Reading Instruction)

The term *leveled books* refers to any group of books that has been organized along a gradient of difficulty. Chapter 12 describes in detail the gradient we use to categorize books for instruction. The purpose of the gradient is to help teachers "match" books to readers. Teachers constantly select books for small-group reading instruction (guided reading) and guide their students' choices for independent reading.

Almost any kind of text can be leveled, but we concentrate on those that are appropriate for guided reading: easy and longer chapter books, short stories, and shorter informational texts. Paperbacks are generally preferred, because multiple copies are needed. Some picture books and illustrated informational books that are available in paperback may also be appropriate for guided reading.

Using a range of text characteristics, we group books along a continuum from A through Z+, representing texts that support reading development from the very beginnings of literacy in kindergarten to the almost adult level of competency that eighth and ninth graders can demonstrate (although we do not include books that have very mature adult themes and content).

The short stories (sometimes called *little books* at the early levels or *leveled readers* at all levels) designed for children to read for themselves as they build processing strategies during reading instruction are a type of picture storybook, in that they involve print (from simple to more difficult) accompanied by illustrations. There are also a variety of "readers" designed for older students who read far below grade level. Many of these are age-appropriate topics but are written to be easy. You can find good books with literary quality among this type of book. Regretfully, there are also many books in this category that do not provide excellent quality. You need to be selective to ensure a high-quality collection. It is quite an accomplishment to write illustrated books that are simple enough to help beginning readers build processing strategies. We discuss texts designed for instruction in Chapter 12.

Poems

No classroom collection would be complete without a large selection of poetry collections. While we would not want to "level" poetry, we can certainly think of a continuum of complexity over the grades. Throughout the world, in many different cultures, children's first acquaintances with the world of poetry usually consist of saying and singing traditional rhymes and verses. Ditties like "I love chocolate, yum, yum, yum, I love chocolate in my tum" are not usually considered true poetry, nor are traditional nursery rhymes such as "Hey Diddle Diddle." These structures, however, are highly appealing to children and provide a foundation for appreciating the sounds of words and the images associated with them. Your children may enjoy the rhyme and riddle in "Little Jumping Joan":

> Here I am,
> Little jumping Joan.
> When nobody's with me,
> I'm always alone.

They may also begin to appreciate poems that depart from verse but still feature repetition and convey visual images and an implied story, such as "The Beach":

> White sand,
> Sea sand,
> Warm sand,
> Kicking sand,
> Building sand,
> Watching sand
> As the waves roll in.

As children become older and more sophisticated, they learn that poems do not necessarily rhyme and that there are a wide variety of poems. They enjoy selecting poetry for themselves. They will be reading more literary, sophisticated poems such as "December Leaves" by Kaye Starbird.

> The fallen leaves are cornflakes
> That fill the lawn's wide dish,
> And night and noon
> The wind's a spoon
> That stirs them with a swish.
>
> The sky's a silver sifter
> A-sifting white and slow,
> That gently shakes
> On crisp brown flakes
> The sugar known as snow.

Poetry provides intense meaning using very few words. There are funny poems, sports poems, dramatic poems, lyrical poems, poems about nature, patriotic poems, poems about heroism, poems on just about any topic. In its infinite variety, poetry can:

- Be listened to.
- Be performed as shared or choral reading.
- Be memorized and shared orally.
- Form the basis for discussion.
- Provide an inspiration for writing or drawing.
- Provide individual satisfaction.

GENRES

Genre simply means type of text. All literature may be divided into poetry and prose, and these media are sometimes used together within a text. For example, in *Bat Loves the Night* (Davies), the writer tells facts about bats in straightforward prose but also uses poetry to help the reader develop a sensory understanding of bats (see Figure 10-7).

Nancy Patz's *Who Was the Woman Who Wore the Hat?* provokes thoughts about the Holocaust in a long "prose poem" that begins

A bat can eat dozens of big moths in a single night — or thousands of tiny flies, gnats, and mosquitoes.

This time she bites hard.
Its wings fall away, like the
wrapper from a candy.
In a moment the moth is eaten.
Bat sneezes.
The dusty scales got up her nose.

18

Most species of bats eat insects, but there are some that eat fruit, fish, frogs, even blood!

Figure 10-7. Bat Loves the Night

Who was the woman
Who wore the hat
I saw in the museum?
What was she like?
Did she lie awake
In the morning and watch
The way I did today
As dawn brushed light through the sky?

Prose may be further divided into fiction and nonfiction. Fiction includes contemporary realistic fiction, historical fiction, traditional literature, fantasy, and science fiction. Nonfiction genres include biography, autobiography, and memoir as well as informational texts on a full range of topics. The two selections mentioned above indicate that the lines between genre are not always clear and that wonderful texts can be created by combining fiction and nonfiction, prose and poetry. In Chapters 13 and 14, we look at genre in more detail.

SPECIAL TYPES OF TEXT

Across the genres you will find other types of text that have features in common. Mysteries, sports stories, survival stories, or adventure stories are examples of special types of books that have common elements. A mystery may be contemporary or historical as can adventure stories. Series books give students a foundation that makes the reading of subsequent books easier and are a favorite for many stu-

dents. Some series books tell a continuing story and call for readers to bring a rich background to bear on the next text.

CONTENT: LITERARY AND INFORMATIONAL

In the past there was some competition between reading literary texts and reading in the content areas. There was only so much time, and students needed to read textbooks so that they could learn all the facts they needed to know. After the primary years, in which students spent time "learning to read," they generally spent a great deal of time reading expository texts, along with some fiction, including "classics." This was called "reading to learn." Often, they studied a few novels in detail and read anthologized excerpts meant to familiarize them with various genres and build their reading skills. These practices, of course, were particularly damaging to struggling readers, who could often go an entire month, or even a year, without actually reading a text with ease and understanding.

We now know that "learning to read" continues as students increase the depth and breadth of the texts they process. We also know that reading a variety of texts for real purposes must start early. Fortunately, the number of high-quality texts in content areas has rapidly increased. Teachers can select from a range of informational texts that extend content areas at their grade levels; they can read

135

them aloud to students or make them available in other ways. Students can choose these texts for independent reading, and they can be used in guided reading. It is important for the classroom collection to add richly to students' knowledge of science, social studies, and mathematics.

DIVERSITY

It is essential that students have access to high-quality texts that in every way reflect the diversity of our world. All students need to see people like themselves in the books they read and hear read aloud. But it is equally important for them to learn about diversity. The fiction and nonfiction texts they read need to reflect diverse:

- Cultures.
- Languages.
- Races.
- Geographic regions.
- Religions.
- Traditions.

It is a good idea to look at all instructional contexts through a multicultural lens.

A wonderful read-aloud for grades five through eight is *Circle Unbroken* (Raven). In this book an African American girl's grandmother tells her the family's history. The grandmother calls it a "circle tale" because she is using an unbroken circle to make a sweet grass basket that is so strong it will hold water. Although the author does not say so directly, the basket is symbolic of the strength of the family, from long-ago generations in Africa to the present ones in South Carolina. The author uses figurative language such as, "And when his fingers talked just right and the wet season came—his basket held the rain, and the men were pleased." Occasionally, the grandmother breaks away from the story and talks directly to the girl: "Just as I am pleased with you. . . ." The story continues into the present day, and at the end of the text, more information is provided about sweet grass baskets, along with a bibliography. A lot of information is also conveyed in the paintings, some of it not mentioned in the text. This story simultaneously informs us about history of a people and a region.

Another good book to read to upper elementary or middle school students is *Alice Yazzie's Year* (Ramona), which includes a short vignette for each month of a year in the life of a Navajo girl. Shonto Begay, the illustrator, who was raised in the Navajo Nation, provides paintings illustrating Navajo art and life. This book shows the cultural perspective of Alice Yazzie. The text is not elaborate but communicates emotion; explanatory notes for each month are provided in the back.

A good book to provoke thinking among second or third graders is *The Name Jar*, by Yangsook Choi. In the text Unhei, a recent Korean immigrant, goes to a U. S. school for the first time. She carries with her a gift from her grandmother—a little wooden block with her Korean name carved in it. Children at school find Unhei difficult to say and poke fun at her, so she says she has not picked an American name yet. Becoming more friendly, the children put many different names in a jar so that she can select one. Finally, she decides to keep her own name. Even younger children can discuss how and why one's name is important.

An interactive read-aloud is an excellent way to help students at any age discuss the strengths and values of cultures different from their own. The sample text sets we provide (Chapter 17) include texts that reflect a wide range of diverse peoples. You'll also want to be sure that diversity is reflected in your leveled book collection and in the books students choose for independent reading. The books do not necessarily have to be *about* the differences among people. Sometimes it is important just to see a mix of people. But some texts can extend students' understanding. (Just be sure they are accurate and authentic.)

Perry Hewitt has written a biography of the poet Pat Mora (*Pat Mora: Two Languages, One Poet*) that focuses on Mora's writing in two languages. A discussion of this text (about third grade level) might focus on the idea of keeping one's own heritage alive while at the same time succeeding in a new language. A more difficult text (about fifth grade level) is *Xuanzang: Chinese Hero,* by Kathleen Ferguson. This text begins with a complex Chinese legend and requires understanding the true nature of enlightenment as taught by Buddha, which means developing qualities such as gentleness and patience in contrast to violence, boastfulness, and anger. These are abstract ideas, and they are revealed in an allegory. Then the text changes to a more straightforward biography. Even upper elementary students will find it challenging.

ACCESSIBILITY

It is important for students to have access to a wide variety of texts, and that will not happen easily if they are simply reading at their own level all the time. So, in providing variety to stretch students' thinking, it is also necessary to think about accessibility to texts.

First, you want to be sure that the books you read aloud are highly varied. Reading aloud is the quickest and easiest way to give all students access to a text, and doing so forms the foundation for discussion. It is worth a regular trip to a good library to keep new texts coming into the classroom.

Most texts today have been recorded on audiotapes, and an increasing number of them are available on compact discs. These resources enable students to listen to a text that they cannot read with ease independently. Students may also want to make use of audio technology to experience a text a second time, either to reflect on what is being said or to prepare for literature discussion. Some texts are available on computer software programs, and you may even want to check out DVD versions of movies based on books or stories.

Ultimately, of course, you want to be sure that students' independent and guided reading includes a variety of texts, but you can greatly enrich their experience by making an even wider range accessible aurally and visually.

VARIETY OVER TIME

The textual variety that students experience during their years of schooling is the basis for flexible processing. It simply does not work to "train" young children on one kind of text and then later expect a processing system that incorporates the full range of strategic reading behaviors. If children encounter only one kind of text, they are likely to form some rigid early theories about what the act of reading is all about.

True, we cannot expect kindergartners and first graders to independently process a wide range of genres in many different content areas. They do not yet have the necessary:

◻ Knowledge of the characteristics of texts.

◻ Background knowledge of content areas.

◻ Processing strategies, including word-solving skills.

They need simple texts to support the building of a reading process, but even with that criterion in mind, we can carefully introduce variety over time. In addition, we must make clear that there are many different ways to experience texts, including hearing them read orally. This principle holds true up through the grades, with students gradually increasing the variety of texts they read for themselves but always having access to texts in other ways as well.

SUGGESTIONS FOR PROFESSIONAL DEVELOPMENT

ANALYZING THE TEXT RESOURCES

1 Pair with a colleague to examine the diversity of texts in each of your classrooms.

2 Make an informal inventory of the texts students currently experience. Without performing an exhaustive inventory, make some estimates of books in several categories.

3 Using the form, Assessing the Classroom Library, (Figure 10-8) (or one you create), use a simple code to judge the adequacy of the collection. You can print this form from the DVD that accompanies this book.

$-$ = not adequate or missing

$+$ = adequate representation

$++$ = excellent representation

4 After this quick assessment, the teacher in this classroom will have a good idea where to allocate resources. For example, if there are very few biographies (or if there are some biographies for students to read but none to read aloud), you will want to make a more focused trip to the school library.

This activity may also help you identify neglected genres or cultural groups, so it can inform instruction as well. If students do not experience a breadth of text, their thinking will not develop as richly as it could.

Assessing the Classroom Library

	PICTURE BOOKS	CHAPTER BOOKS	SHORT STORIES	SHORT INFORMATIONAL TEXTS	POETRY BOOKS
Format					
Genre	REALISTIC FICTION/ HISTORICAL FICTION	TRADITIONAL LITERATURE/FANTASY/ SCIENCE FICTION	BIOGRAPHY, AUTOBIOGRAPHY, MEMOIR	INFORMATIONAL TEXTS	POETRY

Content — *List content areas and literacy content*

Special Types

Diversity — *List cultures/races represented:*

	BOOKS TO READ ALOUD	AUDIOTAPED BOOKS	BOOKS ON CD	COMPUTER RESOURCES	OTHER
Media (Accesibility)					

Figure 10-8. *Assessing the Classroom Library*

CHAPTER ELEVEN

SUPPORTING THINKING ACROSS A VARIETY OF GENRES

We assign students new and more complex texts that make unique demands on readers without helping them to recognize and meet these "text-specific" requirements. We send them to a foreign land without the language, currency and tools to be successful.

—JEFF WILHELM

Knowing about genres is, as Randy Bomer (1995) says, knowing how things tend to go. Literally, genre means *type*. Written texts are categorized as poetry or prose, with any number of subcategories going on from there. These distinctions are very handy for organizing libraries and planning reading programs, but simply naming types of texts does not tell the whole story of how genre functions in our lives. Genre is a strong source of meaning as we attempt to comprehend the world, and it is helpful to think of the definition in broader terms:

> If this chapter were a television show, the opening music would be fading right about now. When we watch television, we expect a piece of music at the beginning. They can't skip it; it has to be there. How else would you be sure you were seeing the beginning? And if we wanted to make a sitcom with our own video cameras, we'd put a song at the beginning, too. Because a sitcom has to have a song. That's how these things go. Our sense of "how this type of thing tends to go" could be called a genre schema, a *scheme* for a *kind* of thing. We have thousands of them: for restaurants and school days and knock-knock jokes and football cheers and New York City taxis and family relationships. (Bomer 1995, p. 116)

The genre, or *kind,* of text lays down a set of rules and creates expectations in our minds. It shapes and constrains predictions. New genres are created all the time. Several years ago, *Survivor* launched a new genre of television now called "reality TV." Real people played out their problem-solving skills, unscripted, in front of millions of viewers. As another example, thirteen million teenagers now use text messaging, with its very specific requirements and forms, to have almost synchronous virtual conversations. As Leila Christenbury, a past president of National Conference of Teachers of English (NCTE), says, "Instant messaging is in and of itself almost a separate, private language, and there is a certain specific pleasure in using this specialized form of communication" (cited in Ebbing 2005, p. 1).

Genre is a powerful factor in helping readers build meaning. It shapes predictions, directs attention where it needs to go, and eliminates possibilities that can be distracting. Genres have "rules," not in the sense of written contracts, but as expectations. Genres describe the way speakers, writers, and musicians organize the work they produce. As Bomer says, the *genre scheme* "lays down a track for reading." We do not learn everything about genres from studying them in school. We are always learning the characteristics and "rules" of genres by experiencing them within social contexts.

When new genres are created (often by breaking the rules), one of the first tasks is to explore them to see how they "work." People who became engrossed in the first season of the popular television series *American Idol* quickly parsed the underlying structure:

- The contestants are like themselves—unknown.
- The viewers sit in the same "power seat" as the judges.
- It is interesting to find out which contestants have talent.
- Some contestants have little talent but are very funny.
- The judges alternatively humiliate, advise, and praise contestants.
- There is a long, drawn-out quest for the "top," during which time the principal characters become familiar and elicit sympathy and allegiance from viewers.
- Leading contestants become increasingly sophisticated; they look and act different.
- The devoted audience members divide into "camps," rooting for their favorites.
- The final episode is a love fest in which everyone still in the running vows undying friendship.

When these dedicated viewers tuned in to subsequent *American Idol* telecasts, they expected the same experience. Other viewers never "got" the genre. They turned the show off as bad entertainment by unknowns showing off. Either they disliked the genre, or they did not spend the time needed to understand it.

We sometimes speak of genres as if they are discrete, but often the lines are blurred. Writers combine genres or, working in one genre, slide in pieces of text that have characteristics of others. As teachers, we need to recognize in pure or combined form the genres our students will likely encounter in grades K–8 (see Figure 11-1). The words *prose* and *poetry*, often used in combination as the title of literature anthologies, describe the whole of literature.

POETRY

Poetry is language that imbues a few words, phrases, and sentences (and sometimes longer combinations thereof) with intense meaning. The poet evokes images and feelings, often speaking ambiguously. Poetry can be nonfiction—a poem written about an outstanding individual or a heroic time, for example; writers can also publish their memoirs and autobiographies as poetry. But in most cases the fiction/nonfiction distinction is sometimes difficult to make with regard to poetry, and is not always useful. The important thing about poetry is how it speaks to the heart.

THE APPEAL OF POETRY

Poetry provides special opportunities for children as they build their processing systems over time. For example, poetry:

- Supports the engagement of emotions—an important way to respond to both prose and poetry—while reading.
- Evokes sensory images, allowing for communication of deeper meanings.
- Lends itself to reading aloud and to reading over and over because of the inherent pleasure the reader or listener takes in the form.
- Incorporates rhythm and sometimes rhyme.
- Captures deep meanings in very spare language from which the reader must make inferences.
- Offers opportunities for many interpretations.

THE ELEMENTS OF POETRY

Poetry is characterized by the elements that make it memorable and enjoyable. These elements include:

- *Compact language that evokes meaning and emotion.* Poets choose unusual ways to express meaning, often compressing it into just a few words, each of which has inherent feelings or images.
- *Figurative language.* Poets often use comparisons to express meaning and emotions: "a little silver slipper of a moon." (See Figure 11-2.)

Figurative language compares two or more things through metaphor (using one object in place of another) or simile (a comparison using *like* or *as*). Figurative language also takes the form of personification, in which an object is given human qualities.

FORMS OF POETRY

Poetry comes in many forms. If we think about the forms of poetry that students will encounter in elementary and middle school, the list is long:

- *Traditional poems and rhymes*, sometimes called *nursery rhymes,* are many children's first introduction to poetry. All cultures have their own rhymes, which originated as oral entertainment and were not reserved for children but were relevant to adult interests and current events.
- *Songs and chants* are usually chanted or sung, often to accompany activities such as dancing, working, jumping rope, or playing certain games. Traditional poems, rhymes, songs, and chants are not true poetry, yet they can introduce young children to the elements in a highly enjoyable way.
- *Free verse* is poetry that does not rhyme.
- *Lyric poetry* expresses direct, personal emotion in a musical or melodic manner.
- *Narrative poetry* tells a story.
- *Limericks* are humorous poems with five lines, lines one, two, and five having three anapestic feet, lines three and four, two anapestic feet, in the rhyme scheme *aabba.*
- *Cinquains* are five-line stanzas that have, respectively, two, four, six, eight, and two syllables.
- *Concrete poems* represent meaning not only with words but also with the graphic pattern of letters, words, or symbols.
- *Found poems* are pieces of poetic writing not originally intended as poems; they are often discovered in newspaper headlines, signs, and similar texts.

Genres of Written Texts

Poetry

Compact writing characterized by imagination and artistry and inbued with intense meaning.

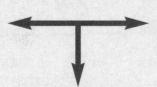

Prose

Language that informs, shows, describes, and explains; prose employs language in a more discursive way.

Fiction

A narrative that is imagined rather than real and includes elements such as characters, a problem or conflict, setting, a plot with events or episodes, and problem resolution.

Nonfiction

A text that is intended to provide factual information through text and visual images; contains ideas, facts, and principles; primary purpose is to communicate information.

REALISTIC FICTION	FANTASY	BIOGRAPHICAL TEXTS	FACTUAL TEXTS
Stories that are drawn from the writer's imagination but could have happened.	Fiction that contains unrealistic or unworldly elements.	Factual works that describe the life of a real person.	Texts that present ideas, facts, and principles related to the physical, biological, or social world.

REALISTIC FICTION

Stories that are drawn from the writer's imagination but could have happened.

Contemporary Realistic Fiction

Realistic fiction in current-day settings. Usually presents problems typical for the age of characters. May highlight social issues.

Historical Fiction

Realistic fiction set in the past. Usually focused on social and political issues of the time and how the characters see them. The setting is important.

FANTASY

Fiction that contains unrealistic or unworldly elements.

Traditional Literature

Stories, with recurring themes and motifs, that have been passed down orally throughout history:
- Cumulative tales
- Pourquoi tales
- Beast tales
- "Noodlehead" tales
- Realistic tales
- Fairytales
- Fables
- Myths, Legends, Epics

Modern Fantasy

Stories that include magic and the struggle between good and evil.
- Animal fantasy
- Magical fantasy
- High fantasy

Science Fiction

A fantasy text that involves and/or is based on scientific principles.

BIOGRAPHICAL TEXTS

Factual works that describe the life of a real person.

Biography

A biographical text written about a person, the "subject," by another person, the "biographer."

Autobiography and Memoir

A biographical work written by the subject about his or her own life. An autobiography usually deals with the writer's entire life or a large part of it; a memoir usually focuses on memories of a particular time, event, place, or relationship.

FACTUAL TEXTS

Texts that present ideas, facts, and principles related to the physical, biological, or social world.

Underlying structural features:
- Description
- Enumeration
- Comparison/contrast
- Cause and effect
- Chronological sequence
- Problem/solution
- Question/answer

Sample content areas:
- History
- Social studies
- Health
- Science
- Sports
- Space
- Technology
- Cooking

Kinds of factual texts:
- Short texts
- Longer informational books
- Articles
- Internet postings

Poetry

TRADITIONAL POEMS	SONGS AND CHANTS	FORMS OF POETRY	
Simple poems that employ rhythm and rhyme; sometimes called *nursery rhymes*.	Poems that represent language that is usually chanted or sung (ditties, jump-rope chants, etc.).	▫ Free verse ▫ Lyric poetry ▫ Narrative poetry ▫ Limericks ▫ Cinquains	▫ Concrete poetry ▫ Haiku ▫ "Found" poetry ▫ List poems ▫ Formula poems

Figure 11-1 *Genres of Written Texts*

December Leaves BY KAYE STARBIRD

The fallen leaves are cornflakes
That fill the lawn's wide dish,
And night and noon
The wind's a spoon
That stirs them with a swish
The sky's a silver sifter
A-sifting white and slow,
That gently shakes
On crisp brown flakes
The sugar known as snow.

Figure 11-2. *December Leaves*

- *Haiku* are three-line poems using simple language with no rhyme and a syllable structure of five, seven, and five.

- *List poems,* which may be rhymed or unrhymed, itemize a series of objects, events, characteristics, and the like.

- *Formula poems* are created by prescribing a sequence or form into which students can place words.

HOW POETRY AND PROSE RELATE

The different forms of poetry help individuals experience and use language in many ways, and as a result, expand their thinking and abilities as readers and writers of prose. Any of the prose genres can be written in poetic form.

PROSE

Prose is language that is organized into sentences and paragraphs. The writer of prose describes, elaborates, and explains. Written language generally follows conventions that readers expect, although there are many variations and the "rules" may be broken for special emphasis. Keep in mind that there can be a "prose poem" that has qualities of poetry, for example, *Who Was the Woman Who Wore a Hat?* (Patz). Prose can be divided into fiction and non-fiction.

FICTION

The organizing structure of fiction is *narrative,* which comes from oral storytelling. Fiction has a number of defining elements:

- *Characters* are the people, animals, or objects that appear in the story. Readers learn about characters through the writer's descriptions, what the characters think or say, what the characters do, and what others say or think about them. Characters change, or *develop,* over a text in response to the events in their lives. They may be *rounded* (fully developed) or *flat* (stereotypical or unchanging). In compelling works of fiction, fully developed characters capture the reader's attention; they seem real. Secondary characters who play minor roles are usually flat. Characters in traditional literature also tend to be flat.

- The *setting* is the time and place in which the action happens. Sometimes the setting is relatively unimportant. For example, certain family stories can take place almost anywhere. At other times, the setting is all-important to the theme and plot. For example, in Karen Hesse's *Out of the Dust,* a family copes with the Dust Bowl of the 1930s.

- *Plot* refers to the action of the story. Every plot includes a *problem.* A straightforward narrative begins by introducing the characters and setting and defining the problem. A series of events then follow, rising to a point of greatest tension as the character(s) take actions meant to solve the problem and either succeed or fail. The action falls rapidly thereafter in the form of a brief ending, or *denouement,* that brings the narrative to a close. Complex narratives may have several plot lines. Also, writers may alter the time sequence; a prime example is beginning at the end of a narrative and then "flashing back" to the events that led there.

- The *theme* is the big idea of the story, the author's attitude toward a significant human concern or issue. A writer may weave several themes into any one narrative. Generally, the theme transcends the particular narrative to reveal something about human problems and issues: growing up, prejudice, school problems, survival, for example. These themes can play out whether the fiction is contemporary realism, historical realism, or fantasy.

- *Perspective* refers to the narrator's point of view. The perspective guides the reader. Usually, we see the problem through the eyes of the main character (protagonist), and our expectations are shaped by this individual's attitudes. We tend to feel sympathy for the protagonist, whose thoughts and ideas are revealed by the writer. The protagonist may be presented in first, second, or third person.

LITERARY QUALITY IN FICTION

Writers of fiction use many different techniques to communicate their message, make characters and setting come alive, and engage their readers. Novelists and short story writers develop their own styles and ways of using language. Like poets, they use figurative language and personification. They create images in the minds of readers and often use symbolism to emphasize meaning. They use fast-paced action to create a sense of danger, suspense, or adventure; they use foreshadowing to help readers predict how a problem or a mystery will be solved. A piece of fiction may also have a tone or mood, such as whimsical, humorous, somber, or menacing.

In literary works for children, illustrations add meaning in all of the ways mentioned above—imagery, mood, powerful symbols, tone. In picture books, the words and illustrations form a cohesive whole to convey the theme, mood, and events of the story. In fact, the quality of all fiction depends on how well the elements work together:

- Is the plot interesting and do events follow logically?
- Are the characters well drawn and believable?
- Are the writing style and language effective and interesting?
- Are the illustrations integral to the text and do they contribute both to meaning and enjoyment?

FICTION GENRES

Fiction can be divided into realism and fantasy, each of which can be further subdivided.

Contemporary Realistic Fiction and Historical Fiction
Realistic fiction can be contemporary or historical. Contemporary realistic fiction is drawn from the writer's imagination. These works are not true, but *could be true*, and so relevance and believability are very important in assessing their quality.

In *Because of Winn-Dixie,* Kate DiCamillo (2000) tells the story of ten-year-old India Opal, whose mother has left her and who moves to a new town with her preacher father. Opal is lonely and shy, but when she adopts a large, ungainly stray dog, whom she names Winn-Dixie after the supermarket where she found him, things start to happen. She finds that people just naturally take to Winn-Dixie, and she makes some unusual friends who help her and, in turn, her father overcome sadness. The characters are eccentric

and colorful but believable. Events happen chronologically, chapter by chapter, and each time Opal feels encouraged by Winn-Dixie to open up to people. The story has the ring of reality, combining sadness with humor and hope (see Figure 11-3).

Historical fiction has all of the aspects of contemporary fiction except that it takes place in the past. It is sometimes difficult to draw a line between contemporary and historical fiction, but in general, books placed in settings prior to the last forty years would definitely be considered historical. The setting is all-important in historical fiction because it cues readers to interpret characters and events in the light of the times. Values, perspectives, and certainly living conditions will be quite different from today, and readers should expect that.

A Single Shard (Park) is set in a small village in twelfth-century Korea. Tree-ear, the central character, received his name because he was an orphan (like the mushroom that grew without seed). With the dream of becoming a master potter himself someday, Tree-ear works for the master potter Minn, who creates the famous celadon ware of Korea. As Tree-ear learns more about pottery, he earns the trust of the master and undertakes a journey to bring two fine pots to the royal court and secure a commission for Minn. Everything depends on his success, although he is afraid of going so far away.

Figure 11-3. Because of Winn-Dixie

Figure 11-4. A Single Shard

Tree-ear is attacked and the vases are shattered, but he perseveres and saves a single shard of a vase to show to the royal emissary, and the master is awarded the commission. Tree-ear finds a home with the master potter and is given a new name that shares a syllable with Minn's, an honor bestowed on siblings.

The writer of *A Single Shard* tells a story set in the far distant past, but the human problems of loneliness and the pain of being without parents is relevant today. In fact, even though *Because of Winn-Dixie* and *A Single Shard* appeal to two different age groups, they have common elements. Both protagonists are lonely and long for parents; each has trusted advisers and friends; both make a journey to a better emotional place.

Traditional Literature, Fantasy, and Science Fiction
Traditional literature, fantasy, and science fiction are highly connected and make similar demands on readers.

Traditional Literature Traditional literature has delighted children for countless generations. These texts were created centuries ago and disseminated by traveling minstrels who went from village to village retelling them orally. The very popular tales, such as *Cinderella,* appear in some version in almost every culture. No one knows their origin; they have no authors. We can categorize them as:

- Cumulative tales, such as *The House That Jack Built* and *The Turnip,* in which previous events are repeated every time a new one is added to the sequence.

- Pourquoi tales, such as *How the Elephant Got His Trunk,* which explain how or why things are as they are.

- Beast tales, such as *The Three Bears,* which involve animals who behave as humans.

- "Noodlehead" tales, such as *The Three Sillies,* which recount the antics of fools.

- Realistic tales, such as *Zlateh the Goat,* which may have grown out of actual events.

- Fairy tales, such as *Cinderella,* which include magical beings.

- Fables, like *The Lion and the Mouse,* which involve animals with human traits and have a moral lesson.

- Myths, like the Iroquois "How Fire Came to the Six Nations," which usually involve a quest and answer questions about things that cannot be explained.

- Legends, like *Paul Bunyan* or *John Henry,* which involve larger-than-life characters who perform remarkable or heroic deeds.

- Epics, such as *Jason and the Golden Fleece*, which are extended stories of a hero's quest.

It is obvious from this list that traditional literature may be very simple, appealing to young students, but it also may be geared to adults. In traditional literature, characters are usually flat. They are stereotypical and are either good or bad. The plots are simple and straightforward.

Traditional literature is very important, not only in its own right, but as a foundation for understanding the complex genre of fantasy. A rich foundation in traditional literature helps students internalize some very important symbolic patterns, or *motifs,* that reappear again and again. Think back on your own experience with traditional literature. Aren't many of the following true?

- Many things come in threes: three wishes, three bears, three tasks.

- The youngest or smallest often becomes the hero, overcoming others.

- There are transformations—people into animals and vice versa.

- There is magic—magic words, magic objects, magic people.

- There are tricksters who triumph over much larger animals or people through their intelligence.

◻ Good triumphs over evil.

These things may seem part of the literature of childhood, but, in fact, you will find these same motifs in an adult fantasy such as *The Lord of the Rings* (Tolkien).

Fantasy Fantasy is fiction that contains unrealistic or unworldly elements. Fantasy has its roots in traditional literature, in that it borrows many of the motifs found there (e.g., the quest, talking animals, and magic objects). At the same time, fantasy's plots are relevant to the issues and problems of today, so they can be linked to realistic and historical fiction. The characters may have magical powers but at the same time have human qualities. Perhaps the best current example is the Harry Potter series. Harry is a boy with whom modern children (especially underdogs) can identify, yet he is a powerful wizard. The Charlie Bone series for younger children is another example.

Simple animal fantasy is especially appealing to young children. The Baby Bear series, by Beverly Randell, is an animal fantasy that first graders will enjoy reading for themselves. In these easy books (*Baby Bear Goes Fishing, Baby Bear's Present, Father Bear's Surprise,* and the like), they can read about the life of three bears that in most ways are like people. These books are not connected to the classic story *The Three Bears,* but many children ask, "When is Goldilocks going to visit them?"

Peaches the Pig is another example of a modern "talking beast" fantasy. A story to read to second or third graders is Alma Flor Ada's *Dear Peter Rabbit.* This book is a series of letters between Pigs One, Two, and Three, Goldilocks, Peter Rabbit, and Baby Bear that make use of readers' prior knowledge of these characters.

For older students, *The Tale of the Swamp Rat* (Crocker) is a fast-paced text about a personified orphan rat that is protected by a large alligator. The text is fantasy, but the writer has woven in information about animals, the swamp in various seasons and during a drought, and much history. Although all the swamp animals talk and have definite personalities, they do not live like people. This fantasy will remind you of *Watership Down* (Richard Adams) or *Mrs. Frisby and the Rats of NIMH* (Robert C. O'Brien).

Science Fiction Science fiction is a work of fantasy that involves or is based on scientific principles. It is often set in the future, and writers make use of technology to create the fantasy. Middle school lovers of fantasy will read voraciously through Orson Scott Card's *Ender* series about war in space (for example, *Ender's Game*).

Although not technically "true," all good fiction holds up a mirror to life. Your students will find universal truths within both realistic stories and fantasy. For many readers, fiction remains a source of enjoyment throughout life. As Dal Mossman said in the documentary *Stone Reader,* it is a "feast that never ends." In *The Child That Books Built* (p. 5), Francis Spufford's memoir of decades as an avid reader, the author confesses, "I need fiction. I'm an addict . . . There is always a heap of unopened paperbacks near the bed, always something current on the kitchen table to reach for over coffee when I wake up . . . Fiction is king." As Frank Conroy said in the documentary *Stone Reader,* "It's like food. There are some pleasures that simply never run out and books are one of them."

NONFICTION

In spite of the appeal of fiction, many readers prefer nonfiction. There is a groundswell of interest in expository texts. We divide nonfiction texts into two categories: biographical texts and factual texts.

Biographies, Autobiographies, and Memoirs
Biographical texts are usually organized in ways similar to fiction. They tell a story. Usually, there is a beginning and a series of events drawing to closure. But unlike fiction, there is not always a central problem or high point. Instead, the text presents crossroads or significant events and accomplishments in the person's life, gradually building a picture of the subject and often providing lessons or models for readers.

A *biography* is a text written by one or more writers to tell the story of another person's life. The subject of a biography is usually someone of accomplishment, whether famous or little known. The point of a biography is that the person has lived a life that will be interesting or informative to others.

An *autobiography* is a biographical text in which a person tells about his or her own life. Autobiography is qualitatively different from biography, of course, because it is told from the subject's own perspective; but in general, all biographical texts have a similar structure. Biographies tend to be written in third person, autobiographies in first person.

A *memoir* is also usually written in first person but is

shorter and tends to focus on a particularly important time period or memory. A memoir may focus on a very brief period—a day or a week. It may focus on a series of experiences in a single place or a long and important theme. It may focus on the writer's experience with one other person. In other words, a memoir is more often a vignette than the whole story. It typically includes thoughtful analysis and self-reflection.

Biographies are available even for younger children (about the middle of first grade). An example is *Sally Ride,* by Elizabeth Schomel, which tells a few simple facts about the astronaut Sally Ride in the sequence they occurred. Biographies can take unique forms. In *If a Bus Could Talk* (Ringgold), a talking bus tells the story of Rosa Parks. As the story begins, a young girl gets on a bus and hears a mysterious voice; by page 3 the bus is telling the life story of Rosa. This biography, wrapped in fantasy, is a good one to read aloud to third or fourth graders (a good example of a hybrid text).

Factual Texts

To help us distinguish between types of nonfiction, we use the term *factual* to refer to texts whose primary purpose is to provide information. Similar terms are *expository,* meaning to set forth the meaning or purpose, or *informational,* and we will use these terms interchangeably in the book. Factual text is different from fiction in a number of very important ways:

- Rather than using the narrative structure described above, factual texts are often organized into sections or categories, indicated by headings and subheadings.
- Factual texts do not have characters and settings, although they may focus on particular people, topics, or places.
- Factual texts often include graphics such as maps, charts, and diagrams that add meaning.
- Writers of factual texts use a range of organizational patterns to provide information to readers.
- It is very important for factual text to be *accurate* or *scientifically true,* which is not always the case for fiction.

Factual texts can be on just about any topic or content area. A couple of decades ago, most expository writing took the form of textbooks, but more recently many informational picture books are being published. *The Bone Detectives* (Jackson), for example, is a factual text with literary qual-

ity (see Figure 11-5). These books may truly be called literature. They contain high-quality illustrations in a variety of media (often photographs but sometimes paintings or drawings). The text is a coherent whole and is well written. The information is scientifically sound.

Writers of factual texts tend to use one or more of several typical organizational patterns, such as description, enumeration, comparison and contrast, cause and effect, chronological sequence, problem/solution, and question/ answer. Understanding these underlying structures helps the reader search for, find, and understand the important information. You can find many more examples in *Leveled Books for Readers, K–8* (Fountas and Pinnell 2006).

HYBRID TEXTS

The lines between genres are not firm. Increasingly, we find very interesting expository "hybrids," often referred to as *literary nonfiction.* Narrative structure is built into factual texts using the writer's distinctive voice. Factual text can also be inserted into fiction—when characters do research or follow maps, for example. Joanna Cole's Magic School Bus series is an excellent example of a text that technically is fantasy but has as its major goal the intent to inform and provides a great deal of factual information. How would we categorize *The Magic School Bus* or *Tell Me, Tree* (see

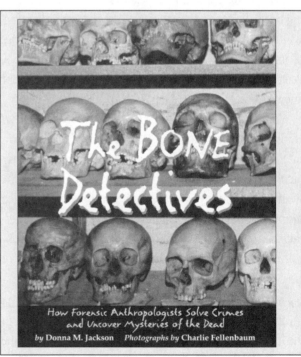

Figure 11-5. The Bone Detectives

Chapter 13)? In a sense, it doesn't really matter. Your students can easily learn to separate fiction from fact if they have experienced many different kinds of texts, and they will soon recognize a mixture of features within texts.

THINKING ACROSS GENRES

Genres make different demands on readers' thinking, which is a good thing! Readers who experience a wide variety of genres as they become literate will have greater flexibility in processing text, but more important, they will have developed ways of thinking within, beyond, and about their reading. Figure 11-6 summarizes ways of thinking across genres. These ways of thinking are explored in more detail in Chapters 3, 4 and 5.

Thinking Within the Text

All genres require that readers:

- Decode and understand the words.

- Monitor and check on their reading to be sure that it is accurate and that they understand what they read.

- Search for and use the important information in a text.

- Summarize information to store it in memory.

- Maintain fluency by integrating sources of information in a smoothly operating process that results in phrased reading.

- Adjust reading for different purposes and types of text.

We began this chapter by stating that knowledge of genres and their forms helps readers use expectations as a road map

THINKING ACROSS GENRES:
Fiction

GENRE	THINKING WITHIN THE TEXT	THINKING BEYOND THE TEXT	THINKING ABOUT THE TEXT
Contemporary realistic fiction	Search for and remember important information about setting, plot, and characters.	Interpret and make connections to characters' motivations and the events of the story.	Notice how the writer uses language to make the story seem real for the reader to think critically about the text.
Historical fiction	Search for and remember important information about the historical setting, the way events are related to it, and the way characters behave in relation to it.	Interpret characters' motivations and story events in light of the historical context and make connections to today.	Critically evaluate the text by comparing it to existing knowledge and other texts; notice how the writer uses features to help the reader understand the historical context.
Traditional literature	Follow simple plots with characters that represent "types" rather than changing and developing over time.	Make connections to other versions of the same text and derive the moral lesson from the text.	Compare different versions of the same tale and notice motifs or common themes across traditional literature.
Fantasy	Follow events of the plot and notice characters within a fantastic world that can be understood by suspending reality.	Understand characters' motivations and make connections to one's own life even though the plot and setting depart from reality.	Notice how the writer uses language to create the fantastic world and considers the deeper meaning of the text for today's real world.
Science fiction	Follow events of the plot and notice characters within a fantastic world built through technology.	Understand characters' motivations and make connections between the unreal world, created through technology, and the real-life world of today.	Notice how the writer uses language and technological concepts to create the fantastic world and considers the deeper meaning of the text for today's real world.

Figure 11-6. *Thinking Across Genres: Fiction, Nonfiction, and Poetry*

THINKING ACROSS GENRES: *Nonfiction*			
GENRE	**THINKING WITHIN THE TEXT**	**THINKING BEYOND THE TEXT**	**THINKING ABOUT THE TEXT**
Biography	Gather and remember important details and events of a person's life.	Infer the importance of the subject and the influence of events on his or her life; make connections to one's own life.	Evaluate the accuracy and significance of the events reported in the text; notice how the writer uses language and details to make the subject's life seem real to readers.
Autobiography and Memoir	Gather and remember important details and events of the writer's life.	Infer the influence of events on the writer's life; make connections to one's own life.	Evaluate the accuracy and significance of the events reported by the writer; notice how the writer uses language and details to make his or her life seem real to readers.
Informational	Read and understand technical words and gather important and new information within categories of knowledge.	Bring existing knowledge and experiences to understand the content as communicated in text and graphics and notice writers' choices in selecting and presenting information.	Notice and understand how writers use text structure and organization (description, temporal sequence, compare/contrast, cause/effect, and problem/solution) to provide information to readers and critically evaluate the content and way of presenting it.
THINKING ACROSS GENRES: *Poetry*			
GENRE	**THINKING WITHIN THE TEXT**	**THINKING BEYOND THE TEXT**	**THINKING ABOUT THE TEXT**
Poetry	Gather important information and language, including figurative use of language.	Infer the deeper meaning of the poem; interpret symbolic references.	

Figure 11-6. *Thinking Across Genres: Fiction, Nonfiction, and Poetry (cont.)*

for reading. The moment proficient readers begin reading a text, they adjust their approach and arrange their predictions based on what they know about the kind of text they are reading. If all six systems of strategic actions listed above are operating in an integrated way, the reader will achieve *literal understanding* of the text. Good literal understanding is the basic foundation for other ways of thinking.

Fiction demands that readers notice and think about characters, gathering descriptive information about how they look, what they think or say, what they do, and what others think or say about them. Readers of fiction will pick up information about the setting and follow the plot line, noticing how one episode follows another. Traditional literature supports young readers in these kinds of strategic actions, because the plots are simple and straightforward and the characters are easy to understand.

Readers of historical fiction engage in all of the ways of thinking that contemporary realistic fiction requires but are especially challenged to notice details of the setting, because all characters and events must be understood in that context. Readers of fantasy must also pick up important information about the setting, because they have to understand an unreal world that is far from being their own.

When you read fiction, you carry in your head a summary of the plot and vital information as you go, reorganizing it as necessary. After reading, your memory of this important information allows you to draw conclusions about the text and to link it to others.

Nonfiction poses similar challenges. Biography, autobiography, and memoir require you to gather and remember important details and events of a person's life. Descriptions of the subject are helpful in thinking about the influences and motivations that lead to accomplishment.

Factual texts provide a large amount of information, requiring that you separate new information from previous knowledge. Just as in fiction, you probably carry a categorized summary of new facts or bigger ideas with you as you read, building one upon the other. Having some prior knowledge helps you strategically acquire more, because you do not have to notice and remember every piece of information—only what you do not already know and what seems significant. Unless one is cramming for a test on the material, no reader of factual texts tries to remember all the information included.

Thinking Beyond the Text

All genres require that readers think beyond the text. Readers of fiction need to interpret characters' motivations, and they may often make connections to their own lives. Readers of historical fiction sometimes have to work harder, because they have to interpret characters in the light of the historical times. Readers of fantasy must use the unreal world of the text to frame their understanding of characters and events. Their predictions deal with what is possible within the fantasy world the writer has created.

In biographical texts, readers use inference to understand the subject of the text and to determine its meaning for their own lives. Readers of factual texts access their existing knowledge as they encounter new ideas, and they constantly adjust their own categories of information. Poetry, too, provides opportunities for readers to think beyond the literal meaning of a text, using symbolism and comparisons to interpret the writer's visions and emotions.

Thinking About the Text

Proficient readers notice and use analytical thinking across all genres. As we've pointed out, knowing genre characteristics supports reading; but readers can turn around and think like writers. In the process, they learn more about the inner workings of texts. For example, you might reread a poem many times to admire the beauty of the language or the way the poet has used imagery. Reading fiction, you could appreciate the way a writer presents characters or keeps your attention. Here is Jackie's comment about *Because of Winn-Dixie*:

> I'm only up to Chapter 7, but I've fallen in love with this book! The author uses such descriptive writing. I'd definitely recommend it to you. Oh, and it's a Newbery Honor Book!

When you consider a text as an object, you might make statements like these:

- "This writer is really keeping me in suspense."
- "This biography makes Thomas Jefferson seem like a real person."
- "I like the way the writer traveled back and forth in the character's memory."
- "The language is beautiful, almost like poetry."
- "The ideas were presented so compellingly that I was persuaded."
- "The text was so well organized that I learned a great deal from it."

Students of literature go deeply into analysis in a scholarly way, but all proficient readers learn to notice aspects of the writer's craft if for no other reason than to develop tastes and preferences as readers. Examining texts in an analytical way can also greatly inform writers.

Readers must also be critical, and that is especially true when reading factual texts. In times past, many readers thought "if it's published, it must be true." In fact, that statement was never true, yet there were publishing constraints that added to credibility. With current technology, anyone can publish just about anything in writing. Readers must learn to analyze texts critically, sorting credible facts from misleading information.

SYSTEMS OF STRATEGIC ACTIONS

We have written about twelve powerful systems of strategic actions that readers use in flexible and integrated ways as they process texts (see Chapters 3, 4, and 5). You will want to think about how a reader's knowledge of the characteristics of a genre helps a reader engage each of the systems of strategic actions.

SUGGESTIONS FOR PROFESSIONAL DEVELOPMENT

Thinking Across Genres

1 Select one book in each of the following categories from your classroom: contemporary realistic fiction, historical fiction, science fiction, traditional literature, biography, autobiography or memoir, factual text, and poetry collection.

2 Meet with your grade-level colleagues and place all books of the same genres in a pile.

3 Use the following chart, Thinking Across Genres, in Figure 11-7 (which can also be found on the DVD that accompanies this book) and refer to Figure 11-6 in this chapter.

4 Discuss each text in each genre and the thinking within, beyond, and about the text it requires.

THINKING ACROSS GENRES:
Fiction

GENRE	THINKING WITHIN THE TEXT	THINKING BEYOND THE TEXT	THINKING ABOUT THE TEXT
Contemporary Realistic Fiction			
Historical Fiction			
Traditional Literature			
Fantasy			
Science Fiction			

THINKING ACROSS GENRES:
Nonfiction

GENRE	THINKING WITHIN THE TEXT	THINKING BEYOND THE TEXT	THINKING ABOUT THE TEXT
Biography			
Autobiography and Memoir			
Informational			

THINKING ACROSS GENRES:
Poetry

GENRE	THINKING WITHIN THE TEXT	THINKING BEYOND THE TEXT	THINKING ABOUT THE TEXT
Poetry			

Figure 11-7. *Thinking Across Genres: Fiction, Nonfiction, and Poetry*

CHAPTER TWELVE

USING A GRADIENT OF TEXT TO MATCH BOOKS TO READERS

It is most useful for teachers to collectively discuss the leveling of texts and to share their knowledge and experience to provide some gradient of difficulty among the books they like to use . . . .

—MARIE CLAY

Your classroom library comprises a wide variety of texts in many genres, texts that provide enjoyment, serve children's varied interests, and are connected to the curriculum. This rich text base is essential not only to build your students' future literacy but also to enable them to lead literate lives in the here and now. There need to be books at a wide range of levels appropriate to the age group and reading ability, but books are not organized by "level." In this chapter we focus on using text levels for small-group reading instruction. These levels are labeled A to Z+, designating texts from easier to more difficult.

Small-group reading instruction helps students expand their reading powers by processing new texts with success. It requires books that readers can read with the support of your teaching. Books for reading instruction, therefore, must be selected with meticulous precision. A gradient of text difficulty is a valuable tool in the process of selecting the "right" books for a particular group of readers. The "right" book provides the appropriate mix of support and challenge to the reader.

The role of the text is critical, as it can support the reader's ability to "learn to read in the text" or it can interfere. The text is important in the development of a reading process because of the supports it provides and the demands it makes.

WHAT IS A TEXT GRADIENT?

Put simply, a *leveled set* is a collection of books in which processing demands have been categorized along a continuum from easiest to hardest:

> Creating a text gradient means classifying books along a continuum based on the combination of variables that support and confirm readers' strategic actions and offer the problem-solving opportunities that build the reading process (Fountas and Pinnell 1996, p. 113).

The "level" of a text is not just a housekeeping detail. It has everything to do with successful processing and the growth of readers' systems for strategic actions. A text that is too difficult does not give the reader the opportunity to learn how to read better. No gradient can be absolute, of course, because readers' background knowledge, habits or attention, and prior reading experiences are so diverse. Nevertheless, each category along the continuum presents new or more complex challenges. The level takes into account a composite of text factors that we describe later in this chapter and in greater detail in *Leveled Books for Readers, K–8*, (Fountas and Pinnell 2006) and *The Continuum of Literacy Learning, PreK–8: A Guide to Teaching* (Pinnell and Fountas 2008, 2011).

The complexity in creating a text gradient lies in the range of factors that need to be assessed. One text might be challenging because of hard words; another might be challenging because its length requires readers to concentrate for longer periods; still another might have very complex or mature themes and ideas.

Figure 12-1 sums up what a text gradient *is and is not*. Notice the emphasis on the value of a gradient as a teaching tool: it provides parameters for selecting books. It would be very difficult to match books to readers using an unorganized collection with hundreds of titles. You can also use the gradient to help you analyze texts in preparation for introducing them to readers and finding teaching points. Finally, the gradient is valuable as background knowledge when you work with students who are having trouble selecting texts for their independent reading.

We do not recommend that students use the levels of a gradient to choose books for independent reading. The levels should be very unobtrusive (if not totally invisible) in your classroom. Students need to learn how to choose books

---

What Is a Text Gradient?

A TEXT GRADIENT IS:	A TEXT GRADIENT IS NOT:
□ A tool for teachers to use in analyzing texts.	□ A tool for students to use in selecting books for independent reading.
□ A tool for teachers to use in selecting books for . small-group reading instruction.	□ A label for book baskets in a classroom library.
□ A support for teachers in guiding readers' choice of books for independent reading (when necessary).	□ A label that students should attach to themselves.
□ A guide to judging below, on, or above grade-level reading.	□ An incentive for students to practice reading.
	□ A label for a grade on a report card.

Figure 12-1. *What Is a Text Gradient?*

---

based on their own assessment of readability, interesting topics or plots, favorite authors, and general appeal. You can teach students how to assess the appropriateness of texts they find interesting for their present reading levels (see Chapter 8). Proceeding through the levels should not be an incentive *per se.* Rather, readers should have goals like these:

□ Reading a variety of texts—genres, authors, topics.

□ Learning how to select books for oneself.

□ Accomplishing a large amount of enjoyable, interesting reading.

□ Thinking deeply about reading.

□ Discussing reading with others in thoughtful ways.

□ Getting better at writing about reading.

□ Taking on new genres, authors, and interests.

Simply moving "up a level" is not a goal that fits into the making of a reader. Children need to (with teacher support) read widely and thoughtfully, with ease and enjoyment, on a given level prior to reading texts at a more difficult text level. We do want children to make vertical progress, reading at grade level or above, but breadth of reading and age appropriateness of content are also factors. The point of reading instruction is to ensure both growth and breadth as well as steady vertical movement. When readers move to levels too far above their current grade level, the content often becomes developmentally inappropriate.

Another important point is that a text level has no place on a report card. First, text levels are narrowly defined in a way that may be complex for parents to understand. There is variation within a level. Parents do need to know whether

their children are reading above, on, or below grade level instructionally and independently (along with your plans to help them), but the gradient reading levels are complex and designed to be used by educators who are making selections for instruction. As a teacher, you may have a very good reason for allowing a student to read below or above his designated instructional level (when introducing a new genre, for example, or when learning about a topic, or when you are providing a high level of support). Parents may see the level as a label, or as a comparison to other children, not a tool for making complex decisions. As adults, we do not read constantly at our highest level; we have many different purposes for reading. If you keep these cautions in mind, the gradient is a powerful tool:

> Children can use their control of oral language and knowledge of the world and as-yet-limited literacy knowledge to move up through a gradient of difficulty in texts. They are aided by teachers who arrange their opportunities and support their efforts. As texts are read and written, different kinds of learning are drawn together, coupled, integrated, or changed. New items of vocabulary are added, frequently constructed from familiar bits, roots, prefixes, patterns, clusters, chunks, and analogies.
>
> In the short time it takes a budding reader to read through many texts on an increasing gradient of difficulty . . . the network of strategic activity gets massive use, expands in range of experience, and increases in efficiency. This happens providing the reader is not struggling. (Clay, 2001, p. 132)

In our view, specific reading instruction is essential throughout the elementary and middle school grades to take each reader from where he is to as far as he can develop as a reader in a school year. Students who make excellent reading progress expand their reading powers with good instruction, which depends on choosing the right selection of books for instruction.

WHEN DOES THE GRADIENT MATTER? WHEN DOESN'T IT MATTER?

We have made a case for the usefulness of the gradient, but we need to sort out when it is important and when we need to think about texts in other ways. Every time students read a text, we need to think in some way about the text's complexity and accessibility, but it is not always necessary to use the finely calibrated gradient (see Figure 12-2).

WILL I NEED TO USE THE TEXT GRADIENT FOR INTERACTIVE READ-ALOUD?

No. Obviously, you heavily scaffold students' text processing when you decode the words, use phrasing and expression to convey meaning, and stop occasionally to discuss what you have read. Listeners are freed from using the visual information because you are processing it for them, but they are very active in every other way. They can give their attention to thinking about the text.

You'll still want to think about the supports and challenges in the text so that you can select appropriate texts to read aloud. There are big differences between the texts you'll read to first graders, third graders, and sixth graders. You will want to consider their background of experience, interests, ability to handle the themes and ideas, the vocabulary challenges, and general complexity of language and text structure.

Most of the texts you read aloud to students will not be part of the leveled collection and will not have a letter des-

Considering the Supports and Challenges in Texts

INSTRUCTIONAL CONTEXT FOR READING	WILL I NEED TO USE THE TEXT GRADIENT?	HOW TO APPROACH TEXT COMPLEXITY
Interactive Read-Aloud	No	Since you are processing the text, factors such as word solving and sentence complexity are not so important. Consider instead: ▫ Students' interests and tastes. ▫ The quality of the text and illustrations. ▫ The opportunities for new content, vocabulary, and attention to writing craft. ▫ The appropriateness of content to the age group. ▫ The maturity of the issues and themes. ▫ The prior experience required to understand the ideas in the text. ▫ The length of the text and the time it will take to read it (one or two sessions). ▫ The vocabulary "load." ▫ Age-appropriate content. Although read-aloud texts are not "leveled," it may help to keep in mind the the kinds of concepts, ideas, and language that are available to children in the texts they are reading for instruction.
Literature Study	Yes and no	Keep in mind the levels of texts that students can read as you select books for literature discussion, but *students will not necessarily be reading at that level.* Instead: ▫ Set up mixed-ability discussion groups. ▫ Make sure students for whom the texts are too hard can hear them being read aloud. ▫ Use age-appropriate material. ▫ Consider students' interests and compelling issues and themes. ▫ Select texts that students will want to discuss with others. ▫ Consider gender preferences.

Figure 12-2. *Considering the Supports and Challenges in Texts*

Considering the Supports and Challenges in Texts (CONTINUED)

INSTRUCTIONAL CONTEXT FOR READING	WILL I NEED TO USE THE TEXT GRADIENT?	HOW TO APPROACH TEXT COMPLEXITY
Shared Reading	Yes and no	Texts for shared reading are poems and other works with print big enough for all students to see (for example, picture books with enlarged print or texts produced through interactive writing). With group support and much rereading, children can read books that are more complex than those they read during reading instruction. In selecting texts for shared reading, consider these characteristics: ▫ Amount of text children can follow. ▫ Supports in terms of repeated phrases or high frequency words. ▫ Meaningfulness of the text to children (familiar experiences, linked to content, product of interactive writing). ▫ Whether the texts will be pleasurable for students.
Guided Reading	Yes	Use the text gradient as a tool in selecting instructional-level texts to introduce to readers. ▫ Select books that children can read with accuracy and understanding *with instructional support.*. ▫ Select books that will help children develop their systems of strategic actions. ▫ Regroup children for effective teaching. ▫ Track students' reading progress over time. ▫ Organize books for efficient instruction.
Independent Reading	Yes and no	Use the gradient as background knowledge when you help readers select texts. You won't know the level of every book, but you can make approximations based on what you know about the texts that *are* leveled. Students do not choose books by levels. ▫ Look for books that interest them. ▫ "Stretch" them by having them try new authors or genres. ▫ Remember favorite authors, series, and genres and reflect on why they like them. ▫ See them as readers who have tastes and preferences. ▫ Try a little bit of a book to know if it is "just right" for their present reading powers. ▫ Think carefully before abandoning a book, reflecting on why it is not a "just right" book.

Figure 12-2. *Considering the Supports and Challenges in Texts (cont.)*

ignation for a text level. However, keeping in mind the text levels that children are reading during guided reading will give you a general sense for the kinds of concepts, ideas, vocabulary, and language they can process. Since one of your goals in reading aloud is to stretch them in these areas, you will select a range of easier and challenging texts. (Interactive read-aloud is discussed in more detail in Chapters 15, 16, 17, and 18.)

WILL I NEED TO USE THE TEXT GRADIENT FOR LITERATURE STUDY?

A qualified yes. You will want to keep students' reading levels in mind when you select texts for literature discussion, because you need to know whether they will be able to process them independently or whether you will need to make the text accessible in other ways, such as an audiotape or a CD. (Alternatively, an adult can read the book to the student at home.) But students will not necessarily be reading at their independent level when they prepare for literature discussion. It is important to use mixed-ability groups for literature discussion. All students need access to age-appropriate, grade-appropriate material and a chance to discuss this material with peers, regardless of their current reading ability.

You may want to begin literature discussion groups using books that you have read aloud to the class. If everyone in a group has a copy of the text, students can then go back through it, marking interesting illustrations and passages they would like to discuss with the group. Post your book club choices, and let students make a selection based on interest. In selecting books, again consider interests, including gender-related preferences, and be sure these books have ideas and themes students will want to talk about. A more detailed description of literature discussion is presented in Chapters 18 and 19.

WILL I NEED TO USE THE TEXT GRADIENT FOR SHARED READING?

Yes and no. Shared reading is an activity for younger students designed to scaffold their early understandings of how printed texts "work." You can use any enlarged text for shared reading. Teachers make great use of poems copied onto chart paper and of texts that they have co-written with students through interactive writing.

In interactive writing, the class constructs text as a group. The students and teacher negotiate the text together; they may write about anything—an experience they've had as a class, a science experiment, an innovation from a book they have heard read aloud, a letter or note, a sign for the classroom, directions and instructions, etc. The teacher works at an easel that all the children can see. The text is usually read many times during the process. While the teacher does most of the writing, sometimes individual students come up to the easel and contribute a letter, word, or punctuation mark.

Teachers also use picture books with enlarged print ("big books") for shared reading. Because texts are read many times, with group support, in unison or with specific children or groups of children assigned parts, children can usually read texts that are more complicated than those they can read during small-group instruction. You will not

need to use the text gradient specifically when you select texts for shared reading. Consider instead the children's ability to deal with the number of lines of text, built-in support through repetition and rhyme, and the familiarity of content. We discuss shared reading in more detail in Chapter 21.

WILL I NEED TO USE THE TEXT GRADIENT FOR GUIDED READING?

A definite yes. The gradient is most useful in selecting texts for guided reading. Text difficulty is a key to selecting and introducing texts in a way that will help students expand their reading powers. We discuss guided reading in detail in Chapters 24 and 25.

WILL I NEED TO USE THE TEXT GRADIENT FOR INDEPENDENT READING?

A qualified yes, which applies to your thinking, not to the students' use. We *have never recommended that students use letter levels as a criterion for choosing books they want to read.* We do not want children to label themselves by level. Rather, we want to help them select a range of books they can read and understand without our help. We see independent reading as "reading for pleasure," meaning that it must have the chance of being enjoyable and intrinsically rewarding. It also serves the purpose of helping students solidify and expand their own processing systems. You will want to spend time teaching students how to become skilled selectors of books (see Chapter 22)

You will want to teach students how to select books in minilessons in the reading workshop (see Fountas and Pinnell 2001). As a teacher, you use your background knowledge of the levels students can process independently and with instruction to help you guide students who need help choosing books. We discuss independent reading and reading workshop in more detail in Chapters 22 and 23.

WHAT IS THE RELATIONSHIP BETWEEN THE TEXT GRADIENT AND GRADE-LEVEL READING?

There is an important relationship between the levels on the gradient and traditional grade levels in elementary and middle school (see Figure 12-3), but the lines are not firmly drawn. Grade-level ranges as indicated on the chart are goals and may not be an appropriate level for instructing a particular child at a particular point in time.

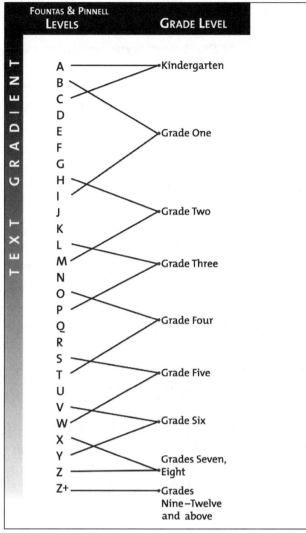

Figure 12-3. *Text Gradient*

We envision kindergarten children independently reading texts between levels A and C by the end of a year of school. Many first graders will be reading at level B at the beginning of the year but progress to at least level I by the end of the year. Second graders who enter at level H have a slight bit of catching up to do but will likely be able to progress to about level M by the end of the year.

You will notice as you move up the levels of the texts that there are fewer gradations at each grade level. That's because texts in the categories become more complex and there is wider variety. (The level-by-level description of text features in Figure 12-6 will make this clear.) The point of the gradient is to help you choose books that particular readers are not able to read independently but will be able

to process successfully with your support. Your teaching and the text you select will help them learn more about the reading process, and they will apply what they have learned as a reader with the "just right" text to other texts they read.

There is probably a limit to how far up the levels you want to take readers at any point in time. This will depend on the individual, of course, but the idea is to help each child become an excellent, flexible, and voracious reader of a variety of texts within any one level before moving to more difficult levels. It is important to notice that good readers will probably select books from a variety of levels that they can access easily when reading independently.

WHAT ABOUT CHILDREN WHO ARE READING BELOW GRADE LEVEL?

There is only one way to gain reading power—by successfully processing continuous texts every day. It is important to match books to readers very carefully and provide daily small-group instruction that ensures they will process these books successfully. Since the book selected for guided reading provides a little more challenge than children can handle independently, reading it successfully will expand their systems of strategies. The gradient and approximate grade-level expectations also serve as a warning. A child who is reading well below expectations will need intervention in addition to good daily teaching at the instructional level.

WHAT ABOUT CHILDREN WHO ARE READING ABOVE GRADE LEVEL?

Many children will exceed grade-level expectations, but you will want to check carefully to be sure that the materials they are reading are age appropriate and interesting to them. It is unwise to encourage students to read "harder" books just to say they can do it. The kind of thinking students engage in with texts is the challenge, not how hard the words are to read. You will find that when students are reading up to about one year above grade level, the content continues to be appropriate.

HOW DO I USE THE GRADIENT TO SELECT TEXTS FOR GUIDED READING?

Briefly, there are three steps in using the gradient:

1 The first task is to find out what the student can read independently with fluency and understanding. To find out, sample some oral reading at several levels. Don't

expect "performed" or "expressive" reading, but notice how the student:

- ❑ Groups words while reading.
- ❑ Moves along with good momentum, solving words easily without losing meaning.
- ❑ Reflects the meaning of the text with the voice.
- ❑ Talks about the text in a way that reflects understanding.

Some systematic ways of assessing oral reading behaviors and text comprehension are provided in Chapters 8 and 9, but you can also tell a great deal by informally assessing students' reading of the books they are choosing as you listen to them read and talk with them about their reading. Remember that you will likely have an idea in your own mind of the book's level from your use of leveled texts as you listen to the child read and talk about the text.

2 After determining the highest level the student can read *independently* with understanding, accuracy, and fluency, think about what he can do with instruction and support. Moving up a level on the gradient will probably give you a good set of texts from which to choose. Once you begin teaching at this level, you can adjust it if necessary.

3 Be sure to consider your students' interests, the genre of the text, and opportunities to learn as you select books to introduce for guided reading from within the level you determine is appropriate for instruction.

HOW DO I FIND THE "LEVEL" FOR BOOKS?

We suggest that you use our leveled book list to label as many books as you can from your book collection. Once you become very familiar with the books at various levels, you will feel comfortable meeting with colleagues and folding in other books you have that are on the list. You can try them out at levels you think appropriate and adjust as needed. You can discuss the specific level-by-level text characteristics described in Fountas and Pinnell 2006 and

www.fountasandpinnellleveledbooks.com. You can find about 18,000 leveled books on the website as well as in a printed book list, *Fountas and Pinnell Leveled Book List, K–8* (2006).

You can pencil in the label designation inside the front or back cover of the book or place it on a sticker on the back cover. Explain that these letters are for your reference. Usually, teachers keep multiple copies of books for use in guided reading lessons in containers by level as in Figure 12-4. These books are not available to children to select for independent reading.

We encourage you and your colleagues to create a school book room in which you have organized many books by level, A through Z+. You can then "shop" in the school book room for books for guided reading and return them when you have finished using them. The book room (see Figure 12-5) is thus a shared resource for the whole school. A middle school book room should include some lower-level books for students who are reading below grade level, but try to see that they incorporate age-appropriate topics and characters.

Complete descriptions for using, acquiring, and storing leveled books, along with level-by-level examples, are presented in Fountas and Pinnell, *Leveled Books, K–8: Matching Texts to Readers for Effective Teaching,* Heinemann, 2006.

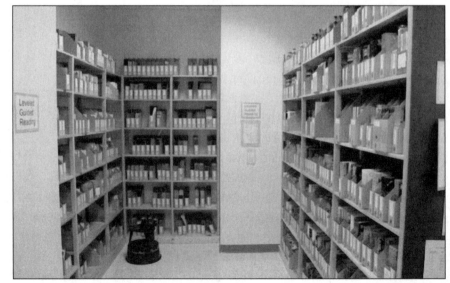

Figure 12-4. *Leveled Book Storage*

Figure 12-5. *School Book Room*

WHAT FACTORS CONTRIBUTE TO TEXT DIFFICULTY?

Figure 12-6 is a concise summary of ten factors to consider in analyzing the supports and challenges in written texts. Looking at all these factors, you can determine the level of a text along the gradient, remembering that in any one text, several factors usually combine to raise the challenge.

Genre

Except for the beginning levels (approximately A–M), every level of the gradient has a full range of genres. After level M, children tend to have a backlog of reading experience and are at ease with realistic narratives, traditional literature, some fantasy, and very simple informational books on familiar topics, and even some historical fiction. In general, they are ready to cope with a wider range.

Books for Beginning Readers

Young readers are just learning about written texts, so they need very simple, highly regular examples. Topics must be very familiar. Because these children are just beginning to build a reading process, they should not also have to struggle with new and difficult concepts. Biography and history would demand much more background knowledge than most kindergarten and first-grade students have.

We can divide lower-level books roughly into simple narratives (realistic and fantasy) with predictable features and informational texts based on familiar concepts. Simple narratives tell a real story in just a few pages. Different kinds of predictability are built into the text:

- The story line may be very predictable. (The character goes somewhere, has a problem, solves it, and returns home.)
- The language is not precisely like oral language but is close enough that children can use the predictability of the syntactic patterns they know.
- There may be some repeating refrains so that children recognize them and use them to gain momentum as they progress through the text.
- The text may be organized around a familiar sequence, such as numbers.
- Fantasy takes the form of very simple stories (such as talking animals) with predictable plots.
- Children may have experienced a version of a traditional tale before.

Informational texts for young readers may look so simple that you would hardly classify them as such, but they have the following characteristics:

- Topics are either familiar or highly accessible (zoo animals, planting a seed, transportation, daily activities).
- Concepts within a text are easily related to one another; concepts build on one another.
- Pictures augment content very clearly and are easy for children to understand (the word *apple* and a picture of an apple in an uncluttered illustration).
- The text contains many high frequency words that children already know (*here is, I like, this is, Mom is*).
- No highly technical information is included (such as *thorax, antennae*).

Books for More Proficient Readers

Each level from I through Z+ contains examples in all genres; however, texts become much more complex at the upper levels. At level I you will find many works of realistic fiction, with more historical fiction after about level M. Remember that setting the story in a world distant in time adds challenge. Some easy historical fiction may be read as a story without much consideration of the setting, but true examples of this genre require background knowledge.

Factors Related to Text Difficulty

FACTOR	DEFINITION
Genre	The *genre* is the type of text and refers to a system by which fiction and nonfiction texts are classified. Each genre has characteristic features.
Text Structure	The structure is the way the text is organized and presented. It may be *narrative,* as in most fiction and biographical texts. Factual texts are organized categorically or topically and may have sections with headings. Writers of factual texts use several underlying structural patterns to provide information to readers: *enumeration, chronological sequence, comparison/contrast, cause/effect,* and *problem/solution.* The presence of these structures, especially in combination, can increase the challenge for readers.
Content	The content refers to the subject matter of the text—the concepts that are important to understand. In fiction, content may be related to the setting or to the kinds of problems characters encounter. In factual texts, content refers to the topic being focused on. Content is considered in relation to the prior experience of readers.
Themes and Ideas	The themes and ideas are the big ideas that are communicated by the text. A text may have multiple themes or a main theme and several supporting themes or ideas.
Language and Literary Features	Written language is qualitatively different from spoken language. Fiction writers use dialogue, figurative language, and other kinds of literary structures. Factual writers use description and technical language. In hybrid texts you may find a wide range of literary language.
Sentence Complexity	Meaning is mapped onto the syntax of language. Texts with simpler, more natural sentences are easier to process. Sentences with embedded and conjoined clauses make a text more difficult.
Vocabulary	Vocabulary refers to the meaning of words and is part of our oral language. The more the words are accessible to readers in terms of meaning, the easier a text will be. An individual's *reading and writing vocabularies* are words that they understand and can also read or write.
Words	A text contains printed words that must be recognized and solved. The challenge in a text partly depends on the number and difficulty of the words that the reader must solve by recognizing them or decoding them. A text that contains a great many of the same common words makes a text more accessible to readers.
Illustrations	The illustrations are the drawings, paintings, or photographs that accompany the text and add meaning and enjoyment. In factual texts, illustrations also include graphic representations that provide a great deal of information readers must integrate with the text. Illustrations are an integral part of a high-quality text. Increasingly, fiction texts include a range of graphics.
Book and Print Features	The book and print features are the physical aspects of the text—what readers cope with in terms of length, size, and layout. Book and print features also include tools like the table of contents, glossary, pronunciation guide, index, and sidebars.

Figure 12-6. *Factors Related to Text Difficulty*

Fantasy is the most challenging fiction genre. You'll find simple fantasy at every level, with traditional literature and fantasies like *Alexander and the Wind-Up Mouse* (Lionni) up through about level L or M. Animal fantasy series such as Frog and Toad, The Littles, and the Arthur books are also included. *Catwings* (Le Guin) is a beginning fantasy with some plot complexities yet easy reading at level N. More complex fantasies appear at about level P; Joy Cowley's *Dragon Fire* and *Dragon Slayer*, the Magic School Bus series, and the Time Warp Trio (which combines fantasy and factual texts) are at this level. The Secrets of Droon series are examples of beginning fantasy books. The popular Help! I'm Trapped series is level Q. *The Castle in the Attic* (Winthrop) is a text that can "hook" readers on more complex fantasy. In it a young boy finds a toy castle and a knight in his attic that become real.

Several of the Harry Potter series are level V, appropriate for about grade five. Of course, many younger readers want to read this series and may be willing to encounter quite a few challenges to process it, but we suspect that most third graders who are carrying it around are "spot reading" or watching the video. One thing about series books, though, is that after you have read the first one, you have an enormous amount of prior knowledge to bring to the next, making it more accessible. You already know the important characters. You know the structure and types of events to anticipate; you know quite a lot of the vocabulary; you get used to the style of writing. Susan Cooper's fantasy *The Dark Is Rising* is level X. Tolkien and LeGuin are level Z. As reflected in the gradient, we expect increased reading of fantasy during the upper elementary and middle school years, but students may need a great deal of scaffolding to deal with the symbolic messages of this genre.

The lower levels of the gradient (through about K) have only a few simple biographies. At level M, there are many easy biography series, such as Picture Book Biography. Upper elementary students usually enjoy reading biographies. After they have read quite a few books and developed some favorite authors, they like reading biographies of these authors as well as their memoirs. All kinds of characters from Harry Houdini to sports figures appeal to preteens. Some autobiographies, such as *Zlata's Diary* (Filipovic, level X), tell of children who have survived times of hard-

ship and war. Children can meet the same biography subject at different levels. For example *Anne Frank,* by Rachel Epstein, is level S; *Anne Frank: Life in Hiding,* by Johanna Hurwitz, is level W; and *Anne Frank: The Diary of a Young Girl,* written by Anne herself, is level Y. Students who find a favorite character will enjoy reading more about them. Biographies are a good way to satisfy gender differences. For example, girls might enjoy reading *Babe Didrikson: Athlete of the Century,* by Rozanne Knudson, while boys could select *The Story of Walt Disney, Maker of Magical Worlds* (Selden, level O), *The Wright Brothers* (Freedman, level Y), or *Orson Welles and The War of the Worlds* (Vierno, level V).

After the early levels, you will find factual texts on a wide variety of topics at every level of the gradient. Topics such as prehistoric and modern animals, the environment, and how things are made are very popular in the middle and upper elementary and middle school grades.

Text Structure

Genres are organized in different ways, and readers' deep knowledge of genre helps in forming expectations that support reading. The structure may be narrative, which consists of an opening, the presentation of a problem, a series of events, a climax in which the main characters solve the problem, and a few more pages or a chapter of "falling action" in which loose ends are tied up. Fiction texts and most biographical texts are narratives. The ease with which readers can follow the narrative depends on how many things are happening. Some texts have lots of plots and subplots, twists and turns. The setting may jump to the past or the future. For beginning readers in general, you want simple and easy-to-follow plots. New concepts and ideas should be explained within the text.

Factual texts are organized categorically, often into sections that have headings, subheadings, and sub-subheadings. In addition, factual texts incorporate underlying structural patterns—*enumeration, chronological sequence, comparison/contrast, cause/effect,* and *problem/solution*—which are described in Chapter 13. Readers must detect these patterns and use them to derive and understand information. The presence of these underlying structures, especially in combination, can increase the challenge for readers.

The structure of factual texts for beginners should be very easy to detect. You wouldn't want each page to switch to a very different topic, which would require having a range of background knowledge and prevent the reader from building knowledge across the text. For all factual texts, you'll want to ask, "What background knowledge will be required for readers to process this factual text with understanding?"

Content

The content or subject matter of factual texts for beginners should be familiar and deal with the everyday. You will want to examine every text for challenges presented by its content. The heavier the content load, the more background experience is required; the more "new" information presented in a text, the harder it is. Factual texts, for example, may be written very simply with only a few lines on each page yet present very difficult content. Such texts do not offer readers the opportunity to process enough text.

Themes and Ideas

In general, themes for beginning readers are very simple and obvious. More proficient readers are ready to encounter several themes or a main theme with many supporting ideas. The more complex the theme, the harder the text. Some texts that are fairly simple to decode have very mature themes, such as sexuality, murder, or rape, that require maturity to understand, so levels X, Y, Z and Z+ include some texts that, on the surface, look unexpectedly easy. Level Z+ books are for mature, high-school level readers.

Language and Literary Features

Written language is qualitatively different from spoken language. Features such as figurative language, dialogue, description, and technical language make literature what it is, but they also increase the complexity. Figurative language in texts for beginners should be very easy to understand and description should be kept to a minimum. Longer descriptions and more technical language are typical of upper-level texts.

Sentence Complexity

Longer sentences are harder than shorter ones. Sentences with embedded clauses are harder than simple sentences. Sentence complexity is more than sentence length. You can get an idea of the level of challenge by sampling about ten sentences from the text in Figure 12-7, counting the words to get an idea of average length, and counting the dependent clauses ("*When she goes to the garden,* Jan likes to see pink and blue flowers") and modifying phrases ("*In the garden,* Jan likes flowers, which may be pink, yellow, or blue"). Also notice compound subjects and adjectives.

In general, books for beginners should have simple sentences or compound sentences that are joined with *and* or have no more than one independent and dependent clause. Dialogue should be very simple, as in sentence 3 in Figure 12-7. As sentence structure increases in complexity, the text becomes harder.

Vocabulary

A person's vocabulary is made up of the words she or he understands. You may know the meaning of a word in oral language, using it when you speak or understanding it when you hear it; that is a known vocabulary word. If a reader already has a word in his oral vocabulary, it is easier to learn to read it or write it. Teachers sometimes talk about a child's *reading vocabulary* or *writing vocabulary,* but these terms refer more to word recognition or correct spelling than to understanding. Here, we use the term to mean knowing a word's meaning.

If possible, all words in books for beginners should already be in their oral vocabulary. As texts become more complex, it is likely that readers will meet new words. You'll want to determine whether these words are clearly defined within the text and also how many new vocabulary words are introduced. We need also to remember that there are shades of knowing a word; that is, you may know a word in the context but not otherwise.

Words

Bottom line, the reader must be able to read the words in a text. Most of the words in a text will be recognized immediately, often without conscious effort. If more than five or ten percent of the words require effort to solve, the text is too difficult for the reader. Too much attention devoted to word solving means that the reader can pay little attention to thinking. Unfamiliar words may be solved using a flexible range of actions, including taking the word apart without losing the meaning and using the context to predict a meaning and check whether that meaning makes sense.

The difficulty of a text partly depends on the number of challenging words. For beginners, texts should have many very easy high frequency words that are repeated many times. The first books children read should have a 1:15 or

Sentence Length and Complexity

1 Jan likes blue.
2 Jan likes blue flowers.
3 "I like flowers," said Jan.
4 Jan likes blue and pink flowers.
5 Jan likes blue and Peter likes pink.
6 Peter and Jan like blue and pink flowers.
7 Peter likes pink flowers and Jan likes blue flowers.
8 Peter likes pink flowers but Jan likes blue. [implied direct object]
9 Peter likes pink, yellow, and blue flowers in the garden.
10 In the garden, Jan likes flowers, which may be pink, yellow, or blue.
11 When she goes to the garden, Jan likes to see pink and blue flowers.
12 When they go to the garden, Jan and Peter like pink and blue flowers.
13 "Oh," said Jan. "What a beautiful garden with its pink, blue, and yellow flowers."
14 When they go to the garden, Jan and Peter like to see pink flowers, but not blue or yellow.
15 When she is planting her garden, as well as when she visits Peter's garden, Jan likes pink and yellow flowers in an interesting combination.
16 When they are planting flowers in the garden, as well as when they visit other people's gardens, Jan and Peter like pink and yellow, colors that to them represent happier times

Figure 12-7. *Sentence Length and Complexity*

1:20 ratio of new to known words. As you progress up the levels, the number of multisyllable words, compound words, homophones, and so on increases. The challenge for writers of these books is to control the words and still produce engaging and natural-sounding text.

Illustrations

The illustrations include drawings, paintings, or photographs that accompany the text and add meaning and enjoyment. Illustrations in factual texts also include graphics that provide a great deal of information, some of which is not in the text. Readers must learn to integrate the information in the illustrations and in the text. Increasingly, readers are encountering hybrid texts that combine fiction and nonfiction and include graphic information.

Illustrations for beginners, especially in factual texts, should be simple and clear rather than cluttered. Factual texts at easier levels should not have too many kinds of information in any one graphic. The more complex the graphic information, the more challenging the text will be. In all texts, illustrations should be of high quality and add meaning and enjoyment to the reading.

Book and Print Features

The book and print features are the physical attributes of the text. They include:

- Length.
- Words and sentences per page, and where sentences start (always at the left margin or immediately after the period of the prior sentence).
- Layout, including the use of white space between words, between lines, and to signal different kinds of information.
- Print size.
- Punctuation.
- Special features of print such as italics or boldface.
- The way sections of the text are indicated by headings, sidebars, insets, and so on.
- Tools such as table of contents, index, punctuation guide.

Producers of high-quality books for beginners take extreme care that the font is friendly and the layout assists young readers in tracking print. Some publishers even divide lines to help readers recognize phrase units, as in Figure 12-8 from *Baby Bear Goes Fishing*. In fiction texts, words in boldface provide special information for readers and suggest emphasis. Boldface words help readers know how the

Father Bear and Baby Bear
went down to the river.

"Come here, fish,"
said Baby Bear.

Figure 12-8. Baby Bear Goes Fishing

text should be read aloud. In Figure 12-9, also from *Baby Bear Goes Fishing,* Baby Bear asserts his independence.

Layout helps more experienced readers find information. In factual texts, a word in boldface might be a "key word" or concept defined in the glossary. Text length is an important factor as well, because the longer the text, the more information that must be remembered in summary form and carried over to additional reading sessions. The density of the text—print size and the amount of print on each page—also makes a difference. We all know that white space can make a text more readable and accessible.

"I'm **not** too little,"
said Baby Bear.

Figure 12-9. *An Example of the Use of Boldface Type to Suggest Emphasis*

WHAT QUESTIONS SHOULD I ASK WHEN CONSIDERING A TEXT FOR STUDENTS?

Whatever the genre or level, you will always want to ask some guiding questions when considering books for your classroom library or for guided reading purposes. At upper levels, there will be more highly technical subjects and topics that take a great deal of experience and knowledge to understand—for example, *The Journey: Japanese Americans, Racism, and Renewal* (Hamanaka), level X, and *I Have Lived a Thousand Years: Growing Up in the Holocaust* (Bitton-Jackson), level Y.

Figure 12-10 lists some questions to ask about text factors when considering books for beginning readers (about levels A–H) and more proficient readers (levels I–Z+). These questions generally address the text factors listed in Figure 12-6. You may find it useful to work with your grade-level colleagues in examining texts for your classroom. In the process, you will learn a great deal more about leveling texts.

WHAT IS IMPORTANT TO LOOK FOR AT EACH LEVEL OF THE CONTINUUM?

We have provided example layouts from several books selected from the continuum (see Figures 12-11 through Figure 12-17). As you look through them, you will notice major shifts in the processing requirements. If you examine the entire book represented by each of these layouts, you will have even more information about the ten text factors that figure into the analysis.

The level-by-level continuum included in *The Continuum of Literacy Learning, PreK–8: A Guide to Teaching* (2008, 2011) looks across instructional contexts to describe the demands on the learner in relation to texts from year to year. This comprehensive continuum includes:

◻ Characteristics of texts to consider at each level.

◻ Lists of behaviors to teach, notice, and support in guided reading instruction for each text level.

FACTOR	BEGINNING READERS	MORE PROFICIENT READERS

QUESTIONS TO ASK ABOUT
Text Factors When Considering Books for Readers

FACTOR	BEGINNING READERS	MORE PROFICIENT READERS
Genre	What is the genre? (In general, narrative genres are easier for beginners. Factual genres should focus on familiar and easily available subject matter.)	□ What is the genre? (As the variety of genres increases, readers will need very clear, simple, straightforward examples of new ones.) □ Does the first part of the text provide enough information to let readers know what to expect?
Text Structure	***Fiction and Biographical:*** □ Does the text tell a real story that will engage children? □ Is the narrative straightforward and easy to follow? □ Are new concepts and ideas explained/shown in the text? □ How many plots are there? (In general, books for beginners should have one main plot.) ***Factual:*** □ Are factual texts organized around single, easy-to-understand concepts? □ How many new ideas, concepts, or topics are presented in a section of text or in the whole text? □ Are underlying factual structures very simply presented and not combined?	***Fiction and Biographical:*** □ Is the structure a straightforward narrative or are there literary devices such as flashbacks and changes in perspective? □ Is the plot or sequence of events easy to follow? □ How many plots and subplots are there? (The more complex the text is, the more difficult it will be to follow.) ***Factual:*** □ What is the density of concepts and ideas? □ Are concepts clearly presented and elaborated? □ Are there new topics, concepts, or ideas on every page or in each section? □ To what degree are underlying structures used to provide information, and how many structures are included in a single text or section of text?
Content	□ What background experiences will be required to understand the content? □ Are concepts and ideas clearly and simply explained in the text and shown in pictures? □ How much unfamiliar content is in the text for this group of children?	□ What background experiences and knowledge will be required to understand the content? □ What information is carried in graphics to be integrated with text? □ How much unfamiliar content is in the text for this group of children? □ Are difficult key concepts and new ideas explained within the text?
Themes and Ideas	***Fiction and Biographical:*** □ Are themes and ideas familiar to children or close to their own experiences? □ Are themes and ideas simple enough for children to grasp? ***Biographical and Factual:*** □ Are historical concepts available to children? □ Are technical ideas and concepts familiar to children?	***Fiction and Biographical:*** □ Are themes and ideas concrete or more abstract? □ What background experiences, including knowledge from reading, are required to derive the theme of the story? ***Biographical and Factual:*** □ Is the subject interesting to students? □ Does the subject's life have meaning for students' lives? □ Are the historical and technical ideas in the text explained and demonstrated in a way that readers can understand?

Figure 12-10. *Questions to Ask About Text Factors When Considering Books for Readers*

QUESTIONS TO ASK ABOUT
Text Factors When Considering Books for Readers (CONTINUED)

FACTOR	BEGINNING READERS	OLDER READERS
Language and Literary Features	▫ Is the story told from a single perspective? ▫ Is there figurative language that increases the level of difficulty? ▫ Is any description simple, short, and easy to understand? ▫ Does the dialogue sound like oral language?	▫ How much figurative language is included in the text? ▫ To what degree does the writer use language symbolically? ▫ Is the language direct or indirect (requiring inference)? ▫ Are signal words easy to notice and use? (Informational structures are signaled by words like *first, second; while, yet; because, since; conclude; the evidence is; furthermore, etc.*)
Sentence Complexity	▫ Are the sentences simple and straightforward? (In general, simple sentences are easier than compound sentences, which are, in turn, easier than sentences with embedded clauses.) ▫ How much dialogue is introduced? Is it clear who is speaking?	▫ What is the general length of sentences and how complex are they? ▫ How much dialogue is included and is it assigned or unassigned? (In general, strings of unassigned dialogue increase difficulty.) ▫ Is the dialogue continuous or are quotations "split" by the words assigning dialogue?
Vocabulary	▫ How many new/difficult words are in the text? ▫ Are new words available to children because they already understand the concepts? ▫ Are there words that are used in new ways that will be unfamiliar to children? ▫ Are there words that are frequently used in written language but scarce in oral language? ▫ Is there varied and interesting word choice? How does word choice affect the text difficulty?	▫ How many new/difficult words are in the text? ▫ Are new words clearly explained or demonstrated in the context of the text and/or illustrations/graphics? ▫ Are there words with multiple meanings that will require interpretation? ▫ How many technical words are included in the text? ▫ What background knowledge or experiences are required to understand the words in the text? ▫ Does the writer use interesting and new words that can be linked to children's existing vocabulary?
Words	▫ How difficult are the words for readers to solve by recognizing them or taking them apart while reading? ▫ How many *different* high frequency words are included in the text? (There must be enough words to make a good story, but, using many of the same words makes a text more accessible.) ▫ What portion of the words in a text are easy, single-syllable high frequency words? ▫ Are "content words" clearly signaled or demonstrated by the pictures?	▫ How difficult are the words for readers to solve by recognizing them or taking them apart while reading? ▫ What proportion of words in the text are high frequency words? ▫ What level of difficulty are high frequency words? ▫ How many content/technical words are readers expected to decode? ▫ How frequently do multisyllable words appear in the text?

Figure 12-10. *Questions to Ask About Text Factors When Considering Books for Readers (cont.)*

Text Factors When Considering Books for Readers (CONTINUED)

FACTOR	BEGINNING READERS	OLDER READERS
Illustrations	**Fiction and Biographical:** □ Do illustrations appeal to children and add enjoyment? □ Do illustrations help children appreciate high-quality art? □ Do illustrations add meaning to the text? How accessible is the added meaning? **Biographical:** □ Do illustrations help students understand and appreciate the subject? **Factual:** □ Are the graphics simple, providing only one or two categories of information? □ Are the graphics very clearly labeled?	**Fiction:** □ Do illustrations add symbolic meaning? □ Do illustrations offer good examples of high-quality art? **Biographical:** □ Do illustrations help students understand and appreciate the subject? **Factual:** □ Are graphics (diagrams, tables, graphs, drawings, illustrations, maps, legends, cutaways) clear and easy to understand? □ Is there a clear and direct relationship between graphics and text? □ Are there organizational features and tools (table of contents, index, glossary, pronunciation guide) that demand readers' attention?
Book and Print Features	□ How many pages does the text have? □ How many words are on each page? □ How many words are in the entire text? □ Is the print size "friendly"? □ Is the print clear and easy to see? □ Are there adequate spaces between words and between lines to help beginning readers track print easily?	□ What is the length of the text? □ How dense is the text? (Check the size of the print and the amount of print on each page.) □ Is the layout of print "friendly" in that it is easy to follow? (When texts switch from starting sentences on the left margin to starting them anywhere after a period, the text difficulty can increase.) □ Are sections clearly marked with white space, with shading, or in other ways? □ Are headings and subheadings clear in size and placement?

Figure 12-10. *Questions to Ask About Text Factors When Considering Books for Readers (cont.)*

□ Kinds of thinking children will do—within, beyond, and about the text.

□ Instructional approaches that are appropriate.

□ Assessment that demonstrates learning.

The continuum is the backbone for using guided reading in your teaching. There are two places you can find a highly detailed look at the text factors for each level of the gradient:

□ In *The Continuum of Literacy Learning, PreK–8: A Guide to Teaching* (Pinnell and Fountas 2008, 2011).

This curriculum document provides detailed goals for literacy learning across interactive read-aloud, shared/performance reading, writing about reading, and guided and independent reading.

□ In *Leveled Books for Readers, K–8* (Fountas and Pinnell 2006). This volume provides detailed descriptions, examples, and page layouts for each level of the gradient as well as much information about acquiring and using leveled texts.

All of this information is designed to support your thinking and decision-making as you select texts for students, read to them, guide their choices, and help them produce their own written texts. Whether you are teaching kindergarten or eighth grade, analyzing and working with texts is challenging but very worthwhile. After all, you are offering riches to your students. These are the resources on which you can draw as you design your teaching.

SUGGESTIONS FOR PROFESSIONAL DEVELOPMENT
ANALYSIS OF TEXT CHARACTERISTICS

It is important for you to develop a lens for analyzing the characteristics of texts on the gradient. When you have spent time analyzing and discussing texts, you begin to internalize the factors and think about how they support and challenge readers. This knowledge will help you select books and use them more effectively in instruction.

1　Gather a group of colleagues. Select three texts you often use at your grade level and analyze the characteristics in depth. You might want to use the blank form Analyzing for Text Characteristics included on the DVD that accompanies this book.

2　Discuss the text characteristics that offer special opportunities for your students to learn.

3　Summarize on chart paper new understandings you have about characteristics of texts and how they will influence your teaching.

"Hen is making soup!" said Pig.
"I will have a sip."

6

So he went in the kitchen
and had a big sip.

7

Figure 12-11. Making Soup *(Level C)*

"The boys and girls at school
like you, Katie," said Joe.
"Your teacher likes you, too."

"No," said Katie.
"I'm not going back to school."

Figure 12-12. Katie's Caterpillar *(Level E)*

"Oh, sure," Mike thought back to Harry, as he caught his father's soft throw. "The great Harry the Airedale. Dog pitcher. Strikes out McGee with the bases loaded. You're out of your mind, Harry."

"Control, man," said Harry. "All you need is control. I'll tell you what to pitch to each guy as he comes to the plate, and you take it from there."

"That'll be fine, except that I don't have control," Mike grumbled. "All I've got is speed."

"Did you say something, son?" his father asked.

Mike shook his head. "Sorry, Dad," he said. "I was talking to myself."

Sometimes Mike forgot to communicate mentally with Harry and started talking out loud. Mike and Harry had made a pact that nobody — not even Mike's parents — would find out their secret, but sometimes that made for embarrassing moments.

24

25

Figure 12-13. The Dog That Pitched a No Hitter *(Level L)*

In the swim of it

Some athletes have far greater challenges to face than beating their rivals on their way to success at the Olympics. To earn her medal, American Shelley Mann had to overcome a terrible disease that almost paralyzed her whole body.

In 1945, the doctors looking after six-year-old Shelley recognized the classic signs of polio. They told her parents that Shelley's case was severe. She could hardly move.

Healing waters
Many doctors recommend exercises in warm water to treat muscular illnesses.

Polio
Polio is a disease that affects part of the spinal cord and causes paralysis. All children should be vaccinated against polio.

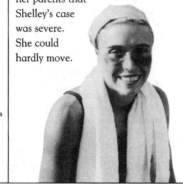

At the age of ten, Shelley's family took her swimming at a summer camp in Maryland. She couldn't play golf or tennis with the other children, but she could mix with them in the pool.

Floating weightless in the warm water, Shelley began to move her weakened limbs.

"Lift your arms, Shelley. You can do it," her mother encouraged her.

Every day in the pool, Shelley worked to get the strength back in her body. It was difficult work, but swimming soon became the most important thing in her life.

By the age of twelve, Shelley had begun competitive training in Washington, D.C. She was a natural at every stroke she tried.

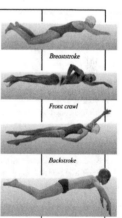

Breaststroke

Front crawl

Backstroke

Butterfly

Racing strokes
When Shelley was training, the breaststroke became the fourth stroke swum in competitions. Shelley swam medleys, where a swimmer does two lengths of each of the four strokes.

16

17

Figure 12-14. Going for Gold *(Level P)*

when he gives it to our cat. Not me. I don't like to eat it, but I love it anyhow. Anyway, we don't have to save leftovers anymore ever since Sam found this restaurant.

He saw the place from the window of the bus a couple of days ago. He said he read a sign on it that said, "Special Today: Broccoli casserole." He got right off and asked the owner if he could have what they throw out. He told about needing to feed our cat. Now the man saves us bits of broccoli and whatever else he doesn't want, and Sam brings it to the lava field in a box like McDonald's.

When I got home from school today, Mom was in her room cleaning out her closet. She never does that. She hates housework worse than anything, worse than I do. She told me once that one of the reasons she went back to work was so she could pay someone to clean for her. She's on leave now, but she was going to send in articles to the newspaper from here. Some of you know that she wrote the "People are Funny" column for the *Boston Star*. Well, she hasn't been at the typewriter once since my grandmother came, and I used to think it was attached to her, like a growth.

About cleaning, only when she's angry or worried does she do it, and we all know it's a sign. We keep out of her way then. Sometimes I don't know what's the matter, but now I do.

I said to her, "I'm going to the lava field, Mom." She knows about the pool, but absolutely not about Broccoli.

She was deep in the closet, so I didn't hear what she said. It wasn't, "It's raining out, don't go," or "Stay and

60

keep me company." I could have told her I was flying to the moon. She's not thinking of me now, which is the reason I slammed the door. She didn't yell; she didn't even notice.

When I peeked in my grandmother's room, she was on her bed taking a nap. She already has her suitcase packed for the hospital, and she doesn't go in until Sunday. It sits on her dresser, and every time I go in to see her it reminds me and flop goes my heart. She still acts like everything is normal in our house, and so do Mom and Dad.

I got Broccoli's milk, put on my sneakers, and changed into my bathing suit because of the rain. It's the middle of February but more like July here.

Eddie was at the rescue rock, sitting in the rain waiting for us. He waits, but when we get there he acts like he doesn't care that we're there.

Today, when I sat down next to him, I said, "Howzzit?" the way I hear kids here say. Just to fool around, you know?

That got him to smile again, so at least he's not mad at me anymore. He said, "Haole talk," like he's disgusted and I said, "Pidgin talk," like I was disgusted, and then we both had to laugh. Did I tell you his voice is deep like a man's? Today I learned that when he laughs it's like a high giggle. The kind that makes you laugh back.

Broccoli doesn't show at all when Eddie is there, and Eddie knows it. When Sam came today with the McDonald's box, Eddie left us and went to work on the pool. Our pool isn't all that far from the rescue rock, and I could hear him grunt when he lifted a rock. Hey,

61

Figure 12-15. The Broccoli Tapes *(Level S)*

This catastrophe terrified the Klamaths and Modocs living nearby. They believed that their warring gods were engaged in their final battle at last. Many expected that their time on earth had ended, and they waited fearfully for the end of the world.

When the smoke cleared, most of the gigantic mountain was gone. Where the peak had been, a giant crater, six miles across, now boiled over with lava and steam. Ash covered the ground twelve inches deep for hundreds of miles. The volcano cooled slowly. Inside the pit, a vast wasteland with ragged and bumpy walls remained.

The local people believed that the area was sacred and dangerous. Some thought that if they even glanced at the spot where the mountain had stood, they would die instantly. So they stayed away from the mountain. Centuries passed, and the mountain remained quiet, apparently lifeless, and ignored by those who inhabited the area. But even today, the Klamath people tell stories of their ancestors' experiences during the eruption of Mount Mazama.

As time passed, water began to collect in the pit. Rain fell into it. Snows built up around its edges and melted into it every spring. Slowly a lake began to form. It took between 700 and 1,500 years for the water to reach its present level. Today, the 4.6 trillion gallons of water in the pit form Crater Lake.

6

Despite its name, Crater Lake is not a crater, but a *caldera*. A caldera has a diameter many times larger than that of a crater. A caldera is formed when a volcanic explosion causes the volcanic cone to collapse inward. The caldera at Crater Lake has a circumference of thirty-six miles. With a maximum depth of 1,932 feet (589m), Crater Lake is North America's deepest lake and the seventh deepest in the world. The Empire State building in New York City could rest on the bottom of the lake and still be 500 feet short of the lake's surface! The water remains at a constant 39°F and is so clear, local people say, that you could read a book if it lay open six feet below the lake's surface.

Scientists have used a deep rover, a kind of small submarine, to explore the lake's floor. The descent takes 30 minutes. The scientists describe the bottom of the lake as a "moonscape of underwater cliffs from 50 to 150 feet tall, scattered rocks, mineral deposits and fields of sediment." When making this journey, they are astounded to find that they can still see the blue light filtering through the water's surface even from as deep as 1,200 feet.

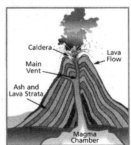

7

Figure 12-16. A Deep Blue Lake *(Level V)*

a baby out before it's umbilical cord has dropped off? What can they be thinking of?" whispered a woman.

"Shhh!" said her companion. "The Spirit Medium has to make up his mind."

"He's strong," Garikayi announced, as the baby squalled and kicked. The old man obviously wanted to hold it, but Tendai knew that would go against custom. No one but the mother and midwives could touch it for several days.

The Spirit Medium inspected the infant. It was clear he was not fond of children, or at least this one. He frowned as he studied the wrinkled little face. The moments passed.

"He's one of us," the man said at last. A collective sigh went around the crowd.

"I have a son," cried Garikayi over the howls of the infant. "Now take it to the safety of the hut!" The old woman, smiling toothlessly, began to hobble back through the villagers. They smiled in return. The anxious feeling Tendai had noticed earlier was gone.

Suddenly a pot crashed. Someone screamed. Everyone froze. Above the rustling fire, Tendai heard a baby—*another baby*—wailing. A girl emerged from the same hut as the old woman had. She, too, carried a bundle. She resolutely approached Garikayi, who looked as though the sky had fallen on his head. His mouth dropped open. The girl drew near and held out the second bundle.

It was Rita!

"No," said Garikayi, waving her away.

"It's your daughter," Rita said.

"I do not accept her. She is an accursed twin."

"She's perfectly healthy," said Rita, whose voice was beginning to get shrill. "The midwife was going to *kill* her."

"It is a weak, unnatural child. It will die."

"Listen to her! She's not weak! Oh, I won't let you kill a tiny baby!" Rita began to cry. Her sobs resounded through the village clearing.

154

"Twins are evil," came the thin voice of the Spirit Medium. "They are against *Mwari*'s order."

"No baby is evil," sobbed Rita.

"One must die and be buried under the floor of the hut where it was born."

"So of course it's the *girl* who has to go," cried Rita. "Let's throw the *girl* away. She's no good! She's worthless! You're all a bunch of *vicious!—rotten!—ignorant!—pigs!*" She was screaming now. Myanda pushed through the crowd and snatched the infant from Rita's arms. The Spirit Medium raised his walking stick, but Tendai wrenched it away before he could strike his sister. The medium was so startled, he let go without a struggle. Tendai flung the stick into the heart of the fire. It burst into flames at once.

The villagers gasped in horror. They pounced on the children and stretched them out on the ground. Someone handed Garikayi a club. Oh, *Mwari*, he's going to kill us, thought Tendai. Garikayi stood over them a long, long moment. Tendai gritted his teeth as he waited for the first blow. But the old man's face suddenly contorted with anguish. He threw the club away and tottered back to his stool. His face was etched with deep lines, and he seemed to have aged ten years.

"Take these little hyenas to the punishment hut," hissed the Spirit Medium. Tendai and Rita were carried off by many hands—it was as if the whole village had risen against them with one thought and one purpose. The last thing Tendai saw before they were flung through a door was Myanda holding the girl baby against her breast.

"Thank you for sticking up for me," said Rita after she had recovered from being thrown down. She shivered violently, and Tendai hugged her. She burst into sobs. He rocked her back and forth as she wept. He knew this wasn't how a traditional brother treated his sister, but he was thoroughly sick of village ways.

155

Figure 12-17. The Ear, The Eye, and the Arm *(Level Y)*

CHAPTER THIRTEEN

UNDERSTANDING THE DEMANDS OF NONFICTION TEXTS

No matter the grade level, when I walk in and out of classrooms, I expect to see classroom libraries brimming with nonfiction. I always look at the amount of space devoted to nonfiction as compared to poetry and fiction.

—SHELLEY HARWAYNE

All nonfiction texts have one thing in common: they are based on documentable facts. Nonfiction offers readers the opportunity to extend, refine, and revise their knowledge. If nonfiction is interesting, well illustrated, and clearly written, it appeals to elementary and middle school students. We classify nonfiction texts as biographical or factual. We recognize that all forms of biographical text, such as autobiography and memoir, are fact-filled, but because they tend to follow a narrative structure, we distinguish them from the sort of nonfiction text one might find in *Newsweek* magazine or on a gardening tips website. Nonfiction poses some special demands that require experience over time. Schoolchildren, from kindergarten through middle school, benefit when they read the full spectrum of nonfiction text.

GENERAL DEMANDS OF ALL NONFICTION TEXTS

Nonfiction texts, both biographical and factual, have a variety of structures, but they have several characteristics in common. First, they all report real information, at least to the extent that the text is of high quality. Second, all nonfiction texts require the reader to think within, beyond, and about the text (see Figure 13-1).

THINKING WITHIN THE TEXT

Readers of nonfiction texts must deal with a wide variety of ways of presenting information. Look at the layouts in Figures 13-2 and 13-3.

Meet Yo-Yo Ma (Goldish) is a straightforward biography about a famous cellist who began playing his instrument at age four. The text starts with a page of information about his present life and his credentials as a musician. On the next page, the writer begins telling about Yo-Yo's early life in Paris. In each of six subsequent sections, readers learn about key decisions Yo-Yo made that influenced his life. For example, he decided to play the cello instead of the

violin; he went to Harvard rather than immediately becoming a full-time musician; he risked having a dangerous back operation; and he decided to spend more time with his family and to appear on children's television. Key to understanding the biography is picking up and interpreting information about these key passages. *Meet Yo-Yo Ma* is presented chronologically. In the layout shown in Figure 13-2, information is presented in pictures and print. The treble clef and heading signal the beginning of a new section discussing a key passage in his life. One picture has a caption that provides more information.

The information in *Butterflies!* (Strummer), on the other hand, is presented in categories: "A Butterfly's Body," "A Butterfly's Life Cycle," "How Butterflies Survive," "The Butterfly's Role in Nature," and "Where Butterflies Live." Readers can turn to a section of interest instead of reading the text in order. Each section is signaled by a heading and illustrated by colorful photographs. The layout in Figure 13-3 shows the life cycle in photographs and drawings, which are labeled.

As you can see, readers extract information from both text and graphics and must integrate the two. Nonfiction texts are likely to use words with meanings that are rooted in science or technology, requiring readers to access background knowledge and derive knowledge from the context to figure out important terms. In informational texts, these particular ways of providing information are basic to understanding and often appear implicitly. Let's examine the two books mentioned above further.

Thinking Within the Text—Meet Yo-Yo Ma
Meet Yo-Yo Ma provides information in narrative form, which makes it accessible to readers; however, background knowledge is required. The analysis in Figure 13-4 is organized around the ten text factors discussed in Chapter 12.

The General Demands of All Nonfiction Texts

READERS THINK WITHIN THE TEXT TO:	▫ Search for and use information that is presented in a variety of ways. ▫ Notice and extract information from illustrations and graphics. ▫ Notice and follow time sequences. ▫ Solve specialized or discipline-specific (history, geography, science, technology, etc.) words. ▫ Get information from readers' tools such as tables of contents, headings, pronunciation guides, legends, indexes, footnotes, and references.
READERS THINK BEYOND THE TEXT TO:	▫ Infer underlying reasons for events and actions. ▫ Bring background knowledge to understanding the information presented. ▫ Gather information from underlying structures: chronological sequence, description, comparison/contrast, cause/effect, problem/solution. ▫ Integrate information from text and graphics.
READERS THINK ABOUT THE TEXT TO:	▫ Notice how the writer has organized the text to present information. ▫ Interpret underlying structures: chronological sequence, description, comparison/contrast, cause/effect, problem/solution. ▫ Make comparisons between the text and others on the same subject or topic. ▫ Critically evaluate the accuracy and authenticity of the text. ▫ Examine the author's credentials and evaluate his or her qualifications for writing the text. ▫ Notice how the writer has used language to make the text interesting to readers.

Figure 13-1. *The General Demands of All Nonfiction Texts*

Growing Up in New York City

When Yo-Yo was seven, the family left France to live in New York City.

In New York, Yo-Yo's new music teacher saw that the young cellist was remarkably gifted. Yo-Yo performed on television when he was eight. He gave a concert at Carnegie Hall when he was nine. That same year, he entered the Juilliard School of Music. It is one of the finest music schools in the world.

Yo-Yo was very small and shy. He had been taught to obey his parents quietly and without question. Now, in the United States, his music teacher wanted him to show his feelings more. At school, he was supposed to speak up. American children were expected to ask lots of questions about everything.

Yo-Yo Ma felt torn. How could he fit in with other American kids and still be a good son?

Yo-Yo continued to study music. His cello playing began to change. It felt freer, more full of feeling.

Carnegie Hall

8

9

Figure 13-2. *Meet Yo-Yo Ma*

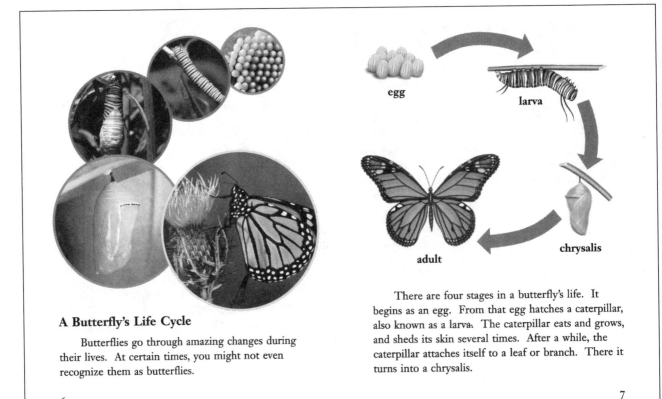

A Butterfly's Life Cycle

Butterflies go through amazing changes during their lives. At certain times, you might not even recognize them as butterflies.

6

There are four stages in a butterfly's life. It begins as an egg. From that egg hatches a caterpillar, also known as a larva. The caterpillar eats and grows, and sheds its skin several times. After a while, the caterpillar attaches itself to a leaf or branch. There it turns into a chrysalis.

7

Figure 13-3. Butterflies!

Readers need to know at least the name of the instrument Yo-Yo plays, the significance of names like Isaac Stern and Carnegie Hall (also shown in illustrations), and the characteristics of classical music. They should follow the time sequence presented and notice and understand the information given at each period of Yo-Yo's life.

Meet Yo-Yo Ma presents some challenges in terms of a technical vocabulary connected to the music world—for example, *perform, cello, composers, audiences, classical*—and the writer also uses some literary language. There are some long sentences with lists of nouns, but most words are defined within the text. There are also many easy high frequency words, but just about every page includes some complex words with inflectional endings (*fulfilling, cheerfulness, regularly*). There is no table of contents or glossary, but information in each section is signaled by a substantive title.

Thinking Within the Text—Butterflies!

This factual text is very much available to readers (see the analysis in Figure 13-5), but they will need to go about

searching for information in ways that are somewhat different from reading *Meet Yo-Yo Ma. Butterflies!* is organized into sections, and the following structures are evident:

- Description of the parts of the butterfly's body and many other aspects of butterflies.
- Comparison/contrast—how butterflies are like other insects but different from them in two ways.
- Problem/solution—butterflies' tricks for survival (including comparing wing spots to the eyes of owls or cats).

Many but not all technical words are explained in the text, and there is a long list of the environments in which butterflies live with no supporting information (*grasslands, deserts,* and *rain forests*). To understand this text, readers would need some prior knowledge of such environments as well as of insects in general. The language of the text is clear; there are some complex sentences on each page.

THINKING BEYOND THE TEXT

Nonfiction books present facts, but readers must think beyond the specific information to truly understand the

174

Analysis of
Meet Yo-Yo Ma (Level R)

Text Factor	Analysis
Genre	▫ Biography
Text Structure	▫ Starts in the present, giving his qualifications, then moves to the subject's early life on the next page ▫ Organized by sections ▫ Straightforward revelation of life events ▫ Clear revelation of life decisions, the reasons behind them, and the consequences
Content	▫ Names and qualities of musical instruments ▫ Classical music ▫ Significance of names like Isaac Stern, Carnegie Hall, and Juilliard School of Music (most explained within the text) ▫ Contrasting cultures and lifestyles ▫ Life decisions
Themes and Ideas	▫ Dedication to a dream—love of music ▫ Decisions in life and their effects ▫ Relationship between music and feelings ▫ Abstract ideas, such as sorrow living in music ▫ Inspiring story
Language and Literary Features	▫ Clearly written ▫ Terms defined within the text ▫ Literary language in describing his feelings about music ("fulfilled life in music")
Sentence Complexity	▫ Some long sentences with lists of nouns ("He was learning how to make the cello come alive with feelings. He was learning to show the fear, dreaminess, joy, hope, and sorrow that live in music.")
Vocabulary	▫ Words related to the music world: *perform, talent, cello, enriches, composers, audiences, classical*
Words	▫ Most words accessible ▫ Many easy high frequency words ▫ Words with inflectional endings: *regularly, completely, finest, warmly, freer, performer, fulfilling, regretted, cheerfulness, constantly*
Illustrations	▫ Color illustrations (photographs) on almost every page ▫ Treble clef marks new sections ▫ Captions for pictures
Book and Print Features	▫ 16 pages and 1,406 words ▫ Plenty of white space to make text "friendly" ▫ Medium-size font
When introducing this text in guided reading, keep this in mind:	▫ The subject has accomplished his goals through dedication and commitment from childhood. ▫ Names may need some rehearsal in conversation. ▫ The writer has revealed some key decisions that made a difference in the subject's life: (1) to get a Harvard education instead of becoming a performer alone; (2) to risk having a dangerous operation; (3) to spend more time with his family; and (4) to appear on children's television. ▫ Discussion can focus on how each of these decisions helped him.

Figure 13-4. *Analysis of* Meet Yo-Yo Ma *(Level R)*

ANALYSIS OF **Butterflies!** (LEVEL O)	
TEXT FACTOR	**ANALYSIS**
Genre	▫ Factual
Text Structure	▫ Four sections with titles, each three to four pages ▫ Information presented in categories
Content	▫ Variety of butterflies ▫ Life cycle of butterflies ▫ Comparison of butterflies with other insects
Themes and Ideas	▫ There are many kinds of butterflies ▫ Butterflies have many ways of surviving ▫ Butterflies play an important role in nature
Language and Literary Features	▫ Clear language with conversational tone ▫ Writer talks directly to the reader (second person)
Sentence Complexity	▫ Example: "Many other insects also have feeding tubes, but a butterfly's tube is tightly coiled when not in use. If you happen to watch a butterfly feeding on a flower, you may see it uncoil this tube to drink the nectar." (p. 4)
Vocabulary	▫ Some technical language ▫ Many but not all technical words explained in the text ▫ Examples: *thorax, abdomen, antennae, scales, coiled, chrysalis, pollen, migrate* ▫ Long list of environments with no supporting information: *grasslands, woods, deserts, mountains, rain forests*
Words	▫ Words formed from base words: *poisonous* ▫ Compound words: *overlapping, butterfly*
Illustrations	▫ Variety of photographs, including close-up of wing ▫ Labels on some photos ▫ Life cycle shown in diagram form
Book and Print Features	▫ 16 pages, with illustration and text on every page ▫ Section titles ▫ Sentences arranged in paragraph form
When introducing this text in guided reading, keep this in mind:	▫ Children can talk about what they already know about butterflies or insects. ▫ Some of the technical language could be used in conversation. ▫ The word *eye* is used in a different way in the text. ▫ After reading the book, children might want to examine comparisons between butterflies and other insets. ▫ Examining the photographs to see how butterflies camouflage themselves would be interesting. ▫ Students could suggest a list of how butterflies play an important role in nature.

Figure 13-5. *Analysis of* Butterflies! (*Level O*)

text. To illustrate this kind of thinking, we'll again use *Meet Yo-Yo Ma* and *Butterflies!*.

Thinking Beyond the Text—Meet Yo-Yo Ma

Readers of this biography should understand (or be able to learn about) the significance of life's decisions and of conflicting cultures and lifestyles. They may make connections between their own dreams and Yo-Yo's dedication to pursuing his dream of becoming a cellist. Or they might recognize him from television appearances.

The major themes of the text are Yo-Yo's dedication to his dream and his willingness to make choices based on values (education, family, health, service to society). The tension in those choices is not fully explained; in fact, the writer makes it sound pretty easy. But thinking readers will infer how difficult some decisions may have been. They will identify the relationships between problems Yo-Yo encountered and the solutions that he chose. Readers will also pick up on and interpret the cultural conflict Yo-Yo may have felt when he left home, where he obeyed his parents quietly and without question, and began showing his feelings more in his life and music. There are also some quite abstract themes communicated by the text—for example, the idea that "fear, dreaminess, joy, hope, and sorrow . . . live in the music" (p. 15).

Thinking Beyond the Text—Butterflies!

To understand this text, readers need to think about what they already know about insects and identify how butterflies are different in some ways from other insects. As they move around in this text, readers will notice information that is new to them—for example, that there are more than 20,000 different kinds of butterflies or that they are camouflaged to look like the eyes of larger animals. Readers might not realize that butterflies play an important role in nature; the underlying understanding to come to here is that species of animals and plants are interdependent. In fact, an underlying theme of the text is that butterflies are not just there to look beautiful but are important in the environment.

THINKING ABOUT THE TEXT

Readers of nonfiction are also called on to notice aspects of the text in an analytical way, and they are certainly required to evaluate the authenticity of these supposedly "true" texts. In fact, thinking about nonfiction texts can help students in their own writing of biographical and factual texts.

Thinking About the Text—Meet Yo-Yo Ma

Students may notice the circular way the information is presented, starting with the present, going back 40 years, and then returning chronologically to the present. They might also notice the particular parts of Yo-Yo's life the writer discusses and think about why (or whether) these were important. Author credentials are not presented in the text (although the photographs are credited), so readers may want to check Internet sources to determine whether the information is accurate. Certainly, you would want readers to wonder whether there may have been more problems in Yo-Yo's life than the writer of this biography was willing to discuss.

Thinking About the Text—Butterflies!

Butterflies! is a simple example of information presented in categories and divided into sections. Readers will notice how each section provides related information and could even make a table of contents for the text. They will also see how graphics are used to extend the text and could hypothesize why the writer selected the kind of information to present.

FACTUAL TEXTS FOR BEGINNING READERS

It is quite difficult for beginners to build a reading process and at the same time learn new ideas and concepts from a text. Therefore, factual texts for beginners must deal mostly with information they already know. Nevertheless, they can begin to become familiar with the organizational structure and characteristics of nonfiction with texts that we sometimes call "factual-like." Some of these texts are not strictly nonfiction, but they are organized in the same way and their purpose is to impart information. An example is *My Cat* (a page spread from the book is shown in Figure 13-6).

This book provides significant support for beginning readers in the repeating patterns that occur on every page and in the highly supportive illustrations. The text contains only ten different words; two are the high frequency words *my* and *can*. Print is placed consistently at the bottom and is separate from the illustrations. There is ample space between words and only one line of print on each page.

In this text, the narrator (who is not the author, since the little girl in the pictures is clearly not Will McGovern)

My cat can play.

4

My cat can sit.

5

Figure 13-6. My Cat

speaks directly to the reader about what cats can do. In addition, the drawings depict a somewhat fanciful cat. The sentences, however, each present a simple piece of information much in the way a factual text would be organized. (For an analysis of the text, see Figure 13-7.) Young readers could understand that on every page they are going to read something new about what cats do. The illustrations depict the behavior mentioned.

Many texts at early levels combine some of the features of factual and fictional writing. The main thing is to help students understand how the text "works" so that they can get used to these features of the text to help them process it.

SPECIFIC DEMANDS OF BIOGRAPHICAL TEXTS

In addition to making the same demands as all nonfiction texts, biographical texts present some unique challenges. Thus, we can divide biographical texts into (1) biography and (2) autobiography and memoir. Each presents specific challenges to readers (see Figure 13-8).

BIOGRAPHIES

A biography like *Meet Yo-Yo Ma* requires readers to understand the importance of culture and geography and the influences they have on a subject's life. For example, Yo-Yo's cultural background as it came into conflict with American life was an influence on his music. Readers need to make some judgments about the important experiences in the subject's life and also try to understand the important lessons that can be learned from this one person. Often, a reader of biography is prompted to consult other sources for more information.

Orson Welles and the War of the Worlds is biographical in nature, although it tells only a small part of the life of Orson Welles (see Figure 13-9). The writer tells the story of the famous broadcast that was so realistic that many people thought Martians had invaded Earth. Orson Welles and the Mercury Theater of the Air are identified on the first page, which ends with a cliffhanger ellipsis as the announcer breaks in with the startling news. The reader

ANALYSIS OF **My Cat** (LEVEL A)	
TEXT FACTOR	**ANALYSIS**
Genre	▫ Factual
Text Structure	▫ New idea on each page
Content	▫ Things cats can do
Themes and Ideas	▫ Cats can do many things ▫ You can tell about what animals do
Language and Literary Features	▫ Same repeating pattern on each page ▫ Actions paired logically
Sentence Complexity	▫ Simple sentences
Vocabulary	▫ Name of animal species ▫ Action words–*run, jump, eat, drink, sleep*
Words	▫ Same high frequency words repeated on each page: *my, cat, can*
Illustrations	▫ Simple, uncluttered illustrations showing one activity per page ▫ Illustrations add information by showing a girl with the cat
Book and Print Features	▫ Eight pages ▫ One line of print on each page ▫ Print in same place on each page ▫ Large font with extra space between words ▫ Capital letters and periods
When introducing this text in guided reading, keep this in mind:	▫ You may want to use action words in context, although it is not necessary to look at every page. ▫ Predict and locate *my,* which begins each sentence. ▫ The illustrations support the text but do not really look like a real cat. ▫ Children can discuss what the book told them the cat "can do." ▫ They can make connections to other animals or other books about cats.

Figure 13-7. *Analysis of* My Cat (*Level A*)

should realize that the audience was not informed that the broadcast was a hoax. In fact, knowledge of text structure should indicate to them that the announcer was using a genuine news format that was quite convincing. (For an analysis of the book, see Figure 13-10.)

To understand this text, the reader needs to follow and understand the sequence of events, presented in the order in which they happened, and understand vocabulary associated with radio broadcasting (for example, *off/on the air, studio,* or *newsreel.* The last section, "The Story Behind the Story," provides further background information.

Some of the concepts are archaic. There are also challenges to decoding (for example, many three-syllable words). Readers get information from the headings of sections and from the full range of punctuation and the varied font sizes. Black-and-white pictures provide further information.

But readers also have to try to imagine what it would be like not having television and depending on radio as the main source of news. They might think it was easy to "fool"

The Specific Demands of Biographical Texts

	Biography	Autobiography and Memoir
READERS THINK WITHIN THE TEXT TO:	□ Search for and understand important information about the setting. □ Understand and remember important information about the subject's life. □ Notice information that tells of the subject's accomplishments. □ Gather information about the subject's experiences over time. □ Gather information that describes how the subject changes over time. □ Identify and remember important events in the subject's life.	□ Understand important details about the setting. □ Understand and remember important information about the writer's life. □ Understand and remember important events in the writer's life. □ Gather information about the time frame (entire life or a brief but important period). □ Gather information that describes the writer's changes over time.
READERS THINK BEYOND THE TEXT TO:	□ Bring to their reading what they already know about the subject or the setting. □ Make connections between the subject and people they know. □ Make connections between the subject's life and the problems of today. □ Hypothesize about the influences on the subject. □ Infer the subject's feelings and motivations.	□ Infer what is important to the writer about his or her own life. □ Speculate why the writer wrote the text. □ Bring to the reading what they already know . about the writer. □ Make connections between the writer's life and perspectives and their own lives and perspectives. □ Make connections between the writer's memories and what others have said about the same setting, problem, or time period. □ Infer what the writer thinks are the major influences in his or her life. □ Infer feelings that are not explicitly stated.
READERS THINK ABOUT THE TEXT TO:	□ Evaluate whether the subject was a good choice. □ Evaluate the writer's choices of events to report. □ Reflect on the importance of the subject's accomplishments and the lessons for today's world. □ Use other biographies and historical information to verify the accuracy and authenticity of the text. □ Evaluate whether the writer has presented an unbiased view of the subject and/or identify the writer's attitudes and biases.	□ Evaluate the writer's choices of events to report. □ Evaluate the writer's honesty. □ Use other biographies and historical information to verify the accuracy and authenticity of the writer's report. □ Reflect on the importance of the writer's story for their own lives and the problems of today.

Figure 13-8. *The Specific Demands of Biographical Texts*

a radio audience because of the imagery evoked by the language, the announcers' voices, and the sound effects. Further, you would want readers to think critically about whether the "trick" was funny or dangerous. They would probably be thinking about how people today, with the current emphasis on terrorism, would react to such a broadcast, and they could predict some very undesirable results, such as mass panic. People might even die. The writer's subtle suggestion that Americans might have "wanted to believe" also prompts thinking beyond the text to grasp that abstract meaning. And what kind of person was Welles that he would not stop even when the police showed up to arrest him?

Readers could notice how the writer changes style and perspective in the last section. In the first section, the writer is trying to help the reader experience the terror that panicked the nation. The black-and-white drawings are fanciful representations of what people might be imagining. When the writer switches to straightforward reporting of information in the last section, the illustrations change to black-and-white photographs.

Finally, readers might speculate about this writer's view of Welles and why this one incident in his life was considered so important. Maybe the writer was fascinated with the biggest Halloween trick of all time (the date of the broadcast was October 30, 1938).

AUTOBIOGRAPHY AND MEMOIR

Reading an autobiography or memoir is a very intimate experience. It is as if someone is telling you personally about his life or a part of it. As in biography, readers need to pick up the important information about a person and what he has done, but thinking about the text becomes much more personal. You are weighing the individual's own account against what you have heard elsewhere, and you are also drawing conclusions about what the person wants you to understand.

What individuals put in and leave out signals how they want to be viewed. Individuals "read between the lines" to learn more about what the writer is really like. They may evaluate the completeness or honesty of the text. They may be inspired and reflect on what they have learned from the writer.

Moments later, another radio reporter came on. He sounded scared. He said that the top of the object had started to open. Then, with a more frightened voice, he described what crawled out. It was Earth's first visitor from another planet!

The creature came out of the dark like a snake. Its skin was like wet leather. It was as large as a bear. It had huge black eyes and a V-shaped mouth.

According to the reporter, the frightened crowd slowly backed away from the creature. People were afraid of what it would do next.

By this point, the telephones at CBS were ringing like mad. Listeners from all over were calling in. Some were angry. Some were frightened. All were curious. Some of the callers wanted to know if the story was a joke. If it was a joke, they said, it wasn't funny! Many other callers, however, were sure that Martians had landed in New Jersey. They wanted to know how to protect themselves. Where should they go to be safe? What should they do if they saw the strange visitors?

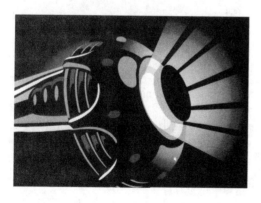

6

7

Figure 13-9. Orson Welles and the War of the Worlds

ANALYSIS OF
Orson Welles and the War of the Worlds (LEVEL V)

TEXT FACTOR	ANALYSIS
Genre	▫ Factual/Biographical
Text Structure	▫ Temporal sequence ▫ Setting communicated briefly on first page (date and time of the broadcast and the CBS radio station on which it aired) ▫ Information at end called "Story Behind the Story" gives straightforward facts
Content	▫ Nature of radio broadcasts in the 1930s ▫ Perspectives of people listening—fear of aliens, envisioning what is described (as opposed to TV) ▫ Background required to understand role of newsreels in people's lives ▫ How radio shows created drama by raising visual images
Themes and Ideas	▫ How writers/playwrights create illusions that are believable ▫ Welles's personality—caught up in the excitement of the moment, refusing to stop, and later expressing some regret
Language and Literary Features	▫ Dialogue used to make it more realistic ▫ Short, rapid-fire sentences create feeling of tension ▫ Conversational, "to the reader" style
Sentence Complexity	▫ Many short sentences ▫ Last sentence on page one has ellipses leading to next page where the story unfolds
Vocabulary	▫ Radio terminology: *broadcast, studio, newsreel, announcements, interviews, eyewitness reports on/off the air, script*
Words	▫ Many place names that could pose challenges to decoding ▫ Many three-syllable words—above 15% ▫ Words like *convincing* that are derived from root words
Illustrations	▫ Black-and-white illustrations on every page ▫ Illustrations show what people were imagining ▫ Illustrations and text integrated
Book and Print Features	▫ Sections marked by headings ▫ Full range of punctuation, including dashes ▫ Medium-size font ▫ White space makes print friendly ▫ Font varies—text and captions
When introducing this text in guided reading, keep this in mind:	▫ Readers need to assume the perspective of people who had never seen TV and depended on radio for news. ▫ Readers need to imagine how hearing a broadcast like *War of the Worlds* could create images in one's mind. ▫ Vocabulary connected to radio broadcasting could be used in conversation. ▫ Some multisyllable words could be examined. ▫ Readers might think Welles played an exciting trick. ▫ Readers should think critically about the consequences and dangers of such a trick—what if this happened today?

Figure 13-10. *Analysis of* Orson Welles and the War of the Worlds (*Level V*)

SPECIFIC DEMANDS OF FACTUAL TEXTS

Factual text, too, has its own unique characteristics over and above the demands of all nonfiction texts (see Figure 13-11). Readers of factual texts are required to process a great deal of topic-specific information, identifying new information and adding it to what they already know.

There is something of a curvilinear relationship between what readers already know about a topic and the potential for a text to be understandable and interesting, which are not always the same (see Figure 13-12). If you know something about a topic, it is easier to learn more and you are more likely to comprehend a text and find it interesting. If the text has just about nothing new for you, however, you may understand it very well but not find it engaging. If you have very little prior knowledge, the potential for both understanding and engagement is low.

In guided reading lessons, you select texts that students can connect with their own experiences and content knowledge, but in the introduction you also scaffold the reading by providing more information. When you introduce the

The Specific Demands of Factual Texts

READERS THINK WITHIN THE TEXT TO:	▫ Gather important information of a technical nature. ▫ Remember concepts, labels, and ideas. ▫ Make note of information new to them. ▫ Use information gained from readers' tools such as tables of contents, legends, headings and subheadings, indexes, pronunciation guides, glossaries, and authors' notes. ▫ Discover the author's qualifications. ▫ Gather information from graphics specific to the topic.
READERS THINK BEYOND THE TEXT TO:	▫ Bring background knowledge to the reading. ▫ Extend the meaning of the text through connections to their own personal experiences or to other texts they have read. ▫ Integrate information from graphics and text. ▫ Make connections between fiction and nonfiction texts.
READERS THINK ABOUT THE TEXT TO:	▫ Notice the writer's choices in selecting information to present. ▫ Evaluate the writer's qualifications to write on the topic. ▫ Think critically about the information in the text by comparing it with their background knowledge and other sources of information. ▫ Notice how the writer has used underlying structures (chronological sequence, description, comparison/contrast, cause/effect, and problem/solution) in presenting information about this particular topic. ▫ Compare the treatment of the topic in this text with other texts.

Figure 13-11. *The Specific Demands of Factual Texts*

Role of Prior Knowledge in Engaging with a Text

LEVEL OF PRIOR KNOWLEDGE	Little or No Prior Knowledge	Some Prior Knowledge	Knowledge of Almost Everything in the Text
POTENTIAL FOR READERS' UNDERSTANDING	Low	High	High
POTENTIAL FOR READERS' INTEREST AND ENGAGEMENT	Low	High	Low

Figure 13-12. *Role of Prior Knowledge in Engaging with a Text*

text, you fine-tune the selection by having students share what they know and provide enough information to enable students to read the text successfully. Of course, if the text is too far beyond students, it will not be possible to provide enough information in the introduction or it will take a long time. The goal is to select a text that students can understand with your input.

DESIGN FEATURES OF FACTUAL TEXTS

Duke (2003) defines "informational texts" somewhat more broadly than nonfiction. This distinction is useful today when children are encountering so many hybrid texts and genre lines are blurred. A factual text, for example, may have an element of fiction, such as a story about a group of friends going through a museum and learning about the artifacts. If the primary purpose of the text is to explain or inform, and if the design features of factual texts are present, then the opportunity is there for readers to learn about the genre.

The design features of factual or informational texts are striking and easy to identify (see Figure 13-13). We have mentioned many of these features previously, but they are summarized here. The five design features of factual texts are (1) text divisions, (2) organizational tools and sources of information, (3) graphics, (4) print, and (5) layout.

Text divisions are how the content is categorized and presented. Readers distinguish between information in the text body and other information on the page. Insets or lists call attention to concisely summarized information. Information about the author provides evidence of his qualifications, which is helpful in evaluating the accuracy of the text.

Graphics in a factual text do more than enhance the reader's visual images; they inform and are an integral part of the text. Readers need to learn how to look at a variety of graphics, including photographs (which sometimes have a more authentic quality than drawings), paintings and drawings, charts that present rows and columns, diagrams that reveal processes, tables and graphs of various kinds, time lines, and captions. Graphics may be circular, linear, vertical, or horizontal. Often, readers will look at them, read some of the body of the text, and then go back to look at them again. They may contain information reported in the body but in a different form, or they may provide completely different but complementary information.

Design Features of Informational Texts

Text Divisions	▫ Chapters or sections ▫ Body copy (paragraphs) ▫ Introduction/Preface ▫ Lists ▫ Insets (print set in a box or other distinguishing area) ▫ Foreword and afterword ▫ Author information
Graphics	▫ Photographs (color or black-and-white, enlarged or zoomed) ▫ Paintings (acrylic, watercolor, pastel, oil) ▫ Drawings (scale, labeled, color or black-and-white, realistic or interpretive) ▫ Charts (rows and columns) ▫ Diagrams (cutaways, cross sections, flowcharts, webs, trees) ▫ Tables and graphs (bar, line, pie) ▫ Timelines and cycles (horizontal, vertical, circular) ▫ Captions
Print	▫ Type size and style (regular, boldface, italic, underlined) ▫ Typeface (font) ▫ Color
Layout	▫ Format of the whole text ▫ Columns ▫ White space ▫ Shading ▫ Insets ▫ Bullets and numbers
Organizational Tools and Sources of Information	▫ Titles ▫ Table of contents ▫ Headings, subheadings, sub-subheadings ▫ Index ▫ Glossary ▫ Pronunciation guide ▫ Appendixes ▫ References

Figure 13-13. *Design Features of Informational Texts*

The *print* itself is a source of information for the reader. More important words may be in a larger font size, in italics, or in boldface. Many factual texts place important ideas in a different color. As children read more and more nonfiction, they will assimilate these clues automatically.

Organizational Tools and sources of information support the reader in accessing the content. Chapter or section headings, as well as subheadings and sub-subheadings, foreshadow the kind of information readers will encounter in the body copy. The table of contents and index provide quick ways to find information. References can be used to authenticate the information in the text. The pronunciation guide supports the reader in decoding difficult words.

Finally, even the placement of information on the page is a design feature of factual texts. Readers gather meaning from the *layout* of the entire text. The use of columns (as opposed to text that continues all the way across the page) makes a difference in the reader's eye movements. White space, shading, insets, bullets, and numbers can make information "pop out" at the reader, and writers and publishers of factual text use them advantageously.

PATTERNS OR UNDERLYING STRUCTURES IN FACTUAL TEXTS

Writers of factual texts also commonly use repeating patterns or underlying structures. The patterns summarized in Figure 13-14 are those K–8 readers will most likely encounter. Each underlying pattern raises expectations in the reader's mind, and readers detect the pattern through what is being said as well as by "signal words" typically associated with the pattern.

Description. Much of factual text is description. The writer is providing information to help the reader learn details and facts about the topic. The reader expects to gather up these details and to put together a visual picture. When writers of factual texts provide descriptive details, accompanied by high-quality illustrations, readers find it easier to understand the content. Posada provides description this way in *Ladybugs: Red, Fiery and Bright:*

> Tiny creatures climb out from creamy white eggs. They have hairy gray bodies and long skinny legs.

Established sequence (also called *enumerative*). Often writers use an established sequence, such as numbers or the alphabet, to organize the ideas in a text. These include "how-to" books with step-by-step directions. Readers detect

this pattern and expect to follow it as they search for information. *Pick a Pet* (Rotner and Garcia) features many different kinds of pets, most of them starting with the same letter as the first name of the owner. Patty, of course, "picks a puppy."

Chronological sequence. Sometimes the events in a text or the directions in a "how-to" book are arranged in the order they occurred or must occur. The reader expects to receive information in order. *Siebert's Cave* tells about life in a cave during the four seasons of the year. Chronological sequence can be quite complex, as when two or more sequences move along together.

Comparison and contrast. As a powerful way of illustrating concepts, writers of factual texts sometimes compare entities in order to clarify one or both. The reader expects to find how entities are alike and how they are different from each other. Arnosky's *All About Frogs* begins with a detailed comparison of frogs and toads.

Cause and effect. Cause and effect is closely related to problem and solution and is signaled by many of the same words (for example, *because* or *as a result*). Sometimes the cause and effect relationship is explicit, as in Romanek's *ZZZ: The Most Interesting Book You'll Ever Read About Sleep,* when she describes what happens when a person gets enough sleep. In Arnosky's *All About Frogs,* readers are expected to infer that environmental dangers may pose a real problem for frogs and that the writer wants to persuade the readers to protect animals like frogs. The reader expects to learn how one entity affects another or a number of others.

Problem and solution. Writers often present a problem and explain it using cause and effect. Sometimes a factual text centers on one problem; others present many problems and solutions. Then, they use the same data to present or propose a solution, or they tell how people solved a problem in the past. In *Ice Cream: Great Moments in Ice Cream History,* Older describes the many problem-solving processes that created today's ice cream industry, including the invention of the ice cream soda. The reader expects to identify a problem and often predicts a solution, confirming it as the writer unfolds it.

Question and answer. A simple format that appears in many factual texts is question and answer. The structure works to raise questions in the reader's mind or address

Patterns or Underlying Structures in Factual Texts

GRAPHIC	TEXT PATTERN	SIGNAL WORDS	DESCRIPTION
	Description	*On, over, beyond, within, like, as, among,* descriptive adjectives, figurative language	Reader expects the writer to tell characteristics.
1-2-3	Established Sequence	Numbers Alphabet Days of the week Months of the year Centuries	Reader expects to follow an established and known sequence in gathering information.
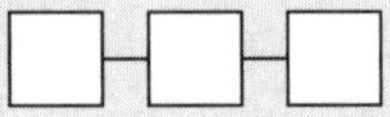	Chronological Sequence	*First, second; before, after; then, next, earlier, later, last, finally; again, in addition to; in the beginning/end*	Reader expects that events will be told in order of the time they happened.
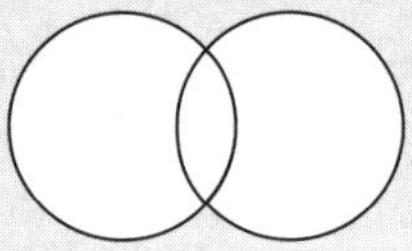	Comparison and Contrast	*While, yet, but, rather, most, either, like, unlike, same as, on the other hand, although, similarly, the opposite of, besides, however*	Reader expects to learn how one entity is like and different from another or others.
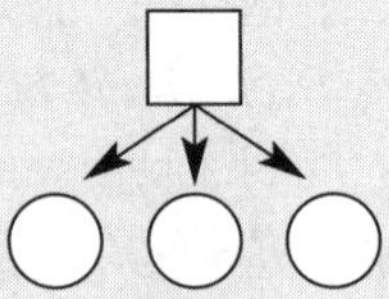	Cause and Effect	*Since, because, thus, so that, if . . . then, therefore, due to, as a result, this led to, then . . . so, for this reason, consequently*	Reader expects to learn the effect of one entity on another or others; reader expects to learn why this effect takes place.
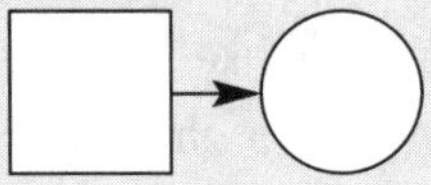	Problem and Solution	All signal words listed for cause and effect; *propose, conclude, the solution is, the problem is, research shows, a reason for, the evidence is that*	Reader expects to identify a problem, predict a solution, and be told a solution or solutions; reader expects to know why the solution is viable.
?	Question and Answer	*Why, what, when, how, why*	Reader expects to consider a question, come up with an answer, and verify the answer.
	Combination	Any and all	Writer uses a combination of patterns within any one text or section of text.

Figure 13-14. *Patterns or Underlying Structures in Factual Texts*

questions readers already have. An example is Berger's *Why Don't Haircuts Hurt?*, organized by questions in categories. The reader expects to consider a question, come up with an answer, and verify the answer. Many factual texts use this pattern explicitly, but it is also often implied.

Combination. Almost never will a reader encounter a single pattern except in very simple texts. Usually, the writer uses the patterns in various combinations.

ANALYSIS OF *OWLS*

Let's look at a variety of organizational patterns in a text. *Owls* is a "friendly" factual text (a two-page spread from the book is shown in Figure 13-15). Notice that pictures illustrate nearby text. Key vocabulary words are presented in boldface and defined within the text. The reader is constantly reminded of important information through a question-and-answer format. At the end of page 12, for example, is the question, "How does an owlet break open its shell?" The reader is expected to recall information from the section to answer the question and verify the answer: "An owlet uses its egg tooth to break open its shell."

To read this easy informational text, readers would have to think about what they already know about owls and would need to learn some new technical vocabulary, such as *nocturnal, prey, camouflage, beak,* and *pellet.* The meaning of many of these words is evident within the context. (For an analysis of the book, see Figure 13-16.) Notice that there are a few complex sentences but that except for the technical vocabulary mentioned above, most of the words are easy to decode. The print is very predictably placed and there are clear section headings.

Readers of *Owls* need to understand that each section presents a different kind of information, but almost no elementary age readers will know everything in this book. Readers should be able to sort out new information and reorganize what they already know about owls.

Now let's look at a much more complex factual text, *Lands of the Rain Forest* by Johanna Alexander. (Two pages are shown in Figure 13-17.) This factual text requires that readers assimilate information about many different parts of the world to derive the nature of the rain forest and

---

4

What owls look like

Owls have large heads with eyes that look forward as they hunt for prey.

Owls' eyes are very big to let in more light. This helps them to see in the dark.

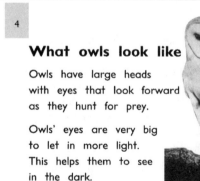

Most owls hunt for their food at night.

5

Owls have an extra eyelid that protects their eyes from dirt and dust.

This extra eyelid also helps keep light out of the owls' eyes during the day when they are asleep.

Why do owls have big eyes?

Figure 13-15. Owls

ANALYSIS OF
Owls (LEVEL M)

TEXT FACTOR	ANALYSIS
Genre	▫ Factual
Text Structure	▫ Nine sections with substantive titles ▫ Each section a different category of information about owls ▫ Question/answer format at bottom of each page
Content	▫ Many facts about owls—parts of body, food, sounds ▫ Names of different types of owls ▫ Concepts related to animals hunting for prey
Themes and Ideas	▫ There are many different varieties of owls ▫ Types of owls look different but have many things in common
Language and Literary Features	▫ Simple, clear language ▫ Description but no figurative use of language
Sentence Complexity	▫ Multiple adjectives: *soft, down edges* ▫ Both dependent and independent clauses ▫ A few longer sentences: "When an owlet is ready to hatch out of the egg, it uses a special hard tooth on the end of its beak to break the egg shell."
Vocabulary	▫ Technical vocabulary relative to owls: *nocturnal, prey, feathers, perching, camouflage, downy, swooping, beak, pellet, digested, owlet, egg tooth, rustle* ▫ Compound word: *eyelid* ▫ Some familiar words with new meanings: *egg tooth* ▫ Key vocabulary words in boldface—explained in the text and shown in illustrations
Words	▫ Mostly one- and two-syllable words with a few three-syllable words on each page
Illustrations	▫ Photographs that are closely linked with the text—one two-page-spread photo of an owl ▫ Map on last page showing where owl types are found; owl names connected to locations
Book and Print Features	▫ Sixteen pages with illustrations and text on each page ▫ Predictable placement of print; easy to see which illustrations fit with the body of the text ▫ Question/answer format always at bottom of pages ▫ Table of contents and index ▫ Section titles indicate content ▫ Some key vocabulary words in boldface
When introducing this text in guided reading, keep this in mind:	▫ Children should understand that each section tells a different kind of information about owls. ▫ Children may say aloud some of the technical names of owls but should not worry about perfect pronunciation of each (most easy to say). ▫ Some key concepts for discussion are *nocturnal, downy feathers* (allowing silent flying), *hunting for prey, owl pellets,* and care of owlets. ▫ Children may want to talk about surprises—information new to them.

Figure 13-16. *Analysis of* Owls *(Level A)*

its importance in the global ecology. (Figure 13-18 is an analysis of the book.)

Readers will need to gather and remember information from the eleven short sections presenting categories of knowledge. There is a fairly dense description of the role of rain forests in taking carbon dioxide out of the air that requires some understanding of the composition of gases that make up the air we breathe. Some language is used figuratively; being able to make sense of rain forests as the "lungs of the world" requires some understanding of the role lungs play in the human body. Vocabulary includes technological words such as *ecology* and *ecosystem,* which could be linked to help students begin to understand their roots.

Underlying structures that are important for the reader to use to organize thinking are comparison/contrast and problem/solution. Above all, readers should leave this text with a good idea of just how important rain forests are on the planet as well as an awareness that we need to preserve

them. Students could also argue whether the writer has presented a balanced view of the problem.

LEARNING—THE PLEASURE FACTOR IN NONFICTION TEXTS

Nonfiction texts are highly appealing to readers because they hold "truth," at least as the writer sees it. For human beings, learning is inherently pleasurable. We may not remember it that way, because much of our learning may have been assigned or required; however, pursuing a topic of interest in texts that are accessible to you is very satisfying. Helping your students grasp this principle early in their school careers will be valuable to them in further study and may lead to careers or avocations that will last all their lives.

SUGGESTIONS FOR PROFESSIONAL DEVELOPMENT
ANALYZING NONFICTION TEXTS

1 Have a discussion with peers of the kinds of nonfiction you like to read. First, you will probably focus more on

Rain forests cover much of the Amazon River region.

6

Most of the animals that live in the rain forest are insects. There are many species of colorful butterflies and moths. More than 40 species of ants can live in one South American rain forest tree. Scientists have counted as many as 1,200 species of beetles living in fewer than 20 tree tops in Panama.

Some large mammals live on the forest floor. A large cat called the jaguar (JAG wahr) lives in the rain forests of Central and South America. Some huge elephants live in rain forests in Africa and Asia.

THE AMAZON RAIN FOREST

The Amazon rain forest is the largest tropical rain forest in the world. About two-thirds of this rain forest is found in Brazil, South America's largest country. The Amazon rain forest also extends into the countries of Venezuela, Colombia, Ecuador, Peru, and Bolivia. There are more species of plants and animals in this rain forest than in any other place in the world.

The Amazon River flows through the Amazon rain forest. The Amazon is one of the mightiest rivers in the world. It begins in the Andes Mountains of Peru and flows 4,000 miles to the Atlantic Ocean on the coast of Brazil. The Amazon is second in length only to the Nile River in northern Africa. The Amazon River is also very wide—up to 6 miles wide in some places. You could not see from one side of the river to the other.

7

Figure 13-17. Lands of the Rain Forest

ANALYSIS OF
Lands of the Rain Forest (LEVEL T)

TEXT FACTOR	ANALYSIS
Genre	▫ Factual
Text Structure	▫ Information on rain forests, categorized into eleven short sections that define rain forests, provide information on animal and plant life, and tell about the different rain forests of the world
Content	▫ Location of rain forests ▫ Description and importance of rain forests ▫ Destruction of rain forests (often implied rather than explicitly stated) ▫ Fairly dense description of the role of rain forests in taking carbon dioxide out of the air and the importance of it ▫ Assumes readers know country names and many concepts such as *equator, species, temperature designations, amphibian, reptiles, mammals, varnish*
Themes and Ideas	▫ Implicit themes—rain forests essential for the ecology and it is necessary to save them
Language and Literary Features	▫ Some language used figuratively: "lungs of the world" assumes scientific knowledge of how lungs work ▫ Much description
Sentence Complexity	▫ Most are simple sentences that follow subject-verb pattern ▫ Multiple items in series ▫ Amplifying information set off by dash, for emphasis
Vocabulary	▫ Technical vocabulary related to rain forests: *ecosystems, carbon dioxide, greenhouse gas, species,* technical names of plants ▫ Many difficult concepts/words not defined in the text: *fossil fuels, resins, varnish, native peoples*
Words	▫ Many multisyllable words ▫ Many place names that will be challenging
Illustrations	▫ Photographs with captions bearing extra information ▫ Map showing rain forests of the world
Book and Print Features	▫ Sixteen pages with illustrations and text on every page ▫ Pronunciation guides in parentheses for difficult words ▫ Captions for pictures
When introducing this text in guided reading, keep this in mind:	▫ Text requires so much background information that it would be impossible to familiarize readers with all content; should be used with students who already know some of the important information. ▫ It might be interesting to discuss the creation of a new word such as *eco-tourism* and connect it to *ecology* and *ecosystem.* ▫ Readers should discuss background information they already have on rain forests. ▫ If countries and native peoples are unfamiliar, the reader can still learn something about rain forests. ▫ This dense text is full of information, so readers should not expect to remember every detail but to learn some important new things about rain forests. ▫ The central idea of the text—that rain forests perform a service for the ecology—is essential for readers to understand.

Figure 13-18. *Analysis of* Lands of the Rain Forest (*Level T*)

topics or content areas than on genres, although some might say they like biography in general. The list might also be much more wide-ranging, including cookbooks, self-help books, magazines, and travel books rather than straight accounts of history. Individuals might be motivated to read biography not because they particularly like the genre but because they are curious about the subject.

2   Make a list of *what* people like to read and then go back and add *why* they like to read those examples of nonfiction. The reasons for reading will be as varied as the types.

3   Then make a list of what engages you as a reader of nonfiction. Link this list, as much as possible, to what teachers think will engage the readers in their classrooms.

4   It might be interesting to invite the group to discuss gender differences. Some writers claim that nonfiction is actually more appealing to boys than fiction is (see Duke and Bennett-Armistead 2003), who argue for an infusion of nonfiction into classroom reading).

5   Look at an array of familiar nonfiction texts for children (K–8). Try to have a balance of biographical and factual texts.

6   Have each person (or pair) select a text and discuss its potential in terms of appealing to students. Then, use the ten factors associated with nonfiction to analyze the text. You may want to use the form, Questions to Ask About Factual Texts, in Figure 13-19 and on the DVD included with this book to guide your discussion.

7   From the analysis, pull out a list of reminders that can be used to plan an introduction to a text in a guided reading lesson.

8   Remember that you would not conduct such a detailed analysis for every book you use in guided reading. What you want to do is build the capacity to analyze texts mentally as you plan introductions.

9   Have participants practice giving a quick oral analysis of several texts.

Questions to Ask About Factual Texts

1 To what extent does the text offer readers the opportunity to add to their own knowledge?

2 Does the text provide aids such as illustrations? How helpful are the illustrations to the reader?

3 Are graphic features (maps, charts, cutaways, graphs, etc.) helpful to the reader in terms of understanding information?

4 To what extent does the text provide readers with definitions and examples to help them understand concepts?

5 Are there a sufficient number of examples to help students understand concepts?

6 Are important relationships (for example, cause and effect) explicitly stated, or does the reader need to infer them?

7 Are concepts summarized, or does the text require the reader to select the important information and remember it?

8 Do paragraphs, chapters, and sections have clear summaries of main ideas?

9 Is the organizational pattern simple, straightforward, and clear, or are there embedded concepts and narratives?

10 To what extent do the titles, headings, and subheadings help the reader find information?

11 What features of this text would make readers want to learn more about the topic?

12 What evidence is there that the text is accurate?

Figure 13-19. *Questions to Ask About Factual Texts*

CHAPTER FOURTEEN

UNDERSTANDING THE DEMANDS OF FICTION AND POETRY

Words are merely words, but real literature for any age is words chosen with skill and artistry to give the reader pleasure and to help them understand themselves and others.

—REBECCA LUKENS

GENERAL DEMANDS OF ALL FICTION TEXTS

All fiction texts make some general demands on readers (see Figure 14-1). Readers are required to suspend reality and enter the story, gathering important information about the characters, setting, and events. As described in Chapter 3, they search for this important information and store it in memory so that they can ground their thinking as they navigate the text.

DIALOGUE

Most fiction includes dialogue, which can be presented in a variety of ways (see Figure 14-2):

- *Simple dialogue* is straightforward and easy to follow. The speaker is identified either before or after the direct speech.

(Jared said, "It's raining." "I know it," said Raphael.)

- *Simple dialogue using pronouns* requires readers to remember the referent for words like *he, she, they, we*. Often after the speaker has been identified, the subsequent dialogue uses pronouns. *("We're going to have a great time," exclaimed Sarah. "You bet," said John. "I wish Grandma could come too," she remarked. He added, "Me too.")*

- *Split dialogue* interrupts the speech to insert assignment or provide narrative. *("Are you leaving?" whined Carrie. "I don't have anything to do." "Are you leaving?" Carrie's eyes filled with tears. "I don't have anything to do.")*

The General Demands of All Fiction Texts

READERS THINK WITHIN THE TEXT TO:	- Gather important information about the characters, setting, and plot. - Gather information across the events of the story. - Remember important parts of the story.
READERS THINK BEYOND THE TEXT TO:	- Understand the setting and relate it to characters and events. - Understand characters by noticing and interpreting how they are described, how they act, what they say or think, and what others say or think about them. - Identify the important characters and secondary characters. - Identify the conflict or problem of the story. - Follow the events of the plot and make predictions as to resolution of the problem. - Understand the prominent theme or author's message. - Relate the primary message or theme to their own lives—make the story their own. - Relate events of the plot to one another—for example, derive cause and effect. - Notice how characters change over time and infer causes. - Make inferences as to the significance of events. - Make inferences as to characters' feelings and motivations.
READERS THINK ABOUT THE TEXT TO:	- Evaluate the importance of the setting to the plot. - Notice how the writer has made characters seem real. - Notice the plot structure and connect it to other texts. - Notice the writer's use of language and connect it to other texts.

Figure 14-1. *The General Demands of All Fiction Texts*

Ways of Presenting Dialogue IN FICTION TEXTS	
DIALOGUE	**EXAMPLE**
Simple Dialogue	Lisa said, "Let's go." "Let's go," said Lisa.
Simple Dialogue Using Pronouns	"Run!" yelled Sarah as she raced toward the barn. Brian tried to follow. "I'm caught," he screamed. "Keep trying," she called.
Split Dialogue	"Come on guys," said Lisa. "Let's get going." The children moved through the doorway slowly. "Where are we going?"–Tracey moved even more slowly–"Are we going to come back?"
Direct Dialogue (first person narrator)	This is the story of my dog Willy. I'll tell you the real story. Listen carefully.
Unassigned Dialogue	"We're in a hurry!" "No we're not." "Don't you want to come?" "What do you think?" "I think you're just being mean."

Figure 14-2. *Ways of Presenting Dialogue in Fiction Texts*

- In *direct dialogue* the writer talks directly to the reader. Quotations marks are not used. (*I want you to know, dear reader, that this is a tale of adventure. It's a true story of my life as a bird.*)

- Dialogue may be *unassigned* in that the writer does not provide any words to identify the speakers. (*"Are you going?" "No." "Why not?" "Because I'm too busy."*)

Split, direct, and unassigned dialogue are more challenging for readers than simple dialogue using characters' names or pronouns. Some high-level texts contain long strings of unassigned dialogue. The reader is required to track the interchange mentally in order to identify the speaker. The writer may provide signals in the form of ways of talking or motivations that are specific to particular characters, so sorting unassigned dialogue may also require insights into character development.

THINKING BEYOND AND ABOUT THE TEXT

Readers also employ a range of thinking beyond and about the text. They learn to interpret characters' motivations, and understand and empathize with them, using:

- The writer's descriptions of characters.
- What characters do.
- What characters say or think.
- What other characters say or think about them.

Much understanding of a character lies in the reader's interpretation. The characters in a fiction text can seem more real than actual people you know.

Fiction texts require that readers identify the conflict or problem of the story and follow the plot to the resolution. Looking across events, readers of fiction make predictions that they later confirm or reject, and ultimately they derive the primary message or "theme" of the text.

Throughout this process, readers of fiction make connections to their own lives. Here we do not mean going off on tangents (noticing that there is a dog in a story and beginning a long daydream about having a dog, for example). Although a discussion can move in many directions, it should keep coming back to the text. A thoughtful reader might think of a particular dog, but the comparison would involve an event or an emotion that extends understanding of the text.

Readers of fiction sort out the events of the story, deciding which are important and have causal effects. In fact, it would seem that reading is a series of thousands of decisions—what to attend to, what to remember, what to puzzle over. These decisions are largely unconscious, although sometimes readers can reflect on them after reading.

Readers of fiction also form opinions as they read. Usually, they can say whether they like a text or not and why. Going beyond simple opinion, readers can think analytically. For example, they can make a decision as to the relevance of the setting; often, in realistic fiction, the setting is not important to the plot. Readers can notice how the writer has used language to make characters become real. They can notice "leads," the way the writer begins a story and captures interest. They can notice the structure of the plot or the writer's style and relate them in an analytical way to other texts.

ANALYSIS OF *WILLY THE HELPER*

Figure 14-3 examines a simple text, *Willy the Helper* (Peters), using the ten text factors introduced in previous chapters as a lens. This text is contemporary realistic fiction. It does have an animal character, Willy, but the dog only does things that dogs really do. The plot is revealed on the first page, and there is an episode for each day of the week. This plot is simple and straightforward. The narrator is talking directly to the readers. Readers can empathize with this little girl who is putting up with Willy but loves her pet. The text is not challenging in terms of literary language or features. The language is very close to natural oral language; nevertheless, the text is a real story with appeal.

The analysis includes some thoughts about the use of the text in guided reading. These are suggestions rather than directions. In any consideration of a text, the decision about what information to bring to children's attention and how to guide the discussion is always yours and will depend on your knowledge of your own students. We would only say this as an absolute: *the talk before and after students read a text must always include a discussion of the meaning.* We discuss guided reading in great detail in Chapters 24, 25, and 26 where we revisit some of these texts.

ANALYSIS OF *HANNAH BROWN, UNION ARMY SPY*

Hannah Brown, Union Army Spy (Crowley) is set during the Civil War. (See the analysis in Figure 14-4.) Hannah and her Quaker family live in the "buffer zone" of Pennsylvania. Although they oppose the war, their sympathies are generally with the North. As Confederate soldiers encroach on the territory, Hannah and her family are forced to feed them, and she overhears their war plans. She gathers her courage to take a coded message (disguised as her arithmetic sums) to warn the Northern soldiers. In the end, Hannah succeeds. The bridges are burned and the city of Washington is saved.

The text is short—just sixteen pages—but it has tension and action. There are short sections or chapters signaled only by a one-word centered heading. There are several black-and-white illustrations, including one map that shows the buffer zone. Almost all dialogue is assigned.

To understand *Hannah Brown*, readers need quite a bit of background knowledge about the Civil War. Because the action is packed into a short text, the writer does not provide very much background to help students understand causes of the war, the stances of the two sides, the idea of a "buffer zone," and Quakers' conscientious objection to the war. The text assumes that readers understand slavery and the concept of a "runaway." Even the wagon with a false bottom is not described but only mentioned.

With adequate background knowledge, the text is easy to follow. The readers need to understand why Hannah was frightened but also why she felt so compelled to warn the soldiers in the North of the impending invasion of Washington. The text contains some challenging vocabulary words, like *pillage*, but most words are easier. Another key idea is that Hannah, because she was a child, was the *only* person who could deliver the warning successfully. The writer expects readers to admire Hannah's conquering her fear to rise to the occasion as well as her cleverness and nerve.

SPECIFIC DEMANDS OF REALISM

Realism includes contemporary realistic fiction and historical fiction. Both genres are set in the real world, as imagined by the author. Realism incorporates the demands of fiction listed above, but each genre makes specific demands (see Figure 14-5).

CONTEMPORARY REALISTIC FICTION

Readers of contemporary realistic fiction set in the present (or near past) are required to detect the problem or central conflict of the story. The problem will be very simple and easy to see in lower-level texts, but highly sophisticated texts may have many interlocking problems and conflicts. In realistic fiction, readers encounter plots that could occur in real life, as well as characters that are realistic but may be far distant (geographically and culturally) from their own experience. Realistic fiction can greatly expand readers' worlds. Readers are required to think beyond the text to interpret characters' perspectives, attitudes, and motivations in the light of their circumstances. They need to predict events and characters' responses to them as well as to think about the ending of the story based on characters' attributes and decisions. They need to identify the main characters and begin to empathize with them, understanding that the characters in realistic fiction may be good, evil, or something in between and that they change over time.

ANALYSIS OF
Willy the Helper (LEVEL C)

TEXT FACTOR	ANALYSIS
Genre	▫ Contemporary realistic fiction
Text Structure	▫ Plot presented on first page (Willy makes a mess) ▫ New episode every page ▫ Surprise at the end
Content	▫ Days of the week ▫ Everyday household chores ▫ Pets
Themes and Ideas	▫ Family and pet relationships ▫ Amusing family incidents
Language and Literary Features	▫ Meaning provided through integration of pictures with text ▫ Expression–*What a mess!*
Sentence Complexity	▫ Told in first person–teller to the reader ▫ Introductory prepositional phrases, "On Monday, Willy…" ▫ Direct speech–*What a mess!*–implied but no quotation marks ▫ Example: "On Tuesday, Willy helped me paint the fence."
Vocabulary	▫ Days of the week ▫ Words for chore *(paint the fence)* clearly signaled by pictures
Words	▫ High frequency words–*on, me, the, a, what*–repeated almost every page ▫ Challenging words on last page
Illustrations	▫ Illustrations provide essential meaning–that Willy is always acting up. ▫ Illustrations show the surprise ending that is not reflected in the text (that Willy has had puppies).
Book and Print Features	▫ Sixteen pages, three lines of print on each, ten to twelve words on each page ▫ Punctuation–period, comma, exclamation point, question ▫ Large font ▫ Larger than usual spaces between words and between lines ▫ Three lines on a page
When introducing this text in guided reading, keep in mind:	▫ The text follows the days of the week. ▫ The pictures provide very important information. ▫ There are some high frequency words that could be located; *what* is the most difficult and begins a sentence. ▫ Content words are signaled by pictures; children may need some labels, such as *garage.* ▫ Discussion could focus on the little girl's relationship with her dog.

Figure 14-3. *Analysis of* Willy the Helper (*Level C*)

ANALYSIS OF
Hannah Brown, Union Army Spy (LEVEL T)

TEXT FACTOR	ANALYSIS
Genre	▫ Historical fiction
Text Structure	▫ Setting explained in first two pages

Content	▫ Key content knowledge required:
	  ▫ Positions of the North and the South in the Civil War
	  ▫ Idea of a "buffer zone"
	  ▫ Transportation—wagons (with false bottoms for runaways), horses
	  ▫ Milk delivered in large metal cans

Themes and Ideas	▫ Courage ▫ Commitment to a cause
Language and Literary Features	▫ Some archaic language (*She fears the Confederates have found her out. . . .*)
Sentence Complexity	▫ Split dialogue ▫ Complex sentences with phrases but only a few embedded clauses ▫ Example: *Limp with relief as well as exhaustion, Hannah turned her horses away from the camp and urged them on toward her teacher's home.*
Vocabulary	▫ Key vocabulary words: *pillage, skirmishes, Quaker, exercise* (an arithmetic problem), *endeavored* ▫ Ironic use of *guests*
Words	▫ Multisyllable words in almost every sentence
Illustrations	▫ Black-and-white drawings ▫ Map of Pennsylvania and Maryland for the period ▫ Ink and quill on title page signaling importance of the message she carried
Book and Print Features	▫ Sixteen pages; six illustrations; many whole pages of text ▫ Dialogue is assigned ▫ Short sections or chapters indicated by a one-word centered heading ▫ No side headings ▫ Most sentences ten to fifteen words ▫ Use of italics
When introducing this text in guided reading, keep in mind:	▫ Students need a good understanding of the "sides" and issues in the Civil War in order to engage with the story. ▫ They need to know how important it was for the Confederate soldiers to capture the city of Washington. ▫ They need to know something about Quakers—why they opposed the war and what their values were in wanting the North to win. ▫ Might use words related to war in conversation—*pillage, skirmish*. ▫ Students may discuss why Hannah felt so compelled to warn the North. ▫ They may reflect on how she could help *because* she was a child; she was the only person who could perform the task with any hope of success.

Figure 14-4. *Analysis of* Hannah Brown, Union Army Spy (*Level T*)

TEACHING FOR COMPREHENDING AND FLUENCY

The Specific Demands of Realism

	Contemporary Realistic Fiction	Historical Fiction
READERS THINK BEYOND THE TEXT TO:	□ Understand characters in the light of current issues and problems. □ Understand characters from the perspective of the characters' problems, issues, and settings. □ Understand different cultures. □ Predict endings based on characters' attributes and decisions. □ Understand complex characters that may be good, evil, or somewhere in between.	□ Understand archaic language that is authentic to time and place. □ Understand the problem in the light of historical events and problems. □ Sort out imaginary characters from authentic historical characters. □ Understand characters in the light of the culture, time in history, and physical setting. □ Distinguish imagined events from authentic historical events. □ Relate present events and circumstances to those of the past. □ Relate historical characters and events to their own lives—the human condition.
READERS THINK ABOUT THE TEXT TO:	□ Take a critical stance toward decisions characters make. □ Discuss alternative events and endings. □ Notice how the writer has revealed the complexities of characters. □ Critically evaluate the authenticity of the text in the light of current issues. □ Make hypotheses about the writer's perspectives and attitudes.	□ Make judgments as to the authenticity of the language and described setting. □ Make hypotheses about why the author has selected the time in history and the setting in order to tell the story. □ Realize how the writer has made historical characters seem real to readers of today. □ Critically evaluate the text in terms of perspective on historical events. □ Make hypotheses as to the writer's interest in or attitude toward historical times.

Figure 14-5. *The Specific Demands of Realism*

To think beyond the text, readers need to take a critical stance toward the characters and their decisions as well as whether the text is truly realistic. Readers should notice how the writer has revealed the complexities of the characters. Realistic fiction also gives readers an idea of the writer's own perspectives and attitudes. *Willy the Helper* is a text for beginning readers. The content is close to typical experiences of first graders, yet there is something to be inferred. Readers can notice how the ending is surprising and reflect whether they ever suspected Willy was female; also, there is plenty of room for prediction as to what might happen next.

HISTORICAL FICTION

Historical fiction makes special demands on readers over and above the general requirements of fiction. In historical fiction, the setting is all important. Readers need to think

beyond the text to understand archaic language that is authentic to the time and place. They are required to understand the problem in the light of the setting and to bring background knowledge to their understanding. For example, readers sort the imagined historical characters from real people who actually lived and imagined events from what really happened.

The Night Crossing (Ackerman) is the story of a Jewish family in Austria in 1938. (See the analysis in Figure 14-6.) Because of the Nazi takeover, they sell everything they own and walk across the Alps to Switzerland. The story is told from the point of view of Clara, who is about six. The writer provides details to illustrate the family's desperate plight— for example, they burn their piano to keep warm. The mother will not give up two candlesticks that have been in her family for generations—all she has left—so she takes them in her petticoats. When the time comes to pass the final barrier, the father knows the clanking candlesticks will give them away. Clara has the bright idea of hiding them inside her two precious dolls, the only things she has saved. The idea works and the family crosses into safety. The text contains an epilogue that tells what happened to the family later. The theme of the book is summed up in the father's regular toast on the Sabbath or a holiday:

> "To freedom," Clara's father would toast, first holding his glass of sweet wine in the direction of the dolls and then to where his daughters sat, "and to the courage required to keep it."

Readers of *The Night Crossing* would need to be aware of what was taking place politically in this time and place in order to understand why the family has to flee. Readers also need to cope with German and Hebrew words and challenging place names. Once they are oriented to the situation, children can identify with a very exciting story in which a little girl shows ingenuity and courage.

They should empathize with the feelings of the family, including fear and loss. It is important to understand the symbolism of the candlesticks (tradition, heritage, generations of a family) and why the mother is willing to risk their lives to keep them. The importance of the candlesticks makes Clara's idea and her bravery in carrying the dolls more significant and is reflected in the father's final toast.

Even though characters of historical fiction are far distant in culture and time, readers must still seek out their essential human qualities and try to relate these people to their own lives. Readers will then derive the author's general message and consider its relevance to themselves.

Readers of historical fiction can reflect on the text in light of their own knowledge in order to make judgments about its authenticity. It is also interesting for readers to notice how the writer has described the settings and characters in ways that make them seem real, and readers can speculate on the author's reasons for creating this historical piece. Readers of *Hannah Brown, Union Army Spy* need to understand why the Quaker family had to provide food for whichever army occupied the buffer zone in which they lived, and they can think about how it might feel to be in the midst of a war, to have sympathies for one side but not to take part because of their beliefs.

SPECIFIC DEMANDS OF FANTASY

In addition to the general demands of fiction, all fantasy involves elements that require readers to suspend their sense of reality and enter a world that can only be imagined. The roots of fantasy can be found in traditional literature (see Figure 14-7).

TRADITIONAL LITERATURE

Traditional literature has been passed down by word of mouth through generations; many versions of the same tales appear all over the world. Traditional literature has a special role in the life of a reader. Readers encounter recurring motifs such as three wishes, tricksters, or journeys. Often in these traditional tales, the smallest or youngest character becomes the hero, overcoming stronger characters through her wits. Readers of traditional literature come to expect repeating refrains and predictable, or "flat," characters that do not change. They can sort the characters easily into good and evil and should derive some kind of moral lesson.

Because the structure of traditional literature is so available, it is easy for even young children to "see." They can follow the plots and make lists of the traits of characters. Also, the major message (often the moral) is easy to determine. Listening to, talking about, and drawing or writing about traditional literature is appealing to young children and provides a strong foundation for reading fantasy later.

A prime example of a very simple traditional tale is *The Little Red Hen*. (See the analysis in Figure 14-8.) Most children will encounter many versions of this tale before they get to first grade. This version of *The Little Red Hen* is categorized as level I. It's a straightforward plot that includes the expected episodes except that the writer has omitted the hen's trip to the mill to grind the wheat. Simply saying that the hen made the wheat into flour greatly simplifies the tale, because the concept of grinding the wheat in a mill requires background knowledge. (Children who have heard a more complex version before may mentally add this information or even wonder why it is not there.)

As background knowledge, readers would understand that they are following the sequence of how to do something and at the same time noticing traits of characters such as hardworking or lazy. The end is highly predictable, so you would expect readers to have it in mind.

ANALYSIS OF
The Night Crossing (LEVEL O)

TEXT FACTOR	ANALYSIS
Genre	▫ Historical fiction
Text Structure	▫ Desperate circumstances of family revealed in chapter 1 ▫ Simple chapter book
Content	▫ Conditions in Austria in 1938–perspective of Jews ▫ Religious prejudice
Themes and Ideas	▫ The triumph of courage ▫ Family loyalties and values ▫ Religious prejudice
Language and Literary Features	▫ Details showing the family's situation (burning the piano to keep warm)
Sentence Complexity	▫ Some simple sentences ▫ Some more complex sentences with dependent clauses ▫ Very few long sentences ▫ Sample: *Both Clara and Marta were surprised that unlike the city, the Austrian countryside seemed untouched by the war.*
Vocabulary	▫ Vocabulary specific to the times: *cobblestones, Nazis, Hitler, swastika* (shown in illustrations), *Jewish*
Words	▫ Some German and Hebrew words as well as place names that may be challenging ▫ Many two- and three-syllable words
Illustrations	▫ Black-and-white charcoal drawings, one in each chapter ▫ Illustrations communicate fear and hardship
Book and Print Features	▫ Fifty-six pages ▫ Medium-size font and ample space between lines ▫ Chapters with numbers and titles
When introducing this text in guided reading, keep this in mind:	▫ Children need to understand background that makes the situation desperate for the family before they begin reading. ▫ Readers should understand what the candlesticks meant to the mother and why the father let her keep them although they sold everything else. ▫ Readers will probably need some conversation about vocabulary specific to the text and some coaching on how to approximate the pronunciation of German and Hebrew words (and then move on rather than dwelling on them). ▫ Students can discuss the mood of the illustrations as well as how they add to the somber tone of the text. ▫ Discussion can focus on the setting and injustice as well as how children would feel in the family's situation. ▫ Discussion can focus on the nature of courage.

Figure 14-6. *Analysis of* The Night Crossing (*Level O*)

The Specific Demands of Fantasy

	Traditional Literature	Fantasy
READERS THINK BEYOND THE TEXT TO:	□ Suspend belief so that talking beasts, magic, granted wishes, and supernatural events are possible within the story. □ Make predictions based on episodes in the plot. □ Notice and make use of recurring patterns of language. □ Categorize flat or stereotypical characters as *good, bad, tricky, lazy, hardworking, timid, brave,* etc. □ Make connections among texts that are different versions of the same story. □ Make connections to texts that have similar themes or characters. □ Make connections to situations in their own lives. □ Use traditional structure and characters to predict events and endings. □ Derive the moral lesson.	□ Enter into imaginary worlds. □ Use imagination to understand plots, settings, and characters. □ Understand different types of fantasy (human characters in fantastic situations; fantasy characters; magical characters). □ Recognize the basic human quality of characters in fantasies. □ Make connections between the events and lessons of fantasy and their own lives. □ Derive understandings about people and life even though the settings are different. □ Recognize the main idea or theme even though the setting is far from reality. □ Understand complex and highly developed characters that may usually be categorized as good or evil. □ Recognize and understand elements related to science and technology in relation to the imaginary worlds.
READERS THINK ABOUT THE TEXT TO:	□ Compare versions of the same tale. □ Compare tales that have similar motifs (threes, quests, villains, tricksters). □ Recognize and appreciate traditional story language (*once upon a time, once there was, …and they all lived happily ever after*). □ Consider whether the moral lesson is worthwhile. □ Recognize the historical origins of traditional literature.	□ Recognize frequently occurring themes and motifs and their relationship to traditional literature (quests, magical characters, talking beasts, tricksters). □ Recognize and reflect on the writer's use of symbolism. □ Consider whether the moral lesson is worthwhile. □ Speculate on the author's goals in writing the fantasy. □ Notice the details the writer used to make the imaginary world seem plausible. □ Critically evaluate the construction of the story and the writer's craft in making a coherent whole.

Figure 14-7. *The Specific Demands of Fantasy*

The text does not use difficult vocabulary, and most words are a single syllable. The greatest challenge will be words that are connected to the characters—"quacked the duck," for example. Readers will need to process some repetitive traditional language.

The print layout guides phrasing, letting the reader pause at the end of lines. Also, some words in boldface provide a guide for expression. The simple illustrations add a great deal of personality to the animals and help readers understand the animals' feelings and motivations.

A great feature of the book is that it also presents the same story as a play for readers to perform. This play incorporates much of the same language as the tale, and the dialogue is color-coded to help readers identify their parts.

FANTASY

Fantasy is a highly complex genre that combines all of the traits of fiction yet has highly imaginary elements as well. Fantasy may involve simple stories that have magical elements. High fantasy incorporates many of the motifs of tra-

ANALYSIS OF
The Little Red Hen (LEVEL I)

TEXT FACTOR	ANALYSIS
Genre	□ Traditional literature
Text Structure	□ Episodic plot that is predictable and repetitive □ Plot proceeds in sequence to the end □ Predictable ending □ Tale is also presented as a play, beginning on page 20
Content	□ Cycle from planting seeds to baking bread □ Animal names and typical behaviors □ Animals behave like people but do not wear clothing
Themes and Ideas	□ Moral lesson: if you want to eat, you must work
Language and Literary Features	□ Traditional language (Once upon a time, there was . . .) □ Repetitive refrains □ Predictable characters
Sentence Complexity	□ Split dialogue, all assigned ("I will plant this wheat," said the little red hen. "Who will help me?") □ Flexible use of dialogue □ Compound sentences using and and prepositional phrases.
Vocabulary	□ Words associated with animals (quacked the duck, grunted the pig).
Words	□ Most words one syllable □ Inflectional endings—ed
Illustrations	□ Simple pictures of animals with great personality □ Illustrations add information about characters' motivations □ Color coding of the narrator, duck, pig, dog, and little red hen dialogue in the play □ Illustrations of real children wearing masks in the play
Book and Print Features	□ Layout signaled by phrasing □ All new sentences start at left margin □ Words in boldface to guide expression
When introducing this text in guided reading, keep this in mind:	□ Students should bring their knowledge of this familiar tale to the reading. □ Some of the traditional literary language ("Not I") can be practiced prior to reading. □ Long embedded clause on page 15 (When the bread was baked and ready to eat, the little red hen took it out of the oven.) may require some practice. □ Some content words (water the wheat, grunted the pig) could be discussed. □ Students should understand the moral of the story. □ They may discuss what characters are like (responsible, lazy, hardworking).

Figure 14-8. *Analysis of* The Little Red Hen (*Level I*)

ditional literature (for example, the quest) and presents a highly complicated text with multiple characters, themes, and events (for example, Susan Cooper's series beginning with *The Dark Is Rising*). Science fiction presents technological and scientific concepts and is often set in the future. A popular variation is to take a traditional tale and turn it into fantasy. (An example is *Ella Enchanted* (Levine), in which the Cinderella story is never directly mentioned but is signaled, tongue in cheek, by things like naming the Prince *Char* and using similar plot elements.)

Readers of fantasy are asked to imagine a past that never existed or a future that perhaps never will. Or they are asked to imagine a completely different world with characters that are very different from humans. Fantasy may involve human characters that have or encounter supernatural powers. Characters may be animals or other beings different from humans. Events may involve time travel, life in space, or seemingly everyday events that nevertheless have magical qualities.

In spite of these challenges, readers must derive the essentially human qualities of the characters as well as the writer's overall message. Most fantasy presents characters as

being either good or evil and there is a struggle between the two, with good usually winning, at least temporarily.

The science fiction novel *Among the Hidden* (Haddix; see the analysis in Figure 14-9) is the first of a series called The Shadow Children. The writer presents a future world in which government control has decreed only two children per family; Luke, about age twelve, a third child, has been hidden since birth. He is never allowed to leave the house or even to show his face in the window. Luke's family loses their hog-raising business because of taxes they cannot pay, so they are forced to sell off lots for luxury housing development. The government even rations food and has forbidden junk food and pets! When the woods surrounding his home are cut down, Luke is even more trapped in the house, and his mother has to go out to work. Then, he spots the face of another shadow child in one of the big houses near his own. He breaks into that house and meets Jennifer, who though she also has to hide, has many more advantages. Luke learns that there are many shadow children who talk with each other via the Internet. Jen organizes a rally to protest population control and free the shadow children but is killed. Jen's dad helps Luke acquire a new iden-

ANALYSIS OF *Among the Hidden* (LEVEL Z)	
TEXT FACTOR	**ANALYSIS**
Genre	▫ Fantasy/Science fiction/Series
Text Structure	▫ Setting and problem revealed in first chapter ▫ Episodes reveal more about government control over the thirty chapters ▫ Main character's problems resolved only partially at the end
Content	▫ Extreme government control ▫ Population explosion and scientific gender control ▫ Takeover of family farms ▫ Development of farmland for luxury housing ▫ Bureaucratic control and propaganda
Themes and Ideas	▫ Dangers of too much government control ▫ Class system whereby one group (*Barons*) gets more than all the others by keeping them in poverty ▫ Importance of critically examining history books and news articles: "There have been too many lies for too long. Our Government is totalitarian, and totalitarian governments never like truth." ▫ Overcoming fear and growing up

Figure 14-9. *Analysis of* Among the Hidden (*Level Z*)

ANALYSIS OF **Among the Hidden** (LEVEL Z) (CONTINUED)	
TEXT FACTOR	**ANALYSIS**
Language and Literary Features	□ The text is in itself a persuasive document □ Futuristic world cued by facts like inflation (a $12,000 door); only the elite have access to computers; Luke doesn't know commonplace concepts like the Internet and surveillance "bugs" and has never seen a fur coat
Sentence Complexity	□ Split dialogue with narrative inserted in addition to words assigning speakers: *"What they're talking about"—she pointed at the computer screen—"is taking on a fake identity permanently."* □ Use of dashes to make complex sentences
Vocabulary	□ Specific-to-the-text use of terms such as *shadow child* and *Baron* □ *Propaganda* is a key vocabulary word □ Differences between *wrong* and *illegal*
Words	□ Multisyllable words such as *infiltrator, adjudication, hydroponics*
Illustrations	□ No illustrations other than cover design
Book and Print Features	□ One hundred fifty-three pages of small print □ Thirty chapters □ Use of italics to show the main character's thoughts, writing that characters do, and Luke's memory of words said by others □ Use of capital letters to indicate power (*Government, Barons*)
When introducing this text in guided reading, keep this in mind:	□ Text could be divided into about five readable segments. □ Group should understand some special meanings of some words within the imaginary world *(population control, shadow children, Barons)*. □ It is important to understand the setting, with background on why a government might try to control children (possible connections to China's policy of one child per family in the 1990's); could this really happen in the future? □ Readers will probably make predictions about what will happen to the character with his new identity and new life. □ From Luke's perspective, the world is very limited, but his world opens up after meeting Jen; children could discuss how he changed in response. □ Group could find details that are convincing in explaining the setting. □ Children could discuss writer's possible attitudes toward government control of environment.

Figure 14-9. *Analysis of* Among the Hidden (*Level Z*) (cont.)

tity. The story ends with his plan to go to a boarding school, setting the scene for further adventures.

This text includes some mature themes and sophisticated concepts, such as government bureaucracy. To fully understand the story, readers must build the image of a world that is futuristic but simultaneously nontechnological for most of the population, who do not have access to it. To understand this setting, readers follow along as Luke recon-structs the history that led to the situation. Because he is kept hidden and his parents are low-status citizens who are not knowledgeable, Luke sees the world in a very limited way in the beginning of the story. The readers should enter into his perspective, as it gradually changes after meeting the more sophisticated Jen. Why was he terrified, for example, to cross the yard? Why are his parents angry when he walks around the kitchen? Why is he not allowed to sit at the table to eat?

Episodes follow each other in logical sequence as the plot builds. Several long sections of "history" are inserted. Readers may be tempted to skip them, but they are essential for understanding the text. Sentences are complex but vary between being very short and having twelve or more words. Dialogue is assigned to speakers but is often split, with narrative inserted using dashes. Dialogue is easy to follow. Readers will notice interesting details, such as Luke's not knowing about the Internet or never having tasted potato chips or a door's costing $12,000, which help readers understand the setting.

The subplot of the narrative is Luke's growing up and leaving home. Readers will probably make predictions about what will happen to the character with his new identity and new life. Readers who enjoy the story will want to read the sequel.

SPECIAL TYPES OF FICTION

When guiding students to read realistic fiction, it will be good to keep in mind the special types of this genre (see Figure 14-10). As they develop tastes and preferences, students will definitely gravitate toward some of these themes and formats, which can occur in realistic or historical fiction or fantasy.

As children you probably didn't talk about genres in the same way we do in this book. You probably said things like:
- "That was a great mystery."
- "I love sports stories."
- "That book was so exciting."
- "I've read all of the Nancy Drew books."

Readers' tastes are often expressed not in terms of fantasy or nonfiction but by type of book. A mystery can be realistic fiction, fantasy, or historical fiction (a historical character who solves mysteries, for example). The specific characteristics of mystery cross genres. Each type of text makes its own special demands on the reader.

MYSTERIES AND THRILLERS

Readers of a mystery or thriller must identify the problem, often a "crime," and gather clues to solve it. Readers tend to notice very fine details and to document them mentally so that they can be organized into a logical solution. Readers may recognize the author's skill in building the mystery. Readers want to solve it, but they do not want it to be too

Special Types of Fiction

TYPE	SPECIFIC DEMANDS ON THE READER READERS:	EXAMPLES:
Mysteries and Thrillers	<ul><li>Identify the problem, sometimes a crime.</li><li>Gather detailed clues.</li><li>Put together clues, as well as use their own imagination, to solve the mystery.</li><li>Identify with the detective or individual seeking to solve the mystery.</li><li>Rely on suspense for unexplained events or actions.</li><li>Recognize the writer's technique in creating suspense.</li><li>Confirm or reject predictions at the end.</li><li>Evaluate the skill of the writer in challenging the reader (mystery solver).</li></ul>	<ul><li>Cam Jansen series</li><li>Nate the Great series</li><li>*Mixed Up Files of Mrs. Basil E. Frankweiler*</li><li>Magic Tree House series</li><li>Something Queer Mysteries series</li></ul>
Adventure Stories	<ul><li>Follow fast-paced plot with hero.</li><li>Recognize main character's courage, strength, or other attributes.</li><li>Recognize the main character's purpose (which may involve a quest).</li><li>Recognize author's ability to create suspense.</li></ul>	<ul><li>Narnia series</li><li>*The Dark Is Rising*</li><li>*The Black Pearl*</li><li>Horrible Harry series</li></ul>

Figure 14-10. *Special Types of Fiction*

Special Types of Fiction (CONTINUED)

TYPE	SPECIFIC DEMANDS ON THE READER READERS:	EXAMPLES:
Survival Stories	□ Identify the specific problems that make survival a problem for the main character. □ Follow the survivor's problem solving. □ Predict chances of survival based on the setting and the character's ingenuity. □ Confirm or reject predictions at the end. □ Evaluate how the writer helped readers know what it was really like for the character.	□ *Hatchet* □ *Dolphin Music* □ *My Side of the Mountain*
Animal Realism (realistic portrayal of animals with no personification)	□ Look at the world from the perspective of a real animal. □ Access background information about the particular animal; use scientific knowledge. □ Predict events based on the real animal's characteristics and abilities.	□ *Willy the Helper* □ *Julie of the Wolves* □ *Where the Red Fern Grows* □ *Old Yeller* □ *Baby Bear Goes Fishing* □ *Frog and Toad*
Animal Fantasy	□ Understand that animals have some of the qualities of people but may also retain some animal qualities.	□ *Watership Down* □ *Peaches the Pig* □ *Charlotte's Web*
Sports Stories	□ Bring to reading background knowledge about a particular sport. □ Follow fast-paced descriptions of sporting events. □ Understand competitive spirit and empathize with the hero, who either is defeated or victorious.	□ Matt Christopher series □ *The Contender* □ *Taking Sides*
Formula Fiction and Series Books	□ Grasp the basic formula to be applied to other books of the same type or in the series. □ Build knowledge of characters and what they are like over time. □ Make predictions based on knowledge of the characters, the series, or the type of text.	□ Henry and Mudge series □ Amelia Bedelia series
Short Stories (related collections with overall meaning)	□ Understand the events, characters, and message of each story. □ Derive how each story is related to the other stories. □ Derive an overall meaning for the text.	□ *Fig Pudding* □ *The View from Saturday* □ *Witch on Fourth Street*

Figure 14-10. *Special Types of Fiction (cont.)*

easy. The perfect mystery is one that has twists and surprises. When children are first being introduced to this kind of text, the mystery must be very simple and obvious. They notice whether the time is present, historical, or futuristic.

ADVENTURE STORIES

All of us enjoy a fast-paced story with lots of action. Readers of adventure stories focus on a main character who performs heroic deeds. The character faces challenges or engages in a quest. Readers may recognize the writer's ability to create an engaging hero and create suspense.

SURVIVAL STORIES

There is something compelling about a story of survival; news stories on television feature them almost daily. Survival can involve triumphing against nature, society's ills (poverty, crime), human evil (war, psychological or physical abuse), or mental or physical illness. Readers of survival stories identify with the main character, evaluate the odds against him, and predict possibilities for survival based on the person's abilities. Readers check the plot against their own knowledge of circumstances.

ANIMAL REALISM

Writing interesting stories about real animals is quite a challenge. Writers must depict a realistic animal, not sliding into personification but staying with real traits, yet create empathy in the reader's mind. Readers of animal realism are required to look at the world from the perspective of a real animal and to access background information based on scientific knowledge.

ANIMAL FANTASY

Writers of animal fantasy may make their characters totally human except in physical aspects, but most choose to combine human and animal characteristics. For example, the animals in *Mrs. Frisby and the Rats of NIMH* (O'Brien) talk, feel fear, are brave, and have true emotions yet have ratlike characteristics. The mice in the Redwall series (Jacques) are heroic characters. Readers of animal fantasy are required to understand this mix of traits, to enjoy the animal-like characteristics, and to detect the essentially human characteristics as well as the overall message of the text. Readers of high fantasy notice its focus on the conflict between good and evil.

SPORTS STORIES

Sports stories have become so popular that they are a type of literature. Readers of sports stories bring everything they know about that sport to the reading of the text; in the process they learn more about reading. They also need to understand the nature of the sport and, more globally, the competitive spirit (why it is important to make an extra effort to win).

FORMULA FICTION AND SERIES BOOKS

Some types of books are very formulaic. You can almost always predict the kinds of characters, the progression of the plot, and the ending. Adult examples are romance novels and gothic romance novels. A gothic novel has a heroine, a large mysterious house, and a somewhat frightening but handsome and sexy "master." The heroine survives many trials and is frightened by the hero but also (often against her will) falls in love with him. They have many romantic encounters, and there are episodes of danger in which the hero saves the heroine and vice versa. The novel ends with the two main characters solving whatever problem exists and being together romantically. You would recognize this type of text anywhere; in fact, they are grouped together in bookstores.

There are parallels in formulaic books for children. The classic example is the Nancy Drew series, which debuted in the 1940s and is still going strong today. (The "author," Carolyn Keene, is a pseudonym for a number of individuals who actually wrote the books.) Nancy, the heroine, with her chums Bess and George, solves mysteries. She has a boyfriend, Ned Nickerson, but he is a secondary character. Formulaic writing appears in many other series books for children: the Baby-Sitters Club, the Hardy Boys, the Cam Jansen series—the list is long.

We distinguish between books that offer a number of sequels over time and formulaic series, although both make similar demands of readers. Betsy Byars's Beezus and Ramona series follows a family as the children get older. The same is true of the Little House series by Laura Ingalls Wilder and Betsy–Tacy series by Maud Hart Lovelace. Another well-loved example is the Earthsea series by Ursula K. Le Guin. These books were written by authors who wanted to develop characters over several years of their lives. The Little House and Betsy-Tacy series were based on the writers' own childhood memories. Series books vary in quality, but all require that readers develop a set of understandings about the characters over time.

Formula fiction and series books are highly supportive in that after reading one or two of them, readers feel a kind of security. Before beginning they know what to expect. They know the types of characters or the actual characters; they know the likely settings and circumstances; they know how the plot will develop and how it is likely to end. It is like going to a well-loved and familiar place. Almost all voracious readers have gobbled up a large number of formulaic and series books.

SHORT STORY COLLECTIONS

Some unusual and highly interesting texts combine the format of the short story with the exposition of a longer text. These texts present a series of short stories that could stand alone yet are combined in a volume with other stories that are integrally linked by characters, setting, and theme.

For example, all the stories might be about people who live in the same place. The classic example for adults is Edgar Lee Masters's *Spoon River Anthology,* poems about people in a small town. *The Stories Julian Tells* (Cameron) is a wonderful example of the genre for second or third graders. Each story or chapter could stand alone but is related to all the other stories about the family. Julian and his brother Huey are always getting into trouble, but the problem is always resolved. *Seedfolks* (Fleischman) is a more sophisticated example. Each chapter is a different story told by a different character. The voice, vocabulary, attitude, perspective, and even the grammar change from chapter to chapter. Yet the stories are woven together, and the reader looks for connections among the characters who are telling the stories. They also build toward the development of an overall plot. To understand this type of fiction, readers draw meaning from the individual stories, derive how they are related, and come up with an overall message.

POETRY

No classroom library is complete without a rich collection of poetry. Poetry is a vital part of interactive read-aloud, and poetry workshop is an important component of the language and literacy framework. Students enjoy making their own personal poetry anthologies, reading and evaluating many poems as they make their selections. So it is important for us as teachers to consider the special demands of poetic texts (see Figure 14-11).

As with other kinds of texts, readers engage in thinking *within, beyond,* and *about* the text. Poetry is a genre that lends itself to analytical thinking, but we should be cautious about asking children to take that stance too quickly.

If they are going to learn to love poetry, they need to feel it and enjoy its language first. Many of us remember learning to hate poetry or a particular poem because of endless analyses in English class.

THINKING WITHIN THE POEM

For people who read poetry for pleasure, the important thing is to enjoy the language and the images and emotions that these words evoke. Many people read poems again and again, often aloud, because of the feelings they generate. They enjoy the response itself.

The same is true for students. Young children respond to rhymes, chants, and songs (not properly called poetry according to the scholars, but an important foundation for appreciating poetry). They love to hear their favorites over and over; they participate. The wonder of childhood is wrapped up in a verse like this:

Twinkle, twinkle, little star,
How I wonder what you are!
Up above the world so high,
Like a diamond in the sky.
Twinkle, twinkle, little star,
How I wonder what you are!

Children enjoy the rhyme and rhythm; it can be sung or chanted. They understand the basic question expressed in the poem.

The Specific Demands of Poetry

READERS THINK WITHIN THE TEXT TO:	□ Gather important information and language. □ Solve unusual or figurative language. □ Use punctuation and text layout.
READERS THINK BEYOND THE TEXT TO:	□ Infer the deeper meaning of the poem. □ Create sensory images in response to the language. □ Make connections between the ideas in the poem and their own lives. □ Generate feelings and emotions in response to the poem.
READERS THINK ABOUT THE TEXT TO:	□ Appreciate aspects of the poem like rhythm and rhyme when appropriate. □ Notice the poet's use of language to create sensory images. □ Notice how the poet uses language to create emotion. □ Infer the poet's feelings and emotions. □ Evaluate the quality of the poem. □ Consider alternative interpretations of the poem.

Figure 14-11. *The Specific Demands of Poetry*

THINKING BEYOND THE POEM

At some time in your life, you may have said something like, "That poem expresses just what I feel about moonlight on water" or some other natural phenomenon. Poetry is most meaningful when it helps us have insights into our own feelings and lives. Poetry contains happiness, affection, sorrow, anger, and beauty, packed into very concise language. Poetry requires that readers bring their thinking to the text. The true meaning of the poem can be called a "transaction" between the reader and the poem (Rosenblatt).

Even young children bring their thinking to poetry. For example, consider this poem, "Who Has Seen the Wind?" by Christina Rossetti:

> Who has seen the wind?
> Neither I nor you:
> But when the leaves hang trembling
> The wind is passing through.
>
> Who has seen the wind?
> Neither you nor I:
> But when the trees bow down their heads
> The wind is passing by.

These words evoke sensory images. Readers (listeners) access their own memories of how trees look. They also need to interpret the poet's use of figurative language in personifying the trees in the second stanza.

Children also enjoy puzzling out riddles. The following poem requires that readers create images in response to the words but also interpret the words beyond their literal meaning:

> I'm a frozen icicle
> Hanging by your door.
> When it's cold outside,
> I grow even more.
> When it's warm outside,
> You'll find me on the floor!

To truly understand this poem, readers have to bring some background knowledge about freezing and melting water to the reading.

THINKING ABOUT THE POEM

Even young children can think analytically about a poem. "Twinkle, Twinkle, Little Star" does not require a great deal of analysis, but children can be aware that the poem made them remember how stars look or prompted them to think about what a star is made of. It is not appropriate to have

young children be more analytical than saying how a poem makes them feel, what they like about it, or what they wonder about, but some discussions may yield some surprising answers.

Older readers of poetry can certainly select language from poems that they find especially meaningful or beautiful. In "Who Has Seen the Wind?" readers can identify with the words that evoke sensory images and discuss the comparisons within the poem. When students have read or listened to a great many poems, they can identify indications of quality in poetry and will also enjoy discussing alternative interpretations of a poem.

VALUES OF FICTION AND POETRY

We cannot leave a discussion of fiction and poetry without mentioning the value of these genres. Often poetry does not occupy a major place in the curriculum, although its presence is growing; however, many conversations today center around the possible "overuse" of fiction to the exclusion of nonfiction in elementary schools. It is interesting that this discussion is taking place right at the time when many appealing works of nonfiction (as opposed to textbooks) are available, and we certainly support the use of nonfiction, as noted in the previous chapter.

But it is imprudent to forget that young children thrive on stories and enter joyfully into the world of poetry. The text structure of narrative is very available to them; that's where they learn to love reading. Good experiences with fiction and poetry can greatly strengthen readers' systems of strategies and can lay a foundation for the act of *reading for pleasure*. While reading for pleasure, individuals actually acquire a good deal of content knowledge, although they must be on guard to verify its accuracy. But also in reading for pleasure, people find new ideas to think about and countless hours of escape into imagined worlds.

SUGGESTIONS FOR PROFESSIONAL DEVELOPMENT

EXAMINING FICTION TEXTS

1 Have a discussion with a group of peers in which you share preferences for types of fiction. Instead of sticking with the traditional genre designations, suggest some very specific characteristics (strong women characters, methodical and clever detectives, for example). Talk over what appeals to individuals about these types of texts.

2 Look at an array of familiar fiction texts for children (K–8). Discuss what might appeal or be off-putting to the readers in your classrooms.

3 Select one work of realism and one of fantasy that everyone will read and discuss.

4 Discuss these texts and list the demands each makes on the reader. (You may want to use the form, Analyzing Text Factors, in Figure 14-12 and on the DVD that accompanies this book.)

5 Remember that you would not conduct such a detailed analysis for every book you use in guided reading. What you want to do is build the capacity to analyze texts mentally as you plan introductions.

6 Have participants practice giving a quick oral analysis of several texts.

ANALYSIS OF _____ (LEVEL ____)	
TEXT FACTOR	**ANALYSIS**
Genre	
Text Structure	
Content	
Themes and Ideas	
Language and Literary Features	
Sentence Complexity	
Vocabulary	
Words	
Illustrations	
Book and Print Features	
When introducing this text in guided reading, keep this in mind:	

Figure 14-12. *Form for Analyzing Text Factors*

TEACHING

The previous sections of this book lay the foundation for designing and implementing effective instruction. This section, the largest, focuses on practical aspects of teaching. We believe it offers rich and practical information for helping every child become a lifelong reader.

As we considered the challenge of teaching for comprehending and fluency, we knew that we could not confine instruction to one context. Good minilessons have a role; so does conferring with individuals. Small-group instruction in the form of guided reading is essential for helping students move forward in developing a reading process; shared and performed reading support both comprehension and fluency. Interactive read-aloud is a context within which students are freed from decoding words, but in every other way they are processing and comprehending texts. Book clubs are essential to helping readers build a deep understanding of texts. Writing about reading in many instructional contexts helps readers expand their thinking.

Chapter 15 introduces the section by exploring interactive read-aloud. We examine the concept of intentional conversation as a way of teaching children to think and talk about texts. The next three chapters also focus on this powerful instructional context. In Chapter 16 we present ideas for creating a literate culture through shared talk about texts. In Chapter 17 we provide guidelines for planning for interactive read-aloud across the grades and present the idea that by working together teachers can create a very powerful series of experiences to support comprehending. Chapter 18 focuses on moving from interactive read-aloud to literature study followed by a chapter on deepening the conversation, and Chapter 20 provides some very specific guidelines for getting started with book clubs, a very productive setting for helping students think and talk about texts.

Shared and performed reading is an important component of instruction throughout the grades. Chapter 21 contains descriptions of many kinds of shared and performed reading—for example, readers' theater and choral reading. Shared and performed reading is highly engaging for students; at the same time, it prompts them to think deeply about the meaning of the texts they are reading together.

Reading is a community activity in the classroom, but ultimately it is an individual experience. Students read independently every day. Chapters 22 and 23 focus on the reading workshop, which includes providing powerful minilessons to support thinking about texts as well as guiding independent reading through conferring and group share.

As important as reading aloud, shared reading, and independent reading are, most students need very specific instruction to become highly proficient readers. Small-group instruction can help all readers expand their reading powers. Three chapters, beginning with Chapter 24, provide some in-depth, practical informational about the use of guided reading to support comprehension and fluency. In Chapter 25 you will find information about the use of guided reading of fiction texts; Chapter 26 focuses on guided reading of nonfiction texts.

The final five chapters of this book move back to a description of teaching that crosses instructional contexts. Chapters 27 and 28 present a large number of ideas for writing about reading. These genres and forms for writing about reading, which are defined and described in the context of examples, may be used in connection with any of the approaches discussed in this book. Chapter 29 examines the very important adjustments we must make to meet the needs of English language learners. These days, we are fortunate to have a highly diverse population of students; in meeting the challenge of teaching them, we simultaneously develop skills that enable us to serve all students better. This chapter provides specific guidelines that may be applied across instructional contexts.

The last two chapters focus on two important elements of reading instruction. We teach for fluency and vocabulary learning in all instructional contexts, but we have pulled out these two areas for specific discussion because they are so important. Chapter 30 focuses on teaching for reading fluency; Chapter 31 provides practical suggestions for expanding vocabulary learning. We conclude the book with our thoughts on teaching for comprehending and fluency throughout the day.

Engaging Readers in Thinking and Talking About Texts Through Interactive Read-Aloud

A well-chosen book will leave students with a residue of learning about their world and the wider world and also a deeper conviction that reading is a manageable and worthwhile activity.

—Margaret Mooney

Carol is reading *Bat Loves the Night* (Davies) aloud to her class:

> Out!
> Out under the broken tile
> into the nighttime garden.
> Over bushes, under trees,
> between fence posts,
> through the tangled hedge
> she swoops untouched.
> Bat is at home in the darkness
> as a fish is in water.
> She doesn't need to see—
> she can hear where she is going. (pp. 11–12)

She pauses and invites the thinking of her students:

> Mrs. K.: I wonder what that means, "she can hear where she is going." What do you think?
>
> Rory: Her ears tell her where to go.
>
> Sara: She can hear things that tell her where to go. She makes screams.
>
> David: It's like being a fish, and she kind of swims around in the dark.
>
> Mrs. K.: Oh, you noticed the writer said she was as "at home in the darkness as a fish is in the water." At the bottom of this page the writer tells something about bats—this might help us think more about the bat's hearing. "Bats can see. But in the dark, good ears are more useful than eyes." So how are you thinking her ears are useful to her?

As Carol reads on, the students learn that bats use echoes to guide them. Though her students are getting information from this factual text, they are gaining much more. They also encounter powerful language :

> Gliding and fluttering
> back and forth,
> she shouts her torch of
> sound among the trees,
> listening for her supper. (p. 15)

Afterward, the students talk about the phrase "listening for her supper," a new way of expressing meaning. They discuss how the bat's high-pitched squeals give her a "sound picture" of leaves, twigs, and even the smallest insects so she can hunt and eat them. But the phrase "listening for her supper" is a "cool" way of describing the bat, as opposed to "hunting for her supper" or "looking for her supper." The children agree that the writer gives the reader information about bats in an interesting way. They even talk about a great new word, *echolocation*, which is easy to understand when you take it apart.

Reading aloud to students is not a luxury but a necessity. We consider reading aloud to be an essential foundation of a good language and literacy program. Reading aloud supports learning in every other area. It is a way of nourishing the intellect of your students, expanding background, vocabulary, and language, developing an appreciation for inquiry, and creating a literary community in your classroom.

If students hear one book read aloud each day over the elementary and middle school years (kindergarten through grade eight), they would experience over 1,600 books— 3,200 if the teacher reads two books a day. In upper elementary and middle school, the "book" might be a section of a longer text or chapter book; however, you will also want to use many picture books appropriate for older readers. If you think about it, a picture book is a short story with exquisite art to add to the meaning. You can select a wide variety of genres in picture book format at all grade levels.

Clay (2004) emphasizes the contribution of reading aloud to children's language development:

> Recognize the importance of reading aloud to children. Let children hear text structures that expose them to language beyond their control. Reading aloud to children of any age will sketch for them a landscape of features into which their own language usage may expand.

215

Hearing a stretch of new language in a rereading or a different context will give access to new features of text language. Repeating it in a drama or a refrain might sow seeds that lead to an alternative rule emerging in a child's grammar. (Clay p. 10)

When students have the opportunity to hear a variety of written language read aloud, it becomes accessible to them, and this access to language is important for students of all ages. Teachers often struggle to find the time to read aloud and sometimes even have difficulty including it in the recognized and approved curriculum, but reading aloud has everything to do with comprehending text and building the vocabulary, language, and fluency of readers.

WHAT IS INTERACTIVE READ-ALOUD?

By *interactive read-aloud* we mean that the teacher reads aloud to students; but both the teacher and the students think about, talk about, and respond to the text (see Figure 15-1). Both the reader (in this case, the teacher) and the listeners are *active*. The teacher is reading the words aloud, but in every other way the students are processing the language, ideas, and meaning of the text. Occasionally, the teacher stops briefly to demonstrate text talk or invite interaction. These pauses are intentional and planned to invite students to join in the thinking and the talking about the text. There is no way to predict what students will say, of course, but that is part of the appeal of this interactive way of working with texts. The conversation is grounded in the shared text.

THE VALUE OF INTERACTIVE READ-ALOUD

A strong argument can be made for using interactive read-aloud daily. For years, advocates of reading aloud have pointed out that it helps children appreciate and enjoy literature. That is certainly true, *and enjoyment is the first goal of interactive read-aloud,* but there are many more benefits.

You will find that every moment spent on interactive read-alouds has a big payoff in other learning contexts. The texts you read to students create shared text resources that contribute to:

- Literature study or book clubs.
- Minilessons on reading and writing.
- Reading and writing conferences.
- Independent reading and writing.
- Guided reading.

The read-aloud levels the playing field, ensuring that readers in the classroom experience rich, interesting texts that are age and grade appropriate, regardless of their independent or instructional reading level. All students can think and talk about the text even if they can't read it for themselves.

CONTRIBUTIONS TO OTHER INSTRUCTIONAL CONTEXTS

In Figure 15-2 we describe in greater detail the important relationships between interactive read-aloud and other literacy contexts. The left-hand column lists the specific "bridges" through which interactive read-aloud provides strong support for your language and literacy teaching.

SUPPORTING THINKING—WITHIN, BEYOND, AND ABOUT TEXTS

Interactive read-aloud is a key context for helping your students develop ways of thinking about texts. The fact that you are doing the reading frees their attention from processing the print to think about what is happening in the text and what it means as well as how the writer communicates the information.

Figure 15-1. *An Example of Interactive Read-Aloud*

Interactive Read-Aloud as a Support for Instruction

INTERACTIVE READ-ALOUD:	INSTRUCTIONAL CONTEXT IT SUPPORTS
□ Provides a context for learning how to talk about texts with others. □ Provides a large amount of practice in talking about texts with others. □ Creates a shared language for talking about texts. □ Builds up a shared repertoire of genres, writers, and specific texts that can be referred to in discussion.	**Literature Study-Book Clubs (small group)**
□ Serves as a source of examples when talking about texts. □ Provides examples for demonstrating any strategic actions or skill related to reading. □ Provides examples for literary analysis, including text structure and language. □ Introduces readers to different genres so that they can notice their characteristics.	**Reading Minilessons (whole group)**
□ Introduces readers to authors or series they might like. □ Provides a model of fluent, phrased reading. □ Introduces readers to new genres from which they can select books. □ Introduces a book that children may want to read again independently.	**Independent Reading (individual)**
□ Builds a shared group of texts that readers can use to make connections. □ Provides shared examples to which new texts can be compared. □ Provides examples of different genres and text structures. □ Builds vocabulary that can be used in reading other texts.	**Guided Reading (small group)**
□ Provides mentor texts that can be used as examples of craft. □ Provides models for different kinds of writing—narrative, expository, poetic, for example. □ Provides numerous examples of texts in the same genre.	**Writing Minilessons (whole group)**
□ Builds a group of shared examples that students can access to help them use writing strategies. □ Expands students' use of interesting vocabulary by providing many examples. □ Provides excellent texts for use by writers to learn from other writers.	**Independent Writing (individual)**

Figure 15-2. *Interactive Read-Aloud as a Support for Instruction*

Thinking within the text. If you carefully select texts with concepts and vocabulary that are within your particular students' ability to understand, they will be able to grasp the literal meaning of the text and gather information as they listen. Freed from the challenge of processing the print, they can concentrate on the language and the meaning. Through discussion you can help them identify important information to remember in summary form. Listening comprehension is built through daily experiences in hearing texts read aloud.

Thinking beyond the text. Listening to and understanding a text together makes it easier to engage in inferential thinking. Interactive read-aloud provides numerous opportunities for listeners to think about what the writer has implied but not explicitly stated. They can get involved in characters' lives, question their motivations, and develop empathy for their struggles. You can demonstrate a wide range of thinking—personal connections, connections to other texts, using background information, noticing new information, and adjusting your views. You can revisit sec-

[handwritten margin note: Must be Interactive]

217

tions of the text that offer evidence to support thinking.

A group listening to *A Single Shard* (Park), for example, can take on the perspective of an orphan in twelfth-century Korea, stretching their thinking to understand what it means not to have food every day. Children listening to *Sitti's Secrets* (Shihab Nye) can imagine how a girl listens to the news and worries about her beloved grandmother in Palestine.

Listening to informational texts like *The Tiniest Giants: Discovering Dinosaur Eggs* (Dingus and Chiappe) can make listeners look at birds in an entirely new way or imagine the thrill of discovering tiny dinosaurs in fossilized eggs. Children listening to *Bat Loves the Night* (Davies) will add information about bats to what they already know but will also have images of how bats behave in their environment.

Thinking about the text. Interactive read-aloud provides wonderful opportunities for helping your students consider aspects of the writer's craft and engage in analytical and critical thinking. You can demonstrate thinking about the text through your own talk and revisit sections of the text to provide examples. For example, listeners can consider how the writer uses details to help readers know about *Bigmama's* (Crews). They, too, can provide examples from the text by revisiting sections: they can notice how on the first page the writer signals that the story took place in the past and move to the last page, which shows the grown-up writer in the city; they can speculate as to why the writer/illustrator included the sign "Colored" in the train car but didn't discuss it in the text.

Interactive read-aloud provides a context in which every student in your class can enjoy age-appropriate material and engage in the kinds of thinking that effective readers do related to written texts. Reading aloud makes it possible, but the talk that surrounds the text provides the support students need to stretch their thinking.

VALUES TO STUDENTS

Besides forming a foundation for your instruction, interactive read-aloud is very valuable to your students as individuals. Hearing texts read aloud makes strong contributions to their reading abilities, particularly comprehension, as well as strengthens their use of oral and written language and vocabulary (see Figures 15-3 and 15-4).

Interactive read-aloud provides consistent, strong demonstrations of how reading should sound, so that students can develop a concept of phrased, fluent reading. In addition, through hearing written texts read aloud, students internalize the complex sentence structures in written language and learn new vocabulary, which benefits reading, writing, and oral language.

Hearing written texts read aloud daily provides many opportunities for students to think inferentially, making connections between their own lives and what they read in books, and to become familiar with different genres. This kind of thinking is exactly what they need to do when they read independently. They also have opportunities to notice how writers craft texts, which contributes both to reading and writing.

Reading aloud does more than promote language and literacy. When you read to a group over time, every text makes it possible for them to share ideas and get to know other people and places in the context of a pleasurable experience. The ideas and images readers meet in texts shape their lives and values. Daily read-alouds create shared meanings among a group and contribute to a sense of community. It is important for every child to experience being a member of such a group. Through texts, the teacher and students get to know one another in a deeper way. In addition, students will read inspiring stories in both fiction and nonfiction, ones on which they can model their own actions.

TEACHER AND STUDENT ROLES IN INTERACTIVE READ-ALOUD

It might seem that the teacher is reading and the students are listening, but both have active roles before, during, and after the reading of the selected text (see Figure 15-5).

Before reading. You select and analyze the text and plan for a few intentional interactions. Students may or may not take part in the selection, but they are active prior to the beginning of the session if they have been taught what to expect of texts and know they will have a role in thinking and talking about them.

During reading. You provide a few opening remarks that engage students' attention and prompt their thinking. Opening remarks sometimes (but not always) focus on the

Interactive Read-Aloud—Benefits to Readers

Interactive read-aloud contributes to the development of students' reading comprehension and fluency.

CONTRIBUTION	SPECIFIC BENEFITS	STRATEGIC ACTIONS—THINKING WITHIN A TEXT
Provides a demonstration or model of phrased, fluent reading	▫ Provides a daily demonstration of how reading aloud should "sound." ▫ Gives children the opportunity to learn the relationship between text meaning and the reader's interpretation through voice, pausing, phrasing, stress, rate, volume, rhythm, and intonation.	*Maintaining fluency*
Expands knowledge and control of written language structures	▫ Exposes children to structures that are not usually found in oral language. ▫ Helps children acquire and internalize new ways of talking and writing.	*Maintaining fluency*
Expands speaking and reading vocabulary	▫ Provides access to words that may not usually be found in children's speaking vocabulary. ▫ Presents new words in a meaningful context—through use. ▫ Often shows children new meanings for words they already know.	*Solving words*
Builds a repertoire of known texts that can be accessed	▫ Provides a rich source of texts in different genres, formats, and writing styles that readers will have opportunities to use in many ways.	*Summarizing*

CONTRIBUTION	SPECIFIC BENEFITS	STRATEGIC ACTIONS—THINKING BEYOND A TEXT
Expands content knowledge	▫ Builds concepts to increase the knowledge children can bring to their own reading. ▫ Promotes discussion of interesting new content to increase students' understanding.	*Synthesizing*
Enables readers to make their own connections to texts	▫ Presents situations—human problems, content—that can be connected to life experiences, background knowledge, and other texts.	*Connecting*
Enables readers to think inferentially about all aspects of texts	▫ Presents written texts that must be interpreted for true understanding.	*Inferring*

CONTRIBUTION	SPECIFIC BENEFITS	STRATEGIC ACTIONS—THINKING ABOUT A TEXT
Expands children's literary knowledge	▫ Exposes children to different genres, authors, illustrators. ▫ Helps students understand how to evaluate the quality and accuracy of a text.	*Analyzing/critiquing*
Develops understanding of the elements of literature	▫ Provides many examples of literature so that students can explore plot, setting, character development, themes, accuracy, and authenticity.	*Analyzing*
Broadens understanding of different genres	▫ Helps children understand how fiction and nonfiction texts are structured. ▫ Provides an opportunity to experience many examples of different genres.	*Analyzing*

Figure 15-3. *Interactive Read-Aloud—Benefits to Readers*

Interactive Read-Aloud—Contributions Beyond Reading

CONTRIBUTION	SPECIFIC BENEFITS
Interactive read-aloud contributes to students' knowledge and use of oral language.	
Expands speaking and listening vocabulary	▫ Offers many opportunities to hear new words in meaningful literary contexts. ▫ Offers opportunities to use new words in discussion.
Expands knowledge of conventional grammar	▫ Provides many models of complex, standardized sentence structures.
Interactive read-aloud contributes to students' writing abilities.	
Expands writing vocabulary	▫ Provides meaningful experiences for learning new and interesting words that students can use in writing.
Expands knowledge of written genres	▫ Provides many examples of the structure and characteristics of genres so that students can more easily learn to write them.
Expands writers' craft	▫ Provides high-quality examples of writing that students can "borrow" as they learn more about the writers' craft.
Interactive read-aloud contributes to students' social values and ability to be a member of a community.	
Helps students develop social values through encountering inspiring examples	▫ Provides examples of achievement, service, overcoming hardship, working with others, sacrifice, love, and other inspiring human traits that students can incorporate into their thinking about life.
Creates shared meaning that contributes to the sense of community in the classroom	▫ Provides a way for students to share meaning with others and to experience a sense of community (including what it means to be a responsible citizen).
Helps students and the teacher get to know one another	▫ Provides opportunities for developing relationships by discussing personal experiences, interpretations, and opinions related to the meaning in texts.

Figure 15-4. *Interactive Read-Aloud—Contributions Beyond Reading*

cover, end pages, dedication, book jacket, author information, or publication date. You read the text in a clear voice with appropriate phrasing, stopping occasionally to make or invite comment, demonstrate ways of thinking about the text, or pose genuine questions. Students share comments with the whole group, in twos, threes, or fours. These brief discussions help students stay alert, think about the text, and share their thinking with others. They know that they are expected to listen respectfully to and build on the comments of other class members (not just the teacher).

After reading. You facilitate student talk, making sure that the group has an opportunity not only to make personal connections and share opinions but also to discuss the overall meaning of the text. You and the students may revisit sections of the text that support their interpretations. After discussing the significance of the themes, you may want to ask students to reexamine the text to learn more about the writer's craft or to think critically about it.

THE STRUCTURE OF INTERACTIVE READ-ALOUD

Interactive read-aloud requires highly intentional teaching. Even though it takes up a relatively short segment of the school day, it has a definite structure (see Figure 15-6). Getting the most from an interactive read-aloud means that it must be:

▫ Planned, with books selected and often sequenced for particular purposes.

▫ Prepared for, with some learning opportunities identified before reading but leaving room for surprises and spontaneous discussion.

▫ Active, eliciting response from students.

▫ Connected across instructional contexts.

Roles in Interactive Read-Aloud

	TEACHER'S ROLE	STUDENTS' ROLE
Before the Reading	▫ Knows the students' backgrounds, strengths, and interests. ▫ Selects a wonderful book, article, or poem or invites the students to make a selection from several possibilities. ▫ Reads the text, thinking about phrasing and expression. ▫ Analyzes the text for points of inquiry and notes or marks a few places to remember. ▫ Establishes a physical environment that ensures all students can see and hear.	▫ May select a text from a group suggested by the teacher. ▫ Anticipate thinking and talking about a text. ▫ Activate background knowledge (content and literary) in anticipation of hearing a text.
During the Reading	▫ May address the cover, end pages, dedication, book jacket, author information, or publication date. ▫ Reads the text with appropriate phrasing, intonation, and expression. ▫ Expands children's understanding by facilitating new and varied interpretations. ▫ Engages in a few brief, genuine conversations about the text or illustrations. ▫ Activates students' thinking and elicits their comments. ▫ Stops occasionally to define or highlight unusual or difficult words. ▫ Builds on children's comments, predictions, questions, or wonderings. ▫ Poses genuine questions and makes comments and predictions. ▫ Relates the text to other texts. ▫ Comments on language or vocabulary as appropriate without interrupting the reading too much. ▫ Draws attention to the writer's craft.	▫ Listen intently. ▫ Actively think about the text. ▫ Talk about thinking in twos, threes, fours, or with the whole group. ▫ Respect one another's ideas. ▫ Pose questions or wonderings. ▫ Make comments and build on the comments of others. ▫ React to the content in the text. ▫ Connect the text to their own life experiences or to those of people they know. ▫ Notice language or vocabulary. ▫ Relate the text to other texts. ▫ Notice and comment on the writer's craft.
After the Reading	▫ Facilitates student talk. ▫ Invites discussion of the overall meaning of the text. ▫ Reflects on the writer's craft. ▫ Links the text to other texts. ▫ May reread a section or the ending. ▫ Evaluates the quality of thinking around the text. ▫ List books read on a large chart to create a reminder of shared experiences.	▫ Respond to the meaning of the whole text. ▫ Look for deeper meaning or themes. ▫ Reflect on the writer's craft. ▫ Link the text to other texts. ▫ Suggest further texts to read. ▫ Sketch or write responses to the text.

Figure 15-5. *Roles in Interactive Read-Aloud*

Structure of Interactive Read-Aloud

Selection and Preparation

Opening

Reading Aloud
□ Embedded Teaching
□ Text Talk

Discussion and Self-Evaluation

Record of Reading

Written or Artistic Response (Optional)

Figure 15-6. *Structure of Interactive Read-Aloud*

In Figure 15-7 we describe part of an interactive read-aloud session. Ms. S., the teacher, selected *Pulling the Lion's Tail*, by Jane Kurtz, to read to her class. The book is a retelling of the Ethiopian folktale *The Lion's Whiskers*, which is about a stepmother who wins her resentful stepson's love by taming a lion and taking three whiskers from his tail. The central character is Almaz, a girl who (after her mother's death) persistently attempts to reach out to her father's new wife. The new wife, who is also lonely, appears to reject all the young girl's attempts to interact, and so the child feels left out but gets advice from her grandfather.

SELECTION OF A TEXT

Sometimes teachers are tempted simply to pick up a handy book and read it, and it is certainly true that students can enjoy and benefit from any wonderful book. But if you want to get the most instructional power from interactive read-aloud, it is important to plan for teaching in a more precise way. Some guidelines are provided in Figure 15-8.

Texts students will enjoy. Select books that you love and it's likely that your students will love them as well. The text should first of all be one that will engage the listeners; it is the job of the reader to make that happen. In general, you want to select high-quality texts, but there are many other considerations. The first is whether the text will be appropriate for your students. Will they be able to grasp the ideas and concepts? Will the text help them think deeply about their own lives and the lives of others?

Texts that connect to the curriculum. Select books to read aloud for purposes that vary according to the curriculum, the type of texts, and your own goals for your particular group of students. Consider linking some texts to the topics that your students are studying in social studies, health, mathematics, or science. Often, there will be excellent read-aloud choices that connect to those topics.

You will want to select texts that can be used to teach writing. Think about texts that can become mentor texts, that you can use in minilessons to help your students learn how to write from wonderful writers. You will also want to select texts to use as examples in reading minilessons about comprehending.

You don't want all read-aloud texts that can be linked to the curriculum content, of course, because you would sacrifice variety and miss books that students really should experience. When good connections are possible, it is beneficial to learning.

Texts that highlight language. Some texts are specifically directed toward helping children enjoy, use, and think about language. *Chicka Chicka Boom Boom,* by Bill Martin, has engaging rhythm and rhyme as it plays with the alphabet. Older students will like the humorous poetry in *Sometimes I Wonder If Poodles Like Noodles* (Numeroff). *The Absolutely Awful Alphabet* (Gerstein) uses word play and alliteration to describe terrible ideas for every letter: You'll find it hard to pause for breath in this one long, connected sentence!

Books like these do not lead to deep discussions of themes—their whole purpose is to enjoy the sounds of language and expand vocabulary, but students will notice interesting words and the humorous ways in which they are combined. Books like *My Momma Likes to Say* or *My Teacher Likes to Say* (Brennan-Nelson) explore English idioms through text and illustrations but also provide background on the origin of sayings like "Don't let the bed bugs bite!" Such books are excellent links to word study minilessons and can also enrich students' writing. Texts that offer interesting language contribute to students' knowledge of syntax and help them to expand the complexity of the sentences they say and write. This benefit is especially important for English-language learners.

Poetic texts. Students of all ages will enjoy hearing poetry read aloud. There are many excellent books of poetry for children—*Seeing the Blue Between*, by Paul B.

EXCERPT FROM THE INTERACTIVE READ-ALOUD OF
Pulling the Lion's Tail

Ms. S.: This story is called *Pulling the Lion's Tail.* It is written by Jane Kurtz and illustrated by Floyd Cooper.

TANISHA: We read another book by Jane Kurtz, *Far Away Home.*

Ms. S.: Yes, we're going to be reading books by Jane Kurtz this week to get to know her stories and to get to know her as a writer. This is called an *author study.* You read many books by the same author, and you start to ask questions such as, "Are there things that are similar in these stories. Are there patterns you notice about this writer and her stories?" [BEGINS READING, AFTER REPEATING THE TITLE] *"In the high mountains of Ethiopia, there lived a girl named Almaz. . . ."*

Ms. S. stops to invite children to examine the phrase "every night when the sun stooped low." Several children offer that it must be in the evening because the sun was low.

Ms. S.: Why do you think Almaz took off her rings and her necklace and had her hair cut short?

JOSHUA: Maybe because they found the necklace belonged to her mom.

DIANA: Because she died.

Ms. S.: Because her mother died?

DIANA: Yes.

Ms. S.: Why would she do that? What would that show?

DIANA: I thought she took off her rings and her necklaces because she was going to bed.

Ms. S.: But why would she cut her hair short? It says that the mourners came. What does that mean?

JOSHUA: Someone has died.

Ms. S.: What are some things people do here to show that they are mourning?

LEA: Have a funeral.

Ms. S.: Sometimes they wear black. Well, this takes place in Ethiopia, so maybe this is how she shows that she is mourning her mother, thinking about her mother who has died.

Reading on, the children learn that Almaz's father has said that he is going to get a new wife. Ms. S. asks them to turn and talk about what they think Almaz might be thinking about. She reads on and the listeners learn that Almaz was happy because she would have a new mother.

Ms. S.: How many of you thought that she would be sad? [SEVERAL CHILDREN RAISE THEIR HAND.] You made predictions, didn't you? But sometimes as you read, you find information that tells you whether your predictions are right or wrong.

Ms. S. reads on, stopping briefly to emphasize the descriptions of the new mother, who always keeps her eyes down.

TONY: She's nervous.

RAINBOW: She might be shy.

ALIA: She's not used to Almaz's family yet.

Ms. S. invites children to notice the writer's way of showing the passing of time by considering the phrase "now it is the rainy season." She also helps them compare the bright outside with the cool, dark interior of the hut. Almaz's grandfather tells her that he will tell her the secret of winning her new mother's love if she will bring him three hairs from the tail of a lion. The children turn and talk again about why he might be asking her to do that. The children continue to use what they know to predict the story events.

Figure 15-7. *Excerpt from the Interactive Read-Aloud of* Pulling the Lion's Tail

Janeczko, or *Beneath the Blue Umbrella*, by Jack Prelutsky, for example. For middle school students you can read several poems and discuss them during an interactive read-aloud session. You can also pair a poem with another text you are reading. Poems like those in Joyce Carol Thomas's *Brown Honey in Broomwheat Tea* are simple but meaningful. You will want to read the poem several times so students can take away more of the meaning each time as they listen.

Sometimes poems are arranged in sequence to tell stories. *Some of the Days of Everett Anderson*, by Lucille Clifton, for example, will appeal to primary age children. A serious example for older students is Hope Anita Smith's *The Way a Door Closes*, a series of poems that tell of a thirteen-year-old's struggle to accept that his father has left home.

Texts to connect to children's lives. It is always important to read books that students can connect to their own lives. We all like to read about problems that are familiar to us. For elementary and middle school students, that might include making friends, moving, playing sports, or fulfilling ambitions. Stories like Jane Dyer's *Little Brown Bear Won't Take a Nap!* explore familiar topics like disobedience and the progression of the seasons using animals with human characteristics. Rose Lewis's *I Love You Like Crazy Cakes* explores the topic of adoption in a way that young children can understand.

Preteens want to hear about children their age or a little older who have overcome difficulties. The picture book *The Dust Bowl* (Booth) tells the story of a family's survival and provides some background to explain the Dust Bowl but links the story to a contemporary drought. Karen Hesse's *Out of the Dust*, written in blank verse, is the emotional story of a young girl as she moves with her family because of the Dust Bowl. *A Single Shard* (Park), set in twelfth-century Korea, is the story of a young boy who grows up and achieves his dreams in spite of being an impoverished orphan.

Texts that reflect our diverse world. Books like *The Dust Bowl* and *A Single Shard* also have the

Guidelines for Selecting Texts for Interactive Read-Aloud

- Look for texts that you know your students will love (funny, exciting, connected to their experiences, able to extend their thinking).
- Select texts appropriate to the age and interests of your students.
- Select texts that are of high quality (award winners, excellent authors, high-quality illustrations).
- Plan selections so that you present a variety of cultures; help students see things from different perspectives.
- Choose texts that help students understand how people have responded to life's challenges.
- Consider books on the significant issues in the age group—peer pressure, friendship, families, honesty, racism, competition.
- Especially for younger readers, select texts that help them enjoy language—rhythm, rhyme, repetition.
- Select different versions of the same story to help students make comparisons.
- Evaluate texts to be sure the ideas and concepts can be understood by your students.
- Plan selections to appeal to both boys and girls.
- Mix and connect fiction and nonfiction.
- Repeat some texts that have been loved by former students.
- Vary genres so that students listen to many different kinds of texts—articles, poems, fiction, informational texts.
- Select informational texts even if they are long; you can read some interesting parts aloud and leave the book for students to peruse on their own.
- Choose texts that will expand your students' knowledge of others' lives and develop empathy.
- Choose texts that will help students reflect on their own lives.
- Select texts that you love and tell students about them.
- Select texts that build on one another in various ways (sequels, themes, authors, illustrators, topics, settings, structure).
- Link selections in ways that will help students learn something about how texts work.
- Select books that provide good foundations for minilessons in reading and writing.
- Consider the curriculum demands of your district; for example, link texts with social studies, science, or the core literature program.
- Select several texts that help listeners learn from an author's style or craft.
- Select texts that develop artistic appreciation.
- Select fiction and nonfiction texts on the same general topics.
- Consider "text sets" that are connected in various ways—theme, structure, time period, issues, series, author, illustrator, and genre.

Figure 15-8. *Guidelines for Selecting Texts for Interactive Read-Aloud*

advantage of expanding students' worlds by helping them understand other cultures and times. You'll want to be sure that the literature that you read aloud to students reflects our diverse world. A book for younger children, for example, is *Sitti's Secrets* (Shihab Nye), the story of a young girl's grandmother who lives "on the other side of the earth" (p. 13). Students today include a great number of immigrants from many parts of the world. We are truly becoming a global society. Books can connect us and expand our understanding of ourselves and others.

Texts to learn more about genres. Variety in genre is also important to consider in selecting books to read aloud. All genres should be represented—fiction, nonfiction, and poetry. In recent years, a lot more "literary nonfiction" is being published. These informational texts have high-quality illustrations and excellent expository writing. *The Tiniest Giants: Discovering Dinosaur Eggs* (Dingus and Chiappe), with its connections between dinosaurs and today's birds, will fascinate readers of any age. *Faces Only a Mother Could Love* (Dewey) deals with a variety of captivating animal mothers and babies.

The lines between fiction and nonfiction are often blurred, and these texts are sometimes referred to as "hybrids." *The Yellow Star: The Legend of King Christian X of Denmark* (Deedy) tells the inspiring (but undocumentable) story of King Christian, who wore the star to support Danish Jews and encouraged his countrymen to do the same. The author's note grounds the story in history. *Bat Loves the Night* (Davies) is a wonderful poetic text that evokes visual and auditory images, but there is also a subtext that provides a great deal of interesting technical information about bats. *Mailing May* (Tunnell) is fiction written in the form of a memoir. It provides a great deal of information about train travel in the 1930s.

Texts to expand thinking. The books you read aloud to children carry profound messages wrapped up in stories and interesting information. Students who work to understand Solomon Singer's loneliness in *An Angel for Solomon Singer* (Rylant) are learning more about the human condition. Younger readers who understand Ruby in *Ruby the Copycat* (Rathmann) will think about how this character wanted so much to be liked that she copied another girl. Children who listen to *White Socks Only*

(Coleman), *The Other Side* (Woodson), and *The Bus Ride* (Miller) will see 1950s segregation and Jim Crow laws from a child's perspective. Students who listen to the chapters in *Flying Solo* (Fletcher), about a day in the life of a sixth-grade class, will switch points of view every chapter and sometimes within chapters, hearing characters' voices and others' thoughts about them.

PREPARATION FOR READING ALOUD

As you prepare for a read-aloud session, we suggest that you create a planned sequence of several texts over a few days or about a week or two, so you can be thinking of how several texts are connected. Be sure that you read the text well ahead of time, thinking about children's previous literary experiences. It is important to be familiar with the text and think about the opportunities it offers your students. Luckily, you will probably enjoy the wonderful texts you choose just as much as your students will!

You may want to examine the artwork, dedication, end papers, date of publication, genre, as well as the author and illustrator information. You will find it helpful to jot down page numbers or mark a few places with stick-on notes to remind yourself to create opportunities for brief text talk during the reading. How often to stop is your decision, but don't make too many. A few targeted or spontaneous stops will enrich the experience. You will not want to stop so often that you interrupt students' comprehension of or engagement with the story, but these brief dialogues have great instructional value. You'll also want to note some places where you are making your own personal connections or have strong feelings about what is being said. Your own engagement as a reader provides a model for students.

Of course, there may be a text that you choose to read aloud from beginning to end without stopping for a particular reason. For example, you may be reading a rhythmic text or a somber one that requires silence to create the tone.

SETTING

The two key factors in a successful setting for interactive read-aloud are: 1) students are comfortably seated; and 2) everyone can hear easily and see anything in the text the teacher decides to show. Beyond that, there are many choices: You may want your third graders to sit as a group on the rug facing you, or you may want to sit in a low chair to be

225

closer to the students' levels. Your students need to be far enough apart so that they can "turn and talk" to each other quickly, and just as quickly turn back to listen to you. You will need to teach them this routine (see Chapter 18).

The setting above works at every grade level. If a cluster of students on the floor is not an option, you may want to have them sit on chairs placed in a circle or horseshoe in the meeting area. A circle is an excellent arrangement for whole-group discussion, but you have to be sure that students sitting near you can see the pictures. You may want the students seated to the left or right of you to move in to face you.

Sometimes students are seated at their desks arranged in clusters, and you can walk around to read the text, achieving proximity with all students at one time or other, but this setting does not have the same sense of community. Students can, however, talk with a partner or with three or four others in the cluster of desks arrangement. This arrangement also works when you simply pull up a chair in front of the room to read.

Sometimes, students may be at their desks and have their own copies of the text. No matter what the arrangement, it is helpful for students sometimes to change where they sit so that they talk with different students.

You will want the room to be quiet except for your voice and for students' discussion when invited to talk. Avoid distractions such as having music playing or groups of children working elsewhere in the room while you are reading. The entire atmosphere should be one of concentration.

OPENING MOVES

Your first words in the session engage the students' interest and activate thinking in various ways. These "opening moves" set the tone for the lesson and should not be the same every time. Your students will learn to listen to what you say when you begin because it communicates expectations for their active listening. For example, you can:

- Prompt children to anticipate a book by a favorite author.
- Ask children to make connections to a previously read text.
- Ask children to think about the writer's style and typical theme or topic.
- Prompt predictions based on the title.

- Prompt brief sharing of personal experiences related to the topic or theme.
- Alert children to unusual features of the text, such as its structure or narrator.
- Share a personal connection you have with the text.
- Raise interest in a topic or theme.
- Provide important background information.
- Draw attention to the setting.
- Lay the groundwork for helping children understand the theme.
- Draw attention to the genre.
- Lay the groundwork for children's understanding of diverse settings and people.
- Raise questions to spark curiosity.
- Draw attention to the language of the text.
- Prompt hypothesizing based on the situation.
- Read some of the text to engage attention.
- Remind children of genre comparisons.
- Activate background knowledge.
- Alert listeners to important signals such as passage of time.
- Foreshadow the problem of the story.
- Alert students to unusual literary structures such as flashbacks, or flash-forwards, or story within a story.
- Invite personal connections.
- Tell the meaning of a key word.
- Prompt the listeners to notice details.
- Draw attention to readers' tools such as charts, maps, diagrams, index.
- Clarify the writer's point of view.
- Raise questions in the readers' minds.
- Draw attention to the writer's or illustrator's craft.

As you can see, the above list has everything to do with helping students think within, beyond, and about a text. The opening moves also reveal the stance you are taking toward the text and let your listeners in on your thinking. On the DVD that accompanies this book, you will find a large number of sample openings (see Sample Openings for Interactive Read-Aloud).

Let's look at a few examples of openings. In Figure 15-9 through 15-15, you can see three different ways you might open an interactive read-aloud session with the same book. These examples reflect various grade levels, so you may concentrate on the ones that interest you most. As you examine the figures, think about:

- What information has the teacher provided to the listeners?

- How does what the teacher knows about the listeners influence decisions?

- What are listeners likely to attend to as a result of the opening moves?

- How do the opening moves start the listeners thinking?

Different ways of framing the texts can have different results. In the *Pulling the Lion's Tail* example, the teacher introduced the book by telling the children the title and the names of the author and illustrator. She raised expectations by inviting them to notice the book had the same author as a previously read story, *Far Away Home*. She noted that this was the second book in an author study that they will be undertaking, explaining that in an author study readers look for similar characteristics in the stories they read. These activities will not only help them notice the details of the texts they read but also support the development of tastes and preferences as readers.

READING THE TEXT

Through your voice and sometimes your nonverbal actions, you bring a text to life for your students. It is not necessary to be overly dramatic, and we all develop our own styles for reading aloud, but it is important that your voice reflect your interpretation of the writer's meaning. If you are new to reading aloud, don't be afraid to tape yourself and practice. Also, the large number of books now available on tape or CD are wonderful examples. Think how the following suggestions for reading aloud can contribute to enjoyment and also to comprehending:

- A dramatic pause, letting stillness fill the air.
- A frightened tone.
- A sudden use of a louder or much softer voice.
- Talking with a character's voice.
- A sarcastic, ironic, or sad tone.
- Modulating the voice up and down, loud and soft.

WAYS OF OPENING INTERACTIVE READ-ALOUD FOR
Firefighters BY NORMA SIMON

OPENING #1	OPENING #2	OPENING #3
"We've been talking about what firefighters do to help us. Today we're going to read another book about what firefighters do. [SHOWS OPENED COVER OF BOOK.] What do you notice? [CHILDREN RESPOND.] This book is funny because it shows dogs as firefighters, but it also tells us what real firefighters do. So listen to find out what firefighters do for work. What kinds of things do you think you will hear about?"	[OPENS BOOK TO END PAPERS.] "Something really exciting is happening here. What do you think? [CHILDREN RESPOND.] Firefighting is dangerous work, isn't it, but firefighters really help us. You know that they fight fires, and this book tells about that. You'll learn how they fight fires but also what they do after the fire is out. What kind of questions do you think firefighters would ask after they put out a fire?" [CHILDREN RESPOND.]	"[OPENS BOOK TO SHOW BOTH FRONT AND BACK OF COVER.] These dogs are firefighters. When the fire alarm rings, firefighters have to be ready to go in just a few minutes. Listen to this: 'Open the firehouse doors. Start the engines. They're off!' We have seen firefighters speeding to put out a fire. They do that over and over, but they have other work to do as well. That's what we'll learn in this book."
In this opening, the teacher:	*In this opening, the teacher:*	*In this opening, the teacher:*
- Activates background knowledge.	- Engages the readers.	- Engages attention.
- Encourages children to notice information in illustrations.	- Draws attention to action in illustrations.	- Draws attention to language.
- Foreshadows factual text.	- Raises questions in listeners' minds.	- Foreshadows circular text structure.
		- Alerts readers to find information.

Figure 15-9. *Ways of Opening Interactive Read-Aloud for* Firefighters

---

WAYS OF OPENING INTERACTIVE READ-ALOUD FOR
What Do You Do With a Tail Like This? BY ROBIN PAGE AND STEVE JENKINS

OPENING #1	OPENING #2	OPENING #3
"The book we're going to read today is *What Do You Do With a Tail Like This?* [SHOWS COVER.] Do you think this could be a tail? [CHILDREN RESPOND.] [OPENS BOOK TO SHOW BACK—FULL PICTURE OF LIZARD.] It's this lizard's tail. This book is all about the parts of animals' bodies and what they are good for—like ears. What do you do with your ears? [CHILDREN RESPOND.] Well, animals do some very special things with their tails. We'll read about some of them."	"I'm going to read you the first page of this new book, and you think what it's going to be about. 'Animals use their noses, ears, tails, eyes, mouths, and feet in very different ways. See if you can guess which animal each part belongs to and how it is used.' (p. 2) [TURNS THE PAGE.] 'What do you do with a nose like this?' [CHILDREN RESPOND TO ILLUSTRATIONS.] Let's choose one of these noses and then we'll turn the page to see what the animal is and what he does with his nose."	"This new book is *What Do You Do With a Tail Like This?* This silver sticker on the front tells us it is a Caldecott Honor Book. What does that let you know? [CHILDREN RESPOND.] Yes, a lot of people like the illustrations. Also, it is an informational book. That means we are going to learn something new and interesting. What kinds of things do you suppose we are going to learn in this book? [SHOWS ENTIRE FRONT AND BACK.] [CHILDREN RESPOND.] I'll read the first page to see if you are right."
In this opening, the teacher: ▪ Draws attention to illustrations. ▪ Invites prediction from information in illustrations. ▪ Provides background information. ▪ Activates children thinking about their own bodies. ▪ Foreshadows information in the text.	*In this opening, the teacher:* ▪ Engages children with the language of the text. ▪ Asks children to think what the text will be about. ▪ Asks children to select information they want to learn. ▪ Models searching for information.	*In this opening, the teacher:* ▪ Draws attention to text quality. ▪ Reminds children of a mark of quality they know. ▪ Tells children the genre and what to expect. ▪ Invites predictions based on the title, the genre, and the illustrations. ▪ Asks children to confirm predictions.

Figure 15-10. *Ways of Opening Interactive Read-Aloud for* What Do You Do With a Tail Like This?

▪ Reading slowly to create suspense.

▪ Slowing down right before an important conclusion.

▪ Commenting on and showing illustrations.

Be sure to make eye contact with children if they are sitting in front of you. Looking at them frequently as you read will be easy if you are familiar with the text, having read it a couple of times beforehand.

Think of reading aloud as a conversation between you and the children. You are, to the best of your ability, bringing the author's message directly to them. We strongly advise that as much as possible, you read books that you find wonderful—or at least very interesting. You may have experienced hearing someone drone through the reading of a speech; it is not engaging and your mind sometimes refuses to follow it. But through a good delivery, you get inside the text.

Remember that you cannot discuss every single thing in a text. Doing so would "beat the text to death" and run four very great risks:

▪ The discussion may lose its grounding in the text and simply become "talk."

▪ Everyone will lose track of the meaning of the story because there is too much interruption.

▪ Children will become disinterested and disengaged.

▪ It will take them too long to get through the text.

A story needs to move along with good momentum. Readers simply don't stop every page or so for a long discussion. They keep going because they want to know what is happening or get the information. All that said, a few brief pauses for quick interaction can greatly enliven a read-aloud session and lift the student's learning.

WAYS OF OPENING INTERACTIVE READ-ALOUD FOR
If You Find a Rock BY PEGGY CHRISTIAN

OPENING #1	OPENING #2	OPENING #3
"When I was your age, I had a rock collection that I loved! I used to find unusual rocks everywhere I went, and I kept them in a special box. This book, *If You Find a Rock*, reminded me of my rock collection because it is about special rocks and things you can do with them. Do any of you have some special rocks at home? [CHILDREN RESPOND.] Let's see if this book has any rocks like yours."	"This book is about all kinds of rocks. I'll read a page and you think about what kind of rock the writer is talking about. 'Then again, you could find a small, rounded rock right in front of your toe as you go down the sidewalk. You have found a walking rock, and you kick it ahead of you and let it lead you home.' [SHOWS PAGE 24.] Have you ever done that? Just kick a little rock as you walk along? How did the writer describe the rock? [CHILDREN RESPOND.] And the writer called it a . . . [CHILDREN RESPOND.] On every page of this book, Peggy Christian is going to tell us about a different kind of rock, and its name will tell us what you do with it."	[SHOWS TITLE PAGE.] "What do you see in this picture? [CHILDREN RESPOND.] Yes, those are different kinds of rocks. Let's look at a few of the pages in this book and see if you can find the rock and talk about what you might do with it. [SHOWS PAGE 4 (CHALK ROCK), PAGE 5 (SITTING ROCK), PAGE 15 (HIDING ROCK).] Peggy Christian has a name for each kind of rock in this book, so be watching for it! You might even think of some new names for rocks. Or, we might write some of the names of these rocks after reading to help us remember them."
In this opening, the teacher:	*In this opening, the teacher:*	*In this opening, the teacher:*
□ Shares a personal connection. □ Invites personal connections.	□ Provides a summary of what the book is about. □ Reads a sample of some of the language. □ Helps children remember description. □ Helps children understand the organization of information in the book.	□ Draws attention to details in the illustrations. □ Asks children to draw conclusions from information in the illustrations. □ Helps children link illustrations with labels. □ Reveals writer's literary devices. □ Prompts children to remember information and go beyond it.

Figure 15-11. *Ways of Opening Interactive Read-Aloud for* If You Find a Rock

DISCUSSION AND SELF-EVALUATION

At the end of the session, it's a good idea to wrap up the discussion in a meaningful way and to prompt students to evaluate their participation in the read-aloud.

Discussion

If you are reading a chapter book or longer picture book, the discussion will focus on what you have learned so far and what might happen in the next reading. If you are at the end of the text, students can reflect on the meaning of the whole text, drawing out significant events or people and comparing what they know now to what they thought earlier. It is appropriate to discuss the deeper meanings and overall messages that the writer is conveying. You might also go back into the text to support students' thinking or to illustrate special aspects of the writer's craft, such as the use of symbolism or the way the writer showed the passage of time.

Sometimes, as part of the discussion, you might quickly record students' thinking on a chart. The kind of writing you do may be related to the opening moves, but that is certainly not a requirement. Nevertheless, looking back at the "Ways of Opening" charts, here are some possibilities:

□ *Firefighters*—map the circular sequence of events (from firehouse to fire and back again, then starting over).

□ *What Do You Do With a Tail Like This?*—make a list of favorite animals that children could use to do their own drawings.

OPENING #1	OPENING #2	OPENING #3
"Remember *Henry and Mudge,* by Cynthia Rylant? Some of you have read other Henry and Mudge books. What do you know about Henry and Mudge? [CHILDREN RESPOND.] We have a new book and I'm going to read it to you. It is *Henry and Mudge Get the Cold Shivers.* What does that title make you think about? [CHILDREN RESPOND.] It could mean several things. Sometimes when you're sick, do you feel kind of shivery?" [CHILDREN RESPOND.] *In this opening, the teacher:* ▫ Activates background knowledge of text. ▫ Invites personal connections. ▫ Draws attention to the title. ▫ Invites predictions. ▫ Foreshadows meaning.	"I have a new chapter book to read to you today, *Henry and Mudge Get the Cold Shivers.* Some of you have read about Henry and Mudge before, but this is the first one we have read together. Henry is a boy about your age and Mudge is his dog. Wow! Just look how big Mudge is! Kind of like Rosie in *My Dog Rosie.* [CHILDREN RESPOND.] Well, Henry and Mudge do *everything* together, because Henry doesn't have any brothers or sisters and there aren't any kids on his street. This time they even get the cold shivers together and they do almost the same things. We'll find out what that means." *In this opening, the teacher:* ▫ Acknowledges connections some readers will be making. ▫ Provides background information. ▫ Draws attention to character traits shown in illustrations. ▫ Makes explicit text connections. ▫ Foreshadows parallel plot.	"Today I'm going to read a new chapter book to you. It's about Henry and Mudge. What do you remember about Henry and his big dog Mudge? [CHILDREN RESPOND.] This book is *Henry and Mudge Get the Cold Shivers.* I'll read you the table of contents and you think about the title of the book and the chapters to predict what might be happening to Henry and Mudge in this book." *In this opening, the teacher:* ▫ Activates background information and invites children to provide summary. ▫ Draws attention to readers' tools. ▫ Invites predictions.

Figure 15-12. *Ways of Opening Interactive Read-Aloud for* Henry and Mudge Get the Cold Shivers

▫ *If You Find a Rock*—list the names the writer gave to rocks and add some that the children think of.

▫ *Henry and Mudge Get the Cold Shivers*—make a list of all the things Henry does when he is sick and beside it put everything Mudge does to show the parallel plot.

▫ *The Islander*—make a comparison chart of how Daniel feels at age ten and how he feels at age seventeen; discuss what made the difference.

▫ *Out of the Dust*—invite students to make a list of memorable words or phrases or language that they found particularly vivid.

▫ *A Wizard of Earthsea*—keep an ongoing list of the writer's use of symbols.

Creating some sort of visual record like the ones listed above demonstrates aspects of comprehending more explic-

itly to the listeners and helps them remember the text. This demonstration will also be useful for students' writing of longer pieces about their reading (see Chapters 27 and 28).

Self-Evaluation

Involving students in self-evaluation raises awareness that interactive read-aloud is a setting in which everyone is supposed to be listening to the writer's thinking and sharing their thinking with each other. You can create a simple list of questions like these:

1 Was the room quiet, except when I was reading or we were having discussion?

2 Did everyone look at the reader and listen carefully during the reading?

3 Did everyone show that they were thinking about the story/information and the pictures?

WAYS OF OPENING INTERACTIVE READ-ALOUD FOR
The Islander BY CYNTHIA RYLANT

OPENING #1	OPENING #2	OPENING #3
"The chapter book we are going to start today is *The Islander,* by Cynthia Rylant. What do you know about this author? [CHILDREN RESPOND.] Many of you have read books by Cynthia Rylant when you were younger, and we have also read picture books. This book is a little different from those you have read because it's longer, but you will find out that Rylant has written many different kinds of books for different ages. One thing that reminds me of her is the dedication. 'My name is Daniel Jennings, and on this day, my twentieth birthday, I wish to make a record of the marvelous things that happened to me when I was a boy. I dedicate this book to my grandfather.' It sounds like a memoir, doesn't it? Does that remind you of any other books by Cynthia Rylant?"	"Listen to the first paragraph of *The Islander.*" 'I was a boy when I met the mermaid, and, of course, no one believed me. It didn't matter. I was a solitary boy–lonely, actually–and had long given up on anyone understanding what I said or how I felt. I had lived with my grandfather for three years, and he was a kind and gentle man, but he could not see into a boy's world and so could not do much more than love me' (p. 3). What are you thinking? [STUDENTS RESPOND WITH IDEAS AND THEORIES OF WHAT THE BOOK WILL BE ABOUT.] One thing I'm wondering is whether he really saw a mermaid or whether he's so lonely he is imagining it. Another thing I'm wondering is whether birds are important in the story, since there is a picture of a pelican on the back."	"The book we are going to start today is *The Islander,* by Cynthia Rylant. Remember we have read some of her picture books, but this is a chapter book. When this book starts out, the main character, Daniel, is remembering a time when he was only ten years old and his parents died in a plane crash. He came to live on an island with his grandfather who hardly talks; the island had only a small number of people on it; he had no friends. He is an outsider, so he doesn't feel like a true *islander.* So he spends a lot of time reading, walking on the shore, and imagining things. How do you think he feels? [STUDENTS RESPOND.] In this book some pretty unusual and special things happen to Daniel. For one thing, a sea otter tosses him a shell and he finds a key inside. Does the title make you think he might become a true islander? Why?" [STUDENTS RESPOND.]
In this opening, the teacher:	*In this opening, the teacher:*	*In this opening, the teacher:*
▫ Activates background knowledge of an author.	▫ Sparks interest by engaging listeners with the language.	▫ Provides details on the setting and main characters.
▫ Invites connections to other books.	▫ Provides information on the setting.	▫ Defines abstract meaning of a term.
▫ Draws attention to a characteristic of a writer's style.	▫ Invites students to hypothesize about the meaning of the lead.	▫ Invites students to infer the character's feelings.
▫ Engages interest through the dedication.	▫ Demonstrates anticipating the text.	▫ Arouses interest by telling something about the plot.
	▫ Demonstrates using the illustrations.	▫ Invites students to consider the meaning of the title.

gure 15-13. *Ways of Opening Interactive Read-Aloud for* The Islander

Did everyone contribute thinking to the group?

Did everyone share their thinking politely with others?

Did everyone build on comments others made?

Did everyone listen carefully to a partner during "turn and talk"?

Did people ask questions when they didn't understand or want to know more?

9 Did people make comments or predictions about what they were hearing?

10 Did people notice things about the writing or art?

You can modify your list of self-evaluation questions to fit the age group. Self-evaluation takes only a minute, but it is an effective way to help students realize that they have a responsibility to contribute to the learning in the classroom.

WAYS OF OPENING INTERACTIVE READ-ALOUD FOR
Out of the Dust BY KAREN HESSE

OPENING #1	OPENING #2	OPENING #3
"You've been reading a lot of poetry, and you know that poetry doesn't necessarily rhyme. The book we are starting today is actually written in poetry, but it is also a kind of journal; it's dated and the girl is telling the story. You'll find that as we read the poems, a story unfolds. This poem begins in August 1920, when Billie Jo is thinking back to when she was born. [READS PAGES 3–5.] How did it sound like poetry? [STUDENTS RESPOND.] What did we learn about the main character? [STUDENTS RESPOND.] In this book Billie Jo is nearly fourteen and her family is living in Oklahoma at the time of the Dust Bowl. Does anyone know what that was? [STUDENTS RESPOND.] It was a time when there were terrible dust storms. Most people moved away. Living with the dust is hard, but Billie Jo loves to play the piano and she loves her mom. So we're going to read about some really serious problems that she and her family have in about 1934."	"When I was your age I remember being in a dust storm, like a snowstorm, only dry with dust swirling all around. You can hardly even see the sun it's so dark. Have any of you been in a storm like that? [STUDENTS RESPOND.] This book is *Out of the Dust,* by Karen Hesse, and you can see that it is a Newbery Award winner. It's a wonderful book about a fourteen-year-old girl who lives in Oklahoma during what they called the Dust Bowl. Listen to how Karen Hesse describes one of the dust storms in the book: '. . . heaven's shadow crept cross the plains, a black cloud, big and silent as Montana, boiling on the horizon and barreling toward us. . . . We watched as the storm swallowed the light. The sky turned from blue to black, night descended in an instant and the dust was on us" (p. 163). Isn't that interesting language? This story is told by Billie Jo in a journal. She begins in 1920."	"We've been studying how people's use of the environment can change things and sometimes have a devastating effect. Remember that one example is the Dust Bowl in Oklahoma in the 1920s and 1930s. What do you remember happened? [STUDENTS RESPOND.] The drought and terrible dust storms made it impossible to grow food or feed animals, so many people went to California. But some stayed, and this is the story of Billie Jo, a fourteen-year-old girl who is telling the story through a kind of journal. She gives us some information about when she was born and her early life, but most of it is just what it is like to experience a year of tragedy with her in 1934–1935. It's both sad and happy. I love the language in this book. Karen Hesse is telling this story through a long poem."
In this opening, the teacher:	*In this opening, the teacher:*	*In this opening, the teacher:*
▫ Asks students to think about their experiences with poetry.	▫ Shares a personal connection.	▫ Makes a connection to content area study.
▫ Makes a connection to the journal as a genre.	▫ Invites personal connections.	▫ Provides information on the setting.
▫ Provides background information.	▫ Communicates an indicator of high quality.	▫ Provides information about the format.
▫ Shares information about the main character.	▫ Provides background information.	▫ Foreshadows the plot.
▫ Grounds the reading in the time of the setting.	▫ Engages listeners by sharing some of the language.	▫ Expresses a personal preference.
	▫ Shares information about the genre.	▫ Draws attention to the writer's craft.

Figure 15-14. *Ways of Opening Interactive Read-Aloud for* Out of the Dust

RECORD OF READING

A highly productive component of interactive read-aloud is to make some kind of record of the books students have shared during the year. Most teachers keep a chart that simply lists titles and authors and sometimes the genre (see Figure 15-16). Such a chart helps you and your students recall previously read texts as you think about:

▫ An author's or illustrator's style.

▫ An example of a genre.

▫ Characters encountered and their similarities to other characters in other books.

▫ Good leads.

▫ Interesting language.

WAYS OF OPENING INTERACTIVE READ-ALOUD FOR
A Wizard of Earthsea BY URSULA LE GUIN

OPENING #1	OPENING #2	OPENING #3
"The book we are starting now is the story of Ged, who was a great sorcerer in a place called Earthsea. This book is the first book in a series that I really love. I've read them several times and I always see something new in Ursula Le Guin's language and imagination. The sorcerer had one name when he was a child, and he saved his village through wizardry and was renamed Ged at age thirteen. Names are very powerful in this story. But he was also called Sparrowhawk, and you will learn why. He had great powers as a wizard, but he misused them. And so he had a long, dangerous quest. Do you know what that means?" [STUDENTS RESPOND.]	"This book is *A Wizard of Earthsea,* by Ursula Le Guin, who is a very famous writer of fantasy. What other fantasies have you read? [STUDENTS RESPOND.] What are some characteristics of fantasies? What can we expect in this book? [STUDENTS RESPOND.] This book has some of those characteristics. Ged, the main character, can change himself into a Sparrowhawk. The mythical world is called Earthsea, and it is a land famous for magic. There are wars, spells, and a school for wizards. Like other fantasies, there is a kind of struggle between good and evil, and you might even find that sometimes the characters have to struggle within themselves."	"In this book, Ursula Le Guin has created a mythical world named Earthsea, and there are other books in this series. The main character is Ged, who is a wizard. This writer really provides some great descriptions to help us imagine the world. I'll read a couple. 'They came out into the courtyard where a last silvery daylight still hung above the soiled, trodden snow' (p. 120). [STUDENTS DISCUSS.] And even though these characters are magic, the writer helps you know how they feel: 'Anger welled up in Ged's heart, a hot rage of hate against all the cruel deathly things that tricked him, trapped him, hunted him down'. What do you know immediately about Ged?" [STUDENTS RESPOND.]
In this opening, the teacher:	*In this opening, the teacher:*	*In this opening, the teacher:*
□ Notifies students that this is a series. □ Shares a personal preference as a reader. □ Foreshadows the significance of names. □ Tells children something about what to expect. □ Identifies a motif in fantasy.	□ Draws attention to the author's credentials. □ Draws attention to the genre. □ Asks children to make predictions based on knowledge of genre. □ Provides information about the setting. □ Provides insights into the theme.	□ Notifies students that this is a series. □ Provides information about the main character. □ Provides examples of the writer's language. □ Invites children to think in advance about the character and his problems.

Figure 15-15. *Ways of Opening Interactive Read-Aloud for* A Wizard of Earthsea

□ Illustrators you're familiar with.

□ Themes.

□ Books about similar cultures.

□ Books on similar topics.

There are many different ways to keep a record of books shared, and students can be active participants. Kristen asks each student to prepare a three-by-five card containing the title, author, and some kind of artistic representation of each book she reads to them. Then, they categorize and display them by genre on a graph of Books We Shared. The result is a growing graph of the shared books in each genre

category (see the photo in Figure 15-17).

You might want to consider some other suggestions for recording reading:

□ Create a graph with a square for each book, organized by genre.

□ Enter book titles on the computer and keep an up-to-date printed list posted.

□ Create a "notebook" on a chart in the room that children add to each time a book is read.

□ Photocopy the cover of the book and make a scrapbook of book covers.

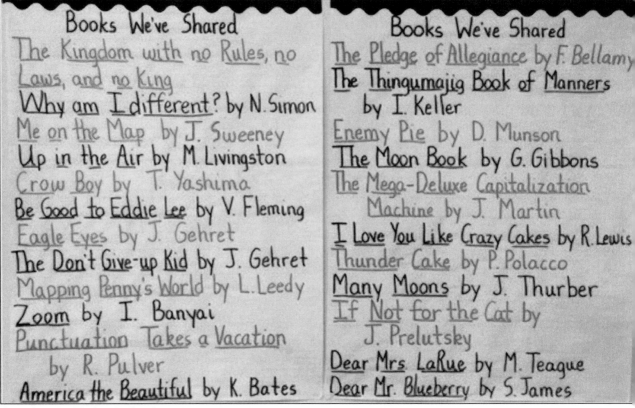

Figure 15-16. *List of Books We've Shared*

- Make a border (like a wallpaper frieze) around the room of photocopied book covers.
- Have students design their own cover for each book and add it to the scrapbook or border.

One of the values of keeping records of books you have read aloud is that you can give next year's teacher the list. Unless you have a special reason, you usually won't want to read aloud a text that most of your class has already heard. There are enough wonderful books to read aloud that you can always find something that most students have not heard. Of course, if they do hear a few more than once, they will always be able to notice more about them and often you will choose to revisit a text for good reason. When a student volunteers that he has read or heard a book before, you can respond with, "That's wonderful. You know what a special book this is, and you will be able to notice things you didn't notice before."

WRITTEN OR ARTISTIC RESPONSE (OPTIONAL)

It is certainly not necessary to follow every text read-aloud with some kind of project or task, but on occasion performance, art, or writing will provide an opportunity to dig deeper into the meaning of a text.

Readers' Theater or Choral Reading

Readers' theater is a type of scripted performance that is very manageable, beneficial, and enjoyable for children who are becoming more proficient readers. It is different from a play, in that memorization is not involved and the emphasis is not on the drama but on the literature. Choral reading is similar in that children read parts. Various lines are assigned to individuals or groups. Children can practice rereading texts in meaningful ways and can participate in heterogeneous groups (see Chapter 21).

The children read their scripts aloud in front of classmates. Their primary goal is using their voices to interpret the text. No costumes, scenery, or props are necessary, and generally there is little movement. If props or scenery are used, they are minimal: signs strung around children's necks with the name of their character or taped-on ears to indicate a cat, for example.

You can select a picture book or a scene or chapter from a longer book and turn it into a choral reading or readers' theater script for children to read. For example, see the following script for Figure 15-18, *If You Find a Rock*. You can assign several children to read each part or assign solos.

There are many books that can be easily turned into choral reading or readers' theater scripts. Karen Hesse's *Out of the Dust* especially lends itself to choral reading. Language selected from the book can be used to tell an abbreviated summary of Billie Jo's experiences during the Dust Bowl years.

Partner or Group Text Talk

There are numerous ways to promote text talk to expand thinking during the interactive read-aloud session. At the end of a story, section, or chapter, invite pairs, trios, or quartets to talk with each other about the text. Their ideas may be shared with the larger group.

At the end of the read-aloud session, sharing may also take the form

Figure 15-17. *An Example of the Classroom Graph on Books We Shared*

If You Find a Rock

PART 1	You might find
PART 2	A skipping rock To trip across the water.
PART 1	You might find
PART 3	A chalk rock To make pictures on the pavement.
PART 1	You might find
PART 4	A resting rock To sit and feel cool moss.
PART 1	You might find
PART 2	A wishing rock To whisper what you want.
PART 1	You might find
PART 3	A splashing rock To make the water jump.
PART 1	You might find
PART 4	Some sifting rocks to slide slowly through your fingers.
PART 1	You might find
PART 2	A worry rock To smooth away your troubles.

PART 1	You might find
PART 3	A hiding rock Where things creep and crawl out of sight.
PART 1	You might find
PART 4	A climbing rock To grip and stretch to the top.
PART 1	You might find
PART 2	A crossing rock To walk over rushing water.
PART 1	You might find
PART 3	A fossil rock With shapes from long ago.
PART 1	You might find
PART 4	A kicking rock And let it lead you home.
PART 1	You might find
EVERYONE	A memory rock, The rock that's best of all.

Figure 15-18. *Script for* If You Find a Rock

of quick writing that students then share with one another (see Chapter 28). Consider having students make a quick sketch or list, or engage in a short write. Linda Rief invites written conversation in a "write around." She distributes a different quote from the text to each group of four students. Each student reads the quote, writes a comment, and then passes it on, until all four have read the quote and added a comment. Then the whole class shares.

Perspective

You can assign students a perspective, or role, to dig deeper into the meaning of the text. They think about the role and then take it on in talking about the story events. For example:

like this!

- For *Henry and Mudge Get the Cold Shivers,* one person might tell the story from Henry's point of view and one from Mudge's.

- For *The Islander,* one person might tell the story from Daniel's point of view, one from his grandfather's point of view, and still another from the point of view of Anna (the dead sister of the grandfather, whom Daniel thinks is helping him).

Taking a perspective is quite a difficult cognitive task for young children, so you will want to be sure their tasks are very simple. They can take roles in stories that are very available to them, such as folktales. But the challenge of switching roles can stretch the thinking of older students immensely.

Focused Text Talk

You can create small groups of three, four, or five children to talk briefly about an open, thoughtful question that gets to deeper aspects of the whole text. They are accountable for keeping their talk focused on that specific question. For example:

1 What was the writer's real message?

2 Why did the character change?

3 What is the symbolic meaning of [an artifact, person, event]?

4 What was the most important moment of the story? Why?

ASSURING TIME FOR TALK

There is simply no substitute for talking about texts. Each reader/listener is able to build a richer meaning for the text than he can build himself. Every time you involve your students in productive conversation about high-quality texts, your students build comprehending ability, expand vocabulary, and learn more about constructing written texts. The time spent will be well worth it, and the outcome will enrich learning in other areas.

SUGGESTIONS FOR PROFESSIONAL DEVELOPMENT

CONSTRUCTING TEXT OPENINGS

1 Collect a set of good fiction and nonfiction texts that you might use for reading aloud across the grades.

2 In grade-level groups, select and read two of the "Ways of Opening" figures (Figures 15-9 through 15-15) that are appropriate for the grade level. Notice what the teacher is doing in each of the three openings.

3 Have grade-level groups take two texts from the collection, create two ways of opening a read-aloud session for each, and present them to the group.

4 If there is time, have groups think of a way to extend a read-aloud session for each text.

5 View and discuss an interactive read-aloud session on the DVD that accompanies this book. Choose from Randy reading *Short Cut* by Crews or Rebecca reading *A Day's Work* by Bunting and Himler. Discuss how the teacher engaged students and supported their thinking.

CHAPTER SIXTEEN

CREATING A LITERATE CULTURE THROUGH INTERACTIVE READ-ALOUD: SHARED TALK ABOUT TEXTS

Nothing a parent or teacher does for a child's intellect or social growth is more important than talking to—and by extension—reading aloud to a child.

—REBECCA LUKENS

Each time you read aloud to your students, you think about teaching and learning opportunities. Questions arise like:

◻ What do my students need to understand about this particular text?

◻ What important aspects of the text can students talk about with one another?

◻ What are the opportunities for teaching or "lifting" students' thinking with this book?

◻ How much should I try to teach using this book (without overdoing it)?

◻ What is most important to help the students think about today, and what should I save for another day?

◻ Is it more important to reread or revisit this text than to have students experience another book?

◻ Should I plan to revisit the text?

These questions can be answered only by the person who asks them! Even in kindergarten and first grade, any text worth taking up your very scarce read-aloud time probably offers many possibilities, so your decisions are critical. You will want to find a good balance between letting students become engrossed in the story or information and doing some intentional teaching. You will want to avoid becoming so focused on teaching about the text (for example, noticing the "lead" or the way the writer uses description) that students miss the point of the story. The first priorities are always understanding and enjoyment.

INTENTIONAL CONVERSATION

An interactive read-aloud should look like a group of people sharing their thinking about a book together—something that we as adults do in book clubs. As we talk, our understanding and the way we look at a text deepen and become more analytical. Each person develops a fuller understanding while benefiting from the interpretations of others. But

your interactive read-aloud differs from adult book groups in an important way: As the "more expert" other, you are guiding and shaping the conversation so that your students learn more about the strategic actions readers use. We use the term *intentional conversation* to represent the use of talk to achieve the goals of your instruction or to "lift the thinking" of your students (see Figure 16-1).

In intentional conversation, you:

◻ Keep in mind the systems of strategic actions that readers must use (see Chapters 4 and 5).

◻ Know the text thoroughly and understand its demands and the opportunities it provides to promote learning.

◻ Provide conversational leads to focus students' attention.

◻ Model and demonstrate behaviors that help students achieve better understanding.

◻ Ask students to share their thinking in a focused way.

◻ Prompt students to listen to and respond to one another rather than always being the center of the conversation.

◻ Keep the conversation grounded in the text.

◻ Turn the conversation back to students, asking for deeper thinking.

◻ Require students to be accountable for their comments, asking for more than opinion and asking them to provide evidence from the text or from personal experience.

◻ Give feedback to students on what they are learning and the kinds of thinking they are doing.

◻ Ask students to evaluate their conversations about the text.

Intentional Conversation

Conversational moves directed toward a goal of instruction.

Figure 16-1. *Intentional Conversation*

The talk is intentional because you always have in mind the reading process and the particular text you are sharing. You know when reading *My Name Is Yoon* by Recorvits, for example, that readers must reach into their own experience to understand what it was like to be a new little Korean girl in an American school. You know you want them to imagine what it is like to wish you were a cat who could hide or a bird who could fly away. You want them to see the contrasts between Yoon's first day of school and her smile on the last page. You want them to understand how teasing hurts and to appreciate the gesture of the girl with the cupcake. Maybe they will even think about Yoon's statement that in Korea she was the teacher's favorite. Maybe she just thought she was because her teacher was so nice. The teaching possibilities are many. The first time you read *My Name Is Yoon,* you may not want to ask students to notice how the author uses comparisons, but that information might emerge as the talk goes deeper.

When reading Deborah Hopkinson's *Under the Quilt of Night,* a challenging text appropriate for older children, you want listeners to feel the terror conveyed by the suspenseful, fast-paced blank verse as the boy and his family run from the slave master. You would not want to ask students to listen for the writer's use of metaphor during the first reading, but in your mind you know that this writer uses language like this:

> But I'll make my steps
> Quick whispers in the dark.
> I'll run where he won't find me,
> Under the quilt of night.

You know that you want students to notice the connection between the metaphoric "quilt of night" that shelters the family and the quilts displayed in homes that are stops on the Underground Railroad, whose blue squares signal that their owners will offer protection. You may want them to notice the terrible darkness in the first illustration and compare it with the bright and joyous portrait of the boy in the last. The students' first response to *Under the Quilt of Night* might be to empathize with the characters, to be glad they were free, and to talk about the situation in general. Then, through intentional conversation, you can probe deeper. (Remember, the texts you select will be well worth revisiting for many different purposes, so don't try to do everything in the same session.)

RELATIONSHIP OF INTENTIONAL TALK TO READING MINILESSONS

The learning potential in interactive read-aloud supported by intentional conversation is exponential over the nine-year span we examine in this book. Although it does not look formal or direct, you are embedding brief, specific teaching in your read-aloud. From an instructional point of view, formal minilessons in the reading workshop and the embedded teaching in interactive read-aloud are alike in that you have specific goals in mind. During an interactive read-aloud, talk will certainly arise from spontaneous student response, not simply your own agenda, but you will find it easy to integrate your points to take the readers beyond what they already understand.

Even after you begin teaching minilessons on reading strategies and skills as well as literary analysis in the reading workshop, you will want to include embedded teaching in the intentional conversation during interactive read-aloud. Intentional conversation begins in kindergarten and continues through middle school: you and your students can simply make a pleasurable habit of it (see Figure 16-2). They will know that each time they listen to you read they are expected to listen to each other and to share their thinking. In kindergarten and grade one, the reading workshop is usually comprised of guided reading in small groups, with the remaining children working independently at reading, writing, or word study.

Beginning in grade two through grade eight, you may want to use a reading workshop structure that includes a minilesson, individual reading, conferences, and group sharing. The reading workshop involves implementing a minilesson, after which students read silently and independently, keeping in mind the reading principle that you have presented. You can confer with individual readers, work with small groups for guided reading, and meet with literature study groups or book clubs. Using intentional conversation during interactive read-aloud sessions makes it easy to implement an additional, explicit minilesson because students have so many shared text resources on which to draw.

AN EXAMPLE OF INTENTIONAL TALK

Let's look at some examples of embedded teaching in interactive read-aloud sessions (see Figure 16-3). The teacher is

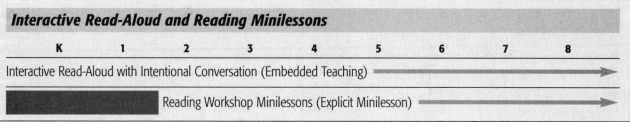

Figure 16-2. *Interactive Read-Aloud and Reading Minilessons*

reading *The Lotus Seed* (Garland 1993), the story of a Vietnamese family who immigrate to the United States by riding on a crowded boat. The girl in the story tells about her grandmother, who as a girl saw the emperor cry and picked a lotus seed from his garden. She wraps the seed in silk and saves it all her life, taking it to the new country. Then the seed is lost because a young child in the family takes it outside and buries it. The surprise at the end of the story is that in the spring, the lotus seed blossoms and the family has new seeds to save.

Ms. S. wants to help children see that the lotus seed has deep, symbolic meaning for the family. It stands for memories of the old life but also for life and hope. If you read the excerpts and look at the analysis on the right, you can see that in this first reading, Ms. S. has established a strong foundation for understanding what the seed means to the family. She can revisit this text in the future as she explores the idea and relates the symbol to the symbolic meaning in other texts—the yellow Cub Scout scarf that Laura leaves on her grandfather's grave in Manzanar in *So Far from the Sea* (Bunting), for example.

DEVELOPING A SHARED LANGUAGE FOR TALKING ABOUT TEXTS

One of the goals of interactive read-aloud sessions is to develop a literate culture in your classroom. Every culture is characterized by a shared language. Language learning takes place through interaction with others. Through intentional conversation over the years, you and the other teachers in your school can help your students acquire a specialized vocabulary they can use to talk with one another about books.

TALK RELATED TO AGE AND EXPERIENCE

When should students start using the technical terms related to literature? Would you really want to talk with kindergartners or first graders about the *plot,* the *conflict,* or the

theme of a story? Should they be talking about *chronological order* or *problem/solution?* They could learn to use the labels, which might be very impressive to the casual visitor to your classroom, but we do not think teaching young children a large number of technical words is appropriate. However, children can develop an understanding of the *concepts*:

- What is happening in the story?
- What are the little red hen and the cat and dog disagreeing about?
- What do we learn from that story?
- What happened first? And then what happened?
- What is the little red hen's problem? What did she do to solve the problem?
- What did you notice about the illustrations?

However, we do want fifth, sixth, seventh, or eighth graders to use a sophisticated vocabulary that includes the names of genres and words like *media, theme, subtopics, style, metaphor,* and *simile.* Developing this kind of language in a meaningful way is learned over time across the grades.

A general rule of thumb is, *Students should first develop a deep understanding of the concept and then take on the label.* When to introduce a technical word is up to you, because you know the understandings that your students already have. Certainly, kindergarten children can talk about the title, writer or author, illustrator, and problem. At all levels, the key is whether students truly understand the words they are using and whether it is a label readers of that age would use in authentic reading contexts. We suggest meaningful terms to use in talking about texts with younger children (or less experienced students) until they are ready to use the specific technical terms when they are older (see Figure 16-4). We will discuss this concept in greater detail in Chapter 19 in relation to planning minilessons.

The Lotus Seed

Ms. S.: *[Opens with information about the setting and gives children a sample of the language.]* Today I'm going to read to you *The Lotus Seed,* by Sherry Garland, illustrated by Tatsuro Kiuchi. This story is told by a girl whose family is from Vietnam and they had to come here because of the war. Listen to how the girl starts the story.

"My grandmother saw
The emperor cry
The day he lost
His golden dragon throne." (p. 20) [PAUSES TO INVITE COMMENT.]

JARED: She's going way back in time to tell about her grandmother.

MARTY: She's dressed like older times.

Ms. S.: *[Foreshadows the importance of the lotus seed and alerts listeners to think about what it means to the grandmother.]* Yes, it says "My grandmother saw," so you know that this story happened in the past. This picture [SHOWS PAINTING OPPOSITE TITLE PAGE] shows the lotus blossom. Isn't it beautiful! You are going to hear about the lotus seed and what it means to the grandmother all of her life. Think about that. *[Prompts children to remember details that establish the symbolic value of the lotus seed.]* [MS. S. READS THE TEXT.] *[Synopsis]: As a girl, the grandmother takes a lotus seed from the emperor's garden and keeps it safe on the family altar and carries it for good luck when she gets married.*

Ms. S.: It seems like the lotus seed means a lot to her, doesn't it? How can you tell?

JAKE: She keeps it wrapped up in a silk scarf.

PETER: She puts it where she prays.

MARSHA: Why did her parents choose the person she married?

JENNIFER: Maybe because it was a long time ago or maybe because they were in that country.

Ms. S.: *[Shares a personal connection regarding an object with symbolic meaning.]* You're noticing a lot. I guess it was pretty special to carry it when she got married. When I got married, I wore my grandmother's ring and that was special to me. It reminded me all day of my grandmother and how happy she would have been. *[Prompts children to infer character's motivations, again working to understand the significance of the seed.]* [MS. S. READS ON.] *[Synopsis]: When her family has to flee from war, she saves the seed. Going to a new land, they work hard. The lotus seed is kept on the family altar. The family works very hard in the new land. One night the little brother steals the seed and plants it in a pool of mud, forgetting where he put it. The grandmother mourns.*

Ms. S.: Why do you think she is so sad?

RACHEL: Because she lost her keepsake.

JAKE: She was missing the seed because she had it all her life.

MARSHA: I think it might have been her memory of her old life and her home.

RACHEL: Remember? It was reminding her of the emperor.

MARSHA: But it was really more than just that. She was thinking of a different time—a beautiful flower.

MARTY: I think it might have been her memory of her old life and her home.

Ms. S.: *[Reaffirms the connection between the seed and memories.]* I'm glad you are thinking of all the reasons that the lotus seed was important to Ba, the grandmother. She even carried it at her wedding before her husband had to go to war. Sometimes something can really hold our memories, like my grandmother's ring. I wonder what might happen.

JAKE: Maybe they find it?

Ms. S.: I'm going to turn the page! [SHOWS PAINTING OF THE LOTUS BLOSSOM.]

JAKE: It grew!

MARSHA: She might just be remembering again, like it's in her heart.

Figure 16-3. *Excerpt from an Interactive Read-Aloud of* The Lotus Seed

EXCERPTS FROM AN INTERACTIVE READ-ALOUD OF
The Lotus Seed (CONTINUED)

Ms. S.: It could be! Because it seems like she is carrying all her memories in her heart. That's a wonderful way to think about it.

Ms. S.: [CONTINUES READING]: *Then one day in spring / my grandmother shouted, / and we all ran / to the garden / and saw / a beautiful pink lotus / unfurling its petals, / so creamy and soft.*   *"It is the flower / of life and hope," / my grandmother said. / "No matter how ugly the mud / or how long the seed lies dormant, / the bloom will be beautiful. / It is the flower / of my country."' (p. 21)*

Ms. S.: *[Elicits thinking from a student who has not yet talked.] [Ms. S. finishes the story, which describes the two children receiving a seed from the new plant. The little girl wraps the seed in silk and hides it, hoping one day to plant it and give the seeds to her own children, telling them about the day her grandmother saw the emperor cry.]* Simon, what are you thinking about the end of the story?

SIMON: It's good that the plant grew. I was surprised. It must have been all dried up and stuff.

MARSHA: Was it magic?

Ms. S.: *[Revisits some language in the text to address a student's question. Selects language that provides more explicit information.]* Well, let's read again what the writer says [READS PAGE 21 AGAIN]. What does that tell you?

SIMON: It's like a seed that can be dead for years and still grow a flower.

MARSHA: The little boy put it in the mud and it woke it up.

BOBBIE: It grew in the new country.

Ms. S.: *[Demonstrates theorizing about the seed.]* I'm thinking that the flower could be a bit like the grandmother and her family. They had a terrible time in the war and had to move here, sort of like being planted in a new place.

SIMON: It's like they became successful because they worked so hard and the flower was beautiful again.

Ms. S.: *[Invites inference.]* I think that this writer is trying to help us understand a couple of things with this flower. You know that the lotus seed is important because it is the title of the story. Why did it mean so much to the family?

JAKE: Because it reminded the girl of home.

ALI: She kept it all that time and now the little girl wants to keep her lotus seed to remind her of her grandmother's story.

Ms. S.: *[Keeps the discussion grounded in the text and supports thinking about the text.]* Yes, it seems like the lotus seed reminds everyone of their family. And remember, she said "It is the flower of life and hope." What do you think the writer meant by that?

SARA: Even though they had a war and had to go in a boat to another country, they still had hope of a better life.

KAREN: And they had their memories, and the seed would bring up another flower.

ALI: It's like they always had hope even though they had to work so hard.

Ms. S.: *[Summarizes the discussion; makes the teaching goal explicit.]* So when we read *The Lotus Seed* we could see that Sherry Garland was helping us understand the family by showing something that was really precious to them—the lotus seed. But it wasn't just a seed, was it? The writer was using it as a reminder of their family and their memories and also of hope because it was dormant. It seemed like it was dead, but it was always there ready to come alive again.

Figure 16-3. *Excerpt from an Interactive Read-Aloud of* The Lotus Seed *(cont.)*

Moving Toward a Specialized Vocabulary in Talking About Texts

MEANINGFUL TERMS TO USE IN TALKING ABOUT TEXTS WITH YOUNGER STUDENTS	TO	SPECIFIC AND TECHNICAL TERMS TO USE WHEN TALKING ABOUT TEXTS WITH OLDER STUDENTS
Person [animal, other being] the story is about	➡	Character
People [animals, other beings] in the story	➡	Characters, main character, supporting characters, minor characters
How [name] changes and why	➡	Character development, "round" and "flat" characters
When and where	➡	Setting
Problem(s) in the story, beginning and ending, what happens in the story	➡	Plot, conflict
What happened first, next?	➡	Chronological order
Feelings you have	➡	Mood
Person telling the story	➡	Narrator, perspective
What the story is about	➡	Theme
What we'll learn about	➡	Topics, categories, subtopics
Stories that might be true	➡	Realistic fiction
Stories that happened in the long-ago past	➡	Historical fiction
Stories like *The Three Bears*	➡	Traditional literature, folktales and fairy tales
Stories that could not be true	➡	Fantasy, high fantasy, science fiction
Books that give us real information	➡	Nonfiction—factual, informational, expository texts
Writer, author, and illustrator	➡	Writer, author, illustrator, biographer, reporter
Poems, rhymes, songs, Mother Goose	➡	Ballads, narrative poetry, lyrical poetry
Scary; wanting to know what's going to happen	➡	Suspense, thriller, cliff-hanger

Figure 16-4. *Moving Toward a Specialized Vocabulary in Talking About Texts*

TEACHING TECHNICAL VOCABULARY

There is a technical vocabulary associated with talking about texts. Throughout the elementary and middle school years, students should become more sophisticated in using it. Let's examine the ways you can ask questions or make comments that help students develop a shared language to talk about fiction (Figure 16-5), biography (Figure 16-6), and factual texts (Figure 16-7). You will need to adjust the language in each to fit the particular students you teach.

Of course, a concept or idea will need to be demonstrated by you before you question students about it. If students can answer questions such as the ones we list, then at some point, they can take on the formal terminology. Notice that the terminology and the questions are different for fiction and nonfiction texts.

Developing a Shared Language for Talking About Fiction Texts

SHARED TERMS	TEACHING POINTS WITHIN INTERACTIVE READ-ALOUD (INTENTIONAL CONVERSATION ABOUT THE TEXT, K–8)
Setting	"Where does the story take place?" "Look at the picture. This story is . . ." "When is the story happening?" "This story happened . . ."
Characters	"Who are the characters [people/animals] in the story?" "In this story we're going to read about. . . . [name or type of character]" "What does the writer say about [name(s) of character or characters]?" "Here the writer is telling us about [a character]. Listen to hear what he is like!" "How does the character look? What does it say [or what's in the pictures] to make you think that?" "What does [name of character] think about [character]? What does the writer say to make you think that?" "Who is the most important character in the story?" "Who are some of the other characters that are not as important? Why do you think the writer included this character?" "Listen to see if [name of character] changes during this story." "Did any of the [characters, people, animals] change in any way?" "What character does the writer tell us most about?" "Who is the character that you like the most or care most about?"
Plot	"What problem does [character] have?" "They are going to take some action to solve the problem. One thing they'll try is . . ." "What is the problem in this story?" "In this story [problem] is going to happen." "How did they solve the problem?" "What helped them solve the problem?" "What were the most important things that happened in the story?" "How does the author show the time or how the time has changed?" "What words does the author use to show the time or how time has changed?"
Narrator and Perspective	"Who is telling this story?" "How do you know [writer, character] is telling the story?" "The writer [name of author] is just telling us this story." [Example from the text.] "In this story, the character [name of person, animal] is telling us what happened." [Example from the text.] "Sometimes the person telling the story talks directly to us as readers." [Example from the text.]
Mood	"How does this story make you feel? What makes you feel that way?" "Sometimes stories just make us have some overall feelings—like surprise, sadness, homesickness. This story makes me feel [mood] because [descriptive details from text or pictures]." "How does the writer make you feel now?" "Did the way you feel change at any point in the story?"
Theme	"Think about the whole story. What is this story really about?" "When you have read a story, you can think about what the writer was really trying to tell you. It might be making friends or having courage. I think that in this story the writer was telling us [theme]. Sometimes the writer tells us more than one important idea."

igure 16-5. *Developing a Shared Language for Talking About Fiction Texts*

Developing a Shared Language for Talking About Fiction Texts (CONTINUED)

SHARED TERMS	TEACHING POINTS WITHIN INTERACTIVE READ-ALOUD (INTENTIONAL CONVERSATION ABOUT THE TEXT, K–8)
Genre	"What kind of story is the author telling?" "How do you know this story is fiction?" "How do you know the writing is nonfiction?" "How do you know this is science fiction [or other genre]?" "Could the story have happened?"
Style (use of language)	"Where does the writer use strong words?" "What words or phrases are memorable? Special?" "What words, phrases, or sentences does the author use to make us see [hear, feel, smell, taste] what it was like?"
Simile	"What words did the writer use to describe/compare the character?" "What did the writer say the person or object was like?"
Metaphor	"What was the writer comparing the [character, object, action] to?"
Personification	"What was the writer trying to say about the person?"

Figure 16-5. *Developing a Shared Language for Talking About Fiction Texts* (cont.)

Developing a Shared Language for Talking About Biography

SHARED TERMS	TEACHING POINTS WITHIN INTERACTIVE READ-ALOUD (INTENTIONAL CONVERSATION ABOUT THE TEXT, K–8)
Setting	"What was it like when this person was young?" "Where did this person live? What was that place like?" "When did this person live? What was that time like?" "How did the times affect the person's life?" "How did the place where the person lived affect her life?"
Subject	"What was the person trying to do?" "Why were the person's accomplishments important to her? To others?"
Themes	"In what ways did the person show courage?" "What about this person's life is important to others?" "What does this person's life teach us?"
Accuracy of Information	"Where did the writer get the information?" "How do we know the writer's information about a person is true?"
Structure	"What part of this person's life does the writer describe?" "Where did the writer begin to tell the story of this person's life?" "Where did the writer end the story of this person's life?"
Illustrations, Graphics Features	"What information do the illustrations give us about this person's life?" "How do the sections and headings help us find information about this person's life?" "What other information does the writer give us?"

Figure 16-6. *Developing a Shared Language for Talking About Biography*

Developing a Shared Language for Talking About Factual Texts

SHARED TERMS	TEACHING POINTS WITHIN INTERACTIVE READ-ALOUD (INTENTIONAL CONVERSATION ABOUT THE TEXT, K–8)
Accuracy of Information	"How do we know the writer has given us correct information?" "How do we know the information is factual?"
Style	"How did the writer make the information interesting?" "How did the writer tell the information in an interesting way?"
Organization	"How has the writer organized the information?" "Has the writer told the information as a story?" "Has the writer given the information in an order?" "Has the writer organized the information in topics?"
Features	"What kinds of features does the writer use to present the information?" "What did the writer do with the print to help us understand more?" "What information do the illustrations [photos, diagrams] give us about the topic?"
Patterns	"How did the writer organize the ideas?" "How did the writer describe the topic?" "How did the writer use time to tell about the topic or events?" "How did the writer compare, or tell how things are alike?" "How did the writer contrast, or tell how things are different?" "How did the writer explain causes for what is happening?" "How did the writer tell about what happened as a result of something?" "What problems and solutions did the writer explain?"

Figure 16-7. *Developing a Shared Language for Talking About Factual Texts*

A SUGGESTED CONTINUUM

When we think about teaching this specialized vocabulary to children, we may need to be quite specific about the use of particular terms at different grade levels. No one can specify exactly at what point you will want to introduce technical vocabulary, but some terms are more difficult than others. Our suggestions (see Figure 16-8) are approximations, and you will need to decide what is appropriate for your particular group of students. Your kindergarten students may be perfectly comfortable talking about "characters" or "authors," but it would be ridiculous to try to get them to understand "round" and "flat" characters. Seventh or eighth graders, on the other hand, might find it useful to make this distinction in a literary analysis.

The first column of Figure 16-8 is a list of terms. It is certainly not exhaustive, but most of the terms used in elementary and middle school are here. A quick definition is in the next column. In the columns headed K–8, you will see arrows and shaded material. The shaded area indicates when the term or concept should be used in conversation, assuming children know it. Don't expect all children just to pick up terms from conversation. The arrow indicates the approximate grade level at which we think most teachers will want to introduce the label or technical term for the concept: At this point, the concept should be well established and the term ready to be explicitly taught.

TEACHERS' FACILITATIVE TALK

You are an important voice in the classroom, but student voices are equally important. Your talk is important simply because it demonstrates ways of thinking and ways to share that thinking. Your facilitation engages students in using talk to share their thinking (see Figure 16-9).

Questioning alone will not facilitate student talk. Facilitative teacher talk includes a full range of conversational moves that includes demonstrating, prompting, and

Acquiring a Shared Literary Vocabulary for Talking About Books

TERM	QUICK DEFINITION	K	1	2	3	4	5	6	7	8
General										
Author	Person who wrote the text.	➡								
Illustrator	Person who provided the illustrations, graphics.	➡								
Cover	Outside design of the book.	➡								
Wordless picture book	A book in which the meaning is created only by pictures.	➡								
Picture book	A book with words and illustrations in which the illustrations show what the words tell and more (the mood, a second story, etc.).	➡								
Series book	Books that have a unifying element such as same characters (Cam Jansen), same setting (Little House), or same subject (One Day in the Tropical Rain Forest).			➡						
Dedication	Author's and illustrator's tribute to an individual or group.			➡						
Endpapers	The material (usually art) just inside the front and back covers.			➡						
Book jacket	The paper that covers the hard cover of the book.			➡						
Title page	The page on which the title and author are given.			➡						
Chapters	Sections of a text that are labeled by number and sometimes labeled with a title.			➡						
Author's note	A note by the author that provides personal information or extra factual information.				➡					
Illustrator's note	A note by the illustrator that provides personal information or extra factual information.				➡					
Single page spread or double page spread	A picture and text on a single page or pictures and text across two pages.				➡					

Figure 16-8. *Acquiring a Shared Literary Vocabulary for Talking About Books*

Acquiring a Shared Literary Vocabulary for Talking About Books (CONTINUED)

TERM	QUICK DEFINITION	K	1	2	3	4	5	6	7	8
Talking About Fiction Texts										
Character	People/animals in the story.	➡								
Problem	The central issue or conflict that characters in the story face.	➡								
Events	What takes place in the story.	➡								
Resolution	The point in the story when the problem is solved (and how it is solved).			➡						
Main character	The character the story is mostly about.			➡						
Setting	Time and place of the story.			➡						
Fiction and nonfiction	The two basic types of texts.			➡						
Poetry	Condensed language arranged to create an emotional response through meaning, sound, and rhythm.			➡						
Fiction genres	Categories of fiction: contemporary realistic fiction, historical fiction, traditional literature (folktale, fairy tale, myth, legend, fable), modern fantasy, high fantasy, science fiction.				➡					
Character development	The way characters change over time and in response to events in the story.					➡				
Point of view	The mind that the writer chooses to tell a story.					➡				
Theme	The main idea or unifying ideas told through the story by the writer.					➡				
Supporting characters	Characters other than the main character that interact with and affect her.						➡			
Plot	The problem of the story and the events that follow.						➡			
Conflict	The kinds of clashes that create the problem—person against person, society, nature, self.							➡		

Figure 16-8. *Acquiring a Shared Literary Vocabulary for Talking About Books (cont.)*

Acquiring a Shared Literary Vocabulary for Talking About Books (CONTINUED)

TERM	QUICK DEFINITION	K	1	2	3	4	5	6	7	8
Tone	The attitude of the writer or illustrator toward the story or toward the reader.							➡		
Symbol	Person, object, or situation that has a meaning beyond its literal sense.							➡		
"Round" characters	Characters that are well developed, in that they change over time.								➡	
"Flat" characters	Characters that do not change (usually supporting characters).								➡	
Plot type	Various kinds of plots—romance, tragedy, satire, irony, comedy, mystery, adventure.								➡	
Plot structure	Various points in the plot—initiating event, rising action, climax, falling action.								➡	
Types of poetry	Various forms of poetry: ballads, narrative poems, lyrical poems.								➡	
Talking About Nonfiction—Biography Texts										
Time line	A representation of the sequence of events in the subject's life—arranged in a list or diagram.				➡					
Caption or legend	An explanatory title or similar information under maps, graphs, or illustrations.				➡					
Accuracy and authenticity	The extent to which the text reflects facts and truth.				➡					
Biographical genres	Categories of biographical writing: biography, autobiography, memoir.				➡					
Events	The important events of a person's life, arranged in time.				➡					
Subject	The person the biographical text is about.					➡				
Life decisions	The critical decisions in a person's life.					➡				
Setting	The characteristics of the time and place the subject lived and their influence on her.					➡				

Figure 16-8. *Acquiring a Shared Literary Vocabulary for Talking About Books (cont.)*

Acquiring a Shared Literary Vocabulary for Talking About Books (CONTINUED)

TERM	QUICK DEFINITION	K	1	2	3	4	5	6	7	8
Talking About Nonfiction—Factual Texts										
Information	Facts and ideas that are in the text and can be learned.			➡						
Chapters or Sections	The divisions of a text; may be chapters.			➡						
Accuracy	The extent to which the text reports correct information.				➡					
Table of contents	A list of the major sections or informational divisions of a text (usually the same as the headings).				➡					
Heading	A phrase in a larger font or boldface, usually set off by white space, that provides information about the topic of the section.				➡					
Glossary	A list of key words and their definitions, usually placed at the back of the text.				➡					
Topic	The subject of a text or the subject of divisions of a text.					➡				
Subheading	A phrase in a larger font than the text (but smaller than the heading) that provides information about the topic of a division of a section.					➡				
Category	A defined division of a classification system.					➡				
Index	A list of topics and names in the text.					➡				
Pronunciation guide	A list of words, phonetically transcribed to help readers say them accurately.						➡			

Figure 16-8. *Acquiring a Shared Literary Vocabulary for Talking About Books (cont.)*

Teachers' Facilitative Talk

Through commenting, demonstrating, and questioning, teachers:

- Show readers how to express interpretations of texts.
- Prompt readers to consider many possible interpretations.
- Demonstrate making predictions and referring to evidence.
- Use evidence from personal experience or the text to make predictions.
- Prompt readers to examine texts closely.
- Ask for open-ended comments and responses.
- Share personal connections to texts.
- Let students in on some information that will help them understand a text.
- Demonstrate connecting texts in many different ways.
- Ask students why they think or feel something related to a text.
- Ask students to talk about any aspect of a text.
- Help students notice the writer's craft or the writer's decision.
- Model the idea that readers have varying responses and interpretations.
- Demonstrate and prompt for using personal experience or evidence from the text to support thinking.

Figure 16-9. *Teachers' Facilitative Talk*

reinforcing the thinking that is shared. It also includes:

- Expressing opinions and ideas.
- Building on another person's ideas.
- Sharing personal perspectives.
- Responding to the comments of others.
- Confirming students' thinking.
- Asking genuine questions to clarify or prompt thinking.

Your goal is to demonstrate, confirm, prompt, and extend thinking and talking about texts. Through facilitative talk, you can help students think and talk about any kind of thinking demanded by the text.

ROUTINES TO FACILITATE TALK DURING INTERACTIVE READ-ALOUDS

You want your students to talk with one another and learn from the experience. Discussing texts with others is learned behavior and needs to be taught. Building some routines into interactive read-aloud will greatly increase both the quality of the talk and efficiency. In addition, these routines will prepare your students for more extended and productive discussions in book clubs or literature circles, which we examine in detail in Chapter 17. Let's think about how the social conventions of talking with each other can be established through interactive read-aloud (see Figures 16-10).

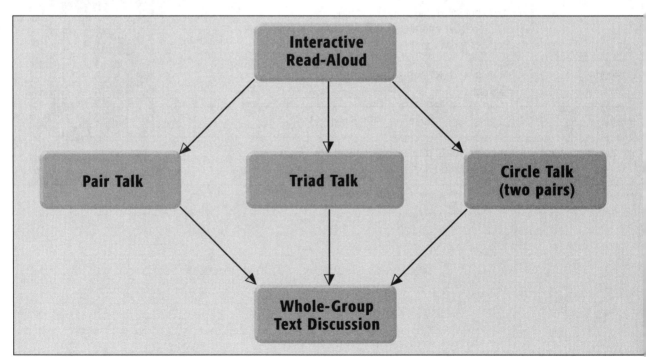

Figure 16-10. *Interactive Read-Aloud Routines to Facilitate Talk*

Even young children can learn to "turn and talk" to one or two other students (Harste, Short, and Burke 1998). Teach this routine explicitly and use it often enough that children can do so with ease. They do not need to talk very long; 30 seconds or a minute will be enough to verbalize their thinking. This activity gives children the opportunity to share their own thinking and "primes the pump" for whole-group discussion. After children have become familiar with the routine, they can do more—talking first in pairs, then threesomes, and then moving to a circle of four (two pairs). The bridge to small-group literature circles or book clubs will have been firmly built.

These routines are not just for elementary children. Seventh and eighth graders will enjoy the opportunity to talk with peers, and these brief conversations will make your whole-group discussions richer.

SUGGESTIONS FOR PROFESSIONAL DEVELOPMENT

SHARED LITERARY VOCABULARY

1 With grade-level colleagues, take a look at the continuum in Figure 16-8.

2 Think about the terminology you are using with your students at your grade level. Ask:

- Do my students understand the concepts or principles underlying the vocabulary they are using?

- What terms do I need to teach them?

- What terms should I wait to teach?

3 Have each person in your group conduct an interactive read-aloud with their students. Afterward reflect on the session. Jot down the vocabulary terms you remember using or that children in your class have used. Ask:

- What terms did I use?

- What terms did students use easily and with understanding?

- Are there terms students should be using easily and with understanding at my grade level?

- How can I teach a shared literary vocabulary?

4 At another meeting discuss specific goals for articulation of terminology across the years in your elementary/middle school.

CHAPTER SEVENTEEN

PLANNING FOR INTERACTIVE READ-ALOUD AND LITERATURE STUDY ACROSS THE GRADES

Because words are essential in building the thought connection in the brain, the more language a child experiences—through books and through conversation with others, not passively from television—the more advantaged socially, educationally, and in every way that child will be for the rest of his life.

—MEM FOX

There is only so much time in the school day. Hearing one text read aloud each day amounts to 180 books (or segments of longer texts) a year. That's not so many, considering the quantity and variety of texts necessary to build a strong foundation for language and literacy. Of course, children read many more books in other instructional contexts (and, we hope, at home), but interactive read-aloud and literature study help you reap a variety of benefits and deserve careful and thoughtful planning.

Look at this quote from Bobby's diary in *Spider Boy* (Fletcher):

> *Which reminds me—I HOPE we don't have to read* Charlotte's Web *in English this year. We studied it last year in Mrs. Sibberson's class, and I've read the book at least five times on my own. It's a good book—well, all right, a great book—but I'm a little sick of it.* (p. 26)

Bobby reminds us that sometimes the same book is read for several years, and we might want to choose with a little more discrimination throughout the grades. With all the wonderful books available, we can achieve variety without narrowness and rigidity.

We are not advocating that certain grade levels "own" certain books, but we do think that some collegial planning can ensure that students:

- Encounter mostly fresh material each year.
- Experience all genres deeply enough to know them.
- Read and listen to texts that build on one another in a variety of ways.

It seems reasonable to come up with six to ten "core" texts or topics for each grade level and four or five authors that students might study, with individual teachers adding many more texts, topics, or authors of their own choosing. This kind of planning leaves plenty of room for a teacher's

preferences, and working together across grade levels K–8 can put more power into the curriculum. We all need to take a "long view."

USING TEXT SETS TO HELP STUDENTS DEVELOP A SHARED LANGUAGE

"Text sets" (Harste, Burke, and Short 1998) are a way of organizing and connecting books (see Figure 17-1) that helps students build understanding from book to book. A *text set* consists of two or more books that are connected in some way—author, theme, topic, illustrator, text structure, genre, or particular aspect of craft. You can create fiction/nonfiction pairs on the same topic or connect texts that illustrate a particular kind of writing style. The first column of Figure 17-1 identifies various kinds of sets that you might put together for interactive read-aloud. For students in grades two through eight, you will want to use these same texts as examples for reading and writing minilessons. In all grades, you can use the same texts as single examples or in sets formed on a different basis, for example, to help your students learn to write from reading multiple texts from a particular writer. The text sets also provide good introductions to topics, themes, or genres that will characterize books students will select for literature study.

For example, you might use *Elizabeti's Doll, Mama Elizabeti,* and *Elizabeti's School* to study their author, Stephanie Stuve-Bodeen. You might later use *Elizabeti's School* as a mentor text to demonstrate how the writer showed Elizabeti's feelings, something young students can do when they are writing about their own lives.

Text sets are characterized by *inquiry* and *versatility.* You can tell students some things to notice about books, but learning is much more powerful if they can learn to take the stance of an *inquirer into literature.* By combining

Text Sets for Interactive Read-Aloud

TEXT SETS FOR UNITS OF STUDY	MENTOR TEXTS FOR WRITER'S WORKSHOP
Texts that:	**Texts that provide examples of:**
□ Have the same *themes*. □ Are on the same *topic* or related topics (content area curriculum). □ Have the same kind of *structure*, for example, cumulative, circular. □ Are of the same *genre*. □ Are by the same *author*. □ Are *illustrated* by the same artist. □ Pair *fiction and nonfiction* on the same topic. □ Contain particular elements of craft—e.g., leads that start with dialogue, stories told in the first person.	□ A particular style of writing. □ Ways to use language (imagery, figurative language, flashback, etc.). □ Perspective taking (first, second, third person). □ Ways to reveal characters. □ How writers use dialogue or punctuation. □ Ways of showing that time has passed. □ Ways to begin and end a text. □ Ways to include graphics or other text features. □ Characteristics of genres like memoirs, biographies, autobiographies, feature articles. □ Level of detail necessary to help readers understand the text. □ Topics writers tell about. □ Making a genre to fit the information the writer wants to convey. □ Considering the purpose and audience for writing. □ Ways to make an informational text interesting. □ How to organize information so it will be clear to the reader. □ How to use organizational tools like table of contents, headings, and subheadings. □ Creating effective titles.

Figure 17-1. *Text Sets for Interactive Read-Aloud*

books in text sets, you make it easy for students to notice what they might miss if they simply encounter one text after another in a random way—no matter how good the texts are! Juxtaposing texts for various reasons makes it possible for students to discover more about authors, genres, illustrators, text structure, craft, and other factors related to reading and writing.

A text set is not a static collection. As you group texts, you will notice that depending on the aspect of text you are noticing, a single text can be part of many different sets. *Bat Loves the Night* (Davies) might be paired with *Stellaluna* (San Diego) as a fiction/nonfiction pair on the topic of bats. But *Bat Loves the Night* might also be used with *The Seasons of Arnold's Apple Tree* (Gibbons) and *What Do You Do When Something Wants to Eat You?* (Jenkins) to compare how writers of factual texts organize

and present information. Once you have used a text set, you will find that students will suggest others that are connected in the same way.

Logistically, you can keep text sets together to be used at a particular time of the year, but you may have other purposes for the individual volumes (for example, using them as mentor texts in a writing workshop or as part of other text sets). Keeping lists of potential text sets rather than assembling them physically lets you use each book with more flexibility. They can easily be assembled in a week or month ahead of your planned use period.

We have provided examples of text sets for use across the grades (see Figures 17-2 and 17-3). It may be a good idea to talk with colleagues at your grade level to discuss and identify strong and productive text sets that you will want to use and share over the year.

TEACHING AND LEARNING ACROSS THE GRADES

Throughout this book, we examine students' learning over the elementary and middle school years. You will notice that we have not discussed using leveled books for interactive read-aloud. The gradient of leveled texts does not apply to books read during interactive read-aloud and need not be a factor in literature discussion because the texts can be made accessible to all students, regardless of their independent or instructional reading level. When you read the text aloud, you make the content available to all students.

Sample Text Sets for Interactive Read-Aloud, K-3

TYPE OF TEXT SET	TITLES	DESCRIPTION
Topic–ants **Fiction/Nonfiction pair**	*Night Visitors* (Young)	A retelling of a Chinese folktale about a young boy who learns to value life, even in small creatures like ants.
	Thinking About Ants (Brenner)	An informational text about ants.
Topic–pets	*A Pup Just for Me* (Young)	A book with two perspectives–the boy who wants a pet and the dog who wants a boy.
	Pick a Pet (Rotner and Garcia)	Realistic story about a girl who is choosing a pet; includes letters of the alphabet that match pets and owners.
	Come Meet Muffin! (Graham)	Realistic story about a cat who wanders around lost and then is adopted by a family.
	The Tenth Good Thing About Barney (Viorst)	Realistic story of the death of a favorite pet cat.
Topic–pets **Genre**–informational	*How to Talk to Your Cat* (George)	Provides factual information about cats.
	How to Talk to Your Dog (George)	Provides factual information about dogs.
Theme–immigration; names; teasing; moving	*The Name Jar* (Choi)	Story of a little Korean girl, new to the U.S., who is teased because children cannot pronounce her name.
	My Name Is Yoon (Recorvits)	Story of a little Korean girl, new to the U.S., who does not like the way her name looks written in English characters and tries to overcome homesickness by changing her name.
Theme–environment; making a difference	*Miss Rumphius* (Cooney)	Story of the life and contributions of a fictional character who made the world beautiful by planting lupines.
	Something Beautiful (Wyeth)	Story of a little girl who makes her urban environment more beautiful and inspires others.
Theme–feelings; problem solving; families	*When Sophie Gets Angry–Really, Really Angry . . .* (Bang)	Realistic story of how a little girl finds constructive ways to deal with anger.
	A Screaming Kind of Day (Gilmore)	Realistic story of how a child who is hard of hearing copes with frustrations.
	Rain Romp: Stomping Away on a Grouchy Day (Kurtz)	A little girl works out her grouchiness by dancing in the rain.

Figure 17-2. *Sample Text Sets for Interactive Read-Aloud, K-3*

Sample Text Sets for Interactive Read-Aloud, K-3 (CONTINUED)

TYPE OF TEXT SET	TITLES	DESCRIPTION
Author Study—Henkes	*Once Around the Block* (Henkes)	Realistic story of a young girl who finds going around the block to be an adventure.
	Lilly's Purple Plastic Purse (Henkes)	Story of a child-like mouse who is distracted by the new purse she brings to school.
	Chrysanthemum (Henkes)	Story of a child-like mouse who is teased because of her name.
	Owen (Henkes)	Story of a child-like mouse who has trouble giving up his blanket.
	Sheila Rae, the Brave (Henkes)	A story of a child-like mouse who is very brave but gets scared when lost and depends on her younger sister.
Text Structure—numbers	*Feast for Ten* (Falwell)	A counting book that presents elements of a family gathering.
	The Baseball Counting Book (McGrath)	A counting book that provides information about baseball.
Theme—elements of art	*Lunchtime for a Purple Snake* (Ziefert)	A little girl visits her artist grandfather, and they paint a picture together.
	Painting the Wind (MacLachlan and MacLachlan)	A boy learns about painting from watching different kinds of artists.
Theme—family; caring for others **Author Study**—Bodeen	*Elizabeti's Doll* (Bodeen)	A young girl in Africa imitates her mother by pretending a rock is a doll.
	Mama Elizabeti (Bodeen)	A young girl in Africa takes care of her little brother because her mother has a new baby.
	Elizabeti's School (Bodeen)	A young girl in Africa goes to school for the first time.
Genre—traditional literature **Illustrators**—Marshall and Galdone	*The Three Little Pigs* (Galdone) *The Three Little Pigs* (Marshall)	Traditional tale told in a straightforward way. Traditional tale with whimsical modern touches in the illustrations.
Genre—traditional literature	*The Three Billy Goats Gruff* (Stevens) *The Three Little Pigs* (Galdone) *The Three Bears* (Galdone)	Traditional tale told in a straightforward way. Traditional tale told in a straightforward way. Traditional tale told in a straightforward way.
Informative fiction text **Fiction/Nonfiction pairs**	*Private and Confidential: A Story about Braille* (Ripley) *Louis Braille, the Boy Who Invented Books for the Blind* (Davidson)	Story about a young girl who was to have private correspondence and learns Braille to communicate with a blind pen pal.

Figure 17-2. *Sample Text Sets for Interactive Read-Aloud, K-3 (cont.)*

Sample Text Sets for Interactive Read-Aloud, K-3 (CONTINUED)

TYPE OF TEXT SET	TITLES	DESCRIPTION
Language Play—rhyming; words that end alike; onomatopoetic words	*Duck in the Truck* (Alborough)	Rhyming book with cumulative structure about a duck getting stuck.
	One Duck Stuck (Root)	Humorous book about a duck stuck in the muck and a series of animals (making sounds) in increasing numbers coming to the rescue.
	My Truck Is Stuck (Lewis)	Rhyming book about a stuck truck and vehicles, making sounds, coming to help.
Mentor Text—use of interesting language	*Rain Romp: Stomping Away on a Grouchy Day* (Kurtz)	A little girl works out her grouchiness by dancing in the rain.
	Come On, Rain! (Hesse)	Children in the city enjoy rain after very hot weather.
Genre—traditional literature	*Zomo the Rabbit: A Trickster Tale from West Africa* (McDermott)	Traditional tale of the trickster.
	Why Mosquitoes Buzz in Peoples' Ears (Aardema)	Pourquoi tale.
Mentor Text—how writers represent sounds	*Hush!* (Ho)	Rhyming story of a mother in Africa hushing animals (who make sounds) so her baby can sleep.
	One Duck Stuck (Root)	"Splish, clomp, pleep, plop, plunk, slosh, slash, slink, ring" are some of the words in this funny rhyming book.
Author Study—Gibbons	*The Seasons of Arnold's Apple Tree* (Gibbons)	A boy explores the seasons through changes in an apple tree.
	Weather Words and What They Mean (Gibbons)	Gibbons's distinctive artistic style illustrates commonly misunderstood weather terms.
Topic—pets **Text Structure**—series about the same family	*My Dog Rosie* (Harper)	Realistic story about a big dog, Rosie, that a little girl takes care of while her grandfather works.
	My Cats Nick & Nora (Harper)	Realistic story about cats as pets in the same family as *My Dog Rosie.*
	Our New Puppy (Harper)	Realistic story about a new addition to the same family as *My Dog Rosie.*

Figure 17-2. *Sample Text Sets for Interactive Read-Aloud, K-3 (cont.)*

Yet we do have to think in broader terms about the appropriateness of texts for readers with different experiential backgrounds. We want the texts we read aloud and that students discuss in literature circles to be accessible in terms of language, concepts, and ideas. We want to consider a range of texts in terms of content and genre as well as age and grade appropriateness. We suggest thinking about curriculum mapping, or planning curriculum experiences across the grades. The plan need not be rigid but can provide a flexible map of rich and varied experiences to guide the learning across the year.

In creating curriculum goals, you will want to consider the texts that students should experience. In general, you will want to use a range of genres at each grade level, but

Sample Text Sets—Grades Four to Eight

TYPE OF TEXT SET	TITLES	DESCRIPTION
Genre—authors' autobiography	On the Bus with Joanna Cole (Cole)	Joanna Cole describes her writing, complete with drafts and dummy pages.
	The World of William Joyce Scrapbook (Joyce)	William Joyce writes about his work (writing and illustrating) in the form of a scrapbook.
	A Letter from Phoenix Farm (Yolen)	Jane Yolen writes about her life.
	The Days Before Now: An Autobiographical Note by Margaret Wise Brown (adapted by Blos)	A memoir by Margaret Wise Brown is put into a picture book.
Topic—bats	Stellaluna (Cannon)	A fictional text about a bat.
	Bat Loves the Night (Davies)	A poetic text that also provides facts about bats.
	Bats (Gibbons)	Informational text about bats.
Author Study—George	Look to the North: A Wolf Pup Diary (George)	An informational text about the early life of a wolf pup.
	How to Talk to Your Cat (George)	An informational book about cats.
	How to Talk to Your Dog (George)	An informational book about dogs.
	Nutik the Wolf Pup (George)	A realistic story about a boy who raises a wolf pup.
Mentor Text—personification to present information	Cave (Siebert)	Informational text, except that the story is told as if the cave is alive.
	Dear Children of the Earth (Schimmel)	Informational text about the environment, told by the earth personified.
Genre Study—biography	Abe Lincoln Remembers (Turner)	A biography of Abe Lincoln told from his point of view.
	Thomas Jefferson: A Picture Book Biography (Giblin)	A straightforward biography.
	The Amazing Life of Benjamin Franklin (Giblin)	A straightforward biography.
Author Study—Bunting **Topic**—immigration	A Picnic in October (Bunting)	A family celebrates the Statue of Liberty's birthday and their immigration to the U.S.
	So Far from the Sea (Bunting)	A Japanese American family visits Manzanar, where their grandfather is buried.
	How Many Days to America? (Bunting)	A family survives a trip to America in a small boat.
Topic—the dust bowl	Angels in the Dust (Raven)	Historical fiction text about a family surviving in the dust bowl.
	The Dust Bowl (Booth & Reczuch)	Realistic fiction combined with historical fiction about families in drought.

Figure 17-3. *Sample Text Sets—Grades Four to Eight*

Sample Text Sets—Grades Four to Eight (CONTINUED)

TYPE OF TEXT SET	TITLES	DESCRIPTION
Text Structure—letters that tell a story **Mentor Text**—using letter format; allusion	*Dear Peter Rabbit* (Ada)	Various storybook characters write letters to each other, weaving a story.
	With Love, Little Red Hen (Ada)	Little Red Hen tells her story through letters that she writes.
	Dear Mr. Blueberry (James)	A little girl engages in a series of letters about an imaginary whale.
Topic—art **Mentor Text**—biography	*My Name is Georgia* (Winter) *The Starry Night* (Waldman)	A portrait of Georgia O'Keefe. A biography of Vincent Van Gogh.
Theme—striving for freedom	*My Freedom Trip: A Child's Escape from North Korea* (Park and Park)	A story of a young girl's escape from North Korea to South Korea, based on the authors' mother's life—biography.
	Under the Quilt of Night (Hopkinson)	A slave family's journey on the Underground Railroad.
	Almost to Freedom (Nelson)	Escape from slavery, told from the point of view of a child's doll.
Topic—slavery and the Civil War **Genre**—historical fiction	*Pink and Say* (Polacco)	Two young boys, one white and one black, struggle to survive during the Civil War.
	Under the Quilt of Night (Hopkinson)	A slave family's journey on the Underground Railroad.
	Almost to Freedom (Nelson)	Escape from slavery, told from the point of view of a child's doll.
Theme—war	*My Freedom Trip: A Child's Escape from North Korea* (Park and Park)	A story of a young girl's escape from North Korea to South Korea, based on the authors' mother's life—biography.
	Journey Home (McKay)	A young girl accompanies her mother to Vietnam, where she was born and lost her family.
	So Far from the Sea (Bunting)	A Japanese American family visits Manzanar, where their grandfather is buried.
Author Study—Arnosky **Text Structure**—informational texts	*All About Frogs* (Arnosky) *All About Deer* (Arnosky) *All About Snakes* (Arnosky)	Informational text about frogs. Informational text about deer. Informational text about snakes.
Topic—wolves; environment	*Look to the North: A Wolf Pup Diary* (George)	An informational text about the early life of a wolf pup.
	Nutik the Wolf Pup (George)	A realistic story about a boy who raises a wolf pup.
	Wolf Watch (Winters)	Informational book about wolves.

Figure 17-3. *Sample Text Sets—Grades Four to Eight (cont.)*

Sample Text Sets—Grades Four to Eight (CONTINUED)

TYPE OF TEXT SET	TITLES	DESCRIPTION
Topic—the Holocaust and World War II **Mentor Texts**—writers' and illustrators' use of symbolism	*The Yellow Star* (Deedy)	Legend of King Christian X of Denmark who wore the yellow star to protect Jews.
	The Harmonica (Johnston)	Historical fiction of a young Jewish boy in a concentration camp.
	Rose Blanche (Christophe, Gallanz & Innocenti)	Historical fiction about a young girl during World War II.
Topic—discrimination **Theme**—courage; one person can make a difference	*If a Bus Could Talk* (Ringgold)	The story of Rosa Parks told through the eyes of a little girl who hears a bus talking.
	White Socks Only (Coleman)	A little girl's grandmother remembers racially segregated drinking fountains.
	The Bus Ride (Miller)	Historical fiction about a young African American girl who has the courage to sit at the front of the bus in the 1950s.
Topic—children and war	*Sadako* (Coerr)	A young Japanese girl has cancer in the aftermath of the atomic bomb.
	Rose Blanche (Christophe, Gallaz & Innocenti)	Historical fiction about a young girl during World War II.
Mentor Text—interesting ways to provide information **Text Structure**—factual texts	*Great Moments in Ice Cream History* (Older)	Informational book on the kinds and history of ice cream; many interesting facts—journal-like appearance.
	Bugs Before Time: Prehistoric Insects and Their Relatives (Camper)	Informational book about prehistoric insects.
	Faces Only a Mother Could Love (Dewey)	Informational book about many different baby animals.

Figure 17-3. *Sample Text Sets—Grades Four to Eight (cont.)*

the examples should become increasingly sophisticated. Format, too, is a consideration. While you want to use mostly picture books at every grade level, consider integrating some longer texts such as chapter books as appropriate.

Some genres, such as high fantasy, will not be appropriate for interactive read-aloud or literature discussion at primary grades. Avoid the temptation to use highly sophisticated texts that are beyond your students' understanding. It isn't worth it. If the books you read aloud are too mature, you run the risk of:

- Superficial treatment of texts that have a deeper meaning.
- Having many students disengage and think that reading is boring.
- Getting students to "put on a show" of talking about something they do not really understand.
- Wasting valuable instructional time in which you could be providing an in-depth experience that will support the development of strategies for understanding more sophisticated texts.

There are many good books that will hit the mark and offer rich thinking and learning opportunities for your students. Stick with them.

We set out a conceptual framework for creating an interactive read-aloud/literature discussion continuum (see Figure 17-4). It is important to think about the *characteristics of texts* and the *formats* that you will want to include at each grade level. Also, it is important to consider the *kind of thinking* that children will be able to do—within, beyond, and about the texts. Keeping this thinking in mind will guide your instruction. With extending thinking as a goal, you will want to consider *instructional approaches*—that is, *how* you use the texts to help students think, talk, and write about reading. Finally, *assessment* is another important goal. You want to think about how students will demonstrate their learning through talking and writing, which, again, changes over time.

THINKING WITHIN, BEYOND, AND ABOUT TEXTS THROUGH INTERACTIVE READ-ALOUD

At all levels, kindergarten through grade eight, interactive read-aloud provides the opportunity for students to engage in thinking within, beyond, and about texts. In your oral reading, you will be decoding the words for them, grouping words into phrase units, and reflecting the author's meaning and your own interpretation. Students can:

- Recognize new and interesting vocabulary.
- Discover new meanings for words they know.
- Follow multiple events in stories to understand the plot.
- Notice and remember important information.
- Make connections among and between texts.
- Make connections to their own lives.
- Infer what the author has not stated.
- Think about major and minor events and characters.

- Notice and understand the organization, or structure, of a text.
- Use graphics to gain information.
- Recognize aspects of the writer's or illustrator's craft.
- Think critically about a text, to include evaluating and forming opinions.

All of these strategic actions are present every time a student effectively processes a text through listening. These strategic actions are engaged daily over years of interactive read-aloud, moving from easier texts to very challenging texts over time. Each time listeners experience a text, they apply these cognitive actions in orchestrated ways. Their efforts are supported by the way you present the material and engage them in talk. Many different kinds of learning take place:

- As they experience variety, they become more flexible in orchestrating their thinking about texts.
- As they experience more sophisticated texts, they expand their thinking.
- As they talk with others, they learn to compose language that expresses their thinking.
- As they write and draw, they put their thinking into texts that they can share with others.

Much depends on the sequence of texts students experience over time. As teachers, we want to provide a strong ladder of

Creating Curriculum Goals for Interactive Read-Aloud and Literature Discussion

Characteristics of Texts: What kinds of texts are appropriate for students?	- What genres should students experience? - What types of examples within genres are appropriate? - What topics should students experience? - What authors or illustrators are appropriate? - What text formats should students experience? - What kinds of examples of each format are appropriate?
Supporting Readers' Thinking: What kind of thinking should students be able to do?	- What kinds of thinking within the text should students be able to do? - What kinds of thinking beyond the text should students be able to do? - What kinds of thinking about the text should students be able to do?
Teaching	- What instructional approaches are appropriate? - What kinds of interactions within instructional contexts power and support thinking?
Assessment	- How can I tell if students are learning? - How can I expect students to demonstrate learning?

Figure 17-4. *Creating Curriculum Goals for Interactive Read-Aloud and Literature Discussion*

support for growth in flexible thinking, and we can do so by selecting, connecting, and sequencing texts.

If you would like to use a highly detailed grade-by-grade continuum for interactive read-aloud, *The Continuum of Literacy Learning, PreK–8: A Guide to Teaching* (Pinnell and Fountas 2008, 2011) provides overall grade-by-grade curricular goals that are consistent with the framework in Figure 17-4. Although specific texts, topics, and content areas are not included (you will want to consult your district or state requirements in establishing these), the goals remain the same. You can use this guide as an overall schematic to set curriculum goals for grades PreK–8, or you can construct your own. Your conversations with colleagues about such guides will be important in developing common goals, but keep in mind how individuals and groups of children will vary in their development and needs.

In the sections below we discuss selecting texts, teaching through intentional conversation, and teaching through extended experiences, while observing for evidence of strategic actions for primary, intermediate, and upper elementary/middle grades.

SELECTING TEXTS

You will want to consider several factors in selecting texts to read aloud to your students. A high-quality text can be enjoyed at several levels, so precise grade-level designations are not possible. We are thinking about a long continuum of development, in which some texts are in general more suited to younger children and some are so sophisticated that it would be better to use them with older students. You do not want texts that are so simplistic that older children will not find them engaging; they need thought-provoking texts focused on issues important to them. You will also be using interactive read-aloud as a way to help your students learn about genre and the craft of authors and illustrators.

In selecting texts for your grade level and particular group of students, consider factors such as the following:

◻ Length of the text and the time required to read it.

◻ Your students' background of knowledge.

◻ Your students' experience in listening to texts.

◻ Topics of interest to the age level.

◻ Accessibility of concepts to the age level.

◻ Maturity of themes and ideas (from concrete stories

about friendship to themes dealing with serious social issues).

◻ Density of the text (amount of print on a page).

◻ Accessibility of the illustrations.

◻ Complexity and accessibility of the language.

◻ Appeal to the age group.

◻ Topics you want to explore with your students.

◻ Opportunities to connect to other texts.

The list is long and selection can become complex. With the wealth of children's literature available, however, probably the hardest decisions will be related to choosing between many good alternatives. Remember that at every level, you can organize text sets to help students make connections across topics, authors, illustrators, styles, and genres.

Primary Grades (K–2)

The realistic fiction texts that you select for reading aloud to primary age children will focus on everyday situations such as families, shopping, pets, and friends. Children ages five to eight also enjoy traditional literature in the form of folktales and simple animal fantasy. Providing a rich experience with folktales and fairy tales will "set the scene" for later enjoyment of complex fantasy. These stories, with repeating patterns, have special appeal for young children, as do cumulative stories, such as *The House That Jack Built*. Second graders who have had a rich previous experience with folktales and fairy tales will enjoy some of the modern "twists," such as *The True Story of the Three Little Pigs* (Sczieska), which is told from the wolf's point of view.

They will also enjoy books of poetry and language play that include rhymes, songs, nonsense poems, and very simple poems, as well as predictable books that have rhyme and repetition. You will also want to use some informational texts with primary children, including ABC books, label books, counting books, and concept books. In general, stick to familiar topics that children can relate to; these books will help them think in deeper ways about the world around them. Also available are some "factual-like" texts that have some of the features of informational text but incorporate fictional characters (such as a child making something and giving directions). Kindergarten and grade one children are fascinated by learning new information about their world. Second graders will enjoy exposure to easy picture biographies of well-known individuals, as well as factual texts on topics such as the human body, insects, sea animals, "how-to" books, electricity and magnets, and other topics that provide interesting information children can connect to and extend their personal background of knowledge.

Most of the texts that you read to primary children will be picture books with large illustrations. You can also use enlarged texts, which will be helpful for shared reading. Many teachers enjoy wordless books because they foster the use of oral language as well as noticing details in illustrations. These books are easy for children to pick up, look at, and discuss on their own. At second grade level, you may want to choose some simple chapter books, such as the Henry and Mudge series. Easy, or "starter," chapter books are quick to read and can start some children reading more books about the characters.

Intermediate Grades (3–5/6)

In intermediate grades, you will gradually expand both the genres and the variety within genres that you select for interactive read-aloud. Realistic fiction will become more complex, with stories that have multiple characters that change over time. Themes, such as friendship, school, teasing, and self-esteem, are appealing to students; there are also some texts with serious and inspiring themes, such as respecting nature, courage, and prejudice. Most plots are linear but have some twists. While you will want to include examples of the diversity of our society from the earliest days of kindergarten, texts in the intermediate grades more directly address issues related to racial, religious, and cultural differences and many texts require knowledge of different cultures. Traditional literature includes more complex tales, legends, and myths from a variety of cultures. Works of fantasy go beyond simple animal ("talking beast") stories to more complex texts that present moral lessons. Factual texts cover a wider range of topics, many well beyond students' personal experiences. Historical fiction presents even more challenge, in that listeners must understand important aspects of setting, which is also true of biography. Autobiography and memoir, which are written in first person, are also added. More complex poetry includes ballads and lyrical poetry.

Formats are more widely varied, to include not only chapter books but many picture storybooks and picture

biographies that include drawings, paintings, and photographs. Students will also enjoy short stories. Illustrated factual texts include simple graphics, easy-to-identify headings, sections that present categories of information, and some readers' tools, such as index, table of contents, and glossary. Across the grades, topics and graphics are more complex. You may also want to select some series books or texts with sequels which have the potential of capturing students' interests in reading more. Plays and enlarged poems can be used to support oral reading.

Middle School Grades (6–8)

For middle school students, you will want to select a full range of realistic fiction with complex plots taking place in highly diverse settings. Texts reflect serious social issues and have potential for expanding listeners' ability to empathize with others whose lives are different from their own. Historical fiction reflects a wide variety of settings that are distant both in time and place from students' own experience; knowledge of history is required for understanding many texts. Many texts, realistic and historical, focus on the problems of growing up, with themes that are appealing to preadolescents and adolescents. Traditional literature reveals cultural icons through legends, myths, and epics. Students enjoy some satirical pieces of fantasy that offer interesting twists on traditional stories. Fantasy involves symbolism, larger-than-life characters, the quest of the hero, and the struggle between good and evil. Science fiction presents even greater challenges, with their complex and fantastic technology in the creation of new worlds. Both fantasy and science fiction reveal universal truths that offer insight into the human condition. A wide variety of biography, autobiography, and memoir is available to expand students' knowledge of the events and individuals who have shaped and contributed to history. Both biographical texts and factual texts can serve to build background knowledge that students need to bring to their independent reading, and you can use informational texts to build knowledge not only of content but of how to read nonfiction and use the full range of readers' tools. Poetry will expand to include ballads and lyrical poetry, some longer poems, prose poems, and high abstract poetry.

Formats include the full range of choices—picture books, short informational texts, short stories, chapter and picture biographies, photo essays, chapter books of all genres, and series books or texts with sequels. You will want to continue to use high-level picture books because of their literary quality and appeal to students. (These texts are really short stories with artistic illustrations that make them into a coherent whole.) Many focus on sophisticated themes such as war, prejudice, and death. You will want to balance chapter books with shorter texts so that students experience a rich array across the year. As with earlier grades, interactive read-aloud is an ideal way to help students learn more about the complexities of genre and literary elements.

TEACHING THROUGH INTENTIONAL CONVERSATION

Teaching through intentional conversation will start your students on a journey of thinking, talking, and writing about reading. Skills build across the years. The conversations students have in the primary grades lay a strong foundation and help to build the habits of good discussion, which you can extend in subsequent grades. If your intermediate grade and middle school students have not had a great deal of experience using routines for interactive read-aloud, examine the suggestions for earlier grades and teach the routines explicitly. You will be adding to students' repertoires as they go up the grades.

Primary children like to join in on refrains when you are reading repetitive texts. Be sure that they have first listened to the text and truly understand it because they expect to join in with their voices. On simple texts with very strong refrains (such as *The Very Quiet Cricket*), this can often happen by the middle of the text. Children soon learn signals from the teacher that indicate they can join in. Older students can also enjoy repeating portions of the language of the text, which may take the form of creating readers' theater scripts and performing them or using poetry as a base for choral reading.

From the very beginning, engage students in conversation about texts. Some principles to consider for engaging your students in intentional conversation at all levels include the following:

- Select high-quality texts.
- Design openings that set the scene for thinking within, beyond, and about texts.
- Open texts in different ways to promote flexibility.

- Engage children in conversation before reading to share and build background knowledge and make predictions.
- Pause to invite conversation with one or more kinds of thinking in mind (that is, within, beyond, and about the text).
- Incorporate "turn and talk" in pairs, triads, and quads before, during, or after reading the text.
- Invite discussion of the meaning of the text after reading.
- End the session with a brief summary.
- Reread favorite stories, books with repetitive language, and poetry, inviting children to join in on refrains.
- Revisit sections of texts to reinforce specific teaching points, and help children develop shared examples.

Once students have learned a set of routines and customs for interactive read-aloud, they are poised to engage in productive discussion daily.

TEACHING THROUGH EXTENDED EXPERIENCES

Each read-aloud text has potential for extended learning. The first goal is to have students process the text and discuss it orally, but you may also want to provide some more extensive experiences connected to the text if you feel your students need to explore the meaning of the text further. You will want to think carefully about implementing these experiences: It is certainly not necessary to extend student understanding with most of the texts you read aloud and discuss. If you choose to do so, be sure that the activity is worthwhile in terms of expanding students' thinking and appreciation of the text and also consider your scarce time. Sometimes it is better to read and talk about many texts than to engage in elaborate extensions. Those that we have listed below for three levels are not time-consuming but have potential for extending oral and written language.

Primary Grades (K–2)

Suggestions for teaching through extended experiences include the following:

- Involve children in responding through drawing, painting, collage, or other art projects.
- Use "sound effects" with hands, feet, mouth, or musical instruments to accompany the reading of the text.
- Use shared and interactive writing to retell or innovate the text.

- Produce artwork to illustrate texts produced through shared or interactive writing.

- Dramatize a text by taking roles, emphasizing repetitive language.

- Dramatize a text using puppets.

- Engage in activities suggested by the text (cooking, walks, etc.).

- Use simple charts to help children remember the events of a story (lists, time lines).

- Use simple charts to help children remember and understand characters (lists of traits with pictures, webs).

- Perform observations/experiments suggested by an informational text.

- Use simple examples of readers' theater to help children re-create a scene or the whole text.

- Encourage children to do some writing about the text and illustrate it.

Intermediate Grades (3–5/6)

Suggestions for teaching through extended experiences include the following:

- Have students engage in dialogue with the teacher about the texts that have been read aloud.

- Have readers do a "short write" to get immediate responses down.

- Have readers explore in their own reading the genres that they have heard read aloud.

- Construct (or have students create) readers' theater scripts that students can perform.

- Have students make textual and visual representations of their interpretations of a text or group of texts (for example, posters).

- Have readers write letters to authors or illustrators.

- Have students select language from the text to illustrate.

- Involve students in extended projects (for example, author study) including visual and written presentations.

- Make charts with readers' contributions: story structure, story retelling, lists of information, character webs, sequence of events.

- Have readers make lists in the reader's notebook (for example, character traits or attributes of the setting).

- Have students make a picture or photo essay of a text.

- Have students write book reviews or book recommendations of texts they have heard read aloud.

- Have students write or draw to represent sensory images formed while listening.

- Invite readers to write a prose text in response to a poetic text or write a poem in response to a prose text.

- Have students write essays on a particular author or illustrator.

- Have students write biographical sketches of the authors, the subjects of biography, or fictional characters.

Middle School Grades (6–8)

Suggestions for teaching through extended experiences include the following:

- Have students engage in a written dialogue with the teacher and individual students about the texts.

- Have the students engage in "short writes," open-ended or focused, to get their thinking down.

- Make a variety of charts with student contributions to record their thinking; record their questions, demonstrate summaries; make lists; show character traits; show the sequence of events; identify plot structure; show important aspects of underlying informational structures (compare/contrast, description, sequence, cause/effect, problem/solution).

- Have students make their own charts in partners or small groups to record thinking; sometimes use individually reproduced graphic organizers to shape thinking in specific ways.

- Invite readers to construct a series of questions and responses that include information about an author or from a text or series of texts.

- Have readers do sketches, "short writes," and take notes to get immediate responses down.

- Have readers make and present textual, visual, or dramatic representations to express their interpretations (posters, photo essays, PowerPoint presentations, readers' theater scripts, etc.).

- Have readers produce a variety of letters, either to other persons about texts or to writers/illustrators.

- Have readers produce a poetic text in response to a prose

text, focusing on any aspect of a text (character, plot, setting, the achievements of a biographical subject).

□ Provide memorable quotes and ask students to respond to them in writing (may also include sketching).

□ Use double-column entry with a quote (phrase, sentence, question) in the first column and student comments/responses in the second column.

□ Prepare readers' theater scripts (and have students prepare them) from a scene or chapter of a book for performance.

□ Have students write essays on authors or illustrators.

□ Have students prepare biographical sketches of the subjects of biography, of authors, or of fictional characters.

□ Have students who have experienced a wide range of analytical thinking and writing bring their skills together to produce literary essays (formal treatises on any aspect of fiction texts).

□ Have students engage in extended research stimulated by response to texts that are read aloud, reading a variety of related fiction and nonfiction texts and producing reports.

You can find more elaborated descriptions of the writing activities mentioned above in Chapters 27 and 28, Writing About Reading.

PLANNING FOR THE YEAR

We have provided a series of curriculum maps (one at each grade level) to show how a number of teachers have thought about categories in planning a year of interactive read-aloud experiences. We have also provided a blank template so you can meet with colleagues and develop your own. We include a partial example here to illustrate the concept (see Figure 17–5), but you can find the other grade levels on the DVD that accompanies this book. Don't simply take them as your own. Rather, think about:

□ The kinds of decisions teachers are making and sharing with colleagues.

□ The ways texts and areas of study build on one another over the years.

□ The variety this ongoing curriculum assures students.

□ The foundation it provides for creating a rich text base.

□ The guidance it offers for purchasing and organizing books.

□ The potential for organizing the interactive read-aloud and literature study curriculum to meet the demands of state standards.

Within each example of a yearly interactive read-aloud plan, you will notice that teachers have included:

1 *Topics or themes.* Topics will be influenced by the district or state curriculum, as well as by the particular interests of children in local areas, but it is useful to specify a few special topics or themes at each grade level. Book collections or text sets for read-aloud and literature study can be organized around these topics. There may be special topics or titles that are ideally related to the social studies or science content at a particular grade level.

2 *Authors or illustrators.* At each grade level, it is useful to identify a few authors or illustrators suitable for author–illustrator study text sets. Author or illustrator study is a powerful way to help students learn to think about texts, because they will attend to the writer's style and language and other aspects of craft.

3 *Genres.* While you will want to have a wide variety of genres, it is a good idea to specify some focused genre studies at each grade level, particularly when you are introducing new kinds of texts. Of course, in kindergarten you will not be using the words *genre study,* but you can make comments like these:

□ "We are reading different kinds of folktales that have talking animals."

□ "This book is an informational book like *What Do You Do with a Tail Like This?*"

□ "This book is like *The Turnip*. On each page you hear everything that happened before."

Most genres are included at all grades, but the examples you share with children become much more complex. For example, poetry is included at every grade level. Kindergartners and first graders may be listening to shorter poems, many of which are the rhymes and verses that lay the groundwork for enjoying poetry. At upper grade levels, students will enjoy a wide range of ballads, narrative poetry, and lyrical poetry.

4 *Craft element.* You may select a number of texts that provide good examples of a writer's or illustrator's craft. For example, you might select a text set that shows how

Planning for Interactive Read-Aloud: Text Sets Across the Year—Grade Two

AUGUST/SEPTEMBER

FOLKTALES (BEAST)	ENVIRONMENT/RESPECTING NATURE	MEMOIRS/PERSONAL NARRATIVES	AUTHOR STUDY—MEM FOX	POETRY
□ Mouse Match (Young)	□ Miss Rumphius (Cooney)	□ Bigmamas (Crews)	□ Koala Lou	□ The Sun is So Quiet (Giovanni)
□ Beat the Story Drum Pum Pum (Bryan)	□ Something Beautiful (Wyeth)	□ Shortcut (Crews)	□ Boo to a Goose	□ Nathaniel Talking (Greenfield)
□ Rabbit Makes a Monkey of Lion (Aardema)	□ Our Big Home (Glaser)	□ Night in the Country (Rylant)	□ Wilfred Gordon McDonald Partridge	□ Cat Poems (Livingston)
□ Foolish Rabbit's Big Mistake (Rafe)	□ Dear Children of the Earth (Schimmel)	□ Goin' Somewhere Special (McKissack)	□ Wombat Divine	
□ The Bremen Town Musicians (Plume)	□ The Great Kapok Tree (Cherry)	□ Now One Foot, Now the Other (dePaola)	□ Hattie and the Fox	
□ The Three Billy Goats Gruff (Brown)	□ Hey! Get Off Our Train (Burningham)	□ Tell Me a Story, Mama (Johnson)	□ Possum Magic	
		□ Ma Dear's Aprons (McKissack)	□ Whoever You Are	
			□ Hunwick's Egg	
			□ Night Noises	
			□ Harriet, You'll Drive Me Wild	

OCTOBER

FAMILY	FOLKTALES (POURQUOI)	HUMAN BODY/HEALTH	FICTION/NONFICTION PAIRS	POETRY
□ All Kinds of Families (Simon)	□ The Great Race (Goble)	□ Actual Size (Jenkins)	□ A Pup Grows Up (Foster)	□ I Like You, If You Like Me (Livingston)
□ Birthday Presents (Rylant)	□ The Great Ball Game (Bruchac)	□ My Dentist, My Friend (Hallinan)	□ Hachiko: The True Story of a Loyal Dog (Turner)	□ Secret Places (Huck)
□ I Love You the Purplest (Joosse)	□ Why Mosquitoes Buzz in People's Ears (Aardema)	□ Gregory the Terrible Eater (Sharmat)	□ My Cat Jack (Casey)	□ Honey, I Love and Other Poems (Greenfield)
□ The Wednesday Surprise (Bunting)	□ How the Guinea Fowl Got Her Spots (Knutson)	□ How the Doctor Knows You're Fine (Cobb)	□ How Kittens Grow (Selsam)	
□ Hairs (Cisneros)	□ How Chipmunk Got Tiny Feet (Hausman)	□ A Book About Your Skeleton (Gross)		
□ How I was Adopted: Samantha's Story (Cole)	□ How the Stars Fell Into the Sky (Oughton)	□ My Friend the Doctor (Cole)		
□ Nettie Jo's Friends (McKissack)	□ How Spiders Got Eight Legs (Mead)	□ My Doctor (Rockwell)		
□ In My Momma's Kitchen (Nolen)	□ How Honu the Turtle Got His Shell (McGuire-Turcotte)	□ The Edible Pyramid (Leedy)		
	□ Why the Sun and the Moon Live in the Sky (Daly)			

Figure 17-5. Planning for Interactive Read-Aloud: Text Sets Across the Year—Grade Two

Planning for Interactive Read Aloud: Text Sets Across the Year—Grade Two (CONTINUED)

NOVEMBER

OCEAN
- Do Whales Have Belly Buttons? (Berger)
- The Magic School Bus on the Ocean Floor (Cole)
- Under the Sea From A to Z (Doubilet)
- The Whales (Rylant)
- What Lives in the Sea (Seymour)
- How to Hide an Octopus and Other Sea Creatures (Heller)
- The Ocean Alphabet Book (Pallotta)

CULTURAL TALES
- Jalapeno Bagels (Wing)
- Bimwili and the Zimwi (Aardema)
- The Paper Crane (Bang)
- Buffalo Woman (Goble)
- The Story of Jumping Mouse (Steptoe)
- The Night the Moon Fell (Ed Young)
- Little Plum (Ed Young)
- Miz Berlin Walks (Yolen)
- Tulip Sees America (Rylant)
- Mirandy and Brother Wind (McKissack)

MEMOIRS/PERSONAL NARRATIVES
- Sweet Sweet Memory (Woodson)
- Fireflies (Brinckloe)
- Tell Me a Story Mama (Johnson)
- Let's Go Home (Polacco)
- We Had a Picnic this Sunday Past (Woodson)

AUTHOR STUDY—GAIL GIBBONS
- The Pumpkin Book
- Apples
- Dogs
- Bats
- Bicycle Book
- From Seed to Plant
- The Season's of Arnold's Apple Tree
- The Reasons for Seasons
- Spiders
- Cowboys and Cowgirls
- The Post Office
- The Planets
- Sea Turtles
- Whales

POETRY
- Dog Poems (Livingston)
- Blackberry Ink (Merriam)
- Beneath a Blue Umbrella (Prelutsky)

DECEMBER

COMMUNITIES
- On the Town: A Community Adventure (Caseley)
- Me on the Map (Sweeney)
- Where Do I Live? (Chesanow)
- City Green (DiSalvo-Ryan)
- Jonathan Goes to the Library (Baggette)
- Night on Neighborhood Street (Greenfield)
- Arthur's Neighborhood (Brown)
- Everybody Bakes Bread (Dooley)
- Community Helpers (Kalman)

INSECTS (FICTION AND NONFICTION)
- Fireflies in the Night (Dawes)
- Spiders (Otto)
- The Big Bug Book (Facklam)
- Spiders (Gibbons)
- How to Hide a Butterfly (Heller)
- My Father's Hands (Ryder)
- Night Visitors (Young)
- Fireflies (Ryder)
- Fireflies in the Night (Hawes)
- The Magic School Bus Inside a Beehive (Cole)
- Butterfly House (Bunting)
- Monarch Butterfly (Gibbons)

CIRCULAR STORIES
- Louis the Fish (Yorinks)
- The Relatives Came (Rylant)
- The Cold Coin (Ada)
- The Woodcutter's Coat (Wolff)
- Two Bad Ants (Van Allsburg)
- The Marzipan Pig (Hoban)
- Ollie Forgot (Arnold)

MEMOIRS/PERSONAL NARRATIVES
- When Grandpa Came to Stay (Caseley)
- Poppy's Chair (Hesse)
- I Don't Want to Go to Camp (Bunting)
- Goodbye Max (Keller)
- Island Boy (Cooney)
- Nana Upstairs, Nana Downstairs (dePaola)

POETRY
- People Poems (Bennett)
- Noisy Poems (Bennett)
- Old Elm Speaks (George)

Figure 17-5. Planning for Interactive Read-Aloud: Text Sets Across the Year—Grade Two (cont.)

writers use language "to show" readers, not tell them what something is like (provide details only when they are helpful to readers) or texts that show how writers show the passage of time.

5 *Specific texts.* You may want to select, in cooperation with colleagues, a few texts that are "too good to miss"—core texts to read at a particular grade level. There are some cautions in taking this approach, however:

◻ The core texts should not be arbitrarily adopted by the principal or any one teacher without communication and consultation across the grades.

◻ Core texts should not become "set in stone" so that nothing changes year after year. Conversation could become static rather than fresh.

◻ Core texts should change in response to current interests of children—not those who are now in high school or college.

Bearing these cautions in mind, identifying a few core texts can ensure that students have access year after year to some very high-quality texts appropriate to the grade level. Moreover, you can count on students' bringing to your classroom the shared experience of common texts, which makes it easier for them to make connections between texts and for you to find examples for mini-lessons (although nothing substitutes for building a large group of shared texts in your own classroom). Inevitably, of course, some students in your class will already have heard whatever text you use.

SUGGESTIONS FOR PROFESSIONAL DEVELOPMENT

OPTION 1: FORMING TEXT SETS

1 Meet with your grade-level colleagues for a series of meetings.

2 Bring one fiction and one nonfiction text set to the first meeting. Share the titles, why you chose them, and a few opportunities for learning that you have marked with stick-on notes.

3 For the second meeting, bring an author text set and an illustrator text set. Repeat the process.

4 For the third meeting, bring a topic text set related to a social studies theme at your grade level and a genre text set. Repeat the process.

5 Have everyone give colleagues a copy of the list of books you have shared.

OPTION 2:

1 Gather colleagues within and across grade levels to discuss the planning of the reading curriculum.

2 If you have *The Continuum of Literacy Learning, PreK–8: A Guide to Teaching* (Pinnell and Fountas 2008, 2011), use the read-aloud guides for the focus of your discussion. Teachers at each grade level can look at the guides specific to their level, but everyone should also look at a couple of grade levels before and beyond just to see the kinds of learning that are going on there.

3 Then, look at the sample yearly plans by grade level on the DVD that accompanies this book (Sample Text Sets, K–8). This sample includes more books than you might be able to read aloud in a year, but it offers a variety for selection. Use the blank planning template included to build a yearly plan based on what you see. Choose authors, topics, genre studies, and so on. The ultimate goal will be for each teacher to have a tentative plan of categories for text sets for the year and to ensure variety across the grades. You may also discuss some specific titles for each category.

4 Discuss how the categories for the sets will support the content area curriculum.

5 Spend some time after your planning meeting searching for excellent titles for each category. When you fill in your tentative titles, meet again to distribute a copy of each curriculum map to colleagues and to have a discussion.

6 Consider meeting again at the end of the school year to evaluate and revise your selection.

CHAPTER EIGHTEEN

MOVING FROM INTERACTIVE READ-ALOUD TO LITERATURE STUDY

Literature can take us out of ourselves and return us to ourselves—slightly different with each book we have loved.

—CHARLOTTE HUCK

Reading workshop is a highly productive structure within which students participate in whole-group, small-group, and individual instruction. It is closely linked to, and rests on, the foundation created by interactive read-aloud and shared literary experiences with common texts on which students base other literary learning experiences. Thus it builds their content and literacy knowledge.

At every grade level, interactive read-aloud promotes whole-group talk oriented toward helping children learn how to discuss texts with others and, ultimately, think on their own in deeper ways. As a teacher, you play a key role in demonstrating, prompting, reinforcing, and observing effective talk about texts. We call this conversation "text talk," as a reminder that the text anchors the discussion. To a great extent, interactive read-aloud and literature study (often called literature circles or book clubs) have many of the same goals; however, their structures are different. Literature study offers opportunities for increased text talk, since there are fewer individuals talking for longer amounts of time. Moving from interactive read-aloud as a whole-group discussion to peer talk in pairs, triads, and circles is a natural progression. By the time students engage in effective talk in threes and fours, they have learned how to engage in the deep discussion of book clubs, or literature circles.

THE INTERRELATIONSHIP OF CURRICULUM COMPONENTS

Interactive read-aloud contributes strongly to learning across the language and literacy framework. As shown in Figure 18-1, interactive read-aloud is the foundation of a variety of literacy contexts throughout the grades.

Daily interactive read-aloud introduces shared texts that become the basis for explicit minilessons in reading (and writing) workshop. Just as important, interactive read-aloud is a forum for helping students learn the interactive skills they will need to discuss literature effectively.

Literature study is one component of reading workshop that is usually introduced in grade two or three. From kindergarten through grade 8, students can discuss literature by way of interactive read-aloud, at some point taking part in more formal small-group discussion groups (book clubs). If students have had a great deal of prior experience discussing books during interactive read-aloud, you can usually begin book clubs in second grade.

We recommend a reading workshop of seventy-five to ninety minutes in the early grades (K–1), that includes a variety of shared reading and writing experiences as well as explicit phonics instruction and word study. You may want children to work at centers while you meet with small groups for guided reading instruction. An alternative is for children to engage in meaningful independent literacy tasks at their seats, a choice that may work well for students at grade two and above. Some teachers prefer the structure on the left side of Figure 18-1 for grade two, while others prefer the structureas shown on the right. You will also want to have about an hour for writing workshop.

At the intermediate and middle school grades, we recommend an hour for reading workshop and an hour for writing workshop. You may find this a challenge at the middle school level, especially as days become divided into increasingly shorter periods; you may need to alternate several days of reading workshop with several days of writing workshop. Intermediate teachers will also want additional time for language/word study (see Fountas and Pinnell 2001).

The reading workshop (see Chapter 23) begins with a brief minilesson on any aspect of reading. After that, students independently (and silently) read books they have selected themselves. Remember, you will already have spent

Thinking, Talking, Reading, and Writing About Texts

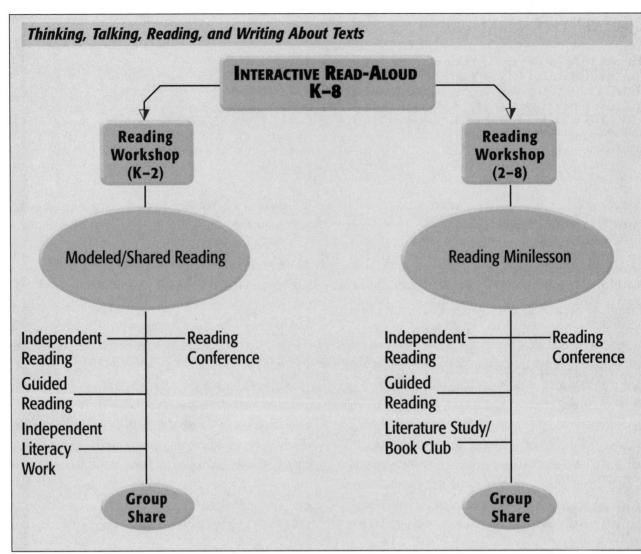

Figure 18-1. *Thinking, Talking, Reading, and Writing About Texts*

a great deal of time teaching the routines of the workshop as well as helping students learn how to select appropriate books—texts they can read with understanding and fluency without your support. At this point, you have several options:

1   You can confer with students individually. These reading conferences allow you to determine how well students are processing and understanding the texts they are reading independently and offer specific support to help them expand their strategic actions. Typically, a reading conference lasts about three to five minutes and may include listening to the student read a short portion of text aloud, discussing the text, demonstrating or showing the student something about effective reading,

and/or helping the student write about reading or reflec on information in the reader's notebook.

2   You can work with one or more small groups of student in guided reading. This small-group instruction lets you work efficiently with students who read at about the same level and can benefit from this focused instruction (see Chapters 24, 25, and 26).

3   You can work with one or more small groups of student in mixed-ability book clubs. Interest in talking about a text, not reading ability, is the criterion.

The sixty-minute reading workshop in grades two through eight might include any one or a combination of the three instructional contexts above. The workshop ends with a brief sharing period, during which students can talk abou their reading and you can reinforce and extend what you taught in the minilesson. It may also include a quick evaluation of how well the group worked.

TEXT TALK

Authors, students, and teachers come together through talk. Noted children's author Katherine Paterson shares her pleasure in bringing students and books together:

> Teaching children to read and providing them with something worthwhile to read is not a job for the faint of heart in this world. But I'll keep at it, and I won't be alone. You'll come too. We're fortunate, you know. Too many people in this world spend their lives doing work that doesn't really matter in the great scheme of things, but bringing children and books together does matter. And we get to do it. (*Hornbook,* 1999)

Interactive read-aloud and literature study abound with *text talk,* the shared talk about narrative, expository, or poetic texts (see Beck and McKeown 2001).

The more we have a chance to do it, the better we all get at text talk. As groups work together, they develop a backlog of shared meanings that increasingly deepens their talk. You may have experienced this phenomenon yourself as a member of a book club over several years' time. A friend of ours recently remarked, "The books we read aren't always my first choice, but I love talking to my friends in my book club." You not only come to understand texts differently, but you get to know each other.

EFFECTIVE TEXT TALK

For your students, text talk is effective because you have demonstrated it during interactive read-aloud. Some productive text talk includes the following characteristics:

- The people in the group have a shared, constantly growing language they use to talk about texts.
- The talk is anchored to the particular texts being discussed.
- The talk is based on the readers' personal experience or information in the text.
- Individuals may connect the text to other texts they have read.
- One idea sparks another, so individuals "piggyback" their comments.
- People in the group listen actively and carefully to one another.

- People in the group ask one another questions to clarify or extend the meaning they are sharing.
- The group maintains ownership of the conversation, but the text is the focus.
- Members of the group stay on a topic long enough to gain depth and get several perspectives.
- The talk of the group often changes the thinking of individuals in some way.
- The talk builds relationships and develops a sense of community among members.
- People in the group really care about what other group members think.
- People know how to disagree respectfully; constructive disagreement is valued rather than avoided.
- Members of the group can change opinions and understandings during the course of a discussion; they do not have to stick rigidly to a position.

Your literature discussions will not possess these characteristics automatically. Even adult groups have to work together for a while before they are able to have rich discussions. Students need to experience these qualities over several years in both interactive read-aloud and book clubs.

TEXT TALK AS EVIDENCE OF THINKING

As a teacher, text talk gives you a great deal of information about the ways in which your students are thinking within, beyond, and about a text (see Figure 18-2). The idea, of course, is not to approach text talk as an exercise. The kinds of talk mentioned in Figure 18-2 will occur naturally during interactive read-aloud and literature study if students are thinking deeply about the text and if you are demonstrating and teaching them how to build a richer understanding of the text together.

Our approach to literature discussion is to engage students' attention but to leave room for open response. Louise Rosenblatt's (1978) distinction between aesthetic and nonaesthetic reading is a useful way to think about the different kinds of reading we do.

In aesthetic reading, the reader is "living through" the text (p. 25), responding in all kinds of ways to the experiences she is having while reading. The reader's purpose, to experience the text, results in her taking a "stance" that influences what she does. When you read a wonderful book

---

Text Talk: Thinking About Texts

Within the Text

- Recount important events from the text.
- Describe characters, setting, events.
- Report or list new ideas or information gained from reading.
- Summarize the story or ideas.
- Provide specific evidence from personal experience or the text to support theories or inferences.
- Draw the group's attention to a specific part of the text or to illustrations that convey specific information.

Beyond the Text

- Express hypotheses, inferences, predictions, or theories.
- Disagree with a statement made by another reader.
- Reconsider ideas.
- Talk about personal responses and connections.
- Contribute prior knowledge for the benefit of the group.
- Interpret illustrations.
- Link evidence from the text with inferences, hypotheses, predictions, or theories.
- Talk about the central theme or meaning of the text.
- Seek many interpretations.

About the Text

- Identify literary elements.
- Use literary terms.
- Attend to the language of a text.
- Draw the group's attention to aspects of the writer's craft using examples from the text.
- Talk about the characteristics of the genre, offering examples from the text.
- Draw the group's attention to literary aspects of the text (symbolism, for example).
- Challenge the accuracy of an author's statement.
- Offer a well-formed criticism of some aspect of the text, using evidence to support the argument.

Figure 18-2. *Text Talk: Thinking About Texts*

like *Reading Lolita in Tehran: A Memoir in Books* (Nafisi), for example, your stance might simply be to experience the book club along with the women and understand how liberating the experience is for them. Your responses might range from curiosity about what their lives are like to empathy with individuals to a comparison with your own reactions to the books these women have read. You might be enthralled by the book, and as a result, make it a work of art.

In nonaesthetic reading, which Rosenblatt labels *efferent*, the reader is more concerned with what she carries away from the reading—the end result. You might pick up *Reading Lolita in Tehran* with the goal of being able to talk about what life in Tehran was like after the Shah left and Khomeini took charge. You might skim and scan, occasionally taking notes. You would tend to disengage from the personal elements in your response. According to Rosenblatt:

> The distinction between aesthetic and nonaesthetic reading, then, derives ultimately from what the reader does, the stance that he adopts and the activities he carries out in relation to the text. (p. 27)

Of course, most reading does not take place on the extreme ends of the efferent–aesthetic continuum. Often you hope to come out with some information or ideas after reading,

but you also settle into reading simply to enjoy and appreciate it.

The very idea that you are going to discuss a book with others means you are conscious of an end result—information or ideas you want to share with others after reading or information you want to seek from others. The knowledge of the upcoming meeting influences your stance. At the same time, your sharing will not be very rich or personal if you are only thinking about what you will say about the book. What makes literature discussion very rich is that individuals first experience the text in an aesthetic way and then reflect on that experience as they share it with others.

It is important to remember that the reader and the reader's purposes determine the stance and have a powerful influence on the experience. We have to be careful as we prepare students for and engage them in literature discussion. Requiring students to focus on only one kind of response can unnecessarily limit their response. Readers have a range of ways of responding to texts. For example, if you ask students to come to the group with three personal connections, you run the risk of setting in motion a search for three items: They may shut down other more appropriate responses and stop doing much thinking at all after the responses are gathered. The task becomes the focus.

When you work with book clubs, we suggest that you participate in or observe the group closely. There may be times when your students will be able to discuss a book on their own, but in our experience, your presence makes a big difference (see Fountas and Pinnell 2001). Your expertise can give the group a "lift," as they are able to learn even more than they would be able to learn from talking to each other. Of course, your role will change over time, from more active to mostly an observer, with only occasional interaction needed.

INTERACTIVE READ-ALOUD AND BOOK CLUB EXAMPLES

Even very young children can engage in meaningful text talk. Figure 18-3 is an excerpt from a read-aloud of the very funny text *Knuffle Bunny* (Willems). We have found that kindergarten children thoroughly enjoy the baby talk in this story, as well as the situation.

Mrs. Marta began by drawing children's attention to the endpapers, which feature many repetitions of a picture of Knuffle Bunny (a child's special stuffed animal) peering out from inside a washer at a laundromat. She then drew attention to the title page, which features a sequence of picture frames showing two people getting married, the same couple with a baby, the same couple walking with a baby in a snugglie, and, finally, the main character, Trixie, hugging Knuffle Bunny. Mrs. M introduced Trixie and her stuffed bunny and drew attention to her family. Several children talked about their own special stuffed animals or blankets.

The teacher was skillful in setting up a situation in which children could find it easy to notice and remember Trixie's attachment to the animal and to use that information to interpret the little girl's actions as well as the story's happy ending. Notice how she not only asked the children questions but also made comments herself to demonstrate her thinking. At one point, she summed up the children's thinking so far, thus helping them remember the prediction so they could confirm it. The way she drew their attention to critical information made it easier for them to make inferences about the character's motivations, make connections to their own situation, and predict the ending.

In the next example (see Figure 18-4), Mr. Glazer interacted with third graders around *In the Small, Small Night* (Kurtz), a story in which two traditional African tales are embedded and in which he saw a good opportunity to help

---

EXCERPT FROM INTERACTIVE READ-ALOUD DISCUSSION OF
Knuffle Bunny

MRS. M.: [READING] *"Then they left."* There they are. They put everything in the washing machine and they are going to walk home. [SHOWS CHILDREN THE PICTURE.]

YUKI: Is the bunny in the machine?

MRS. M.: It looks like Knuffle Bunny's eyes, doesn't it? [READING] *"But a block or so later . . . Trixie realized something."* She looks really surprised, doesn't she? [READING] *"Trixie turned to her daddy and said, 'Aggle glaggle klabble!' 'That's right,' replied her daddy. 'We're going home.'"* [Continues to read several pages showing Trixie's frantic attempts to communicate with her daddy.] She is really unhappy, isn't she? I'm wondering why.

SAM: Maybe she needs to go to the bathroom! [LAUGHTER]

JEREMY: She's just a baby and cries a lot.

LATOYA: She doesn't have her blanket, I mean her bunny.

MRS. M.: I was thinking that too, LaToya. I wonder if her daddy was supposed to stick Knuffle Bunny in the wash! So she's just screaming and crying . . .

YUKI: And she's a baby so she can't really talk.

MRS. M.: The author said that, didn't he, right at the beginning. He said it was before she could even speak words. So, maybe that's why she was using all that baby talk and crying, and waving her arms, because she missed Knuffle Bunny and couldn't tell her daddy what was wrong. What do you think?

CHILDREN: Yes that's why.

YUKI: Maybe she'll learn to talk.

MRS. M.: Let's read on and see if we are right. [Reads the next page, where Trixie's mother opens the door and asks, "Where's Knuffle Bunny?" and then to the end where Trixie speaks her first words, which are, of course, "Knuffle Bunny."] You were right, Yuki. She did start to talk!

Figure 18-3. *Excerpt from Interactive Read-Aloud Discussion of* Knuffle Bunny

---

his students notice the text structure and become familiar with some traditional literature from another country at the same time. He also wanted children to empathize with the two children and see the strength in their relationship—the older sister taking care of her younger brother. He briefly reminded them that they had heard other stories by the author and then "set the scene" by telling a little bit about the setting.

An older sister and little brother from Ghana are spending one of their first nights in America. The little brother crawls into the sister's bed and says he is cold, but she knows that he is really afraid. To distract him, she tells two stories from their homeland— one about tricky Anansi and the other about a turtle. Afterward, her brother helps her address her own fears about being in a new place.

MR. G.: This story is by Jane Kurtz, who also wrote *Pulling the Lion's Tail*. Remember that one?

NOAH: That was from Ethiopia and she was trying to make her new mother like her.

MR. G.: This is a story about two children who have just moved to America from Ghana, another place in Africa. The older sister is named Abena and the younger brother is named Kofi. Just imagine what it would be like to be in a completely different country on the other side of the world. Would you like remembering the place you left?

SARA: I maybe wouldn't, because it would be kind of sad.

KWAMI: I did come from another country, but I was too little to remember.

DWAYNE: Did their cousins come with them?

MR. G.: Abena's and Kofi's grandmother and cousins still live in Ghana. Sometimes you can remember a place by remembering stories, or by using your imagination, and that is what happens in this story.

MR. G.: *[Reads the text to page 5, where Abena says, "Once upon a time," and Kofi whispers "Time." At this point in the story Abena has asked Kofi to imagine that her new flashlight is the moon over their old home and she herself imagines that she hears a storyteller. She begins to tell a story to Kofi about Anansi.]* When I read those words, "Once upon a time," I knew that Abena was using her imagination to help Kofi. What were you thinking?

DWAYNE: She's trying to get him to go to sleep by telling a story.

NOAH: She's thinking about the story to remember it.

KWAMI: It's going to be the start of a story that she's telling.

MR. G.: I think you are right, and maybe Abena is homesick for the old place and wants to remember it. *[He reads to the end of the Anansi story.]* That was a good story. I noticed that Abena even changed the way she was talking. Maybe she became like the storyteller in her old village. Now turn and talk with your group of three about what you think that story meant to Abena and Kofi.

Children turn and talk in small groups of three for about two minutes. Afterward, they comment that:

▫ Abena told the story to make herself less homesick.

▫ Abena and Kofi do storytelling often, as evidenced by the way they start.

▫ She has a very good imagination.

▫ Abena must have heard the story a lot in her home village.

▫ Sometimes it seems like she is talking like a storyteller and sometimes like a girl.

▫ She is kind of scared, too, and so she doesn't really mind when Kofi comes into her bed.

▫ She's a good big sister.

▫ There are really two stories here.

Figure 18-4. *Excerpts from Interactive Read-Aloud of* In the Small, Small Night

After reading past the first embedded tale, Mr. Glazer used a routine called "turn and talk" (Calkins 2002), also known as "say something" (Harste, J. Short, K, and C. Burke 1988) in which the children quickly share their thinking with one or two others before discussing the text as a group. He shared the way the words "Once upon a time" signaled that the text was changing and they were now hearing a story within story. Right before "turn and talk" he shared his own obser vation that even Abena's way of talking changed when sh became the storyteller. His teaching helped the childre make inferences about the characters' attributes and thei motivations, as well as notice the change in text structure.

At the end of the story, when Kofi reassured Abena, the children learned that he was really listening. Their discussion reveals that they recognize the characters' apprehensions and how their traditions and relationships help them deal with these apprehensions.

A group of students talking about *Maniac Magee* (Spinelli) (see Figure 18-5) provides a third example of text talk, but with a more sophisticated text. These readers have agreed to read the first part of the book during independent reading and at home and then come together to talk about it before reading the next part.

In this example, the teacher's voice was not as evident (she supported and encouraged the group with just one question), but she had worked with the students on how to talk to one another about books and they were very able to control the discussion, with only an occasional comment from their teacher. Notice how the students were working with each other to understand Maniac and empathizing with him.

EVIDENCE-BASED TEXT TALK

Text talk is based on evidence, which means that participants in literature discussion do not simply offer opinions. They ground their statements in evidence from the text or from personal experience. In a good literature discussion, you will often hear the readers make connections to real evidence. Even young children can learn how to support their thinking. You simply ask the question, "What made you think that?" and soon they learn to always tell "why."

For example, here are some comments related to Jacqueline Woodson's *Coming on Home Soon*, a story about a little girl and her grandmother who waited to hear when the girl's mother would come home. The mother went to Chicago, where she had heard they were hiring "colored" women since the men were off fighting in the war. A long time passed with no word. Meanwhile, even though they had little food and the grandmother told the girl not to get attached to a small black kitten, the grandmother ended up letting the girl adopt it and (the author implies) even grew fond of it herself. At the end of the story, they got a letter and money from the mother, so they knew the venture had been a success. On the last page there are no words, but we see the mother arriving at the country house in the snow.

EXCERPT FROM LITERATURE DISCUSSION OF
Maniac Magee

JESSE: Maniac reminds me of a crazy, but independent, person. He never goes with the crowd. He doesn't think like other characters do, that black is black and white is white. He's always trying to figure out where he belongs.

MRS. L.: Even though he doesn't need many physical things, does he have any emotional needs?

GAYLA: I think Maniac just needs a family. He keeps changing. From his parents, to his aunt and uncle, to the Beals and then Grayson. I think he needs not just a family but the same one—something to fill the empty spot in his heart.

JESSE: It's really kind of a mixture of emotions and stuff. First, he's upset because of the confetti incident and then he's happy with the buffalos. Then Grayson finds him and brings him to the bandshell. The more they spend time together the more links of friendship they add on to the chain. Then when the last link is in place at Christmas, he dies. Then the link is broken. I feel so bad for Maniac.

KARLA: On page 114 when Jerry Spinelli says, "Five days later the old man was dead," I jumped in my chair. It was so shocking. Just like a fly getting hit with a swatter. Bam! It really made me think. Now the book is so somber. I hope it will have a happy ending and Maniac will find where he truly belongs.

Figure 18-5. *Excerpts from Literature Discussion of* Maniac Magee

---

▫ "I knew the grandmother was going to let her keep the cat **because** even though she said they couldn't, she poured the milk for it."

▫ "The grandmother is really worried, too. **For instance,** it says 'her eyes are sad.'"

▫ "The grandmother is a survivor. **For example,** she knows how to hunt for possum and rabbit."

▫ "I think the girl doesn't really like her grandmother to kill rabbits. Here **the author said,** 'A little bit of me hopes we find one. A little bit of me hopes we don't.'"

▫ "They are so happy at the end when they read the letter. She says her mama loves her more than rain or snow because that's what they always said to each other. **Earlier it said** that the girl would say 'more than rain' and the mother would answer 'more than snow' and that they had done it a hundred thousand times."

- **"From the book I know that** the grandma loved the cat, because she put it in her coat to keep it warm."

- **"Let me explain** why I think the grandmother was as worried as the little girl. She was always watching for the postman, and when they finally got the letter, she said, 'Thank you, Lord.' And she put her hand to her face. She looks like she's about to cry."

- "The mother loved her daughter and her mother a lot. She went away, but **think about** that she had to leave home and work hard cleaning trains and she sent her money back."

- **"When I think about** the mother not being able to get a job unless all the men were away fighting the war, it makes me realize how unfair some things were back then."

- "The grandmother wants the mother to come home. **On the last page** she said, 'Well, she needs to take a mind to go.'"

THE SOCIAL CONVENTIONS OF TEXT TALK

Students learn how to engage in text talk that incorporates important social conventions. These socially appropriate conventions help group members show respect for one another and develop the ability to engage in productive and enjoyable discussions. Some examples of language that is helpful include the following:

- "Building on what ____ said . . ."
- "I agree with ____ because . . ."
- "I disagree with Annie because . . ."
- "Help me understand that."
- "What made you think that?"
- "Say more about that."
- "Talk more about your thinking."
- "I see why you might say that, but . . ."
- "I'm thinking from another point of view that . . ."
- "I agree, but look at page ___, where . . ."
- "I disagree because . . ."
- "How is that different from what ____ said?"
- "Can you say more about why you think that?"
- "Where in the book did the author show us that?"

- "That surprises me. Tell me more about it."
- "I think we have two good possible explanations (theories) here."
- "I'll keep that in mind when I'm reading."
- "I've been thinking differently about that because . . ."
- "That helps me understand this in a different way."
- "Is it all right to change the topic now?"
- "I'm confused about something. What do all of you think about it?"

There are hundreds of ways in which people use language socially to establish relationships and express agreement and disagreement. This behavior is learned through many experiences discussing topics with other people. Participants learn that they are more receptive to others' statements when they are couched within the language of social conventions and they start to use such language themselves.

At the appropriate time, you will want to bring these language constructions to students' attention. Younger children can learn to say "I agree/disagree with John because . . ." or "I like what Annie said because . . ." Simply using this kind of language communicates that it is important to listen to and build on others' comments and tell why you think the way you do. Older children can consciously become much more sophisticated with their language while talking about texts. You can model the language as you participate, and have them reflect on the specific language that "opened up the conversation" or kept the conversation going in your evaluation after the discussion.

THE ADVANTAGES OF TEXT TALK

Text talk is genuine conversation through which individuals get to know more about one another and their world while at the same time deepen their understanding of text. Through text talk, your students can:

- Make meaning that is grounded in a text.
- Work through their thinking as they explain what they understand.
- Seek a richer meaning of a text together.
- Discover other interpretations.
- Revise their thinking.
- Reach for higher-level thinking.
- Learn from and about one another.

- Become more engaged and motivated.
- Become more independent.
- Take responsibility for their own learning and the learning of others.

In addition to expanding children's knowledge of the world and others, text talk about good books makes an important contribution to the development of a sense of community. It enables students to know one another in new ways as they live a literate life together in the classroom (see Figure 18-6).

DEVELOPING THE ABILITY TO TALK ABOUT TEXTS

Interactive read-aloud plays an important role in preparing students for small literature discussion groups. Language extends students' understanding. "Intentional conversation" (see Chapter 13) lets you guide talk in a way that not only allows for a range of student responses but also provides learning opportunities. Because text talk is so important, we need to be sure that the ability to engage in it is developed in explicit ways throughout elementary and middle school.

WHOLE-CLASS DISCUSSION OF THE SAME TEXT

In small-group literature discussion, you will want your students generally to have a choice about what they read, and you will want different groups to read different selections most of the time. But it is also important for the class to have some opportunities to read and discuss a single text. Either you can read the text aloud, or each student can read the selection individually. (In the latter case, some students will need to access the text through other means, such as a CD or another person reading it to them.) Sometimes you may want to read a text aloud while each student follows along in his or her copy.

According to Bomer and Bomer (2001), whole-class reading and discussion of the same text accomplish a number of goals:

- It makes it possible for the group to talk about the text in great detail, because they have all read it or heard it read.
- It makes it easier to use a shared language, shared references, and shared examples.
- All students experience the same conversations and are moving toward the same instructional goals.
- The shared text can be the basis for writing or sketching, which, again, can be shared as a whole group.
- Even though everyone has read the same text, there can be flexibility in the way the discussion proceeds (pairs, threesomes, circles, small groups)—"a fluid combination of smaller social structures."
- Teachers can work in small groups with students who are having more difficulty understanding the text, providing more support before moving to the whole-group discussion.
- The process of working with a shared text builds community among the readers in your classroom. Students learn to be part of a democratic classroom.

When you first begin interactive read-aloud in kindergarten, you will want to invite children to participate in whole-class discussion and continue this throughout the grades. You can encourage students to talk by asking some questions, but you also need to make genuine comments yourself to demonstrate the many ways of talking about texts.

Another goal of whole-class discussion is to encourage your students to listen and talk to *one another* rather than simply to you. Many whole-class discussions tend to follow this pattern:

Figure 18-6. *Literature Discussion Group*

- Teacher question.
- Student one answers the teacher.
- Teacher repetition of student one's answer and/or comment or question.
- Student two answers the teacher.
- Teacher repetition of student two's answer and/or question.
- Student three answers the teacher.
- Etc.

In the situation above, students learn that the most important person to talk to is the teacher, who is also the only important person to listen to. Some ways to change this pattern are:

- Establish expectations that students will respond to one another's comments.
- Ask other students to respond to student one's comment, rather than doing it yourself.
- Instead of repeating each student's comment and then commenting yourself, ask other students to comment on what the student said.
- Ask student one to call on another student to respond or make a comment.
- Write comments on a chart as many students respond.
- Seat students in a circle so that they are looking at one another rather than all facing you. Go around the circle for comments.
- Teach some of the routines that encourage peer talk.

Also, it is important to ensure the widest participation possible. Otherwise, the more talkative students will inevitably dominate. You can encourage quieter students to participate by:

- Calling on them based on something you know they have to say.
- Seating them in a more central position so that they are closer to you.
- Encouraging them to participate in routines that involve peer talk before asking them to talk in the larger group.
- Helping students become aware of the importance of wide participation; over time, they should assume responsibility for ensuring that everyone gets a turn (but rigid turn taking becomes tedious).

- Occasionally asking for comments from students who have not yet spoken.
- Helping students understand that part of being a good participant is to listen carefully to others and comment constructively.
- Requiring that students avoid criticizing or shutting down others' talk and teaching them how to respectively disagree and say why.

ROUTINES TO ENCOURAGE PEER TALK

You can easily build routines for talking about texts into interactive read-aloud by teaching these routines one at a time. To teach a routine (see Figure 18-7):

- Be sure that you choose a wonderful text that you know students will have a lot to say about.
- Prepare them for the first use of the routine by letting them know the expectations. (Students need to turn quickly, talk, and then turn back at a signal. They need to know they will be talking only a short time, that they need to get right into it.)
- Working with one or two students, quickly demonstrate the "turn and talk" action yourself. Be sure that you show "taking turns." Then have students describe what they saw (see Figure 18-8).
- Assign partners or threesomes before you begin reading so that students will know to whom to turn.
- Quickly practice the physical actions of the routine several times. (Have students turn toward partners and back to the whole group.)
- On the first day you use a routine, use only one routine and avoid other lengthy discussion.

Steps in Teaching a Routine

1 Select a text that students will understand and find it easy to talk about.
2 Establish clear expectations.
3 Demonstrate the routine thoroughly.
4 Assign partners or threesomes.
5 Practice the actions.
6 Use only one routine per session.
7 Have students evaluate themselves afterward.

Figure 18-7. *Steps in Teaching a Routine*

Figure 18-8. *Turn and Talk*

❑ Have students evaluate themselves afterward.

We suggest you teach the routines in the following sequence:

❑ *Pair talk.* Students talk in preassigned pairs. At a preplanned point in the text, you ask them to "turn and talk to your partner." You may want to guide their discussion ("Turn and talk to your partner about how the grandmother and little girl felt when they didn't hear from the mother") or allow it to be more open-ended.

❑ *Threesome talk.* Students talk in preassigned groups of three. The routine is similar to pair talk, but students need to know how to pace their discussion so that each person has a chance to participate in the short talking time.

❑ *Circle talk in two pairs.* Two pairs turn to each other and talk. You can teach this routine step-by-step. First, have pairs talk. Then have them share what they were thinking with another pair. Soon you will be able to move directly to circle talk if desired.

These three routines can be used effectively from kindergarten through grade eight. They provide the opportunity for individuals to engage in more talk than would otherwise be possible in whole-group discussion. Inserting these routines into your interactive read-aloud sessions will make whole-group discussion more lively and productive.

SUGGESTIONS FOR PROFESSIONAL DEVELOPMENT

PLANNING FOR "TURN AND TALK"

1 Bring together groups of grade-level colleagues.

2 Give each group a selection of appropriate read-aloud texts.

3 Have each group select two or three texts that build on one another in some way or are related by theme, author, content, type of text, or in some other way.

4 Have each group read each text and identify two points at which it would be productive to "turn and talk." Ask them to place a "turn and talk" stick-on note at the appropriate points.

5 Have groups share their decisions, talking about how they made their choices and about the discussion they would expect as a result.

CHAPTER NINETEEN

DEEPENING COMPREHENSION: ENGAGING STUDENTS IN SMALL-GROUP LITERATURE DISCUSSION

Children grow into th
intellectual li
around then.
—LEV VYGOTSH

There are many different names for small-group literature discussion: book clubs, literature groups, literature circles, book groups, reading clubs (Daniels 2002; Peterson and Eads 1990; Raphael and Day et al. 2002). All these terms describe a context in which children engage in shared talk as they examine and explore one another's thinking about narrative, expository, or poetic texts.

Whatever the name, a well-executed program of literature discussion can be very motivating for readers. They are able to talk about books that are of particular interest to them. Their opinions are valued rather than evaluated. And, since they are in charge of their own thinking, talking, and writing, they are very involved in their own learning. Book clubs offer all students the opportunity to expand their understanding of a rich array of texts. Participants have the opportunity to think within, beyond, and about a text, always grounding their thinking in evidence from the text or from personal experience.

Book clubs have specific benefits for below-grade-level readers. Of necessity, in small-group instructional reading (e.g., guided reading), these students are processing texts at reading levels they can handle, with some teacher support, but they also need to experience age-appropriate, grade-level-appropriate material. Because they can access the text, they will be expected to discuss upon hearing it read aloud (on tape, via a computer, by an adult) if needed; these students can think and talk about any text that interests them. In our experience, these students have no difficulty discussing a text they have found interesting. They can think and talk about a text even if they cannot read it for themselves. We have written extensively on this topic in *Guiding Readers and Writers* (Fountas and Pinnell 2001), where we provide many book club models for younger and older children. In this chapter, we explore the potential of book clubs and discuss some practical point related to implementation.

BOOK CLUBS AS SHARED INQUIRY

The name *book clubs* makes it sound as if students are going to have a good time together talking about a book, and that is true. But much more is going on. Whe students participate in book clubs, they talk, read, and ofte write in highly interactive ways. The central idea is tha greater insight can be achieved when several people shar their thinking, thus benefiting from each other's under standings and perspectives. The discussion takes the form of an investigation as participants try out tentative idea: search for information to confirm or refute their thinking and build on one another's ideas.

The book club context eliminates the search for th "right answer," substituting instead the search to under stand your own thinking, the author's thinking, and th thinking of your fellow readers. As opposed to tradition postreading discussions, in which students answer a bar rage of questions, in book clubs students are encouraged t ask questions, which help them clarify and expand the thinking and clear up confusion. They probe for deepe understanding and invite the interpretations of other Students understand that they are expected to ask ques tions. It is interesting that when the twin specters of havin the right answer and being evaluated on those answers ar removed, students reveal their misunderstandings quit honestly, and members of the group learn from the proces of seeking clarification.

Inquiry is present when students read texts in prepara tion for book club and when they probe the meaning of text as they talk together. Students are expected to brin their own thinking to the text; they don't read searching fc answers to the teacher's preplanned questions. But if there are some particular features of the text that the teacher or group wants to discuss, the teacher may ask the students to read with something in mind and take notes in a reader's notebook or on a "thinkmark" (see Fountas and Pinnell, 2001). The key is to ask for "light attention," not to interfere with the enjoyment of the text.

Anticipating the discussion, students tend to "dig a little deeper" and question themselves more as they read. They may reread to check their understanding or be more aware of nuances in the text that will be interesting to others in the group. If the club discusses a segment of the text at a time, the previous discussion will influence students' further reading.

Inquiry also takes place as students share their thinking and question one another. An effective book club discussion is not a series of static reports by students taking on assigned roles. It is freewheeling, full of unexpected comments that are nevertheless grounded in the text and related to one another. A line of reasoning will surface; participants may change their perspectives in response to the logic that is building.

Inquiry is supported by the writing or sketching that students do in preparation for or as a result of book club. Writing in preparation for discussion, the emphasis is on examining one's own thinking before sharing it with others, organizing one's thoughts so that they are more easily and clearly presented to the group, or taking notes on specific portions of the text that are the nucleus of ideas and the basis for hypotheses. Writing after the discussion, students are able to express ideas that have been richly explored, even rehearsed, orally.

As an example, let's look at an excerpt from a more extended discussion a group of intermediate grade students had about the picture book *White Socks Only* (Coleman) (Figure 19-1). Clearly, the students were using systems of strategic actions as they read or listened to *White Socks Only*. The reflections of their peers and the support of their teacher helped them share and extend their thinking: They were able to think beyond and about the text.

Notice how all four students jumped right into the discussion, expressing their opinions, bringing up important details from the story, and drawing some conclusions

(*summarizing and synthesizing*). It is obvious that they were *making connections*, and they *drew some inferences* as to the writer's purposes. Maria revealed her understanding of the writer's voice when she said, "I could hear in her words that she could really remember the pain of it." Luke and Ronaldo commented on the writer's voice as well. All three students were taking an *analytical* stance. The teacher made encouraging comments to "talk more" and prompted them to make specific references to the text. By going to the precise pages to ground their comments, everyone developed richer shared understandings. The teacher followed up by confirming these comments and then signaled that she was changing the topic. This time, she directly drew students' attention to the structure of the text. Susan and Luke responded with comments that indicated their ability to take this analytical stance and think *critically* about it.

At first glance, the teacher's job here may seem pretty easy. The students are obviously self-motivated. But consider these factors:

- The teacher had previously provided explicit instruction, including demonstrations, to help students learn how to conduct a literature discussion, as well as how to build on one another's ideas.

- The students' discussion was based on several months of learning how to talk with others about books and how to participate in book clubs.

- The teacher was intentionally holding back and only stepping in for very specific purposes.

Let's look at a discussion by some primary grade children who were just learning how to participate in book club (see Figure 19-2). Four children and their teacher were discussing *Owen* (Henkes). These students already understood some of the basic routines of book club, and they were learning to back up their comments with evidence from specific pages of the text. Throughout the discussion, you can see that students *inferred* Owen's motivations and feelings. It is evident, too, that they had made some personal *connections* with the idea of having a special blanket. The teacher played an active role in the discussion even though the children made most of the comments. She prompted them to "take us to places in the text" and probed with questions like "how

---

BOOK CLUB DISCUSSION OF
White Socks Only (COLEMAN)

MARIA: It was hard to believe that a man would beat a little girl for drinking water. Wouldn't that be against the law?

RONALDO: Those were the things that happened in Mississippi during segregation when there was a lot of prejudice in the South. The people just did whatever they wanted to all the black people until someone stopped them.

SUSAN: And that's what happened in this story. One person was brave enough—had the courage to cross the line.

LUKE: Really a lot of people did it, but Mr. Chicken was the one who made the man stop because he was scared of him.

MRS. B.: Talk more about that.

SUSAN: The line between black and white. White people would not have allowed any black people to drink from that water fountain. They put up this sign that said "Whites Only." It might not have been really the law, but people just did what they said because they were afraid.

LUKE: The little girl was really innocent in the story. She thought the sign meant that you could only wear white socks to drink. This writer made me think about how prejudice is taught by the adults. Kids learn to discriminate because adults want them to do it. It's not something you are just born to do.

MARIA: I think it's interesting that the author based the story on her own memories of discrimination when she was a little girl. I could hear in her words that she could really remember the pain of it. Maybe she wrote this to help her remember and sort of deal with it.

MRS. B.: What did the author say that made you feel that way?

MARIA: On page 15, she describes the people staring at her and says, "Seeing all the people made me real scared, and I cried louder." And on page 18, she said, "I knew the man was gon' yell at her, and he did." Also, look at page 19, where she describes how the man's face got red as fire and he was snorting through his nose like a bull when "it's gon' charge."

RONALDO: The author describes the scenes so exactly that you know she was right there. You can see it.

LUKE: I agree with what you are saying. It's like the writer brings you with her into the story. You can see, hear, and feel what is happening.

MRS. B.: So you're describing the writer's talent as a storyteller and her strong voice. I want to change the topic. Did you notice how the writer starts the story with the voice of a young girl and uses italics? Then on page 3 she switches to a story told by the grandmother when she was young.

LUKE: And she's not using the italics any more.

SUSAN: It's like a story starts and then there is another story inside the story.

MRS. B.: So you are ntoicing the way the book is organized. That is the *structure* of the story. Do you think it works well?

SUSAN: I think it's a good way for the writer to show that one generation learns lessons from another. The grandparents learn and then pass it along to their children and they pass it along to their children. If she just told the story instead of making it show that she's telling it to her granddaughter, it wouldn't be as good.

LUKE: It makes me think how stories of our grandparents help us kind of understand the times—the history. The story shows history from the viewpoint of people who really lived it, not just read about it or remembered it. You have to know it and feel it to write about it.

Figure 19-1. *Book Club Discussion of* White Socks Only

do you know?" She also modeled thinking about the handkerchief as a symbol for the blanket, explaining the term. She summed up children's remarks about the ending by rephrasing their language as a "satisfying ending." She modeled wondering about the illustrations and the author's motivations. Finally, she prompted the children to assess their own participation as book club members.

Over time, children become more and more skilled at book club participation. Several things are happening simultaneously:

BOOK CLUB DISCUSSION OF
Owen (HENKES)

SELENA: It seems like Owen just wanted some comfort. I wonder why Mrs. Tweezers kept minding someone else's business. Owen is not her kid and she shouldn't be interfering. She should let his parents decide.

MATTHEW: She was trying to help because she didn't want him to be embarrassed.

MS. P.: Can you take us to parts where you thought she was helping?

MATTHEW: On page 4 she says, "Isn't he getting a little too old to be carrying that thing around? Haven't you heard of the blanket fairy?" The parents didn't know about how to have a fairy come in the middle of the night to take the blanket.

LEAH: Well, it didn't work anyway.

MS. P.: Are there other places where Mrs. Tweezers tried to help?

RAFAEL: On page 11 she told her about the vinegar trick.

SELENA: I don't understand what a vinegar trick is.

MARK: I think it means that you can put vinegar on it and it will smell bad and Owen won't want it.

MS. P.: The author doesn't say that, so how do you know?

MATTHEW: On pages 12 and 13 the author tells how Owen kept smelling it, so it must have smelled bad. He picked a new corner and rubbed the smelly corner in dirt. The author says it was smelly.

LEAH: It wasn't smelly anymore after the dirt and then it wasn't fuzzy either.

MS. P.: So what do you think made Owen's parents decide to say no to him?

SELENA: Mrs. Tweezers told them to say no.

MS. P.: Can you take us to that part?

SELENA: It's on page 16. Mrs. Tweezers filled them in. That means she told them.

RAFAEL: Mrs. Tweezers tried to help, but Owen's parents are the ones who figured out what to do.

MARK: I like how the handkerchiefs look like the blanket.

LEAH: It's like he still has his blanket only it's a tiny blanket now! And it fits in his pocket.

MS. P.: I think the writer created another symbol—a handkerchief for a blanket! Same shape, same color, same comfort! I know you like Kevin Henkes. I was wondering what you think about his writing in this story. Would each of you share something you noticed about the writing or the illustrations that Kevin Henkes did?

MATTHEW: I like it when he said on page 18, "It was an absolutely wonderful, positively perfect, especially terrific idea." He shows that Owen's mother was sure she figured it out.

RAFAEL: The ending was really good—the way Henkes says Mrs. Tweezers didn't say a thing. I wanted her to quit and she did.

MS. P.: So you are saying it was a satisfying ending for you.

SELENA: I like looking at the pictures of the blanket. You can tell how Owen feels by what he does with Fuzzy.

MS. P.: I wonder if Fuzzy is in every picture.

MARK: Kevin Henkes uses good words to describe all the things he did with his blanket. He twisted it, and sucked it, and hugged it, and stuff like that.

LEAH: This story reminded me of when I used to have a blankie and I remember that I liked it.

MS. P.: I wonder if Henkes had a blanket or knew someone who did. We have talked a lot about how writers get ideas from their own lives. Think a bit about what Kevin Henke's story is really about—what is he trying to say? Then we will end our talk today by having each of you saying something about how you think we did in our talk together about the book *Owen*. We'll talk about what went well and what we could do better.

Figure 19-2. *Book Club Discussion of* Owen

- Texts are becoming more sophisticated and demanding, prompting richer discussion.

- Children are developing as conversationalists who know how to talk with one another about texts.

- Children's reading abilities and interests are changing.

The process stimulates individual thinking, so that children leave the group with richer understandings than they could have achieved from reading and thinking about a text independently.

BOOK CLUBS THROUGHOUT THE GRADES

Book discussion should be a rich, continuous element of every child's literacy program. As discussed in Chapters 12, 13, and 14, we believe interactive read-aloud is an ideal context in which to demonstrate, support, and engage children in all aspects of effective text talk from kindergarten through grade eight. We suggest you add small-group discussions in grade two, depending on how effective your interactive read-aloud "turn and talk" segments have been.

In kindergarten and grade one, you can create the following situations for children to talk with one another about books:

1 *Whole-group–small-group talk*. Read a text aloud, or have the children listen to a CD or tape, or ask children in higher grades to read the text to their "buddies." Then have the children meet in groups of four to talk about the text for ten or fifteen minutes as you rotate from group to group. (There should be at least one copy of the book per group to which they can refer.) They can also draw or write about their thinking.

2 *Small-group choice*. The children have wordless books or simple picture books from which they can choose to read. Children with similar books talk to one another about their books for fifteen minutes.

3 *Text set small groups*. The children each have a version of a folktale to read. Students who have read similar folktales then form groups. Each child in the group tells a little bit about the version he has read and then they ask one another questions and share their thinking. (The

Figure 19-3. *Book Club Discussion*

same can be done with books by the same author or the same illustrator.)

4 *Pair share*. Pairs of children select the same book. They talk with each other about the book for ten minutes and prepare to share something about their talk with the whole group.

BUILDING DEEPLY SHARED MEANINGS

As teachers, we think a great deal about the kinds of interactions we want our students to have during book discussions, and we are also aware that we need to prompt for particular types of thinking to expand what our students are able to do. But students should not just "do" discussion by the numbers. We want them to lose themselves in the conversation, to be intensely interested in what others are saying as well as motivated to express their own views. We want them to be thinking about the book, about something that matters to them, rather than the techniques they are using. As they learn discussion routines, the behaviors should become unconscious and automatic.

Although most of the time her students participated in mixed-gender discussion groups, Mrs. R. occasionally organized all-boy or all-girl groups to discuss books that had particular gender appeal. Jack, Rob, D.J., Forest, and Joyner chose to discuss *Private Captain: A Story of Gettysburg,* by Marty Crisp, a fast-paced story about a young boy who goes looking for his older brother in the middle of the Civil War (Figure 19-4). They identified with

EXCERPT FROM DISCUSSION OF
Private Captain: A Story of Gettysburg

JACK: *Private Captain: A Story of Gettysburg,* by Marty Crisp. Well, it's about the Civil War. We left off when the Reb attacked Ben and we left off when he was running away because Captain had attacked him. On the first page, it kind of sounded like Ben and Captain had already . . .

ROB: He was more protective of Ben. And it was like he was forgetting about Reuben and we said that at the beginning of the book; we said he got more attached to Ben than Reuben.

D.J.: I think that in the very beginning the dog was really fuzzy about where to go, but kind of where we left off, he really knew that he was going to go with Ben and try to help him. And Captain was really raising Ben's spirits I think . . . and spots where he thought he was about to give up, the dog would make him go on . . . and find the house.

FOREST: On the next page, it's kind of like Ben does want Captain (READING). *"Trouble was, it was a lie. Ben wanted Captain the same way he wanted to keep the pocket watch that, by rights, belonged to Reuben; the same way he wanted the war to be over and life to get back to normal.* (p. 157)

D.J.: I really completely agree with that because he really got attached to that pocket watch. And I think that throughout the book . . . more and more towards the end . . . the dog and Captain [meaning Ben] became attached to each other. And I think it's the same with Danny and him, because Ben and Danny. At the very beginning Ben really, really doesn't want Danny, but then more to the middle, he was kind of getting used to having him around, and then at the end I think he almost wants him there.

JOYNER: The whole dog thing was how . . . that one part where he messed up because he thought that—I forget what his name was—he found this guy in the battles with all the bodies and stuff and he thought it was Reuben. So he kind of messed up there but still . . .

SAM: I agree with D.J. on Ben and Danny because at the end of the book, I think I remember saying that he actually kind of needed him because of, you know, with Mavis and everything—he didn't know how to milk it and take care of it. [Mavis is a cow that the two boys acquired.]

D.J.: I think this book really just kind of brought them closer together, but it's also bringing them farther because Ben is trying to find Reuben in the very beginning and he won't let anything stop him. And now towards the middle when they are with the cow and everything, it's almost like he's not looking for Reuben anymore. It's almost like he's just trying to stay alive. But at the very beginning, he's still looking for Reuben. But it's not much.

JOYNER: I don't like remember exactly the page, but in the prison scene where we it started off on the 170 when Nate dies . . . the guy . . . I thought that was pretty sad.

D.J.: I can imagine how that would feel if you're in a house and there's somebody next to you in a bed and you think they are asleep, still or something, and you try to shake them and try to wake them up and all that, but they won't wake up. And someone else comes over and is saying he's dead. Well, even if I don't know the person, it's still kind of really freaky. You're trying to wake them up.

JOYNER: A couple of pages after it says that Ben wants Captain. It looks like Captain wants Ben to stay alive.

MRS. R.: Can I interject here on a comment you made—both of you actually—about the eighteen-year-old and being dead and that whole horror of that. Rob, you had mentioned in your reading letter [Reader's Notebook] the reality that these soldiers are so young, and you're not that far away from their age. And war is not all that glamorous by any means. I guess we saw that even in other books you have read. That seems to be a very, very important issue. I think Rob, that you have more to say.

ROB: That was one of those . . . similar to *My Brother Sam Is Dead.* Because it's like more real now that the war is over and everyone is all happy, but back then we didn't know if we would win and we didn't know if it was the right thing to do.

D.J.: And also the war was back and forth, so actually at one point—just like in this book—how Ben would go to the one side and then to the other—it's almost like in reality you don't know who to back. Because one battle, one side would win. Then the very next battle, the other side would win and it will go back and forth like that. So you really have no idea who is going to win the war, who is going to win the battles. You don't know who to back. And if you are backing the wrong person, you could get killed.

Figure 19-4. Excerpt from Discussion of Private Captain: A Story of Gettysburg

the protagonist, Ben, who was just a little older than they were. They found the text, with its descriptions of the horrors of war, compelling; often, they wondered what they would have done in similar circumstances. Throughout the discussion, they referred often to another favorite book they had read, *My Brother Sam Is Dead.* By the end of the discussion, they were talking about the complexities of war and its implications for humankind.

You can hear some of this discussion of *Private Captain* and a discussion of *When She Was Good* on the DVD that accompanies this book.

Using Close Reading of a Text to Build Understanding

Book clubs are a wonderful opportunity for students to undertake close reading of a text. You can identify sentences or paragraphs that you want students to give particular attention to and think about deeply. After reading, they can go back to those paragraphs, think about them, and discuss them with others. They may even do some quick writing or drawing in response to these passages.

Let's look at some paragraphs from books that lend themselves to close reading for deeper understanding of the author's message. Here are a few from *A Year Down Yonder,* by Richard Peck:

> When Mrs. Abernathy touched his shoulder, he turned toward her. Then you could tell he was blind. He turned his head away.
>
> Nobody spoke. There was nothing to say. Grandma and Mrs. Abernathy stood together for a minute—a minute like the morning. Then we left.
>
> We went in a hurry past the coffee cans on the kitchen table because Grandma didn't want thanks. Outside, I was surprised it was still daylight, surprised the world was still there. (p. 52)

With close reading, students might notice that the writer has created a moment of tension and the feeling of silence with the short sentence, "Nobody spoke." The description goes further to say, "a minute like the morning," illustrating how time seems very long in a space like this, and the feeling is extended with "surprised the world was still there."

Here's a passage from *Love That Dog,* by Sharon Creech:

> I am sorry
> I took the book home
> without asking.
> I only got

> one spot
> on it.
> That's why
> the page is torn.
> I tried to get
> the spot
> out.
> I copied that BEST poem
> and hung it on my bedroom wall
> right over my bed
> where I can
> see it when I'm
> lying
> down. (2001, pp. 42–43)

With close reading, students may notice the layout of text that communicates the poignant and poetic, hesitant delivery of strong emotions masked in everyday language.

Here is a section from *Baseball Saved Us,* by Ken Mochizuki:

> One day, my dad looked out at the endless desert and decided then and there to build a baseball field.
>
> He said people needed something to do in camp. We weren't in a camp that was fun, like summer camp. Ours was in the middle of nowhere, and we were behind a barbed-wire fence. Soldiers with guns made sure we stayed there, and the man in the tower saw everything we did, no matter where we were.
>
> As Dad began walking over the dry cracked dirt, I asked him again why we were here.
>
> "Because," he said, "America is at war with Japan, and the government thinks that Japanese Americans can't be trusted. But it's wrong that we're in here. We're Americans too!" (1993, p. 2)

With close reading, students may notice the contrasts—the idea of a "fun" summer camp and the kind of concentration camp the characters are experiencing. They may also think about "baseball," the American sport, and these Japanese Americans who love their country but are not accepted or trusted.

This is from *The Night Crossing,* by Karen Ackerman:

> "We had to leave everything behind and run for our lives," Grandma had said. "But Gittel and Lotte were very brave, and they wanted to go along. So my mother let me carry them over the mountains and all the way to Austria."
>
> "On your night crossing," added Clara.
>
> "Yes, *maydel,* on my night crossing to freedom," Grandma replied as she put the two dolls in Clara's arms.
>
> Now, as Clara drifted back to sleep in the dark, she hoped Papa would let her take Gittel and Lotte with her to wherever he planned to take the family to escape the Nazis. (1995, pp. 12–13).

With close reading, students may notice the parallels between Grandma's story about carrying the dolls over the mountains and young Clara's intention to take the dolls on her escape from the Nazis. The dolls take on symbolic significance for the family.

And here's part of *The Great Gilly Hopkins,* by Katherine Paterson:

> That cans it, thought Gilly. At least nobody had accused Mr. or Mrs. Nevins, her most recent foster parents, of being "nice." Mrs. Richmond, the one with the bad nerves, had been "nice." The Newman family, who couldn't keep a five-year-old who wet her bed, had been "nice." Well, I'm eleven now, folks, and, in case you haven't heard, I don't wet my bed anymore. But I am not nice. I am brilliant. I am famous across this entire county. Nobody wants to tangle with the great Galadriel Hopkins. I am too clever and too hard to manage. Gruesome Gilly, they call me. She leaned back comfortably. Here I come, Maine, baby, ready or not. (1987, p. 3)

With close reading, students may notice Gilly's voice—tough, experienced, confident but sad.

All of the above insights might arise during close reading of the selections noted here; but readers will probably notice even more. Selections like these help students go deeply into the critical events, notice important information, realize aspects of the writer's craft (like the use of symbols), or understand characters. The close analysis of selected segments lets students ponder significant information together, learning how to think beyond and about a text. It becomes a model for the kind of analysis students will be able to do on their own as readers.

LEARNING HOW TO TALK ABOUT TEXTS

Literature discussion provides the opportunity for even the youngest child to benefit from the thinking of others. The talk in book clubs is not casual; it is grounded in and lifted by the text. Students enjoy talking with peers about books, and doing so helps them understand the value of reading. Literature discussion is the truest form of teaching; these are discussion-based lessons "geared toward creating richly textured opportunities for students' conceptual and linguistic development" (Goldenberg 1992, p. 317). The idea of bringing students' own thoughts into the learning conversation is as old as Socrates and represents an educational ideal. Goldenberg describes a learning conversation as "deceptively simple" on the surface (p. 318). The talk that

surrounds children's literature has great depth because it is about *text.*

First, students are learning a *common language* for talking about texts. This may include some of the labels (such as *endpapers, chapters, leads, flashbacks*) that can aid understanding and thinking (Sipe 1998). If considering picture books, they can develop an in-depth appreciation for illustrations that, in turn, aid thinking about symbolism and larger themes. Sipe describes the picture book as "the principal format in which preschool and primary age children experience literature" and believes that "every part of the picture book is meaningful" (p. 66). The text, of course, is important, but the *peritext* (anything in a book other than the printed text) is equally important, as it adds to the total meaning of the text. Here are just three dimensions of picture books that have direct implications for comprehension:

- Readers can discover a sequence in connected illustrations: chronological order, cycles of action from home to an adventure and back home, flashbacks, embedded stories. Attention to the illustrations can support understanding of text structure (thinking about the text).

- Readers can learn to notice the jacket flaps, which provide a great deal of information about the illustrator and author, as well as a summary of the book. A summary can help readers grasp the overarching theme of the story, and author information can help them think beyond the text to the author's motivation for writing.

- Readers can learn to look for recurring elements, or *motifs*, that the illustrator is using throughout. These recurring elements often have great significance. For example, Patricia Polacco often uses photographs of her own family or repeats patterns in clothing from one generation to the next, symbolizing strong connections. Understanding symbolism in art can help readers think about the craft of writing and illustrating.

Second, students' conversations are grounded in the text. On the surface, they have all of the elements of a good conversation (Goldenberg 1992). People are responsive to and respectful of one another. They listen and take turns talking. There are few "known answer" questions, and one comment tends to build on others, creating a series of connected ideas rather than random comments or answers to questions. The atmosphere is supportive rather than threatening, and participants feel that they can safely extend themselves.

At another level, however, the participants are being challenged to connect their talk to a specific text and to engage in a highly focused discussion. They are expected to stay on the topic, to focus on exploring this particular text, and to work at including everyone in the conversation. The teacher demonstrates, directly teaching when necessary, so that students expand their understanding. The expectation is that students will base their statements on specific evidence that turned their thinking in the direction described. Generally, the process promotes using more complex language and sharing background knowledge, which expands students' understanding.

LEARNING HOW TO ENGAGE IN LITERARY ANALYSIS

Because students are engaged in deep thinking about the text, they are inevitably drawn into literary analysis. Thinking analytically about books involves a whole range of thinking beyond and about fiction, biography, and factual texts. The degree to which children's discussion reflects content is the true measure of success in literature discussion. In saying this, we do not mean that children have to use words like *plot* and *perspective,* although such terms will enter their vocabulary as they work with texts over time. We do mean that we should be able to see evidence that students are thinking and talking about the content. They explore the lives of characters and talk about how they change and develop. They search for turning points in the lives of biographical subjects. They speculate on the writer's purpose and underlying message and notice the style and tone. They talk about the impact of important historical events. Otherwise, the book club may amount to no more than a display of using big words, meaning that participants are playing the roles and taking turns but the talk is empty.

You can demonstrate attention to content in your own remarks, reinforce these concepts as students go deeper into the content, and prompt content discussion with questions and comments. Remember that the goal is not to get a lot of "talk" or to get children to use labels, but to have them genuinely discuss content.

Content Analysis of Fiction Texts
Readers can learn how to think about big elements of a fiction text. With the appropriate age group, you can help

readers think about the characters, plot, setting, theme, language, tone, mood, point of view, or illustrations, and symbols (see Figure 19-5). Your understanding of these elements will enable you to help children attend to them in stories they read.

Content Analysis of Biography
Writing an interesting and engaging biography is challenging. In discussing a biography, members of book clubs can focus on aspects of craft just as they do with fiction, but the process is even more interesting because the writer is telling about a real person. What the writer selects to tell reveals the reasons for writing the biography as well as attitude towards the subject. In Figure 19-6, we outline big elements to consider when analyzing biography.

Students can talk about why the subject was important and about the events and decisions that shaped the author's life. Sometimes the discussion of a biography is "dry," with students simply recounting events as if they were inevitable. Deep discussion of the content of biography will help students understand that accomplishments are related to critical decisions, and that many of them are difficult. They can also help one another understand the subject within the attitudes and culture of the particular time or setting. Critical thinking about biography involves considering the biographer as well—his or her purpose and point of view, as well as the degree to which the text accurately portrays the subject.

Content Analysis of Nonfiction Texts
In the past, nonfiction was not considered "literature," but in recent decades so many factual texts of high quality have been produced that scholars of children's literature have placed them within that category (Freeman 2001). According to Freeman, it is just as important for students to notice features of nonfiction as it is to appreciate features of fiction.

A content discussion of nonfiction can focus on how, and perhaps why, the writer has organized and presented the information in this particular way. Readers can talk about the writer's style and tone. Critical discussion of factual texts also focuses on accuracy or on the writer's attitude; readers should be able to understand the writer's biases or critique a persuasive argument. Informational texts also have many illustrations; students can talk about the information in graphics and also notice and discuss how the author has selected particular information to represent visually.

The Content of Literary Analysis–Fiction

ELEMENT	DEFINITION	CHARACTERISTICS TO KNOW
Characters	The people, animals, or personified objects in a fiction text–realistic or fantasy.	▫ Revealed by description of appearance, what they do, what they say or think, what others say or think about them. ▫ May be "flat" (unchanging) or "round" (developing and changing. ▫ Includes main characters (usually more round) and supporting characters (sometimes flat). ▫ May be strong or weak, good or evil, mixed.
Plot	The problem of the story and the events that flow from it.	▫ Unfolds in a series of ordered events. ▫ May unfold in order of their happening (chronological) or may juggle time as in flashback. ▫ Involves conflict, which may take several forms– for example, person against (1) person, (2) self, (3) society, or (4) nature. ▫ May involve suspense, cliff-hanger, sensationalism, or inevitability. ▫ May involve several patterns of action–foreshadowing, flashback, rising action, climax, and falling action.
Setting	Where and when the story takes place.	▫ May be integral to the plot or merely serve as a backdrop. ▫ May be the source of conflict or the adversary (e.g., people against nature). ▫ May communicate the mood or tone. ▫ May be symbolic (represent good, evil, home, alienation).
Theme	The central message or messages of the text or what the story is really about.	▫ May be explicitly stated or implied. ▫ May involve multiple themes–a main theme and secondary themes. ▫ Usually related to a central truth about the human condition. ▫ Sometimes involves a moral or inspirational lesson. ▫ May provide a comment about human nature or society.
Style/Language	Particular ways that writers use language to communicate about the characters, plot, setting, and theme.	▫ May involve figurative language such as simile, metaphor, or personification. ▫ May involve imagery. ▫ May involve poetic language such as onomatopoeia. ▫ May involve symbolism. ▫ May involve using words in a playful, whimsical, or connotative way. ▫ May involve allusion. [e.g., *Dear Little Red Hen*]
Tone	The writers' communication of an overall feeling about or attitude toward the book's subject, content, or topic.	▫ May include descriptive words. ▫ Requires understanding connotative meanings of words. ▫ May involve explicit or implicit communication of meaning. ▫ May be carried through selection of information to include.

Figure 19-5. *The Content of Literary Analysis–Fiction*

The Content of Literary Analysis—Fiction (CONTINUED)

ELEMENT	DEFINITION	CHARACTERISTICS TO KNOW
Mood	The underlying and pervasive feelings the reader gains from reading a text.	□ May be serious or involve humor or absurdity. □ May be somber or light and happy. □ May involve descriptions of the setting or people's actions. □ May be carried through dialogue. □ May involve readers' connection to their own lives.
Point of View	The perspective from which the story is told.	□ May be an anonymous outsider who reveals everything about the main and supporting characters through actions, dialogue, and thoughts (third person, *he, she, they*). □ May be an anonymous outsider who mostly reveals the main characters' point of view through actions, dialogue, and thoughts (third person, *he, she, they*). □ May be the main character telling the story directly to the reader (first person, *I*). □ May be the main character telling the story and engaging in dialogue with the reader (first person, *I*, and second person, *you*). □ May be an objective point of view that offers only description and leaves interpretation to the readers.
Illustrations	All graphics that accompany a text—drawings, photographs, paintings.	□ Communicates information about the setting. □ Contributes to the mood or tone. □ Assists the reader in forming visual images. □ Can be related to revealing the point of view. □ May be matched to the style of language. □ Reveals characters.
Symbols	Persons, objects, actions or situations that have more than their literal meaning.	□ Can help readers understand the theme. □ Are particular to a story. □ Connects to some aspect of the story meaning.

Figure 19-5. *The Content of Literary Analysis—Fiction (cont.)*

We present key elements of nonfiction for you to consider when analyzing nonfiction (see Figure 19-7).

LEARNING TO THINK CRITICALLY ABOUT FICTION AND NONFICTION TEXTS

We want to bring critical thinking to bear whenever we read something. Critical thinking may begin with students simply saying whether or not they liked a book and why. They may also compare the book to others. When Rob said that *Private Captain* was his "second favorite book," he supported that statement by comparing it to *My Brother Sam Is Dead*, with the resultant discussion centered around critical thinking about war. This kind of thinking, particularly when focused on informational texts, may question the attitudes or qualifications of the authors or the scientific or historical accuracy of the text. Finally, students can think critically about the quality of the writing in either fiction or nonfiction.

You can use book clubs as an effective technique for helping your students deepen their understanding of a variety of worthwhile texts. In the next chapter, we will provide practical information for getting your students started in small group discussion.

The Content of Literary Analysis—Biography

ELEMENT	DEFINITION	CHARACTERISTICS TO KNOW
Subject	The person the text is about.	▫ Why the subject is important. ▫ How the subject's life sheds light on the time. ▫ How the subject was able to achieve the accomplishments. ▫ Important characteristics of the subject that are related to accomplishments.
Chronology of Events in the Subject's Life	The actual events, over time, that the subject experienced.	▫ How the events in the subject's life occurred. ▫ What the subject accomplished in chronological order. ▫ How to identify the significant events in the subject's life. ▫ When the biographer begins and ends the story and why. ▫ Important facts about the subject. ▫ Critical decisions that the subject made that influenced his/her life.
Setting	The place(s) the subject lived and the times of his/her life.	▫ Circumstances that influenced the subject's life. ▫ Aspects of the times in which the subject lived that influenced him/her. ▫ Perspectives (related to setting) of the subject and people who influenced him/her. ▫ Characteristics of the setting in which the subject lived and how they influenced him/her.
Author's Point of View	The writer's attitude toward and perception of the subject of the biography.	▫ Information about the writer's own background as a basis for hypothesizing attitude toward the subject. ▫ Evidence from the text that reveals the author's point of view—selection and reporting of facts, interpretation of facts, statement of opinions, description, etc. ▫ Accuracy or objectivity of the writer.
Tone	How the writer uses language to reveal his/her thinking about and attitude of the subject.	▫ How the writer shows feelings about the subject through language. ▫ How the writer shows sympathy or compassion for the subject. ▫ Authenticity of the writer's style—sentimentality, exaggeration, etc.
Accuracy	The authenticity of the information provided by the writer.	▫ The writer's personal qualifications related to knowledge of the subject. ▫ The sources cited by the writer to authenticate the biography. ▫ The consistency of facts reported here with other sources. ▫ What the writer selected to report and what the writer left out.

Figure 19-6. *The Content of Literary Analysis—Biography*

The Content of Literary Analysis—Nonfiction

ELEMENT	DEFINITION	CHARACTERISTICS TO KNOW
Organization	How the information is organized and presented.	▫ The presentation of key ideas and supporting information. ▫ How the information is presented—narrative, categorical, sequential, etc. ▫ Organizational structures used to present ideas (compare/contrast; problem/solution; description; cause/effect; sequence).
Style	How the writer uses language (distinct from the ideas expressed—manner of speaking, choice of words).	▫ How the writer uses language to convey ideas and important information. ▫ How the writer selects particular words to convey precise information. ▫ How the writer uses language to increase the reader's interest. ▫ The clarity with which the writer presents information.
Tone	How the writer uses language (choice of words, phrasing) to indicate his attitude/feelings toward the topic.	▫ How the writer selects information to reveal the subject in a certain light. ▫ How the writer reveals a perspective on the subject through descriptive language.
Illustrations/ Graphics	The art that accompanies and is related to the text.	▫ How illustrations/graphics are used to convey important ideas and information. ▫ How illustrations/graphics are used to compare ideas. ▫ How illustrations/graphics are connected to the body of the text. ▫ What information is provided in illustrations/graphics as compared to information provided in the body of the text. ▫ What kind of information is provided in varying kinds of illustrations/graphics—photographs, drawings, diagrams, cross-sections, maps. ▫ Why the writer selected particular kinds of illustrations/graphics to convey different kinds of information.
Accuracy/ Evidence for Statements	The authenticity and integrity of the content presented.	▫ The writer's credentials for providing information on the topic. ▫ The writer's citations supporting the accuracy of information on the topic. ▫ Whether the writer provides supporting details for generalizations and conclusions. ▫ Whether facts are consistent across the text. ▫ The writer's purposes for producing the text. ▫ Which facts the writer selected to present and which have been omitted. ▫ The writer's objectivity in producing the text. ▫ The presence of persuasive arguments or propaganda and the degree to which arguments are supported by facts.
Mood	How the writer makes the reader feel about the subject.	▫ How the writer uses language to make the reader sense important underlying emotions or feelings. ▫ How the writer uses language to make the reader care about and understand the information being presented.

Figure 19-7. *The Content of Literary Analysis—Nonfiction*

SUGGESTIONS FOR PROFESSIONAL DEVELOPMENT
ANALYZING BOOK CLUB DISCUSSIONS

1 Gather your grade-level colleagues. Listen to the three segments included on the DVD that accompanies this book: *Rechenka's Eggs, Private Captain,* and *When She Was Good.* The transcript for the discussion of *Private Captain* is presented on page 285. As an alternative, look at one or more of the transcripts of discussions included in this chapter.

2 Using the Systems for Strategic Actions Observation chart on the DVD, make notes about the talk within, beyond, and about the text that the students engage in.

3 Notice the language the students use to discuss the text with each other. What social conventions have they learned?

4 Discuss with your colleagues the implications of your teaching with a book club approach.

CHAPTER TWENTY

GETTING STARTED WITH BOOK CLUBS: THINKING AND TALKING ABOUT TEXTS

What is the use of a book,
thought Alice, without
pictures or conversations?
—LEWIS CARROLL

In this chapter, we will provide the nuts and bolts for getting started with book clubs. We will help you think about how to help your students engage in the process step-by-step and gain worthwhile literary analysis skills.

BOOK SELECTION

Book clubs that engage students in inquiry start with good book selection. In Figure 20-1, we have listed some general suggestions for selecting books for discussion.

CRITERIA FOR SELECTING BOOKS

It is important to choose books that are developmentally appropriate for your students as well as interesting to them. Children like to read about people their own age or a little older. Select books that focus on issues and topics that your students find intriguing and that will provoke talk. No one wants to talk about an issue that he just doesn't care about. A great book will result in great talk!

Choose books that are well written and have excellent qualities as works of literature. Don't be afraid to include some books that you personally love! Your own enthusiasm will increase students' motivation. The problems, characters, and settings should be within your students' reach in terms of grasping the major issues. Although reading level is not a criterion, you will want to consider readability in a broad sense. Select books at a range of reading levels, but choose books that most of the students in your class can read independently. At all grades, be sure to select wonderful picture books by great authors. At the intermediate and middle school level, there are many picture books that are very sophisticated and engaging. You will also want to include a variety of novels. *The Horn Book* provides lists and summaries of books to guide your selection as you add to your classroom collection each year.

If you want everyone in your class to read the same book, you'll need a copy for each student. Otherwise, you will need about six to eight copies to accommodate the number of children in a small group. Books can be "cycled through" more than one group so that, over time, several groups will have read and discussed the same book.

TEXT SETS

Discussion groups can read several books in a "text set" and make connections between them. (See Chapter 17 for information on text sets.)

Selecting Books for Book Clubs

- Select great books that are appropriate for the age and level of sophistication of the students in your class.
- Include books that you love yourself!
- Choose high-quality texts that are well written and have layers of meaning.
- Find texts that have significance and good potential for discussion (include issues, questions, or topics that students will want to talk about).
- Consider readability in broad terms (texts should be in the range that most students can read independently, but you can offer more support to those who need it).
- When appropriate, consider selecting texts related to the social studies and science curricula in your school or district so that readers can make connections.
- Select beautifully illustrated picture books for all grades.
- Select novels or longer texts for the appropriate grades, but don't eliminate picture books.
- Vary the topics or themes so that you have a better chance of meeting diverse needs.
- Put together sets of texts with similar themes but different reading levels so that you accommodate a diversity of students.

Figure 20-1. *Selecting Books for Book Clubs*

The following list is just a sampling of the types of categories:

- Author study (for example, books by Babbit, Avi, or dePaola).

- Genre study (informational books, biographies, historical fiction, traditional literature, realistic fiction).

- Books on the same theme (books that show the human condition over time and cultures in relation to such issues as family closeness, friendship, courage, war, prejudice, death).

- Paired fiction and nonfiction selections (informational books about an animal and fantasies with the same animal as a character; works of historical fiction and factual books about the same time period).

- Picture books and novels by the same author or that have the same theme.

- Biographies (children's book illustrators and authors, artists, sports figures, explorers, revolutionary figures, scientists, inventors, public figures, courageous people).

- Turning points (books showing critical events, hard choices, or momentous decisions that changed people's lives).

- Different versions of the same story (historical fiction; informational account; folktale).

- Content (a range of factual books on the same topic— period of history, animal, scientific process).

- Characters (books that have similar characters—for example, strong girl characters, characters who have overcome handicaps, characters who have fought for the same causes, rebellious characters).

- Text structure (books that have similar organizational patterns or structures, such as flashbacks or stories within stories).

- Series (books that relate the adventures over time of the same characters—*The Dark Is Rising* and *The Grey King; Sarah Plain and Tall, More Perfect Than the Moon, Skylark,* and *Caleb's Story*).

- Books with similar plots (for example, quests or fantastic journeys, such as *The Phantom Tollbooth* and *The Book of Three*.)

You can even include picture books that you have read to the entire group and novels that several students have read

independently and would like to have a chance to discuss.

On the DVD provided with this book, we have listed a number of text sets for literature study, linked in many different ways. The first column identifies the way the texts are connected. The second column gives examples of a few titles you might use in interactive read-aloud to introduce a topic. You can continue to read these titles aloud while your students also prepare for and participate in book clubs. As you can see from this list, you can connect texts in a great many ways. The connection might be as simple as reading a series of texts in the same genre. In addition, we have provided some lists of great Books for Text Talks that you might find useful for book club selections (see the DVD that accompanies this book).

There are many resources to help you put together text sets for book clubs. Start with your school librarian if you have one; if not, visit your community library. The proprietor of your local children's bookstore (if you're lucky enough to have one) can also help. Some schools have core text sets for literature discussion for each grade level, kept on movable carts so that the classroom collections can be constantly replenished. Finally, your students are also a resource. They may discover books during reading workshop that they like well enough to discuss further in book club.

FORMING GROUPS FOR BOOK CLUBS

Forming groups for book club discussions will depend on your purposes, on the particular books you have selected, and on the experience of your students.

GROUP SIZE

Most book clubs work well with four to six students. In the intermediate grades or middle school, they can be as large as seven or eight. Groups of this size have enough diversity to make the discussion interesting while providing plenty of opportunity for all students to participate. When there are only four students, it is easier for the group to get to know one another's point of view and for everyone to have more opportunities to talk. Also, since you will have been working with pairs (and then combined pairs) as part of interactive read-aloud, students will find literature discussion groups or book clubs of four members an easy transition.

You don't need to be rigid about group size, however. Sometimes it is more important for students to have their first choice than to stick to even numbers in groups. When students are very experienced in book discussion and have been talking together over time, groups can be larger.

GROUP COMPOSITION

Book clubs are heterogeneous. All students in your class need the opportunity to experience and discuss age-appropriate texts of their own choosing. The more diversity in the group, the better the discussion. Students are capable of understanding and discussing texts that may be more difficult than those they can read independently, and they will benefit greatly from talking about these ideas. Remember, they will also be reading many books independently, as well as books at their instructional levels in guided reading. With so many books now on tape or CD, you can often make a text available that way; alternatively, a parent or another person can read the book aloud to a student.

Composition of groups can also vary by interest. For example, a group of students who are interested in a particular author, topic, or genre may meet several times during the year, building their knowledge as they explore different works. You may also want to consider all-girl and all-boy groups who read books on gender-specific topics or authors who appeal particularly to boys or girls.

SCHEDULING BOOK CLUBS

There are many possibilities for scheduling book clubs. In Chapters 15 and 16 we discuss interactive read-aloud as a context for teaching students many of the interactive skills they need to engage in successful literature discussion groups. It is important to incorporate these routines and conversational strategies into every lesson, every day, every year; literature discussion is not exclusive to reading workshop. It takes place in interactive read-aloud in every grade. In kindergarten and grade one, most literature discussion will take place during interactive read-aloud as children learn to talk with one another about books, but in grade two and up, you will want your students to have additional time to talk with one another about books in small groups.

Just when and how often you schedule book discussion groups during a reading workshop depends on several factors:

1 *Class size.* It is important for all students to participate in literature discussion. If you have a small class, you can have fewer groups and they can meet more often.

2 *Group size.* If your groups are slightly larger, you can do more in a short time period; however, if groups are too large, they will not be as productive for individuals.

3 *Nature of the text.* Picture books usually require only one meeting, though sometimes the group may want to meet again to discuss a particular aspect. If a group is discussing a longer chapter book that requires several meetings *during* the reading of the text, you will need to schedule groups so that there is time in between group meetings to read assigned segments but not so much time that the book is dragged out.

In Figure 20-2 we present some examples of schedules for book clubs. Each example comprises one month, and the teacher is always working within a sixty-minute reading workshop. Book club meetings may range from about fifteen minutes for younger children to as long as thirty or more minutes for older and/or more experienced students. At the middle school level, when students are experienced in book clubs, it is possible for more than one group to meet simultaneously within the same time period while you rotate from one to another. In these six examples, whenever the teacher is not working with a book club, the time is available for guided reading groups or individual reading conferences. Students should know their book club meeting date well in advance so that they can complete the required reading.

- Example 1. The teacher meets with one book club on Mondays and a second book club on Wednesdays, meeting with four different book clubs each month.

- Example 2. The teacher schedules four different book clubs, each on the first Thursday and Friday of each month (any day is possible).

- Example 3. Every Friday, a book club meets, making it possible for four groups to meet over a month's time. Each student meets in a book club once a month.

- Example 4. Every other week, one book club meets each day, Monday through Thursday. Over the month, each student has met in a book club twice.

- Example 5. Two book clubs meet each Friday, alternating groups so that each student participates in a meeting twice during the month.

- Example 6. Book clubs meet several times over a two-week period. This example works well when students are

Sample Options for Scheduling Book Clubs

EXAMPLES (ONE MONTH)	MONDAY	TUESDAY	WEDNESDAY	THURSDAY	FRIDAY
Example 1					
week 1	Group 1	–	Group 3	–	–
week 2	Group 2	–	Group 4	–	–
week 3	–	–	–	–	–
week 4	–	–		–	–
Example 2					
week 1	–	–	–	Groups 1 & 2	Groups 3 & 4
week 2	–	–	–	–	–
week 3	–	–	–	–	
week 4	–	–	–		
Example 3					
week 1	–	–	–	–	Group 1
week 2	–	–	–	–	Group 2
week 3	–	–	–	–	Group 3
week 4	–	–	–	–	Group 4
Example 4					
week 1	Group 1	Group 2	Group 3	Group 4	–
week 2	–	–	–	–	–
week 3	Group 1	Group 2	Group 3	Group 4	–
week 4	–	–	–	–	–
Example 5					
week 1	–	–	–	–	Groups 1 & 2
week 2	–	–	–	–	Groups 3 & 4
week 3	–	–	–	–	Groups 1 & 2
week 4	–	–	–	–	Groups 3 & 4
Example 6					
week 1	Groups 1 & 2	Groups 3 & 4	–	Groups 1 & 2	Groups 3 & 4
week 2	Groups 1 & 2	Groups 3 & 4	–	–	–
week 3	–	–	–	–	–
week 4	–	–	–	–	–

Figure 20-2. *Sample Options for Scheduling Book Clubs*

reading a longer text that you have divided into three or four segments. Groups meet three or four times.

Many more schedules are possible. You may want to plan a couple of months ahead or even make a predictable schedule for the entire year so that your students know when to expect to participate in book clubs.

THE STRUCTURE OF BOOK CLUB

Like every other element of the reading workshop, book club has a particular structure (see Figure 20-3). You will want to select a set of books (picture books and/or novels)

and introduce the books to the students through short book talks. (If a picture book does not have page numbers, number the pages by hand.) Then have your students make a selection from the group of texts. Give each student a slip of paper with the option to indicate a first, second, and third choice. Most usually can get their first or second choice, but even if they do not, remember that members of a book club often find that reading something they might not have chosen on their own is still very satisfying because of the interesting discussions they have about the text. If you have made good selections and choose with your students' inter-

Structure for Book Clubs		
Prepare	Read, think, mark	Students read during reading workshop and at home during the days preceding the book club meeting. They are asked to think about what they want to discuss. They may be asked to mark the text with stick-on notes, or write page numbers or notes on a "thinkmark" or in their reader's notebooks, so that they do some documentable, individual thinking before the meeting.
Discuss	Talk and listen	For 20 to 30 minutes, students share their thinking through talk, listen to others, add to the thinking of others, challenge the thinking of others, and ask questions, always supporting their thinking with personal experience or evidence, from the text.
Summarize and Evaluate	Summarize and reflect	Students make summary comments and briefly evaluate what went well in the group. They set goals for how they can improve in book club discussion. If they need to read more, they make plans for how much more to read and when to meet.
Extend (Optional)	Extend	Students may be asked to reflect in writing to extend and demonstrate their thinking after reading and discussing the text. Occasionally, members of the book club may create a larger project to share their thinking with others in the class.

Figure 20-3. *Structure for Book Clubs*

ests in mind, you can probably count on a high level of engagement.

Most often, students in a group will be reading and discussing the same title. In the "jigsaw model," however, children in a group each read a different book. When they get together, they spend a few minutes telling one another about their books and responding to questions. Then they explore how the titles are related.

PREPARATION

In the days preceding the meeting, students read and prepare for book club discussion while reading independently at school or home. This reading is qualitatively different from much of the other reading students do. Either consciously or unconsciously, they are selecting information and ideas to share later. You may ask them to bookmark the text or jot down page numbers so that they can quickly take the group to the pages to which they wish to refer.

You might have them use a "thinkmark," a type of bookmark on which they note page numbers (see Fountas and Pinnell 2001). Susan Davis has her students fold a piece of 8-1/2" × 11" paper in half and write notes and page numbers as they read a section. When they read a new section,

they turn it over and then inside out. By the time they finish, there are notes on all four sides. Your students may also take some notes or do some writing in the reader's notebook they bring with them to the group. Lengthy writing assignments, however, can detract from the book club discussion, especially if it takes away from the momentum and enjoyment of the book or if students then just read their notes or essays aloud. The point of book clubs is genuine interaction, not simply taking a turn. Also, assignments should not be so prescriptive that they limit students' responses—having one person write about characters and another about setting, for example. The best discussions are those prior to which participants have reflected thoughtfully, raised their own questions, and identified specific examples from the text that they want to discuss with the group. A "light" assignment that helps them gather their thinking gets the conversation started. If they have done some short writing, such as notes or a paragraph, it can be the source for longer writing later.

DISCUSSION

For the designated time (twenty to thirty minutes, sometimes longer), students discuss the text. When students are first learning discussion techniques, they may tend to "run out of things to talk about" after five or ten minutes. Your prompts and genuine questions can help the group move ahead. Teach them not to be afraid of a few moments of silence while members gather their thoughts. Often, the discussion goes to a deeper level right after such moments.

At least in the beginning, it can help to teach students to use temporary hand signals to guide the discussion. One student begins talking. Others who want a turn hold out two fingers or hold up a thumb. Two fingers means, "I want to add to what the speaker is saying." A thumb means, "I want to change the subject or focus." The speaker calls on the students with two fingers out first. This helps to maintain a coherent sequence of comments around a topic. When no one is holding out two fingers any longer, the speaker calls on a person holding up a thumb, and the exploration of a new topic begins. (You may want to read more about the "fish bowl" technique or other suggestions for facilitating book clubs in Fountas and Pinnell 2001.)

EVALUATION

At the end of the meeting, it is useful for students to take just a few moments to evaluate how things went and set goals for how they can improve during their next discussion. As a teacher you may wish to use your own assessment tools to evaluate groups and individuals, but the real goal is for students to become self-aware. As they do, they will better understand your expectations.

We have included examples of two kinds of self-assessment charts (see Figure 20-4). Blank forms can be found on the DVD that accompanies this book. The first chart can be used with a group as a self-assessment guide. It's a good idea to involve students in creating charts like this one. As you teach minilessons in the reading workshop, you will be teaching them the processes or social skills involved in group discussions. Devote one minilesson to creating an assessment chart together, which you can modify from time to time, adding expectations. Be careful, though, not to make the list so long that students find it difficult to use as a guide.

The second chart is a prompt for individual self-assessment. This can be a written form that is turned in to you after each discussion, or students can use it as a guide for writing a reflective comment in the reader's notebook. Involving your students in self-evaluation is more about teaching than about evaluation; the goal is learning. Here

are some evaluative comments made by a group of boys after a discussion of *Private Captain* (Crisp).

- Paul: "I think I came prepared and I stayed on topic, and I said a lot. I thought I contributed and we really had a good discussion."

- Ben: "I think the group did really well with the hand signals. We had two or three interruptions, and I've got to work on that. I think I came well prepared—more than usual. I really tried not to interrupt people."

- David: "I was way more prepared than usual. I think we didn't just discuss war but lots of other ideas. "

Occasionally, you may want to have students do a "quick write" at the end of a book discussion so that you can see how their thinking has been extended or changed by talking with others. These quick writes can be included in the reader's notebook as part of response to reading, or they can be used as the basis for group assessment.

EXTENSION PROJECT (OPTIONAL)

Students will often write briefly or draw as an integral part of their preparation for and quick reflection on book club discussions. But occasionally you may want students to extend their understanding in a more formal and elaborated way. The purpose of an extension project is to deepen understanding by responding to the whole book and to the conversation that took place around it.

Individual Extensions

To extend the text, individuals can:

- Select a quote that is significant and tell why.

- Make a T chart in the reader's notebook—on the left side "What I Think" and on the right side "Evidence from the Text/Personal Experience." In this way they will not only give their thoughts but also tell what the author said to make them think that.

- Write a book review or book recommendation.

- Write a letter to the author.

- Assume the role of a character and write a diary entry or letter.

- Draw or sketch something from the text that shows a significant event or development.

- Learn more about the author, the topic, or the setting (using reference materials or the Internet).

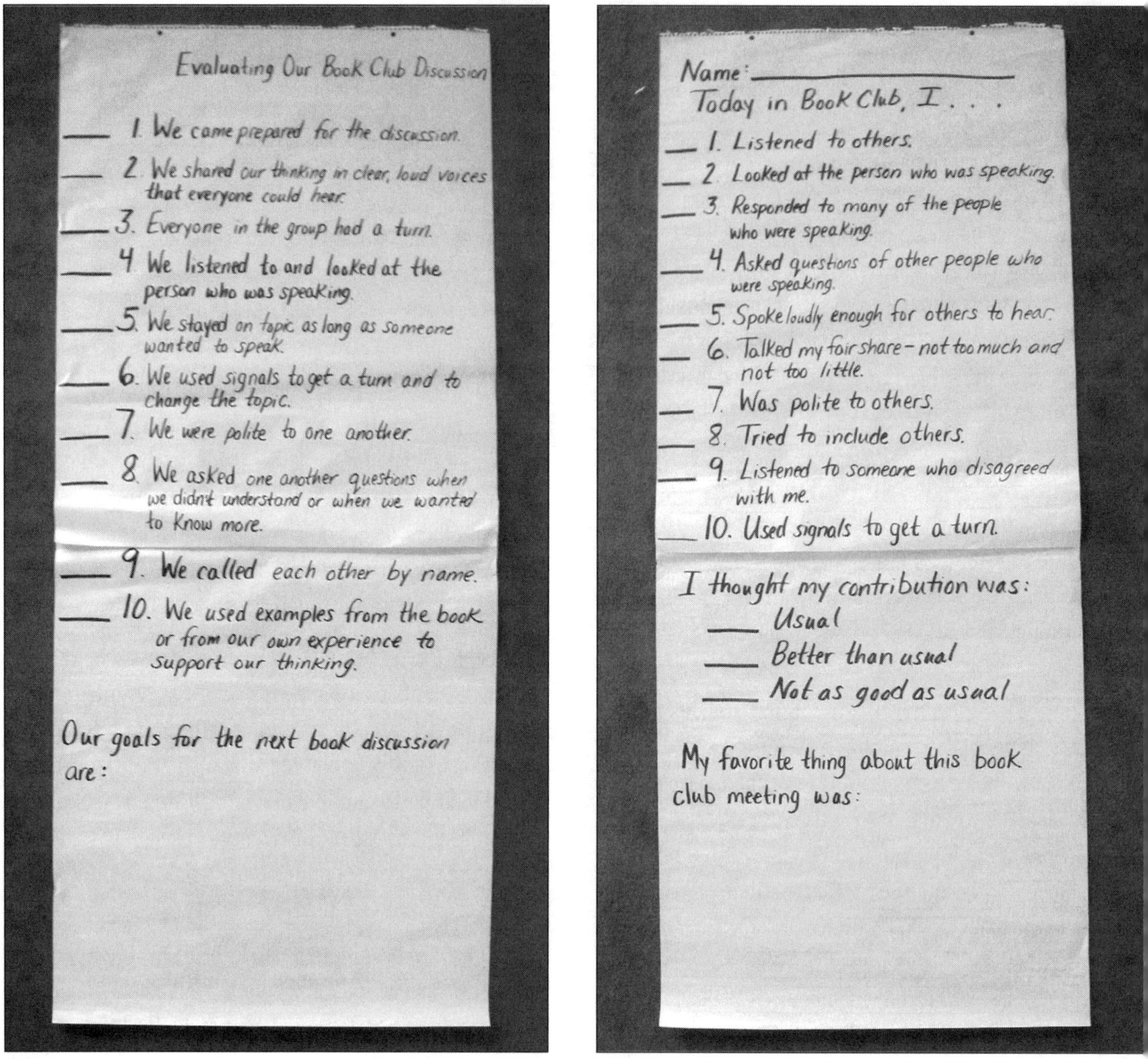

Evaluating Our Book Club Discussion

_____ 1. We came prepared for the discussion.

_____ 2. We shared our thinking in clear, loud voices that everyone could hear.

_____ 3. Everyone in the group had a turn.

_____ 4. We listened to and looked at the person who was speaking.

_____ 5. We stayed on topic as long as someone wanted to speak.

_____ 6. We used signals to get a turn and to change the topic.

_____ 7. We were polite to one another.

_____ 8. We asked one another questions when we didn't understand or when we wanted to know more.

_____ 9. We called each other by name.

_____ 10. We used examples from the book or from our own experience to support our thinking.

Our goals for the next book discussion are:

Name:_____

Today in Book Club, I . . .

_____ 1. Listened to others.

_____ 2. Looked at the person who was speaking.

_____ 3. Responded to many of the people who were speaking.

_____ 4. Asked questions of other people who were speaking.

_____ 5. Spoke loudly enough for others to hear.

_____ 6. Talked my fair share—not too much and not too little.

_____ 7. Was polite to others.

_____ 8. Tried to include others.

_____ 9. Listened to someone who disagreed with me.

_____ 10. Used signals to get a turn.

I thought my contribution was:

_____ Usual

_____ Better than usual

_____ Not as good as usual

My favorite thing about this book club meeting was:

Figure 20-4. *Examples of a Book Club Assessment Chart and a Student Self-Evaluation Chart*

You will not want to assign an extension project simply to give children something to do. Each time you ask students to extend meaning through writing or drawing, have in mind the strategic actions you are trying to support. For example, writing about a character requires understanding basic information from the text (what the person thinks, says, or does and what others think about him); these tasks also require inferring the character's motivations and inner feelings—thinking *within and beyond the text.* Writing a letter to an author or a book review or recommendation prompts thinking *about the text*—the writing style, the use of language, or the organization. An extension project is an opportunity for further analysis of the meaning of the text.

Group or Partner Extensions

Conversations can be extended when members of book clubs work as a group or with partners. For example:

▫ They can make a "jackdaw," a collection of artifacts that represent the events, settings, themes, or characters in the book. (The word "jackdaw" is used metaphorically for good reason! Jackdaws are birds that like to collect shiny objects like pieces of broken glass, foil, and white paper to deposit in their nests.) The jackdaw collection can be presented to the class and displayed for a time as a representation of the group's understandings and an incentive for others to read the book.

- They can produce a poster that focuses on several books by the same author or on the same topic. The poster might include quotes, summaries, and drawings that represent the themes.

- They can prepare a brief drama or piece of readers' theater showing a significant event in the story and perform it for the entire class.

- They can closely examine one significant scene from a fictional, biographical, or historical text and create a tableau by placing themselves in the appropriate positions and assuming appropriate expressions for a minute or two. (A narrator can set the scene.) A "live picture" like this can help them think about what people in the story must have been feeling at the time.

As with individual extensions, you are always working to help students to think within, beyond, and about the text.

Even though students may enjoy extension projects, don't let them take up too much time. For example, elaborate costumes, long periods of drawing, painting, or coloring, and many rehearsals consume time that is better spent reading and discussing another book. The real point of book clubs is the talk.

School-to-Home Extensions

Certainly, students at appropriate grade levels can do extension projects as homework; this has the added benefit of letting parents know what their children are learning. You can also organize parent–child book discussion groups. Sometimes the librarian makes this kind of discussion a school project. Picture books work well for these discussions, since many parents have limited time to read. These discussion groups operate the same as classroom book clubs and can be held after school or in the early evening. Once parents understand the process, they can hold book discussions in their own homes as part of the students' homework.

THE TEACHER'S IMPORTANT ROLE IN LITERATURE DISCUSSION

Your role as a teacher is key to student success in learning to talk about texts and developing strategic actions for understanding those texts. Expressing one's thoughts aloud

requires that the speaker be more precise and specific. Daily text talk will foster this ability, which is often also required in the writing they do for assessment and test taking. As a teacher, you play many different roles (see Figure 20-5). Also, your role will change over time as your students take over more of the process.

- As the *leader,* you open and guide the discussion and work to help participants keep their talk grounded in the text. As students become more experienced, they may take over some of the leadership functions.

- As the *facilitator,* you invite and support discussion but allow participants to work more independently. You remain closely involved through observation and often intervene at key points to help the group stay focused and grounded in the text.

- As a *participant,* you become a member of the group. Having a highly sophisticated member can "lift" the discussion.

- As an *observer,* you observe group behavior and make notes for future work with students.

- As an *evaluator,* you assess the quality and content of the discussion and use the information to inform teaching. Often, you also prompt students' self-evaluation.

ASSESSMENT AS AN INTEGRAL PART OF BOOK CLUBS

Student self-assessment is an important part of their learning. You will also assess students' work in book clubs for your own reasons. Assessment should include both *process* and *content.* Process includes the desired interactions and conversational routines. But remember that students can be having a discussion that looks very good from a process point of view but is still empty in terms of content. The discussion is interactive but you are not hearing good thinking that is clearly expressed; students aren't learning how to participate in book clubs just to be able to participate in book clubs. Rather, they are learning how to examine the meaning of texts. There are few "right" answers in book club discussions—you want the thinking to be the students' own. But you will want to assess the depth of your students' thinking, the degree to which they can summarize the text and think beyond it, and their ability to ground the talk in the texts and in their own experience. We have developed a comprehensive checklist for assessing the quality of a litera-

The Teacher's Roles in Literature Discussion

ROLE	RESPONSIBILITIES	ADVANTAGES
Leader	▫ Opens the discussion. ▫ Establishes expectations and occasionally remind students of them. ▫ Teaches routines. ▫ Guides the discussion through comments and questions. ▫ Helps students summarize and conclude the discussion. ▫ Keeps the discussion grounded in the text.	▫ Provides strong support to help students get started. ▫ Provides teaching to help students understand the expectations of book club. ▫ Demonstrates text talk. ▫ Helps students become clearer about what they are learning. ▫ Helps children focus their talk and use more complex language.
Facilitator	▫ Sets the scene for discussion. ▫ Invites discussion. ▫ Withdraws from the group but stays nearby. ▫ Occasionally steers the conversation by asking critical questions. ▫ Intervenes to help the group remain focused. ▫ Intervenes to ask individuals to clarify points. ▫ Intervenes to help students get a turn if this is not happening. ▫ Establishes beginning and ending points.	▫ Provides the support necessary to help students learn to discuss texts more independently. ▫ Keeps the discussion from rambling or going off on tangents. ▫ Provides enough support that the discussion is productive. ▫ Helps students as they learn responsibility for taking charge themselves.
Participant	▫ Acts as a member of the group, contributing occasionally. ▫ "Lifts" the discussion with personal contributions. ▫ Occasionally steers the discussion so that all students have a chance to speak. ▫ Models all the interactive moves—verbal and nonverbal—that students will be expected to use. ▫ Models the expression of many ways of thinking about a text—"text talk."	▫ Gives students a good model of participation. ▫ Helps students gain the benefit of a sophisticated participant's contributions. ▫ Provides a light level of support as students learn to take responsibility for managing the group. ▫ Provides a presence that reminds students of expectations. ▫ Provides a good model from which students can learn.
Observer	▫ Withdraws from the group but stays nearby. ▫ Listens but does not usually participate. ▫ Occasionally leans in and offers a comment or question. ▫ Takes notes to document information for future teaching plans.	▫ Provides information that is valuable for the teacher. ▫ Communicates to students that their discussion is important. ▫ Provides the opportunity for students to work independently.

Figure 20-5. *The Teacher's Roles in Literature Discussion*

The Teacher's Roles in Literature Discussion (CONTINUED)		
ROLE	RESPONSIBILITIES	ADVANTAGES
Evaluator	□ Evaluates the quality of the discussion. □ Evaluates student comments as evidence of learning. □ Compares evidence of learning to curriculum goals. □ Occasionally provides feedback to the group on the quality of their discussion. □ Prompts students' self-evaluation. □ Gathers information for future teaching in minilessons.	□ Provides information for assessing quality of discussion students are able to achieve independently. □ Provides information for further instruction. □ Documents evidence of learning. □ Provides feedback to students on the way they used routines and social conventions as well as the quality of their discussion. □ Helps students understand expectations so that they can grow.

Figure 20-5. *The Teacher's Roles in Literature Discussion (cont.)*

ture discussion (see Figure 20-6). You can use the Checklist for Evaluating Literature Discussion to assess individuals or the entire group. You may want to focus on items from this list one at a time. (You can print a copy for your use from the DVD.)

Additionally, in order to have a record of an individual's progress over time, you can include in students' portfolios samples of any writing they do in preparation for or after a book club discussion, as well as your notes on their individual participation. Catherine took the following notes when she evaluated the all-boy and all-girl groups described on page 284 (see Figure 20-7). She took these simple notes on shipping labels so she could peel them from their backing and stick them on the appropriate sheet in each student's folder. Notice that Catherine was paying attention to both process and content as she observed the members of the book club.

MINILESSONS TO HELP STUDENTS LEARN

You will want to present a minilesson at the beginning of each reading workshop. Most of your minilessons will address the routines of the workshop, reading strategies and skills, and literary elements; however, once you introduce book clubs, your minilessons can also stress the routines of book club and the content of student talk. We have developed a list of minilessons you may want to teach to help children learn how to talk about texts throughout the year (see Figure 20-8). You can show students explicitly how to demonstrate their understandings through the kinds of talk

they do in book club; however, these minilessons will also help them as they read independently, participate in discussion in guided reading lessons, or write about reading in the reader's notebook.

GETTING STARTED WITH BOOK CLUBS

To help get you started with book clubs, we have ordered a list of minilessons for the first couple of months of school (see Figure 20-9). The first column identifies the topic or concept, and the second column states the principle in clear language. You may want to write this principle on a chart so that you can use it in your teaching and your students can keep it in mind. You can embed some of these minilessons in interactive read-aloud by stating the principle and telling students they will be trying them out in twos, threes, and fours when you ask them to turn and talk. Alternatively, you may teach the lesson at the beginning of the reading workshop and have children apply the principles in their book club discussions that day.

This list focuses mostly on the processes of literature discussion, which is necessary to get the book clubs under way. It also includes some content and literary analysis lessons. When students have good control of the process skills, the content of discussions is richer and more productive for all group members. But at the same time, you are helping students notice memorable language or notice perspectives, skills that support a higher level of discussion. As students gain these understandings, their talk about books in all

Checklist for Evaluating Literature Discussion

ASPECT	NAME(S):
Preparation	___ Read the assigned pages.
	___ Made notes and/or identified pages or parts in the text.
	___ Completed a writing or drawing assignment if assigned.
Discussion–Process	___ Came to the group prepared.
	___ Attended to and looked at the speaker.
	___ Spoke clearly, loudly enough for others in the group to hear.
	___ Spoke to other members (not just the teacher).
	___ Contributed an appropriate amount, taking turns with others.
	___ Asked others for clarification when needed.
	___ Asked follow-up questions.
	___ Built on the comments of others.
	___ Encouraged others to share their thinking.
Discussion–Content	___ Contributed accurate information from the text.
	___ Showed familiarity with the text by providing specific examples to support thinking.
	___ Used prior knowledge to extend understanding of the text.
	___ Identified and discussed literary features of the text.
	___ Recognized and discussed examples of the writer's style or craft.
Discussion–Strategies	___ Provided evidence of literal understanding of the text through summary and important information.
	___ Went beyond the text in thinking to make inferences.
	___ Went beyond the text to make personal, world, or text connections.
	___ Went beyond the text to make predictions.
	___ Went beyond the text to incorporate or synthesize new information and ideas into their thinking.
	___ Noticed aspects of the text such as language, structure, or writer's craft.
	___ Provided evidence of critical thinking about the text.
Assessment	___ Noticed aspects of the discussion that were productive.
	___ Identified areas of needed improvement, providing specific examples from the discussion as evidence.
	___ Assessed self as individual participant.
Comments:	

Figure 20-6. *Checklist for Evaluating Literature Discussion*

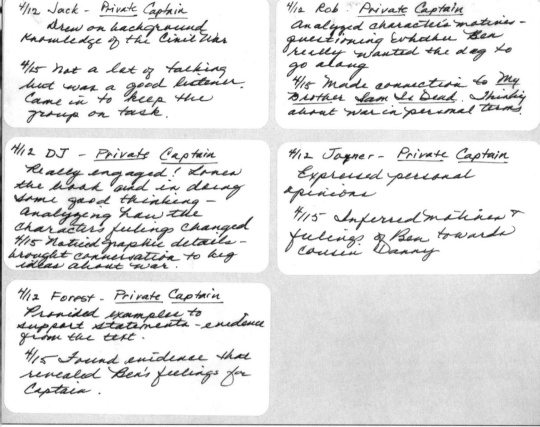

Figure 20-7. *Catherine's Notes on Literature Study*

contexts will be richer and more effective. You will find that they will crave another book about the character, request another book in the genre, and look forward to more frequent book club discussions.

SUGGESTIONS FOR PROFESSIONAL DEVELOPMENT
FORMING BOOK CLUBS

1 Start your own book club! There is no better way for you to understand the process. Bring together a group of colleagues at your grade level or several grade levels. Collect multiple copies of wonderful picture books or novels.

2 Outline the procedures for book club and invite participants to read and prepare.

3 Schedule meetings during several lunch periods or before or after school.

4 Follow the procedures outlined for book clubs. Even though most adults do not need the hand signals, try them out and notice how they help the discussion stay with and develop an idea.

5 Ask several participants to observe the group and take notes before they join in.

6 At the end of the session, ask the note takers to talk about the process and the content of the discussion.

7 Talk about the potential of literature discussion for your students.

Minilessons to Support Literature Discussion

Process: Procedural Minilessons
Lesson Goals.

- How to select a book for literature discussion.
- How to prepare for a discussion.
- How to take notes, make sketches, write questions, or reflect in a reader's notebook before discussion.
- How to get the discussion started.
- How to respect one another's thinking.
- How to participate in a discussion.
- How to encourage one another's thinking.
- How to keep the discussion moving.
- How to respect one another's ideas.
- How to make the discussion interesting (build on one another's ideas).
- How to disagree politely.
- How to listen actively (use positive body language, make eye contact).
- How to take turns speaking in a discussion.
- How to ask questions.

- How to vary language.
- How to summarize and evaluate a discussion (what went well, goals for next time).
- How to seek clarification ("I am confused"; "I don't understand what you mean").
- How to write in the reader's notebook after discussion.
- How to use language that facilitates discussion.
- How to use language that helps others understand better or clarifies:
  - "What do you mean?"
  - "Talk more about that."
  - "Say more about . . ."
  - "Why do you think that?"
  - "What did the author say that made you think that?"

Content: Strategies and Skills Minilessons
Lesson Goals

- Noticing important information in the text or art.
- Making predictions as you read.
- Connecting your personal experiences and knowledge to the text.
- Connecting other texts, authors, and illustrators to the text.
- Using evidence from the text or personal experience to support your thinking.
- Noticing interesting or new vocabulary.
- Recognizing clues provided by the author.

- Predicting the story ending or events following the story.
- Judging the believability of the story.
- Summarizing the story.
- Identifying unanswered questions.
- Analyzing the story title.
- Synthesizing the greater meaning of a text.

Content: Literary Analysis Minilessons
Lesson Goals

- Recognizing the narrator.
- Identifying the author's perspective.
- Identifying the challenges characters encounter.
- Identifying the choices characters have.
- Analyzing how a character affects others.
- Recognizing the most important event in the story.
- Recognizing the shape of the story—circular, linear, triangular.
- Recognizing the order of events as they are told (sequence, flashback).
- Noticing how the author makes the story realistic.
- Finding memorable words or phrases.
- Noticing strong verbs.
- Noticing figurative language: simile, metaphor, personification.

- Identifying and analyzing the lead or how the author engaged the readers.
- Recognizing the high point or climax of the story.
- Recognizing the problem in the story and attempts to solve the problem.
- Recognizing the genre—realistic fiction, historical fiction, fantasy, science fiction, folktale, myth, legend, tall tale, biography, autobiography, informational (factual) texts, poems.
- Responding to the text in writing and drawing.

Figure 20-8. *Minilessons to Support Literature Discussion*

Getting Started: The First 35 Days

TOPIC/CONCEPT	STATEMENT OF PRINCIPLE
1 Making Good Book Choices	Readers can listen to book talks and look through books to help them make good book choices.
2 Preparing for Book Club	Readers prepare for book club by reading and thinking about the assigned pages so they can contribute to and learn from the discussion.
3 Getting Started Quickly	Readers quickly and quietly take their chairs and books, get in a circle, and start the discussion so they can make the best use of time.
4 Respecting Group Members	Readers look at the speaker and show their attention so the speaker feels they value each other's thinking.
5 Respecting One Another's Thinking	Readers show respect for one another's thinking so others will feel good about sharing.
6 Participating Actively	Readers share their thinking by making comments and posing questions so others can learn from, add to, or challenge their ideas.
7 Listening Well	Readers listen to the thinking of others so they can understand and learn from their ideas.
8 Taking Turns	Readers wait for a person to finish speaking before they start speaking so that everyone can hear and understand.
9 Building on Ideas	Readers build on one another's ideas so they can make the discussion more interesting. Readers add to the comments of others so they can examine one another's thinking more deeply.
10 Disagreeing Politely	Readers disagree in polite ways so they can help one another understand more.
11 Encouraging Group Members	Readers encourage one another to share their thinking so they can feel good and learn a lot from the discussion.
12 Marking Sentences or Passages	Readers jot down or mark sentences or passages that they want to discuss in the group so they can find them quickly and easily.
13 Noticing Memorable Language	Readers notice the language (words, phrases, or sentences) writers use so they can think about their meaning.
14 Noticing Important Information in the Text	Readers notice important information as they read so they can understand the author's message.
15 Noticing Important Information in the Art	Readers notice the information in the art or illustrations so they can fully understand the meaning of the text.
16 Using Stick-on Notes to Mark Places	Readers use stick-on notes to mark places in the book that they find interesting or confusing, so they can go to the places quickly during group discussion.
17 Making Notes for Discussion	Readers make notes and list page numbers so they can go to the places in the book quickly during group discussion.
18 Using a Thinkmark to Make Notes	Readers use a thinkmark to note places they want to discuss so they can find them quickly in group discussion. (A thinkmark is simply a bookmark with lines on which to make notes or list page numbers.)
19 Writing Personal Reflections and Questions	Readers write their own thoughts or questions before group discussion so they can do their own thinking before hearing the thinking of others.
20 Reflecting After Discussion	Readers write about or sketch their thinking after group discussion so they can examine and extend their understanding.
21 Supporting Your Thinking with Evidence	Readers support their thinking with personal experience or evidence from the text so others can understand the reasons for their statements.

Figure 20-9. *Getting Started: The First 35 Days*

Getting Started: The First 35 Days (CONTINUED)

TOPIC/CONCEPT	STATEMENT OF PRINCIPLE
22 Searching for Information	Readers ask questions so they can better understand the thinking of other speakers. For example: ▫ "What do you mean by that?" ▫ "Say more about that." ▫ "Why do you think that?" ▫ "What did the author say that made you think that?"
23 Sharing Your Thinking	Readers tell about their thinking so others can learn from their ideas.
24 Summarizing the Learning	Readers comment on what they learned at the end of the discussion so others can understand what they thought was important.
25 Evaluating the Discussion	Readers discuss what went well and what needs to work better and set goals so discussions can improve.
26 Making Choices for Book Club	Readers list their first-, second-, and third-choice books so the teacher can make groups and try to assign each person one of their best choices.
27 Having a Good Discussion	Readers listen, talk, and ask questions so they can learn from and contribute to a good discussion.
28 Making Predictions	Readers think about what they know and make predictions so they can understand a text better.
29 Noticing Perspectives	Readers notice the writer's attitude or point of view about a topic so they can share it in group discussion.
30 Identifying Genre	Readers notice the characteristics of a genre so they can know what to look for or expect as they read.
31 Using a Good Voice Level	Readers share their thinking in a soft voice that can be heard clearly by all group members but does not disturb the other readers in the classroom.
32 Asking Questions	Readers ask questions so they can learn more about one another's thinking.
33 Asking Follow-up Questions	Readers ask follow-up questions so they can get further information about something they asked about.
34 Requesting Evidence	Readers ask other group members to support their thinking with evidence by asking what made them think that.
35 Noticing What Made the Text Interesting	Readers notice how the writer made the text interesting to readers so they can understand more about how writers craft their stories.

Figure 20-9. *Getting Started: The First 35 Days (cont.)*

CHAPTER TWENTY-ONE

PROMOTING SHARED AND PERFORMED READING: FLUENT ORAL PROCESSING OF TEXTS

The style of teaching . . . might be called invitational—an enthusiastic invitation to participate, contribute, take over the operation.

—DON HOLDAWAY

Performing in concert with others increases the enjoyment of many tasks: singing, playing in a band, dancing, or synchronized swimming are only a few. In some cases, working in unison with a group even helps an individual perform with greater skill. The group provides support. Singing alone, your performance might not be noteworthy, but as one of a fifty-member chorus you produce something audiences will flock to see. For the young child, shared reading provides easy entry into behaving like a reader. As readers grow proficient, they may no longer need the support of the group to read a text, but their understanding and enjoyment can be greatly enhanced through performed reading.

Three group contexts have particular value for teaching comprehension and reading fluency: shared reading, choral reading, and readers' theater (see Figure 21-1):

- *Shared reading* usually refers to young children's reading from a common enlarged text—a large-print book, a chart, or a projected text. When children are first beginning to learn to read, the teacher leads the group, pointing to the words or phrases. Reading is usually in unison, although there are adaptations, such as groups alternating lines or individuals reading some lines alone.
- *Choral reading* usually refers to any group of people reading from a common text, which may be written on a chart, projected on a screen, or printed in individual

Contexts for Performed Reading

In performed reading, students read aloud for their own pleasure and that of others, paying attention to expression and interpretation.

CONTEXT	DESCRIPTION	APPROXIMATE GRADE LEVELS
Shared Reading	Led by the teacher, students read in unison from a shared text on a chart or in a book. The teacher uses a pointer to guide the reading and help children follow the print. The emphasis is on enjoyment and experiencing a large number of texts together. As children become more proficient at following the print, the teacher actively supports phrasing, fluency, and other strategic actions.	K–2
Choral Reading	Students read aloud from a chart, a projected text, or individual copies of a prose or poetry text. The reading includes unison sections and solos, and the emphasis is on interpreting the text through expression, tone, volume, and rhythm.	2–8
Readers' Theater	Students use a script (usually based on a story) prepared by the teacher or themselves or read dialogue from a story. Parts (individual characters and often a narrator) are assigned. The emphasis is on interpreting the text vocally. Readers' theater does not require props, costumes, or memorization. Readers' theater may be performed for others.	1–8

Figure 21-1. *Contexts for Performed Reading*

copies. The text is usually longer than that used for shared reading. The emphasis is on interpreting the text with the voice. Some reading is done in unison by the whole group or subgroups, and there may be "solos" or "duets."

- *Readers' theater* usually refers to enacting a text by reading roles. The scripts (which are usually adaptations of stories and do not start out as plays) are generally not memorized nor performed with costumes and props. The emphasis is on vocal interpretation. Usually, the parts are read by individuals, although some roles may be read by small groups.

Shared and choral reading are essentially the same activity—reading in unison from a common text—but they are used in different ways. All three contexts involve reading aloud for the pleasure of oneself and others. Common characteristics include:

- Processing print in a continuous text.
- Working in a group.
- Using the voice to interpret the meaning of a text.
- Reading in unison with others or in "parts" that interact.
- Providing opportunities to learn more about the reading process.
- Collaborating with others to show the interpretation of a text.

SHARED READING

All shared reading of enlarged texts involves a group of children looking at a common text. Shared reading is generally considered a useful technique for working with younger children. In 1979, Don Holladay introduced shared reading pedagogy that he called the "shared book experience." Prior to that, young children had frequently practiced reading in unison from charts and even some big books that were part of basal reading programs, but Holladay brought shared reading to the fore as an instructional technique. His goal was to re-create elements of the "lap story" that children experienced at home:

- Clear view of the print and pictures as the book is read.
- A warm and accepting social experience.
- Collaboration with others in reading.

- An experience highly supported by the adult, enabling the children to take on the behaviors of a reader.
- The opportunity to experience more sophisticated language and content.

According to Holladay:

> The major purpose from the parents' point of view is to give pleasure. . . . From the child's point of view the situation is among the happiest and most secure in his experience. The stories themselves are enriching and deeply satisfying . . . , thus the child develops strongly positive associations with the flow of story language and with the physical characteristics of the books. (pp. 39–40)

As much as possible, Holladay (1979) wanted the elements of the lap story to be duplicated in the classroom:

- The adult models effective reading behaviors.
- The text is usually read many times.
- The adult and child progress to reading the text in unison, with the teacher sometimes dropping out and letting the child finish a line or read alone for stretches.
- The child can see the text (large-print book, large-print chart, projected text).
- The adult provides various levels of support to direct the child's attention to the print.
- The adult engages the child in the reading process.
- The adult discusses the meaning of the text with the child.
- In addition to elements mentioned above, the teacher works in a highly intentional way to teach aspects of the reading process. For example, the text may be revisited for many different reasons—to locate words, notice patterns in words, locate and discuss punctuation, find expressions or language patterns.

VALUES OF SHARED READING

With the support of the teacher, children can do more and, as a result, learn more (Vygotsky 1978, 1986). Specifically, shared reading:

- Provides a demonstration of the reading process.
- Builds phonemic awareness (individual sounds, syllables, onset and rime, words and parts of words).
- Builds letter knowledge.
- Develops understanding of letter/sound relationships.

- Develops understanding of concepts of print (directionality, word-by-word matching, return sweep, punctuation, spacing).

- Develops word-recognition and word-analysis skills by providing the opportunity to teach a range of word-solving strategies.

- Provides social support to a heterogeneous group of readers.

- Builds language skills and enhances vocabulary.

- Builds knowledge of high frequency words.

- Promotes fluent phrased reading.

- Builds students' understanding of different types of texts, formats, and structures.

- Encourages personal and critical response to texts.

- Develops comprehending strategies for a wide variety of texts.

- Helps develop understanding of print and text features.

Selecting Texts for Shared Reading

According to Holdaway (1979), "The language of the books used by parents, even with infants below the age of two, is remarkably rich in comparison with the caption books and early readers used in the first year of school" (p. 40). A key to success in shared reading is the selection of a suitable text. Just about any kind of text can be used for shared reading, provided it is appropriate to the children's experience. The texts used for shared reading should:

- Be immediately interesting to children.

- Often have rhyme, rhythm, and repetition.

- Include a variety of text types, one of them being informational texts.

- Sometimes be texts that children have helped write.

Shared reading can be done of songs or "raps," poems, chants, and all kinds of stories, including traditional tales with repeating refrains and simple realistic or fantasy stories. Shared reading can also focus on informational texts, either commercially published or produced by children and teachers through interactive writing.

No one format is best for shared reading: using a variety of formats will develop flexibility in young readers. Through shared reading, children learn some foundational things about texts:

- Books and other writing have a "right side up."

- You search the page to find the print and that's what you actually read.

- Pictures provide some good information that will help you understand the story.

- You need to read the print on a page and then turn the page to read more.

- You read the left page before the right page if it has print.

- You start on the left and read to the right; you go back to the left to read the next line.

- There are spaces between words.

- You say one word for each printed word.

- Words are made up of letters.

- You can notice the letters in words to help you read.

- When you read, you see some words over and over; you can recognize the word by looking at the letters.

- Some words start alike; some words end alike.

- If you don't know a word, you can reread up to the word and think about what would make sense and how it starts.

- You can reread to check whether what you read was right.

- You need to think about the story (or poem) and remember information to help you understand it.

- You can use parts of words to solve them.

- You read a story or poem in a way that sounds like talking.

- You use punctuation to help you read.

- You can reread to get more information.

- You can think about what word might come next as you read (using language, structure, and meaning).

- Some language is repeated throughout the text; some of the language is fun to remember and use again.

Any of the understandings listed above may be learned implicitly while children are participating in shared reading of a text. The teacher may also select to demonstrate or highlight any of these concepts in instruction.

Children learn a lot about words in shared reading; for example, they become familiar with parts of words, learn some specific words to use as anchors, and begin to associate sounds and letters. Teachers provide a great deal of phonics instruction during shared reading:

◻ Predicting the word by looking at the first letter.

◻ Finding the first part of the word; finding the last part.

◻ Thinking of a word you know like that.

◻ Rereading the sentence and "getting your mouth ready for it."

◻ Looking at the first part (or the last part) of the word.

◻ Covering up the word and predicting the first letter; checking by uncovering the word.

◻ Locating the word after saying what letter you will expect to see.

◻ Finding common words that you see a lot.

However, shared reading has broader goals than learning about letters, sounds, and words. It provides a pleasurable introduction to reading and helps children build efficient initial processes. They learn how to engage in the reading process and take the understandings to guided reading lessons and independent reading. Through shared reading, children:

◻ Experience many texts that they can draw on as examples of written language.

◻ Acquire new vocabulary.

◻ Learn the structures of written language.

◻ Learn a core of high frequency words that they recognize instantly.

◻ Develop word-solving strategies by making connections among words and by noticing letter/sound relationships and visual aspects of words.

◻ Hear and participate in phrased fluent reading of continuous text so that they learn how oral reading should sound.

A STRUCTURE FOR SHARED READING

Shared reading lessons have five key elements (see Figure 21-2). Each element of the shared reading lesson has particular implications for the development of strategic actions (see column 3):

1 *Introducing the text.* Briefly introduce the text in a way similar to the "opening moves" listed in Chapter 15 for interactive read-aloud (see page 226). This brief introduction arouses readers' interest and may provide some

important information that will support children's interpretation of the text.

2 *Modeling the reading of the text.* Usually, you will first model the reading of the text. Be cautious about having children join in before they have even heard the text. They can become so focused on joining in that they "mumble along" and lose the meaning. Set up some clear verbal or nonverbal signals for when and how the children should join in. With a very simple text that has a repeating refrain, they often can join in successfully after several pages have been read. But with complex texts, it may be better for them to hear the whole text the first time. For some texts, you may want to lead them in a small amount of problem solving during first or subsequent reading (for example, covering a few words or word parts and inviting their predictions).

3 *Reading the text together.* After one or two readings, you and the children can read the whole text or parts of the text in unison, using a large number of enjoyable variations. Children can read the text in parts, one group reading one line or page and another group reading the next. Children can join in only on the dialogue or can read roles. Reading like this provides maximum opportunity for all children in the class to "get the feel" of good reading. It promotes phrasing and use of punctuation. By rereading words many times, children not only learn new vocabulary but also become familiar with the visual features of words. They increase their knowledge of high frequency words that they recognize immediately.

4 *Discussing the meaning of the text.* Just as in guided reading or interactive read-aloud, you and the children will discuss the meaning of the text. This discussion is essential, because children think more actively during reading when they know they will be expected to comment afterward. As in interactive read-aloud, discussion can take place at a useful stopping place and/or after the reading. However, since shared reading texts are usually shorter than those you read aloud and because you want to keep the momentum going, you will not want to stop too often. There is always something to talk about— even a repetitive text that plays with language rather than has a plot will raise questions in students' minds about interesting words or ideas.

Elements of A Shared Reading Lesson

ELEMENT	DESCRIPTION	OPPORTUNITIES FOR TEACHING AND LEARNING
Introducing the Text	The teacher piques the students' interest in the text with a brief opening statement that involves them in some conversation.	▫ Prompt children to make connections. ▫ Build background knowledge. ▫ Use vocabulary in conversation. ▫ Provide important information about setting or characters. ▫ Connect to other texts. ▫ Set the children up to anticipate the meaning of the text.
Modeling the Reading of the Text	The teacher reads the text expressively to the children while pointing to the words. Sometimes the teacher pauses so readers can think about how to solve specific problems.	▫ Demonstrate fluency and phrasing. ▫ Demonstrate interpretation of the text. ▫ Pause for problem-solving opportunities. ▫ Talk about what to notice about print or punctuation. ▫ Show how to check on yourself as a reader. ▫ Show how to take a word apart.
Reading the Text Together	The children and teacher read the text in unison, with variations for different purposes.	▫ Prompt children to track print, first word-by-word and then in phrases. ▫ Support children in reading with fluency and phrasing. ▫ Prompt children to attend to punctuation. ▫ Encourage children to read with expression related to the meaning of the text.
Discussing the Text	The children and teacher discuss the meaning of the text.	▫ Help children remember and summarize important information. ▫ Help children infer characters' motivations. ▫ Help children notice the language or story structure. ▫ Invite children to form opinions about the text.
Teaching Points	The teacher makes specific teaching points related to the reading process; often specific pages are revisited.	▫ Demonstrate or reinforce any aspect of a strategic processing system. ▫ Revisit pages of the text to show how to solve words, make inferences, make connections, make predictions, notice and synthesize new information, analyze the text, criticize the text.

gure 21-2. *Elements of a Shared Reading Lesson*

Making teaching points. After reading a text, you will want to make a few explicit teaching points directed at any aspect of the reading process. If children like it enough to reread many times, the shared reading text will become quite well known and a rich resource for examining multisyllable words; looking at parts of words such as letter clusters; and linking words by how they start, how they end, and how they sound. They can think about what the writer is implying but not telling, go beyond the text to make predictions or inferences, or discover and remember new information. Reading and discussion of a familiar text is a good context for demon-

strating early problem-solving strategies such as rereading, with the goal of gaining a clear feeling for semantic and syntactic information in the sentence as a backdrop for reading an unfamiliar word. As the reader holds more information in short-term memory, problem solving and self-correction take place closer to the word. You can also draw readers' attention to information in the pictures, from which they can derive meaning.

ROLES IN SHARED READING

Figure 21-3 clarifies your role and the students' role in shared reading. Before reading, you are responsible for selecting and analyzing the text for its instructional value

Roles in Shared Reading

	TEACHER'S ROLE	STUDENTS' ROLE
Before the Reading	<ul><li>Select an appropriate text for the age group and experience level.</li><li>Ensure the print can be seen clearly (large print, chart, book, or projected images).</li><li>Provide a brief introduction to the text, type, and author.</li><li>Build interest in the text.</li><li>Elicit background or related literary knowledge.</li><li>Encourage predictions.</li><li>Link the text to other texts as appropriate.</li></ul>	<ul><li>Actively respond to the introduction.</li><li>Anticipate the text.</li><li>If a rereading, remember something about the text to use in shared reading.</li></ul>
During the Reading	<ul><li>Model/demonstrate the processing of the text.</li><li>Lead the students in processing on subsequent readings.</li><li>Model fluent, phrased reading with attention to punctuation.</li><li>Varie pointing according to the level of the group:<ul><li>Point crisply to each word.</li><li>Slide pointer below each line of text.</li><li>Place pointer at the beginning of each line.</li><li>Do not point.</li></ul></li><li>May pause briefly for teacher or student comments or predictions (at the word level, phrase level, or sentence level).</li></ul>	<ul><li>Enjoy and understand the text.</li><li>Make brief comments or predictions at pauses.</li><li>Listen actively to the text or participate in reading part or all of the text.</li><li>Engage in the reading process, using the meaning, language, and print information.</li><li>Notice phrase units and punctuation.</li><li>Intentionally use the voice to reflect the meaning of the text.</li><li>Stay in unison with other readers, following the teacher's guidance.</li><li>Gradually gain control of following the text without the teacher's precise pointing.</li></ul>
After the Reading	<ul><li>Discuss the meaning of the text.</li><li>Help readers notice the text structure or organization as appropriate.</li><li>Make teaching points related to letter/word analysis, fluency, language, comprehension, and writer's craft.</li><li>May revisit the text for close reading of a sentence or paragraph.</li><li>May use a whiteboard, Magnadoodle, or masking device to help readers attend to print features.</li></ul>	<ul><li>Think about and share comments about the text meaning.</li><li>Notice vocabulary and language.</li><li>Notice elements of the writer's craft.</li><li>May dramatize the text.</li><li>May engage in response through drawing or painting.</li><li>May reread the text independently.</li><li>May listen to a recorded version of the text at the listening center.</li></ul>

Figure 21-3. *Roles in Shared Reading*

these students and for providing an introduction that will engage readers. Students are expected to participate actively in the conversation before reading; if this is a repeated reading, they should be able to remember something about the text.

During reading, your role is to demonstrate fluent, phrased reading and other aspects of the reading process and to support students in doing the same. You may pause so that students can make predictions, confirm them, or interpret the text. Students are expected to read in unison with you and the other students and to watch the print closely. On a first reading, you usually point to the words. As children become more proficient, you may slide the pointer below the words, place the pointer at the beginning of a line, or use no pointer at all.

After reading, you and the students think about and share comments about the text. You may revisit the text for explicit teaching, using a whiteboard or other devices such as word masks, a highlighter marker, or highlighter tape to highlight features of words, and also help children notice aspects of the writer's craft. Shared reading texts may be extended by listening to a recording (either a professional tape recording or one made by the class), reading the text independently or with a partner, drawing, or innovating on the text (putting in different characters, more words, or different words).

SHARED READING EXAMPLE OF A FICTION TEXT

The Promise (Hughes) is a modern retelling of the traditional tale about the princess who promises to kiss a frog. As you can see from the text in column two of Figure 21-4, *The Promise* is longer and more complex than early shared reading texts. In this example, the teacher read the story to the children (reading #1) and they discussed the meaning of the text. During reading #2 (column three), the teacher again did most of the reading but stopped several times to have children "echo" her reading of dialogue. After reading, the teacher guided children to discuss information in the pictures and also revisited pages 6 and 7, to look at how the writer presented a list, and page 10, to discuss the mother's underlying reasons for forcing Ana to keep her promises.

By reading #6, the children were very familiar with the text. This time, they read the text as a piece of readers' theater, with attention to interpretation. As they assigned roles,

they discussed why the frog and prince should be read by the same person, but several children suggested that the voice should change just as the frog had. Page 8 was revisited to talk about Ana's conflicting feelings (her own selfishness versus her dislike of the frog) and to look at how the writer constructed dialogue.

Even though this text is fairly long for shared reading, it will go quickly if children are reading fluently. Also, when they know the text, you may want to reread only a portion of it in a session.

SHARED READING OF INFORMATIONAL TEXTS

Shared reading of informational texts takes readers into this new kind of genre so that they can become familiar with the features of nonfiction. To read informational texts, readers need to:

- Use background knowledge and experiences to help them understand new information.

- Understand the features of nonfiction texts.

- Understand the sentence patterns of informational texts.

- Know how to select specific parts to read.

- Know how to read photographs, maps, diagrams, charts, etc.

- Know how to use organizational features and print features—table of contents, index, glossary, headings, subheadings, and sidebars.

- Understand technical vocabulary.

- Develop a range of strategic actions for reading factual texts.

For example, look at the page layouts of a challenging informational text, *Is This a Moose?* (Armstrong), shown in Figure 21-5. Each right-hand page has a picture of an animal and the one-line question, "Is this a moose?" You turn the page to see the answer. If it is no, there is a sentence identifying the animal at the top of the page and two lines of information about the animal at the bottom of the page. Until page 14, the answer is always no. This book has wonderful pictures, nice large print, and interesting ideas that will engage children. It is challenging because:

- A different concept (animal) with related facts is presented every two pages instead of focusing on one animal throughout.

SHARED READING OF
The Promise

PAGE	TEXT	TEACHING AND LEARNING		
	Reading #1 (Teacher to Students)	**Reading #2**	**Reading #4**	**Reading #6**
2	Princess Ana was tossing her golden ball. "Will you play with us?" asked the girls. "No!" said Princess Ana.	Teacher read. Children echoed teacher on line 3.	Teacher read, with children joining in on dialogue.	
3	Her golden ball went up and down, up and down. Then . . . splash! It fell in the pond.	Teacher read. Page revisited to talk about what kind of person Ana really was.	Teacher called attention to how to use the voice on ellipses.	Teacher read the narrative. Children read dialogue as in readers' theater. Different children read the roles of:
4	"Oh, no!" said Princess Ana. "My ball!" "Help me! Now!" she commanded. But no one came.		Children practiced split dialogue and noticed punctuation.	–the girls –Ana –the mother –the frog
5	Princess Ana heard a little voice. "I'll help." Princess Ana looked down. She saw a frog. "Ugh!" she said.	Teacher read. Children echoed teacher on line 2 and 5.	Children practiced variation between princess and frog voices.	
6 & 7	"I'll get your ball," the frog said. "But you must make three promises. One: I can eat at your table. Two: I can sleep in your room. Three: You will kiss me goodnight."	Teacher read. Children echoed teacher on frog voice and three promises.	Pages were revisited to notice the way the writer showed the list.	
8	"Ugh!" said Princess Ana. She looked at her golden ball. She looked at the frog. "All right," she said. "I promise."	Teacher read. Children echoed teacher on line 4.	Teacher read, with children joining in on dialogue.	Children read dialogue in roles. Page was revisited to discuss the conflicting ideas in Ana's head.
9	The frog gave Princess Ana her golden ball. "Bye, bye," said Princess Ana. She took her ball and she left.	Teacher read.	Teacher read, with children joining in on dialogue.	Children read dialogue in roles.
10	It was dinnertime. Knock, knock, knock. "You promised," said the frog. "Go away!" said Princess Ana. But her mother was there.	Teacher read. Children echoed teacher on frog voice, princess voice, and line 5.	Page was revisited to discuss why Ana's mother wanted her to keep a promise.	

Figure 21-4. *Shared Reading of* The Promise

SHARED READING OF
The Promise (CONTINUED)

PAGE	TEXT	TEACHING AND LEARNING		
	Reading #1 (Teacher to Students)	Reading #2	Reading #4	Reading #6
11	"You made a promise?" asked the Queen. "Then you must keep it." "Come in," said Princess Ana.	Teacher read the page, then had children read with her.	Teacher read, with children joining in on dialogue.	Children read dialogue in roles. Page was revisited to look at the way the writer showed dialogue (split).
12	They all ate dinner together. Princess Ana yawned. "Time for bed," she said.	Teacher read with children echoing dialogue.		
	The text continues in the same manner through the other two promises made by the princess. Each time, reminded by her mother, she keeps her promise, finally kissing the frog.	Teacher read with children echoing dialogue.	Teacher read narrative parts and children joined in on dialogue.	Children read dialogue in roles.
20	"Now you'll marry me," said Princess Ana. But the Prince said, "No. You're not nice. And you don't keep promises."	Teacher read with children echoing selected lines.		
	The story ends as Ana and the Prince promise to play together and Ana gets a whole new attitude.	Children discussed how Ana had changed and revisited several pages (see above).	Children discussed details in the pictures (such as consistently present cat, the Queen, servants).	Children discussed why the frog and the Prince had to be read by the same person *but* the tone of voice could vary.

Figure 21-4. *Shared Reading of* The Promise *(cont.)*

- Technical vocabulary such as *bowl* and *flippers* is included throughout.

- It requires considerable background information that many children will not have.

- Readers need to understand and follow the question and answer format.

- Once the text says, "Yes. This is a moose," there are several more pages with information about moose, so the text structure changes. Also there are four to five lines of print on each page.

To use this text successfully for shared reading with children, one teacher invited them to join in only on the question and answer lines and encouraged them to listen carefully and learn about the animals in the other parts of the text. After several readings, children could also join in on the two lines of information about each animal and learned some interesting new vocabulary that they could use in discussion.

Through shared reading of informational texts, students can learn how to locate information in texts. You can demonstrate skimming through the text to find answers to questions, and then discuss why the page or section is helpful. You can show students how certain words and ideas are connected to the information they are reading—for example, how animals sound, how they protect themselves, or

No. This is a seal.

Is this a moose?

Seals have flippers to help them swim.

Figure 21-5. Is This a Moose?

what they eat. You can invite them to scan photographs for information that is important for understanding the topic.

CHORAL READING

The term *choral reading* usually refers to more sophisticated vocal interpretations of prose or poetry texts. Choral reading is performance. Participants are generally not in the emergent phase of learning to read; they can process several lines of print and follow it with their eyes. The text may be on a chart or projected on the wall, but participants may also have their own individual copies.

The emphasis in choral reading is on the interpretation of text through the voice. Readers are required to notice phrases and punctuation and to think deeply about the meaning of the text. They read in unison with others, although the group may be divided into several sections. There may be "solos" and "duets" or alternating responses. A great deal of creativity is necessary to divide up the parts, establish phrasing and expression, and indicate changes in volume or tempo for emphasis. Choral reading provides an enjoyable experience with written language for readers of any age. Through choral reading, they:

- Study a text closely to interpret it.

- Practice expressive reading.

- Become more aware of phrases, ways to stress particular words or phrases, and all elements of fluent reading.

- Develop new vocabulary and language structures.

- Become aware of complex literary texts.

PROCESS VERSUS PERFORMANCE

You will not want to put undue emphasis on the *performance* of choral reading because you do not want to encourage nervousness and stress. It is more important to concentrate on the *process* of interpreting the text. Sometimes you will want students to memorize a particular poem or other text and keep it in their repertoire. In that case, it is important that students have some choice in the matter and really like the material you are asking them to learn.

Basic to the process, students must deeply understand the text they are performing. They should be able to talk about the characters, if appropriate, and the ideas. They should examine the language closely and discuss the writer's meaning. The presentation should be discussed and planned.

When you first start working with children on choral reading, be sure they understand what is expected. Work with the whole group at first using a poem or any other text that you have read aloud to them. Once they understand the process, students can work in groups to select and prepare pieces. For example, after a middle school teacher read Karen Hesse's *Out of the Dust* (which is written in blank verse) aloud to her class and two small groups read and discussed the book in book club, those groups each selected a chapter to prepare and perform. The class then discussed the different interpretations.

If no memorization is involved, you will not need to devote a large amount of class time to preparation. Students may prepare some nonverbal gestures and very minor symbolic props, but most of their preparation should be spent on discussion and interpretation. After choral reading, children can discuss the performance and critique their interpretation.

READERS' THEATER

Plays have long been a source of pleasure for readers. Readers' theater is a fast and engaging way of making any literary text a type of play. The "script" is composed from the dialogue and narrative of the text. Often plays based on traditional literature are provided in young children's reading books. Older readers enjoy memorizing and performing short plays and even preparing some of their own scripts. Returning to a text in this authentic way makes rereading and reconsidering text more enjoyable. In the process, students internalize language that they might not have otherwise. Usually, no memorization is involved. Once older readers have experienced readers' theater, they will enjoy preparing and performing their own scripts.

PROCEDURES FOR READERS' THEATER

In readers' theater, participants read a script that has usually been constructed from a longer text. Readers' theater is a little like a traditional play, but it has the advantages of not requiring memorization, costumes, or extensive rehearsal. Participants simply hold the scripts in their hands. (Alternatively, children can use copies of the book and agree who will read each part. This saves having to create a separate script.) Participants are assigned parts and concentrate on using their voices to interpret the text. There may occasionally be some unison reading. After the students have reread the script several times, it is usually ready to be performed for an audience.

BENEFITS OF READERS' THEATER

Readers' theater allows children to experience a text in another way, one that provides an authentic purpose for oral rereading. It engages and motivates readers. Readers' theater is especially effective for English language learners, who need these opportunities to read and reread the syntax of the language. Through readers' theater, all students:

- Use background information from the longer text to interpret oral language provided in the script.
- Study characters in order to use the voice to interpret their feelings.
- Develop ease with new vocabulary words and language structures by using them in the role of characters or a narrator.
- Practice expressive reading.
- Pay close attention to phrases and all elements of fluent reading.
- Self-assess their own reading performance.
- Build self-confidence through reading for an audience.
- Build oral expression and speaking skills.
- Build a sense of community with others.
- Strengthen their word-analysis skills.
- Practice meaningful reading.
- Practice reading loudly and clearly.

CREATING A SCRIPT FOR READERS' THEATER

You can create scripts easily (see the steps outlined in Figure 21-6). Just remember to keep it simple and enjoyable. Trade books can be adapted into scripts without much effort. You can use poems or stories featuring lots of dialogue, intriguing characters, and interesting problems. You can create a script of a complete story or a scene from a longer story.

An appropriate text may be any favorite story or a short segment from a story. Fairy tales, folktales, and legends work well. Mother Goose rhymes and other poems can also be used, as well as a wide range of other genres. Look for texts that have lots of dialogue or from which it will be easy to create dialogue.

Then, select characters and a narrator. You do not need to include all the characters in a text—eliminating minor ones keeps it simple. Two to six characters works very well. The narrator introduces the story and adds important information to move the story forward. If there's a lot of narration, you may want to spread it among more than one narrator.

Eliminate unnecessary text and decide the parts to turn into dialogue and narrative. Keep only what makes the story interesting. Consider critical events in the text or "action sequences" in which the dialogue is short and snappy. Assign the lines to different characters and the narrator.

Decide if you will use any props or costumes. Characters can wear labels with their name or a simple costume piece suggesting who they are. In general, though, props and costumes are not essential.

Have children practice reading the parts. They can work as partners or in small groups to give one another feedback

---

STEPS IN
Creating a Script for Readers' Theater

Select an appropriate text.
Select characters and a narrator.
Decide the parts to turn into dialogue and narrative.
Decide if you will use any props.
Have the children practice reading the parts.
Perform for an audience!

Remember to make it fun and keep it simple!

Figure 21-6. *Steps in Creating a Script for Readers' Theater*

on their interpretations. The process will promote discussion of meaning as well as fluency and confidence. Finally, have the students perform for an audience of their peers in the classroom, or present the piece to another class (see Figure 21-7).

On the DVD that accompanies this book is a readers' theater performance of *Frog and Toad Together* (Lobel) (see Figure 21-8). It calls for a narrator, Frog, Toad, and as many background voices as you want. The voices add significantly because they "announce" Toad's "acts." To perform the piece, children must understand that it is taking place in Toad's imagination (it's a dream) and that he wants to stop dreaming if he's going to lose his friend, Frog, because of it. Frog doesn't really know what Toad is dreaming, but he is a true friend.

Figure 21-7. *Readers' Theater*

We also share a scene from Mitchell's *Pocketful of Goobers* to illustrate how students can reread a section of a longer text to develop understanding and fluency (see Figure 21-9).

Figure 21-10 offers some examples of how scripts can be developed from different genres. Every genre has possibilities, and there are many variations in the way you can prepare scripts. You will also find scripts for the following texts on the DVD that accompanies this book. You can involve children in rereading these texts following an interactive read aloud. You might have them reread a text as readers' theater in guided reading or after a literature discussion.

GENRES FOR PERFORMED READING
There are a variety of genres that are suitable for performed reading (see Figure 21-11).

NARRATIVES
Stories are excellent texts for performed reading. Through authentic oral reading of narratives, children learn about the structure of stories (beginning, episodes, ending). When they read dialogue during shared or choral reading, they must interpret how the individuals' voices would sound, reflecting traits and feelings. Stories for young children often contain repeating refrains. Older students enjoy poetic

language that evokes imagery in narratives. Onomatopoetic words are especially delightful when read aloud.

POEMS
Including as they do rhythm, rhyme, repetition, and interesting language, poems are ideal material for performed reading. Many poems are meant to be performed aloud. Young children can begin by reading very simple poetry—just a few lines. Thousands of children have relished chanting:

> I love chocolate.
> Yum, yum, yum.
> I love chocolate.
> In my tum.

This one is a little more abstract:

> The Bus
>
> There is a painted bus,
> With twenty painted seats,
> It carries painted people
> Along the painted streets.
>
> They pull the painted bell,
> The painted driver stops,
> And they all get out together
> At the little painted shops.

Here, readers need to imagine a painting with the objects depicted. This poem could be read by two alternating groups, each reading two lines.

As they grow as readers, children will enjoy exploring even more sophisticated and complex poems. For example, Lucille Clifton's *One of the Problems of Everett Anderson* tells the story of a young boy who has watched one of his friends being physically abused:

> . . . and Everett tries to understand
> that one of the things he can do right now
> is listen to Greg and hug and hold
> his friend, and now that Mama is told,
> something will happen for Greg that is new.

Older students will enjoy performing poems in a wide variety of genres:

- Fast-paced, action-packed ballads that tell a story.
- Humorous poems that enable performers to use their voices in interesting and amusing ways.
- Lyrical poetry that enables performers to use their voices to evoke imagery.
- Unrhymed poetry that enables performers to use their voices to express emotion.

A wonderful example of mature poetry for older students is

A Readers' Theater Script Derived From Frog and Toad Together BY ARNOLD LOBEL

Chapter 5 "The Dream"   **Time:** 3–5 minutes   **Suggested Grade Level:** 1-2
READERS (4): Narrator; Voices (all children); Frog; Toad

SCRIPT

NARRATOR: Toad was asleep and he was having a dream. He was dreaming he was on stage wearing a costume. Toad looked out into the dark and Frog was sitting in the theater. Then strange voices said:

VOICES: PRESENTING THE GREATEST TOAD IN THE WORLD!

NARRATOR: Toad took a bow. The Frog shouted:

FROG: Hooray for Toad!

NARRATOR: And the strange voices were heard again.

VOICES: TOAD WILL NOW PLAY THE PIANO VERY WELL.

NARRATOR: So the Toad played the piano and did not miss a note! Then he cried:

TOAD: Frog, can you play the piano like this?

FROG: No, I cannot.

NARRATOR: Toad thought Frog looked very small sitting in his chair. Then the voices were heard again.

VOICES: TOAD WILL NOW WALK ON A HIGH WIRE, AND HE WILL NOT FALL DOWN.

NARRATOR: Toad walked on the high wire and shouted to Frog:

TOAD: Frog, can you do tricks like this?

FROG: No.

NARRATOR: Peeped the Frog as he seemed to be getting smaller and smaller.

VOICES: TOAD WILL NOW DANCE AND HE WILL BE WONDERFUL!

NARRATOR: Said the voices.

TOAD: Can you be as wonderful as this Frog?

NARRATOR: Asked Toad as he danced around. There was no answer. Toad looked all around the theater. Frog was so small that he could not be seen or heard.

TOAD: Frog, where are you?

NARRATOR: Asked Toad. There was still no answer. Toad cried:

TOAD: Frog, what have I done?

VOICES: THE GREATEST TOAD WILL NOW...

NARRATOR: Toad screamed:

TOAD: Shut up! Frog, Frog, where have you gone? Come back Frog. I will be lonely without you!

FROG: I am right here,

NARRATOR: Said the Frog. Frog was standing near Toad's bed.

FROG: Wake up, Toad.

TOAD: Frog, is that really you?

FROG: Of course it is me.

TOAD: Are you your own right size?

NARRATOR: Asked the Toad.

FROG: Yes, I think so.

NARRATOR: Toad looked through the sunshine coming through the window. Then he said:

TOAD: Frog, I am so glad that you came over.

FROG: I always do.

NARRATOR: Said the Frog. Then Frog and Toad ate a big breakfast. And after that, they spent a fine, long day together.

Figure 21-8. A Readers' Theater Script Derived from Frog and Toad Together

---

A READERS' THEATRE SCRIPT DERIVED FROM
A Pocketful of Goobers BY BARBARA MITCHELL

READERS (3): Narrator; George Washington Carver; Students

Time: 2 minutes

Suggested Grade Level: 3-5

SCRIPT

NARRATOR: George met his thirteen students.

STUDENTS: Most students come here to get away from farming.

GEORGE: Come, we are going to take a walk.

NARRATOR: The students looked at him.

STUDENTS: What for? We came here to learn agriculture.

GEORGE: You cannot learn agriculture without a lab.

NARRATOR: George took them around the neighborhood knocking on doors. They came away with old jars, bottles, and other throw-aways. Tuskegee had a lab.

NARRATOR: Not long afterward, Professor Carver took his class for another walk.

STUDENTS: Where are we going this time?

GEORGE: To the dump.

NARRATOR: The school dump had sprouted a glorious pumpkin vine.

STUDENTS: It's 37 feet long, Prof!

GEORGE: You see, there is no finer fertilizer for the soil than the food scraps we throw away. Now you will be able to show the folks back home how to feed their gardens for free.

Figure 21-9. *A Readers' Theater Script Derived from* A Pocketful of Goobers

The Way a Door Closes, in which Hope Anita Smith explores family relationships in unrhymed poetry. Here is an example, from the poem "Prodigal Son":

> No one actually heard the door
> open
> but we all heard it close.
> And I breathe a sigh of relief
> because
> I know Daddy is home to stay.
> Trust me,
> I can tell a lot by the way a door closes. (p. 51)

Poems can be adapted to readers' theater by preparing a script with parts marked. For example, you can create a script of "The Crocodile's Toothache", by Shel Silverstein.

You can assign three parts: the Narrator, the Dentist, and the Crocodile. It can be performed by three students, or a group of students can read the Narrator, leaving the Dentist and Crocodile as "solos."

SONGS

Songs are easily learned because of the rhythm, rhyme, and melody. Once children have learned an engaging song like "Happy Birthday to You" or "Itsy Bitsy Spider," they will be fascinated to see it in print and find that they can follow it easily. Older students can learn how to vary their vocal tone to interpret the song in different ways, making a new work of art. For example, a song like "America the Beautiful" or "Lift Every Voice" could be read by a series of groups alternating stanzas or lines. Ballads (songs that tell stories) can easily be turned into readers' theater pieces. Humorous songs, such as "The Other Day I Saw a Bear" (an "echo" song), are fun to perform. Songs can also be performed through a combination of singing and choral reading.

SCRIPTS

You can purchase books of plays: some stories include a script version at the end of the book. You can easily create a readers' theater script from just about any fiction or nonfiction text, as long as it's one that students understand and find interesting. For example, if they know the story of Chicken Little and already have opinions about the characters, they can more easily use their voices to express those meanings. Readers' theater is an excellent context for developing reading fluency, but it provides many other benefits as well. Reading a role helps children reconsider their understandings and deepen them.

BIOGRAPHY AND INFORMATIONAL TEXTS

Through shared and interactive writing, children often produce lists, sets of directions, descriptions, story summaries, and other texts. They will enjoy reading these aloud from charts, and doing so is a way for them to experience informational texts that are more complex than they can read independently. Informational texts can be used as the basis for readers' theater or can be transformed into more poetic texts. Books like *A Drop of Water* (Wick) and *If You Find a Rock* (Christian) have poetic language that can be enjoyably performed as a choral reading. The following sentences are from *In America's Shadow* (Komatsu and

Examples of Scripts for Readers' Theater

GENRE	SUGGESTIONS FOR SCRIPTS	EXAMPLES OF TEXTS
Traditional Literature	▫ Use dialogue to create roles for human and animal characters. ▫ Select dialogue used throughout the tale. ▫ As an option, add some repetition of dialogue for interest. ▫ Have one or several narrators read nondialogue parts of the story.	▫ *The Three Billy Goats* ▫ *The Great Big Enormous Turnip* ▫ *The Three Little Pigs* ▫ *The Gingerbread Man* ▫ *The Little Red Hen* ▫ *John Henry* ▫ *Paul Bunyan*
Fantasy	▫ Talking animals are the characters. ▫ Select dialogue throughout the book or within one scene or chapter. ▫ Have one or several narrators read nondialogue parts of the story.	▫ *The Lazy Pig* (Randell) ▫ *Fox and His Friends* (Marshall) ▫ *Peaches the Pig* (Riley) ▫ *Baby Bear's Present* (Randell) ▫ *Mrs. Frisby and the Rats of NIMH* (O'Brien)
Memoir	▫ Create a narrator's part that focuses on the memories. ▫ Switch the "scene" to characters who read roles within the memoir. ▫ Turn some of the reflections of the writer into dialogue that characters from the memoir read.	▫ *Tales of a Gambling Grandma* (Khalsa) ▫ *Don't Tell the Girls: A Family Memoir* (Giff) ▫ *So Far from the Sea* (Bunting) ▫ *Sister Anne's Hands* (Lorbiecki)
Realistic Fiction	▫ Construct a brief narrator's part for transitions. ▫ Select dialogue throughout the text or concentrate on one very important scene. ▫ Select books with characters that use interesting and memorable language or are humorous.	▫ *Nate the Great* (Sharmat) ▫ *A Year Down Yonder* (Peck) ▫ *The Great Gilly Hopkins* (Paterson) ▫ *Meet M&M* (Ross) ▫ *Pinky and Rex and the Spelling Bee* (Howe) ▫ *Missing May* (Rylant) ▫ *Because of Winn-Dixie* (DiCamillo)
Historical Fiction	▫ Have one narrator who only provides interesting information about the setting as background for the action. ▫ Have another narrator who provides transition material to understand the events. ▫ Create several character roles. ▫ Portray one exciting scene or several important ones.	▫ *Lizzie Bright and the Buckminster Boy* (Schmidt) ▫ *The Night Crossing* (Ackerman) ▫ *Under the Quilt of Night* (Hopkinson) ▫ *The Star Fisher* (Yep)

Figure 21-10. *Examples of Scripts for Readers' Theater*

Examples of Scripts for Readers' Theater (CONTINUED)

GENRE	SUGGESTIONS FOR SCRIPTS	EXAMPLES OF TEXTS
Biography	▫ Have one narrator or a series of narrators tell about important periods or events in the subject's life. ▫ Have the subject as a character and/or have other people talk about the subject. ▫ As an alternative, construct questions that an interviewer reads and have the subject and other people in the story answer using language from the text.	▫ *A Pocketful of Goobers: A Story About George Washington Carver* (Mitchell) ▫ *Coming Home: From the Life of Langston Hughes* (Cooper) ▫ *Rap a Tap Tap: Here's Bojangles—Think of That!* (Dillon & Dillon) ▫ *Sacagawea* (Erdrich) ▫ *If a Bus Could Talk: The Story of Rosa Parks* (Ringgold)
Informational Texts	▫ Create a script like an "infomercial" in which several narrators provide important facts and ideas from the text. ▫ Create an interview with an "expert" who uses language from the text to answer questions.	▫ *All About Frogs* (Arnosky) ▫ *Bat Loves the Night* (Davies) ▫ *Tell Me, Tree: All About Trees for Kids* (Gibbons) ▫ *Wolf Watch* (Winters) ▫ *Ice Cream: Great Moments in Ice Cream History* (Older)

Figure 21-10. *Examples of Scripts for Readers' Theater* (cont.)

Komatsu), a true story of Japanese Americans' internment during the Second World War:

> I will tell this child that you cannot imprison a spirit that refuses to be imprisoned.
>
> This is the promise I make to keep the past alive. To honor those who lived through it and to honor those who died because of it. This is something I can do for them.
>
> I look into my grandfather's eyes and deep down in my heart I understand.
>
> America is still a good place. It is still a good place because in our own way we have helped to make it so.
>
> Grandfather takes my hand in his and together we walk beyond the barbed wire. (pp. 89–90)

The Harmonica (Johnston), based on the true story of a Holocaust survivor, has the quality of a memoir and language that will work effectively for choral reading or readers' theater. *American Boy: The Adventures of Mark Twain* (Brown) uses some of Mark Twain's own words and tells a series of adventures that can easily be adapted for choral reading or readers' theater.

Once you learn to be on the lookout for material suitable for choral reading and readers' theater texts, you will find that they are very easy to construct. Older students will enjoy creating, rehearsing, and performing their own.

CHANGE OVER TIME IN SHARED PERFORMANCE READIN

Looking at the variety of texts and activities described in th chapter, it becomes obvious that although the central prem ise is the same, this activity for upper elementary and midd school students is very different from the experience in th primary grades. In *The Continuum of Literacy Learning PreK–8: A Guide to Teaching* (Pinnell and Fountas 2008 2011), you will find a detailed description of the texts an important behaviors to notice and support for each grad level, PreK–8. You can use this continuum to guide text sele tion and teaching.

We have listed formats to use for shared and perform ance reading and designated an approximate grade lev (see Figure 21-12). In general, work in shared/perform ance reading moves:

▫ From simple to complex texts.

▫ From teaching a wide range of early literacy behavio to interpretations of a text.

▫ From activities that are planned, directed, and led by th teacher to a more independent work by the students.

▫ From playful texts with rhyme and rhythm to matu prose and poetry that reveal complex issues.

Genres for Performed Reading

GENRE	DESCRIPTION
Narratives	The traditional narrative structure involves a beginning, characters and setting, a problem, a series of events, and a conclusion. Stories for shared and performed reading are usually simple for young children and grow more complex for older students, although they remain relatively short. Often, they contain repeating refrains (as found in traditional literature) and/or memorable or poetic language. They are especially constructed to read over and over. Readers are challenged to interpret them with their voices.
Poems	Poems for young children are simple—just two to four lines—and they usually rhyme and have repetitive refrains and alliteration. Poems for older children are more complex, with memorable language and literary forms such as metaphor and simile. Poems may focus on nature, everyday life, and emotions. Poems are often especially suitable for choral reading or shared performance.
Songs	Songs are simply poems set to music; they are a form of shared reading many of us often do. Young children learn simple songs and then are delighted to find them in printed form. Even if you read rather than sing them, songs have an inherent rhythm that helps move the reading along. Older children will enjoy creating and reading innovations on all kinds of songs and performing them in choral reading.
Scripts	Scripts are meant to be performed. Plays are the traditional form; there are many simple plays for younger readers that children enjoy reading. There are also more complex scripts that older children can perform. Readers' theater scripts are created from longer texts and may condense the whole text or zero in on a significant part.
Informational Texts	A wide range of informational texts are appropriate for shared reading. Young children enjoy rereading the texts that they have created through shared or interactive writing—lists, records of their experiences, summaries of stories or scientific experiments. Older students might read a scene from a biography. They might also perform persuasive arguments that incorporate scientific information.

Figure 21-11. *Genres for Performed Reading*

In general, charts and enlarged books are used more frequently with young children, because the teacher can gather them closely around her and help them follow the print. Texts enlarged using an ELMO document camera, an overhead projector, or on PowerPoint slides are appropriate for children who have had quite a bit more experience with print. Individual copies are used more frequently for readers' theater and plays.

LARGE-PRINT BOOKS

For young children, sharing the reading of a "big book" or the slightly smaller but still large-print "lap book" is an active, pleasurable experience. Teachers successfully use shared reading from the very first day of kindergarten. At first, children are probably responding to the appeal of the text in terms of language and story. But as they become more experienced in shared reading, supported by strong teaching, children begin to notice print and learn how it "works." Because they are working with a book that is the same kind of text they will be reading—only bigger—they get a powerful demonstration of what readers do.

Enlarged books for shared reading should be "lap size," about 12" by 18" or larger. They should include:

- Print in a clear, simple font.
- Print large enough for children to see from about fifteen feet away.
- Clear space between words and between lines of print.
- Uncluttered rather than "busy" pages so that pictures and print are accessible "on the run" while children are reading.
- Large, clear pictures that are closely related to the print.

Text Formats for Shared and Choral Reading

TEXT FORMAT	DESCRIPTION	RECOMMENDED APPROXIMATE GRADE LEVELS
Large-Print Books	Led by the teacher, the children read together from an enlarged book. The teacher points to words or slides the pointer (as appropriate to the group's level of development) and demonstrates turning the pages. Eventually, no pointer is needed, or the pointer may simply be placed at the beginning of the line to guide the readers.	K–2
Large-Print Poems, Songs, or Other Texts (on Posters or Charts)	Led by the teacher, the children read together from an enlarged version of a poem. The teacher points to words individually, slides the pointer, or places the pointer at the beginning of each line (as appropriate to the group's level of development). They may read in various ways (subgroups or individuals reading alternating lines, for example).	K–2
Large-Print Shared or Interactive Writing Texts	Led by the teacher, children revisit enlarged texts they have produced through interactive or shared (group) writing. Children will have contributed to the composition of the text. During its construction, they will have reread part or all of the text many times.	K–2
Projected Texts— Overhead Projector or ELMO Document Camera, PowerPoint Slide	Machines can instantly enlarge any text—poem, narrative, or script. After children can track print easily with their eyes and can process several lines of print, you can put print on transparency film for group reading or lay print on an ELMO document camera. (Retype small, dense print so that it is easier to follow.)	2–8
Individual Copies— Books, Poems, Songs, and Scripts	Students each have their own copies of the text. They read in unison, using their voices to interpret the text. The teacher or another student may lead the shared reading.	1–8

Figure 21-12. *Text Formats for Shared and Choral Reading*

- An engaging story, often with rhyme and/or a repetitive text.
- A text that is long enough for children to become highly engaged in the story but not so long that it will be very hard to remember or tedious to finish.

To point to the print, use slim pointers of various lengths. You will want to avoid overly fancy pointers that interfere with a clear view of the print. The most important feature of shared reading is each child's ability to attend to print. Every single child must be able to see clearly (see the photo in Figure 21-13).

An enlarged informational text will help draw children's attention to features of factual texts. The text in Figure 21-14 is certainly not for kindergartners, but first graders will be ready to notice and talk about a bulleted list,

designation of measures, labels for pictures, signal word like *next* that indicate a sequence, and the format for series of directions. All of these are important demands informational texts that they may not be encountering i the texts they read independently. Shared reading can hel them begin to comprehend these features.

ENLARGED-PRINT CHARTS

Many poems are published as enlarged charts or poster and these can be used for shared or choral reading. You ca also print your own versions. Charts have the advantage helping you focus children's attention on print because it easy to use a pointer. Charts can be laminated and use throughout the year. They can also be placed in centers f children to read independently using the pointer. Childre often revisit a well-known poem for help in spelling a wor

These charts are also useful to revisit in reading, writing, and word study minilessons.

PROJECTED TEXTS

Enlarging text with an overhead projector, an ELMO document camera, or on a PowerPoint slide works well with texts that have "friendly fonts," but is less effective for texts with small print and many lines of text. You may need to retype dense text to put space between lines. The print children read should always be in a "friendly" and easy-to-read font and layout.

INDIVIDUAL COPIES OF SHARED TEXTS

Many teachers begin with poems that are enlarged on charts and that children read together. (After children become very familiar with a poem, they will enjoy gluing an individual version in their personal poetry books.) They can illustrate the pages. They can then read them together in a shared way. Older students will also enjoy having individual copies when they practice their choral reading and readers' theater pieces.

Remember that shared/performance reading should not be "hard" for students. It will be supported in reading challenging texts, often more complex than they can read independently, but no text should require a struggle or long

Figure 21-13. *Shared Reading*

hours of study. This learning context must be one of the most enjoyable.

SUGGESTIONS FOR PROFESSIONAL DEVELOPMENT
CREATING SCRIPTS FOR READERS' THEATER

1 Readers' theater is a context that can be used at just about any grade level. Even kindergarten children can play the animals in *The Little Red Hen*. Select some

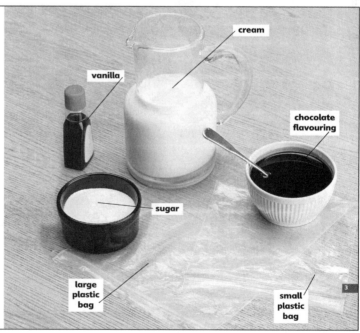

You can turn cream into ice cream!
You will need:
- 125 mL of cream
- 15 mL of sugar
- 5 mL of vanilla or 15 mL of chocolate flavouring
- a little plastic bag with a zipper top
- a big plastic bag with a zipper top

Figure 21-14. *An Example of an Informational Text from* Making Ice Cream

books and work in grade-level groups to prepare several readers' theater scripts that can be used in your classroom. Plan a script for whole picture books or a few scenes from a novel.

2 Then, over a period of about two weeks, have everyone on the grade level make a teaching plan and implement the scripts.

3 Meet to debrief the experiences, comparing different teachers' experiences with the same scripts. They can share adaptations they made and the different benefits to students.

4 Use *The Continuum of Literacy Learning, PreK–8: Guide to Teaching* (Pinnell and Fountas 2008, 2011 to reflect on your teaching and identify principles yo want to include in your teaching using shared and pe formed reading. Or, use your district curriculum guid to discover goals that can be addressed through share performance reading.

5 Finally, for each grade level, collect a list of books th can be easily adapted to readers' theater. Select and us some before the next meeting, this time identifying pa ticular teaching points you want to make.

CHAPTER TWENTY-TWO

MAXIMIZING INDEPENDENT READING: HELPING STUDENTS THINK WITHIN, BEYOND, AND ABOUT TEXTS IN A READING WORKSHOP

Reading catatonically wasn't something that I chose to do, it just happened.

—FRANCIS SPUFFORD

With passion and humor in the above quote from *The Child that Books Built: A Life in Reading,* Spufford (2002) creates a vision of a truly literate life, one within which reading holds a firm and central place. As teachers, we know that while it usually seems so to the reader, in fact, it doesn't just happen. A literate life is carefully constructed from early experiences in settings that have characteristics like these:

People whom children respect and who are close to them provide powerful models of reading behavior and express an interest in and a love of reading.

Reading is seen as a productive and valued activity in the places children live and work. People expect to spend time reading.

People in children's lives talk with one another about their reading. They have some favorite authors and just can't wait to get new books by them!

Wide varieties of books and other texts are readily available. People recommend books to others.

People own books. Books are treasured and some are read over and over.

If we could, we would give every student we teach the gift of a literate life. Even though it may seem unattainable within the constraints of modern society, we can reach for it by creating classrooms in which reading is a constant daily presence. Independent reading is a context within which children can see themselves as readers and build habits that can last a lifetime.

Hargreaves (2005) challenges educators to ask how we can improve the *literacy* of all our children rather than how we can improve their *literacy scores*. He says that if we improve children's literacy, scores will improve. Learning first, he says, then achievement, then testing—not in the reverse order. Good teaching that improves literacy will take care of the scores, because those who read a lot of many kinds of texts read fluently, and reading with understanding results in higher scores (Pinnell et al. 1995). We can make all of that happen in independent reading every day. While choice is an essential characteristic of independent reading, a strong instructional frame is also important. Texts that are right for readers provide intrinsic rewards.

THE GOALS OF INDEPENDENT READING

An important part of teaching literacy is providing daily opportunities for students to read, on their own, books they have selected themselves. Through independent reading, students:

- Learn to exercise choice as readers, selecting from a wide variety of texts.
- Develop favorite books, types of books, genres, topics, writing styles, and authors.
- Develop the habit of spending a significant amount of time reading.
- Build a "reading agenda" that includes books, authors, and types of books they want to read in the future.
- Gain "mileage" as readers by processing a large number of texts on a regular basis.
- Engage in fluent reading daily (including well-paced silent reading in which they are processing syntactic structures).
- Learn about themselves as readers.
- Become part of a community of readers.

KINDERGARTEN AND GRADE 1

Even beginning kindergartners can spend some time revisiting picture books that teachers have previously read to them. They may remember language and "reenact" the texts. This activity is like independent reading and is well worth doing. Children:

□ Behave like readers.

□ Remember and think about the ideas in the texts.

□ Internalize the language.

□ Expand their vocabulary by using words from the texts.

Very soon, however, they begin reading simple texts by attending to the print.

For emergent and early readers, independent work includes a variety of reading, writing, and word-study activities that they perform while the teacher is working with small guided reading groups. Often, there is a sharing period at the end so that students can talk about what they have been doing. Independent reading activities may include:

1 *Rereading poems students have experienced in shared reading.* They read from charts or have individual copies. Many teachers have children glue the familiar poems into a personal poetry anthology that they can illustrate.

2 *Rereading books previously experienced in shared reading.* Students may have small copies of large-print books they have read with the teacher.

3 *Reading from individual book boxes.* These boxes or baskets contain books that students have previously read in guided reading groups with the teacher's support or books at easier levels that they have not read before. New books are regularly added and old ones removed. Students keep the book boxes at their desks or on a designated shelf.

4 *Reading from group book boxes.* The teacher creates browsing boxes from which groups of children select their books for independent reading. Each group is assigned a particular box because it contains books they have previously read in guided reading. The teacher may also include some easy books that students will be able to take on independently. A typical independent work assignment would be: "Go to your browsing box and choose three books to read. Read all three books and then go to your next activity."

5 *Reading with partners.* Using individual or group book boxes, children read with a buddy. A typical independent work assignment would be: "Choose three books and then meet with your buddy. Take turns reading your

books until you have read three books and your partner has read three books." Buddies should be reading at about the same level so that they will be interested in and learn from each other's reading.

6 *Reading with a partner—single texts.* Another way for children to do partner reading is to have them take turns reading the same text and then talking about it. You can also teach children to take turns reading every other page, which promotes collaborative behavior.

7 *Reading selections from the classroom library.* Children select books they can read from baskets in the classroom library organized by topic, author, genre, etc.

Independent reading activities usually last between ten and twenty minutes, depending on the length of the text and the students' ability to sustain their reading. During the year children should gradually increase the time they are able to sustain reading.

Late Grade 1 Through Early Grade 2

Children are now beginning to read much longer texts, some that cannot be finished in a single guided reading lesson or in one independent work period. Expectations and scheduling are gradually adjusted so that more time is spent on reading and writing. Some students still use browsing boxes and some of the other earlier activities, but they should also be choosing many books directly from the classroom library, reading longer texts, and doing some connected writing in response.

Some students will still be reading lower-level texts and having trouble sustaining their reading for the expected amount of time. You can support these students by providing

□ Daily guided reading instruction.

□ Assignments at the listening center to give them exposure to higher-level texts.

□ Individual book boxes and browsing boxes with an assortment of books that they can read—both familiar and new.

□ Support from older children or paraprofessionals.

Grade 2 Through Grade 8

In grade 2 we encourage teachers to make a transition to a sixty-minute reading workshop, as discussed in Fountas and Pinnell (2001), using the following structure (see Figure 22-1):

Independent Reading in a Reading Workshop

ELEMENT	ADVANTAGES
Book talks and minilesson The teacher demonstrates and helps students become aware of something important they need to think about as readers.	• Students receive explicit demonstrations that help them learn more about processing a variety of texts. • Students apply what they have learned. • Students think in new ways about their reading.
Reading, conferring, and writing about reading Students read silently and independently. The teacher has individual reading conferences and also works with small groups. The entire period is spent reading with the exception that they write about their reading (texts read or listened to) at least one time per week in a reader's notebook.	• Students choose books and enjoy reading for a sustained period. • In brief conferences, teachers provide individual instruction on any aspect of reading or writing about reading. • Teachers review a student's accomplishments and interests. • Teachers interact with students in ways that help them extend their understanding of the text they are reading. • Students apply what they learned in the minilesson. • Students share their thinking on an individual basis. • Students reflect on their reading through writing. • Students get written feedback from the teacher in their reader's notebook.
Sharing Students share their thinking with one another in the whole group (or in partners or small groups).	• Students build a community of readers. • Students recommend books to others. • Teachers reinforce and extend the minilesson principle. • Students can talk about their thinking in relation to specific aspects of the reading process (for example, predictions or connections they made, memorable language, what they liked or disliked, an interesting character, etc.).
Evaluation The group talks together about what went well in the workshop and formulates goals for improvement as needed.	• Students take responsibility for their own learning.

Figure 22-1. *Independent Reading in a Reading Workshop*

• *Book talks and minilesson.* At first the teacher gives short book talks to introduce books to students and motivate their reading. Then the teacher begins by providing a brief, explicit lesson on any aspect of the reading process.

• *Reading, conferring, and writing about reading.* Students read books of their own choosing, silently and independently, and spend some time writing about the reading. In grade 2, the teacher may assign a few other quiet work options at a listening center or word-study center. The teacher may confer with individuals during this time, teach small guided reading groups, or meet with book clubs.

• *Sharing and evaluation.* Students share something about their reading and evaluate their work in a brief session at the end of the period.

An important tool that students can use to collect their thinking about books is a reader's notebook (Fountas and Pinnell 2001). We suggest they write thoughtfully at least once a week about the books they are reading independently (independent reading choices, literature study books, guided reading books) or are hearing in interactive read-aloud (see Chapters 27 and 28 for forms this writing may take). This is a way for students to:

• Reflect on particular texts.

- Keep a record of reading and reflect on progress over time.
- List their preferences and specific books they want to read.
- Engage in a written dialogue with the teacher.
- Keep a record of their thinking.

CONSIDERATIONS FOR DEPARTMENTALIZED LITERACY PROGRAMS

Middle schools are usually departmentalized, with teachers working with different groups of students throughout the day. This kind of schedule benefits the teaching of math, science, history, and the social sciences, but it can make it difficult for English and language arts teachers to teach comprehension and to get to know their students well as readers and writers in a short period once a day.

If your school uses a departmentalized structure, you might join forces with colleagues to create fewer, longer blocks of time instead of more, shorter blocks. You may consider trying to teach a reading workshop for several consecutive days and then a writing workshop for several consecutive days.

If you are locked into a fifty- or sixty-minute period and must teach all aspects of language arts and literature within it, you'll need to be flexible. You can still use the *minilesson, reading and conferring, sharing* structure, just not every day. Some options are listed in Figure 22-2. The bottom line is for students to read continuously and think, talk, and write about their reading. Expectations must be high.

The typical student load in departmentalized programs (some teachers have over a hundred students a day) makes it difficult to respond to weekly student writing in a reader's notebook; paradoxically, it is even more important for students at this age to have these written conversations with their teachers. Sometimes students can write letters about their reading to each other, but nothing will substitute for the lift you give students with your own feedback and dialogue. If you can manage written exchanges in a reader's notebook, you will get to know your students better. At the very least, try to read and write brief comments on a regular basis. Here are some options:

- Have students write letters (or other genres) about their reading each week. Respond to half of them one week,

the others the next week. You can respond to both student letters at the same time.

- Respond to half or a third of the students each week with only a brief comment on all the writers since you last commented.
- Have students send you emails; they're easier to respond to. (But make sure they save and print them and your responses so that they can reflect on them over time.)
- Select one class to respond to each week and vary the classes systematically. Respond to all the writing for each student with brief comments.
- Alternate student–teacher responses with peer dialogue. Teach students effective ways to write good responses to each other in your minilessons.

Try to find a schedule and method that works for you. Substitute written responses to your students with time that was spent on the tasks that were less beneficial. Don't worry if you do not have an ideal schedule. Any time you work with a large number of students, some compromises must be made, and chances are your students' writing will be so interesting you will make the time to respond! Also, with experience, you will find you gain ease and speed in responding.

TEXTS TO SUPPORT INDEPENDENT READING

A good classroom library is essential for supporting independent reading. This is not to disparage the role of the school library or community public library. The library is the heart of the school, and the librarian is an important partner in all aspects of reading instruction. Regular visits to the school and public library are important, but a classroom library is also necessary:

- In classrooms, as in homes, students need to be surrounded by a variety of accessible books at all times— not just during library period.
- When students finish a book, they must be able to start another book immediately. Usually, through book talks and browsing, they have a list of books they plan to read. They need to be able to find them in the classroom immediately.
- In most schools, students can't go to the library whenever they need to. In any case, much time is wasted going back and forth.

Options for Providing Reading and Writing Workshops in Limited Time Periods

OPTION	ADVANTAGE
Conduct a reading workshop and a writing workshop each day if the schedule allows. Consider linking the reading and writing work through specific units of study some of the time and promoting self-selected reading and writing topics in between.	Students receive consistent daily teaching in reading and writing, allowing for momentum and depth. Several units of study can be related but there will also be ample time for independent reading and writing.
Alternate the reading and writing workshop. Have the reading workshop for one or two weeks to include interactive read-aloud and independent reading, with minilessons sometimes focused on a particular genre, author, topic, literary element, or the reading process. Follow up with one to two weeks of the writing workshop to focus on units of study such as writer's craft, convention, writing process, writing genre, author study, or topic focus. Specific reasons or genres for writing about reading are provided (e.g., letters, two-column entry, literary essay). During those weeks students do not have reading or writing workshops, but students continue to read and work on writing at home.	Students have opportunities to engage in intensive reading on a consistent basis. You can link some areas of reading with writing, for example, listen to and read a variety of biographies or memoirs in reading workshop and write a biographical sketch or memoir in writing workshop. You can transition from reading to writing workshops at an appropriate time without feeling fixed on a particular number of days for each. Students also learn how to respond to texts in a variety of genres in the reading workshop.
Provide a reading workshop for one quarter and then a writing workshop for one quarter. In addition to self-selected reading and writing, include several units of study. For example, focus on reading memoirs, personal narratives, and informational texts in one quarter and follow with writing in these genres the next quarter. Students continue to read and work on writing at home.	Students have much opportunity to develop their tastes as readers and interests as writers but also have focused opportunities to learn about specific types of reading and writing. A full quarter allows for momentum and in-depth work. For example, focus on author study, historical fiction, biography, informational reports in reading and link writing units the next quarter. Students will learn how to write about reading in a variety of genres in the reading workshop.
Conduct a language/word study workshop to include word study, interactive read-aloud, and a poetry workshop on Monday. Follow with a reading workshop and a writing workshop on each of the other four days of the week.	Students have the opportunity to develop a set of shared literacy experiences that can be built on in the reading and writing workshop. The texts used for interactive read-aloud serve as mentor texts for the minilessons. There is dedicated time to develop vocabulary and spelling skills. Experiences can include reading, writing, and sharing of a variety of poetic texts. Students can continue spelling/vocabulary work across the week in class or as homework.

Figure 22-2. *Options for Providing Reading and Writing Workshops in Limited Time Periods*

Students need both school and classroom libraries if they are to have the necessary richness and variety of texts.

You may be able to supplement your classroom library with collections of books on loan from the school or public library, exchanging them from time to time. If you have a single copy of a book that is becoming very popular, the school librarian may be able to supply a few more copies so that all students who want to read it can do so.

You will want to be sure that the classroom library includes a full range of genres (see Chapter 11). Although students will not choose books by level, you want to be sure the available texts meet the needs of the whole range of readers in your class. The classroom must include many books on topics that are of interest to the age level you teach—children like to read about others of their own age or a little older. For students who are reading below grade level, you'll want to try to find easier texts on age-appropriate topics. We provide a detailed description of classroom libraries in *Leveled Books for Readers, K–8* (Fountas and Pinnell 2005), along with suggestions for getting started and acquiring more books over time.

Also, most of the time when we refer to independent reading, we mean reading books. There is a place for reading magazines, journals, Internet articles, comic books, and other popular written materials, and you may want to include magazines such as *Kids Discover, Muse,* or *Ranger Rick* in your classroom. Most of the time, however, you want to guide students to read books in the reading workshop. Completing texts that require a longer attention span must be a goal of independent reading. For many children, this will happen only in school.

In connection with your classroom library, you may want to place book reviews or articles about favorite authors on a bulletin board or in a three-ring binder. Some websites that feature book reviews are *www.kidsreads.com* and *www.gigglepoetry.com*. Sites that features book reviews by kids, for kids are *www.spaghettibookclub.org* and *www.worldreading.org,* (Many author websites are listed on the DVD that accompanies this book. In general, it is a good idea to try the author's name, followed by ".com.", for example, *www.jerryspinelli.com*. You will either get a site or a link to one.). Students can also find excellent articles at sites like *www.stonesoup.com* or *www.zoobooks.com*.

It is important to organize the classroom library in ways that attract students to books and make it easy for them to select them. Think of a good bookstore in which you have spent a lot of money! It has the following characteristics (note that sections grouped by specific reading level is not one of them):

- New books are featured in some way—on a central table, on bookracks that you can't miss as you enter the store.
- Best sellers are identified.
- Books on common topics (travel, history, finance, self-help) are clearly labeled and easy to find.
- Book reviews are featured.
- "Staff favorites" or "must-reads" are identified.
- Many books are face-out so that the covers and authors are visible.

- Posters or other information featuring famous author is visible.
- At the checkout, there are books on shelves that have been reserved or special-ordered for individual readers.

Your overall goal is to make books in the classroom library accessible and inviting to your students (see Figure 22-3). The system should be well organized in a way that students understand; then, in minilessons, you can demonstrate how they are to select and return books.

WHAT MATTERS IN INDEPENDENT READING

The independent reading described in this book is different from the "free reading" or "sustained silent reading" typically done in schools. At all levels, it is surrounded by a strong instructional frame (see the description of reading workshop in Figure 22-4). Children read books of their own choosing selected from a well-stocked classroom library. Usually, they read seated at their own desks, although sometimes teachers provide some comfortable chairs that students take turns using.

From the beginning of the school year, you will want to provide procedural minilessons that help students learn the routines and expectations of a reading workshop. (*Guiding Readers and Writers,* Fountas and Pinnell 2001, include scripts for minilessons for the first couple of months of school to help you get started with a reading workshop.) In the earliest grades, rereading familiar texts is supported by guided reading lessons. Students have received instruction in reading the text, which they can apply in subsequent readings. The teacher has also created some structures such as browsing boxes, to provide a range of good choices in addition to the baskets in the classroom library.

For kindergarten and grade one, children should read and talk in soft voices. For grades two and up, you will want to establish a *completely silent* classroom for independent reading before you begin small-group work. The only voices that should be heard are the soft voices of the teacher conferring with one student at a time. The "voice chart" in Figure 22-5 is one way to communicate your expectations. After workshop routines have been established, you can begin to work with small groups in guided reading and literature discussion, but, again, the classroom should remain quiet. Reading workshop is a time for students to

Figure 22-3. *Examples of Classroom Libraries*

ngage as a community in thinking, talking, and writing bout books. With good organization and explicit expectations, the time spent is highly productive. Students learn what it feels like to read for an extended period of time.

Reading with fluency and understanding is not possible f students cannot spend extended time processing text. The outines of the reading workshop set the scene for possibilities. *In developing competent readers:*

- *Quantity matters.* How *much* students read makes a difference. They need to process thousands of words within continuous texts each year to accumulate the kind of experiences with texts they need. We can require home reading and do everything possible to make it happen.

- *Time matters.* No one becomes a reader without spending a great deal of time doing it. Real readers crave time to read, and they make time for it. To reach that mind-

set, students need to have many experiences reading pleasurably for extended periods of time.

- *Variety matters.* People become readers by sampling a wide variety of genres, topics, and writing styles. Variety develops flexibility in processing many different types of texts. Variety is also necessary to stretch readers' powers of comprehension so that they apply systems of strategic actions in different ways and learn to adjust their reading. Variety also helps readers develop informed preferences that they will carry with them all their lives.

- *Choice matters.* Real readers choose the books they read. It is important that early in their lives as readers, children learn the power of choice. Only through choice can they develop tastes and preferences, learn that they like some writers better than others, and experience finding a *great book* that they can recommend to their friends. Many people never have that experience.

□ *Fluency matters.* Readers need to process a large number of texts at their independent reading level (or even easier) so that they develop fluency. It makes sense that doing something competently over and over creates ease and fluency.

□ *Conversation matters.* Reading is much more interesting when surrounded by talk. In reading workshop, there are many opportunities for conversation about books—with the teacher during read-aloud and in reading conferences, with other students during sharing, guided reading, and literature discussion.

HELPING READERS CHOOSE BOOKS

The teacher's key role in independent reading is to ensure that students consistently select books they can read with understanding and fluency and to have conversations with them about those books. The more students read, the better readers they can become, but there is also the additional factor of comprehension.

Readers must be interested and active. They need to feel anticipation as they begin reading a text, an anticipation that heightens as they read more. They need to emerge from the reading with a satisfying feeling of having enjoyed a text as well as some expectations regarding the genre, the topic, the writing style, or the author. As a reader, you may have said:

□ "I'm going to read the next book in the series!"

□ "I love this writer. Has he [she] written anything else?!"

□ "I have read many books of this type, but I'm going to read more!"

□ "Why haven't I read books like these before? I'm going to look for more!"

□ "The ideas in this book are so interesting! I'm going to read more on the same topic!"

The exclamation points are intentional. Independent reading should get students excited about reading, and that cannot happen without choice. Choice is the key ingredient.

Unless readers are processing texts with understanding and fluency, they will not be building a network of effective strategic systems. A major challenge for teachers is fostering good book choice. You may be tempted to prescribe book choices, asking student to progress through a sequence provided by a publisher or choose by level, but this only results in a mechanical approach to reading as a "task." Without genuine choice, they will never experience the authentic role of a reader.

Guidelines for Reading Workshop

1. Read a book or write your thoughts about your reading.

2. Work silently so that you and your classmates can do your best thinking.

3. Use a soft voice when conferring with a teacher.

4. Select books that you think you'll enjoy and abandon books that aren't working for you after you've given them a chance.

5. List the book information when you begin and record the date when you finish.

6. Always do your best work.

Figure 22-4. *Guidelines for Reading Workshop*

Think About Your Voice

0	1	2	3	4	5
Independent Reading	Conferences	Group Work	Sharing	Readers' Theater	Outside
No talking at all	Whisper	Quiet voices	Clear, loud voices	Loud voices	Very loud voice

Figure 22-5. *Think About Your Voice*

The ability to choose books is not something you can expect your students to know. It is something you need to teach. What you are enthusiastic about and recommend is very powerful. Some suggestions for helping students choose books are listed in Figure 22-6.

The first step in helping readers choose books is to have a good collection at an appropriate range of reading levels that includes many books that will appeal to both genders and is so well organized that students can find books very quickly. Asking older students to sort the books and set up some of the book boxes will help them become familiar with the system. You can always sort books by genre, but think in terms of more specialized categories that, once your students understand them, will pique their interests. Some favorite categories are:

- Award-winning books (Newbury, Coretta Scott King, Caldecott).
- New books.
- Books that feature word play.
- Books we've shared (through interactive read-aloud).
- Interesting characters or a series (Ramona, Joey Pigza, Anastasia)
- Books of a particular period (colonial times, the Civil War, etc.)
- Book pairs (same title, similar characters, same theme or setting) for partners to choose, read, and discuss.
- Informational topics (dinosaurs, the ocean, storms, space, sports).
- Authors (Cynthia Rylant, Gary Paulsen, Katherine Paterson).
- Series books (M&M, Arthur, Harry Potter, Boxcar Children).
- Biographies on the same person.
- If You Liked _____, You'll Like _____.
- Class [Genre] picks.
- Books with sequels (put a rubber band around a set and number them).
- Poetry.
- Must reads!

Many teachers set up a special rack or shelf where students place their own recommendations with short reviews

Helping Readers Choose Books

- Have the collection well sorted and labeled by topic, genre, theme, author, illustrator.
- As you observe student interests, create more baskets for particular topics, authors, or types of books.
- Have a "book recommendations" rack.
- Have students help set up new-book baskets.
- Put books you have used in book talks on display so that they are easy to find.
- Create book baskets that connect books: "If you liked _____ , you'll love ____."
- Create "exclusive" baskets of selections for individual students if needed.
- Give book talks that motivate and legitimize student book choices (e.g., easy books, more difficult).
- Provide as many minilessons as needed to help students understand how to choose just-right books.
- Communicate to the entire class that choosing a just-right book, not a difficult book, is the expectation for reading workshop.
- Through conferences, help students learn to evaluate their own choices.
- Share book reviews from journals or websites.

Figure 22-6. *Helping Readers Choose Books*

designed to interest other students.

There are some important ideas to get across when helping students choose books. Through minilessons and individual conferences, you can teach students how to look at books. Making an informed book selection is part of a proficient reading process. On page 146 of *Guiding Readers and Writers* (Fountas and Pinnell 2001) you can find a sample minilesson for helping students choose books. Some important techniques to teach are:

1 Think about the topic of the book or the kind of story it seems to be. Does it sound interesting?

2 Look at the illustrations if there are any. Do you like them? Do they make you want to read the book?

3 What do you already know about this book? Have you read this book before? What makes you interested in reading it again? Is this book popular in your class? Why? Is this book a part of a series? Is this book a sequel to a book you have read? Has anyone else recommended this book to you? What did they say about it?

4 Look at the front cover. Does it look interesting? What are you going to expect based on the picture? Does it have an interesting title?

5 Look at the back cover. What have other people said about this book? Does it sound like you would like it for the same reasons?

6 Look inside the back (or front) cover. What does it say about the author?

7 Think about the author. Do you know any other books by this author? What have people told you about this author?

8 Try the beginning and read a little from the middle. Do you know most of the words? Can you understand what is going on? Is it very easy or are there just a few problems to solve? Does it seem really hard? Think about whether it will be:

   □ Easy—you know almost all the words and understand it very well.

   □ Just right—you read it smoothly but need to slow down to figure out just a few words or think about the meaning. (Choose "just right" books whenever you can!)

   □ Hard—you have trouble reading many of the words and you don't understand most of what you are reading.

Students need to know that thicker books with smaller print are not necessarily harder. Sometimes just the look of a book can intimidate them, and they will reject it without trying. If the topic or plot sounds interesting, they will need to sample the text. Students need to learn how to recognize the complexity of texts and to think about much more than the words. Some short texts can require very complex thinking, for example:

□ *Rose Blanche* (Innocenti).

□ *Through My Eyes—Ruby Bridges* (Bridges).

□ *Love That Dog* (Creech).

As they grow more sophisticated, students can reflect more on their own choices and deliberately expand their repertoires as readers.

USING BOOK TALKS TO HELP READERS MAKE CHOICES

WG Nothing is quite so helpful as the recommendation of another reader! As adults we recommend books to one another all the time. You can do this for your students by providing book talks at the beginning of reading workshop.

A book talk is a very short "commercial" that tells just enough about a book to interest readers. Most of the time, you will have read the book yourself and can communicate enthusiasm and make some very specific recommendations about what might interest students; however, you can also give a book talk on a new book that you have not read yet simply by discussing the author and the topic: "I've heard about this author, and it sounds like this might be a very good book for some of you to try!" As adults, we do this pretty often—the student who first reads the book can tell everyone a little more about it later.

Let's look at a book talk designed to interest students in reading the first book in a new fantasy series (see Figure 22-7). The teacher identifies the book as a fantasy and discusses the main character and the setting. She sets up the conflict in the story by talking about the main character's traits.

Let's look at a book talk on a book for mature readers, *Speak* (Halse Anderson) (see Figure 22-8). The teacher provides information that should appeal to middle school stu-

---

BOOK TALK FOR
The Dark Hills Divide (THE LAND OF ELYON BOOK 1)

One of our new books is the first of a fascinating fantasy series by Patrick Carman. The book is called *The Dark Hills Divide*. When I read that title, it made me think of something dangerous and sinister that kept people imprisoned or separated.

The main character is Alexa Daley. You can see on the cover that she is holding something that glows, and a squirrel is sitting on her shoulder. Alexa lives in a city that is completely surrounded by a high wall. Even when she travels to the three other cities in her land, she travels on roads that have high walls on either side.

This map shows Bridewell, the central city, and the roads to the three other cities, like spokes on a wheel. So you might be wondering right away, "What is on the other side of the wall?" All the people are afraid of evil that lurks in the forests and the dark hills outside the wall. But Alexa, whose father is one of the governors of the cities, is very curious. She's always trying to see over the wall and to find out what is on the other side. If you like this book, you'll be able to read more in the Land of Elyon series.

Figure 22-7. *Book Talk for* The Dark Hills Divide *(The Land of Elyon Book 1)*

Speak (HALSE ANDERSON 1999)

Melinda is a ninth grader, and it's her first day in high school. She used to have lots of friends, but it seems that now everyone–even her ex–best friend Rachel–hates her. Rachel is now in another crowd and calls herself Rachelle. Melinda meets a new girl, Heather, from Ohio, who sort of becomes her friend but is always trying to get in with the popular kids. Melinda made good grades last year, but this year she just hates school and her grades are terrible. She doesn't talk very much; she doesn't join things; other kids are mean to her; she doesn't get along with her parents.

It's kind of mysterious why she changed over the summer, but we know right away that it has something to do with a party she went to. She called the police from this party and all the other kids got mad, but there is definitely more to it than that. As you read this book, you will find out what really happened and why Melinda is having such a hard time talking to people.

Figure 22-8. *Book Talk for* Speak

dents who are concerned about making and losing friends, being popular, getting good grades, and getting along with parents. She also sets the scene for the mystery of the story.

Finally, let's look at two short book talks on two very different texts (see Figure 22-9). The first talk, *Ten True Animal Rescues* (Betancourt) focuses on an informational book that the teacher says will be "easy or just right" for most of the kids in the class. The second is on a realistic fiction survival story, *Hatchet* (Paulsen), which she categorizes as "challenging or just right." The teacher is validating two texts at different levels of difficulty (without identifying the levels) and appealing to children who like different genres and topics.

In summary, book talks:

- Get the readers interested in the topic, author or genre.
- Speak directly to the readers.
- Are very short usually, taking less than a minute.
- Give children important information about the genre, title, topic, and author.
- Provide a thumbnail sketch of the plot so that readers can anticipate the text.

- Sometimes provide some information about how challenging the book will be.

But they do more than simply motivate students to read the books, although that is important. Book talks are also a model for how a reader thinks about a book *before reading it*, which is related to the stance the reader takes. You can teach your students to give book talks to the class. The teacher's comments are models of real readers' questions and predictions when beginning to read a text. You can look at a few different book talks on the DVD that accompanies this book.

REFLECTING ON INDEPENDENT READING THROUGH WRITING

Writing about their independent reading is a powerful way for children to expand their powers of comprehension. Kindergartners and first graders can respond to texts they have experienced in interactive read-aloud and small-group instruction by drawing and by participating in shared and interactive writing. These experiences prepare them to write about texts independently. Students at every grade level can use writing or drawing as a tool for thinking, before, during and after reading. Chapters 27 and 28 discuss a range of authentic opportunities for students to draw and write about reading.

Ten True Animal Rescues AND *Hatchet*

I have a couple of books I want to share with you.

The first one is *Ten True Animal Rescues,* by Jean Betancourt. This is a collection of short stories about how animals have helped people in different situations. So if you are an animal lover or a short story lover, this would be a great choice for you. This will be easy or just right for most of the kids in our class.

The other book, *Hatchet,* by Gary Paulsen, is a survival story. It's about a young man named Brian Robeson, who is going on summer vacation to visit his dad, in Canada. And he has to go in a tiny plane because his dad lives in a small town in the far north. During the flight the pilot has a heart attack, and the plane crashes. If you are interested in finding out how Brian survived his adventure, this would be a great book for you. This is going to be just the right book for many of you.

Figure 22-9. *Book Talks for* Ten True Animal Rescues *and* Hatchet

USING A READER'S NOTEBOOK AS A REFLECTION TOOL

A reader's notebook is a powerful tool for supporting reading during the year, helping students organize their thinking and collect it in one place. We prefer a reader's notebook to any workbook or set of exercises as students engage in meaningful opportunities to collect and organize their thinking about books. The notebook has several sections, each of which supports the reading process (see Figure 22-10).

You can foreshadow the notebook and start kindergarten and grade one children on the way to written responses to reading by providing simple notebooks with plain pages. Invite your students to draw and/or write in response to text they have heard or read. In second grade, you may want to use a version with lined paper and add a section for students to list the books they've read. The version of the reader's notebook discussed here is suggested for use from grade two through grade eight.

READING REQUIREMENTS

This section of the notebook specifies the year's reading requirements (see Figure 22-11). It is important for students to explore a range of genres so that they become flexible as readers. Reading is never "just reading." You need to adjust to the genre, taking a stance that leads to rich comprehension. Notice that students have a great deal of "choice" on this list, but there are some very specific requirements. The students tally each type of book they read.

BOOKS TO READ

Proficient readers are always anticipating their next book. People who make reading a part of their lives are always saying, "Oh, I've been wanting to read that book!" A good way to teach students this process is to guide them in recording their reading interests and identifying potential texts they want to read next. On their reading interests list (see Figure 22-12), students can write down genres, topics, and authors that interest them. On their books-to-read list (see Figure 22-13), they can write down specific titles of books gleaned from peer recommendations, book talks, or their own exploration and check them off when they've read them.

Thinking about and making these lists helps students focus their attention on books that are appealing. Chapter 11 stresses the importance of knowing the characteristics of

Figure 22-10. *A Reader's Notebook*

Reading Requirements

Book Minimum: _40_

Requirement	Genre	Tally
3	Traditional Literature	//
5	Realistic Fiction	##–
5	Historical Fiction	///
2	Fantasy	/
2	Science Fiction	/
8	Informational	##–
3	Biography	/
12	Choice	##– //

Figure 22-11. *Reading Requirements*

the various genres, a kind of road map of what a text will be like. This allows you to take a stance toward the text, adjust your strategic actions in anticipation of what you're going to find in terms of:

Reading Interests

Topics That Interest Me	Genre/Types of Books That Interest Me	Authors That Interest Me
cars	informational	Harry Mazer
dirtbikes	H.F.	
motorcycles	biography	
monkeys		
World War II		
video games		
computers		
Alaska		
Australia		
famous People		

© 2002 by I.C. Fountas and G. S. Pinnell, *Reader's Notebook*, NH: Heinemann

Figure 22-12. *Reading Interests*

Books to Read

Title	Author	Check When Completed
Tonight on the Titanic	Mary Pope Osborne	✓
Polar bears past bedtime	Mary Pope Osborne	✓
Fly away home	Eve Bunting	✓
Everything Cat	Marty Crisp	
Every thing Dog	Marty Crisp	✓
Baby Sitters Club (4th grade)	Ann M. Martens	✓
Captin Underpants	Davey	

© 2002 by I.C. Fountas and G. S. Pinnell, *Reader's Notebook*, NH: Heinemann

Figure 22-13. *Books to Read*

- Structure (which is related to genre and content).
- Writing style (if you've already read something by this writer).
- Known versus new information (related to content or topic).
- Purpose (getting information, enjoying a story, etc.).

Good comprehension requires some advance thinking. It's quite different from simply picking up any book, starting with page one, and "doing the reading" in order to win a pizza or a little plastic trophy.

READING LIST

It is not practical for very young children to keep a list of the books they've read. Because it sometimes takes longer to copy the title than to read the book, listing can become a meaningless exercise. But when students are more proficient writers and are reading longer texts, keeping a reading list (see Figure 22-14) can be an important tool in self-reflection and self-assessment. It is also an assessment tool for you.

Reading List

Select a book to read. Enter the title and author on your reading list. When you have completed it, write the genre, and the date. If you abandoned it, write an (A) and the date you abandoned it in the date column. Note whether the book was easy (E), just right (JR) or a difficult (D) book for you.

#	Title	Author	Genre	Date Completed	E JR,D
1	The Witches	Roald Dahl	F	10/1	D
2	Death comes to Dinner	Marvin Millar	RF	10/23	D
3	Mustard	charlotte Graber	RF	10/31	JR
4	Let's play Soldiers Gorge Washington	Peter and connie Roop	B	11/8	JR
5	Stories about Aberham Lincoln to read aloud	Mary Darty	B	11/21	JR
6	Papa's Parrot	Gynthia Rylant	RF	11/25	JR
7	The forth floor twins and the fouchon cookie chase	David A. Adler	RF	12/6	D
8	Stone fox	John Reynolds Gardiner	RF	12/19	JR
9	Post cards from Pluto	Loreen Leedy	I	12/23	JR
10	loser (A)	Jerry Spinelli	F	1/7 (A)	D
11	Little wolfes Book of bad ness	Lan Whybrow	TL	1/8	JR
12	Flat Stanly	Jeff Brown	F	1/11	E
13	charles web	E.B. White	F	1/21	JR

Figure 22-14. *Reading List*

It's a simple procedure. The student numbers and lists each book read, including the author, the genre, the date completed, and whether the book was easy (E), just right (JR), or difficult (D). Over time, the reader—and you, and her parents—will have a picture of her reading development—quantity, variety, and the degree to which she is making good choices. (It is also important to note when a book has been abandoned and to give a specific reason.)

Just by looking at the list in Figure 22-14, you can see:

- How often the student finishes a book.
- The quantity of reading the student has accomplished.
- The range of difficulty levels of the books the student is reading.
- The variety of genres the student has read (this can be compared with requirements at various points in the year).
- The topics or authors that interest the student.
- The degree to which the student is sticking to books and finishing them rather than abandoning them.
- The student's experience in reading several related books to develop depth in reading, e.g., books on the same topic, by same authors, same genre.

Once they understand the importance of the reading list, parents can learn to support home reading and see it as important "homework" rather than recreation. Work with parents to:

- Be sure that time is set aside for reading at home and that there is a quiet place to do it.
- Create a spot to keep the independent reading book, since it must go back and forth between home and school every day.
- Encourage children to talk about the books they are reading.
- Take their children to the public library in order to expand their reading choices.

The reading list can also play an important role in collaborative assessment and goal setting as you talk with students. Look at the partial transcript of Ms. W.'s reading conference with Jason (Figure 22-15). After briefly discussing the new book he had chosen, they looked at his reading list. Jason, who had participated in reading workshop for two years, demonstrated a great deal of self-awareness as he discussed his love for fantasy. He was "reading like a writer." Notice how Ms. W. helped him set a goal to broaden his reading preferences to include more realistic fiction. In doing so, she shared some of her own thoughts as a reader and made specific suggestions.

In the reading conference in Figure 22-16, Mrs. S. is talking with Carl about his reading goals. Carl is interested in stretching himself as a reader by finding more time to read at home. Mrs. S. helps Carl think about the kind of choices he is making and about trying not only to read more but also to extend himself by choosing more just right books. They look at a letter he has written in his reader's notebook. Mrs. S. encourages Carl to move from retelling the story to writing more about his own thinking and she guides him toward a specific example.

SURROUNDING READING WITH WRITTEN CONVERSATION— LETTERS IN A READER'S NOTEBOOK

The conferences above illustrate the importance of having conversations about reading and of using a reader's notebook. Letters in the notebook are another form of dialogue

---

Ms. W.'s Reading Conference with Jason

Ms. W.: Can you tell me what book you are reading?

JASON: I'm reading *Sammy Keyes*. It's a mystery book. It's by Wendelin Van Draanen.

Ms. W.: And you just chose that today?

JASON: No, I chose it yesterday.

Ms. W.: Did you read any other books in the series before you picked up this one?

JASON: No.

Ms. W.: There are more books in this series–different books about Sammy Keyes. I introduced it at the circle. What made you choose this book?

Figure 22-15. *Ms. W.'s Reading Conference with Jason*

Ms. W.'s Reading Conference with Jason (CONTINUED)

JASON: Well, I haven't read any mysteries yet this year. So I decided I wanted to read it. The cover seemed interesting. And then you read us the prologue, and kind of like we were talking about strong leads—you really made me want to read the rest of the book.

Ms. W.: Can we take a look at your reading list? You've done a lot of reading this year. What do you notice about the genres you've been focusing on? Let's just look through and see.

JASON: Well at the beginning of the year I read a lot of fantasy. I've been reading a lot of fantasy and adventure fiction.

Ms. W.: You have a lot of fantasy.

JASON: Some realistic fiction and lots of fiction. I've read a few biographies—Sacagawea, Walt Disney.

Ms. W.: And you've read or tried just a few realistic fiction books. Is that something you would like to try more of?

JASON: Yes.

Ms. W.: There are lots of great realistic fiction books. You've read a lot of fantasy and a lot of adventure. And you've read a lot of nonfiction, too. What is it about fantasy and adventure that drew you to those genres?

JASON: It started last year when my teacher—Mr. Tugwall—he read for read-aloud *The Lion, the Witch, and the Wardrobe*. So I wanted to read the rest of the C. S. Lewis series. So when I finished that series, I just wanted to read more fantasy because I was used to it and I liked it.

Ms. W.: What did you like about it?

JASON: I liked first of all how it's much different from real life, of course, because anything can happen. The most unexpected can happen.

Ms. W.: That's very different from realistic fiction, isn't it. Now which realistic fiction book have you read? I noticed that you read a Beverly Cleary book. Did you like that?

JASON: What started me to read some Beverly Cleary books was reading *Dear Mr. Henshaw* in reading group. After that I read *Strider* and then I read these two.

Ms. W.: What did you notice about realistic fiction?

JASON: Well, even though it's fiction, you think things happened. It's possible it could have happened. I could relate to it.

Ms. W.: That's what I like about realistic fiction. When I read realistic fiction, it makes me feel I have something in common with the characters and I really get to know these characters as people. And I can relate to them and connect or compare my life to theirs. That's a genre you might want to explore a little bit more, because you haven't read that many of those books. Let's see. I'm trying to think of some authors. Beverly Cleary has done a lot of realistic fiction. You might want to stick with her since you feel comfortable with her. Judy Blume is another realistic fiction writer. Do you know *Tales of a Fourth-Grade Nothing* or *Superfudge*?

JASON: I started reading *Tales of a Fourth-Grade Nothing* last year but I didn't really like it.

Ms. W.: You didn't like it? You might want to give it another try, because you are thinking about the genre in a new way.

JASON: I think I didn't like it because it was kind of hard for me.

Ms. W.: Yes, try it again, because it is about a boy and his family and there are a couple of books that come after it. Let's see . . . what are some others? Do you know John Fitzgerald? He's written a lot of stories in the Great Brain series. Those are fun. It's about a boy . . . it's actually a lot of adventure. He has a brother and they are with their friends and getting into trouble or adventures with each other.

JASON: So there actually could be two kinds of adventure fiction—one could be fantasy and one could be realistic fiction.

Ms. W.: A lot of times when you have a book, it doesn't have to be just one genre. You could have a realistic fiction book that has some mystery in it. I don't know about this particular Sammy Keyes book. It might be just fantasy because it would never happen, or it might be more realistic, so that's a good point. So it's just something to think about as you are reading and exploring genre: what makes a book a certain genre? and could there be more than one genre in a book? So try to read some realistic fiction, because that would also be good for you to read in the summer.

Figure 22-15. Ms. W.'s Reading Conference with Jason (cont.)

Mrs. S.'s Reading Conference with Carl

MRS. S.: So you are reading the "book talk" book. How is it going? As funny as I said?

CARL: Yeah. The morals in the book—they are very funny. One that I was just reading, it was about a skunk and a musk oxen and a cabbage. Then they smelt this very spooky smell. "Whoa," said the skunk. "Is that you, musk oxen?" And the musk oxen asked the cabbage if it was a cabbage, and the cabbage said, "Uh-uh." Then they both started looking at the skunk. It said that the skunk got quickly very interested in tying his shoe. And the moral said, "He who smelt it dealt it."

MRS. S.: So what are you thinking about his style of writing? What were you noticing?

CARL: I'm thinking he is good at making the funny kind of morals and interesting morals. They are interesting but they are funny . . . they are good morals, but they are funny at the same time.

MRS. S.: And remember, too, when we were talking about voice and personality in our writing. Can you see his personality coming through so strongly? It's interesting. I wonder where he got his ideas. Do you remember the part I read aloud to you, where it said he gets a lot of ideas from people he knows? So I'm wondering who some of these people are. What are you thinking about that?

CARL: I'm thinking he probably gets his ideas from seeing things happening. Maybe, like in this one, he's seen a cat chasing a pigeon. This one is about a pigeon and a lion, I think.

MRS. S.: And we were talking about that, right? Being really observant because you never know what you are seeing that you will want to write about? Let's look at your reading list. How has that been going for you? What is your current goal in reading workshop? What have you been working toward?

CARL: To read more at home, more than usual, just thirty minutes—maybe forty-five minutes or an hour. I tried that yesterday and I thought I did pretty good with my book.

MRS. S.: What made you do well yesterday and not necessarily other times?

CARL: I had nothing to do until I remembered that I needed to read my book, so I just went to read my book, and after a while, I just got stuck in my book and I kept on reading.

MRS. S.: So, I hear you saying it's about finding really good books that you want to read.

CARL: Yes, that's what I'm trying, to read more so I can read longer and get better and so I can read the fourth-grade goal of forty books.

MRS. S.: I also see that you are reading different genres and that's good; you are really aware of that. I am seeing a lot of easy books. What do you think about that?

CARL: I should try to read more just-right books instead of easy ones.

MRS. S.: We sometimes read easy books to take a break, but we shouldn't have that many, so I'm going to write that goal right here. One other thing I wanted to talk to you about was your letters. Look at this right here: "Right now Meiko was having a hard time. Just two weeks ago an atom bomb dropped. It seemed like it was the end of the world. She was shielding her face when a piece of glass gave her a big gash in her hand. Sounds pretty nasty. Now she thinks she lost the fifth treasure, beauty in the heart, so now she only has four of the treasures." See how you are retelling what the book is about? But what I wanted to know—because I already read that book—I wanted to know what you were thinking when you wrote that. So what could you have said there? What could you say instead? Think about that part you wrote about.

CARL: Maybe I could say that when the glass hit her and gave her the gash, it must have been bleeding really badly because glass can be very sharp.

MRS. S.: Okay. If that had happened to you, how might you feel, or if you had seen that happen to someone, how would you feel?

CARL: I would probably feel bad if it was my friend. I would also feel bad if it happened to me, because then I would be in the hospital and I wouldn't be able to do much. I wouldn't be able to use my hand, especially if it's my left hand, because I'm a lefty.

MRS. S.: What I want to hear about is what you were thinking about that part, not just telling me about that part. So you could say, "When the atom bomb dropped and Meiko got hurt, I was thinking . . ." and just get right into it. So I'm going to be looking to see that and I'm going to be looking to see fewer easy books. Why don't you write a little stick-on note so you will remember the two things we were thinking about.

Figure 22-16. *Mrs. S.'s Reading Conference with Carl*

between student and teacher or student and student (a written conversation). *Guiding Readers and Writers* (Fountas and Pinnell 2001) includes many management suggestions as well as suggestions for specific minilessons that will help your students exchange thoughtful letters with you and with their classmates about the books they are reading.

Your goal in using a reader's notebook is to help students extend and express their thinking about reading. Being expected to write about their thinking places an extra layer of consciousness on readers. They are more likely to remember details and to store up responses they feel deeply about and want to include in their writing. Letters between you and your students are a collection of thoughts over time as they develop as readers. Think of them as a written conversation about books. You can help children better communicate their thinking in several ways:

1. You can model and demonstrate ways of expressing thinking through minilessons. Write a series of letters yourself and share them, letting students notice places where you have written about your thinking in various ways—noticing the language of the text, critiquing the text, making personal connections, comparing and connecting texts, and so on.

2. You can talk with students about their letters during conferences, providing specific feedback, as illustrated in the conference in Figure 22-16.

3. Students can bring their notebooks to the community meeting, finding places in their letters where they demonstrated their thinking and sharing selected paragraphs from their journals with partners or in small groups.

4. You can lift or scaffold student's thinking through your ongoing written exchanges with them.

Once you begin using reader's notebooks, you'll find that responding to students is fascinating rather than arduous. If you enter into a genuine conversation, keeping strategic actions in mind, you will inevitably stretch your students' thinking. Don't expect breakthroughs in one or two letters; this is an ongoing process. Figure 22-17 illustrates a teacher/student exchange over a six-week period. Notice how Maddie's responses are changing as a result of the minilessons and conferences she is having, as well as Carol's written feedback.

Take time to read these letters; together they tell a story. Maddie loves the Ramona series, by Beverly Cleary. While she recognizes Maddie's enjoyment of this popular writer, Carol gently nudges her to vary her reading. Maddie persists in gobbling up the series, and Carol doesn't force the issue. Finally, Maddie seems to realize on her own that she is ready to try something new. Meanwhile, she has completed five or six books over the six weeks—reading she has enjoyed and learned from. She has also moved from telling about the story to writing more articulately about her own thinking. Overall, these letters:

- Are very personal but stay focused on reading.

- Are open-ended in that Carol and Maddie can write about any thoughts related to reading.

- Are conversational and friendly.

- Reveal that Carol and Maddie care about each other's opinions and enjoy sharing.

- Indicate an ease of expression on the part of both Carol and Maddie.

- Contain advice and suggestions from a more experienced to a less experienced reader.

- Indicate Maddie's growth as a reader.

The reader's notebook provides an enormous amount of valuable data that will inform your interactive read-aloud, minilessons, guided reading lessons, and individual conferences. To make time for writing about reading, you will need to reduce some other homework, such as worksheets, writing assignments, and book reports.

Keep notebook writing open-ended at first rather than give specific assignments. This will help students learn that they have good thinking to share and don't need you to tell them what to think about. Once they are well on their way to understanding the many ways of responding, you can occasionally make specific requests related to your minilesson, such as asking them to comment on characters or predict outcomes. You can assign your students to write one paragraph related to the minilesson principle in their letters; they can write on topics of their own choosing for the rest of the letter. We address letter writing in greater detail, as well as other genres for writing about reading in a reader's notebook, in Chapter 28.

Dear Ms. Won,
The book I am reading is Ramona Forever. I love it so far. As you know I love Ramona books. I'm going to tell you what has happened so far. Well... right now Ramona is talking with her big sister Beezus. Beezus thinks their mother is going to have a baby because she hasn't been eating dessert and when their aunt was at their house she kept asking how she was feeling. I don't think she's going to have a baby. I don't know why, I just don't think she is! Another thing that's happening is Ramona's best friends Uncle Hobart came. Ramona thinks he's mean because he is teasing her. (sort of!)

Love,
Maddie

P.S. I just finished it and, they do have a "baby named "Roberta.

P.P.S Beezus and Ramona's aunt got married to Howie's Uncle Hobart and Ramona (his new niece) thinks he's nice now, and they are friends!

Dear Maddie,
Oh, I remember loving Ramona when I was growing up. I still like her so much. I just remember feeling that I was a lot like her character and that if we could be friends, we would really understand each other.
Through Beverly Cleary's writing, I knew a lot of Ramona's thoughts. She seemed to have a lot that she worried about, was scared about, and wondered. I liked knowing all of those things, and I enjoyed reading about how Ramona would act in different situations. How do you feel about Ramona? What do you think about her?
I looked at your reading list and am wondering what books you will try next. Is there another series or author that you would like to try?

Love,
Ms. Won

Dear Ms. Won,
Well..... you asked me how I feel about her and what I think about her, I sort of feel the way you do I like her and sometimes I picture myself in her shoes. I also think she has a very creative imagination and it would be cool to be her!
I don't really want to read any other series soon but I will try some a little later!
I started a new book called "Ramona Quimby age 8" it's great so far there's nothing I really have to tell you about but when I do... I'll let you know!

your student,
Maddie

Dear Maddie,

Once you start a series, it does take a while to get through all the books. It is often worth it, but it can keep a reader from exploring and trying new kinds of books and authors. What are you thinking in terms of the next books you'd like to try? What kind of book would you like to read next? I can help you find something during Readers' Workshop!
How is Ramona Quimby Age 8 coming along? You've probably moved on to your next book by now. You are doing a lot of thinking (Reading is thinking ☺). That's what I'd like for you to share with me - your thoughts as you read!

Love,
Ms. Won

Figure 22-17. *Maddie's Letters and Her Teacher's Written Feedback*

Dear Ms. Won,

You're right! I did finish Ramona Quimby age 8. Now I'm reading... Ramona and her Mother. But I'm only on p. 43. I am doing a lot of thinking when I'm reading and I usually just think about what I'm reading. I don't really think about anything else! Just what the story is about and what the characters are doing.

I'm not sure what other kinds of books I'm going to read next, but I still want to read 2 more Beverly cleary books after the one I'm reading now. Those books are... Ramona and her Father and Ramona's World.

Love,
Maddie

Dear Maddie,

Thank you for your letter. The second one is much more detailed than the one before. The more specific your details and ideas, the better I can understand your thoughts.

I understand what you mean about how it seems that Ramona just tries so hard sometimes, but things don't always work out for her, do they? I always felt badly for her, too. I felt she was misunderstood a lot and that she just needed some attention at times.

I also really like the stories that Beverly Cleary comes up with. Wow! Look at all of the Ramona books she's written, and we like them all! ♥ I think it would be neat for you, Maddie, to read one of Beverly Cleary's memoirs. You can learn more about her as a person and writer and find out more about how she comes up with ideas for her books.

Love,
Ms. Won

Dear Ms. Won,

The part of Ramona and her Mother I'm on right now is when Ramona is using the sewing machine and is making slacks for her stuffed elephant. She finished the slacks but they wouldn't fit him! She tryed so hard! I feel bad for her! I think she deserves better than that!! She's a sweet little girl that was just trying to make slacks! Well anyway, I think Ramona and I have a lot in common with eachother for one thing, we are both very picky! She is a very picky eater and so am I. I really like Ramona books they are just so funny and I like the idea of the stories. Ramona is a really funny character. Beezus is very serious and their parents are serious too.

Love,
Maddie

P.S. Let me know if I didn't write enough details.

Figure 22-17. *Maddie's Letters and Her Teacher's Written Feedback (cont.)*

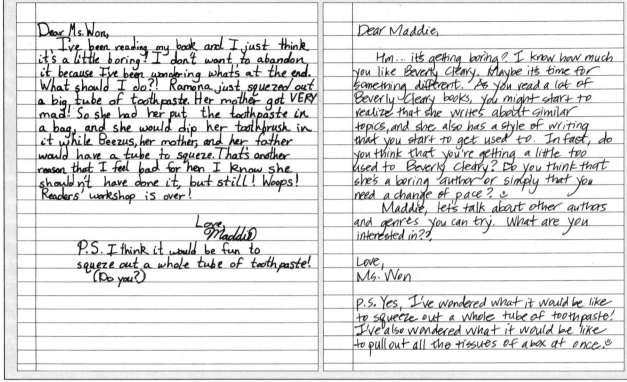

Figure 22-17. *Maddie's Letters and Her Teacher's Written Feedback (cont.)*

TALKING WITH STUDENTS ABOUT READING—INDIVIDUAL CONFERENCES

There are no substitutes for individual interactions with students around their reading lives. Having regular one-to-one conferences with students is a scheduling challenge, but they are well worth it.

CONFERENCES WITH YOUNGER CHILDREN

Conferences with younger children can take place during independent work and usually consist of a short "check in" on some aspect of that work. If you are meeting with children in guided reading groups, you will listen to them read individually, one at a time, right after the text introduction. Additionally, sampling oral reading while students are reading independently and having a brief conversation about the book reinforces and expands student thinking while at the same time lets you gather valuable information.

Two examples of these brief interchanges in a first-grade classroom are shown in Figures 22-18 and 22-19. Lisa (Mrs. D.) first talks with Morgan, who is rereading books in the browsing box her teacher created with her guided reading group. Notice that she briefly discusses the meaning of the story before listening to Morgan read. Next,

---

MRS. D.'S READING CONFERENCE WITH MORGAN
Peaches the Pig

MRS. D.: Hi, Morgan. Are you enjoying the books from the browsing box?

MORGAN: Yes. I'm reading *Peaches* again.

MRS. D.: I love that book *Peaches the Pig*. What was an interesting part?

MORGAN: Where they wallow in the mud.

MRS. D.: That was important wasn't it? Are you thinking why?

MORGAN: Because she's a pig and that's what pigs can do and she couldn't do the other kinds of things, like kittens.

MRS. D.: She was happy when she found those other pigs. Read a little bit to me. Remember to make it sound like talking when she meets those animals.

Figure 22-18. *Mrs. D.'s Reading Conference with Morgan—Peaches the Pig*

she talks with Temple, who is reading longer text. He is making his way through the volumes of the Henry and Mudge series. During this brief conference, Lisa learns that he is monitoring and self-correcting his reading and grasping literary language.

MRS. D.'S READING CONFERENCE WITH TEMPLE
Henry and Mudge Under the Yellow Moon

MRS. D.: Hi, Temple. I see you are reading another Henry and Mudge book. Do you like it as well as the others you've read?

TEMPLE: I'm just in the first chapter, but it's kind of funny that they do the same things but not really the same.

MRS. D.: What's an example?

TEMPLE: Well, like they both like leaves but Mudge eats them.

MRS. D.: I'm glad Henry doesn't eat leaves! Read a little just right where you are.

TEMPLE: [READS] "Henry put on a coat and Mudge grew one. And when the fall wind blew, Henry's ears turned red and Mudge's ears turned outside, in, inside, outside [REPEATS] Mudge's ears turned inside out. [CONTINUES READING TO THE END OF THE CHAPTER]

MRS. D.: That was a good chapter. Let's go back to something you found tricky.

TEMPLE: It was on this page [TURNS BACK TO THE PAGE WHERE HE MADE THE SELF-CORRECTION].

MRS. D.: Read it again.

TEMPLE: [READS THE PAGE ACCURATELY.]

MRS. D.: I noticed that you were kind of connecting *inside* and *outside,* but you were looking really closely at the words. Does *inside out* make sense to you? It's an expression. What does it mean?

TEMPLE: Like if you pull off your coat and the sleeve turns inside out. And his ears—you can see inside them.

MRS. D.: Yes, that wind is blowing so hard, it's blowing them back. So you said they do things kind of alike but also different. Henry's ears turned red in the wind and Mudge's ears . . .

TEMPLE: . . . turned inside out!

MRS. D.: They both like fall, don't they?

Figure 22-19. *Mrs. D.'s Reading Conference with Temple*—Henry and Mudge Under the Yellow Moon

CONFERENCES IN GRADES 2–8

Individual conferences during reading workshop will vary in time and purpose (see Figure 22-20). During the first two or three weeks of school, you will establish the routines of the reading workshop. For a detailed description of mini-lessons for the first twenty days of reading workshop, see *Guiding Readers and Writers* (Fountas and Pinnell 2001). During the weeks, you'll make time to confer with every student individually to be sure that they know how to choose and are reading a just-right book. These conferences may also involve a benchmark assessment to determine initial reading levels for the guided reading group (see Chapter 8). After several reading conferences, you usually know students' present strengths and have established some reading goals.

At this point you need to establish a system for holding conferences. Many teachers keep a list of the students on a clipboard with spaces for notes. Using the list, you can keep track of the children who have had a conference and those whom you still need to see. Depending on the size of your class, you should try to have short conferences with each student as often as possible. You may need to meet more often with students who are struggling and less often with students who are making good progress.

Figure 22-20. *Individual Conference During Reading Workshop*

You'll supplement these short conferences with quick "check-ins" to offer encouragement and help you keep track of what individual students are doing and make sure they are getting started. You will want to do this only with students who need a strong level of support. (On your list, place an asterisk by the students with whom you want to have these quick interactions.)

Look at the transcripts of two reading conferences Linda (Mrs. T.) had with students in her class (Figures 22-21 and 22-22). She first had an exchange with Tony, referring to the day's minilesson. Next, she spends some time with Samantha, talking mostly about personal connections and what we can learn from reading. All in all, she accomplished a lot!

EFFECTIVE CONFERENCES

Looking at the conferences with younger and older students that we have explored in this chapter, you will notice the following characteristics:

- They were one-on-one and had the feel of a real conversation.
- The student did a lot of the talking.
- They took place at the student's desk.
- The teacher and student sat side-by-side at the same eye level (the teacher didn't lean over the child).
- The teacher listened to the student read a section of the text orally.

Mrs. T.'s Reading Conference with Tony

MRS. T.: Hi, Tony, how's your reading work going?

TONY: Okay.

MRS. T.: What are you reading?

TONY: *Herbie Jones and the Class Gift.*

MRS. T.: And who's that by?

TONY: Suzy Klein.

MRS. T.: Have you read anything else by Suzy Klein?

TONY: Mm-hm. Horrible Harry books.

MRS. T.: Horrible Harry books. And what are you thinking about this book? Is it easy or just right for you? How is it for a match?

TONY: Just right.

MRS. T.: So talk to me a little bit about what is happening

TONY: I'm up to where Herbie and Ray, . . . they got two dollars to add to the gift that they are giving their teacher and then they get to sign a card, but then Ray spent it on food because he was hungry. And now they got another two dollars and they gave it to her, to Annabel, but she says she already bought the gift.

MRS. T.: So you are talking about the problem in the story. So what do they want to do? They want to buy a gift?

TONY: Yes.

MRS. T.: For who?

TONY: For their teacher. It is the end of the year, and they wanted to buy her something really nice like a fancy gift. And she likes owls so they are getting her a ceramic owl.

MRS. T.: Do you ever go shopping for gifts for teachers?

TONY: Yes.

MRS. T.: Does it make you think about that a little bit? How do you think it's going to end up?

TONY: I think that they're gonna pay for it. They're gonna get the money and give it to her. And, then they might buy something else with the money to add to the owl—like candy or something.

MRS. T.: Okay. Have you noticed anything about the author's use of language?

TONY: It's pretty just like regular.

MRS. T.: So it's pretty clear. We talked in the minilesson today about why you think characters do things and what their actions make you think about them. So what does one of the characters do in your book?

TONY: Ray spends the money on food.

MRS. T.: So why is he doing that?

TONY: Because he was hungry.

MRS. T.: All right, what does that make you think about him as a character?

TONY: He was selfish, like he only thinks for himself. So, when Herbie told him not to spend the money, he did, on himself.

MRS. T.: So now you're talking about character traits like he's selfish. That's what readers do. They think about how different characters react to others in a book and it helps you really get to know the character a little bit better. Well, you enjoy your reading. I'll be listening to you in group share.

Figure 22-21. *Mrs. T.'s Reading Conference with Tony*

Mrs. T.'s Reading Conference with Samantha

MRS. T.: Samantha, how are you doing today?

SAMANTHA: Good.

MRS. T.: How is your reading work going? Talk to me a little bit about your book. What are you thinking about?

SAMANTHA: The name is *Judy Moody*. And she's not in a good mood but it's a bad mood. Judy Moody is starting third grade and she didn't want the summer to be over and she doesn't want to be older. And when she goes to school, she finds that it isn't so bad.

MRS. T.: Does that ever happen to you?

SAMANTHA: Yes.

MRS. T.: So why do you like this book so much?

SAMANTHA: Because, like, it has a lot of details. You just, you know, you don't want to stop reading it.

MRS. T.: You don't want to stop reading . . . . You're really engaged in it. That's great! So talk to me about Judy as a character.

SAMANTHA: She sometimes can be very snotty—like to her brother. But with her friends she can be the nicest person ever. So her moods change around different people.

MRS. T.: So what does that tell you about her as a person?

SAMANTHA: [Pause.]

MRS. T.: Would you want to be her sister or her friend?

SAMANTHA: [Laughing] Her friend.

MRS. T.: It kind of reminds me a little bit of my daughters. Do you have anyone in your family that she reminds you of?

SAMANTHA: Well, I do kind of, with my sister sometimes.

MRS. T.: Oh, so you are reading a little bit about yourself there. What does it make you think about then. Is there something you can learn?

SAMANTHA: I don't know. Maybe back off my sister a bit.

MRS. T.: It's interesting, isn't it, how we can just read a book and if we really think about how we react to people, we can learn something and maybe change. Would you recommend this book to others in the class?

SAMANTHA: Yes.

MRS. T.: How did you pick this book?

SAMANTHA: I read one Judy Moody book before and I kind of liked it but I wasn't sure if I really liked it. So I tried another one, and I noticed I really started liking it.

MRS. T.: That's interesting. So now do you feel that you know the character much better now that you have read another book about her?

SAMANTHA: Yes.

MRS. T.: And are you thinking that you might be interested in reading another book about her?

SAMANTHA: Yes.

MRS. T.: That's the interesting thing about reading books in a series, because you get to know the characters really well and see how they act in lots of different situations. And you almost become friends.

SAMANTHA: Mm-hm.

MRS. T.: That's great. Well, enjoy your reading.

SAMANTHA: Okay.

Figure 22-21. *Mrs. T.'s Reading Conference with Samantha*

- The student talked about the story.
- The teacher encouraged the reader and affirmed good thinking.
- The teacher sometimes helped the student clarify thinking about the text.
- The teacher sometimes prompted the student to make connections, make predictions, or extend thinking in different ways.
- The teacher sometimes applied labels to the student's thinking (for example, the *problem of the story* or *character traits.*)
- The teacher sometimes helped the student understand difficult language.
- The teacher sometimes worked on word-solving strategies.
- The student and teacher sometimes reflected together on the reading list or on writing about reading in the reader's notebook.
- The student and teacher sometimes set reading goals.
- The teacher gained information about the student's understanding and fluency.
- The teacher gained valuable information to inform instruction.

The key to effective instruction is interaction, both oral and written, around texts. Through interaction with your students, you support deeper comprehension of texts they read independently.

SUGGESTIONS FOR PROFESSIONAL DEVELOPMENT

OPTION ONE: ANALYZING READING CONFERENCES

1 Working in cross-grade-level groups, think about the oral language used in conferences.

2 Re-read the transcripts of conferences in this chapter (or watch the reading conference on the DVD that accompanies this book).

3 Make a list of "instructional moves" that you observed and that would be useful in other conferences.

4 Have each participant audio- or videotape one five-minute reading conference during the next two weeks.

5 Then meet again to share and discuss the conferences. Ask:

- □ What evidence of processing is gained by observing the oral reading?

- □ What evidence of processing is gained by what the student says about reading?

- □ How did the teacher help the student extend thinking?

- □ What new understandings does the student gain during the conference?

OPTION TWO: ANALYZING WRITTEN CONVERSATIONS

1 After a group of teachers have been using reader's notebooks for several months, have them bring some samples to a meeting.

2 Working in pairs (at the same grade level), share notebooks and discuss evidence of thinking within them. Be sure to talk about the change you see in each reader over time.

CHAPTER TWENTY-THREE

DESIGNING MINILESSONS TO SUPPORT THINKING ABOUT TEXTS IN A READING WORKSHOP

We want our students to make a lifetime commitment to reading and writing. And so we begin by painstakingly caring about the literary landscape and then we proceed to do the best teaching imaginable.

—SHELLEY HARWAYNE

Minilessons are brief, highly focused group lessons that help readers learn more about any aspect of an effective processing system. The goal of all reading workshop minilessons is to help children become independent readers for life, functioning as fully literate people in today's world. You're probably thinking, "How can I do that in one short lesson?" and you're right. The daily minilesson is important, but it is certainly not the only context in which you are teaching students about reading. Minilessons will be effective or ineffective to the degree that students can apply principles in many different reading contexts.

SIX KEY IDEAS ABOUT MINILESSONS

Below we present and discuss six key ideas about minilessons in a reading workshop.

1 *The purpose of a minilesson is to "teach the reader." Your goal is to help children think like readers.*

Everything children learn how to do as readers must be integrated into a smoothly operating processing system. If the student is reading a book proficiently, all systems are working together to meet the demands of the text. The processing system then expands to meet the demands of more challenging texts (Clay 2001). Simply by reading a text well, one learns more about how to read, especially if texts offer different kinds of challenges. In instruction you highlight one aspect of reading. The goal is to help readers notice, understand, and use the information, strategy, or skill effectively when they encounter it in other texts, thus expanding their general ability to read.

When teaching minilessons on strategies and skills:

- Keep the language grounded in good texts so that students understand that their goal is to understand and notice more rather than to "do" a strategy.
- Avoid labels and jargon, especially with younger chil-

dren. Keep the language focused on understanding what the writer is doing for the reader.

- The goal is not naming a strategy, but applying it to the reading of text. Students can learn to repeat the names of strategies without learning a single thing about how to read proficiently, and you will have engaged them in a meaningless (and possibly confusing) exercise.

2 *The purpose of reading minilessons is to help the reader build effective processing strategies while reading continuous text.*

Whenever you highlight a particular aspect of the reading process, it is important that readers be able to apply it to continuous text as part of an orchestrated system.

The structure of reading workshop (minilesson, reading and conferring, sharing) provides an immediate opportunity for students to apply minilesson principles to their own reading of just-right books, collecting examples at a level they can process well and understand. Sharing brings them back together as a community to revisit and extend the understanding presented in the minilesson principle.

3 *Whole-group lessons are effective as part of a reading workshop for grades two through eight. Briefer lessons can be embedded in an interactive read-aloud for children of any age.*

In Chapter 13 we explore the idea of "intentional conversation" during interactive read-aloud, an instructional technique that can be effective at any grade level. But turning an interactive read-aloud into a heavy-handed lesson is counterproductive. A general rule of thumb is to engage in a great deal of intentional conversation focused on exploring the deeper meaning or other aspects of the text you are reading aloud. After children have explored a concept in everyday language during an interactive read-aloud, they will better

353

understand the same concept as the topic of a minilesson (see Figure 23-1). That is, for example, after children have spent a great deal of time talking about "the writer's message" and they can identify several important ideas, they will have the underlying foundation they need to understand terms such as "main ideas" or "themes." We are talking about years of developing a variety of understandings about the reading process and texts. By the time children experience more "formal" minilessons in grade two, students will have had many daily intentional conversations around texts.

4 *Some reading minilessons must be directed toward the routines that will support efficient teaching and learning.*

Until the routines of reading workshop are firmly established, it will be impossible to be effective in whole-group, small-group, or individual instruction. When you provide a whole-class minilesson, students need to apply what they are learning while reading independently; they also need your support through individual conferences and guided reading. So when you launch reading workshop, procedural minilessons as described in *Guiding Readers and Writers* (Fountas and Pinnell 2001) will be a priority. Once the workshop has been established, you can focus the minilessons on:

- Applying the strategies and skills of reading, with an emphasis on comprehension.
- Engaging in literary analysis.
- Responding to texts (talking and writing about reading).
- Engaging in critical thinking.
- Analyzing the writer's craft.
- Understanding characteristics of each genre.

Several potential minilessons within each category are listed later in this chapter. You will want to select and plan your minilessons to address the specific needs of your students.

5 *Precise and explicit language will help students understand minilesson principles.*

When you plan your minilesson, it is helpful to write the principle or understanding you want to teach in one or two sentences that will turn your students' thinking in the right direction. It is a good idea to formulate the statement in terms of what readers do. Whatever approach you take, it will be helpful to state the principle in the same (or very

similar) language every time you refer to it. You want your students to easily be able to remember the principle as they read, to reflect on their reading, and prepare for sharing. Remembering and eventually internalizing this language will help them read and think about texts with a new lens. In addition, they will have a shared language for talking about texts. From grades five through eight you may want to consider having your students write the concept and an example or take notes in a section of their reader's notebook (or another blank notebook) that they can use as a reference. They can make a table of contents at the front and use it as a reader's tool. We have provided examples of specific language you may find helpful for talking with students about texts in reading minilessons (see Figure 23-2).

Once you have a clear statement of the minilesson principle, you can record it on a chart, along with the examples you want to show and those you add as you work with the students. You can quickly refer to examples from texts you have read to students, as they will provide shared literary background. The visual reminder in Figure 23-3 will help support students in reading, writing, and talking about their reading.

6 *Being able to apply the principle with teacher support helps readers make a link to their own thinking.*

You will want to invite children to share their examples during the minilesson, as can be seen in Figure 23-4. Many will come from the texts you have read together. It is also very helpful if you can give them an opportunity to "try it out" with you before they go to their seats to try it on their own. For example, they can talk in partners or threes or do some quick writing in their reader's notebooks so they have had some opportunity to apply the new principles.

MINILESSONS IN ACTION

Let's look at two examples of minilessons, one used with younger children and one used with older children. In each lesson, you will see how the teacher uses a shared text to illustrate the points that are being made.

NOTICING THE PROBLEM IN THE STORY

Mr. T. wants to help his students learn to be more precise in identifying the problem in a story (see Figure 23-5). Identifying the problem is central to comprehending fiction. Often, readers can follow a plot line or series of events

Sample Language for Embedded Instruction and Minilessons

	SAMPLE TEACHING POINTS DURING INTERACTIVE READ-ALOUD	SAMPLE PRINCIPLES IN AN EXPLICIT MINILESSON
Elements of Fiction		
Setting	"Where does the story take place?" "When is this story happening?" "Think about whether the place or time is important in this story." "Why?"	"Readers notice the time and place of the story and their importance to the story." "The setting is the time of the story and where it takes place. Sometimes the setting is very important to the story."
Characters	"What does the writer say about [name of character]?" "Listen to see if [name of character] changes during the story." "Why did [name of character] change?"	"Readers think about what the writer says about the characters." "Readers notice that some characters in a story change." "Readers think about what makes a character change."
Plot	"In this story, [name of character] has a problem. It is_____." "What problem does [name of character] have in this story?" "How do you think [name of character] will solve the problem?"	"Readers think about the problem in the story." "Readers think about what might happen to solve the problem in a story."
Narrator and Perspective	"Who is telling this story?" "[Name of character or author] is telling us this story."	"Readers notice who is telling the story." "Readers notice when a narrator is telling the story." "Readers notice the character who is telling the story."
Mood	"How does this story make you feel?" "What makes you feel that way?"	"Readers notice the mood of the story." "Readers notice how the writer makes them feel." "Readers notice how the writer uses language/illustrations to create a mood."
Theme	"Think about the whole story. What was the writer really trying to tell us?" "In this book, the author might be trying to help us know that____." "What is the writer's message?"	"Readers think about what the writer of a story is really trying to say." "Readers think about the writers' messages or themes." "The theme is what the writer is trying to help us understand. There might be more than one theme."

Figure 23-1. *Sample Language for Embedded Instruction and Minilessons*

Sample Language for Embedded Instruction and Minilessons (CONTINUED)

	SAMPLE TEACHING POINTS DURING INTERACTIVE READ-ALOUD	SAMPLE PRINCIPLES IN AN EXPLICIT MINILESSON
Elements of Nonfiction		
Accuracy	"This is a factual text. Let's look at what the writer did to be sure the information is right."	"Readers check the writer's credentials and sources to be sure the information is accurate."
Style	"What did you find interesting?" "How did the writer make that interesting to you?"	"Readers think about the way the writer has presented information to make it interesting."
Organization	"What do you notice about the kind of information the writer tells us first [next]?" "How is the writer organizing the information?"	"Readers notice how the writer has organized the text [sequence, category]." "Readers notice how sometimes writers use more than one way to organize and present information."
Text Features	"What do you notice about the print? How does that help you read this book?"	"Readers notice different sizes and types of print [italics, bold] and think about how it helps them understand the text."
Text Patterns	"The writer is telling how two things are alike and how they are different. How are [items] alike?" "In this book the writer is showing us something that happened in a sequence. What happened first? Next?" "In this book the writer tells us about a problem and also how to solve it. What's the problem?" "In this book the writer uses language to help us know how something [looks, sounds, etc.]. Listen to some of the language." "In this book the writer helps us understand what causes something."	"Readers notice when the writer is comparing and contrasting two things." "Readers notice when the writer is presenting a sequence." "Readers notice when a writer is solving a problem and the solution to a problem." "Readers notice when the writer is describing something." "Readers notice when the writer is showing what causes something."
Elements of Biography		
Setting	"What was it like when this person lived [or was young]?"	"Readers think about the setting and how it influenced the subject's life."
Subject	"What was important about this person?"	"Readers think about why the writer chose the subject."
Theme	"What can we learn from reading about this person?"	"Readers think about what they can learn from a subject's life."
Accuracy	"Let's look at what the writer did to be sure the information about this person was right."	"Readers look at the writer's research and credentials to get information about the accuracy of a biography."

Figure 23-1. *Sample Language for Embedded Instruction and Minilessons (cont.)*

Sample Language for Embedded Instruction and Minilessons (CONTINUED)

	SAMPLE TEACHING POINTS DURING INTERACTIVE READ-ALOUD	SAMPLE PRINCIPLES IN AN EXPLICIT MINILESSON
Elements of Biography (continued)		
Text Structure	"What did the writer tell you first about the person? Next?"	"Readers notice how the writer has organized information about the subject."
Illustrations, Graphic Features	"Let's look at the [pictures, charts] to see what they tell us about this person."	"Readers find important information in the pictures or charts."

Figure 23-1. *Sample Language for Embedded Instruction and Minilessons (cont.)*

Using Explicit Language to Communicate Minilesson Principles

FICTION

LITERARY ELEMENT	TEACHING POINTS IN A MINILESSON
Setting (time and place of story)	Readers notice the time and place (setting) and the importance to the story. Readers consider how a story would be different if it happened in another time and place.
Characters (identification and development)	Readers notice who are the most important characters (main characters) in the story. Readers think about the ways the writer helps them get to know the characters. Readers notice that some characters are not important to the story. Readers notice what the author or other characters say about how the characters look and what these descriptions tell you about the characters. Readers think about what characters say and what their words tell you about them. Readers think about why a character does something in order to understand the character. Readers think about what characters do and what their actions tell you about them. Readers notice what other characters say or think about a character. Readers notice that some characters change in a story and some do not. Readers think about how and why characters change.
Plot (problem and events that follow)	Readers think about the problem in the story. Readers think about how the problem in a story is solved. Readers think about the important events in a story. Readers think about the choices characters have. Readers think about the order of events in a story. Readers think about what might happen in a story. Readers think about whether the story could have happened. Readers predict how a story will end. Readers think about how the author shows time in a story.
Narrator and Perspective (point of view, person telling the story; all-knowing third person; third person focusing on one character; second person—writer speaking directly to reader)	Readers think about who is telling the story. Readers notice when an outside person (writer) is telling about the people in the story. Readers notice when the writer focuses on the actions and feelings of one character in the story. Readers notice when a character is telling the story. Readers notice when the writer is speaking directly to them.

Figure 23-2. *Using Explicit Language to Communicate Minilesson Principles*

Using Explicit Language to Communicate Minilesson Principles (CONTINUED)

FICTION (cont.)

LITERARY ELEMENT	TEACHING POINTS IN A MINILESSON
Mood *(overall feeling developed throughout the text)*	Readers think about how a story makes them feel (notice the mood). Readers think about how and why their feelings toward characters or events change as they read.
Theme *(main message or messages the writer is trying to convey)*	Readers think about what the writer of a story is really trying to say. Readers think about what the story means to them. Readers think about why the writer wrote the story. Readers think about whether the title tells something important about the theme. Readers understand that there may be more than one theme in a book.
Genre *(the type of text)*	Readers notice the characteristics of a book so they can identify its genre. Readers identify the genre of a book so they can know what to expect as they read.
Language *(the way the writer selects words and puts them together in phrases, sentences, paragraphs, and the whole text)*	Readers notice how writers use words carefully to communicate meaning. Readers notice memorable phrases and sentences writers use to communicate meaning to the reader. Readers notice the language that writers use to help them form images—what they can see, hear, feel, taste, or smell. Readers think about how writers use words to help them see, hear, smell, feel, or taste. Readers think about the language writers use to make comparisons that helps them understand the meaning and enjoy reading. Readers notice how writers give some objects or animals human characteristics in order to interest them.

BIOGRAPHY

LITERARY ELEMENT	TEACHING POINTS IN A MINILESSON
Setting *(time and place of story)*	Readers notice how the time, place, and circumstances influenced the subject of the biography. Readers notice how people influenced the subject.
Character *(information on the subject)*	Readers think about what the subject was trying to accomplish. Readers think about why a person's accomplishments are important to society (to others, to the world).
Theme *(message as conveyed)*	Readers notice how a person showed courage in overcoming obstacles. Readers notice how a person's life contributed to society. Readers make connections among people who have shown courage and made outstanding contributions.
Accuracy and Authenticity *(qualifications of the writer; grounded in fact)*	Readers notice the source of information used to describe a person's life accurately. Readers think about the accuracy of information about a subject's life. Readers notice what information writers include or omit.
Text Structure *(organization of the information)*	Readers notice and think about the way the writer selected events in the subject's life to describe. Readers think about the time periods described in a subject's life.

Figure 23-2. *Using Explicit Language to Communicate Minilesson Principles (cont.)*

Using Explicit Language to Communicate Minilesson Principles (CONTINUED)

BIOGRAPHY (cont.)

LITERARY ELEMENT	TEACHING POINTS IN A MINILESSON
Perspective	Readers think about why the writer selected events in the subject's life. Readers think about what the author wants us to think about the subject of a biography.

NONFICTION

LITERARY ELEMENT	TEACHING POINTS IN A MINILESSON
Accuracy and Authenticity of Information *(qualifications of the writer; grounding)*	Readers judge the accuracy of information about a topic that writers provide. Readers notice the source of information in nonfiction texts so they can think about the accuracy and authenticity. Readers notice the qualifications of the writer when they are judging the accuracy and authenticity of the text.
Style *(writer's way of making information available and interesting)*	Readers notice how writers present information in interesting ways. Readers notice how writers make information interesting. Readers notice words writers have selected to get them interested.
Organization of the Text *(narrative, sequential, categorical)*	Readers notice how the writer has presented the information in the text: ▫ Things that are like a story (narrative). ▫ Things that happened in time (sequential). ▫ Things that go together (categorical).
Features *(specific features of nonfiction that guide the reader–graphics, print features)*	Readers notice how writers label information. Readers notice how illustrations/graphics show the information in a different way. Readers notice how illustrations and graphics add more information. Readers notice how the print changes to communicate information (italics, bold, different sizes). Readers notice the information in photographs, drawings, and paintings.
Underlying Structural Patterns for Presenting Information *(description, comparison/ contrast, chronological sequence, cause/effect, problem/solution)*	Readers notice how writers use description to give information. Readers notice how writers compare and contrast ideas or events to provide information. Readers notice how writers provide information in a chronological sequence. Readers notice the way writers show how one thing causes another. Readers notice how writers present a problem and a solution to the problem. Readers notice how writers use several different ways of presenting information.

Figure 23-2. *Using Explicit Language to Communicate Minilesson Principles (cont.)*

without thinking about the true significance of the problem in relation to the character's circumstances or how it is important to understanding the character's perspective and motivations. Sometimes the solution to the problem has symbolic importance that leads to the reader's larger understanding of the human condition.

Mr. T. began by expressing the principle and showing it at the top of a chart. He moved quickly to a well-known

Readers think about the problem in the story when they read.

Figure 23-3. *Minilesson Principle*

Figure 23-4. *Teacher Conducting a Minilesson*

why. By the end of the minilesson, she had completed the chart shown in Figure 23-8.

Look at a brief excerpt from the sharing session at the end of Linda's (Mrs. L.) reading workshop (see Figure 23-9). It didn't take very long for Linda to revisit the minilesson principle, have students share their own observations in partners, and then have a few students say something to the whole group. In all, about seven or eight children shared with the whole group, but notice that Linda did not stop and engage in a longer discussion of any one book that the other students would not have read.

shared text, *The Name Jar* (Choi), with which the students were very familiar. Several said that Unhei was new to the school or felt strange, but Mr. T. wanted them to dig deeper to get to the significance of the problem. Mr. T. guided them to recall more details from the text and to think about why Unhei's name was so significant. By the end of the lesson, he had finished the chart shown in Figure 23-6.

UNDERSTANDING CHARACTERS

Linda wants her fourth graders to learn how to engage in deeper character analysis so that they can infer characters' motives (see Figure 23-7). Inferring characters' motivations is essential for understanding fiction and often for understanding biography. Only by seeing from the characters' point of view can the reader understand the writer's message in terms of characters' overcoming difficulties.

Linda began by connecting her lesson to the students' letters and stating the minilesson principle clearly. She used two familiar mentor texts, *Lester's Dog* and *The Wolves in the Walls*, to illustrate her points, writing something on the chart about each of them as the students engaged in discussion. They explored two actions on the part of the storyteller in *Lester's Dog*, both of which required overcoming fear. Then they explored two actions on the part of Lucy in *The Wolves in the Walls*. During the lesson, Linda provided several examples to allow her and the students to demonstrate thinking about characters' motivations. She then turned the task over to the students, who (if reading fiction or biography) were asked to come to the sharing session ready to discuss something a character did, with a hypothesis about

MINILESSONS FOR DIFFERENT PURPOSES

Readers need a wide variety of understandings, which you introduce through minilessons in a number of categories. The lessons in each category contribute in different but related ways to your students' development of effective reading systems.

MINILESSONS ON STRATEGIES AND SKILLS OF READING

Many specific skills are directly related to effective comprehending. Strategies and skills in four categories are listed in Figure 23-10. This list could be many pages long! There are hundreds of reading strategies and skills, even if we name only the obvious ones. The topics on this list contribute directly to reading comprehension. There are four categories.

- Vocabulary—for a text to be comprehensible, a reader should know the meaning of at least 90 percent of the words (Carver 2000). While students will and must learn many new words through extensive reading, specific lessons on vocabulary are also needed.

- Thinking within the text—readers must gather and remember essential information necessary to understand the literal meaning of the text as a foundation for thinking beyond it.

- Thinking beyond the text—readers need to think beyond the literal meaning of a text to comprehend it.

- Perspectives as a reader—an important element of comprehension is the reader's stance toward the text formed by his knowledge of genre and his attitudes, opinions, and purpose. A reader needs to know his own preferences and think about the basis for them.

MINILESSON:
Noticing the Problem in the Story

MR. T.: Have you ever noticed that pretty soon after a good story begins, the writer tells how the people or animals in the story have some kind of problem?

STUDENTS: Yes. [READERS THINK ABOUT THE PROBLEM IN THE STORY.]

MR. T.: You remember this story, don't you? *The Name Jar,* by Yangsook Choi?

LISHIE: It's about a girl from Korea who is new and strange to the school.

MR. T.: The main character is Unhei, and she was new to the school. What was Unhei's problem?

SHANA: She was new and felt strange.

ROBERT: She maybe didn't speak English yet very well.

LISHIE: Yes she did, because she got what they were saying and what the teacher was saying.

MR. T.: How did you know, Lishie, that she could understand English?

LISHIE: Because when her mother asked her what was wrong and could she understand the teacher, she said yes. And her mother said she was proud.

MR. T.: You are noticing the details to explain your thinking. Now let's think more about the specific problem Unhei has in the story.

SEELEY: It's her name. They couldn't say it right.

MR. T.: It was hard for the children to say her name. That's a problem, isn't it? Why was that a very important problem for Unhei to solve?

CLIFF: She really liked her Korean name but she was afraid the kids would just keep teasing her and stuff.

FARA: It was too hard to say.

LISHIE: She could get called Amanda or Laura or names like that, because she wanted to be like the other kids.

SEELEY: She could be called Grace, because that's what her name means.

MR. T.: How did you know that?

SEELEY: That's what the man in the store said—she was graceful. So it's Grace.

MR. T.: I'd forgotten that—that's really good thinking. So the problem in this story is that Unhei feels some conflict, doesn't she. How do you know her Korean name means a lot to her?

ROBERT: She had the name stamp from her grandma in Korea. It says her name and is beautiful. It kind of reminds her of her grandma.

MR. T.: Yes, her name is important to her. The writer told about the name stamp at the beginning of the story and helped us understand how important her Korean name was. But she also wants the other kids to like her—just like all of you do. So her problem was to find a way to make a decision about her name that would be satisfying to her.

LISHIE: And she did it! She kept her Korean name and the other kids learned it.

MR. T.: Right, she did solve her problem in the story with the help of . . .

ROBERT: Her friend.

MR. T.: Her friend Joey, who took the name jar. So today when you are reading, think about the important problem in the story you are reading. There might be more than one problem, or there might be a problem in the chapter you are reading. When you have found the problem in your story, think about it so you can share it with the class. You might want to put a stick-on note in the part to help you remember.

Figure 23-5. *Minilesson: Noticing the Problem in the Story*

MINILESSONS ON LITERARY ANALYSIS

Comprehending is intricately related to understanding the literary quality of a text (see Figure 23-11). Literary analysis involves stepping back and considering the text as an object—thinking about it as a work of literature.

MINILESSONS ON ANALYZING THE WRITER'S CRAFT

When you use minilessons to help your students engage in literary analysis, you can decide to go one step further to

Unhei liked her Korean name, but she wanted the American kids to like her.

Unhei needed to make a decision about her name

Figure 23-6. *Readers Think About the Problem in the Story*

MINILESSON:
Understanding Characters

MRS. L.: Readers think about what characters do and why they do it to help them understand the character. We all do things for a specific reason, and usually it is because of the kind of person we are. So we need to be thinking about the characters in our stories that way, too. Let's think about *Lester's Dog.* Remember that great story? Why did the boy, the one who was telling us the story, actually go with Corey past Lester's dog? We know how frightened he was of Lester's dog. Why do you think the boy went with Corey?

KAREN: Because Corey talked him into it, and, really, he didn't really have a choice.

DEREK: He felt braver with his friend.

MARK: When he was coming back with the kitten, he was sort of brave.

MRS. L.: This was at the very beginning of the story, and we know that he didn't want to go past Lester's dog but he went anyway. What was the relationship between the boy telling the story and Corey?

ANTHONY: They were best friends.

MRS. L.: So why do you think the boy was willing to go with Corey across and in front of Lester's dog?

KATE: Because he knew he could trust him.

MRS. L.: So it's because they were such good friends, right? [WRITES "GOOD FRIENDS" ON THE CHART.] And maybe he thought Corey was going to protect him. [WRITES "COREY WOULD PROTECT HIM" ON THE CHART.] In another part in the story, the narrator stands up to Lester's dog. Why did he do that?

MARK: He was protecting the cat and he didn't want the cat to get hurt.

ANTHONY: Because he didn't even think about the dog maybe. He just went past it because knew he had the cat and he was trying to save it.

MRS. L.: Great, so he was strong because he was thinking about that cute little kitten in his hands, wasn't he? [WRITES "BECAUSE HE WAS PROTECTING THE KITTEN" ON THE CHART.] Let's think about another book together. This is *The Wolves in the Walls*. Remember the main character, Lucy? Remember that first time when they had gotten chased out of the house by the wolves? But Lucy went back and got her pig puppet. Why did she do that?

KATE: Because that was like her favorite thing.

DONNA: Because she wanted to be brave and stand up to the wolves.

BRIAN: So she saw that all the other wolves were playing with her brother's toys and her dad's tuba and stuff and she didn't want anyone to play with her pig puppet.

MRS. L.: What do you think about her pig puppet? How did she feel about her pig puppet?

MARK: She loved it.

MRS. L.: So it was her friend, wasn't it, and she loved it. [WRITES "HER FRIEND AND SHE LOVES IT" ON THE CHART.] Then, Lucy decided to get the wolves out of her house, didn't she? Why do you think she did that?

Figure 23-7. *Minilesson: Understanding Characters*

MINILESSON:
Understanding Characters (CONTINUED)

DAVID: Because she couldn't take it anymore.

ANNA: Because the house was getting wrecked and she didn't want her house to be like that.

MIKE: Because she wanted her toys back and her house.

ALLIE: So her family can get back in the house.

MORGAN: Also she didn't really understand because they said when the wolves go into the walls, it's all over. She didn't really understand it and she didn't want it to happen.

MRS. L.: And she didn't want it to be all over, did she? And she wanted her house back, didn't she? [WRITES "SHE WANTED HER HOUSE BACK" ON THE CHART.] Remember they talked about all the different places they could move and she said, "Absolutely not. We are going back in." And she convinced her parents and her brothers to go back in with her and get the wolves out. So readers think about what characters do, and today in reading workshop, I want you to think about the characters in the story you are reading. When you think about something that happened, ask yourself, "Why did that character do that? What does that tell us about the character?" I want you to mark the place in the book where something happened, and then I want you to be ready at group share to talk about it with us—about what happened and why the character did that. Does everyone understand what we are doing in reading workshop now?

Figure 23-7. *Minilesson: Understanding Characters (cont.)*

Figure 23-8. *Readers Think About What Characters Do In Order to Understand e Characters*

EXCERPT FROM SHARING AFTER THE MINILESSON ON
Understanding Characters

MRS. L.: Readers think about what characters do and why they do it to understand the character. So today look at your stick-on notes and talk with a partner about what your characters did and why. Then we will share with the whole group. Turn and talk to your partner and share your thinking around it. [STUDENTS TALK WITH PARTNERS.]

MRS. L.: Now let's come back to the whole group. When you share, we want you to tell us what the character did and then share your thinking about why the character did that.

SAMANTHA: She started her own club because she wanted to be cool like other people in her class.

FELICIA: The babysitter had the kids eat magic cookies so she could get back at them for tricking her.

MRS. L.: A little bit of active revenge!

MARK: My character in the book tried to run away.

MRS. L.: Why did he do that?

MARK: Because he was afraid of living with his mom.

MRS. L.: So it's important for you to be thinking about the characters in the books you are reading. When they do something, it is very helpful to you as a reader to think about why they did that. That way you can really understand your character.

Figure 23-9. *Excerpt from Sharing After the Minilesson on Understanding Characters*

MINILESSONS ON
Strategies and Skills of Reading (Emphasis on Comprehension)

CATEGORY	MINILESSON TOPIC
Vocabulary	□ Solving the meaning of a word by using context. □ Noticing interesting or new vocabulary. □ Noticing words that have new meaning in new contexts.
Thinking Within the Text	□ Identifying dialogue as communication between characters. □ Identifying assigned, split, and unassigned dialogue. □ Identifying the speaker in unassigned dialogue through thinking about the story meaning. □ Understanding how to follow dialogue to know what is going on. □ Understanding the differences between narration and dialogue. □ Distinguishing between what a character says and what the narrator says about a character. □ Noticing pronouns that signal point of view and choice of "person" (*I, you, he*). □ Summarizing the story. □ Recognizing the use of print features—italics. □ Recognizing the use of print features—bold. □ Recognizing the use of print features—larger and smaller font. □ Understanding the use of symbols. □ Understanding how to read punctuation to aid in the construction of meaning. □ Understanding when you need to read a whole text and when you can "dip in." □ Understanding how readers' tools (table of contents, glossary, or index) help you as a reader. □ Following the passing of time in a plot. □ Recognizing that texts have a chronological pattern. □ Using the features of nonfiction texts to locate specific information. □ Understanding how to rapidly read for and highlight specific information (scan a text). □ Understanding how to skim text to get a general understanding.
Thinking Beyond the Text	□ Understanding that some information is stated and some is implied. □ Understanding how to use what you know about the series (characters, setting) to help you understand a new book in the same series. □ Identifying unanswered questions. □ Connecting the text to personal experiences and knowledge. □ Connecting the text to other texts, authors, and illustrators. □ Using evidence from the text or personal experience to support your thinking. □ Understanding what you know about a writer's style to understand a new text by an author.
Perspectives as a Reader	□ Understanding that readers have special genres that they like and why. □ Understanding that readers find authors that they like and why. □ Understanding that readers find illustrators that they like and why. □ Understanding that there are special types of books that readers like (mystery, adventure, humorous) and why. □ Understanding that readers can share their thinking about a text through talking or writing. □ Understanding that readers support their thinking with evidence from the text or their own personal experiences.

Figure 23-10. *Minilessons on Strategies and Skills of Reading (Emphasis on Comprehension)*

MINILESSONS ON
Literary Analysis

ELEMENT	MINILESSON TOPIC
Characters	<ul><li>Noticing the physical, mental, and emotional traits of characters.</li><li>Learning about characters through descriptions of what they are like, what they do, what they say or think, what others say or think about them, and what the writer seems to think about them.</li><li>Recognizing the main character.</li><li>Noticing how characters change or develop.</li><li>Empathizing with characters—how they feel, what they want or need.</li><li>Predicting characters' actions or behaviors.</li><li>Recognizing character traits and providing specific evidence from the text.</li><li>Noticing whether a character stays the same or changes.</li><li>Noticing how the writer provides details to help readers imagine and understand the character.</li></ul>
Plot/Problem	<ul><li>Recognizing the problem in the story.</li><li>Identifying the challenges characters encounter.</li><li>Identifying the choices characters have.</li><li>Recognizing how characters affect one another.</li><li>Recognizing the most important events in the story.</li><li>Recognizing the order of events as they are told—sequence.</li><li>Recognizing patterns of action—foreshadowing.</li><li>Recognizing patterns of action—flashback.</li><li>Recognizing patterns of action—rising and falling.</li><li>Recognizing patterns of action—climax or high point.</li><li>Predicting the story ending from the events and characters' traits.</li><li>Recognizing how the writer uses language or symbolism to foreshadow the events and conclusions.</li><li>Noticing how the writer shows time passing.</li></ul>
Setting	<ul><li>Identifying the setting from the writer's description.</li><li>Understanding the relationship between the setting and characters' thoughts and feelings.</li><li>Understanding the relationship between the setting and the events of the plot.</li><li>Understanding the relationship between the setting and the mood or tone of the story.</li><li>Noticing how the writer reveals the setting.</li><li>Noticing how the writer helps readers understand the significance of the setting.</li></ul>
Theme	<ul><li>Identifying the main idea or "big idea" of the story.</li><li>Identifying what the writer is trying to say.</li><li>Distinguishing between the plot and the theme</li></ul>
Style/Language	<ul><li>Finding memorable words and phrases.</li><li>Noticing strong verbs and their effect on meaning.</li><li>Noticing figurative language and its effect on meaning (simile, metaphor).</li><li>Noticing surprising language and its effect on meaning.</li><li>Recognizing alliterative language and its effect on meaning or mood.</li><li>Noticing onomatopoetic language and its effect on meaning or mood.</li><li>Recognizing personification and its effect on meaning.</li><li>Noticing how the writer uses language to appeal to the senses (see, hear, touch, taste).</li><li>Noticing how the writer has used dialogue (assigned, split, or unassigned).</li></ul>

gure 23-11. *Minilessons on Literary Analysis*

MINILESSONS ON *Literary Analysis* (CONTINUED)	
ELEMENT	**MINILESSON TOPIC**
Mood/Tone	□ Understanding how language shows mood and tone. □ Identifying the mood or tone of a text. □ Identifying and recognizing the "lead," or how the author engages readers. □ Noticing how the writer uses language to create a mood, tone, or feeling in the reader.
Point of View	□ Identifying the point of view from which a story is told. □ Understanding who is telling the story—the narrator. □ Understanding that a story is usually told in first or third person. □ Understanding texts that are told in second person (directly to the reader). □ Understanding the events from a different perspective (different character, different group of people, different setting).
Illustrations	□ Noticing and thinking about important information in the art. □ Identifying questions you would like to ask the illustrator. □ Seeing the relationship between the art and the words. □ Gaining the meaning of the text through art and words. □ Noticing how the illustrator provides additional information or reflects the mood or the spirit of the text. □ Noticing how the art and the narrative are integrated.
Text Organization and Structure	□ Understanding the shape or structure of a text. □ Understanding how the writer compares and contrasts information. □ Understanding how the writer presents problems and solutions. □ Understanding the writer's use of descriptive language. □ Understanding how the writer organizes events in chronological sequence. □ Understanding the writer's use of language to reveal cause and effect.

Figure 23-11. *Minilessons on Literary Analysis (cont.)*

help them "read like a writer." Understanding the text from the writer's point of view or the decisions the writer makes will help students think about the text in complex ways that will contribute both to their reading and their writing skills. Exploration of any of the topics listed in Figure 23-12, for example, will reveal what effective writers do. For example, identifying and noticing the "lead" and how it affected readers will, over time, suggest to students how they might begin their own pieces of writing.

The process of "reading like a writer" is outlined in Figure 23-12.

You also want your students to learn how to "read like a writer." Understanding the text from the writer's point of view will help them think about the text in complex ways that will contribute both to their reading and their writing skills.

Noticing the Writer's Craft

1 Help students notice any aspect of a text as a literary quality.
2 Build students' understanding of literary quality over time through encountering many examples.
3 Invite students to "think like a writer" by exploring what writers do and discussing why they make their choices or decisions.

Figure 23-12. *Noticing the Writer's Craft*

MINILESSONS ON CRITICAL THINKING

An effective reader thinks critically about texts. With the plethora of written material available to them, it is important for students to begin to take an evaluative stance toward texts. Minilessons on critical reading are listed in Figure 23-13.

It takes years for readers to become sophisticated enough to think critically about the texts they read, but

MINILESSONS ON
Critical Thinking

ELEMENT	MINILESSON TOPIC
Quality of Writing	▫ Evaluating the quality of the writing and providing evidence to support points.
Believability of the Text	▫ Judging the believability of the text. ▫ Providing evidence that the text is believable (or not).
Authenticity of the Text	▫ Evaluating the qualifications of the author to write on a topic. ▫ Distinguishing between fact and theory. ▫ Evaluating the timeliness or currency of the information.
Integrity of the Text	▫ Evaluating the writer's use of stereotypes. ▫ Evaluating the inclusiveness of the text to reflect diversity. ▫ Noticing a variety of viewpoints in an informational text. ▫ Evaluating the objectivity of the writer in reporting on the topic.

gure 23-13. *Minilessons on Critical Thinking*

oing so is an important aspect of comprehension. Critical inking is more than opinion. Readers need to make judgents about what they are reading, judgments that are oughtful, grounded in the text, and well founded. Most dividuals need a wide range of experiences and many pportunities to develop as critical readers.

MINILESSONS ON GENRE

or further discussion of the key role that understanding enre plays in proficient reading, see Chapter 11 of this ook. As we have discussed, knowledge of the characteristics f the genre provides strong support for comprehending (see igure 23-14).

MINILESSONS ON RESPONDING TO A TEXT

ou will want to provide explicit demonstrations to help ur students learn how to respond to a text through talking, writing, and sometimes drawing. Response cannot mply be assigned if you expect thoughtful, high-quality lk and writing. In Figure 23-15 we have listed potential inilesson topics in this area.

Students will not automatically know how to respond to text by talking, drawing, or writing. We've all opened a discssion only to find that students don't have much to say or e have asked them to provide a written response and been isappointed. Students need some powerful demonstrations nd examples, as well as specific directions and a great any opportunities, before they will be able to provide the inds of responses we want.

In general, the more you engage children in talking about texts, the better written responses you will get. If they are talking about interesting books in a variety of ways, they will write about the books in an interesting way. You also need to show children you value their thinking. Sketching and drawing are ways to support both talking and writing (Rief 1992). More specific suggestions for helping students with a variety of written responses to reading are included in Chapters 27 and 28.

SELECTING MINILESSONS

Although we want you to use shared texts as resources in reading workshop, we have avoided suggesting a single text or even a few texts as "good" for teaching one strategy or one kind of analysis. Rather than picking up a book because it is "good for teaching inference," you'll want to decide what you want to teach and then look at any good text through that lens—that's basic to *teaching readers* rather than *teaching texts*. In fact, you can use a rich shared or mentor text that students understand and love as a resource for minilessons on a whole range of topics. A rich text offers numerous opportunities for learning. While you do not want to ruin a text by too much analysis, you do want a variety of examples; reconsidering known texts helps students understand your points clearly.

Given the large number of potential minilesson topics, it is easy to be overwhelmed. Remember that minilessons are focused. You will not be teaching more than one prin-

MINILESSONS ON *Genre*	
ELEMENT	**MINILESSON PRINCIPLE**
Fiction	□ Understanding that there are different kinds of fiction texts. □ Understanding the characteristics of all fiction texts. □ Learning how fiction and nonfiction are different.
Realistic Fiction	□ Learning what realistic fiction is. □ Learning how realistic texts are different from fantasy.
Contemporary Realistic Fiction	□ Recognizing realistic fiction. □ Differentiating realistic fiction from historical fiction. □ Differentiating realistic fiction from fantasy and science fiction. □ Understanding the characteristics of realistic fiction. □ Understanding the implications of realistic fiction for understanding oneself and others. □ Recognizing bias or stereotyping in realistic fiction texts—culture, gender, race, age, treatment of the impaired, religion. □ Recognizing common themes in realistic fiction—survival, courage, death and dying, poverty, upward mobility, persistence, family relationships, tragedy. □ Recognizing and understanding common types of realistic fiction—humor, animal stories, sports, school, and mysteries.
Historical Fiction	□ Recognizing historical fiction. □ Recognizing the lesson in historical fiction for today's world. □ Recognizing the values of historical fiction. □ Recognizing the settings in historical fiction—prehistoric times, stories of the old world (e.g., ancient, Medieval); stories of the new world (e.g., Colonial, revolutionary America, Native Americans, frontier, Civil War (slavery, war); Twentieth Century (immigrants, African Americans, war). □ Recognizing and understanding recurring themes in historical fiction—clash of cultures, search for freedom, overcoming handicaps, effects of war, effects of natural disasters, struggle against evil or tyranny.
Fantasy	□ Recognizing the characteristics of fantasy. □ Understanding and recognizing the elements of fantasy. □ Learning how fantasy is different from realistic texts. □ Evaluating the believability of fantasy.
Traditional Literature	□ Noticing the characteristics of traditional literature. □ Recognizing traditional literature by its structure. □ Recognizing language associated with traditional literature. □ Recognizing the types of characters in traditional literature. □ Recognizing motifs in traditional tales: shape changing, power of naming, magical powers, transformations through love, magic objects, wishes, trickery, clever young or smaller person, important numbers—"threes" or "sevens." □ Recognizing common themes across traditional literature: Cinderella, the magic pot or stone soup, generous versus greedy person, helpful companions, magic beans—Jack and the Beanstalk, clever young or smaller person. □ Understanding types of folktales—*cumulative, pourquoi, beast, wonder,* and *realistic.* □ Understanding that there are variants of folktales from different cultures and regions. □ Recognizing relationships between the culture or region and the way the folktale is told.

Figure 23-14. *Minilessons on Genre*

MINILESSONS ON
Genre (CONTINUED)

ELEMENT	MINILESSON PRINCIPLE
Traditional Literature (cont.)	<ul><li>Recognizing and understanding Native Americans (Plains, Woodland, Southwest, Northwest, Southeast, Eskimo).</li><li>Understanding the source and characteristics of fables.</li><li>Understanding the source and characteristics of myths and legends—creation, nature, hero.</li><li>Understanding the characteristics of epics and legendary heroes.</li></ul>
Simple Modern Fantasy	<ul><li>Understanding the text as fantasy related to reality.</li><li>Understanding and recognizing types of fantasy—personified animals, toys, or other inanimate objects; humorous or eccentric characters; preposterous situations; extraordinary worlds; magical or supernatural powers; time shift.</li><li>Understanding the human traits of nonhuman characters such as animals.</li><li>Understanding the setting and its relation to the plot.</li><li>Making connections between modern fantasy and traditional literature.</li><li>Evaluating the logic and common sense in a fantasy.</li><li>Evaluating originality of plot in a fantasy.</li><li>Noticing details that make the plot believable.</li></ul>
High Fantasy	<ul><li>Identifying the text as a highly complex fantasy.</li><li>Understanding the characteristics of high fantasy (recurring themes and motifs, often a series).</li><li>Understanding the motifs of high fantasy—quest, hero, struggle between good and evil.</li><li>Becoming familiar with the characteristics of language in high fantasy.</li><li>Understanding the setting and its relation to the plot.</li><li>Making connections between high fantasy and traditional literature.</li><li>Evaluating originality of plot in high fantasy.</li><li>Noticing details that make the plot believable.</li><li>Identifying the unvoiced truth that is the metaphor of fantasy.</li><li>Comparing a work of fantasy to other works by the same or different authors.</li></ul>
Science Fiction	<ul><li>Understanding the characteristics of science fiction—fantasy with technological component, often futuristic.</li><li>Distinguishing between fantasy and science fiction.</li></ul>
Nonfiction Genres	<ul><li>Understanding the features of nonfiction texts.</li><li>Understanding the structures of nonfiction texts.</li><li>Understanding the characteristics of literary nonfiction.</li><li>Understanding when an author is giving facts or interpreting facts in informational books (both biographical and factual).</li><li>Understanding that when information is not known, the writer often uses words like *perhaps, some say, possibly, it is likely that,* or *probably.*</li><li>Understanding how sequential information is presented in graphics—illustrated timeline, flowchart, graph timeline, quotation timeline.</li><li>Understanding and using authors' notes to gain insights regarding the authors' motives, discoveries of information, or the historical context.</li></ul>
Biographical Texts	<ul><li>Understanding the characteristics of biography.</li><li>Understanding why a subject is selected.</li><li>Revealing the writer's attitude toward the subject.</li><li>Understanding the organization of a biography (chronological sequence or other).</li><li>Understanding how the writer reveals the setting.</li></ul>

ure 23-14. *Minilessons on Genre (cont.)*

MINILESSONS ON *Genre* (CONTINUED)	
ELEMENT	**MINILESSON PRINCIPLE**
Biography	□ Understanding the nature and features of biographical texts.
	□ Understanding authentic biography and fictionalized biography.
	□ Understanding the structure of biographical texts (linear, flashback, selected events, or characteristics).
	□ Evaluating the elements of biography—choice of subject, accuracy, authenticity, style, characterization, and theme.
	□ Understanding the types and characteristics of picture book biographies, autobiographies, and memoirs—shorter, more simplified biographies, partial or complete, one subject or a collective, real images (photos) or imagined images that reflect reality as much as possible (paintings, drawings).
	□ Understanding the setting in a biography and how it influences the person's decisions.
	□ Understanding how a person's decisions affected his/her life as described in the biography.
	□ Recognizing and understanding the turning points in a person's life when important decisions were made.
	□ Understanding what might have happened if different decisions had been made by the subject.
	□ Recognizing and noting information sources, motives, biases, or inconsistencies in a biography.
	□ Distinguishing between reporting facts and historical interpretation in biography.
	□ Understanding how an author's or illustrator's note adds to understanding of a biography.
	□ Understanding how to identify the primary sources used for biography as a means of judging accuracy in interpretation.
	□ Analyzing and comparing several biographies of the same subject to interpret perspectives on the past.
	□ Understanding how biographers shape and structure information, use captions, use details and anecdotes, and use information from primary and secondary sources.
	□ Understand how biographers select art to build interest in the subject.
Autobiography	□ Understanding the characteristics of an autobiography.
	□ Understanding why a person would write an autobiography.
	□ Hypothesizing why an individual would select particular information to report.
	□ Noticing the specific details a person provides about his or her life.
	□ Noticing the organization of the autobiography (chronological sequence or other).
Memoir	□ Understanding the characteristics of a memoir.
	□ Thinking about why a person would write a memoir.
	□ Understanding a writer's reasons for selecting a particular time of his or her life.
	□ Noticing the writer's use of language to convey an intense or poignant memory.
Factual Texts	□ Understanding the features of factual texts.
	□ Understanding the overall structure of factual texts (categorical, logical organization).
	□ Understanding underlying structures that writers use to present information—enumeration, chronological sequence, comparison and contrast, cause and effect, problem and solution, and description.
"How-To" Books	□ Understanding the nature of "how-to" books.
	□ Noticing how writers make sequence understood.
	□ Noticing how writers use language to make directions clear.

Figure 23-14. *Minilessons on Genre (cont.)*

MINILESSONS ON
Genre (CONTINUED)

ELEMENT	MINILESSON PRINCIPLE
Readers' Tools	□ Understanding how to read a table of contents. □ Understanding how to read a glossary or index. □ Understanding the differences between a table of contents and an index. □ Understanding how to use a variety of readers' tools such as pronunciation guides, scales, legends, labels, forewords, epilogues, author's notes.
Poetic Texts	□ Identifying the features of a poetic text. □ Understanding the characteristics of poetry. □ Understanding the elements of poetry–rhythm, rhyme, repetition, figurative language. □ Recognizing the shape of a poem and its distinction from prose. □ Understanding the underlying meaning in poems.
Poems from Diverse Cultures	□ Recognizing that poetry can reflect a culture or group of people. □ Using poetry to learn the feelings of a group of people.
Traditional Rhymes, Songs, Verses	□ Understanding the role of traditional rhymes, songs, and verses in history. □ Identifying the features of traditional rhymes, songs, and verses.
Narrative Poetry	□ Recognizing that poems can tell a story. □ Recognizing a ballad (narrative poem that can be sung). □ Recognizing that narrative poetry can be fiction, historical fiction, biography, or history.
Lyrical Poetry	□ Recognizing poetry that has a singing quality. □ Recognizing elements of poetry such as rhyme, rhythm, and imagery.
Blank Verse	□ Recognizing the characteristics of blank verse. □ Seeing the poetic quality in poetry that does not rhyme.
Specific Text Formats	□ Understanding how to look at text features in different formats: picture books, letters, advertisements, posters, reviews, etc. □ Understanding the relationship between format, content, purpose, and audience.
Mystery	□ Understanding the characteristics of mysteries. □ Identifying the problem and searching for clues.
Adventure	□ Understanding what makes an adventure story. □ Understanding that an adventure can be fiction or nonfiction. □ Noticing how a writer uses language to build suspense or show tension.
Content Reports	□ Understanding the characteristics of a report. □ Understanding that writers use content-specific language.

Figure 23-14. *Minilessons on Genre (cont.)*

MINILESSONS ON	
Responding to a Text (Talking and Writing About Reading)	
ELEMENT	**MINILESSON PRINCIPLE**
Talking	□ Understanding how to express ideas about a text.
	□ Understanding how to present ideas orally in an organized way.
	□ Understanding how to share ideas in a way that a listener can understand.
Writing	□ Understanding how to respond to specific quotes from the text.
	□ Knowing how to take notes or mark a text quickly and efficiently.
	□ Creating a timeline or chart to record thoughts.
	□ Using an organizer or notes to write a longer piece in response to reading a text.
	□ Writing a poem in response to a book.
	□ Writing a short summary statement (plot summary) of a text.
	□ Understanding that readers can mark a text or make notes to help them remember something.
Drawing	□ Understanding how to make quick sketches to capture information or express mood.
	□ Understanding how to use drawing as a basis for talking.

Figure 23-15. *Minilessons on Responding to a Text (Talking and Writing About Reading)*

ciple in a lesson, and you may return to that principle several times to reinforce it in other reading or writing contexts. You may want to revisit some principles several times with different examples. You will also want to teach several related minilessons rather than jumping around so that you can build deeper understanding. With a limited number of days in the school year, you will want to be selective, focusing your instructional time on principles that expand children's thinking about texts.

As you select minilessons to teach, there is only one consideration: what do your students need to learn how to do as readers? Of course, you'll want to consider your required curriculum (state or district) and/or the kinds of questions and language students will be expected to understand and use to show their competencies on tests. Basic cognitive strategies such as predicting, inferring, and analyzing appear on most curriculum guides and state standards at almost every grade level—just at increasingly sophisticated levels. For students who are struggling, curriculum requirements and testing will be important, but you also need to consider foundational understandings that students need to acquire. They will need many, many opportunities to apply the strategies to texts they can actually read and understand, which happens every day in a rigorous reading workshop.

SUGGESTIONS FOR PROFESSIONAL DEVELOPMENT: ANALYZING A READING MINILESSON

1 Work with a group of colleagues. Observe and discuss Rosemary's and Rebecca's minilessons on the DVD that accompanies this book. What makes their lessons effective? Plan to tape one minilesson related to the topics listed in the chapters.

2 As a group, watch each taped minilesson.

3 After watching the minilesson, discuss:
- □ How did the teacher use specific language to help students understand the principle?
- □ How did the teacher use examples from the shared text to help students understand the principle?
- □ How did the teacher engage students in thinking more deeply about the minilesson principle?
- □ How did the lesson start and end?
- □ How did the teacher communicate expectations for independent reading?

4 Have a general discussion of the components of minilessons that should be considered in planning them.

5 Then look at the lists of minilessons in this chapter (Figures 23-10 through 23-15). Discuss what your students already understand and what they need to understand.

CHAPTER TWENTY-FOUR

USING GUIDED READING TO TEACH FOR COMPREHENDING AND FLUENCY

The ultimate goal in guided reading is to teach the students to use reading strategies independently so that they can read texts and discuss them critically.

—NEW ZEALAND MINISTRY OF EDUCATION

Guided reading plays a particular and very important role in reading workshop. Its purpose is to help readers develop systems of strategic actions for processing increasingly challenging texts. Extensive reading, even in connection with individual conferences, as important as it is, will not necessarily produce systematic and continuous reading progress. Reading minilessons, while also important, are not sufficient. Most students require systematic small-group reading instruction. They need to learn how to read, with comprehension and fluency, across a gradient of texts that makes ever increasing demands. In our view, this means they need teaching.

The discussion here does not go into detail about the "nuts and bolts" of guided reading instruction: our books *Guided Reading: Good First Teaching for All Students* and *Guiding Readers and Writers: Teaching Comprehension, Fluency, and Content Literacy* provide a great deal of detailed information about this instructional approach. We will start with some brief descriptions but move to the central goal of small-group instruction: teaching for comprehending and fluency.

THE ROLE OF GUIDED READING IN READING WORKSHOP

Guided reading is an instructional approach in which you bring together a small group of students who are similar enough in their reading development that they can be taught together for a period of time. You select a particular text that provides opportunities for them to expand their processing powers.

Within reading workshop, you can provide this small-group instruction while the other students engage in silent, independent reading or writing in a reader's notebook. For children in kindergarten and first grade, you may want to

provide a variety of meaningful literacy experiences at centers while you meet with the guided reading groups. Alternatively, you can give them two or three specific literacy tasks to complete while you are providing guided reading instruction. They can work at these activities at their own pace.

A guided reading lesson has the following characteristics:

- You work with readers who are alike enough in their reading development and can be taught in a small, temporary group.

- The group is not static; its composition will change periodically according to student growth. You move students into or out of this group as a result of your observations and systematic assessments.

- Students read the same text, selected by you, and receive explicit instruction that will help them expand their reading processing systems.

- The text is "just right" in that students can read it successfully with the support of your teaching. It offers a small bit of challenge to allow the processing system to expand.

- You select the text using a gradient of difficulty (see Chapter 12) that matches the readers' development. You gradually increase text difficulty to provide more varied demands as appropriate.

When students are focusing on the same text in a small group, you can provide very specific instruction directed toward all aspects of the reading process. You can help students engage with a text that is at an appropriate level and provides opportunity for them to learn more about the reading process. Your goal is for students to do a great deal of reading accompanied by instruction that supports successful processing and expands systems of strategic actions. The more successful readers are and the more text they read, the better readers they become (Stanovich 1986).

THE STRUCTURE OF A GUIDED READING LESSON

Guided reading lessons have the same basic structure from kindergarten through grade eight. Each component of the guided reading lesson has implications for students' learning. If you plan your teaching based on the twelve systems of strategic actions and take advantage of students' responses as they arise, you can teach for effective processing throughout the guided reading lesson. Remember, your goal is to teach the reader, not just to get them through the book. This means you are helping readers learn how to do something with this text that they will be able to do while processing other texts.

Overall, the guided reading lesson is *all* about helping individual readers build their systems for processing texts. Although the framework is structured and supportive, the conversations you have with children will vary according to their responses. In fact, no two guided reading lessons— even if they involve the same text—are alike, because the lesson is interactive. In any lesson, there are numerous opportunities to teach for comprehending and fluency (see Figure 24-1). Here we focus specifically on teaching with a "lens" for comprehending across the lesson. Notice that even word work supports the reader's ability to comprehend successfully.

Selecting the Text

Select a text that readers will enjoy and find entertaining and that will also present opportunities to learn more. Though you will sometimes need to choose books that are above a student's grade level, don't reach too far. Texts that are more than one or two years above age and grade level can be uninteresting or hard to understand in depth. You can challenge students thinking about texts and broaden their genre knowledge without simply climbing up levels. Also choose a text that allows the readers to use what they know about reading and learn a little bit more, one that provides the right level of support and challenge for the reader's processing abilities. Think about particular factors such as:

- Print layout and spacing.
- Familiarity and sophistication of content.
- Known and new high frequency words.
- Support provided by illustrations and other art.
- Length.
- Familiarity of language or syntax.
- Amount of new vocabulary.
- Graphic or other text features.
- Organization of information.

Introducing the Text

The text introduction is critical: you need to provide just enough information to ensure that the students will be able to problem-solve or process this slightly challenging text successfully. Your job is to unlock the text, make it more accessible, and then to allow the readers to use their processing systems to think about and problem-solve their way through the text. There are numerous opportunities for you to help readers use effective reading strategies.

The introduction should be conversational. The way you shape the conversation can help you attend to anything your students need to know how to do relative to this text. You want to provide scaffolds that will enable readers to access the full meaning, the language, and the print. As you plan your brief introductions, think about the reading process, the demands of the text, and the readers' strength and needs. You might:

- Call attention to a few difficult words in context.
- Explain a few concepts or vocabulary.
- Foreshadow a problem.
- Build interest in the text.
- Activate background knowledge (about a topic, theme, genre, setting, characters).
- Get students wondering about something in the text.
- Invite students to make predictions, raise questions, and anticipate the text.
- Point out something unusual in the print or layout.
- Show the organization of the text or how it works.
- Point out unusual language structures—have them hear them and sometimes say them.
- Show how to recognize—break apart—two or three new words.
- Point out unfamiliar text features such as bold type, italics, ellipses.

Teaching for Comprehending and Fluency Across a Guided Reading Lesson

LESSON ELEMENT	TEACHING MOVES TO SUPPORT COMPREHENDING AND FLUENCY
Introducing the Text You provide the readers with an understanding of the overall meaning of the text, pointing out aspects that may be new, involving them in a conversation that gets them thinking about the meaning, language, and print, and encouraging their interest in the book.	□ Explore important concepts and ideas. □ Guide the readers to think about important aspects of the text. □ Help readers understand how the text works. □ Activate the content and literary knowledge readers bring to the reading experience. □ Encourage personal connections and help readers make them. □ Help readers make connections. □ Provide essential new information that readers need to understand the text. □ Help the readers understand the organization of the information. □ Enable readers to hear (and sometimes repeat) new language structures or new words. □ Point out text or print features and tools that parallel or add to the meaning of the text. □ Help readers discover information in the art or illustrations or other graphics such as maps, charts, graphic cutaways. □ Draw attention to accuracy or authenticity of the text, writer's credentials, references, presentation of evidence as appropriate. □ Help readers think about ways to solve a few new words if appropriate. □ Get readers to think about qualities of the writer's craft.
Reading the Text The readers engage in a variety of strategic actions to process the whole text or a unified part of it. You may listen to one individual at a time process part of the text, or listen in on all of them if they are whisper reading (emergent readers). You may also engage in brief teaching interactions to support effective reading actions.	□ Prompt readers to initiate problem-solving actions. □ Demonstrate effective ways to search for and use the information in the text. □ Demonstrate effective reading. □ Reinforce effective problem solving of words using the meaning, language, and print. □ Confirm the reader's attempts at problem solving on their own. □ Demonstrate, reinforce, or prompt using self-monitoring or checking strategies to ensure meaning making. □ Demonstrate, reinforce, or prompt self-correcting errors that interfere with meaning making. □ Observe effective reading behaviors. □ Interact with individual readers very briefly around the text meaning. □ Demonstrate, reinforce, or prompt using punctuation to aid meaning, reading with phrasing, pausing appropriately, stressing the correct words, or using expression.

Figure 24-1. *Teaching for Comprehending and Fluency Across a Guided Reading Lesson*

Teaching for Comprehending and Fluency Across a Guided Reading Lesson (CONTINUED)

LESSON ELEMENT	TEACHING MOVES TO SUPPORT COMPREHENDING AND FLUENCY
Discussing and Revisiting the Text You and your students participate in a brief, meaningful conversation about the text. Students may also revisit the text to clarify or locate information or to provide evidence for their thinking.	▫ Invite personal response and sharing of understanding. ▫ Model and promote response to the meaning and language of the text. ▫ Encourage readers to search for new information. ▫ Probe readers to support thinking with personal experience or evidence from the text. ▫ Demonstrate or prompt students to explore the writer's deeper message. ▫ Encourage readers to make predictions and inferences. ▫ Encourage readers to express their opinions and clarify their thinking. ▫ Prompt readers to make connections with their own lives and with other texts. ▫ Demonstrate and prompt students to analyze and critique the writer's craft. ▫ Encourage readers to listen to and build on one another's thinking.
Teaching for Processing Strategies You provide a brief, explicit teaching point focused on any aspect of the reading process. Teaching is grounded in the text students have just read, but readers go beyond it to understand something important and useful.	▫ Revisit the text to demonstrate any aspect of reading, including all systems of strategic actions: ▫ Solving words ▫ Predicting ▫ Monitoring and checking ▫ Making connections ▫ Searching for and using information ▫ Inferring ▫ Remembering information—summarizing ▫ Synthesizing ▫ Maintaining fluency ▫ Analyzing ▫ Adjusting reading—purpose and genre ▫ Critiquing ▫ Explicitly reinforce or demonstrate strategic actions using any part of the text that has just been read.
Working with Words (optional) You provide one or two minutes of work with words. Teaching may focus on any aspect of word solving and is not related to words in the text that have just been read.	▫ Teach any aspect of taking words apart—letter/sound relationships, using analogy, using word parts. ▫ Students work with words in a "hands-on" way ▫ Students develop flexibility and fluency in using word solving strategies. ▫ Have students sort letters according to specific features.
Extending the Understanding of the Text (optional) You invite students to extend understanding of the text through further talk, drawing, or writing. Often, you will work with students to demonstrate ways of writing about texts.	▫ Use writing, drawing, or extended talk to explore any aspect of understanding about the text, (structure or literary elements). ▫ Use writing or drawing as a basis for further talk about texts.

Figure 24-1. *Teaching for Comprehending and Fluency Across a Guided Reading Lesson (cont.)*

Introducing Texts Through a variety of models you will want to introduce the whole text when students can read it in one session. Short texts are very useful because you can teach students how to process a new text and they can take what they learn to a longer text. Figure 24-2 summarizes a variety of ways to introduce whole short texts and parts of longer texts. You will notice that when you use a longer text for instruction you will want to foreground the entire text but introduce each section. The exception is when the students have developed the background from most of the text and you feel they can now process the last section independently.

Reading the Text

Following your introduction, the readers will independently process the whole text or a unified part of it. Students in grade two and above will usually read silently; students in kindergarten and grade one will usually read out loud, very softly, so you will get immediate feedback on the effectiveness of your introduction! (If they are too loud, tell them to "whisper read.") Because they are reading at their own pace, they probably will not finish at exactly the same time. Give them some writing to do in their reader's notebooks or have them read their independent books. If you teach young children, have them reread the text or choose a book to read from a browsing box of similar-level books during the brief time they wait for the discussion to begin. If one student consistently finishes much more slowly than the rest, the level of the text may be too difficult. (An alternative explanation is that the student is reading accurately but has a habit of reading slowly, in which case, you will need to teach intensively for fluency.)

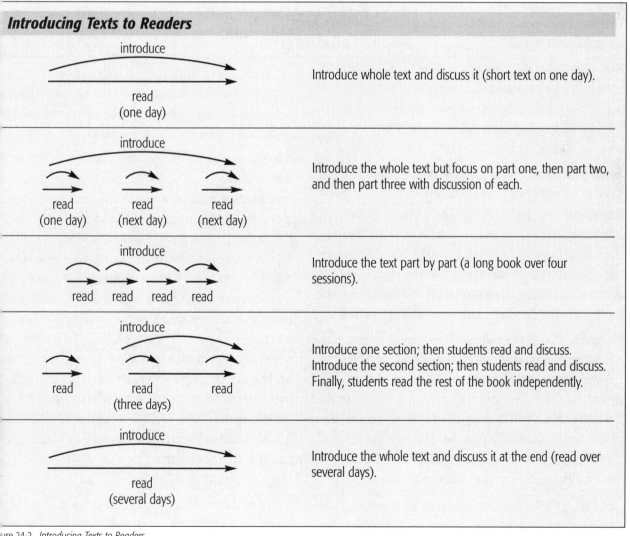

Introducing Texts to Readers

introduce / read (one day)	Introduce whole text and discuss it (short text on one day).
introduce / read (one day) read (next day) read (next day)	Introduce the whole text but focus on part one, then part two, and then part three with discussion of each.
introduce / read read read read	Introduce the text part by part (a long book over four sessions).
introduce / read read (three days) read	Introduce one section; then students read and discuss. Introduce the second section; then students read and discuss. Finally, students read the rest of the book independently.
introduce / read (several days)	Introduce the whole text and discuss it at the end (read over several days).

Figure 24-2. *Introducing Texts to Readers*

As students read the text silently to themselves, you may want to listen to one or more read aloud for a brief time. Just tap the reader's shoulder, or say his name, as a signal to read aloud. Listen as long as you need to to get a feel for how the student is reading the text. This information will inform your teaching after the reading.

As the students read, collect evidence on the effectiveness of the text you selected and your introduction. Observe students' precise reading behaviors so you can think about what aspects of the processing systems they control, almost control, or do not yet control. The level-by-level continuum (*The Continuum of Literacy Learning, PreK–8: A Guide to Teaching*) can serve as a guide to goals for each text level A–Z+. Make notes in a notebook or on a clipboard so you will have the information for assessment and planning. To help you take notes on individuals, you can use the form Systems of Strategic Actions for Processing Written Texts: Observational Notes in Figure 24-3 and on the DVD that accompanies this book.

Teaching During the Reading of the Text You may want to engage in some brief teaching interactions on the spot that will demonstrate, prompt for, or reinforce effective processing (see Figure 24-4), or to talk very briefly with the children about their thinking.

Demonstrating or Teaching When you demonstrate, you teach in an explicit way, "showing how" to process or problem-solve the text. You say things like the following: "Listen to how this reading sounds" (to demonstrate fluency). "The picture can help you think about the words" (to demonstrate using illustrations). "When you come to a tricky part, start the sentence again, think about what would make sense, and say the first sound of the word" (then demonstrate the action).

Prompting for Effective Actions When you use language to remind readers to do something they already know how to do, you are prompting them to initiate problem-solving actions for themselves. It is important that they really do know what you mean by the prompt and can perform the action. We suggest that you use the same language in your demonstration that you will use in your prompt. Figure 24-5 lists useful prompts to support readers' effective processing.

Reinforcing Effective Actions When you see that readers are beginning to initiate effective problem-solving actions on

their own, you will want to reinforce or confirm the actions. The reinforcement will foster further use of effective reading behaviors. For example, instead of saying "Good reading," say something very specific, like "You put your words together," or "You took a short pause at the commas," or "You made your voice go up at the end of the sentence to show that was a question."

Observing Effective Processing If your teaching is effective, you will be able to observe the reader's ability to problem-solve their way through the text independently. You will also want to observe how easily and smoothly problem solving operates. You want your readers to engage in these actions "on the run" while sustaining attention to meaning.

Discussing the Meaning and Revisiting the Text It is important for students to have a chance to discuss the meaning of the text with one another as well as with you. Sometimes you may want to ask questions, of course, but students should know that they are expected to share their own comments or questions. They can ask questions about what they do not understand and build on one another's comments. This authentic exploration of the text is what readers do. As you listen to their comments, you will also gain a great deal of information about the degree to which they understood what they read.

Teaching for Processing Strategies After the discussion, you may need to focus explicitly on one or more aspects of the processing system, for example, making predictions, thinking about what the writer has implied (inferences), analyzing the text, or taking apart words. You can attend to any of the systems of strategic actions. Of course, you need to be selective rather than try to teach everything at once. If students learn (or learn more about) one or two new ways of thinking every time they read a text, their knowledge will grow continuously over time. If they are effectively processing the text, the entire system is getting a massive workout. Base your selection of teaching points on your observations of the students' processing of the text. You may also need to demonstrate fluent reading and have students revisit a section of the text to consciously reflect the meaning through pausing, phrasing, intonation, and stress on words.

Working with Words (Optional)

An optional part of the guided reading lesson is one or two minutes of "word work," a preplanned exploration of the

Systems of Strategic Actions for Processing Written Texts: Observational Notes

Student Name: _____ **Dates Recorded:** _____ **Context:** LD ____ SR ____ GR ____ IR ____

SYSTEMS OF STRATEGIC ACTIONS FOR PROCESSING WRITTEN TEXTS	OBSERVATIONAL NOTES		OBSERVATIONAL NOTES
Strategic Actions for Sustaining Reading		**Strategic Actions for Expanding Thinking**	
Solving Words Using a range of strategies to take words apart and understand what words mean.		**Predicting** Using what is known to think about what will follow while reading continuous text.	
Monitoring and Correcting Checking on whether reading sounds right, looks right, and makes sense and. working to solve problems.		**Making Connections** □ Personal □ World □ Text Searching for and using connections to knowledge gained through their personal experiences, learning about the world, and reading other texts.	
Searching for and Using Information Searching for and using all kinds of information in a text.		**Inferring** Going beyond the literal meaning of a text to think about what is not stated but is implied by the writer.	
Summarizing Putting together and remembering important information and disregarding irrelevant information while reading.		**Synthesizing** Putting together information from the text and from the reader's own background knowledge in order to create new understandings.	
Maintaining Fluency Integrating sources of information in a smoothly operating process that results in expressive, phrased reading.		**Analyzing** Examining elements of a text to know more about how it is constructed and noticing aspects of the writer's craft.	
Adjusting Reading in different ways as appropriate to purpose for reading and type of text.		**Critiquing** Evaluating a text based on the readers' personal, world, or text knowledge and thinking critically about the ideas in it.	

379

Levels of Teaching Interactions in a Guided Reading Lesson

Demonstrate	Show the reader how to take a specific action using simple clear language and providing an explicit demonstration.
Prompt	Use language that calls for the reader to take an action to problem-solve.
Reinforce	Confirm an effective strategic action.
Observe	Notice how the reader processes effectively.

Figure 24-4. *Levels of Teaching Interactions in a Guided Reading Lesson*

Prompting Readers to Monitor, Correct, and Construct Meaning During Reading

READER IS LEARNING HOW TO	TEACHER DEMONSTRATES OR SUPPORTS THE FOLLOWING STRATEGIC ACTIONS
	Self-Monitoring
Check for understanding or a mismatch in meaning, language, or print	Were you right? Does that make sense? Would that make sense? Does that make sense and sound right? Check it. Does that make sense and sound right to you? You said _____. Does that make sense? Check it. Does that look right and make sense to you? Read that again to see if you were right. Check that again. Check it. Does it sound right and look right to you?
Confirm language structure and check for meaning	That looks right, but does it make sense?
Check one source of information with another	That makes sense, but does it sound right? That makes sense, but does it look right? That looks right, but does it make sense?
	Self-Correcting
Predict what makes sense	Try that again and think what would make sense.
Predict what sounds right	Try that again and think what would sound right.
Reread to check and confirm understanding	Try that again. I like the way you worked that out.
Self-correct using multiple sources of information	Something wasn't quite right. You almost got that. See if you can find what is wrong. You're nearly right. Try that again.
Work to make all sources fit together	You figured that out. You're very good at figuring it out. You worked hard at that.
Reread to check and search for print information	Check it. That makes sense, but does it look right?

Figure 24-5. *Prompting Readers to Monitor, Correct, and Construct Meaning During Reading*

Prompting Readers to Monitor, Correct, and Construct Meaning During Reading (CONTINUED)

READER IS LEARNING HOW TO	TEACHER DEMONSTRATES OR SUPPORTS THE FOLLOWING STRATEGIC ACTIONS
	Self-Correcting (continued)
Reread to check and search for language structure	Check it. That makes sense, but does it sound right?
Reread to check and search for meaning	Check it. That looks right, but does it make sense?
Notice and correct error at the point it is made	You fixed that fast. You worked that out quickly.
	Searching for and Using Information
Use information from pictures	Check the picture. Look at the picture. Can the picture help you?
Use story information to solve unknown words	Think about the story. Try that again and think what would make sense?
Predict what would make sense	Are you thinking about the story? Think about what would make sense. Try that again and think what would make sense. Try _____. Would that make sense?
Use language structure as a source of information	Try _____. Would that sound right? What would sound right? Think of what would sound right.
Use pictures to predict meaning	Can the picture help you think about the story? Does that fit the picture? Try that again and look at the picture.
Notice mismatches in meaning and print information	Try _____. Would that make sense and look right? You said _____. Were you right?
Use all sources of information simultaneously	Check it. Does it make sense, sound right, and look right to you? You found [two, three] ways to check whether you were right.
Predict what will come next	What do you think will happen next? (Or, What do you think _____ will do?) Based on what you know, what do you think will happen?

Figure 24-5. Prompting Readers to Monitor, Correct, and Construct Meaning During Reading (cont.)

features of letters or how words are taken apart. For young readers, this is usually a necessary component. You might use magnetic letters or a whiteboard to demonstrate how to use word parts and help the students become better word solvers. Students can manipulate the letters or write words on a whiteboard or piece of paper. Your goal is to develop fast, fluent recognition of letters or words or the ability to take words apart with ease while reading continuous text.

Extending Understanding of the Text (Optional)

Finally, another option is to extend the students' understanding of the text by talking, drawing, or writing about what they have read. This activity speaks directly to the kinds of responses that students are expected to make on tests, but it has value beyond that. Extending the meaning of a text involves representing or reflecting on the text in some way, which, in turn, extends thinking. Students will just have processed a more challenging text, which means they are in an optimal position to extend their understanding. Some possible extensions are listed in Figure 24-6.

Because you are always working with different texts, these suggestions have endless variations. Extending the meaning may also depend on whether the text is fiction or nonfiction (see Figure 24-7). You will not want to engage your students in tasks after reading unless you have evidence that they need to explore the meaning further or can benefit from the activity as they apply strategies to further reading.

ANALYZING GUIDED READING LESSONS

The guided reading lesson is a context you can use to help your students think within, beyond, and about a text. The most important goal is to help each reader build an effective processing system. Within this broader goal is fluent and accurate reading with literal comprehension; without

Ten Suggestions for Extending the Meaning of Texts

1 Discuss the book in pairs or threesomes.
2 Diagram the internal organizational structures in texts—comparison/contrast, problem/solution, cause/effect, sequence, question/answer, story map.
3 Prepare graphic organizers (a character web or a timeline, for example) to reveal the author's craft.
4 Comment on the text in interactive or shared writing.
5 Describe characters, summarize sections of the text, or make a list of key ideas in interactive or shared writing.
6 Respond with "quick writes" that can be shared later.
7 Respond with "quick sketches" that support thinking and can be used as a basis for more talk or writing.
8 Present a readers' theater piece using portions of the text.
9 Write a poem about the book.
10 Collect favorite quotes from the text and tell why they chose them.

Figure 24-6. *Ten Suggestions for Extending the Meaning of Texts*

Extending the Meaning of Fictional and Factual Texts

Extending the meaning of a text means going beyond the literal meaning to perform some kind of analytical thinking and to represent it in a way that helps others understand it.

FICTIONAL	FACTUAL
□ Making hypotheses as to characters' motivations and thoughts.	□ Identifying and using the organizing structure or structures of the text.
□ Predicting actions and events based on past events.	□ Using information in the text to interpret subsequent information as it is given.
□ Identifying the organizing structure of a text.	□ Understanding how ideas, events, or steps in a process are organized in a sequence—how one leads logically to another.
□ Identifying evidence that points to conclusions about the meaning of the text.	
□ Describing relationships among elements of the text—for example, setting (time, place) and the attitudes and motivations of characters or the events of the plot.	□ Identifying comparisons that reveal the properties or characteristics of matter or human events.
□ Identifying the overarching theme of a story—for example, friendship or love, triumphing over fear, loneliness, family, and pets.	□ Identifying causes for phenomena—why physical or social events happen.
□ Identifying how events in a narrative happen in a sequence and how one is connected with another.	□ Identifying and interpreting language that describes important characteristics of natural or social phenomena.
□ Identifying the problem of a narrative and generating alternative possibilities for solving it.	□ Identifying main and subordinate categories of information (and linking to headings, subheadings, and sub-subheadings when necessary).
□ Drawing conclusions about a character and evaluating his or her actions.	□ Identifying and interpreting natural or social problems and their solution.

Figure 24-7. *Extending the Meaning of Fictional and Factual Texts*

at, the processing is not successful. But the second and even more important goal is thinking beyond and about the text. You plan your introduction to ensure readers will be able to engage with all aspects of processing that the text demands, and you select teaching points following the reading based on the aspects of the processing system that you want your students to develop.

Sometimes you may want students to think about how authors present information in expository texts:

Describe ideas and events.

Tell the sequence or order of events.

Compare and contrast ideas or events, showing how they are the same or different.

Give explanations or reasons for events (causes and effects).

Identify problems and their solutions (or questions and their answers).

Any of these ways might be highlighted in the introduction to the text, discussed after reading the text, or be the focus of a teaching point after reading. Each is an opportunity to help readers think about the organization of an informational text. Sometime you can consider the elements of fiction texts in the same way; for example, you can map the time sequence or identify problem and solution.

Vocabulary and language are important to unlocking understanding. Don't be afraid of "telling too much" in the introduction. Readers need to have a good understanding, or at least familiarity, with the vocabulary and language structures in a text, as well as the content and organization, or even the overall theme. When you attend to new words and language patterns, you may want to have students locate them in the text and perhaps read or say some of them. In addition, informational texts may require using "signal words," such as *first* or *next, in addition to, because of, whenever,* that signal the reader to use cognitive actions to anticipate how information in the text will be provided.

Often, the structure of the text is a critical factor in reading comprehension. The way the writer has organized the text is a kind of internal structure that supports understanding. For example, over time readers will learn to detect:

How events are sequenced.

How the passage of time is shown.

When information is presented in categories and how the categories are identified.

Who is telling the story—narrator as person in the story (first person) or narrator as anonymous third person.

When there are literary devices, such as flashbacks or stories, within stories.

When important concepts are explained within the text.

Writers organize texts in infinitely varying ways, which helps readers develop flexibility in the way they approach, process, and understand texts.

EXAMPLES OF GUIDED READING LESSONS

To illustrate the framework of a guided reading lesson and how your teaching actions can contribute to students' development of comprehending strategies and fluency, below are three examples of guided reading lessons.

A GUIDED READING LESSON USING ROSIE'S POOL (LEVEL G)

Introducing the Text

In her introduction (see Figure 24-9), the teacher (Ms. N.) shared the title, author, and illustrator of this easy fantasy and related *Rosie's Pool* (Riley) to a previous text the children had read—*Rosie's Tea Party*. As she built interest in the story, she invited predictions about the character and plot, enabled the children to hear the language of the story,

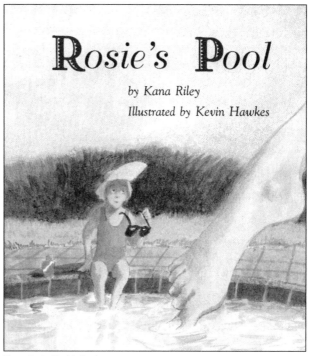

Figure 24-8. Rosie's Pool

and used new structures or vocabulary such as "You're welcome." As she guided the children to look at information in some of the illustrations, she helped them understand how the story works: Rosie's neighbors (two giants) come to visit, make several requests, behave poorly, and then leave to go home. The problem in the story is evident in the pictures: each time Rosie offers the giants something, it causes a problem. Ms. N. also calls the children's attention to one or two words in the print, so when they meet them they will be familiar with how they work.

Reading the Text

As the children read the whole text, Ms. N. observed the processing and interacted with individual readers, showing them how to problem-solve, prompting them to do something they knew how to do, and reinforcing the good reading work. Here are samples of the facilitative language she used as the children read the story:

- Find the tricky part.
- I like the way you fixed that.
- It starts like *sweating,* but look at (pointing to beginning of *sitting*).
- Go back and see if that all makes sense.
- Cover the ending and see if that helps you.
- Are you stuck there?
- Does that make sense?
- It sounds like si-, *sit,* but what would make sense?
- Does that make sense? Try again.
- Do you need help?
- You sure worked hard on that.
- Does that work?
- Could that be _____?
- Does that look right and make sense?
- Put your words together.
- I like the way you fixed that.

This kind of very specific language supports each reader's independent problem solving by revealing the action that is required.

Discussing and Revisiting the Text

After the reading, the children discussed the text. Some of the children's comments were:

- "They splashed all the water!"

- "They need to learn a good lesson."
- "I'd teach them to drink tea."

The students' discussion focused on what they had learned about these characters by reading both of the books about Rosie. They had internalized the idea that even though they say words like "please" and "thank you," the giants are very rude people. Several suggested that another book should be written about teaching the giants manners! Ms. N. did not use the word "character," but through conversation, she helped these children to express a beginning understanding of characters' attributes.

The conversation later turned to the story structure when Ms. N. asked the children which Rosie story they liked better. They unanimously chose *Rosie's Pool,* saying that their favorite part was when the giants jumped into the pool and splashed out all of the water (the climax of the story). They also identified the giants' large burp as their favorite part of *Rosie's Tea Party,* again, the climax of the story. This conversation reveals an implicit understanding of plot structure.

Teaching for Problem Solving

After the short discussion, Ms. N. makes a specific teaching point based on her observation of the group. During reading, several of the children made this error:

sweating
Rosie was at her pool   sitting   in the sun.

They read the word *sweating* instead of *sitting.* It was clear they were using the syntax and some of the visual information in a two-syllable word.

Using a whiteboard, the teacher showed them how to solve words ending in *-ing* by looking at the first part of the word, *sit.* All children in the group then located the word *sitting,* noticed the ending and the first part of the word and read it in a sentence.

Working with Words

Ms. N. had noticed in the past several lessons that the children needed to become more fluent and flexible in solving contractions as they read. In the final minute of the lesson, she used the whiteboard to do some quick work with contractions.

A GUIDED READING LESSON USING *CAM JANSEN AND THE MYSTERY OF THE CIRCUS CLOWN* (LEVEL M)

Erik, the teacher, used a simple chapter book (part of the Cam Jansen detective series) with a group of transitional

GUIDED READING LESSON:
Introduction to Rosie's Pool

Ms. N.: *[Prompts memory of another text.]* I'm going to give you the cover of the book, and I just want you to look at the cover right now. Do you remember Rosie?

JOANNE: There's a giant.

Ms. N.: Do you remember Rosie and *Rosie's Tea Party*? This is *Rosie's Pool*.

CAMILLA: It's like *Rosie's Tea Party*.

Ms. N.: *[Draws attention to author.]* It's just like *Rosie's Tea Party*. Do you think it's going to be the same author?

ALL STUDENTS: Yes.

Ms. N.: Let's check. Kana Riley. Is it Kana Riley again? *[Draws attention to illustrator.]* Do you think the illustrator's going to be the same?

SHARLA AND CAMILLA: Illustrated by Kana Riley.

Ms. N.: Is it the same? Do the pictures look similar?

JANELLE: Yes.

JANELLE: No.

CAMILLA: Illustrated by Kana.

Ms. N.: Kana Riley and illustrated by Kevin Hawkes. Let's look just at the cover for now. Guess who comes to visit Rosie at her pool.

ALL STUDENTS: Giants.

Ms. N.: *[Draws attention to characters.]* The giants. How many giants were there? Let's just look at the cover.

ISAAC: Three.

Ms. N.: *[Invited discussion of character traits.]* There were three. Do you remember something about the giants last time?

JANELLE: They're greedy.

CAMILLA: And the food was for all of them. But one ate the sandwich, one ate the cookies.

JANELLE: And one ate the cheese.

Ms. N.: What about at the end of the tea party? How did they behave?

SHARLA: They were bad.

Ms. N.: And how was that kind of behaving?

CAMILLA: They didn't say "excuse me." And they didn't say "please."

Ms. N.: Was that polite?

ALL STUDENTS: No.

Ms. N.: *[Invites prediction based on character traits.]* You know what? In this book, do you think they're going to be polite? Or do you think they're going to be not polite again?

ISAAC AND CAMILLE: *[Explains the problem of the story.]* Not polite.

Ms. N.: You're right. This time the giants come over. Rosie does not invite them. They come over and surprise her at her pool. They barge right in.

CAMILLA: Oh, my God!

Ms. N.: Is that polite, to barge right in without being invited?

ALL STUDENTS: No, it sure isn't.

Ms. N.: *[Invites further prediction and discussion of the problem.]* And they come over in their bathing suits, expecting to go swimming. Now wait a minute. Think about that. Think about the giants getting in the pool that's Rosie's size.

Figure 24-9. *A Guided Reading Lesson: An Introduction to* Rosie's Pool

GUIDED READING LESSON:
Introduction to **Rosie's Pool** (CONTINUED)

CAMILLA: Oh, my God!

SHARLA: They'll splash it.

Ms. N.: Oh, my gosh.

ISAAC: Squish it. They'll squish Rosie.

Ms. N.: Yeah.

CAMILLA: They'll drink all of the water.

Ms. N.: Oh, my gosh, they might do that. That would be something not very polite, wouldn't it? And splashing Rosie would be not very polite, would it?

ISAAC: Squishing Rosie.

Ms. N.: Or squishing Rosie.

JANELLE: He might wear her shoes.

Ms. N.: *[Invites attention to language.]* Now, boys and girls, remember from last time, Rosie is very polite in the way she talks to the giants. Do you remember some of the words she used last time?

ISAAC: "You're welcome."

CAMILLA: "Thank you."

Ms. N.: She does say, "you're welcome." Last time she said, "please have some sandwiches." What do you think she might say this time? Please . . .

SHARLA: "Come in."

Ms. N.: "Please come in?" Let's turn the page and look.

Ms. N.: *[Invites attention to information in pictures.]* Let's not read right now; let's look at the pictures. Turn the page again. Let's see what she might be offering them. What might she offer them first?

JANELLE: Some tea.

Ms. N.: And what would they say?

Ms. N.: *[Invites prediction based on character attributes.]* Ah, turn the page again. Now, Rosie offers this first giant a chair. Turn the page again. Oh, there might be a problem with that. Don't turn the page past that page, okay? One of the things she offers is her chair. Now, do you think he's going to be very polite about it?

CAMILLA: No.

Ms. N.: *[Invites attention to language and print.]* Hmm. He takes the chair and he says thank you, and what is she going to say?

ALL STUDENTS: "You're welcome."

Ms. N.: Find the words "you're welcome" on that page, and get a good look.

ISAAC: "You're welcome."

Ms. N.: *[Connects language and print.]* Would you run your finger under those words? Now don't turn the page, but I'm going to tell you something else she offers them. Iced tea. Now, knowing you know about the giants, do you think they're going to do the right thing with the iced tea?

CAMILLA: No, they're going to just drink it all.

Ms. N.: *[Foreshadows ending.]* Maybe they'll drink it all without sharing or something. And something else she offers them. Because they're by the pool, she offers them some suntan lotion to put on their bodies. And guess what. They do something kind of silly with it. And at the end, they do something again that doesn't make me think they're very polite. I won't tell you. It's now time to start, and I'm going to start with Isaac reading.

JANELLE: They're going to break the bottle.

Ms. N.: Go ahead and read about Rosie.

Figure 24-9. *A Guided Reading Lesson: An Introduction to* Rosie's Pool *(cont.)*

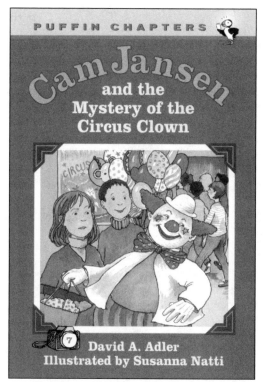

Figure 24-10. Cam Jansen and the Mystery of the Circus Clown

readers. One of the benefits of the book is to be able to help students better understand the mystery genre and how to approach it. The clues are clearly highlighted: the central character, Cam, takes a "mental picture" of an event by saying "click" and is then able to recall explicitly every detail of the action. There are repeating characters who play certain parts. None of the characters really change over the series. The plots are quite predictable, but the setting and the exact nature of the problems vary.

In *Cam Jansen and the Mystery of the Circus Clown*, the setting is important for several reasons:

- Many technical terms are associated with the setting, creating a challenge to decoding and vocabulary.

- Readers need to understand how crowds, such as those found in this setting, can make it easier to steal.

- The ability to use disguise helps the culprits commit the crime.

- Close observation (such as a detective might be capable of) is the only way to solve the crime.

Introducing the Text

Mr. B. began his introduction (see Figure 24-11) by prompting the children to remember other texts in the Cam

Jansen series, and they shared their background knowledge. He then zeroed in on the character of Cam Jansen and her ability to remember clues, a concept that is key to following the plot. Notice that he summarized and restated the important background information. A lesson of this introduction can be viewed on *Guided Reading: The Primary Literacy Video Collection* by Fountas and Pinnell.

One student, Barbara, noticed the cover of the book, and that gave Mr. B. another opportunity to repeat background information and foreshadow the plot. He drew attention to the setting as well, since there are important new words related to it. He mentioned *acrobats* early in the introduction but went on to have children locate the word in the text, where he again explained it. He also points out some proper nouns (*Mexico, Milwaukee,* and *Minnesota*) that he thought might be tricky. Another word he highlighted was *troupe;* the children may have understood the word in another context but not as the proper noun, *Elkans Troupe,* a group of circus performers. The underlying concept here is that words can have multiple meanings and that context is important in thinking about the meaning of a word. Mr. B. ended the introduction by foreshadowing the first part of the story, summarizing some of the background information about the setting, and reminding students that they are supposed to find out what the mystery is. He also gave them a simple writing assignment ("After chapter three, I think . . .") to help them think ahead.

Reading the Text

After the students began to read, the teacher listened to some oral reading and interacted briefly with each reader. The other students continued to read silently at their own pace. Figure 24-12 is a transcript of Mr. B.'s brief and highly focused interaction with Raquel. He listened to her oral reading, noting that her reading was accurate but that she largely ignored the punctuation, running one sentence right into another without stopping and letting the voice fall at the period.

Mr. B.'s decision to intervene was based on the strong connection between phrasing and comprehension. His first prompt ("start again and look carefully at all the commas and periods") did not have the intended result. Raquel seemed a little confused and hesitated slightly at the period, but she did not change her intonation pattern and contin-

A GUIDED READING LESSON:
An Introduction to Cam Jansen and the Mystery of the Circus Clown

Introducing the text

MR. B.: *[Prompts memory of another text in the series. Checks the group.]* Today we are going to read another Cam Jansen book. Have you all read a Cam Jansen book already?

SAMANTHA: I haven't.

MR. B.: *[Asks students to share background information.]* You never have? Who can tell Samantha about Cam Jansen?

JOSEPH: She's a detective.

ELVIS: Like Nate the Great.

MR. B.: *[Probes to make connections explicit.]* Oh, she is a little like Nate the Great. In what way is she like Nate the Great?

ELVIS: A detective.

MR. B.: *[Probes for more background information.]* And what do detectives do usually?

ELVIS: She solves mysteries.

BARBARA: Cam Jansen has a mental camera.

MR. B.: *[Asks for clarification.]* Ah—what do you mean by a mental camera?

STUDENTS: She can remember things by saying "click."
She can remember a picture . . .
She can just look at your face and go "click," and she remembers a picture like in ten hours.

MR. B.: *[Summarizes and restates important background information.]* So she has what they call a photographic memory. When she says "click," it's like she's taking a picture of whatever is in front of her, and she can always remember it, right?

JOSEPH: Right!

MR. B.: *[Repeats deduction.]* And that's why they call her Cam. Remember that?

BARBARA: When she's looking at the clowns, she's taking a picture and she can remember [pointing to the cover of the book].

MR. B.: *[Reinforces Barbara's noticing of the front cover and repeats important background information.]* So, you're already thinking about the title and what might be happening in this book. So Cam Jansen is a girl who solves a lot of mysteries.

ELVIS: With her friend Eric.

MR. B.: *[Reinforces Elvis's memory of another character in the series and foreshadows what to expect.]* Yes, with her friend Eric. And in this book there are going to be some other characters, at least one I think you've read about, Aunt Molly.

JOSEPH: Aunt Molly . . . where there was a flight.

MR. B.: *[Draws attention to the setting.]* Yes, Aunt Molly, in *The Mystery of Flight 54.* And where do you think this story is going to be taking place? I think Barbara already . . .

SEVERAL: At the circus.

MR. B.: *[Checks for background information about the setting.]* Has anybody ever been to the circus? [CHILDREN NOD, RAISE HANDS.]

MR. B.: *[Checks for background information about the setting.]* What's it like at the circus? What happens at the circus?

BARBARA: Oh, I hate the clowns, they're like [MIMES JUGGLING].

JOSEPH: They think they're funny.

ELVIS: They go on the trapeze.

JOSEPH: Juggling things.

MR. B.: *[Provides information about the setting and checks further for background knowledge.]* But basically at the circus, it's very crowded. And people do tricks. Do you know what a trapeze is?

MARCUS: They carry things [MIMES WALKING A TIGHTROPE].

Figure 24-11. *A Guided Reading Lesson: An Introduction to* Cam Jansen and the Mystery of the Circus Clown

---

A GUIDED READING LESSON:
An Introduction to Cam Jansen and the Mystery of the Circus Clown (CONTINUED)

MR. B.: *[Provides background knowledge.]* Well that's a tightrope, where they use a very high rope and they try and balance. And a trapeze is where they swing on something and they try to do tricks. Can you please open to page 3, because there are a few tricky parts that I want to get you ready to read. *[Says and explains tricky proper nouns; has children say and locate.]* On this page Aunt Molly is saying something reminds her of a circus she saw in Montana. And then she says, "Well maybe it was Mexico or Milwaukee." She gets all these M places mixed up. These are all names of countries or cities or states—Mexico, Montana, Milwaukee. Can you put your finger on the word *Milwaukee* on this page? Say it.

CHILDREN: Milwaukee.

MR. B.: *[Checks for understanding of vocabulary.]* Now up above, you'll see Mexico. Point to *Mexico*. That's a word I think you've probably seen before. Now turn the page to page 6. On this page you'll see the word *acrobats*. Do you know what acrobats are?

CHILDREN: No.

MR. B.: *[Explains vocabulary by using in conversation and draws attention to words in the text.]* Acrobats are people who go on the flying trapeze and spin in the air and do lots of flips and turns and things like that. And these acrobats are in a troupe. A troupe is a group of people who perform in the circus and this is the Elkans Troupe. Can you point to those two words—the Elkans Troupe? Sometimes circus troupes are from families and this group is called the Elkans family. *[Foreshadows first part of the story, summarizes information about the setting, and reminds readers of the purpose.]* In the first three chapters you find out what the mystery is. I'm not going to tell you. But you will find out what the mystery that Cam Jansen needs to solve is. They go to the circus with Aunt Molly. Eric is going to buy some popcorn.

JOSEPH: And he disappears!

MR. B.: *[Reinforces the prediction, explicitly describes the writing extension task, and checks for understanding.]* Well, maybe he disappears. But you will see what the mystery is. When you are done, take a pencil and paper [HOLDS UP THE PENCIL CONTAINER AND A PIECE OF PAPER]. I want you to write your name. I want you to write, *Cam Jansen and the Mystery of the Circus Clown*. And then write, "After chapter three, I think . . . ," and you are going to write who you think did it—how Cam is going to solve the mystery. Does everyone know what you are going to do?

Figure 24-11. *A Guided Reading Lesson: An Introduction to* Cam Jansen and the Mystery of the Circus Clown *(cont.)*

---

ed to ignore the punctuation. Mr. B. became more explic-, directing her attention to the period, telling her to stop, nd telling her why it is important (that it will help her nderstand it better). This time, Raquel read with appropri-te phrasing and intonation. The teacher asked her whether er reading sounded better and was easier to understand. hen he listened to a little more oral reading and encour-ged her for stopping at periods. He made a brief note before noving on to another student.

iscussing the Text, Teaching for Processing Strategies, and orking with Words

fter about fifteen minutes, during which the children read le three chapters and completed the brief piece of assigned riting (those who finished early also read from the brows-g box in the middle of the table), Mr. B. drew them into a

discussion of the story (see Figure 24-13). It is obvious that these students understood they were expected to provide their opinions about the story. In the introduction, the teacher had primed them to find out what the mystery was, and that led naturally to trying to solve it, as evidenced by Elvis's theory "that the clown bumped people and stole the wallet."

Mr. B. asked clarifying questions (which are different from questions designed to find out how much students remember of the story) to determine what students were really thinking. At one point, he "corrected" students' assumptions about the setting but accepted their comments when he realized they were recalling Aunt Molly's story of another time. This understanding was important to learning about the character. He listened intently to see what students brought to the reading.

A Guided Reading Lesson:
An Interaction with Raquel While Reading Cam Jansen and the Mystery of the Circus Clown

Mr. B. begins by listening to Raquel read.

Raquel: *[Ignores the punctuation.]* [Reading] *Aunt Molly said, "I do seem to lose things. Once, while I was reading in the library, I took my shoes off."*

Mr. B.: *[Prompts to reread, noticing and using the punctuation.]* Okay. Start again with "Aunt Molly said," and I want you to look carefully at all the commas and periods. And when you come to a comma, pause, and when you come to a period, stop a little bit longer. Start again with "Aunt Molly said."

Raquel: *[Some improvement but still largely ignoring the punctuation.]* [Reading] *Aunt Molly said, "I do seem to lose things. Once, while I was reading in the library, I took my shoes off. I didn't remember them until I stepped in a puddle on the way home."*

Mr. B.: *[Provides feedback to the reader and explicitly directs attention to the period.]* Okay. You said, "Aunt Molly said, 'I do seem to lose things once. . . .'" But what is there after things?

Raquel: A period.

Mr. B.: *[Provides explicit instructions and tells why it is important.]* Yes, will you stop there? And that's going to help you understand it better. Start again with "Aunt Molly said."

Raquel: [Reading] *Aunt Molly said, "I do seem to lose things. Once, while I was reading in the library, I took my shoes off."*

Mr. B.: *[Prompts reader to self-monitor.]* Does that sound better? Did you understand that better?

Raquel: [Nods.]

Mr. B.: *[Reinforces reading behavior.]* Good. Keep reading. *[Listens to Raquel read several more paragraphs. Reading shows use of the punctuation.]* Great job stopping for every period.

Figure 24-12. *A Guided Reading Lesson: An Interaction with Raquel While Reading* Cam Jansen and the Mystery of the Circus Clown

---

Discussion and Teaching Points in Guided Reading Lesson:
Cam Jansen and the Mystery of the Circus Clown

Mr. B.: *[Provides direction and opens the discussion of the meaning of the story.]* Okay, I'd like you to close your books. Put the browsing box books away. Put your paper flat in front of you. What did you think of that?

Barbara: The clowns stole the jacket.

Joseph: And the money.

Mr. B.: *[Asks a clarifying question.]* Wait a minute. What's the mystery?

Andrea: The clowns—

Joseph: Everything's disappearing!

Mr. B.: *[Summarizes thinking and asks for other opinions.]* And it seems that everybody thinks the clowns did it. Is that what you think? Did anyone think something else?

Elvis: Yes.

Joseph: Or the woman that passed.

Mr. B.: *[Encourages clarification.]* Or the woman that passed?

Roberto: What woman?

Andrea: At the zoo.

Elvis: Cam Jansen said she lost her sweater at the zoo.

Figure 24-13. *Discussion and Teaching Points in Guided Reading Lesson:* Cam Jansen and the Mystery of the Circus Clown

MR. B.: *[Asks for clarification.]* At the what?

SEVERAL: At the zoo?

MR. B.: *[Corrects children's assumptions.]* At the circus.

ANDREA: *[Characters referred to another time.]* In the zoo. She and Aunt Molly.

MR. B.: *[Realizes children were right and clarifies their comments, then moves on.]* Oh, she was talking about another time. Next time we are going to find out.

ELVIS: I think I know how it happened.

MR. B.: *[Encourages thinking.]* All right, what do you think?

ELVIS: Well, when he bumped, his hand went into the pocket and he steals the wallet.

MR. B.: *[Reinforces thinking.]* You know, you should be a detective. You have it all figured out—right, Elvis? *[Provides a demonstration of reading over punctuation and then points out the period.]* I want you to turn to page 16, please, because there was a really good example of why it's so important to stop at every period. Page 16—everybody should be on page 16. Look at the bottom of the last paragraph starting with "Aunt Molly said." Do you remember this, Raquel? Everybody reading with me? [READS THE SENTENCE WITHOUT STOPPING AT THE PARAGRAPH.] But what is there after *things*?

STUDENTS: A period.

MR. B.: *[Invites student demonstration.]* A period, so it's really different—right? [TURNS TO RAQUEL.] You want to read it this time?

RAQUEL: [READING WITH APPROPRIATE INTONATION AND PAUSING] *Aunt Molly said, "I do seem to lose things. Once, while I was reading in the library, I took my shoes off. I didn't remember them until I stepped in a puddle on the way home."*

MR. B.: *[Prompts children to consider syntax.]* Now, didn't that sound better? *[Demonstrates reading again.]* It's a very different thing.

ELVIS: She's silly.

CHILDREN: [LAUGHING AT AUNT MOLLY.]

ANDREA: She lost her shoes like that.

MR. B.: *[Responds to children's comments by encouraging thinking.]* What do you think about Aunt Molly? I mean what kind of person loses her shoes in the library and doesn't notice until she steps in a puddle?

ROBERTO: She lost her sweater.

MR. B.: *[Summarizes information about character traits.]* So she lost her sweater at the zoo. She lost her shoes at the library.

JOSEPH: She lost her wallet at the—

ANDREA: Circus.

MR. B.: *[Asks for opinion and draw attention to character traits.]* What do you think about Aunt Molly?

ELVIS: She's very silly.

MR. B.: *[Describes character.]* But the important thing is that we know Aunt Molly is a little bit silly. She loses things. She sometimes doesn't have it all together. Sometimes we could say, "Her elevator doesn't go all the way to the top floor."

CHILDREN: [LAUGHING.]

The discussion and teaching were followed by two minutes of word work on homophones.

Figure 24-13. *Discussion and Teaching Points in Guided Reading Lesson:* Cam Jansen and the Mystery of the Circus Clown *(cont.)*

After the brief discussion of the mystery, Mr. B. focused on an aspect of processing that appeared to have benefit for the group as a whole. He took them back to the page that Raquel had read aloud and demonstrated reading without noticing punctuation. He pointed out the period, and then asked Raquel to provide a demonstration for the group, which she did very competently. He was explaining that using punctuation made your reading sound better and you understand it in a different way when the students expressed their amusement about Aunt Molly. Finally, Mr. B. summarized Aunt Molly's character traits. After he worked for a couple of minutes on homophones (word work that was preplanned), the session ended.

Analyzing the Lesson

In this guided reading lesson, the teacher and students were able to:

- Bring background knowledge of texts and content to their reading.
- Follow a series of events and gather important information.
- Make predictions based on information.
- Infer the solution to a mystery.
- Notice and report important traits of two characters and relate those traits to the plot.
- Notice and use punctuation to read with phrasing.

Mr. B. was focused, explicit, and intentional. He used this text as an instrument for helping students play out their growing reading strategies. They read almost half of *Cam Jansen and the Mystery of the Circus Clown,* and they finished it the next day, using what they already knew to gain momentum.

A Guided Reading Lesson Using *Seedfolks* (Level W)

Seedfolks is a complex text. In it Paul Fleischman presents a series of stories, each one told in a different character's voice, set in a lower-economic Cleveland neighborhood where many groups of immigrants live. The chapters are quite short, demanding that readers infer a great deal of information from brief pieces of text. Characters represent many different social and ethnic groups and range from about eleven years old to elderly. They come from completely different backgrounds, and their ways of talking, their vocabularies, even their use of sentence structure is different from each other. What these people have in common is that they live in the same depressed neighborhood and all, each in his or her own way, are reaching for a better life. They begin to come together around a vacant lot full of unsightly trash when a little girl plants some beans and is observed by two older neighbors. The overall theme is that diverse people who have formerly been in conflict can work together and take small steps to make the world better and more beautiful.

This carefully crafted novel raises a few challenges for upper elementary and middle school readers. The reader must switch perspectives every few pages. The narrator shifts with each chapter and tells a different story, but it

Figure 24-14. Seedfolks

would be a mistake simply to see *Seedfolks* as a series of stories. To understand the author's message, the reader must keep tying the threads together, making predictions about the outcomes and inferring characters' feelings and motivations, as well as the way people and events affect them. Some of the themes are mature; for example, one character is an unwed mother who is giving away her baby.

Introducing the Text

Ms. W., the teacher, introduced the book (see Figure 24-15) by telling the title and author and then provided a very explicit explanation of the structure of the text. It was critical that students understood this concept, because the entire plot hung on it. Understanding the structure of *Seedfolks* is a good example of what cannot be left to "see if students get it." This complex structure must be foregrounded. Otherwise, students might flounder through a big part of it with only superficial understanding at best. Notice that Ms. W. had them turn to three chapters in their own copies of the book. She taught them how to use the pictures and chapter titles as cues to the needed switch in perspective and voice. This lesson (*Seedfolks)* may be viewed on the DVD that accompanies this book.

392

A GUIDED READING LESSON:
An Introduction to Seedfolks

Ms. W.: *[Introduces title and author.]* We're going to read a new book together today, and I'm actually going to go ahead and give it to you. It's called *Seedfolks,* and it's by Paul Fleischman. *[Connects to content area study.]* Now, we've been studying immigration and moving in social studies, and this book is actually nice because it relates that topic with what we are going to be reading. Look at the cover. *[Draws attention to the cover as a basis for prediction.]* Look at the pictures on the cover. What are some things you are thinking about this book based on the pictures on the cover?

MADDIE: All the pictures on the cover are different races.

Ms. W.: *[Confirms prediction.]* Okay, so we are going to be seeing that they are from different races.

JASON: Maybe the items, like the binoculars and whatever else is shown in the pictures—maybe they are like their possessions, so I'm thinking that they all have different possessions.

Ms. W.: *[Reveals and demonstrates text structure.]* Okay. In this book at the beginning of every chapter there is actually a picture of a different person. Turn to page 1. The first chapter is told by one of the characters, and her name is Kim. And there is a picture of her. And as we read this chapter, you can hear Kim's voice as you are reading it. She's telling the story. These are her words. So look at the second chapter. Turn to page 4. Who is telling the story now?

MADDIE: Anna.

Ms. W.: *[Elaborates on text structure and checks for understanding.]* Anna. And do you see the picture of Anna? That's what she looks like. And this chapter is told by Anna. She's telling this chapter. She is telling the story of her life in this chapter. And what do you think you will find next?

MADDIE: Another person.

Ms. W.: *[Checks for understanding.]* Okay, and who do we find?

JASMINE: Wendell.

Ms. W.: *[Elaborates on text structure and summarizes.]* And do you see a picture of him? So that's what he looks like and he's telling the story in this chapter. Each chapter starts off with a picture and the name of the person who is telling the story in that chapter. *[Provides background information.]* And what's really neat about this book is that they are all related in some way. Now, they are not family members, but they are related in some ways. *[Provides background information.]* They have all come from different places. Some of them are from Puerto Rico. There's a woman in here from Vietnam. Actually, Kim, the one that started this book is from Vietnam. There's someone from North Korea. There is someone from Haiti, Mexico—all these different places. *[Checks for understanding.]* Look at the first chapter and we see the picture of Kim. So what do we know?

TONY: She's telling the story.

Ms. W.: So let's look at the first chapter. Who is telling the story? *[Checks for understanding.]*

STUDENTS: Kim.

Ms. W.: *[Prompts to listen for voice—attention to the writer's craft.]* Kim. So let's try to listen for her voice as we read this. Maddie, read the first paragraph for us.

MADDIE: [READING THE FIRST PARAGRAPH] *"I stood before the family altar. It was dark. . . . I was nine years old and still hoped that perhaps his eyes might move, might notice me."*

Ms. W.: *[Checks for understanding of a vocabulary word.]* Okay, so that's Kim speaking. What's a family altar? What does that mean?

JASMINE: I think it's where people get married.

Ms. W.: *[Prompts readers to figure out meaning from context.]* Okay, that's one kind of altar, a wedding altar where people get married. Now, what do you think this kind of altar is, from the description here? Have you ever heard of this before?

Figure 24-15. *A Guided Reading Lesson: An Introduction to* Seedfolks

A GUIDED READING LESSON:
An Introduction to Seedfolks (CONTINUED)

Ms. W.: *[Clarifies meaning of a vocabulary word within the context and draws attention to cultural factors.]* Okay. Actually, this altar is a family altar. It can be just like a table where they put some things. So what's on this altar? There's a picture of her father—her father's photograph—and if you continue reading, there are some other things on this table like some candles and some other things. Her father has passed away. Actually, when she was very young, he passed away. So this is kind of just remembering him, giving him respect. Does everyone understand that? So that's one kind of altar. She's from Vietnam and in this culture that's how they might pay respect to someone who has passed away. Any questions about that?

STUDENTS: [SHAKE HEADS.]

Ms. W.: *[Reminds readers to use background knowledge.]* As you read, you are going to learn more about Kim and what she has to do with all the other people in this book. And they all come from different places so don't forget that as well. As you are reading, think about what we've talked about in social studies about moving and the kinds of difficulties people face. *[Provides directions and reminds readers of two purposes—how the writer shows characters' voices and how their stories are connected (plot).]* You are actually just going to read the first three chapters, Kim, Anna, and Wendell. As you are reading it, think about each person and try to listen to their voice, listen to how they are telling their story, and listen for how they are connected to each other in some way. *[Gives directions for response in writing.]* After you read the first three chapters, you are going to write in your reader's notebook about the characters and how they are connected to each other. Does everyone understand? So start reading, and when you are done with your writing, you can just read your independent reading book.

Figure 24-15. *A Guided Reading Lesson: An Introduction to* Seedfolks *(cont.)*

Ms. W. then had Maddie read a paragraph aloud from the first chapter. This turned out to be an important move, because it gave them the opportunity to talk about how important culture is in each story, to find out a little about Kim's (the character who plants beans), and to get a good start on the reading.

Ms. W. also provided some background information about the word *altar,* which most students had heard or seen before in a different context. Ms. W. simply told them the meaning of the word in this context and in doing so, helped them begin to understand Kim's story better. Notice that she reminded them of the text structure several times. Her expectations were clear—students should:

□ Notice how the writer shows the characters' different voices.

□ Think about how the characters' stories are connected.

Reading the Text
Ms. W. then left the table to have some individual reading conferences with other students. Students finished reading three chapters, wrote a short response, and then read their self-selected books independently until Ms. W. came back to discuss the text with them.

Discussing the Text
After about fifteen minutes, Ms. W. returned to the table and began the discussion (see Figure 24-16). The students were active participants, doing most of the talking as Ms. W. invited and confirmed their responses, probed, summarized, restated to move the discussion along, redirected the conversation, and questioned. Based on the information from the first three chapters, she asked them to make predictions about what would happen, and she drew attention to the title as important information.

Jason's comment that "they are so short and they always leave me thinking about something" is important. After Ms. W.'s probe, he explained that the chapter is short and gives so little information that he found himself wanting more. Jason was reflecting the kind of tension that a text like this one can bring—a tension that demands that the reader seek the satisfaction of closure.

The students often answered one another's questions rather than waiting for the teacher. They had learned how to discuss texts with one another following reading. Jasmine explained to Jason her understanding of why Kim wanted to be like her father. Both Maddie and Jason responded to Jasmine's question about why all the white

DISCUSSION OF *Seedfolks*

Ms. W.: *[Checks progress and invites response.]* Did everyone get a chance to finish the first three chapters? Did everyone write? *[Checks quickly.]* Do you want to just talk a little bit about what you were writing about?

JASON: Sure.

Ms. W.: *[Invites response in the form of talk.]* Let's just talk about the characters and how they are connected to each other.

JASON: Well, should I read it?

Ms. W.: *[Invites response in the form of talk.]* No, don't read it. Just talk about your thinking.

JASON: I was thinking . . . well first of all how each chapter had a different person telling it and how the story takes place in Cleveland. All the people who lived nearby lived near each other, but they don't all know each other.

MADDIE: Anna says that they all live really close to her, and in a way they kind of know each other. They've all seen each other. Anna, she saw Kim planting the seeds. And Wendell is friends with Anna and they both see Kim planting seeds. They all—

Ms. W.: *[Probes for deeper response.]* So how are they connected with each other?

TONY: They all live in the same apartment.

Ms. W.: *[Summarizes responses.]* So they all lived in the same neighborhood, and what Maddie was saying about the planting.

TONY: Kim never saw Anna. She only—

MADDIE: She might have, but—

TONY: Anna thinks Kim might have seen her, but she doesn't know for sure.

Ms. W.: *[Invites predictions.]* So based on the first three chapters, and as we read more chapters, what do you think is going to continue to happen? What do you think? What are some predictions you could make?

JASON: I think if there are twelve chapters, one of these pictures will be about each one of them. If there are less than twelve chapters, then maybe one or two of them will be in one of the chapters. And if there's more than twelve, they will probably use some of the pictures.

Ms. W.: *[Confirms student response and then turns the discussion to invite predictions.]* What do you think will happen in the story? Any predictions about what will happen? You're probably right, and we can continue looking at the pictures and thinking of how they are related to the story, but based on the first three chapters, what do you think will continue to happen as we hear from different characters? Jasmine?

JASMINE: I think they will meet each other. Like, someone will be planting something or taking out the trash, or whatever, and meet another person, and then the list will go on and on and the person will introduce one person to another.

Ms. W.: *[Draws the title to their attention as a basis for prediction.]* Do you have many more ideas about the title?

MADDIE: I think that maybe they'll all—that's happened so far, because Anna and Wendell watched Kim planted her beans— maybe all of them are going to meet each other.

TONY: I agree with Maddie, because I think they are going to get to know each other—like someone is planting seeds and the person comes over to him, and they don't really know each other. They just saw each other.

MADDIE: I think that maybe these things on the back . . . I think all of those things will be the reasons that show that they all need each other, and maybe sooner or later they will all become friends because of each object.

JASON: I want to come back to what Maddie said just now and to what I had said before that. I think that all the things on the back—a branch on a tree with leaves on it, beans and flower and things—are what Kim was talking about. I think that all the people in the book will meet each other and they will turn the vacant lot into a big garden.

Ms. W.: *[Invites another student into the discussion.]* Do you agree?

JASMINE: [NODS] I do.

Ms. W.: *[Asks for discussion on another topic.]* And did these first three chapters make you think about anything else unrelated to the garden?

Figure 24-16. *Discussion of* Seedfolks

DISCUSSION OF **Seedfolks** (CONTINUED)

JASON: Yes, how they are so short and they always leave me thinking about something.

Ms. W.: *[Probes further for clarification.]* What?

JASON: For example, in this first chapter, the last paragraph of Kim.

Ms. W.: *[Asks for page number so all students can closely examine the section.]* Can you tell us what page it is on?

JASON: I'm on page 3, last paragraph, where it talks about how Kim planted lima beans in paper cups and how she placed the beans in the hole now and she covers them up and she opened her thermos of water. I was wondering what was the point of it. The two paragraphs before that came off. It's on page 3 at the end of the second paragraph. I didn't know what was going to happen next. It says, "I would show him I was his daughter." That was the end of this chapter. At this point I wondered what was going to happen next. Why would she want to show him she was his daughter? I was thinking that this chapter should be longer because it hardly gives any information.

Ms. W.: *[Recognizes another student.]* [RESPONDING TO JASMINE] Go ahead.

JASMINE: Jason, when you said you didn't understand why she wanted him to know that she was his daughter it was because she was born eight months after he died. And when other people like her mother and her older sisters cried about him, they knew who he was, but she didn't, so she couldn't cry about him or anyone she didn't know. The only thing she knew was that he liked to plant and all of that, so I guess she just wanted to show him that she had his ability and she could do what he did.

JASON: When it was talking about . . . when she was at the family altar, maybe after that she decided she wanted to do what he did when he was alive and maybe his spirit would rise and watch her or something.

MADDIE: She never met her father so she wanted her father to know that she was his daughter because they never met each other and he didn't really know her that well. She wanted him to know that she was his daughter.

Ms. W.: *[Recognizes student comments and summarizes the discussion.]* I'm really glad you brought that up, because even though we are thinking about how all these characters from different backgrounds and places around the world are connected to each other, they are also stories in each chapter about each character, separate from all the other characters, and what's going on in each person's life. It's good you are focusing on that.

JASON: So, it sounds like even though they are all connected in some way, they are also very different in other ways.

Ms. W.: *[Encourages further discussion.]* Did you have anything to add about that?

JASMINE: I have a comment on a different topic.

Ms. W.: *[Recognizes another student. Invites student to student conversation.]* Okay, go ahead.

JASMINE: Like Anna, in the part that Wendell said that him and Anna are the only two white people left, I didn't get in Anna's story where it said how all of her family and all of the white people left as soon as the other countries and places started coming in. I didn't get why.

MADDIE: I think I may be able . . . because when the other countries came into that kind of apartment thing, her family and friends might have felt uncomfortable around other races. Maybe they wanted to leave because most of that apartment was—most of the people there—other races were living there now and they might have not liked the other races and maybe they just wanted to leave because they didn't want to be around them.

JASON: I disagree with Maddie. I think that during Anna's story it said how that neighborhood was just a place like a hotel until they had enough money and they were able to move somewhere else and get a decent job. It probably just happened to be coincidence that about the time those people got enough money and they were able to leave and find better jobs and stuff, other cultures and races came in.

Ms. W.: *[Affirms student comments.]* It's interesting to think about differences. You are bringing up this issue of differences and how people might feel uncomfortable about the differences. *[Ends with reference to the plot.]* As we continue reading about the people in this neighborhood, there are some things, again, that bring them together and connect them in some way.

Figure 24-16. *Discussion of* Seedfolks *(cont.)*

people left the neighborhood when other cultures and races came in. Each had a viable theory: Maddie's, that maybe they were uncomfortable around other races, and Jason's, that the neighborhood was like a hotel and every group left as soon as they could get a better job. Jason refers to a specific place in the text as his evidence. At the end, Ms. W. recognized children's comments and set the scene for further reading.

Analyzing the Lesson

Let's stop and analyze this guided reading lesson through the lens of thinking within, beyond, and about the text (see Figure 24-17). There is plenty of evidence that these students were engaging in a wide range of thinking, some prompted or modeled by the teacher and some spontaneous. Some of their discussion simply helped them sort out and remember the details of the text, so that they would have enough information to understand the literal meaning (within the text). The discussion was also rich in inference and hypothesis; with Carol's support they connected background information with the story and synthesized

new information (beyond the text). They also paid attention to the writer's craft—how the text was organized and how the writer used point of view to tell a larger story (about the text).

This lesson is a good example of students' helping one another expand their thinking. They answered one another's questions; they understood there might be more than one answer to a question; they built on one another's understandings. They often used language like:

- "I agree with Maddie because. . . ."
- "I disagree because. . . ."
- "I'd like to go back to what Maddie was talking about."
- "When Jason said. . . ."

Students achieve this level of sophistication, not because they had a few lessons focused on comprehending strategies or because they can name strategies, but because they are actively engaged in processing and discussing texts every day over the years of elementary and middle school. Deep thinking cannot be generated through exercises, but it can be supported through authentic conversations surrounding

---

A GUIDED READING LESSON—*SEEDFOLKS*:
An Evidence of Thinking Across the Lesson

Within the Text
- Clarified whether two people knew each other.
- Looked at the relationships among characters.
- Understood vocabulary–the meaning of the word *altar* in this context.
- Understood the use of *hotel* in this context.
- Provided evidence for their thinking by using evidence from the text.
- Brought up confusions for clarification–noticing when something didn't make sense and they didn't have all the information.

Beyond the Text
- Hypothesized what the story would be about–predicting.
- Connected with their own experiences and knowledge about immigration and moving and how this story relates to that knowledge.
- Took on the point of view of a character.
- Synthesized information–the whole is greater than the sum of its parts. Answered the question, What is the greater meaning and implications?
- Questioned events in the text–asking why.
- Inferred characters' internal motivations.

About the Text
- Thought about why the author chose a certain title to communicate to readers.
- Analyzed point of view the way the author used it.
- Noticed the voice of individual characters.
- Noticed features of the text such as short chapters and change of perspective.
- Noticed how the author structured the text–different perspectives for different people.

Figure 24-17. *A Guided Reading Lesson of* Seedfolks: *An Evidence of Thinking Across the Lesson*

texts. Students learn how to explore the meaning of texts with each other and with the support of the teacher. They "own" the discussion rather than thinking they are proving to the teacher that they read the book or are using strategies. At the end of a good discussion, all participants feel as though they have a better understanding of the text.

These children brought to the table years of experience in discussing books—not just in guided reading but in interactive read-aloud and literature discussion groups. Together, they were able to support one another's exploration of the meaning within the text.

A CONTINUUM OF TEACHING AND LEARNING FOR READING AND RESPONDING TO TEXTS

The ability to think, talk, and write about reading develops over a long period of time. Our teaching support in kindergarten through grade eight represents a continuum of progress. The continuum is presented in detail with level-by-level goals and can be found in *The Continuum of Literacy Learning, PreK–8: A Guide to Teaching* (Fountas and Pinnell 2008, 2011). As teachers, we must take a long view of the development of the reading process. Too often, reading instruction becomes isolated exercises, which result in "hit or miss" learning. Attending closely to students' reading behavior will help you chart this complex development of a reading process over time.

SUGGESTIONS FOR PROFESSIONAL DEVELOPMENT

TEACHING FOR COMPREHENDING AND FLUENCY ACROSS THE GUIDED READING LESSON

1 Gather a group of colleagues. Watch the guided reading lessons on the DVD that accompanies this book. Notice how the teacher and students are interacting around the meaning of the text.

2 After viewing the two lessons, discuss what new insights you have about the role of the teacher and the role of the students in making meaning together. Regardless of the grade level, the principles for teaching will be similar.

3 Divide into grade-level partners. Select a text you might use with your students. Make a list on a chart of the demands on comprehending that readers will need to meet. Talk about whether you will need to address the demands in the introduction or the discussion.

4 Plan for some of your colleagues to tape one of their guided reading lessons. In a subsequent session, watch the lessons. Discuss what you learn about teaching for comprehending from observing the lessons.

5 Set goals for making your lessons more effective and share them with the group.

CHAPTER TWENTY-FIVE

Using Guided Reading to Teach for the Comprehending of Fiction Texts

Book introductions are an authentic social interaction about the new book; but when they provide an orientation to stories and their features they are also a kind of teaching.

—Marie Clay

There's nothing like a good story. As teachers, we have the privilege of bringing children and fiction together. Many of us remember the stories we first heard and read as children, and the characters we felt we knew. Fiction is pleasurable. Fiction allows us to introduce children to the joys of reading, something that is essential if they are to have the opportunity to become lifelong readers. As educators we are required to justify the reading experience in more than pleasurable ways, but enjoyment should always remain a prime goal.

The Values of Fiction

Fiction genres include realistic fiction, historical fiction, traditional literature, fantasy, and science fiction (see Chapter 11). Each genre makes a special contribution to our reading lives. Realistic fiction helps us understand and appreciate the current human problems and the diversity in our world today. Historical fiction helps us understand perspectives of people in places and times far different from our own. Traditional literature includes the simple characters and plots that are so accessible to younger children and the sweeping sagas whose moral lessons instruct older children and adults. Fantasy and science fiction present the human condition in the context of imaginary worlds. But all fiction texts:

- Engage readers in plots that add to life experiences.
- Present characters and situations that elicit empathy and help readers understand diversity.
- Allow for vicarious experiences that help in learning human truths.
- Provide moral lessons.
- Help in understanding human problems.
- Provide an escape or release from tension.
- Provide examples of reasoning and problem solving.

- Provide examples of heroism and overcoming difficulties.
- Present memorable characters that we seem to know.
- Inspire readers to persist in overcoming obstacles.
- Help readers understand themselves and others.

The Potential of Fiction

What readers know about the different genres of fiction is an important factor for comprehending fiction texts (see Chapter 10). Each genre makes slightly different demands on readers. Guided reading can help children learn to appreciate and realize the potential benefits of all fiction genres. The framework and prompts in Figure 25-1 will help you think about your teaching in guided reading lessons with fiction texts. You want to demonstrate or teach students to notice before probing for them to think in these ways.

Provided you have chosen a work of high quality that is matched to your group's present ability, every text has the potential to help students learn more about the many aspects of reading fiction. It's simply not true that one text is good for teaching inferring, another predicting, and still another synthesizing new information. A single text will provide a variety of learning opportunities, but you can't "teach it all" with one text at a single point in time. Planning for your teaching in guided reading lessons means keeping in mind:

- Important aspects of processing related to fiction texts.
- What you want your students to be able to do as readers of fiction.
- The potential learning opportunities in reading this particular, more challenging text.
- Student responses to features of the text that create a "teachable moment."

Planning for Guided Reading Lessons Using Fiction

Thinking within the text:	DEMONSTRATION TO SUPPORT THINKING IN TEXT INTRODUCTIONS [SHOW EVIDENCE IN THE TEXT.]	PROBING (OR RELATED COMMENTS) [SHOW EVIDENCE IN THE TEXT.]
▫ Follow the events of the plot.	▫ Let's think about what happens first in the story. ▫ Let's think about what happens after that. ▫ The thing that is going to happen first in this story is _____.	▫ What happened first in the story? ▫ What happened next?
▫ Gather important information about the characters (main and secondary) and the setting and remember it.	▫ When you are reading this kind of book, look for information like _____ so you can get to know the characters. ▫ You can look for information like this [example] so you can understand where and when the story takes place. ▫ In a fiction text, readers notice the most important character. In this book it is _____. ▫ There are other characters in the story. Some are _____.	▫ What is [name of character] like? ▫ What does [name] look like? ▫ How can you tell what [name] is like by what she does? ▫ Who is this story about? ▫ Who is telling the story? ▫ Who else is in the story? ▫ Who is the most important person in the story?
▫ Get to know characters (how they are described, what they do, what they say and think, and what others think about them).	▫ Writers show what the character is like by telling what they do, what they say or think, and what others say about them. ▫ In this story you can tell what _____ is like by _____. ▫ You will want to notice _____ about _____.	▫ How is _____ described by the writer? ▫ What does _____ do? Say? Think? ▫ What do others say about _____?
▫ Notice how characters change over time.	▫ At the beginning of the story _____ was like this _____. But he is going to change. You'll find out that _____. ▫ You will notice that at the beginning of the story _____. Now _____.	▫ What was _____ like at the beginning of the story? At the end of the story? Is _____ changing? ▫ Did _____ change during this story? How?
▫ Identify the conflict or problem.	▫ In a fiction text, there is always a problem or many problems. In this story, the big problem is _____.	▫ What problem does _____ have? ▫ What is the problem in the story?
▫ Solve words	▫ This word is _____. Can you find it? ▫ This word means _____.	▫ Have you seen this word before? ▫ [After reading sentence] What do you think it means?

Figure 25-1. *Planning for Guided Reading Lessons Using Fiction*

Planning for Guided Reading Lessons Using Fiction (CONTINUED)

Thinking beyond the text:	DEMONSTRATION [SHOW EVIDENCE IN THE TEXT.]	PROBING [SHOW EVIDENCE IN THE TEXT.]
▫ Infer characters' motivations and inner feelings.	▫ The author doesn't tell how _____ feels [or what she wants], but readers will know because _____. ▫ The author doesn't tell us why _____ is doing that, but readers have an idea because _____.	▫ How does _____ feel? ▫ Why does _____ behave as he does? ▫ What do you think _____ wants to do? ▫ How would you feel if you were _____?
▫ Infer causes for characters' change over time.	▫ _____ changed maybe because _____. ▫ There might be several reasons why _____ changed. For example, _____.	▫ Why do you think _____ changed? ▫ Why do you think _____ changed in that way?
▫ Connect the text to other texts, to background knowledge, and to personal experiences.	▫ This book may remind you of _____ because _____. ▫ To understand this book, you will want to think about _____. ▫ I've read other books like this one. [Provide example.] ▫ Think about what you already know about this topic/place/time. [Provide example.] ▫ This character (or plot or setting) is like _____.	▫ Does this book remind you of any other text? Which one? ▫ Does this book remind you of anything in your own life? ▫ What do you already know about this topic/time/place? ▫ In what ways does the character remind you of someone you know? ▫ In what ways does the character remind you of a character [plot or setting] in another book?
▫ Make predictions as to resolution of the problem.	▫ Readers are always thinking what might happen next. For example, think about _____. ▫ Based on what you know about the character, you will want to think about _____.	▫ What do you think will happen? Why do you think that? ▫ What do you think will happen to _____? ▫ If you were _____, what would you do in this situation? ▫ What advice would you give _____ at this point?
▫ Understand the prominent theme or author's message.	▫ _____ makes me think that the writer is really trying to say _____. ▫ Readers can think about what the writer is really trying to say. Think about this as you read.	▫ What do you think the writer is really trying to say in this book? ▫ Why do you think that?
▫ Relate the theme, plot, or characters to one's own life.	▫ This story makes me think about _____. ▫ The writer makes me think about _____. ▫ This character reminds me of _____.	▫ Does this story make you think about anything in your own life? What? ▫ What does this writer's message mean to you? ▫ Does _____ remind you of anyone you know? What about him/her?

Figure 25-1. *Planning for Guided Reading Lessons Using Fiction (cont.)*

Planning for Guided Reading Lessons Using Fiction (CONTINUED)

Thinking beyond the text:	DEMONSTRATION [SHOW EVIDENCE IN THE TEXT.]	PROBING [SHOW EVIDENCE IN THE TEXT.]
▫ Make inferences as to the significance of events.	▫ One of the most important things about this book is _____. ▫ A very important thing happens here. [Provide example.]	▫ What do you think is important about _____? ▫ Why was this [event] important?
▫ Notice new ideas or information, and revise previously held ideas.	▫ I didn't know that _____. That was surprising to me, and I changed the way I think about _____. ▫ This helped me know more about _____, and I'm thinking in a different way now.	▫ Were there any new ideas in this book that made you change your thinking? ▫ What did you learn from this text? How did that change your thinking?

Thinking about the text:	DEMONSTRATION [SHOW EVIDENCE IN THE TEXT.]	PROBING [SHOW EVIDENCE IN THE TEXT.]
▫ Evaluate the importance of the setting to the plot.	▫ The time (and/or place) of the story is important because _____. ▫ This book would not be the same in another place (and/or time) because _____. ▫ The time (and/or place) had a big influence on the characters' lives (or decisions) because _____. ▫ When _____ moved from one place to another, it made a difference because _____.	▫ How important was the time (and/or place) of the story? Could it have happened in the same way in another time or place? Why or why not? ▫ Did the place change in the story? How did that affect the character? ▫ Did things change over time? How did that affect what happened?
▫ Notice how the writer has made characters seem real.	▫ _____ seemed real to me because _____. ▫ The writer really makes me feel that I know _____. Here's an example.	▫ Did _____ seem like a real person to you? What made you feel that way? ▫ How did the writer make _____ seem real? Give an example.
▫ Notice the plot structure.	▫ The story is organized in this way. ▫ The writer shows that time was passing. Listen to this: _____. ▫ The writer started telling a story here and finished here. ▫ _____ was remembering something from the past here.	▫ How was the story organized? ▫ How did the writer show that time was passing? ▫ How did the writer show us that _____ was remembering back in time (or telling a story)?
▫ Notice aspects of the writer's craft.	▫ Notice this kind of language in this book. Here's an example. ▫ This language helped me realize _____.	▫ What are some examples of language that you liked (or that made you understand _____)? Why?
▫ Critique the quality or authenticity of the text.	▫ I think this book is highly accurate because _____. ▫ I think this writer is qualified to write about this topic because _____.	▫ What makes you think this book is accurate? ▫ How can you tell whether the writer is qualified to write on this topic?

Figure 25-1. *Planning for Guided Reading Lessons Using Fiction (cont.)*

you remain aware of these factors, you can plan the intro-
uction to, and discussion of, the text with some teaching
oints in mind but also be flexible enough to take advan-
ge of your observations and student-initiated learning.

Embedded in Figure 25-1 are two important types of
aching moves: (1) samples of language used in demon-
ration or teaching that support thinking before reading
ction; (2) probes to support thinking following the read-
g. These two concepts are self-evident but warrant further
scussion.

EMONSTRATING YOUR THINKING

 often we forget that readers who are working with a
ore challenging text need to be taught how to think about
text in more sophisticated ways. As a more expert reader,
u can provide a powerful demonstration of how to think
out a text. First, read and think about the text yourself
hile keeping your group of readers in mind. You can
unt on your own systems of strategic actions for process-
g texts to guide you. Then select some principles that
ur students will need to engage as they read the text and
monstrate or teach in a way that helps students think
out them either in the introduction or during the discus-
on after reading.

For example, Ms. E. was working with a group of first
aders reading *Willy the Helper* (Level D) (see Chapter 14,
195). The events in the story took place on successive
ys of the week, and she wanted them to notice the struc-
re. In her introduction, she said:

In this story, the little girl tells what her dog Willy does to help
her each day of the week. She says, "On Monday, Willy helped
me do the laundry." Then on the next page she tells about the
next day. "On Tuesday . . ." Turn the page again and she tells
about the next day. "On Wednesday . . . " So think about the
days of the week to help you start to read each page.

s. E. also wanted her students to realize that the informa-
on in the pictures will help them understand the story. She
id,

You need to look at the pictures to understand what really
makes this book funny. The little girl says that Willy helped
her rake the leaves. What do you notice? [Children respond.]
Notice that Willy is just rolling around in the leaves and
messing them up and that he really isn't helping! On every
page, the girl says Willy helped her to do something, but you
will need to take a close look at the pictures to see whether
that is really true.

One of Mr. G.'s guided reading groups was discussing *The
Devil's Arithmetic* (Yolen) (Level X). This work of fantasy
by Jane Yolen begins in the present as 13-year-old Hannah
objects to going to Seder with her grandparents at the
beginning of Passover. Hannah doesn't see why her grandfather (who lost everyone but his sister Eva in the
Holocaust) has to keep bringing up old stories. Yet, Hannah
seems to share a special bond with Eva, and it is especially
strong when her aunt says the prayers over the candles.
Hannah drinks a little wine and pours her entire glass into
Elijah's cup—no real sacrifice since she doesn't want it.
But her grandfather is so pleased that he asks her to open
the door to welcome the prophet. As she opens the door, the
story changes completely. Hannah finds herself not in New
Rochelle but in a village in Poland, speaking and understanding Yiddish in 1942.

Mr. G. wanted the readers to put together important
information from the first three chapters as background for
understanding the meaning of the fantasy. Background
knowledge would also be important to set the scene. He
said:

When Hannah turned around and her family had disap-
peared, I was surprised and I knew right away that her whole
world had changed. She was seeing fields with furrow—
meaning that it had been plowed—and she saw a man with
a hoe. That made me think that maybe she had gone back to
another time. Hannah seemed a little spoiled and selfish to
me, and she didn't seem to value the past. She thought that
Seder was boring and was tired of her grandfather talking
about the war. Remember when she whined, "I'm tired of
remembering." So I wondered if this might teach her a lesson of some kind, and I was really anxious to read on.

Notice that some of Mr. G.'s remarks were "question-like."
He was wondering aloud but still demonstrating how a
reader might think about a text as he reads.

You don't want to dominate the discussion, but sometimes readers need to hear how more experienced readers
think about books. The statements above may at first seem
didactic. Why not just ask questions? This is always your
decision, but sometimes students do not know what to say.
You may feel you are dragging information out of them.
They often resort to searching for the answer they think you
want to hear. Mr. G. is sharing his own thinking rather than
saying he has "the" answer. His own comments demonstrate how a reader might be thinking. After comments, he

can then ask the students what they are thinking.

PROBING YOUR STUDENTS' THINKING

If students already have some ways of thinking about fiction in their repertoire, then *questioning* and *commenting* are effective ways to invite discussion. You may ask a few questions that require students to recall information, but in general, we are not talking here about closed questions such as, "Where did the story take place?" A closed question has a right answer that the teacher already knows. It might be just as well to ask whether everyone understands where the story takes place and clarify any misconceptions.

If you do ask closed questions, have a purpose in mind, such as reminding readers of valuable information that will be necessary as a foundation for thinking. Open-ended questions are much more productive, because students' thinking is so interesting and provides a great deal of information about them as readers. For example, asking open-ended questions such as, "Why do you think this person is acting so angry?" and "What does this statement make you think?" elicits discussion.

In the discussion of *The Devil's Arithmetic* described earlier, Mr. G. might have included more open-ended questions to get students to make comments. For example:

- Let's talk about the kind of person Hannah seems to be. What did you learn about her in the first three chapters?

- Hannah opens the door, expecting to see the doors of apartments. How do you know something has really changed?

- Is there anything about the scene that makes you think she is in a different time as well as a different place?

MAINTAINING A FLEXIBLE BALANCE

It is not a matter of demonstrating or probing and commenting. Within an intentional conversation, there will always be both. You will try to raise the level of students' contributions by modeling or demonstrating your thinking; at the same time, you do not want to choke off your students' thinking with a deluge of your own ideas. A flexible balance of interactional approaches is needed, and the interactions should feel like conversation. You can:

- Demonstrate your own thinking and then ask students to do the same.

- Make comments and invite reactions.

- Respond to students' thinking with ideas of your own.

- Provide some demonstration in the introduction but ask open-ended questions in the discussion.

- Encourage and build on students' comments.

- Provide demonstrations as explicit teaching points after reading.

- Let open-ended questions arise from the group.

- Invite students to ask their own questions.

- Wonder aloud to model questioning the text.

- Explicitly summarize and/or communicate information and then ask students what they think.

- Ask some questions during the introduction that prompt students' thinking and then come back to the questions and ask for their thinking during the discussion.

INTRODUCING AND DISCUSSING FICTION TEXTS IN GUIDED READING

The introduction you provide to a work of fiction sets the scene for successful comprehending. Below are some excerpts from teachers' introductions, followed by the teaching points they made after the reading. These examples are drawn from lessons based on realistic fiction, historical fiction, and fantasy at several grade levels. There is usually a relationship between the introduction and the discussion after reading. Notice how each teacher connects students to the meaning of the text before they read and brings them back to the meaning of the text following the reading. Think about how explicit the teachers are about the aspects of fiction and how they prompt students to think within, beyond, and about the text.

REALISTIC FICTION

Dr. Green (Leveled Readers) (level G) is a good example of an "information-like" text. It presents a very realistic picture of a visit to the doctor. There is a twist at the end, though: Dr. Green takes the boy home, because she is his mother!

Mr. S. framed his introduction so that children would be able to read the text with understanding. He began his introduction (see Figure 25-2) by inviting children to connect the text with their own experiences in visiting a doctor's office and then drew their attention to the sequence of actions in the pictures. Several times, he had the children

A GUIDED READING LESSON:
An Introduction to **Dr. Green** (LEVEL G, REALISTIC FICTION)

MR. S.: *[Prompts use of background knowledge.]* (PLACING A COPY OF THE BOOK IN FRONT OF EACH CHILD) What do you do when you visit the doctor's office?

JESSE: My doctor lets me play games. I like him.

PETER: My doctor tells me how tall I am and how much I weigh.

MARIANA: I like to look at all the things there.

MR. S.: *[Draws attention to important information in text or pictures.]* (POINTS TO CHILD ON COVER) This little boy tells about his visit to Dr. Green's office. Turn to pages 2 and 3 in your book. You can see that the little boy likes to play with things, too.

CARL: He is making a puzzle.

MR. S.: *[Draws attention to specific words.]* Yes, he seems to be enjoying that. Turn the page. Then he sees the doctor. Say *then*.

CHILDREN: *Then.*

MR. S.: *[Draws attention to specific words and to important information in the pictures.]* It starts just like *the*. Can you find the word *then* on page 4? You found it. Look at some of the things the boy does with Dr. Green.

MARIANA: On page 4, he gets weighed.

MR. S.: *[Draws attention to important information.]* Yes, just like Peter. He gets on the scale. Now turn the page and you can see that the doctor can measure how tall he is.

CARL: My doctor has a table like that one.

MARIANA: So does mine.

MR. S.: *[Draws attention to important information.]* Can you see how he is trying to get on the doctor's table so the doctor can check him? Turn to page 9. When the doctor looks in his mouth, he says . . .

JESSE AND PETER: Ah!

MR. S.: *[Draws attention to important information and to specific words.]* Yes, he does. And sometimes he listens to his heart. Say *sometimes*.

CHILDREN: *Sometimes.*

MR. .S.: *[Draws attention to specific word and important information.]* Think about the letter you would see first and find *sometimes* on page 10. You found it. Turn the page. You can see other things the doctor does before the boy goes home with his mom. Now close your book and go back to the beginning. Read all about the boy's visit to Dr. Green.

Figure 25-2. *A Guided Reading Lesson: An Introduction to* Dr. Green *(Level G, Realistic Fiction)*

say and locate a particular word (*then* and *sometimes,* for example).

In the teaching points after the lesson, Mr. S. invited children to discuss the story's end—why the boy went home with his mom and also went home with Dr. Green. Here the teacher was prompting them to follow the events of the plot. He also had them summarize by listing the kinds of things that happened during the visit, which will help them remember important information.

Let's look at an introduction to a level J fiction text, *Henry and Mudge: The First Book* (Rylant) (see Figure 25-3). Mrs. M. began by introducing the author and mentioning that this is a chapter book. One of her goals for the group was to help the readers understand that the text will be divided into chapters and that they will need to keep previous chapters in mind as they read. Getting a good start in a chapter book provides automatic background knowledge for reading subsequent chapters.

Mrs. M. referred to another book by the author that students had heard in an interactive read-aloud and helped the students understand that in addition to being a chapter book, this book is the first in a series. She referred to the

---

A GUIDED READING LESSON:
An Introduction to Henry and Mudge: The First Book (LEVEL J, REALISTIC FICTION)

MRS. M.: *[Introduces the format of the text, makes connections to another text by the same writer, and draws attention to the title.]* Your new book is called *Henry and Mudge: The First Book*. It's very exciting because this is a chapter book. The author is Cynthia Rylant. Remember the book *The Relatives Came?* Cynthia Rylant wrote that book, too. *Henry and Mudge: The First Book*. What do you think it might mean to say "The First Book"?

SHADA: Are there more books about them?

MRS. M.: *[Draws attention to the title's significance.]* That's right. This is the first book, but there are more books about Henry and Mudge, and you might like to read some of them later.

LIN: It's like *Clifford*. There are lots of books about him.

MRS. M.: *[Draws attention to character traits and invites readers to infer characters' emotions.]* Yes, a series of books about the same people or animals. Look at the front cover. There's Henry, and there's his big dog, Mudge. Turn the page and you see the title. And it says *Henry and Mudge: The First Book of Their Adventures*. There's another picture of Henry and Mudge. How do you think they feel about each other?

LIN: They like each other.

SHADA: They love each other. I have a dog like that.

MRS. M.: *[Explains a reader's tool showing how the text is organized.]* They do. Maybe some of you have pets that you play with and take care of, and that's what Henry does for Mudge. Turn the page. Do you see the word *contents* at the top? That means there are chapters in this book and the table of contents tells us the names of the chapters and the page. What's the name of the first chapter?

QUIANA: Henry.

MRS. M.: So the first chapter is going to be about Henry. And what page will it be on? Run your finger across to the number. *[Shows readers how to use the table of contents, indicating how the text is organized.]*

ISAK: Page 5.

MRS. M.: *[Shows readers how to use the table of contents, indicating how the text is organized.]* What is the next chapter and the page?

QUIANA: Mudge, on page 9.

MRS. M.: *[Shows readers how to use the table of contents, indicating how the text is organized.]* And that chapter will be something about Mudge. Let's check that. Turn to the next page. Do you see the chapter title *Henry?* What's the page?

ISAK: Page 5.

MRS. M.: *[Shows readers how to use the table of contents, indicating how the text is organized.]* Now turn to page 9. Do you see the chapter title *Mudge?*

WYATT: Yes.

MRS. M.: *[Summarizes how the text is organized and prompts readers to infer characters' motives.]* So all through this book, you'll see chapters and the title helps you think what the chapter will be about. You get to read the first three chapters today. You find out why Henry wants a dog and you read about how he gets Mudge. Just look at page 11. On the left you see Mudge.

ISAK: He's a puppy! He's really little.

MRS. M.: *[Draws attention to character traits.]* Then on the right, you see some collars. Those are all the collars Mudge wore. What happened?

QUIANA: He grew really big!

Figure 25-3. *A Guided Reading Lesson: An Introduction to* Henry and Mudge: The First Book

A GUIDED READING LESSON:
An Introduction to Henry and Mudge: The First Book (LEVEL J, REALISTIC FICTION) (CONTINUED)

MRS. M.: *[Draws attention to character traits.]* Listen while I read on page 11. "He grew out of seven collars in a row. And when he finally stopped growing . . . [TURNS THE PAGE], he weighed one hundred eighty pounds, he stood three feet tall, and he drooled."

SHADA: He's bigger than my dog!

MRS. M.: *[Draws attention to character traits.]* Yes, he's really big. Look back at page 11. Do you see the three little dots? That means that you pause and then keep going to the other page to finish the sentence. Cynthia Rylant was helping us really notice how big Mudge got. Okay, read the first three chapters, and if you have a little time when you finish, you can just take out some paper and do a quick sketch of anything this story reminds you of.

Figure 25-3. *A Guided Reading Lesson: An Introduction to* Henry and Mudge: The First Book *(cont.)*

relationship between Henry and Mudge, indicating its importance, and then showed students how the table of contents works. She had students do some specific work with the table of contents, turning to the indicated pages. She directed their attention to the fact that Mudge grows to be very big, and he drools (character traits). Finally, she explained the use of ellipses to help students understand this cue to keep going to the next page rather than stop. During the discussion after the reading, she invited children to describe Henry and Mudge, which helps them get to know the characters, and asks them to talk about how Henry and Mudge feel about each other, which prompted them to infer characters' feelings.

Now let's review some excerpts from Mr. P's introduction of *Pinky and Rex* (Howe), a level K fiction book, to a guided reading group (see Figure 25-4). He mentioned that this book is the beginning of a series and drew the children's attention to the characters' names and some of their personality traits. These traits set up the problem of the text very well, because both of the characters really like dinosaurs and want the same stuffed animal when they go to the museum. They always want everything to be the same, but there is only one stuffed pink dinosaur; thus tension is created. Mr. P. pointed out two long words related to the names of dinosaurs and ended by prompting the readers to search for more details about the problem.

In the discussion after reading, he asked children to explain the problem in the story, thus helping them to identify the problem, and prompted them to think about what Pinky and Rex were like and about their friendship and to

use that information to predict how the problem might be resolved.

Finally, let's review an introduction to a higher-level (level T) fiction text, *The Islander*, by Cynthia Rylant. (See Chapter 15, p. 231.)

Notice that Mr. H. drew students' attention to specific language signaling that this was a memoir and then labeled the genre, clarifying that Cynthia Rylant was presenting a fictional character who is writing a memoir. He also helped them grasp the particular meaning of the word *islander* as it was used connotatively in this text. In the discussion after reading, children commented about how they imagined Daniel felt putting their inferences into words. They also talked about whether the mermaid was real. Mr. H. followed up on Rylant's choice of Daniel's memoir to tell the story. He asked students to point out language that made the memoir seem real, again drawing attention to the writer's craft.

Finally, we share an introduction to *Buddha Boy*, by Kathe Koja, a level W fiction text (see Figure 25-6). In *Buddha Boy* the central character, Justin, has few friends and tries to stay out of the way of the high school's supposed sports star and cool guy, who is really a bully. When a new kid who doesn't conform or even care what others think moves into the school, Justin has to face up to his values.

Notice that Mr. C. began by asking students to think about their own experiences with teasing someone who might have been different and then provided a great deal of information about the characters in the book. In teaching points after the reading, Mr. C. asked the readers to discuss Justin's character and to provide evidence from the text to

---

GUIDED READING LESSON:
An Introduction to Pinky and Rex (LEVEL K, REALISTIC FICTION)

MR. P.: *[Indicates type of book (series) and draws attention to the title and characters.]* Today we are going to start reading *Pinky and Rex,* by James Howe. This is the first book of a series, so you might be interested in reading more books about these two best friends. Pinky is a boy and Rex is a girl. Does that surprise you?

CARLA: Rex is really a boy's name, but it doesn't matter because sometimes people have different names.

BAILEY: Bailey can be a girl or a boy.

MR. P.: *[Discusses character traits.]* Pinky is a boy and he lives with his family. He has a little sister named Amanda. He has twenty-seven stuffed animals!

DESHAWN: That's a lot.

ALENA: I have almost fifty.

SHANDI: I have about thirty I think.

MR. P.: *[Discusses character traits and draws attention to vocabulary.]* He likes stuffed animals and so does his friend Rex. Rex is crazy about dinosaurs. She also has a lot of stuffed animals, but her favorite ones are the stuffed dinosaurs, and she also has clothes that have dinosaurs on them. Look at page 4. She's trying to decide what to wear. Can you find the word *tyrannosaurus* on this page? Say the name *tyrannosaurus.*

ALL: *Tyrannosaurus.*

MR. P.: *[States the problem of the story.]* Say the word *stegosaurus.* Find it. Those are really long words, aren't they? But they are pretty easy when we know they are the names of dinosaurs. You will find out that Pinky and Rex are best friends. They like to have *everything the same.* So do you think that might mean that sometimes they want the same thing? And remember, they both really like stuffed animals.

SHANDI: They might want to wear the same T-shirt with a dinosaur.

BAILEY: They might want the same kinds of stuffed animals.

MR. P.: Read to page 17 and see if you can figure out what they might both want.

Figure 25-4. *A Guided Reading Lesson: An Introduction to* Pinky and Rex

---

show what kind of person he was, including doubts and fears. He also called attention to the way the writer used first person to show the Buddha Boy through Justin's eyes, helping students recognize aspects of the writer's craft. He followed up on the hyphenated words the writer has created.

When readers explore realistic fiction, they are always thinking about whether something could have happened, and they often discover insights that apply to their own lives. Choose books that have issues that are important to your students. Themes like families, visits to the doctor, pets, friends, loss, loneliness, bullying, popularity, and teasing appeal to students at different ages in the elementary and middle schools.

HISTORICAL FICTION

In processing historical fiction, readers must understand the story or problem in the light of historical events, per-

spectives, and circumstances. Even though all or some of the characters may be imaginary, the setting should be authentic. Historical fiction can help students better understand past times but also present real human problems. Courage is the same whether shown in contemporary or historical situations, for example, but it may be shown in different ways. A real benefit of historical fiction is that children can learn to understand that people just like themselves were involved in the events and accomplishments of the past. Often, serious human issues such as war, immigration, and survival can be better understood through the eyes of fictional characters who are about the same age as the readers.

Notice some of Miss P.'s decisions in a portion of an introduction to *A Lion to Guard Us* (Bulla), a work of historical fiction at level M. *A Lion to Guard Us* is a simple

A GUIDED READING LESSON:
An Introduction to **The Islander** (LEVEL T, REALISTIC FICTION)

MR. H.: *[Draws attention to the main character and the setting.]* At the beginning of this book, Daniel, the main character, is remembering when he was only ten years old and his parents died in a plane crash.

HOPE: That would be awful.

YVONNE: Does he live on an island or go there?

MR. H.: *[Provides background information and some traits of another character.]* After the crash, Daniel came to live on the island with his grandfather, who hardly ever talks. Just imagine this. His grandfather is nice but doesn't talk to him. He's just lost his parents. He has no friends. *[Explains how a term is used in the text.]* This is a very small island and everyone knows each other. They are *islanders.* Daniel feels that he is an *outsider,* not an *islander.* So he spends a lot of time alone, reading and walking on the beach, and some pretty unusual things start to happen to him. *[Prompts readers to make predictions.]* Turn to page 3. [READING.] *I was a boy when I met the mermaid, and, of course, no one believed me.* What does that make you expect?

RICHARD: This is going to be a fantasy story.

FOREST: Maybe he meets a mermaid and she tells him something about his parents. Or maybe the mermaid is really an angel or something.

JENNIFER: But he's not going to have anyone believe him so he will be alone even more because he won't have any friends.

MR. H.: *[Points out key words helping to understand the genre and the setting.]* Yes, also notice that the first few words—*I was a boy*—tell you that he's older now, looking back on this time. What does that make you think about?

MONTEL: He's a lot older now and he's doing a memoir.

JENNIFER: It kind of has the feeling like looking back a long time, like when we wrote about a memory of a person in our family.

MR. H.: *[Clarifies the genre and draws attention to the writer's craft.]* This is written as if it is a memoir. I think it's a fictional memoir, but Cynthia Rylant is creating a character who is writing a memoir. Just turn back two pages. Cynthia Rylant has created a dedication to make this character seem more real: *My name is Daniel Jennings, and on this day, my twentieth birthday, I wish to make a record of the marvelous things that happened to me when I was a boy. I dedicate it to my grandfather.* Doesn't that make the story seem real?

YVONNE: Yes.

MR. H.: *[Provides background information.]* This story starts three years after Daniel's parents' crash, so he's been this lonely for three years. Turn to page 5 and read silently from the top to find out a little about the island. The name of the island is Coquille, and it is in Canada in the western part—off the coast of British Columbia, a province of Canada.

ALL: [STUDENTS READ THEN COMMENT ON THE CHARACTERISTICS OF THE ISLAND.] There is no electricity; there are few visitors; only about thirty families live on the island; the world outside doesn't interest the islanders.

MR. H.: *[Draws attention to character traits.]* You also learned a little bit about Daniel here, too, didn't you.

HOPE: He really wants to get off the island and do things like watch TV and stuff.

MR. H.: *[Sets up the problem of the story.]* So Daniel really wanted something unusual to happen. He is so lonely that he is really imagining a lot of things, and then he finds something that looks like a mermaid's comb—something a mermaid would use to comb her hair—and he really wants to meet the mermaid. You might be like I was—not sure if the mermaid was in his imagination or whether this was really happening. So read from page 3 to 53, the first four chapters, and when you finish reading, write what you think about that and then we'll talk about it.

Figure 25-5. *A Guided Reading Lesson: An Introduction to* The Islander

---

A GUIDED READING LESSON:
An Introduction to Buddha Boy (LEVEL W, REALISTIC FICTION)

MR. C.: *[Makes connections to personal experiences.]* Think in your mind if you have ever known a situation in which someone was a little different from everyone else—maybe dressed differently or looked different—and the other people didn't like them or teased them.

ALL: [STUDENTS NOD.]

MR. C.: *[Provides background information and character traits and clarifies a concept.]* That's what is going to happen in *Buddha Boy,* by Kathe Koja. Justin is in high school and he has two friends, Megan and Jakob. His parents are divorced. Justin isn't really a popular kid, but he isn't unpopular either. He just keeps to himself and his two friends, and he avoids a character named Mark McAnus. McAnus and his crew—that's his friends, guys named Magnur, Winston, and Hooks—are the "cool guys." Do you know what that means?

LARRY: They are the popular guys. They do things and everybody wants to do it, too.

GENO: They might be the football players or something like that.

MR. C.: *[Provides background information and character traits.]* They are sports stars and very popular, but there is something else about Mark that you need to know. Justin doesn't like him, and in fact, he is kind of scared of him, because McAnus is really mean. He is always teasing and fighting and beating up other kids. He doesn't do it himself; he gets his crew, Magnur, Winston, and Hooks, to do it for him. None of the teachers seem to notice.

KAVI: When there are guys like that, you just try not to get noticed by them.

JACLYN: I hate it when people are always teasing—like jerking your hair or putting gum on your chair and stuff.

MR. C.: That is a very bad way to be, and Justin just tries to stay out of Mark's way. But then a new boy moves into the school, and he is really, really different. His head is shaved; he wears weird, big T-shirts. Look at pages 6 and 7 and listen to this description. [READING.] *Then as he got closer and I got a look at his face, I saw that he wasn't Special Needs at all, he looked perfectly normal, except that he was smiling. Not a nervous smile, or that tight bottled-up grin you grin when you're really humiliated and trying not to show it; no, it was a real sunny regular all's-right-with-the-word smile, which meant that he was either high, or crazy, Or—closer now, coming right up to our table, big ears and tilted, sleepy eyes, not bald but shaved, you could see the blond stubble poking up on his scalp. But you could tell he wasn't a skinhead, or anything sick like that, just—just strange, the way a platypus is strange, or one of those deep-sea plants, waving waxy fingers on the ocean floor. "Excuse me," he said to us, very politely. "Do you have any change?"*

"What?" said Megan in spite of herself, and then looked away, mortified that she'd said anything at all, that she'd even acknowledged this kid standing there with his hand out, even the biggest moochers didn't go about it as blatantly as this. "What's the matter?" I asked. "Forget your lunch money?"

His smile went wider still; for a second I thought of Humpty-Dumpty, that bald head smiling all around itself. "Oh no," he said. "I'm begging. Like a monk, you know?" **[Sets up the problem of the story and provides specific language related to character traits.]** What do you think about that?

JACLYN: He's really weird. Why's he begging for money?

GENO: He must be really poor.

MR. C.: The new kid, whose name is Michael, is really different and Justin and Megan and Jakob don't even want to be around him. They start to call him *Buddha Boy* because he seems like a Buddhist monk. Have you ever heard of that? *[Elicits background knowledge and provides information about characters' perspectives.]*

LARRY: Yes, they do shave their heads and they might beg. I saw that on television. Is he really one?

MR. C.: I don't know if he is a real monk, but he does some things like a monk—shaving his head and begging and other things. As you read this book, you will find out why he does that. Look at the part I just read. You will notice that Kathe Koja uses a lot of hyphenated words. Can you find one and tell what it means? *[Draws attention to a particular way of creating words that is an aspect of the writer's craft.]*

Figure 25-6. *A Guided Reading Lesson: An Introduction to* Buddha Boy

---

A GUIDED READING LESSON:
An Introduction to **Buddha Boy** (LEVEL W, REALISTIC FICTION) (CONTINUED)

KAVI: *Humpty-Dumpty*–like he looks like Humpty-Dumpty.

GENO: Also *all's-right-with-the-world.* She made that up.

MR. C.: What do you think it means?

KAVI: It's a kind of smile he had–like a real smile that says everything is okay.

MR. C.: *[Draws attention to the writer's craft and to punctuation.]* So the author sometimes puts words together with hyphens just to show you what something is like. Also, notice on lines 3 and 4 that she puts in dashes to help you know how to pause. Her sentences are really long, so sometimes you just have to keep going. Read that long sentence silently with the dashes. [STUDENTS READ.] Okay, now read the first four chapters.

---

ure 25-6. *A Guided Reading Lesson: An Introduction to* Buddha Boy *(cont.)*

apter book that might be one of the first historical fiction xts that children read for themselves, but they will have eard many others during interactive read-aloud. Once ildren understand the setting and the circumstances nder which the children live, the text is a straightforward ory of overcoming obstacles.

Miss P. began by drawing children's attention to the cover, which provided the basis for thinking about times past. She made the link to "the first Thanksgiving," with which children were familiar. Miss P. then provided background for the story by explaining the characters' circumstances. She encouraged children to compare the life of the

---

A GUIDED READING LESSON:
An Introduction to **A Lion to Guard Us** (LEVEL M, HISTORICAL FICTION)

MISS P.: *[Draws attention to the title, author, and cover as foundation for understanding the genre.]* Take a look at the cover of this book, *A Lion to Guard Us,* by Clyde Robert Bulla. What do you notice?

MADELEINE: It's long ago because they are wearing old-fashioned clothes and on one of the old ships. It might be about coming to America, about when George Washington was here.

MISS P.: *[Provides background information on the setting, time, and circumstances of the characters.]* It is a story that took place long ago, even before George Washington. It was about the time of the first Thanksgiving, when Jamestown was settled by the English. This girl is named Amanda Freebody, and she has a little brother Jemmy and a little sister Meggie. They are on a ship, but the story starts before that. Amanda works for a lady named Miss Triplett. Even though she is only about ten or eleven, she works full time in the kitchen. Her mother is sick, and she is trying to take her place and also take care of her brother and sister.

GRAYSON: Didn't kids have to work a lot in those times?

JAIMIE: They had lots of people working in big houses to cook all of the food.

MISS P.: *[Provides background information on the setting, time, and circumstances of the characters.]* Kids often had to work. In Amanda's case, she just worked so that she and her family would have somewhere to live and something to eat, and her mother is really sick.

MADELEINE: What happened to her father?

MISS P.: *[Provides background information on the setting, time, and circumstances of the characters; invites comparison to modern times; prompts predictions.]* Her father's name is James Freebody, and three years ago he went to America to try to find a better life. They haven't heard from him in three years! So Amanda is very excited when a stranger comes to the door with news of her father. Read the first three chapters, to page 19. As you read, keep in mind that things were really different for children in those days. They just had to survive any way they could until the father came back or could send for them. When you finish, go back and mark a place that surprised you or made you think about how Amanda's life was different from yours.

---

ure 25-7. *A Guided Reading Lesson: An Introduction to* A Lion to Guard Us main character, Amanda, with their own as a foundation for understanding this character's perspectives.

In the discussion after the lesson, Miss P. had children remember details showing what Amanda's life was like. She helped them to notice information and identify the problem of the story. She also had students talk about what kind of person Amanda was and provided evidence from the text to help them notice character traits.

Next, we share an introduction to *Number the Stars,* by Lois Lowry, a level R historical fiction text (see Figure 25-8). *Number the Stars* deals with hard issues. Set in Denmark during the Second World War, it is the story of Annemarie, who lives upstairs from a Jewish family. Annemarie's family is connected with the Resistance.

Notice that Miss V. provided information on the genre and the setting and made the connection to a book children had heard read aloud, *The Yellow Star,* which will be useful in understanding *Number the Stars.* She also prompted them to infer what the characters are feeling and write about it.

After the reading Miss V. invited the children to talk about how Annemarie is feeling in the story, prompting the use of inference as a background for understanding the character's motivations, and she worked to help children understand the setting.

In general, helping students read historical fiction effectively will require much attention to the setting so that culturally bound perspectives can be understood. In addition, you will want to help students see that human problems are similar even though they occur in different times and circumstances. As students become more sophisticated in reading the genre, it will be important for them to make a habit of critiquing a work's authenticity.

FANTASY

Fantasy demands that readers enter into imaginary worlds or understand characters who have superhuman or mystical characteristics. Here, as in historical fiction, the setting is quite important, because children need to understand the parameters of those fantasy worlds as boundaries for the characters: they cannot act outside them, suddenly behaving as though they live in a realistic world.

Fantasy can take many different forms, among them:

▫ Supernatural characters living in a real world.

▫ Settings that change back or forward in time.

▫ Realistic characters who enter unreal worlds.

▫ Fantasy worlds with a variety of superhuman creatures.

Often, works of fantasy depict a conflict between good and evil. The characters are sometimes less complex than in works of realistic fiction (where they frequently display a mixture of strong and weak traits) because they play the role of hero.

Young children enjoy traditional literature or simple animal fantasy, both of which deal with simple, often patterned stories and characters that have definite traits but do not develop much over time. Reading and understanding many traditional stories and simple works of fantasy will provide a foundation for understanding highly complex literature (see Chapters 10 and 11 for a fuller discussion of the genre).

Let's examine an introduction to *Miss Hen's Feast,* a level I animal fantasy (Leveled Reader) (see Figure 25-9). This story is a version of the traditional tale "Stone Soup," in which everyone contributes a little bit to a pot of soup and it turns out to be wonderful. In the tale, however, no trickery is involved. Notice that Mr. M. helps children understand the central problem of the story—that the animals do not have much food left.

In teaching points after the reading, Mr. M. returned to the connection between *Stone Soup* or *Nail Soup* and this story, helping children make a connection between texts. He also had students read Mr. Owl's statement and talk about what it means, repeating some of the language of the text and the central theme. They then looked more closely at the words *arrive, arrived,* and *arriving* and discussed meaning as signaled by the endings.

SCIENCE FICTION

Finally we will take a look at excerpts from an introduction to, and a discussion of, *Among the Hidden* (Haddix), work of fantasy at level Z (see Figure 25-10). *Among the Hidden* is set at some point in the future; the reader required to assume an imaginary history that led to the circumstances in the book. Society is divided into two groups the "Barons," who rule, and everyone else, who is poor. On penalty of death, families are allowed to have only two children. The central character, Luke, is a third child who must remain hidden, a "shadow child." This is the first book a series about the "shadow children."

A GUIDED READING LESSON:
An Introduction to Number the Stars (LEVEL R, HISTORICAL FICTION)

MISS V.: *[Introduces the genre.]* Our new book today is *Number the Stars,* by Lois Lowry. This fictional story takes place in Denmark during the time of the Second World War. So what kind of fiction is it?

ERIC: Realistic fiction?

VALERIE: Historical realistic fiction?

MISS V.: *[Prompts the readers to link the text to another of the same genre.]* It is historical fiction, and yes, it's realistic, too, because it *could* have taken place. But we'll just call it historical fiction. This story might remind you a little of *The Yellow Star,* which I read to you a couple of months ago. Does anyone remember that book?

KALINDA: The king wore a yellow star to show the Nazis that he didn't want them to tell who the Jews were.

DESIREE: He rode through the city on a horse wearing the star and everyone else did too.

MISS V.: *[Confirms the readers' knowledge and prompts them to infer the characters' feelings.]* Yes, King Christian wore that yellow star, because the German Nazis wanted to know who the Jews were–even the children–so that they could treat them badly. And, eventually, they took them away to camps that were like prisons. Wouldn't that be scary?

VALERIE: It would be very scary.

ERIC: He was a Christian?

CHRIS: That's just his name, but he might be.

MISS V.: *[Introduces the setting and plot.]* Well, his name was Christian–King Christian. This story is about Annemarie and her family who live in Copenhagen, Denmark. The Germans have captured the city and there are soldiers everywhere. Annemarie lives with her father and mother and little sister Kirsti in an apartment house. She had an older sister, Lise, and you will find out what happened to her. Her best friend, Ellen, lives downstairs in the building and her family is Jewish. Annemarie and Kirsti often go on Friday nights to see Ellen's mother light the candles, so the girls are learning about each other's customs. Turn to page 2. Do you see a word in italics? *[Introduces the readers to treatment of vocabulary.]*

FRANCIE: Halt?

MISS V.: Yes, that's a German word, but it looks like the English word *halt,* which means . . .?

FRANCIE: Stop!

MISS V.: *[Prompts the readers to notice vocabulary.]* Yes. In this book you will find some German and Danish words. You don't have to pronounce them perfectly, because you are reading silently, so just notice them and think whether they are names of people or places or other words. You'll read that Annemarie and Ellen are really scared of the German soldiers, but they know that the Danish people are still fighting them. Look on page 8. Annemarie's parents read the Danish newspaper, which is illegal, and then they have to burn it.

DESIREE: So the soldiers won't arrest them.

CHRIS: It's saying that they used bombs.

MISS V.: *[Introduces new vocabulary.]* The Danish people were fighting back in all the ways they could. But they had to be secret about it. They used *sabotage.* You'll find that long word in the sixth line from the top–*sabotage.*

CHRIS: Kind of using bombs in secret.

KALINDA: Or doing the newspaper.

FRANCIE: It's anything against the Nazis, to make it hard for them to keep control.

MISS V.: *[Confirms readers' predictions and focuses attention on characters.]* You're right. It is just about anything that undermines the Germans or weakens them. You'll find out in this story that Annemarie's family sabotages the Germans in lots of ways. Read to page 26, the first four chapters. When you are finished, write something about how one of the characters feels.

Figure 25-8. *A Guided Reading Lesson: An Introduction to* Number the Stars

---

An Introduction to Miss Hen's Feast (LEVEL I, FANTASY)

MR. M.: *[Draws attention to the title and prompts children to make connections.]* This book is called *Miss Hen's Feast.* What does that title make you think about right away?

HENRY: It might be about the Little Red Hen.

LILY: She's doing soup this time.

MR. M.: Well, it is a hen and she does look like she has some good hot food in the bowl. Look at page 2. Can you see that it is winter and it's very chilly? There she is watching the snow fall. She says *Brr!* right there at the beginning. Do you ever say that when you are really cold—*Brr!? [Provides information on the setting and calls attention to the writer's craft.]* Miss Hen is thinking about all her friends, the Skunk family, and Mr. Fox, and the Rabbit family, and the Chipmunk family. So she went to the kitchen to make some hot soup for her lunch. Look at the picture. Do you see the bubble with the little dots above her head?

CHILDREN: Yes.

MR. M.: *[Points out a print convention.]* That means she has an idea—she's thinking of something. What does it look like she might be thinking about?

MARTHA: Vegetables.

DAVID: Carrots and potatoes.

MATTHEW: And maybe celery.

MR. M.: *[Uses vocabulary words.]* In the picture you see carrots and turnips, things you might put in soup, and you might put in spices, too. Do you know what spices are?

HENRY: My mom puts in spices to season it.

DAVID: Kind of like salt.

MR. M.: Spices make soup taste better. Like salt and pepper but better. *[Clarifies vocabulary words.]* Well, Miss Hen's idea is to have a feast. Do you know what a feast is?

DAVID: It's like Thanksgiving.

LILY: A big party.

MR. M.: *[Uses vocabulary from the story and provides background.]* Yes, a feast is a special party with lots of good food to eat. Look at page 4. Miss Hen went to the shed and got a heavy pot and some wood to build a fire. Then she invited her friends to the feast. There's Mrs. Skunk and she is saying that she will bring some food, but Miss Hen told them not to bring too much. *[Provides reasons for a character's actions.]* The reason she told them not to bring too much is it's almost the end of winter. Soon it will be warm and sunny and they can plant gardens, but right now, she knew none of them had much food left.
Turn to page 6. Next, Miss Hen filled a huge pot with water and put carrots in it. Say *next.*

CHILDREN: *Next.*

MR. M.: *[Calls attention to a key word and invites interpretation of the pictures.]* Find the word *next* on page 6. [CHILDREN LOCATE THE WORD.] Look at page 7. Now what is happening in the story?

LILY: There's the skunks.

MATTHEW: Look at the little ones!

HENRY: They are bringing something to eat.

MR. M.: *[Uses language from the story and prompts remembering important information.]* The Skunk family is the first to arrive. Those are turnips, and they say, "The turnips aren't much," but remember, Miss Hen told them not to bring much and she will say, "That's just what we need!"
Turn to page 8. There's that important word *spices.* What two letters would you expect to see at the beginning?

CHILDREN: *Sp.* [CHILDREN LOCATE THE WORD *SPICES*.]

Figure 25-9. *A Guided Reading Lesson: An Introduction to* Miss Hen's Feast

---

A GUIDED READING LESSON:
An Introduction to **Miss Hen's Feast** (LEVEL I, FANTASY) (CONTINUED)

MR. M.: *[Makes a connection to another text.]* Pretty soon all the rest of the animals arrive. Well, they had some fun and then Miss Hen served the feast, and they had plenty to eat even though each of them only brought a little food. This story reminds me of the story of *Stone Soup,* or *Nail Soup* is another name for it. Do you remember that story?

HENRY: That's when he tricked them and they put in just a little of this and a little of that and then they had soup.

MR. M.: *[Alerts readers to a character's traits.]* That's right. So watch for what Mr. Owl, who is very wise, says about that. Turn to the beginning of the story and read about Miss Hen's feast.

Figure 25-9. *A Guided Reading Lesson: An Introduction to* Miss Hen's Feast *(cont.)*

Mr. L. introduced the book on day one by describing the setting. He engaged children in an in-depth discussion of Luke's situation, and he demonstrated his thinking as described earlier in this chapter. After the reading on day one, Mr. L. asked the students to further describe what they learned about Luke's situation. He was prompting them to remember and summarize important information from the story. He then asked them to think about why there might be rules like this, comments that required inferring cause and effect. Finally, he asked readers to think about why rules might sound good but how they could also have bad effects, which required critical thinking.

On day two, Mr. L. asked children to remember what Luke's life was like and to see his situation from the character's perspective. Only with that perspective can the reader know how Luke feels. After reading on day two, he asked readers to talk about Luke's world and how he saw his own situation. This action prompted them to share information about the setting and the character and to infer the character's feelings.

Fantasy is a rich world for readers. Many individuals become lifelong readers of fantasy, exploring universal truths by entering another world. We have only to look at the popularity of Tolkien's *Lord of the Rings* or the Harry Potter series to see the appeal that fantasy can have. Yet many people never learn how to read or appreciate it.

A GUIDED READING LESSON:
An Introduction to **Among the Hidden** (LEVEL Z, SCIENCE FICTION)

DAY 1 Introduction

MR. L.: *[Clarifies a key concept.]* Your new book today is a very mysterious book called *Among the Hidden,* by Margaret Peterson Haddix. The main character, Luke, is called a "shadow child." That means that his family has to pretend that he doesn't even exist. He has to stay inside all of the time and stay hidden. No one can know about him. He can't even go near a window.

SAUNDRA: I'd hate that!

JEROME: Why does he have to do that?

JEFFREY: Maybe someone is looking for him to kill him, like in the witness protection program.

MR. L.: *[Draws attention to the setting.]* You'll be reading to find out why. The society is pretty different from ours, too, and you'll see some of the ways it is different. For example, Luke's family lives on a farm and they do not have many things like computers or televisions. But there is another group called "the Barons," and you will read about them.

CANDACE: They could be the rulers or the rich people.

MR. L.: *[Prompts thinking about the setting.]* Luke hates being hidden. Be thinking about how he feels and what he wants and also about what his world is like and how it is different from ours. Read the first three chapters and then make a note or two about what Luke's world is like.

Figure 25-10. *A Guided Reading Lesson: An Introduction to* Among the Hidden

---

A GUIDED READING LESSON:
An Introduction to **Among the Hidden** (LEVEL Z, SCIENCE FICTION) (CONTINUED)

DAY 1 Discussion

MR. L.: *[Asks for recall of, and opinions about, the setting.]* What were you thinking about Luke's life?

CANDACE: He's really in a very bad position. He can't do anything.

JEFFREY: I don't see how he can even keep living like that. What about when he gets older and wants to go places and stuff and even get a job?

DAWN: Can he ever leave and get married?

MR. L.: *[Asks for cause and effect.]* Did you get an idea why he has to stay hidden?

JEFFREY: Because there's a law and there can't be more than two kids. And it would have been better if he was one of the two oldest kids, because his brothers are both mean.

MR. L.: *[Probes thinking about the setting.]* What are you thinking about the time and place of the story?

SAUNDRA: It seems like it might have been a long time ago because they live on a farm and don't have many machines. Or it could even be now, but something like this hasn't happened, so I don't know.

MR. L.: *[Shares a personal connection. Models questioning the text.]* It's actually in the future, but only some people have modern machines. All the time I was reading this book, I wondered how society could make a rule that is so harsh. When I was traveling in China, I learned that there was a rule there about having only one child per family! The reason was that there were just too many people. There weren't enough jobs or food for everyone, so they wanted to reduce their population. They didn't actually kill people, but families had trouble getting benefits like health care and education if they had more than one child. But i was a hard rule to follow. I found myself wondering then and again when I read this book if making rules like that really works. And I also wondered why the Barons live like rich people and Luke's family is so poor. It seemed unfair, and I wondered if they really needed to be so harsh about families having more than two children or if some people were just being greedy. As we read on, think about why they have this rule and whether it is fair. I'm also wondering if there are a lot more hidden children and somehow they will get together to do something about their situation. So we'll read more tomorrow.

DAY 2 Introduction

MR. L.: *[Prompts summary of information.]* Remember what Luke's life was like in *Among the Hidden*?

SAUNDRA: He was the third child so he just had to stay hidden.

DAWN: I think he's going to find that there are other hidden children, because he saw a movement in a window in the big house.

MR. L.: *[Prompts thinking about the setting and inferring character's feelings.]* Yes, he watches all of the time, so he really knows what is going on. It was okay when no other house was near his, but now the houses are close. So as you are reading today, think about Luke's world—why it could be very dangerous for him and his family even to show his face. That will help you understand his feelings. Read to chapter 6 and when you come back, we can talk more about how Luke's world makes his life so difficult.

Figure 25-10. *A Guided Reading Lesson: An Introduction to* Among the Hidden *(cont.)*

LEARNING FROM READING FICTION

Your students will be reading a great deal of fiction if you take into account their independent reading as well as your work with them in guided reading, book clubs, and interactive read-aloud. It is important for them to balance fiction and nonfiction in their reading diets, but variety within fiction genres is equally important. As they move into high school and college, their required reading will increasingly dominated by nonfiction (except for literat courses). Having had good experiences with fiction c ensure that they continue to explore these genres duri their recreational reading. The way you work with th texts daily can help your students build strategic systems expanding their knowledge of all types of fiction.

SUGGESTIONS FOR PROFESSIONAL DEVELOPMENT:

PLANNING TEXT INTRODUCTIONS TO FICTION TEXTS

Work with a group of cross-grade-level colleagues.

As a group, select one of the fiction genres to explore across the grades. We suggest challenging yourselves by choosing a fiction genre that you have not worked with very much in guided reading.

Have each participant choose a book from the genre that will be appropriate for a guided reading group in his classroom.

4 Work together to analyze the text characteristics, using Chapter 12 and the examples in this chapter.

5 Share your analyses of the texts and compare them. How do the requirements of easier texts provide a foundation for reading higher-level texts?

6 Plan an introduction to a fiction text that each participant will use in the classroom.

7 Demonstrate and discuss each introduction.

8 Summarize what each of you has learned about introducing fiction texts to readers.

CHAPTER TWENTY-SIX

USING GUIDED READING TO TEACH FOR THE COMPREHENDING OF NONFICTION TEXTS

In this information age, the importance of being able to read and write informational texts critically and well cannot be overstated. Informational literacy is central to success, and even survival, in schooling, the workplace and the community.

—NELL DUKE

Readers of fiction regularly report being "transported" to other worlds, but nonfiction can also have this delightful time-travel quality. Through nonfiction, we can become intimate with people who will never be personally available to us—people with qualities to appreciate, admire, abhor, or marvel at. We get to know them and learn about their lives and times. Through nonfiction, we can feel the joy of learning new things and visit places and times we could not otherwise.

Guided reading can build a reader's ability to process expository texts, whether biographical (biography, autobiography, and memoir) or informational. (Biographical and factual texts are very different in purpose, structure, language, and topic.) As teachers of reading, we want to be sure that students not only read a wide variety of nonfiction texts but also comprehend them in a way that helps them grow in their ability to learn from informational texts. Many adults continue to use factual texts for self-education throughout their lives, and this is what we want for our students. Reaching that goal means providing effective small-group reading instruction based on nonfiction texts.

WHY USE NONFICTION IN GUIDED READING?

A commonly held reason for teaching students how to read nonfiction is that this is how they will be expected to learn about their world during upper elementary and subsequent years of schooling (Chall 1990). Though true, we do not subscribe to the theory that students first *learn to read* and then *read to learn*. We cannot divide literacy learning into discrete stages. Students learn by reading from the very beginning, and they continue learning to read throughout all their years of schooling.

Perhaps the greatest benefit to students in reading nonfiction is that it is real. While the accuracy of nonfiction is sometimes an issue, it is very satisfying to read about events that really happened, or are happening now, to add to our knowledge of the world, or to learn more about the lives of people of achievement. But children need specific instruction in how to process nonfiction genres, which are as varied as fiction. This chapter focuses on books, but you can apply the same instructional techniques to reading the newspaper, Internet and journal articles, instruction manuals, and many other kinds of nonfiction texts.

BIOGRAPHICAL TEXTS (BIOGRAPHY, AUTOBIOGRAPHY, AND MEMOIR)

The special appeal of biographical texts is that they present us with stories of real people's lives. These stories can inspire us. Through them we can learn about making critical life decisions, overcoming obstacles, and displaying courage and being persistent in the pursuit of goals. As genres:

- Biography refers to a text written about a subject by another person.
- Autobiography refers to text written about a subject by himself/herself.
- Memoir refers to a text written about an individual's life either by himself/herself or by another person who was part of the experience. A memoir often does not cover the individual's whole life but focuses on a particular person, place, or episode. It includes the writer's reflections on the experience. While both autobiography and memoir deal with an author's personal experience, memoir is less encompassing.

All biographical texts tell about a person's life, but each of the above genres does so in a special way. The biographer judges and selects the events, circumstances, and actions that he or she thinks are the most important to understand about the subject. The biographer may make the subject unadulterated hero or a sleazy villain or present a highly analytical, balanced picture, sometimes even helping us understand someone who has performed evil deeds. Biographers cannot escape bias. Autobiographers do the same but find it even harder to present an objective picture because they are explaining themselves and their actions. The writer of memoir seeks to evoke emotions or insights based on an intense memory, suspended in time.

PLANNING FOR GUIDED READING LESSONS USING BIOGRAPHICAL TEXTS

We outline some of the teaching possibilities you have when working with your students in guided reading using biographical texts (see Figure 26-1). The first column lists the demands on readers for thinking within, beyond, and about a biographical text.

As in fiction, readers need to follow, understand, and remember a series of events through which the subject's life is revealed. An added demand of biographical texts is to truly understand the setting—the place and the times as well as the life circumstances—that affect the subject, as well as the critical decisions that reveal the writer's purpose. Biographers do not write just to tell a story; there are reasons for selecting the subject. Usually, the subject's life tells some overarching story—inspirational or cautionary—that the writer wants to convey. As in fiction, readers must notice how

Planning for Guided Reading Lessons Using Biography

Thinking within the text:	DEMONSTRATION [SHOW EVIDENCE IN THE TEXT.]	PROBING [SHOW EVIDENCE IN THE TEXT.]
□ Follow and understand the events in the subject's life.	□ This biography tells about ____'s life. It starts when he was ____. □ Then ____.	□ This biography is about ____'s life. Look at page ____. What did the writer begin by telling us?
□ Gather important information about the subject and the setting.	□ When ____ was born, ____. □ This person lived in ____, which was important because ____. □ This person lived at a time when ____.	□ What did you learn about ____'s life? □ What was important about where ____ lived? □ What did you learn about the times in which ____ lived?
□ Notice the important decisions the subject makes over his/her life.	□ ____ decided to ____, and that made a difference in his life because ____. □ ____ made some important decisions in his/her life, for example ____.	□ What are some of the important decisions that ____ had to make?
□ Notice how the subject changes over time.	□ When he/she was young, ____ was ____. But ____ changed in this way:____. [provide example]	□ What was ____ when he/she was young? □ How did ____ change during his/her life?
□ Identify the challenging circumstances in the subject's life.	□ This person had many obstacles to overcome. Some were ____. □ This person met some challenges, for example, ____.	□ What obstacles did ____ have to overcome to succeed? □ What challenges did ____ have to meet to succeed?
□ Solve words and take on new vocabulary related to the subject's life.	□ There are some new words in this book that you need to know to understand ____'s life.	□ What does ____ mean? How is this word important to the story of ____'s life?

Figure 26-1. *Planning for Guided Reading Lessons Using Biography*

Planning for Guided Reading Lessons Using Biography (CONTINUED)

Thinking beyond the text:	DEMONSTRATION [SHOW EVIDENCE IN THE TEXT.]	PROBING [SHOW EVIDENCE IN THE TEXT.]
▪ Infer the subject's feelings and motivations.	▪ When this happened, the writer is helping readers know that ___ felt ___.	▪ How do you think ___ felt when ___?
▪ Infer how life circumstances were related to the subject's decisions.	▪ The writer is telling readers that ___ made this decision because ___.	▪ Why do you think ___ made that decision?
▪ Infer which decisions made the critical differences in the subject's life.	▪ Think about the most important decision ___ made. ▪ I think that one very important decision was ___.	▪ What do you think the most important decision(s) were that ___ made in his life?
▪ Connect the text to other texts, to background knowledge and to personal experience.	▪ This person's life may remind you of ___. ▪ This biography may remind you of some other biographies and stories, for example, ___.	▪ Does this person's life remind you of anything in your own life? ▪ Does this person's life remind you of anything you know? ▪ Does this biography remind you of other books or stories?
▪ Make predictions as to what the subject will decide and do.	▪ When you read, think about what might happen.	▪ What do you think will happen in ___'s life?
▪ Understand the prominent theme of the text or what is to be learned from the subject's life.	▪ Think about what you can learn from this biography. ▪ In writing this biography, the writer wanted us to learn that ___.	▪ What did you learn from reading about ___'s life? ▪ What do you think the writer wanted us to learn from reading about ___'s life?
▪ Relate the overall lesson of the subject's life to one's own life.	▪ The story of this person's life helped me understand ___ in my own life. ▪ I think the writer of this biography wanted to help readers understand ___ in our own lives.	▪ What can you learn from ___ that will help you in your own life? ▪ What do you think the writer wanted you to understand about your own life?
▪ Notice new ideas or information and revise previously held ideas.	▪ From reading this biography, you can learn ___. ▪ Some new information that not many people know is included in this biography, for example, ___.	▪ Did you learn something new from reading this biography? What? ▪ Did you learn something about ___ that you didn't know before? What?

Figure 26-1. *Planning for Guided Reading Lessons Using Biography (cont.)*

Planning for Guided Reading Lessons Using Biography (CONTINUED)

Thinking about the text:	DEMONSTRATION [SHOW EVIDENCE IN THE TEXT.]	PROBING [SHOW EVIDENCE IN THE TEXT.]
▫ Evaluate the authenticity of the biography.	▫ This biography is true because ____. ▫ This writer did ____ to be sure that the biography would be factual.	▫ Do you think this biography is true? What makes you think that? ▫ How do you know that the writer got true information about ____?
▫ Hypothesize why the writer selected the subject.	▫ I think the writer might have wanted to write this biography because ____. ▫ The writer says that she wanted to write about ____ because ____.	▫ Why do you think the writer chose to write about ____? ▫ Was there anything in the book that helped you realize why ____ wrote it? What?
▫ Notice what the writer has done to make the subject seem interesting.	▫ The writer really made ____'s life seem interesting by ____. ▫ I became interested in the biography because the writer ____.	▫ How did the writer make ____'s life seem interesting to you? Give an example.
▫ Notice how the writer has chosen to present the subject's life—chronological order or other.	▫ The writer might have chosen to present ____'s life in this order because ____.	▫ Why do you think the writer chose to present this part of ____'s life first? Last?
▫ Hypothesize why the writer selected these life events to describe.	▫ Think about why the writer selected these events in ____'s life.	▫ Why do you think the writer told us ____ about ____'s life?
▫ Evaluate whether the biography is accurate or well written.	▫ I think that this biography is well written, for example, ____. ▫ I think the information is accurate because ____.	▫ Do you like the way this writer described ____'s life? Why? Give an example.
▫ Evaluate whether the biographer has been objective or fair to the subject.	▫ I think this biographer has presented a fair picture of ____'s life because ____.	▫ Do you think that the writer was fair in reporting ____'s life? ▫ What is the writer's attitude toward ____?

Figure 26-1. *Planning for Guided Reading Lessons Using Biography (cont.)*

e subject changes over time; tension is inherent because e story is real. Often, too, technical vocabulary is included ated to the subject's profession or accomplishments.

Readers are also required to think beyond the text. The l value of biographical texts is that readers infer from the folding events the feelings of subjects and the reasons for eir decisions, which are often tough ones. We do not want ng readers simply to experience an individual's life as if vere a predetermined story told by someone else. Readers biographical texts need to know that without the individ-

ual's courage or persistence at turning points, the story could have been different. These inferences can make the subject seem real to readers and inspire them. They can relate their own lives to those they read about. Readers of biography usually learn something new about a subject; otherwise, the text will be uninteresting. They may even achieve new perspectives on and attitudes toward individuals. Readers of memoir may "live in the moment," enjoying the vicarious experience of a brief time or only one component of a writer's memories.

Finally, readers of biographical texts are required to think critically. The account of a subject's life purports to be true, and as such it can have a huge influence on the reader. But the critical reader is always questioning the text's authenticity by examining the writer's credentials and comparing the information with other sources. In a sense, all biographies are biased, but the reader must think about what those biases are. We all remember the sugary sweet stories of famous people such as George Washington, written not as true biography but to teach moral lessons. When the text is autobiographical, readers must constantly remind themselves that the writer has one perspective and that there may be other views.

The second column in Figure 26-1 illustrates some language you might use to demonstrate or directly teach how readers meet these demands in the introduction to a text. As noted in the previous chapter, sometimes it is necessary to model the behavior to clearly communicate your expectations before you ask students to perform it. Once the behavior is learned, your questions and invitations become a powerful way to elicit students' thinking.

Use the items in this chart to plan text introductions and think about critical content in text discussion. Each text will offer many possibilities, many more than you can teach in a single lesson. Think about what your students need to know as well as some of your grade-level goals when deciding where to concentrate your efforts.

SAMPLE INTRODUCTIONS AND TEACHING POINTS

Let's look at several book introductions and the teaching that followed in the discussion after the reading. You may want to compare these introductions and teaching points to the demands in Figure 26-1.

Next, we share an introduction to *A Picture Book of Martin Luther King Jr.*, a level N biography by David Adler (see Figure 26-2). Notice that Ms. P. began by asking students what they remembered about Dr. Martin Luther King and then shared personal experiences to provide information about the setting of the biography. She also pointed out some characters from history who influenced King and that students might not know.

In teaching points after the reading, Ms. P. asked students to share their thinking about what was most impor-

tant about Dr. Martin Luther King's life, thus drawing attention to important information from the text. She also asked students to talk about what they learned from reading about Dr. Martin Luther King's life which would lead to expressing personal connections.

Let's examine an introduction to *Rachel Carson* (Leveled Readers), a level B biography (see Figure 26-3). Biographies of writers can sometimes interest readers in learning more about them or reading their works. While Rachel Carson's books may be too difficult for these students right now, it adds to their reading lives to know her name, and they can explore picture books based on her work, like *Rachel Carson: Preserving a Sense of Wonder* (Locker, Joseph, and Bruchac), or other books about nature, such as Locker's *Where the River Begins*.

In this introduction, Mrs. S. presented Rachel as a real person, helped children attend to the decisions a biographer makes, and explained some key vocabulary words. In teaching points after the reading, Mrs. S. asked readers why Carson became so interested in writing about nature, which required them to infer the subject's motives and influential life events. She also prompted readers to list some specific life events that influenced Rachel's decisions.

An introduction to *Meet Yo-Yo Ma* (Leveled Readers), level R biography about a world-famous cellist, is presented in Figure 26-4 (also see Chapter 13).

Notice that Ms. F. began by identifying the genre and familiarizing students with the cello as an instrument and as a word. She also unlocked a particularly tricky page that had a picture of the classical composer Bach. Since there are words from languages other than English in the text, she helped the group learn how to use the pronunciation guide, a readers' tool. She explicitly talked about the decisions Yo-Yo made in his life and had students turn to key parts of the text that refer to them. This familiarity will make it easier for readers to notice these key passages.

After reading, Ms. F. asked readers to identify the important decisions that Yo-Yo made in his life and to identify the outcomes of those decisions. This teaching drew attention to structures such as problem/solution and cause/effect.

An introduction to *Nikki Giovanni* (Leveled Readers), a level T biography of a contemporary poet, is provided in Figure 26-5. Notice that in the introduction, the teach-

---

An Introduction to A Picture Book of Martin Luther King, Jr. (LEVEL N, BIOGRAPHY)

Ms. P.: *[Elicits background knowledge.]* I know that all of you have heard of Dr. Martin Luther King, Jr. What do you remember about him?

BAXTER: He was a leader of civil rights and he was shot. He marched for the rights of African Americans.

MARY: Before Martin Luther King, there were a lot of laws that said we couldn't stay at some hotels or eat at some places. He organized a lot of people from his church or through the churches and they protested.

Ms. P.: *[Elicits background knowledge.]* Do you remember how they protested?

BAXTER: They marched in long lines.

Ms. P.: *[Shares personal connections and provides information about the subject.]* Yes, I remember when I was about your age I would see Martin Luther King marching on television, and I remember seeing some *White Only* signs on drinking fountains and benches. On buses in many places, African American people had to sit in the back of the bus and leave the front seats for white people. One of the very important things I remember about Martin Luther King is that he protested by peaceful marching. He stood up for his rights, but he did it without violence. He used to say, "We must meet hate with love."

MARY: Why were they treated that way?

DERORA: There was a lot of prejudice going back to when slaves were brought over.

TRENT: It wasn't right for people to try to own other people.

EMERY: But it was also wrong to say everyone had to just sit in one place on the bus or wherever. That was prejudice, but sometimes people just thought that was the way it always was and they didn't really think about it.

Ms. P.: *[Shares personal connections and makes comments about why the subject's life was important.]* I remember thinking that it wasn't right to have *White Only* signs, but Martin Luther King really did something about it. *[Draws attention to the illustrations.]* Turn to page 8. I've numbered your pages. Do you see the three photographs there? Do you recognize any of those names?

EMERY: Harriet Tubman.

Ms. P.: *[Provides background information and connects to other texts.]* Yes, Harriet Tubman was a woman who led many slaves to freedom. The other two names are Frederick Douglass and George Washington Carver. You are going to read here about how Martin read books about black leaders. Turn the page. The woman being arrested is Rosa Parks. We've read about her, too.

MARY: She wouldn't get up and move to the back of the bus.

Ms. P.: *[Provides background information.]* That's right and when that happened, Martin Luther King, Jr. led a protest. Black people walked instead of riding the buses. In the rest of this book you are going to read about how Martin Luther King led many marches and won the Nobel Prize. *[Restates personal connections and invites readers' judgment.]* The *White Only* signs came down because new laws were passed. Read the whole book. Remember how I told you what the most important thing about Martin Luther King was for me? It might be different for each of you. *[Prompts readers to notice important information and think about what it means to them.]* Make a note about what you thought the most important thing about Martin Luther King was and we'll share our thinking.

Figure 26-2. *A Guided Reading Lesson: An Introduction to* A Picture Book of Martin Luther King, Jr.

A GUIDED READING LESSON:
An Introduction to Rachel Carson (LEVEL J, BIOGRAPHY)

MRS. S.: *[Identifies author and subject, provides information about writer's intentions, and draws attention to a key vocabulary word in the context of the text.]* This book is about an author named Rachel Carson who loved nature, especially the sea. She decided to write about Carson so people would understand this author better. Her books were a special gift to the world. What does this writer mean by *nature?*

MEGAN: The trees and animals.

PAUL: The woods.

PATRICK: The flowers and rivers.

MRS. S.: *[Draws attention to where the writer begins the biography in time.]* Yes, all those things are part of nature. Turn to page 2 and you can see Rachel when she was young.

SKYLER: She's standing in the ocean and writing.

MEGAN: There's a starfish.

SLADE: She might be drawing things she wants to put in her book.

MRS. S.: *[Draws attention to where the writer begins the biography in time.]* She might be. Turn to page 4 and 5 and you can see the farm where young Rachel lived. She liked to help out on the farm.

SKYLER: Like feed the animals?

MRS. S.: *[Draws attention to events in the biography and what the writer selected to tell.]* Yes, and also to plant things. Turn to pages 6 and 7.

MEGAN: She liked to walk her dog.

MRS. S.: *[Draws attention to events in the biography and what the writer selected to tell.]* Yes, she did. She liked to go hiking or walking for exercise with her dog.

MEGAN: My mom and I go walking with my dog.

MRS. S.: *[Draws attention to and explains a key vocabulary word.]* Walking is the same as hiking. Say *hiking.* Can you find *hiking* on page 6? Put your finger under it and say *hiking.*

ALL: *Hiking.*

MRS. S.: *[Provides background on the subject and draws attention to a key vocabulary word, asking readers to think about what they know already.]* Turn to page 8. When Rachel was older, she went to the sea and loved to learn about all the animals in the tide pools. Have you ever heard of or seen a tide pool?

SKYLER: I've heard of it. Is it a pool of water left when the tide goes out?

KAMERON: I think I have heard about it.

SLADE: It's at the ocean.

MRS. S.: *[Defines a key vocabulary word.]* A tide pool is the shallow water that the waves or tide leaves at the edge of the sea. It gets trapped in rocks.

KAMERON: There are animals in it—little fish and crabs.

MRS. S.: *[Explains subject's motivations—cause/effect.]* On page 10 you can see now in this picture that Rachel is getting older and she wants to learn more about the sea. She wants to write more books because she is worried people will hurt the sea and the animals in it.

MEGAN: They might throw trash.

KAMERON: Put things in the ocean that shouldn't go there, like cans.

Figure 26-3. *A Guided Reading Lesson: An Introduction to* Rachel Carson

---

A GUIDED READING LESSON:
An Introduction to Rachel Carson (LEVEL J, BIOGRAPHY) (CONTINUED)

MRS. S.: *[Draws attention to aspects of the subject's life.]* People love to read Rachel Carson's books. On the last page you can see some of the books she wrote. Some titles are *The Sea Around Us* and *Under the Sea Wing* and *The Silent Spring* and *Sense of Wonder.* Don't those sound like books she would write?

KAMERON: She's taking care of the environment!

MRS. S.: *[Asks readers to consider the author's motivations.]* Now turn to the beginning of the book and read and think about why the author calls Rachel's books a gift to the world.

Figure 26-3. *A Guided Reading Lesson: An Introduction to* Rachel Carson *(cont.)*

A GUIDED READING LESSON:
An Introduction to Meet Yo-Yo Ma (LEVEL R, BIOGRAPHY)

MS. F.: *[Identifies genre, introduces subject, and begins exploration of a topic-related vocabulary word.]* We're going to read a biography today about one of the finest cellists in the world. That's Yo-Yo Ma on the cover of this book, *Meet Yo-Yo Ma,* by Meish Goldish. He is playing his cello. Have you heard someone play a cello?

KENDRA: I heard a violin. It looks like a big violin or kind of like a guitar.

SALIH: Somebody came to the school and played one of these last year.

ERIC: Yo-Yo is a funny name.

MS. F.: *[Provides background information on the subject and draws attention to a topic-related vocabulary word.]* Yo-Yo is a Chinese name because his family is Chinese, but they lived in Paris, France. Turn to the title page and you'll see a bigger view of the cello. Turn to page 1. The first sentence says, "Yo-Yo Ma is playing the cello." Do you see the word *cello*?

QUINLIN: It starts with a *c* but it sounds like a *ch*.

MS. F.: *[Provides information on a key vocabulary word and alerts readers that they will be meeting words from other languages.]* It does sound like it should be *ch*. That word is from another language. In this book you are going to find some names and other words that are from other languages. *[Provides background information on the subject.]* Turn to page 4. That is Paris, France, where Yo-Yo grew up. He started playing the cello when he was just a little boy—not even five years old. *[Provides information to help readers understand vocabulary and concepts.]* Now you see a really good picture of the cello. It is a stringed instrument like the violin. Look at page 6 and find the word *composer*. Do you know what a composer is?

SALIH: Somebody that writes songs?

MS. F.: *[Provides information to help readers understand vocabulary and concepts as well as background information on the subject.]* Yes, anyone who writes a song is a composer. All of the popular songs you like now were written by a composer. Right after the word *composer* is the name of a great composer, Johann Sebastian Bach. He was a great composer and Yo-Yo played his music when he was only five years old. *[Draws readers' attention to a readers' tool and shows how to use it.]* Right after that is a pronunciation guide that shows you how to say his name. [MODELS USING THE PRONUNCIATION GUIDE.] Try it. [CHILDREN TRY OUT THE PRONUNCIATION GUIDE.] So you see it's written just the way you say it, and the part that you say louder than the rest is in all capital letters. Now look at this picture of Johann Sebastian Bach.

KENDRA: He looks funny.

ERIC: Sometimes in old-fashioned times men wore wigs like that, like Benjamin Franklin or George Washington.

Figure 26-4. *A Guided Reading Lesson: An Introduction to* Meet Yo-Yo Ma

---

A GUIDED READING LESSON:
An Introduction to Meet Yo-Yo Ma (LEVEL R, BIOGRAPHY) (CONTINUED)

Ms. F.: *[Provides background information on the subject and on vocabulary and concepts.]* Johann Sebastian Bach composed very difficult music. We call it classical music. Yo-Yo liked playing the cello and he was starting to love great classical music like Bach composed. Look at page 8. Yo-Yo moved to New York with his family and went to a famous music school called the Juilliard School of Music. He played in a famous hall called Carnegie Hall. *[Draws readers' attention to cause/effect—the decisions that the subject made related to his accomplishment.]* In this book you will read that Yo-Yo had some very important decisions to make. First, he decided to play the cello; that was an important decision. *[Draws attention to graphics and labels.]* Turn to pages 10 and 11. That's Harvard University in the picture; you can see the label.

CARLIE: I've heard of Harvard. Did he go there?

Ms. F.: *[Alerts readers to think about the decisions that the subject made related to his accomplishments.]* Yes, and that was an important decision. Turn to page 16. In this part of the book, the writer tells about a serious health problem that Yo-Yo faced; and, again, he had to make a decision. In the last part of the book you will learn about another decision Yo-Yo made that influenced his life. *[Foreshadows information that readers will find in the text.]* You'll find out how Yo-Yo Ma feels about young people and music today and how he spends a lot of his time. *[Communicates expectation that readers will identify and think about decisions and the way they affected the subject's life (cause/effect).]* Today you are going to read about the life of this musical superstar. Be thinking about the decisions that led to his success and made it possible for him to contribute so much. When you are finished, go back and put a stick-on note at a place where you think the writer is describing an important decision Yo-Yo made that changed his life.

Figure 26-4. *A Guided Reading Lesson: An Introduction to* Meet Yo-Yo Ma (cont.)

---

stirred up interest by reading the poem "The Reason I Like Chocolate," clarified the definition of a biography, drew attention to the graphics, and invited interpretation.

After reading, Mrs. O. asked readers to talk about what they learned about Nikki's life, prompting them to recall important information from the text. As prompted in the introduction, she also asked them to talk about how Nikki's writing changed and why.

The next informational text is something of a "hybrid" that is hard to categorize. We include it here as a bridge to the next section. *Orson Welles and The War of the Worlds* (Leveled Readers), by Matthew Vierno, is divided into two sections. The first section is a historical account of the radio-drama incident for which Orson Welles became famous. This section could be called a factual text; it is a dramatic narrative and includes dramatic black-and-white drawings. The second section is the "story behind the story" told as a biography of Welles. The text also has the quality of a memoir because it allows the reader to relive one brief period of time and presents only a single aspect of Orson's life (see Chapter 13 for an analysis of this text).

Ms. W.'s introduction is shown in Figure 26-6. S[he] began by introducing the title and general gist of the sto[ry]. She gave some attention to building background know[l]edge of the setting and helped students understand what [it] must have been like when people didn't have TV and reli[ed] on radio for everything. She guided the readers to imagi[ne] the impact of the trick, using words like *ventriloquist* [in] her conversation. Ms. W. also signaled the switch in the te[xt] to the "story behind the story," drawing attention to the te[xt] structure, and ended by asking them to think critica[lly] about whether Orson's trick was a good thing to do.

After reading, Ms. W. asked readers whether they thoug[ht] Orson's trick was good or not so good and to give reaso[ns] why, which required critical thinking. She also asked rea[d]ers to predict what would happen today if a radio show h[ad] a "War of the Worlds" hoax. She drew attention to the te[xt] structure and writer's craft by asking readers to talk abo[ut] the two sections of the text that are different.

INFORMATIONAL TEXTS

Duke (1993, 2003) makes an eloquent case for including [a] large amount of informational reading (at least thirty p[er]

A GUIDED READING LESSON:
An Introduction to Nikki Giovanni (LEVEL T, BIOGRAPHY)

MRS. O.: *[Identifies the genre and asks students to define it.]* We're going to read a biography today. Do you remember what a biography is?

AESHA: It's a book about a person.

MONTANA: A real person.

MRS. O.: *[Clarifies the definition of a biography.]* Yes, a biography is a true story that someone has written about a real person. Usually, it's someone who has been very successful or done something good for other people. *[Identifies the subject and provides an example to interest readers in the subject.]* This biography is about Nikki Giovanni, and it is written by Aeisha Hubbard. The author has almost the same first name as yours, Aesha! Nikki Giovanni is a poet who has written many poems for children. Here's one from our classroom library. [READS "THE REASON I LIKE CHOCOLATE."] What does that make you think about?

AESHA: It's just like chocolate tastes.

MRS. O.: *[Provides background information on the subject.]* Nikki Giovanni likes to write poetry about just some of the ordinary things that you enjoy every day. She thinks that children hear too much about violence, and she likes to write about happy things for them. *[Draws attention to graphics and invites interpretation.]* Look at the title page, and you'll see a picture of Nikki when she was young. Nikki has written poetry all of her life, and in this biography you will find that her poetry changed as her life changed and she was interested in different things. Look at page 5. What do you see in the photo?

BRAD: An African American and white girl on the bus.

MONTANA: They're holding hands through the window.

MRS. O.: *[Provides information on the setting in which the subject lived and checks for understanding.]* Nikki was born in 1943, in Knoxville, Tennessee, but she moved to Ohio. When she was old enough to go to school, the schools were segregated. Do you know what that means?

AESHA: Black and white kids went to different schools. The black kids weren't allowed to go to school with white kids.

BRAD: But these kids on are the bus together.

MRS. O.: *[Provides information on the setting in which the subject lived.]* In about 1954, when Nikki was just about to start high school, the schools were being integrated. You see these girls on the bus going to the same school. But Nikki went back down to Knoxville to stay with her grandparents and go to an all-black high school.

PETER: She didn't want to go to the white school?

MRS. O.: *[Repeats information from the text.]* The author tells you that Nikki felt safer in the all-black school that was more familiar. *[Provides background information and draws readers' attention to the decisions the subject made as well as how she changed.]* But Nikki later went to college at Fisk University and became very active in the struggle for civil rights. Dr. Martin Luther King was the leader. Her writing focused on the civil rights movement. But then, when she became a mother, her writing changed and she began to write about families. You will find two more times in her life that her writing changes, so look for them as you read this whole book. When you finish, write down at least two of the circumstances in Nikki's life that made her writing change.

Figure 26-5. A Guided Reading Lesson: An Introduction to Nikki Giovanni

nt) in elementary age students' reading (see Figure 26-7). us a truly compelling argument is that many children pre- reading informational texts (Duke 2003). Adults' reading eferences vary widely, so we should not be surprised at diver-y in children's tastes. They find topics that interest them d read to find out more. In a study of first-grade class-

rooms, Duke (2000) found that the average amount of time spent with informational texts was only 3.6 minutes each day (in low-socioeconomic classrooms, only 1.4 minutes each day). This is a big mistake. If we do not include a substantial amount of informational text, we may not be fully engaging a large number of students.

A GUIDED READING LESSON:
An Introduction to Orson Welles and the War of the Worlds (LEVEL V, HYBRID)

Ms. W.: *[Provides information about the topic and setting.]* We're going to read something very exciting today–*Orson Welles and the War of the Worlds.* This book is about a real person named Orson Welles and a trick he played on thousands of people. *[Provides information about the setting.]* You know when you listen to radio, you just have to imagine what people look like and what they are talking about.

HOLDEN: I like TV better because you can see it.

BRYCE: Sometimes the same people are on TV and then they sing on radio and you know what they are like.

DARLENE: I like the music on radio in the car but not anything else. There's too much talking.

Ms. W.: *[Provides information about the setting.]* Well, in these times, people didn't have TV at all. They depended on radio for all the news and their entertainment. They would sit in the living room and listen to the radio. There were news shows and variety shows, music, and plays, sort of like TV is now. *[Provides background information and information about the setting and asks for personal response.]* As this story starts, it was October 30, 1938, and many people all over America were listening to a show called *Mercury Theater of the Air.* The show began and a conductor named Ramon Roquello and his orchestra were playing music. Suddenly the music stopped! An announcer came on and said, "Ladies and gentlemen, we interrupt our program . . ." What would you be thinking?

BRYCE: Something like a disaster or a bomb or something.

DARLENE: Someone attacked the United States.

ELLEN: There's going to be a war maybe or something like a plane crash.

Ms. W.: *[Acknowledges connection to today's world.]* We see that happening on TV now a lot, don't we? *[Provides background information.]* This announcer said that an astronomer had just seen bright explosions on Mars and there was a jet of blue fire shooting toward Earth. Wow!

AMY: They're firing on earth from Mars?

Ms. W.: *[Provides background information and asks for responses.]* The program started back up again and then interrupted again to say a large flaming object had dropped on a farm near Grovers Mill, New Jersey. And a little later there was more news–an army of Martians was taking over the earth! What do you think?

DARLENE: Is this the trick?

BRYCE: It couldn't be real because that didn't really happen. He might have been just making people think that.

Ms. W.: *[States the problem of the story, mentions vocabulary, and foreshadows plot.]* It was a trick, but lots of people didn't really realize that. It sounded so real. People switched from another show–a ventriloquist Edgar Bergen–and they thought it was real. Hundreds of people panicked and ran through the streets. *[Provides information about text structure–how the text "works."]* So you are going to read about that. Turn to page 15. On this page you get the "story behind the story." You'll learn how Orson Welles got the idea for *The War of the Worlds.* You see the picture of the story by H. G. Wells in a magazine in 1927. You'll also get an idea how and why people were so easily fooled. *[Asks readers to engage in critical thinking.]* Read the whole book. Afterwards, write a little bit about why Orson's idea might have been a good one or not so good.

Figure 26-6. *A Guided Reading Lesson: An Introduction to* Orson Welles and the War of the Worlds

---

In making the case for informational texts, we must also exercise caution when it comes to the early grades. Informational texts often include vocabulary and concepts that are well beyond young children's ability to understand. When a word is not in one's speaking vocabulary, it is very hard to decode, remember, and make meaning from it. Learning challenging new content while they are just beginning to build a processing system places a heavy cognitive burden on young children. That obstacle can be overcome by careful selection of the texts you use (see Figure 26-8). You can also ensure that young children experience a large quantity and variety of informational texts in interactive read-aloud and shared reading.

For example, we might not think of *Getting Dressed*

Values of Informational Text

- Readers can acquire valuable content knowledge that will enable them to be good citizens and to know about the world.
- Proficient reading of informational texts is required for school success and most professions.
- Informational texts expand vocabulary related to domains of knowledge.
- Informational texts can provide perspectives on today's problems and issues by teaching about past mistakes and successes.
- Many readers prefer nonfiction because it addresses their interests and questions.

Figure 26-7. *Values of Informational Text*

Selecting Informational Texts for Emergent and Early Readers

- Select true informational texts that have concepts and vocabulary that are familiar to children—clothing, food, pets, families, everyday events.
- Select texts that may have elements of fiction (such as talking animals), but use the *structures* of informational text.
- Select texts that may have a narrative form but have some graphic features that will provide a foundation for reading informational texts.
- Select "hybrid" texts that have combined fiction and informational strands.

Figure 26-8. *Selecting Informational Texts for Emergent and Early Readers*

an "informational" text (see Figure 26-9). If you look at it from a six-year-old's point of view, however, this simple book has content vocabulary organized into a category—items of clothing. Each page presents a different piece of information. If we look for books that have very simple concepts and vocabulary, students can experience a kind of informational text even as beginning readers.

You can also find books that are not true informational texts but have some of the features of the genre. For example, *My Cat* (Leveled Readers) has a very simple text that focuses on what the cat can do ("My cat can jump"). The structure of the text is informational, yet the illustrations show a very fanciful cat with facial expressions doing things that cats simply do not in reality do. Technically, this text is fantasy, but students can still have an experience similar to reading an informational text. As you move up the levels, you will find "hybrid" texts that may include a fiction strand (such as an imaginary child visiting an aquarium) alongside an informational strand (simple sentences with information about fish).

We need to place a greater emphasis on informational texts in schools because nonfiction is the most frequently read kind of text outside schools—over ninety-six percent of texts on the Internet are expository (Duke 1993, 2003). Informational texts help build students' knowledge of our world. One simply cannot be an informed citizen without reading a great deal of informational text. Even if you only listen to the news on TV, you are still processing written

Look at my hat.

Look at my backpack.

Figure 26-9. Getting Dressed

expository texts as a read-aloud. We want our students to have access to the wonders of the world all their lives.

PLANNING FOR GUIDED READING LESSONS USING INFORMATIONAL TEXTS

The specific demands informational texts place on readers are discussed in Chapter 13, and you will want to think about these as you introduce texts. The language illustrated in Figure 26-10 may be useful in planning your introductions and teaching during discussions when you work with informational texts in guided reading.

In order to understand material, readers must gather and remember important information from both the text and the graphics. Often, this information is in categories; identifying these categories helps one remember. Readers of informational texts do not try to remember every single detail; they know that facts they already know do not have to be remembered, so they identify new information. Then

they pick up what is interesting to them and/or important to understanding the text. They import interesting, new information into their existing stores of knowledge. Just as in fiction, readers of informational texts make connections to their own experiences, to their previously acquired content knowledge, and to other texts they have read.

Understanding some specific underlying structures is a critical part of comprehending informational texts—for example, description, temporal sequence, cause/effect, problem/solution, and comparison/contrast. Writers use these structures to provide information, and they may do so through either text or graphics or both. In general, informational texts make more demands than fiction does in terms of using readers' tools (table of contents, headings, index, glossary, pronunciation guides, words in boldface or italic). Knowing how to use these tools can greatly enhance children's understanding, but they need to start with simple examples and move to more complicated ones.

Planning for Guided Reading Lessons Using Informational Texts

Thinking within the text:	DEMONSTRATION [SHOW EVIDENCE IN THE TEXT.]	PROBING [SHOW EVIDENCE IN THE TEXT.]
□ Gather and remember important information from the text.	□ From this book, you will learn that ____. □ Something important in this text is ____.	□ What did you learn from reading this book? □ What was important that you remember from this book?
□ Gather and remember important information from the illustrations/graphics.	□ Look at ____ so you can learn ____. □ Look at ____. From this graphic, you can learn ____.	□ Look at the illustration on page ____. What does it tell you? □ What did you learn from the graphics?
□ Use readers' tools to locate and use information (table of contents, headings, sections, words in bold or italic, print connected to graphics, index, glossary, pronunciation guide).	□ Readers use ____ to help them understand an informational text. In this text, the ____ will help you ____. □ This is a ____. Here's how you can use it to help you.	□ What do you see on this page? How can you use that to help you get information while reading this text? □ Remember, you can use the ____ to help you ____.
□ Solve words, including topic-specific vocabulary.	□ This word is important in understanding this topic. It means ____. □ This is an important word. Here's how you can figure out what it means.	□ Do you know the meaning of ____? □ What is this word? Read and think about what you think it means?

Figure 26-10 *Planning Guided Reading Using Informational Texts*

Planning for Guided Reading Lessons Using Informational Texts (CONTINUED)

Thinking beyond the text:	DEMONSTRATION [SHOW EVIDENCE IN THE TEXT.]	PROBING [SHOW EVIDENCE IN THE TEXT.]
◦ Identify new information and incorporate it into one's existing knowledge.	◦ You will be surprised to learn that ____. ◦ You will learn that ____, and you may change your understanding of ____.	◦ What new information did you learn from this book? ◦ How did you change your ideas after reading this book?
◦ Make connections between the text and background knowledge, personal experience, and other texts.	◦ When you read this book, think about ____. ◦ When you read this book, it may remind you of ____. ◦ You know something about this topic already. [Example.]	◦ What did this book make you think about? ◦ What did you already know about this topic? Did you change any of your ideas after reading? What? ◦ Did this book remind you of any other books you have read on this topic? What?
◦ Infer cause and effect [text and/or graphics].	◦ The writer wants readers to understand that ____ *causes* ____ to happen.	◦ What happened because of ____? ◦ Why did ____ happen? ◦ What caused ____ to happen?
◦ Understand the relationships between problem and solution [text and/or graphics].	◦ Readers think about problems and try to predict solutions. ◦ Readers think about the relationships of problems and solutions. ◦ In this text, there is a problem, which is ____. The writer is telling readers that ____ is the solution to the problem.	◦ What is the problem described by the writer? ◦ What do you think is the solution? ◦ What is the solution described by the writer?
◦ Analyze a temporal sequence to understand it [text and/or graphics].	◦ Readers notice when things are happening in order in time. ◦ Writers sometimes describe things in the order that they happen.	◦ Do you see a series of things happening in order? What information can you get from this sequence?
◦ Analyze description to understand important information [text and/or graphics].	◦ Writers provide lots of descriptive detail to help readers understand something. In this text, ____. Here is an example.	◦ What details have you learned from the description? ◦ What examples of description did you find in the text?

Figure 26-10 *Planning Guided Reading Using Informational Texts (cont.)*

Readers of nonfiction texts must also think *about* the text, analyzing how the writer presents information. Close examination of informational texts will help students improve their own expository writing, a skill that is related to school success. Finally, readers must be critical, questioning the accuracy of the text, the credentials of the writer, and the objectivity with which it is written. Any of the requirements in Figure 26-10 can be the basis for your planning the introduction or for teaching during discussion in guided reading lessons. You can demonstrate and model, as indicated in column 2, or question and invite, as indicated in column 3.

Planning for Guided Reading Lessons Using Informational Texts (CONTINUED)

Thinking about the text:	DEMONSTRATION [SHOW EVIDENCE IN THE TEXT.]	PROBING [SHOW EVIDENCE IN THE TEXT.]
□ Recognize the writer's use of underlying structures such as cause/effect, problem/solution, description, temporal sequence, comparison/contrast.	□ When you read this book, notice how the writer is describing the topic. □ Notice how the writer is comparing and contrasting ___ and ___. □ The writer is telling about something that happened and also what caused it. □ The writer is describing something that happened over time. □ The writer is showing a problem and its solution.	□ What did you learn from the kinds of descriptive details the writer provided? Why do you think the writer included these details? □ What did the writer compare to provide information? How were these things alike? How were they different? Why did the writer use compare/contrast? □ What outcomes or effects did the writer describe? What caused these outcomes? What was the writer trying to help us understand about cause and effect? □ Why is this a good solution to the problem? (How did the writer support his/her ideas?)
□ Evaluate the authenticity and accuracy of the text.	□ It is important for readers to think about whether an informational text is true or accurate. I think this text is accurate because ___.	□ How can you tell whether this text is true or accurate? □ How can you find out?
□ Evaluate the writer's credentials for producing a book on the topic.	□ It is important for readers to think about whether the writer is qualified to write about the topic. This writer ___.	□ What makes you think that this writer is qualified to write about this topic? □ Where can you go to find out?
□ Evaluate the writer's treatment of the subject—objectivity, bias, etc.	□ It is important for readers to think about the writer's own opinions about a topic. This writer seems to ___. For example, ___.	□ What do you think the writer's own opinions are about this topic? □ Do you think the writer is being fair in telling us about this topic?
□ Evaluate the degree to which the writer has made the topic interesting.	□ Readers notice what writers of informational texts do to make a topic interesting. This writer ___.	□ What did this writer do to make the topic interesting? □ What are some specific examples of how the writer interested you?
□ Analyze the way the writer has selected information to include in graphics.	□ Readers notice the particular information that the writer includes in the graphics. In this text, the writer ___. I think the writer put this information in graphics because ___.	□ What information did the writer choose to put in the graphics? □ What do you think is important about the information in the graphics? □ Why do you think the writer chose to put that information in graphics?

Figure 26-10 *Planning Guided Reading Using Informational Texts (cont.)*

SAMPLE INTRODUCTIONS AND TEACHING POINTS

Look at an introduction to a very simple level B informational text, *Clothes* (PM Plus Starters) (see Figure 26-1). Miss P. began by telling children the main idea of the text—that the boy is looking for his clothes. She gave the children a chance to pay close attention to the cover and rehearse some of the vocabulary to be encountered in the book. Since these children were just building a set of high frequency words, the teacher had them locate several and

also rehearse some language, for example, "Here it is." She taught them a strategy for remembering a word by drawing their attention to the visual information. She ended by reminding them to think about some of the kinds of clothing the boy would be looking for, which would help them predict the content-related words. Finally, she reminded the readers to point under each word.

After reading, Miss P. had readers remember some of the items of clothing the boy found, helping children remem-

---

A GUIDED READING LESSON:
An Introduction to Clothes (LEVEL B, INFORMATIONAL)

MISS P.: *[Describes what is happening in the story, uses a key word* clothes, *draws attention to the cover, and invites children to name items within a category.]* In this story a little boy is looking for his clothes. The cover can help you think about what clothes he might be looking for.

RON: His shoes, his socks.

SARAH: His hat.

LIZ: His shirt.

MISS P.: *[Uses language from the text, including key vocabulary.]* Turn to page 2. He says "I am looking for my T-shirt." Can you say that?

CHILDREN: I am looking for my T-shirt.

MISS P.: *[Helps children say a high frequency word.]* Say the word *am.*

CHILDREN: *Am.*

MISS P.: *[Helps children locate a high frequency word using visual information.]* Am has two letters and it starts with an *a.* Can you find *am* and put your finger under it? [CHILDREN POINT UNDER *AM*.] You will find *am* on lots of pages in this book. Turn the page.

RON: He found it.

MISS P.: *[Helps children become familiar with language from the text.]* Yes, he did. And he says, "Here it is!" Can you say that?

CHILDREN: Here it is.

MISS P.: *[Draws attention to visual features of words.]* What letter do you expect to see first in *here?*

CHILDREN: H.

MISS P.: *[Draws attention to visual features of a word.]* And you can see that *Here* starts with uppercase *H* because it comes at the beginning. Put your finger under *Here* and say *here.* Turn the page and see what he is looking for. Now turn again to see if he found it. He says . . .

CHILDREN: Here it is.

MISS P.: *[Reminds readers of the category of information they will be using and prompts rehearsal of vocabulary.]* Yes, he does. Now turn back to the beginning and read the book softly. Find out what clothes the boy is looking for, like . . .

RON: Hat.

SARAH: T-shirt and socks.

LIZ: Shoes.

MISS P.: *[Reminds readers of a print convention.]* That's right. Now begin and be sure to point under each word as you read.

Figure 26-11. *A Guided Reading Lesson: An Introduction to* Clothes

ber the vocabulary and reinforcing the category of knowledge. She also supported word solving by having readers locate several high frequency words as well as a tricky content word.

Let's examine an introduction to *Butterflies* (Leveled Readers), a level N informational text (see Figure 26-12). Even though it is a clear and friendly text, *Butterflies* is quite a step up from *Clothes*. There are scientific or technical words in the text and labeled drawings, as well as

description, problem/solution, comparison/contrast, ar cause/effect patterns.

Ms. L. began by asking a question that focused reader attention on information they probably did not previous know and that she thought would get them interested. Sl drew attention to the graphics in the text, often explicit explaining them. She called attention to places in the te where the writer used underlying organizational structur such as problem/solution and asked readers to make pr

---

A GUIDED READING LESSON:
Introduction to Butterflies (LEVEL N, INFORMATIONAL)

Ms. L.: *[Communicates interesting information and provokes thinking.]* Did you know that there are more than 20,000 different kinds of butterflies?

SHAWNEL: How did you know that?

Ms. L.: *[Calls attention to readers' tools.]* Jose Strummer, the writer of this book, *Butterflies,* tells the most interesting information. On page 3, the dark black print tells you what this part of the book is about—a butterfly's body. *[Directs attention to graphics and prompts readers to get information.]* At the top you see a drawing of a butterfly, and it's labeled with the names of the body parts. Find the word *abdomen* and then put your finger on that body part. Now find the thorax and put your finger on it. What else do you see?

LILY: There's the legs.

GREG: I see the antennas!

Ms. L.: *[Directs attention to graphics and prompts readers to get information.]* Yes—quick, point to the antennae, the legs, the abdomen, and the thorax. These labeled drawings can help you understand more about the butterfly's body. Now turn to pages 4 and 5. The writer says butterflies are different from other insects in two ways.

BEAU: The butterfly is on the flower. Is she eating it?

Ms. L.: *[Provides description from the text.]* She's sucking up the nectar—like sugar water. That's the first way butterflies are different from other insects. They have a long feeding tube like a straw to suck up the sweet nectar from flowers. You'll read about the second way on page 5. Turn to pages 6 and 7. What is the writer showing?

TALISHA: The way a butterfly grows from caterpillar to a butterfly.

SHAWNEL: No, from eggs to a caterpillar and then to a butterfly.

LILY: Is it a cocoon?

Ms. L.: *[Helps students read and understand technical vocabulary.]* In this book we learn that it is called a chrysalis—you say that. [STUDENTS SAY THE WORD.] *[Repeats description from the text and helps students read and understand technical vocabulary.]* The writer explains that there are four stages in a butterfly's life and there are words from each. As I say them, point to the picture—eggs [CHECKS TO SEE THAT STUDENTS ARE POINTING], larva (you sometimes call that a caterpillar), larva attached to a branch, chrysalis, and butterfly.

SHAWNEL: This is like a life cycle.

GREG: There's another diagram on the right.

Ms. L.: *[Calls attention to a temporal sequence, provided in graphics.]* The diagram on page 7 shows you the same life cycle. Who wants to name the stages?

TANISHA: Egg, larva, chrysalis, adult.

Figure 26-12. *A Guided Reading Lesson: An Introduction to* Butterflies

A GUIDED READING LESSON:
Introduction to Butterflies (LEVEL N, INFORMATIONAL) (CONTINUED)

Ms. L.: *[Calls attention to information in the text; focuses on problem/solution.]* Butterflies try many different ways to survive. In this part, starting on page 9, the writer tells how they protect themselves from enemies.

LILY: Look! The butterfly looks like a leaf.

Ms. L.: *[Asks for prediction based on the information so far; asks readers to draw on background.]* What other important information do you think the writer tells about butterflies?

SHAWNEL: The butterfly's role in nature.

Ms. L.: *[Asks readers to draw on background knowledge.]* And what does that mean?

GREG: The butterfly has a job?

Ms. L.: *[Foreshadows information that readers will find in the text.]* Yes, it could mean jobs and it could mean just other ways butterflies help nature just by being there. You will also learn what butterflies do in the winter. Some of them hibernate in their chrysalis.

TANISHA: Like bears?

GREG: They sleep in them?

Ms. L.: *[Draws attention to a topic-specific vocabulary word.]* Bears don't exactly hibernate. They sleep in caves. But the idea is similar. Find the word *hibernate* on page 15 and say it. [STUDENTS SAY *HIBERNATE* AND LOCATE IT.] *[Foreshadows information readers will find in the text and invites them to identify new information and synthesize it.]* And some will fly or migrate many miles to another place for the winter. You will learn a lot of interesting facts about butterflies in this book. Turn to the beginning and start your reading. When you finish, write one or two new things you learned about butterflies to share with the group.

Figure 26-12. *A Guided Reading Lesson: An Introduction to* Butterflies *(cont.)*

ctions based on the information they already had. She explained some of the content-specific vocabulary and invited children to notice new information and bring it back to the group to share.

After reading, Ms. L. asked readers to talk about how butterflies were different from other insects, specifically on pages 4 and 5, engaging the children in understanding the compare/contrast pattern. She also drew attention to the writer's use of temporal sequence (life cycle) and asked readers to report something new they had learned about butterflies, encouraging synthesis.

Lastly, we analyze an introduction to *Bats* (Holmes), a level O informational text (see Figure 26-13). This text communicates a great deal of information presented in categories. Headings provide a clue to understanding the organization. Mrs. D.'s major purpose in helping students read this text was to help them notice the different kinds of information related to the headings. She also drew attention to the connection between the text and the graphics (like the diagram of a bat), and she untangled a very long

and technical key word in the text because it described something unique about bats—*echolocation*. She directed students to use writing as a tool for remembering information from the text.

After the reading, Mrs. D. asked readers to consult their notes and share some new information that they found interesting, prompting for synthesis. Then she returned to the word *echolocation*, asking students to talk about its meaning, as well as to break it down into *echo* and *location* as a way to remember it. She was helping them learn a strategy for solving technical vocabulary words. Finally, she had readers quickly find several different kinds of information using headings as a readers' tool.

As they learn to skillfully use the features of informational texts, your students will find that they can pursue their interests and enjoy a very wide range of high-quality informational writing. No longer are informational texts dull textbooks or dry encyclopedic references. Within the last fifteen years, an enormous number of very interesting texts have been published, so your classroom library can be a rich

---

A GUIDED READING LESSON:
An Introduction to Bats (LEVEL M, INFORMATIONAL)

MRS. D.: *[Probes background knowledge.]* Bats are very interesting animals for many reasons. There are over 800 kinds of bats. What do you already know about them?

RAOUL: Bats have little eyes and big wings. I saw a bat.

PAUL: I saw a bat once, too. I know a lot about bats.

MRS. D.: *[Draws attention to the connection between the text and graphics.]* Then, you will find lots of things you know when you read this book. Turn to pages 4 and 5. On the left is a diagram of a bat. The lines point to the parts. On the right you will learn many facts, such as where they live, or their habitat, and what they eat.

SERENA: They live in dark places.

SAM: And in the attic. They like the dark and the night. They look like birds when they fly.

MRS. D.: *[Helps readers get an idea of the kinds of information they will be learning–prediction that helps in searching for and using information.]* They can fly, but they are not birds. They are mammals. On page 1, the writer introduces us to bats. What kind of information will we find out about bats on page 7?

RAOUL: Appearance.

MRS. D.: *[Identifies information in the text.]* Here, the writer tells all about how they look.

PAUL: On page 11, the writer tells us where they live.

MRS. D.: *[Asks readers to search background knowledge.]* Did you know they hibernate, or take a deep sleep, in the winter?

SERENA: I didn't know that.

SAM: Me neither.

PAUL: Look at how funny the little baby bats look.

MRS. D.: *[Directs attention to another category of information.]* Turn to page 13.

SAM: Sights and sound.

MRS. D.: *[Helps with a technical word.]* They hunt objects and food with a special sense they have called *echolocation.* Can you say *echolocation?*

CHILDREN: *Echolocation.*

MRS. D.: *[Explains a technical word and directs attention to readers' tools.]* Echolocation is using sound to locate food or find objects. The bat sends out high-pitched signals that echo, and only the bat can hear the echoes. You will learn more about echolocation. Look at the headings and see what else you will learn about bats.

SAM: Enemies, young bats.

MRS. D.: *[Asks readers to predict categories of information.]* Yes, bats have lots of enemies, including people who spray pesticides, a chemical that kills insects. What else will you learn about?

RAOUL: Bats and people.

MRS. D.: *[Directs readers to use writing as a tool for remembering information.]* There are so many interesting things to learn. Now turn back to the beginning and begin reading. If you finish, make a list of phrases or sentences to help you remember what you found interesting about bats.

Figure 26-13. *A Guided Reading Lesson: An Introduction to* Bats

source of knowledge. Building expertise in expository reading takes time. If your readers are inexperienced or have difficulty reading informational texts, look for very simple, uncluttered, and clear examples on topics within their reach.

A FINAL CAUTION

Biographical and informational texts offer many teachin and learning opportunities. However, we do not incorpora biographical and informational texts into guided readir ssons in order for students to learn in content areas, and ͻ do not select books because they are on topics related to e required curriculum in science or social studies. Will ere be content learning? Inevitably yes, provided readers n process texts successfully. Will we sometimes have the ance to make links to our content areas of study? solutely. But the primary purpose for choosing texts in ided reading is to help students expand their systems of ategic actions. The goal in reading one informational ˥t is not to study it for a test on, let's say, butterflies. The al is to learn how to process informational texts in a way at will help students read many more such texts.

SUGGESTIONS FOR PROFESSIONAL DEVELOPMENT

PLANNING TEXT INTRODUCTIONS TO NONFICTION TEXTS

Work with a group of cross-grade-level colleagues.

2 As a group, select either biographical or factual genres to explore across the grades.

3 Have each participant choose a book from the genre that will be appropriate for a group in her classroom.

4 Work together to analyze the text characteristics, using Chapter 12 and the examples in this chapter.

5 Share your analyses of the texts and compare them. How do the requirements of easier texts provide a foundation for reading higher-level texts?

6 Plan an introduction to a nonfiction text that each participant will use in the classroom.

7 Demonstrate and discuss each introduction.

8 Summarize what each of you has learned about introducing fiction texts.

CHAPTER TWENTY-SEVEN

WRITING ABOUT READING: MOVING FROM TALK TO WRITTEN CONVERSATION ABOUT TEXTS

Images at any age are part of t

serious business of making meaning—

partners with words f

communicating inner design

—RUTH HUBBA

All human communication is powerful. Communication by way of written language is even more powerful. In times past, the only way friends and family members could communicate with each other long-distance was by writing letters. And written communication is even more important and frequent today as email and text messaging allow people to communicate quickly and easily.

Drawing is also a powerful form of communication, another tool for thinking about a text and composing oral and written texts. A drawing represents one's thinking in images. Many writers keep sketches as well as notes in a special notebook. Teachers encourage children to consider character traits and plot elements by having them draw detailed depictions of characters (skin color, features, clothing), the setting, or important events and details in stories. They can reflect on their reading through sketching or drawing. They can also make drawings or sketches to collect information for informational writing.

Our understanding is enhanced when we communicate with others about our thinking. Oral language as the primary support for thinking leads naturally to written communication, which, in turn, helps readers expand their thinking and use oral language with greater skill. It is a way for readers to construct knowledge, generate new thinking, clarify their own thinking, and rehearse thoughts for writing. If we ask young children to write (and draw) in response to their reading from the beginning, they will be able to use this tool in response to reading and to expand their own thinking about texts. Understanding reading begins with thinking, talking, and representing ideas.

VALUES OF WRITING AND DRAWING ABOUT READING

Students' written responses to reading provide evidence of their thinking and show they have read and understood a

text, but these are not good enough reasons to have stu dents spend their time writing a response. Writing ar drawing in response to reading are vehicles for explorir and communicating one's thinking. Let's look at son examples of how readers have shared their thinking images.

Sybil shared her vision of *Knuffle Bunny,* an engagir text about a child's favorite stuffed animal that is left at tl laundry (see Figure 27-1). Brandon showed his thinking a visual response to the events in Rosa Parks' life as he re her biography (see Figure 27-2).

And now, let's take a look at how three readers also sha their thinking in words. Theodore reflects on a read-aloud *Ira Sleeps Over* (see Figure 27-3). Molly reacts to *The Mou and the Motorcycle,* a text she is reading independently (s Figure 27-4). Maria shares her thinking about her ind pendent reading of *Hatchet* in a quick short write about h

Figure 27-1. *Sybil's Drawing of* Knuffle Bunny

438

dependent reading book (see Figure 27-5).

In each of these examples, readers are sharing their thinking in writing. Writing and drawing about reading make particular demands on students. They must:

Reflect on the text in a focused way.

Reconstruct the meaning and present it in new ways.

Compose language or images to express thought.

Search the text for evidence to support their thinking.

Explore new thinking or reflect on understanding.

Writing and drawing lead thinking about texts in new directions.

SHARED WRITING AND INTERACTIVE WRITING

Shared writing and interactive writing offer a high level of support to help children learn how to write about reading.

These approaches offer a context in which you can demonstrate how written language works (McCarrier, Pinnell, and Fountas 2000). You can use interactive writing and shared writing to demonstrate the characteristics of just about any form of writing about reading using a common text experience in a large- or small-group context. The students will be able to try for themselves the forms they learn as they respond to their own reading.

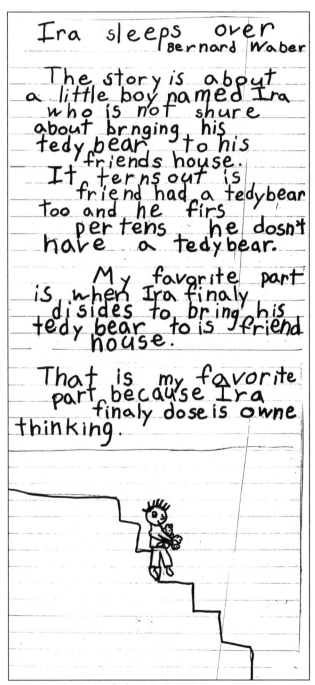

Dear Rosa,

It made me feel great that you finnally stuck up for yourself. I do not think you should have gone to jail—you did nothing wrong. When you went to jail I felt really bad about it beacause if you were still alive now you would not have been treated like you were them. Sometimes I just stop and think about how you people were treated and it makes us feel sorry!!

Sincerely,
Brandon

[white] [black] Police Office

Figure 27-2. *Brandon's View of* Rosa Parks

Ira sleeps over
Bernard Waber

The story is about a little boy named Ira who is not shure about brnging his tedy bear to his friends house. It terns out is friend had a tedybear too and he firs pertens he dosn't have a tedybear.

My favorite part is when Ira finaly disides to bring his tedy bear to is friend house.

That is my favorite part because Ira finaly dose is owne thinking.

Figure 27-3. *Theodore's Reflection on* Ira Sleeps Over

Dear Miss A,
    On page 45, I would have felt the same way to not want to go in a cage. I would have also wanted to go in his pocket where there were crumbs to eat. I can understand why Ralph is worryed abought his motorcycle It's like his child at the top of page 46. I would have been embarresed with three girls stareing at me and calling me darling and saying oh isn't he sweet Would you!

from,
Molly

Figure 27-4. *Molly's Reaction to* The Mouse and the Motorcycle

SHARED WRITING

In shared writing, the teacher and students work together to compose particular kinds of text—lists, summaries, letters, short writes, etc. The teacher is the scribe. Often, especially with younger children, the teacher works on a chart displayed on an easel and uses a dark-colored marker to write the words. Sometimes a teacher working with older students uses chart paper or acetate on an overhead projector, especially when demonstrating a longer piece of writing. Charts have the advantage of being able to be posted in the classroom as a reference or model. In today's classroom, you can find some teachers using the computer and projecting their writing on a large screen.

Shared writing is similar to but should not be confused with "language experience," in which the teacher writes down everything that individual students say. In shared writing, the teacher and students discuss what the text should be saying, with the teacher helping the students put together ideas, so it is truly a group composition. When sharing writing with young children, the text is reread several times during the construction (or actual writing), so the students become very familiar with it and can read it later.

Once produced, a piece of shared writing might be illustrated by students and remain as a reading resource in the classroom for several months. Students sometimes "borrow" ideas from the shared writing piece and/or use it as a kind of "boost" for their own writing. The steps in shared

I have noticed differences in the ways Gary Paulson and Jean Craighead George write adventure storys. Jean Craighead George's writing is exciting but since you know that Sam can go home if he wants it isn't quite as suspensful. Gary Paulson creates suspense and feeling for the character.
    In Hatchet, I'm really glad that Brian finally made fire. I'm wondering what Brian will do for food if he's not found by the time the raspberries run out. I think that these eggs sound disgusting. I don't think I'd eat them. It was dissapointing when the fish spear didn't work and pure agony when the plane didn't see Brian. If I were Brian I would've completely fallen apart. I think that if I had to go through anything like this, I'd probably never survive because I know nothing about surviving on my own and I couldn't stand being separated from my family and friends.

Figure 27-5. *Maria Shares Her Thinking About* Hatchet

writing usually include:

1 Participating in some kind of shared experience—reading aloud, scientific experiment, field trip, etc.

2 Talking about the experience.

3 Deciding the appropriate genre or type of writing in light of their purpose and audience.

4 Talking about the specific text to write.

5 Deciding the exact wording of the text (or part of it).

6 Scribing the text. (Done by the teacher, with student input on spelling; may be scribed in sections.)

7 Reading and rereading the text, sometimes revising.

8 "Publishing" the text by displaying it in the room or making copies, perhaps after adding illustrations.

Ms. M. involved her students in shared writing during their author study of Eric Carle (see Figure 27-6). Notice the collective summarizing they did and the variety of understandings they gained as they recorded what they know, what they wanted to know, how they found out, and what they learned.

INTERACTIVE WRITING

Interactive writing, an approach for use with young children, is identical to and proceeds in exactly the same way as shared writing, with one exception: occasionally the teacher while making teaching points that help children attend to

Eric Carle

What we know...
- He is an illustrator/artist.
- He is an author.
- He uses tissue paper collage.
- He uses lots of colors.
- He writes mostly about animals and insects.
- He is grown up

How will we find out?
- Write him a letter
- Send him an e-mail
- Look on the Internet
- Read the backs of his books

What we want to know...
- How does he get his pictures into the books?
- How does he make the covers of the books?
- How does he get all of his ideas?
- How else does he make his pictures?
- Does he have a family?
- Where does he live?
- What was his first book?

We decided to go to www.eric-carle.com and read the backs of books.
✗ We joined his mailing list!

We learned that...
- His second book was The Very Hungry Caterpillar.
- He lives in Massachusetts.
- His wife's name is Barbara.
- He loves nature. • He was born in New York.
- He grew up in Germany. • He has 2 grown-up kids.
- He opened a museum in 2002.
- His first book was 1, 2, 3, to the Zoo.
- His newest book is 10 Little Rabbits.

Figure 27-6. *An Example of Shared Writing*

various features of letters and words, will invite a student to come up to the easel and contribute a letter, word, or part of a word. The parts of the text written by children are very valuable instructionally, give children more ownership in the piece, and capture their attention. Very often, kindergartners and first graders can tell you exactly which letters or words they wrote, but the technique should not be overused, because it can slow down the production of a text.

Rereading interactive writing and deciding where to put the next word helps young children develop early reading strategies such as word-by-word matching and directionality. Teachers can emphasize the spaces between words, always a challenge for kindergartners. With the enlarged text, children can see and even put their hands in the spaces. Interactive writing is a way to engage children in composing and learning about different genres or forms for writing about reading well before they are expected to produce them independently.

Sometimes during the grade one year, many teachers shift to using mostly shared rather than interactive writing because they want children to compose longer texts. By then, most children can write many words for themselves and have the early strategies well under control. Their time is better spent writing independently. But interactive writing may still be used in small groups for particular purposes—for example, to help English language learners who need strong scaffolding through oral language and hands-on activity or to help small groups of children learn about specific aspects of reading or writing.

AN EXAMPLE OF INTERACTIVE WRITING: *DEAR BEAR*

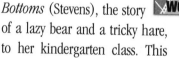

Ms. N. had read *Tops and Bottoms* (Stevens), the story of a lazy bear and a tricky hare, to her kindergarten class. This story is a wonderful concept builder, illustrating over and over the edible "tops" and "bottoms" (or roots) of certain vegetables. In their discussion, children revealed conflicting feelings. Many thought Bear deserved what he got because he was lazy, but they also thought Hare had been unfair.

After they had heard the story a couple of times, they decided that Hare really should write a letter of apology to Bear and that they would produce one together. In their conversation (see the excerpt in Figure 27-7), they also issued a warning to Bear. The teacher was able to incorporate several suggestions into a coherent text that the children could read.

Then they began to write the text. (The final letter is shown in Figure 27-8.) All the children knew that the letter should begin with the opening *Dear Bear*. As the teacher wrote the words at the top of the letter, many children noticed that both words end in *-ear*, and they made the point that although the words look alike, they don't rhyme.

Composition of a Letter from One Character to Another

Ms. N.: Remember that Hare and Bear weren't getting along very well.

JAMAL: He could tell Bear what he should do next.

Ms. N.: What could he say to Bear to make him feel better? If you were Hare and you wanted to say something to Bear, what would it be?

SARAH: Can we be friends?

JAMAL: You can have all of the vegetables.

CHUCK: I'll take all the bad parts of the vegetables.

VIANA: I'm sorry.

Ms. N.: He wasn't trying to be mean, was he?

RENAJA: No, he really likes him.

Ms. N.: Some of you have said something about being sorry. Some of you have said something about sharing the vegetables. You know when you want to send a message to someone, how would you write that?

RENAJA: A letter. He could write a letter to say I'm sorry for tricking you.

TERRENCE: I saw it on TV. This man got mad at this lady and he wrote a letter, a note, with some chocolate and they sent it.

Ms. N.: He wrote a letter. That's a good idea. Let's get back to the letter from Hare to Bear. How would we start?

CHILDREN: Dear Bear!

Ms. N.: You all know how to start a letter. "Dear Bear." Then you want to say, "I'm sorry for tricking you."

CHUCK: And giving you the bad parts of the vegetables.

Ms. N.: "I'm sorry for tricking you and giving you the bad parts of the vegetables." Is that right? And Jesse, you wanted to add something?

JESSE: P.S. Next time don't be so lazy!

JULIE: And say, Love, Hare.

Figure 27-7. *Composition of a Letter from One Character to Another*

It was easy for the children to identify the *b* sound at the beginning of *bad*. Jamal hesitated at the next letter. He knew it was a vowel, but was unsure which one. Ms. N. put *bed* and *bad* on the Magnadoodle. On the word *sorry,* which Ms. N. wrote up to the *y,* she called the children's attention to the long *e* sound of the *y*. When they came to the word *parts,* she reminded them that they knew anothe word that sounds like *parts,* and Jamal came up with *ca* which Ms. N. wrote on the Magnadoodle. From there, the easily spelled *parts,* and Trenecia wrote it on the char They also generated the first part of the word *vegetable* and the teacher wrote the rest, with several children volun teering that there is an *s* on the end. Ms. N. called attentio to the commas after *Love* and *Bear* in the letter. Writing th P.S. quickly, she also pointed out the apostrophe in *don* and the sound of *y* in *lazy*. They practiced reading a sen tence ending in an exclamation point. Finally, they rerea the entire letter with fluency and expression. (You can view this final group rereading of the "Dear Bear" let- ter on the accompanying DVD.)

GUIDED WRITING

Sometimes you will want to pull together a small group o writers who have similar needs. You may have introduced type of writing about reading to the whole group but notic that there are a few students who need reteaching or extr support. When you work with them as a small group i guided writing, you can observe them closely and provid specific guidance.

INDEPENDENT WRITING

Children enjoy responding to books they have read inde pendently or have listened to in interactive read-aloud. Yo can model a variety of forms for writing about reading i interactive writing or as a whole-group minilesson tha become possibilities for their individual responses.

One young writer, Tyrese, responded to *Charlie th Caterpillar* (De Luise) by writing the piece in Figure 27-9 Tyrese derived the central theme of *Charlie the Caterpilla* related it to her experience, and gave some advice tha would be good to follow: "Andres is my best friend. Nothin can break our friendship. It doesn't matter what's on th outside. It matters what is inside." Another young write Theodora, took on the task of writing to a character in *Top and Bottoms* (see Figure 27-6). Both of these pieces revea deep thinking about the texts as the readers take on th characters' roles. Theodora provides a rationale for Hare behavior and infers that Bear's "hobby" is sleeping. Sh goes on to tell her own hobbies as well as give reasons wh she likes Bear.

USING A READER'S NOTEBOOK—FORMALIZING THE DIALOGUE

A reader's notebook[1] is a useful tool that can be used by readers to collect their thinking and record it in a variety of types or forms. As a tool for readers, the notebook is a place to:

Keep a record of books read.

Plan for future reading.

Gather thinking about texts (through drawing or writing).

Write notes, plans, and drafts of thinking.

Engage in a conversation about texts with other readers.

Collect and organize thinking for oneself and to share with others.

Write about thinking in a variety of forms.

Plan for longer writing or future talk about reading.

Gather resources for writing about reading.

The notebook is a collection of thinking that reflects a stu-

Figure 27-8. *An Example of Interactive Writing:* Dear Bear

dent's reading life. It houses a variety of authentic responses to reading and the teacher's responses to thinking expressed by students.

GETTING STARTED WITH WRITTEN CONVERSATION: LETTER WRITING

Even though any kind of written response can be recorded in a reader's notebook, we suggest that you begin with a dialogue between you and the individual student. It is not hard to make the transition from the oral conversation that is integral in reading conferences and interactive read-

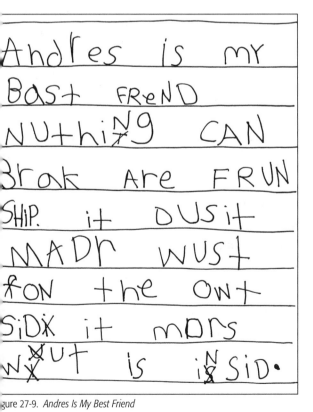

Figure 27-9. *Andres Is My Best Friend*

Figure 27-10. *Dear Bear*

aloud to the written conversation that is integral to using the notebook. We recommend introducing the reader's notebooks with organized sections for writing in grades two or three. By this time, students are able to capture their thinking in writing and explore a range of genres for thinking and writing about texts. For grade two, entries in a blank notebook will be mostly drawings and short pieces of writing, but the range of forms for writing about reading expands as students get older and are introduced to a greater variety of types of writing about reading. In kindergarten or grade one, consider a blank notebook for drawing or writing. An unlined version works well, as young children learn how to use the space on a page. You can expect drawing and one or two sentences early on, and longer writing as the children become more confident.

Begin by introducing procedures for independent reading in the reading workshop so that students learn to select just-right books and read silently and independently for a sustained period (thirty to forty minutes in grades three or above). Start younger children with about fifteen or twenty minutes of independent reading and build from there. Some of the workshop will be devoted to the opening book talks or minilesson and the final sharing, and many students will be involved in small-group lessons (guided reading or literature discussion) during the period as well. You will want to conduct regular individual reading conferences with students as time allows. Younger children may also listen to stories at a listening center or engage in other independent literacy work while you meet with guided reading groups.

After a couple of weeks devoted to establishing these routines, you will want to introduce the reader's notebook through a variety of minilessons that demonstrate many ways of thinking about and responding to the author's and illustrator's craft. This way, you can be sure students are focused on thinking and talking about *reading* rather than primarily thinking about what they will be required to write. After the notebook is introduced, have students write one thoughtful letter a week in it, to which you respond, also in the notebook. (For teachers with large numbers of students, biweekly responses may be more feasible.) Teachers in middle schools may want to write very brief comments on a rotating basis. The important point is that students know their writing is read and get some feedback on a regular basis. Students can write or draw about or refer to any text they have heard read aloud, read in a guided reading lesson, discussed in book club, or read independently.

Letters exchanged in a reader's notebook have many advantages in helping students learn to write about their reading:

- Readers can transition easily from talking about reading to conversing about reading in writing (written conversation).
- Readers are writing to an authentic audience for an authentic purpose. Unlike a "book report," the letters are an authentic dialogue between you and the student.
- The content of the letters is mostly open-ended. Students (most of the time) focus on any kind of thinking about reading that is meaningful to them. Sometimes they are required to include a focused or prompted response as part of the letter.
- Readers know that they are expected to reflect on their reading, so intensity is added to the reading experience.
- Readers have the opportunity to organize and present their thinking in continuous text (in contrast to short-answer questions).
- The format of the letter is easily learned; students can concentrate on the central task of reflecting on the meaning of a text.
- Readers receive authentic feedback that confirms, creates reaction to, and extends their thinking.
- Readers have the opportunity to ask questions and receive a response that includes the information they requested.
- Because the dialogue is ongoing, readers have the opportunity to follow up or build on their thinking.
- Students have regular, weekly opportunities to write about their thinking.
- Readers are writing for a real purpose—to communicate their thinking to another reader.
- Letters have a built-in audience; when students are expressing their thinking, they have in mind another reader who is listening and responding.
- Readers have a record of their own thinking over time and the benefit of someone else's thinking.

Readers gain vast amounts of practice organizing and presenting their thinking in response to a specific prompt, a task required by many state proficiency exams. A reader's notebook that is full of letters, sketches, and other forms of writing at the end of the school year is a treasure. It is a collection of thinking and a record of conversation between two readers as they talk together about texts and benefit from each other's thinking throughout a prolonged period of time.

Once students have learned to write basic friendly letters and have become accustomed to writing about their reading, we suggest that you expand the task so that students learn how to write on particular topics (a prompt) as part of their written response (for example, focus them on the development of characters over time, or reporting new information and how it has changed their thinking). Through interactive read-aloud, group share, literature circles or book clubs, minilessons, and reading conferences, students experience many demonstrations of how to talk and write about their thinking You will want to move from letter writing to include a greater range of types from which they can choose once they have developed a strong voice in their letters.

LOOKING AT LETTERS FOR EVIDENCE OF THINKING ABOUT TEXTS

Let's look at several responses by children who are just learning how to write about their reading in a friendly letter format.

Look at the simple letter to a teacher about *The Carrot Seed* (Krauss) (see Figure 27-11). Notice that the young student has included thinking in a drawing and has also summarized the story accurately and identified the theme. She has clearly demonstrated thinking beyond the text.

Children enjoy drawing and writing in response to texts they hear or read. They learn that their thinking is valued and that it needs to be grounded in the text. Think about the written conversation between Maddie and Ms. Won during the first several weeks of school in Chapter 22 (see Figure 22-17). Think about how Maddie's thinking about the text changed over time, moving from retelling the text to thinking about it in diverse ways. Interactive read-aloud, book clubs, minilessons, conferences, and sharing, as well as the instructional scaffolds of Ms. Won's responses, influ-

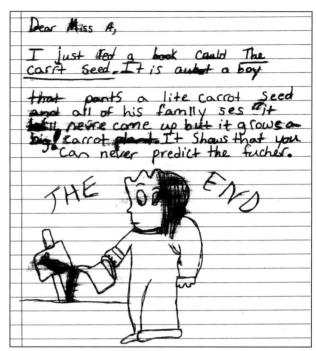

Figure 27-11. *Letter Reflecting Thinking Beyond* The Carrot Seed

enced her ability to think about texts (see Figure 27-12). They provided a "lift" to the thinking and helped her expand her ways of responding to texts. She moved from thinking mostly within the text to thinking about and beyond the text.

We have examined Maddie's thinking for evidence of thinking within, beyond, and about the text. Notice how her thinking has moved from retelling the story to a higher level of response to the text.

Let's also think about a response by Matthew to a nonfiction text he has read (see Figure 27-13). Notice how he shared the way his reading had changed his thinking about sharks. In his teacher's response, she confirmed his feelings and expressed her interest in gaining specific information.

Morgan's letter (see Figure 27-14) is about two texts she is reading, *A Lion to Guard Us* (Bulla) and *A Series of Unfortunate Events: The Reptile Room* (Snicket). Notice that while Morgan devoted most of her letter to *The Reptile Room*, she also dealt quite competently with *A Lion to Guard Us*.

Her comments about the Lemony Snicket book indicate the strength readers gain when reading or listening to texts that are part of a series. They know the characters and follow them through many volumes. This series, in particular, seems to captivate upper elementary or middle school students.

Evidence of Prompting for and Encouraging Thinking

DATE OF LETTER/DESCRIPTION	. . . WITHIN THE TEXT	. . . BEYOND THE TEXT	. . . ABOUT THE TEXT
October 4— Maddie to Ms. Won *Mostly retells the story.*	"I'm going to tell you what has happened so far. Well . . . right now Ramona is talking with her big sister Beezus. Beezus thinks their mother is going to have a baby because she hasn't been eating dessert and when their aunt was at their house, she kept asking how she was feeling." "Another thing that's happening is Ramona's best friend's Uncle Hobart came. Ramona thinks he's mean because he is teasing her. P.S. I just finished it and they do have a baby named "Roberta." P.P.S. Beezus and Ramona's aunt Beatrice got married to Howie's Uncle Hobart, and Ramona (his new niece) thinks he's nice now, and they are friends!"	"I don't think she's going to have a baby, I don't know why, I just don't think she is."	
October 5— Ms. Won to Maddie *Demonstrates making personal connections; prompts thinking about texts.*	"Oh, I remember loving Ramona when I was growing up."	"I still like her a lot. I just remember feeling like I was a lot like her character and that if we could be friends, we would really understand each other." "She seemed to have a lot that she worried about, was scared about, and wondered. I liked knowing all of these things, and I liked to read about how Ramona would act in different situations. How do you feel about Ramona? What do you think about her?"	"Through Beverly Cleary's writing, I knew a lot of Ramona's thoughts." "I looked at your reading list and am wondering what books you will try next. Is there another series or author that you would like to try?"
October 20— Maddie to Ms. Won *Provides details about new book, imitates the teacher in inferring character traits; doesn't respond to prompt about other texts; expresses preference for sticking to the same books.*	"I started a new book called *Ramona Quimby, Age 8*. It's great. So far there's nothing I really have to tell you about, but when I do...I'll let you know." "I don't really want to read any other series soon, but I will try some a little later."	"Well . . . you asked me how I feel about her and what I think about her, I sort of feel the way you do. I like her and sometimes I picture myself in her shoes. I also think she has a very creative imagination and it would be cool to be her."	

Figure 27-12. *Analysis of Maddie's Letters: Evidence of Prompting for and Encouraging Thinking*

ANALYSIS OF MADDIE'S LETTERS:
Evidence of Prompting for and Encouraging Thinking (CONTINUED)

DATE OF LETTER/DESCRIPTION	. . . WITHIN THE TEXT	. . . BEYOND THE TEXT	. . . ABOUT THE TEXT
October 22– Ms. Won to Maddie / *Inquires about her book; prompts writing about thinking; explains reading process.*	"How is *Ramona Quimby, Age 8* coming along? You've probably moved on to your next book by now."	"When you read any book, I know you are doing a lot of thinking. (Reading is thinking). That's what I would like for you to share with me—your thoughts as you read!"	"Once you start a series, it does take a while to get through all the books. It is often worth it, but it can keep a reader from exploring and trying new kinds of books and authors. What are you thinking in terms of the next books you'd like to try? What kind of book would you like to read next? I can help you find something during reader's workshop."
November 1– Maddie to Ms. Won / *Provides information about reading; addresses thinking but does not really share it; expresses preference for sticking to the same books.*	"You're right! I did finish *Ramona Quimby, Age 8.* Now I'm reading . . . *Ramona and Her Mother.* But I'm only on p. 43. I am doing a lot of thinking when I'm reading and I usually just think about what I'm reading. I don't really think about anything else! Just what the story is about and what the characters are doing." "I'm not sure what other kinds of books I'm going to read next, but I still want to read two more Beverly Cleary books after the one I'm reading now. Those books are . . . *Ramona and Her Father* and *Ramona's World.*"		
November 7– Maddie to Ms. Won / *Provides details from story; makes inferences about characters; makes personal connections; mentions writer's style.*	"The part of *Ramona and Her Mother* I'm on right now is when Ramona is using the sewing machine and is making slacks for her stuffed elephant. She finished the slacks but they wouldn't fit him!" "P.S. Let me know if I didn't write enough details."	"She tried so hard! I feel bad for her! I think she deserves better than that! She's a sweet little girl that was just trying to make slacks! Well, anyway, I think Ramona and I have a lot in common with each other. She is a very picky eater and so am I. Ramona is a really funny character. Beezus is very serious, and their parents are serious, too."	"I really like Ramona books. They are just so funny and I like the idea of the stories."

ANALYSIS OF MADDIE'S LETTERS:
Evidence of Prompting for and Encouraging Thinking (CONTINUED)

DATE OF LETTER/DESCRIPTION	. . . WITHIN THE TEXT	. . . BEYOND THE TEXT	. . . ABOUT THE TEXT
November 7— Ms. Won to Maddie. Confirms Maddie's improvement; explains why details are important evidence of thinking; demonstrates inferring character traits and underlying causes; mentions writer's craft; prompts for broader reading.	"Thank you very much for your letter. The second one is much more detailed than the one before."	"I understand what you mean about how it seems that Ramona just tries so hard sometimes, but things don't always seem to work out for her, do they? I always felt badly for her, too. I felt she was misunderstood a lot and that she just needed some attention at times."	"I also really like the stories that Beverly Cleary comes up with. Wow! Look at all of the Ramona books she's written, and we like them all. I think it would be neat for you, Maddie, to read one of Beverly Cleary's memoirs. You can learn more about her as a person and writer and find out more about how she comes up with her book ideas."
November 13— Maddie to Ms. Won *Provides detail as evidence for thinking; makes personal connection; comments on writing style.*	"Ramona just squeezed out a big tube of toothpaste. Her mother got very mad! She had her put the toothpaste in a bag, and she would dip her toothbrush in it while Beezus, her mother, and her father would have a tube to squeeze."	"That's another reason that I feel bad for her. I know she shouldn't have done it, but still! Woops! Reader's workshop is over!" "P.S. I think it would be fun to squeeze out a whole tube of toothpaste! (Do you?)"	"I've been reading my book, and I just think it's a little boring! I don't want to abandon it because I've been wondering what's at the end. What should I do?"
November 13— Ms. Won to Maddie *Demonstrates thinking about a writer's style; demonstrates personal connection in response to the student.*	"Yes, I've wondered what it would be like to squeeze out a whole tube of toothpaste. I've also wondered what it would be like to pull out all the tissues of a box at once."		"Hmm . . . it's getting boring? I know how much you like Beverly Cleary. Maybe it's time for something different. As you read a lot of Beverly Cleary books, you might start to realize that she writes about similar topics and she also has a style of writing that you might start to get used to. In fact, do you think that you're getting a little too used to Beverly Cleary? Do you think it's that she's a boring author or simply that you need a change of pace? Maddie, let's talk about other authors and genres you can try. What are you interested in?"

Figure 27-12. *Analysis of Maddie's Letters: Evidence of Prompting for and Encouraging Thinking (cont.)*

Dear Mrs. Rogers,

I am reading a book called Ripley's Amazing Sharks by Christina Joie Slager. This book fascinates me with amazing facks about sharks. But I had no idea that sharks could be so large and so peaceful. But sharks have such an awful reputation. Before I read this book I was terrified of sharks. But this book makes me feel a lettle sorry for them and now I'm not afraid of sharks anymore.

                    Sincerely,
                    Matthew
                    Cleveland

Dear Matthew,

I grew up in a little place called Gulf Breeze, Florida. It is by the Gulf of Mexico. When I was a little girl some movie people made the film JAWS there. It is a fiction fantasy movie about a killer shark. Ever since I have been totally terrified of sharks. I will have to read that book to ease my fears. What are some things you read that made you feel better about sharks? I wonder if there is any book out there that will help me be less afraid of snakes?
    Keep on reading!

                    Love,
                    Mrs. Rogers

Figure 27-13. *Matthew's Letter and His Teacher's Response*

Dear Ms. D,

I love A Lion to Guard Us. It is a wonderful book. When I got to the part where Amanda can see Mistress Trippet with her wig off, I wondered if she is bald. I also thaugt about how Mistress Trippet keeps interupting Amanda. I think if she does that to everyone it might ruine her life. When the two men are fighting they should work it out with kind words instead.

I am also reading A Series of Unfortunate Events: The Reptile Room. I read the first one. Now I'm reading the second one. Count Olaf is an evil person pretending to be an uncle to the Baulaire orphans to get their personal parents fortune. He lost the first time but... he comes back. This time he is trying to be Uncle Monty's assistant. Uncle Monty is their phoster parent. He studys and discovers never before seen reptiles. They are going on a trip to Puru to find and discover new things. What I think is really cruel is that Count Olaf keeps a VERY sharp knife with him so if any of the children try to tell Uncle Monty who he really is he'll slit their throats.

I have found a bunch of great phrases in this book. Lik: hatched a plan. That made me think of a lightbulb cracking out of an egg all lit up. The strech of the road makes me imagine a road all stretched out like a rubber band. When the book reads there was a warning I could feel their pain. My book is fantasy so if it was reall it would probably take place now. It mostly takes place in conversation in the reptile room.

                    Sincerely,
                    Morgan

Figure 27-14. *Morgan's Letter*

ven though she enjoyed the thrills of the book, Morgan lso thought about the text, as evidenced by her comments bout phrases she found interesting. As her teacher, in your sponse you might:

Acknowledge Morgan for clarifying her understanding of homophones.

Ask what she thinks about the character of Amanda or Mistress Trippett after reading *A Lion to Guard Us*.

Comment on her enjoyment of Lemony Snicket, especially the phrases that she has identified and interpreted.

Ask if she plans to read another Lemony Snicket book.

Kelsey's letter (see Figure 27-15) is about a book her teacher is reading aloud to the class—*Safari,* by Robert Bateman. This gorgeous text has beautiful photographs and captivating text about Africa. Obviously, it has made an impact on Kelsey. Her letter provides ample evidence that she has responded personally to the text and noticed the power of the writing. As a teacher, in your response you might:

□ Appreciate Kelsey's feelings about killing an animal.

449

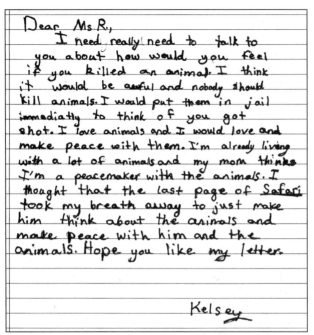

Dear Ms R.,
I need really need to talk to you about how would you feel if you killed an animal. I think it would be awful and nobody should kill animals. I would put them in jail immediatly to think of you got shot. I love animals and I would love and make peace with them. I'm already living with a lot of animals and my mom thinks I'm a peacemaker with the animals. I thought that the last page of Safari took my breath away to just make him think about the animals and make peace with him and the animals. Hope you like my letter.

Kelsey

Figure 27-15. *Kelsey's Letter*

- Tell Kelsey how you feel about killing animals.
- Tell your own feelings about the last page of the book.
- Suggest related books she might enjoy.

Haylea has been writing letters about her reading for several years in school. In the letter in Figure 27-16, Haylea discusses four books she has been hearing in class or reading over the past week: *Love That Dog* (Creech), *Maniac Magee* (Spinelli), *Walk Two Moons* (Creech), and *Mr. Lincoln's Way* (Polacco). She provides evidence of:

- Thinking critically about *Maniac Magee*.
- Making personal connections to *Love That Dog*.
- Considering Spinelli's quality as an author.
- Being aware of Creech's style as an author.
- Comparing the characters in *Walk Two Moons*.
- Predicting and confirming the plot of *Walk Two Moons*.
- Thinking critically about *Walk Two Moons* (some parts are confusing).
- Inquiring into the thinking of the author of *Walk Two Moons*.
- Inferring characters' motivations in *Mr. Lincoln's Way*.
- Inferring cause and effect in *Mr. Lincoln's Way*.
- Identifying the main theme of *Mr. Lincoln's Way*.
- Making connections among books by Patricia Polacco.

Ms. W. responded by agreeing that some parts of *Walk Tw Moons* might be confusing and shared her own readin experiences. She prompted Haylea to notice similaritie between the two characters and made a recommendatio for Haylea's next book. She asked her to think about wh Sharon Creech includes sad moments in her books and t compare this writer with other writers. She shared her ow opinion of *Mr. Lincoln's Way*, acknowledges the student analysis, and encouraged Haylea to keep writing!

EXPANDING THINKING THROUGH WRITTEN DIALOGUE

Dialogue letters provide rich opportunities for genuin reader-to-reader conversation. Think of the interchanges a similar to a reading conference, in which the teacher an student talk together about the meaning of a text. Studen learn that there is no single way to share their thought They learn that the personal response is valued and tha they need to support their thinking with personal exper ence or examples from the text. You will notice how you responses and lessons influence your students' thinkin and are revealed in talk and writing.

HELPING STUDENTS IMPROVE WRITTEN CONVERSATION ABOUT TEXTS

Sometimes when children begin writing letters, they lear the form for the writing but have a long way to go befor they can genuinely express their thinking. You may reco nize comments like these:

- "You are a great teacher. I love you."
- "You are very pretty and a very nice teacher."
- "This is a good book."
- "This book is interesting. You should read it."

While comments like these may be gratifying, they show li tle evidence of thinking about reading! The students hav simply taken on the form of a friendly letter. You will wa to be sure your students are reflecting on the content their reading. Figure 27-17 itemizes six goals for helpin students improve their letter writing.

The first step is to be sure students do a lot of reading. students encounter great fiction and nonfiction tex through interactive read-aloud, independent reading, boc clubs, and guided reading, they will have more to say their letters or other genre writing. If they do not like (c cannot understand) the texts they encounter, or if they hav

Dear Ms. Winkler,

I agree that when Jack, in the book Love That Dog by Sharon Creech, becomes a poet without really knowing it because he thinks he's not good at it. I never thought that I would be good at math, but I'd find myself figuring out daily-live math problems and getting them right!

I thought the ending of Maniac Magee by Jerry Spinelli was good, but it could of had more to it. I'm glad he came back to the Beacles, and I did suspect it. I did not suspect Maniac to work out his problems with Mars Bar, though, I thought that it was a great book, and would like to read more books by Jerry Spinelli.

I just finished Walk Two Moons by Sharon Creech. I like Sharon Creech's style, it comes out a lot in the book. I think they call it Walk Two Moons because Phoebe and Salamanca are so different, yet the same. What happens is that two girls meet eachother, and both lose mothers. It's like a half and half story because Salamanca half

the time is telling a story, and half the time driving to Bylanks, Kentucky. I did not like the murder-talk part. I think it was scary. I thought it was confusing when Phoebe's mom was acting as if her son was her date! I predicted that she would come back, but never like that! I think she was depressed, just like Salamanca's mother was. I didn't think that her "Gram" would die. That was very sad. I've realized by reading Sharon Creech's books that she has put sadness in them, I wonder why she writes like that? Maybe she likes sad stories. I think some of them are things she might have experienced. I really like this book, and look forward to reading more books by her.

For the books we've read I picked Mr. Lincoln's Way by Patricia Polacco. I think that the reason Eugene Esterhause was mean was because of his father. Since his father was so prejudiced against blacks, that's why he did not like Mr. Lincoln. He did not want his dad to be mad at him. By asking Eugene to help him with the birds, he sort of cured Eugene out of being mean. I liked

the way Mr. Lincoln did that. He never was mean. This book teaches people not to solve problems in a mean way, but in a kind way. It teaches people that no matter what color you are, you are equal. Yes, I would recommend this book. It's filled up with great pictures that help tell the story. It's a great book, just like all the books by Patricia Polacco are.
Sincerely,
Haylea

Dear Haylea,
I am thrilled that you enjoyed Walk Two Moons. I agree that there are some parts of the book that are confusing — I have read this book several times and I learn something new every time! Did you notice a lot of similarities between Phoebe and Sal? I think you should read Chasing Redbird as your next Sharon Creech book. You're right — there are sad moments in many of Sharon Creech's books. A lot of writers have sad parts in their stories, but they share them differently. Can you think why that might be so? Is it similar to or different from the way Sharon Creech writes about sadness?
Mr. Lincoln's Way is my favorite Patricia Polacco book. I am so glad that you enjoyed it. You shared the main themes in your letter with clear examples. You also did a fabulous job telling what you thought was the purpose of the story. Keep up the great thinking — you are writing your letters EXACTLY how you should!
Love,
Ms. W

Figure 27-16. Haylea's Letter and Ms. Winkler's Response

How Do You Improve Your Students' Letter Writing?

GOAL	INSTRUCTIONAL CONTEXT
1 Ensure opportunities to read or listen to great fiction and nonfiction books.	▫ Interactive read-aloud, independent reading, guided reading, book club.
2 Ensure numerous opportunities for text talk.	▫ Text talk in interactive read-aloud, reading minilesson, reading conference, group share, guided reading lesson, and book club.
3 Provide regular, explicit teaching on thinking, talking, and writing about texts.	▫ Embedded lessons in interactive read-aloud, reading minilesson, reading conference, and response letter from teacher.
4 Provide regular modeling of writing about reading in a variety of genres.	▫ Reading minilesson, model of genre for reference on chart or in scrapbook, teacher response to student's letter.
5 Provide regular feedback on writing about reading.	▫ Letter of response from teacher or peer, group share, partner share, triad share, reading minilesson, reading conferences, small-group instruction.
6 Provide specific opportunities for students to engage in focused or prompted talk and writing.	▫ Letter writing, "short writes", partner share, triad share, reading conferences, small group instruction, reading minilessons.

Figure 27-17. *How Do You Improve Students' Letter Writing?*

only a "thin" foundation of texts, it will not be possible for them to produce good writing about reading.

The second goal is to provide numerous opportunities for text talk. Reflect on a day of your teaching, asking,

▫ How am I scaffolding the talk to confirm and extend thinking?

▫ How much opportunity have the students had for demonstration of thinking within, beyond, and about texts?

▫ How much did students get to talk about texts today?

▫ Did they talk with peers or only with me?

▫ Did all students have opportunity to talk or only a few?

▫ What did I do when the text talk was especially rich?

You can also provide regular, explicit lessons on how to think and talk about texts. Teaching means intentionally calling students' attention to how they might talk or write about their thinking during interactive read-aloud, in reading minilessons, in individual reading conferences, in book clubs, during group share, and in your responses to students' letters. In these same settings, you can provide

regular demonstrations using your own thinking or students' letters from previous years.

You will want to provide many minilessons on writing thoughtful letters. We provide a comprehensive list of suggestions for improving students' writing about reading in letter form (see Figure 27-18).

Each of the thirty ways we suggest is a separate minilesson you will want to teach at various points in the year to the whole group if needed, to a small group of students, or to individuals as you confer with them. Think about how each suggestion provides a scaffold to extend student responses.

Finally, you will want to provide regular feedback to students on their letters. Make them a point of discussion during individual conferences, or call a small group together to help them work on their responses, adding to or revising them. Your written responses to texts will enhance your students' thinking about the texts. Your scaffolds will direct their attention to a variety of ways to think within, beyond, and about texts. We have developed a list of suggestions for how to pro-

Ways to Help Students Write More Thoughtful Letters in Their Reader's Notebooks

1 Read aloud a text, engaging the students in thinking about the meaning and the author's craft. Following the reading, use modeled writing to compose a letter about the group's thinking. You may want to address it to another class at the grade level, and encourage your teacher colleague to do the same. Use the process with an appropriate picture book and also with a longer text you read over several days

2 Using an enlarged version of a good letter on a chart, invite the students to read each paragraph and describe the type of thinking the reader shared (for example, he tells how the book reminds him of another book, comments on the author's use of language, compares the book to others in the genre, tells why he liked it). Write the description in phrases on stick-on notes or cards and place them alongside each paragraph on the letter with arrows. Summarize by reading the notes and encouraging students to vary their responses by thinking about the type of thinking in each paragraph they write.

3 Using a transparency on the overhead projector or enlarged print on a chart, show students a sample letter you wrote about a book you read to them with statements that do not have supporting evidence. Rewrite the letter with their input, adding specific evidence from your experience or from the text to support thinking. An alternative to rewriting is to mark with an asterisk and number the place to insert and tape the additions along the side of the letter.

4 Show and read three to five student letters (from a previous group of students with names removed). For each letter, ask your students to point out places where the reader shared good thinking. Use a highlighter pen to mark the sentences that show best thinking.

5 Invite students to select two or three of their letters and mark the sentences that show their good thinking. Have them read the selected sentences at group share. Make a list of the kinds of thinking they did so they can refer to it when writing new letters.

6 Invite students to choose a letter they have written that shows their best thinking. Have them write a few sentences or a paragraph telling why they think it is a thoughtful letter.

7 Create a bulletin board or chart of memorable sentences from letters that show the readers' thoughtfulness. Invite students to notice good thinking in each other's letters and to suggest sentences to add to the display.

8 Have students talk with a partner about the book they are reading. Give them two or three specific topics for the discussion, for example, the author's message, the significance of the title, thoughts about one of the main characters. Then send them to write their letters about what they just shared with their partner.

9 Model writing one thoughtful paragraph about a book you have read to the students. In the paragraph, focus on one type of thinking, e.g., a description of the genre and what you think about it or how the character reminded you of someone else and why. Then tell students to include one paragraph of the same type in their letters that week.

10 Write an uninteresting letter to the class about a book with which many of the students are familiar. Contrast it with an interesting letter about the same book. Have students tell what made the second letter interesting to read.

Figure 27-18. *Ways to Help Students Write More Thoughtful Letters in Their Reader's Notebooks*

Ways to Help Students Write More Thoughtful Letters in Their Reader's Notebooks (CONTINUED)

11 Read aloud a wonderful picture book or short story. Invite all students to write a letter about it. At group share, have them take turns reading their letters to each other in groups of five. Following the reading of each letter, have each student in the group read a place where he did some good thinking. Have the group choose one letter to be read to the large group and be prepared to tell what was good thinking in the letter.

12 Create groups of three. Read aloud a short story or picture book for three consecutive days, having children write one paragraph of good thinking after each reading. Each day, have the groups read their paragraphs to each other, giving comments about the thinking. Encourage them to make one statement about what was good and make one suggestion.

13 Keep an ongoing list of many possible topics for letters. On a particular day instruct students to choose three of the topics on the list and write a paragraph about each.

14 Invite students to choose a good letter from the previous month. Photocopy the letters and make a book of them for others to read. An alternative is to make a transparency of each to show and read, or simply to read each to the class over a period of a week in group share. Invite positive, genuine comments about each letter.

15 Tape-record your conference with a student, encouraging the student to share thoughts and feelings about a book. Give the child the tape recorder to listen to the talk again so he can write about the thoughts in the response letter. As an alternative, jot down some phrases on stick-on notes to remind the student of the discussion. The student can use the stick-on notes to prompt writing the letter.

16 As you read a text aloud to your students, mark three or four places where you had some thoughts, feelings, predictions, or questions. Then write a letter to the class using the stick-on notes to remind you of the parts you wanted to write about. Invite the students to do the same with their books that day.

17 With your students, make a list of the most essential elements of a good letter. Include conventions, but be sure to focus mostly on content. With each characteristic, create a scale from one to four, with one indicating the least of the characteristic and four showing the most, (e.g., no evidence for thinking to always provides evidence for thinking). Have students self-evaluate their letters with the rubric for a few weeks so they will think more about the criteria.

18 Select an interesting book. Read a chapter or the first part of a story aloud. Stop and invite the students to write a paragraph to share their thinking. Have your students read their paragraphs to each other in group share or in a small group. Read the next part and have them write another paragraph. Repeat the process for a few days. Have the students proofread the final letter.

19 Have students use a highlighter pen to mark the questions you ask in your response letter to them. Encourage them to respond to each question in the next letter.

20 Have students participate in a book club for several consecutive days prior to writing their letter, making some notes after each discussion. Encourage them to include the content they shared in their weekly book club discussion in their weekly letter.

Figure 27-18. *Ways to Help Students Write More Thoughtful Letters in Their Reader's Notebooks (cont.)*

Ways to Help Students Write More Thoughtful Letters in Their Reader's Notebooks (CONTINUED)

21 Have students read two or three books of the same genre, about the same topic, written about the same time period or by the same author. In small groups, have them talk about how the two or three books were similar or different. Then have them write letters about the books to an assigned peer who was not in their group.

22 In social studies, promote meaningful discussion about issues. Assign a choice of historical fiction texts as a focus for independent reading and/or book clubs for a period of time (e.g., two weeks). After talking with one partner about issues in their books, encourage students to write letters about their book to a new partner. Repeat the process with other topics or genres.

23 Using a text you read aloud, model the writing of a paragraph, telling your students what you noticed about the author's craft and your thoughts about it. Assign children to write one paragraph telling what they notice and how they feel about the author's writing in each letter they write.

24 Explain to your students that when you talk about "voice" in writing it means that you feel like you can "hear the writer talking." Voice is the author's personality or the person behind the words. Help them notice voice in your letters to them, and show them places in their letters where you can hear the personality of the writer. Remind your students to be sure their readers will hear their voices in their letters. In group share, invite them to comment on each other's writing by noticing places where the writer's voice comes through.

25 In a letter to the class, model how to get beyond a simple retelling by briefly reporting something that happened in the book. In a different colored marker, tell your thoughts or feelings about what happened. When the letter is finished, the second color will clearly dominate, so students have a concrete image of the distinction between retelling and responding.

26 To help students learn the importance of giving specifics or details in their letters, write a letter to them about a text you have read aloud. Write a letter scant with detail. Using stick-on notes and numbered asterisks with pieces of paper taped to the side of the letter, show them how to add more specific information. Then reread the more informative letter, reminding the students how much more interesting it is to the reader.

27 As you return the notebooks to your students, share specific examples where the students did good thinking. Read those parts aloud and ask the class what made the comments good.

28 Have children bring their independent reading books, reader's notebooks, a clipboard and pencil or pen to a community meeting. Explain that "good readers think about how characters change as they read." Ask the students to notice how the character changes as you read today's story. Read a picture book that includes a character who changes in response to story events. When you are finished, invite partners to talk about how the character changed and why. Then ask them to write the first paragraph of their weekly letter explaining how and why the character changed in the story they heard, and what they thought about it. Invite them to read their paragraph to a different partner. Then ask them to include a paragraph about character change in their next letter. Repeat the process with other topics to expand the kind of thinking they are using.

29 During a read-aloud, stop two or three times and at the end, and ask students to tell what they are thinking. Write their comments quickly on a chart. When finished, give them phrases such as "makes you feel," "makes you wonder," "reminds you of." Ask them to write a paragraph that addresses each. Then ask them to do the same in their weekly letter about their independent reading book.

30 Teach students how to evaluate the author's and illustrator's craft by using books you have read aloud as models. Engage them in a discussion of particular aspects, for example – Does the title work? Is the language appropriate? Are the characters believable? Was it written in an interesting way? Require that one paragraph of their weekly letter address the questions you discussed.

Figure 27-18. *Ways to Help Students Write More Thoughtful Letters in Their Reader's Notebooks (cont.)*

WRITING RESPONSES TO READERS:
React, Reinforce, and Expand a Reader's Thinking

1 Highlight or notice the questions a reader asks and be sure to respond to them.

2 As you read the letter, think about what the writer is saying to you and react as you read. Then pick up your pen and share those reactions.

3 Think about the type of text a student is reading. How can you use your knowledge of genre characteristics and elements to expand the reader's understanding?

4 Share the thinking the writer brings out in you. In other words, how are you personally connecting with the reader's thoughts?

5 Think about what you would say in a conversation with a reader in a conference. React precisely to the student's comments in writing as you would in the conference conversation.

6 Confirm the reader's good thinking and inquire genuinely about what you don't understand so you can understand better.

7 Relate your own experiences as a reader to those the student shares. Write your reader-to-reader thoughts.

8 Help the reader get to know you as a reader and try to get to know the student as a reader.

9 Think about the genre of the text the student is reading. What characteristics are important for understanding the text and having expectations for it? Nudge the reader to think about these characteristics.

10 Read a student letter and look at the chart of systems of strategic actions (especially strategies for expanding meaning). Notice what aspects the reader is attending to and what aspects would expand the child's thinking about the text. Make comments that will help the reader think in new ways.

11 Think about the student's perspective about a text and add yours. If you haven't read the book, share how you think you would see things.

12 Think about what aspects within the text the reader is thinking about. How can you confirm the thinking, and what further information do you want to know? Does the reader need to clarify statements about information in the text?

13 Think about how the reader is thinking beyond what the writer states in the text. How can you confirm or respond to the student's thinking beyond the text and prompt the reader to think further?

14 Think about how the reader has analyzed aspects of the text or the writer's craft or evaluated it. What is your thinking about the student's analyses or critique? How can you prompt the reader to become more analytical of the content or craft? How can you foster more analysis or critique with some of your own examples?

15 What books, topics, authors, or genres might you recommend to the reader?

16 What do you notice about the student as a reader as evidenced by the reading list, interest list, or previous writing about reading? Share your thinking about the student's accomplishments and nudge the reader to expand them.

17 Consider how you can help the reader link the book to other books you are reading as a whole group or in a small group.

18 Think about how you can get the reader to provide examples or evidence for statements he makes.

19 Invite the student to use what he knows to anticipate what will follow. Get the reader to think ahead.

20 Encourage the reader to share how this is influencing his independent reading life.

Figure 27-19. *Writing Responses to Readers: React, Reinforce, and Expand a Reader's Thinking*

vide scaffolds in your written responses (see Figure 27-19) and improve your students' reflections over time. Remember to react genuinely, reinforce good thinking, and look for one or two opportunities to lift or expand the reader's thinking.

EXPANDING WRITING OVER TIME

The range of writing students use to respond to their reading changes over time with teaching and experience. In this chapter we have described a range of writing in two categories:

- In *interactive/shared writing,* the teacher works the whole group or a small group to produce a common text. Interactive writing involves "sharing the pen" and is most useful with early writers. Shared writing may be used with students of any age and may be applied to any genre of written response to provide explicit demonstrations of the process. The teacher may also used *modeled writing.* Here, the teacher composes and produces the writing but shares and discusses it with students.

- In *independent writing,* students produce individual written responses to their reading. Through minilessons, the teacher demonstrates different genres for sharing thinking about reading and helps students understand how to write in response to reading. Through conferences and the dialogue of letters, teachers help individual students grow in their ability to express their thinking about texts. The teacher broadens the students' knowledge of types of writing through whole-group minilessons to enable the student to select from a repertoire of authentic possibilities for their own reading responses. Teachers frequently bring together students who can benefit from small-group work called guided writing. The teacher focuses on any aspect of written response to reading that all members of the group need to expand.

In *The Continuum of Literacy Learning, PreK–8: A Guide for Teaching* (Pinnell and Fountas 2008, 2011), you will find a detailed continuum of development for writing and drawing about reading. The continuum is organized level-by-level and grade-by-grade. It is designed not as a prescription but as a tool to guide your planning and decision-making. In this continuum document, you will find specific goals for learning at each level and for each context. As a way of thinking about progress over time, we provide the following summary (see Figure 27-20), with each

genre or type categorized as *functional writing* (supporting memory, research, or communication), *narrative writing* (representing stories), *informational writing* (reporting), and *poetic writing* (responding in poetry).

PRIMARY (K–2)

Even kindergarten children can begin writing in response to reading immediately! Using shared and interactive writing, teachers first engage children in discussion of a text and then help them compose and write in response. An example is the letter from Bear to Hare (drawn from the book *Tops and Bottoms*) presented earlier in this chapter and shown in the DVD provided with this book. Group composition and shared writing help to extend children's ability to write about reading. With teacher and group support, children in kindergarten, grade one, and grade two can participate in the composition of lists, letters, and summaries. They can make diagrams or complete graphic organizers showing aspects of texts (for example, character webs, compare/contrast charts, time lines). Often, individual children contribute illustrations to these documents.

In independent writing, primary children move from drawings with just a few letters or words worked out in approximated spelling to writing simple stories, summaries, and letters about texts. Most of the responses of young children are through talk and drawing, but as writing becomes easier and more fluent, they can take some notes in preparation for discussion and even begin to produce a variety of letters and short pieces of independent writing about texts (for example, the summary of *The Carrot Seed,* which was presented earlier).

ELEMENTARY GRADES (3–5)

Shared writing is still of great benefit to children in grades three to five. In whole-class or small-group instruction, you can engage students in discussion surrounding the composition and production of a wide variety of types of writing about reading. Graphic organizers are most effectively used when a great deal of talk surrounds their production. You can draw graphic organizers on charts and students can participate in completing them; you can guide their conversation to reflect a wide variety of thinking. Teachers of older students sometimes use a transparency on an overhead projector, but charts are appropriate for all ages and

Change over Time in Responding to Texts Through Writing

For younger children, genres and forms are demonstrated through many examples of *interactive* and *shared writing.* Across time, they take on approximated versions of the genres and forms in their *independent writing.* As students grow more sophisticated, teachers continue to demonstrate through *modeled* or *shared writing* on charts or projected images. After experiencing the genre or form several times with group support, students select from these options to reflect on their reading in a reader's notebook.

K–2	3–5	6–8
Functional writing:	**Functional writing:**	**Functional writing:**
□ Notes to remember something about a text or to record interesting information or details, or record interesting language or words	□ Notes to be used in later discussion or writing	□ Notes to be used in later discussion or writing
□ Lists to support memory (characters, events in a story, etc.)	□ Notes representing interesting language from a text or examples of the writer's craft (quotes from a text)	□ Notes representing interesting language from a text or examples of the writer's craft (quotes from a text)
□ Written directions (sometimes with drawings) that show a simple sequence of actions based on a text	□ Sketches to represent a text and provide a basis for discussion or writing	□ Sketches to represent a text and provide a basis for discussion or writing
□ Directions or "how to" descriptions drawn from a text	□ "Short writes" responding to a text in a variety of ways (for example, personal response, interpretation, character analysis, description)	□ "Short writes" responding to a text in a variety of ways (for example, personal response, interpretation, character analysis, description)
□ Sketches that assist in remembering a text, interpreting a character or event, or representing content of a text	□ Letters to other readers or to authors and illustrators	□ Letters to other readers or to authors and illustrators (including dialogue letters in a reader's notebook)
□ "Short writes" responding to a text in a variety of ways (for example, opinion or an interesting aspect of the text)	□ Labels and legends for illustrations (drawings, photographs, maps, etc.)	□ Letters to newspaper or magazine editors in response to articles
□ Letters to other readers or to authors and illustrators	□ Graphic organizers—comparisons, time lines, webs that show relationships among different kinds of information or that connect more than one text	□ Graphic organizers—comparisons, time lines, webs that show relationships among different kinds
□ Labels for photographs or any kind of drawing	□ Grids that show analysis of a text or of more than one text	□ Grids that show analysis of a text (a form of graphic organizer)
□ Simple charts (graphic organizers) to show comparisons, time lines, or character traits	□ Poster/advertisement that tells about a text in an attention-getting way	□ Poster/advertisement that tells about a text in an attention-getting way
□ Grids to show relationships among different kinds of information	**Narrative writing:**	**Narrative writing:**
Narrative writing:	□ Cartoons, comics to present a story or information	□ Cartoons, comics to present a story or information
□ Drawings showing the sequence of events in a text (sometimes with speech bubbles to show dialogue)	□ Plot summaries	□ Plot summaries
□ Simple statements summarizing a text	□ Summaries	□ Summaries
□ Predictions as to what will happen in a text	□ Scripts for readers' theater	□ Scripts for readers' theater
□ Innovations on known texts (for example, new endings or similar plots with different characters)	□ Storyboards to represent significant events in a text	□ Storyboards to represent significant events in a text
Informational writing:	**Informational writing:**	**Informational writing:**
□ Lists of facts from a text	□ Outlines that include headings, subheadings, and sub-subheadings to reflect the organization of the text	□ Outlines that include headings, subheadings, and sub-subheadings to reflect the organization of the text
□ Sentences reporting some interesting information from a text	□ "How to" articles that require the writer to be an "expert," who	□ Author study, reflecting knowledge of biographical information and/or response to one or more books by a writer

Figure 27-20. *Change over Time in Responding to Texts Through Writing*

Change over Time in Responding to Texts Through Writing (CONTINUED)

K–2	3–5	6–8
• A few sentences with information about an author • A few sentences with information about an illustrator • Labeling of drawings that represent interesting information from a text **Poetic writing:**	explains to readers how something is made or done • Author study, reflecting knowledge of biographical information and/or response to one or more books by a writer • Illustrator study, reflecting knowledge of biographical information and/or response to one or more books by an artist • Biographical sketch of an author or the subject of a biography • Book recommendations • Drawings or photographs with labels or legends illustrating information from a text • Projects that present ideas and opinions about texts or topics in an organized way (text and visual images) • Reports that include text and graphic organizers to present information drawn from text **Poetic writing:** • Poetic texts written in response to a prose text • Poetic texts written in response to poems (same style, topic, mood, etc.)	• Illustrator study, reflecting knowledge of biographical information and/or response to one or more books by an artist • Biographical sketch of an author or the subject of a biography • Interviews with an author or expert (questions and responses designed to provide information) • "How to" articles explaining how something is made or done (based on one or more texts) • Photo essay or picture essay explaining a topic or representing a setting or plot • Book reviews • Drawings with labels or legends illustrating information from a text • Projects that present ideas and opinions about texts or topics in an organized way (text and visual images) • Reports that include text and graphic organizers to present information drawn from texts • News or feature article based on reading one or more texts • Critiques or analyses of informational articles • Literary essays that present ideas about a text and may include examples and a short retelling of the text **Poetic writing:** • Poetic texts written in response to a prose text • Poetic texts written in response to poems (same style, topic, mood, etc.)

re 27-20. *Change over Time in Responding to Texts Through Writing (cont.)*

ve the advantage of remaining on display to remind stu-nts of their thinking. Through group-composed charts, u can record interesting words, quotes that prompted stu-nts' thinking, and quotes representing aspects of craft. u can involve students in summarizing a text, listing portant ideas, and you can demonstrate how to write od letters or any other kind of written response. Students

will also enjoy creating innovations on known texts (for example, their own versions of wacky folktales).

Students in the upper elementary grades will produce an increasingly sophisticated range of independent writing in response to reading. Each new genre of writing is demonstrated through shared/interactive writing, and students then take it on to produce independently. Over time, they build a repertoire from which they can choose ways to write about reading, for example, notes and lists, response to quotes, letters, summaries, "short writes" as open responses, "short writes" to prompts, book recommendations and reviews, and many others. Students can also use graphic organizers independently (or working as partners) to create their own representations of text structure, character analysis, and other. On the DVD provided with this book, you will find one hundred graphic organizers. But we caution that these should not be used as "worksheets" for students to fill out. Organizers are effective only as much as they are surrounded by productive talk.

MIDDLE SCHOOL (GRADES 6–8)

The degree to which middle school students can produce highly sophisticated written responses to reading depends on the experiences they have had in previous years. They can still benefit from group composition in whole-class and small-group settings. As in upper elementary grades, every genre of written response can be demonstrated through shared writing on charts or using a transparency on an overhead. You can use graphic organizers of all kinds. These demonstrations provide explicit models that students can apply to their own writing.

Students in grades six to eight who have had considerable experience in writing about reading can produce highly sophisticated written responses in a wide range of genres. They write thoughtful letters and can produce literary essays that reflect critical analysis of a text or of the works of an author. They can compare texts or write critiques and book reviews. You can expect middle school students to take notes purposefully for a variety of purposes. If your students are inexperienced, provide more support in the form of demonstrations, guided writing, and individual conferences. You can also move back to having them produce shorter pieces in response to the kinds of demonstrations used in upper elementary so that they build a backlog of experience. It is very helpful also for students to talk and to sketch in response to reading before they are expected to write.

READING AS PRIORITY

This chapter and the next focus on writing and drawing, but remember that we are discussing a particular use for writing. You will always be engaging your students in a writer's workshop in which students work on self-selected topics; writing about reading takes place within reading workshop and has the particular purpose of helping students learn how to extend and express their thinking about texts in a variety of genres. The writing will not be rich or serve this purpose if reading is limited. A high priority is to engage students daily in reading (and listening to you reading) a variety of high-quality texts that they discuss orally.

SUGGESTIONS FOR PROFESSIONAL DEVELOPMENT

A. PRIMARY OR INTERMEDIATE

1 Meet with colleagues at your grade level or across grade levels.

2 Looking at the summary chart for writing about reading, focus on the grade level you teach.

3 Compare you own observations of what your students can do to the two or more levels of the continuum that are applicable. (Remember, the chart reflects expectations by the end of the highest designated grade level.)

4 Select two important genres or types of writing that you want to develop through helping students write in response to reading. You may have them write as part of interactive read-aloud, guided reading, literature discussion, or independent reading.

5 Plan two weeks of instruction, incorporating minilessons on writing about reading that are appropriate to your students' current level of development. Include several days of demonstration through shared or modeled writing.

6 Plan a follow-up meeting to discuss the results.

B. INTERMEDIATE OR MIDDLE SCHOOL

1 Examine and discuss with a colleague the attached letter by a third-grade student.

2 Ask:

   □ What does this student know about the conventions of written language? And, what does he need to know next?

   □ What kinds of thinking does the letter reveal—thinking within, beyond, and about the text?

3 Outline the points you would make in a reply to this letter. Ask:

   □ How would you help the student become more articulate in his thinking?

Dear Ms. Duffield,

My Literature study book is The Table Where Rich People Sit. In this book I think her dad isn't talking about that kind of rich. But the girl does not get it yet. The father is talking about the inside riches and the things around them not about money. Do you think that inside riches are more important than money riches?

I agrey with her mother when she thinks that if all the rulers of the world could get together at a table in someones kitchen they would solve arguments in half the time instead of fighting and doing wars because fighting doesn't solve anything. Do you think that?

It would be great if more people wanted to work outside because the world would be more peaceful. I would LOVE to camp outside again and again espeshuly where they would go i would just love to live there! When she said her first sight was a motens I wonder what it would be like for me to see as

my first sight. I love her phrases like, a place where ocean touches jungle. The pictures in this book are so creative. I mean the are pictures in the pictures! Like on one page there is a house in the sky. I didn't see it intill we had our lit. group.

When her mother says, "We don't just take our pay in cash, you know. We have a special plan so we get paid in sunsets, too." the part I love about it is that her mother and father care more about outside instead of money.

I learned a cactus grows flowers. I also learned that a lot of things are worth more than money like family a friends. I think the other chose the title because it's about her family meeting and she discovers that some things are worth more then money. and

I think the message in this story is that lots of things are worth more that money. and to be thankful for what you have. I love this book. I think byrd Baylor did a great job writing it and Peter Parnall did a

great doing the pictures.

Happy readings!

Sincerely,
Taylor

re 27-21. *Taylor's Letter*

☐ Are there any conventions that you would like to address?

Your goal is to react genuinely to the reader, reinforce the reader's thinking, and nudge the reader to expand his thinking. You can become very efficient in your responses, making just a few comments if you are a middle school teacher with several classes of students, or taking five minutes per student to write a more expanded response each week or every two weeks if you are an ele-

mentary teacher. Your responses will change the way students think and write. We suggest you begin by reacting genuinely to the reader.

---

[1] *In* Guiding Readers and Writers: Teaching Comprehension, Genre, and Content Literacy *(Fountas and Pinnell 2000), we introduced the reader's notebook as an effective tool for helping students write about their reading. You may want to refer to that text for detailed information (including a series of minilessons) about how to teach students to use a reader's notebook.*

CHAPTER TWENTY-EIGHT

WRITING ABOUT READING IN A VARIETY OF GENRES

Once we can get children to comprehend a

respond thoughtfully to texts in conversation a

in short jottings to record their thinking, we c

then work on the muscles of writing wel

authentic genres of writing about read

—JANET ANGEL

From its beginnings as a way of taking inventory and recording transactions, written language has been a support for, and a tool for, recording and exploring thinking. Written language supports memory, allowing human beings to record and preserve events in a way not possible through oral histories alone. Just about every person in modern society uses written language. Think about the many ways you use written language every day without even thinking about it:

- Writing notes to family members, co-workers, and even to yourself!
- Noting hard-to-remember numbers and dates.
- Putting items on your calendar, and consulting the calendar to remember your schedule.
- Writing and receiving email messages.
- Making lists of things to do or buy.
- Reading directions, maps, and signs.
- Looking at prices or information about fabrics while shopping.
- Reading newspapers and/or written information shown on television and computer screens.
- Listening to language read aloud.
- Listening to language spoken on television.
- Reading informational books or novels.

If you belong to a book club, you might make a few notes in preparation for a discussion with friends. If you keep a writer's notebook, you regularly use written language to record your observations and thoughts.

As Clay has said, "For children who learn to write at the same time as they learn to read, writing plays a significant part in the early reading process" (*What Did I Write* 1975, p. 70). For many of us throughout our lives, reading continues to be a resource for our writing. We encounter new ideas that we incorporate, we learn new and interesting

words, and we notice new ways of organizing texts and p senting information in a clear way.

It makes sense that we can use writing to enhance understanding and enjoyment of reading. In classroo we want to integrate writing and reading and teach s dents how to use a wide range of genres for writing ab reading. Writing increases readers' engagement with a te helping them become involved with characters, feel em tions, and think in more organized and analytical ways

TYPES OF WRITING ABOUT READING

We describe four broad categories of writing that will h you expand your students' ability to use writing to comn nicate their thinking about reading: functional, narrati informational, and poetic.

1 *Functional* writing is undertaken for communication to "get a job done." A great deal of functional writi takes place around reading; for example, we make no to ourselves about written texts that we can, in turn, as a basis for oral or written discussion or for a lon piece of writing. We may diagram or outline in attempt to better understand written texts, or we may wi letters to communicate our thinking to others about tex

2 *Narrative* writing "tells a story." When writing about reading, we might retell some or all of a plot or reco significant events in the life of a subject of a biograp In making personal connections, we might relate a se of events from our own lives.

3 *Informational* writing organizes facts into a coher whole. To compose an informational piece, the wri organizes data into categories and may use underly structures such as description, comparison/contr cause/effect, time sequence, and problem/solution provide information. Examples of writing about read

in this category include reports, news articles, interviews, and essays. The writer may also use this genre to analyze or compare several texts.

Poetic writing entails carefully selecting and arranging words to convey meaning in ways that evoke feelings and sensory images. Poetry condenses meaning into shorter language groupings. It lends itself to repeated readings and to being read aloud for the pleasure of listening to the language.

ch type of writing places different demands on the writer, ves a different purpose, takes a specific form, and is ected to a specific audience. We have found that lots of k about reading as well as notes or phrases on stick-on tes or in a notebook are a good beginning. These can be

modeled in whole group interactive read-aloud sessions. Over time you can move to more formal types. Be sure to consider age-appropriateness in your selection.

Many genres are used by students year after year with increasing sophistication. When students are learning how to write in a particular form, you will want to immerse them in it until they have internalized the characteristics. Provide demonstrations with texts that are well known by the group. Eventually, your students will be able to select from a wide range of possibilities to share their thinking about reading.

Within these broad categories, there are a large number of specific forms of writing along a continuum, from formal to informal (see Figure 28-1). In general, younger students will take on the informal approaches, and as they grow they learn to use more formal genres.

Writing and Drawing About Reading

The types of independent writing listed below may be open or focused with a prompt and may be used for individual reflection or as a group response.

	DESCRIPTION	EXAMPLES
Notes and Sketches	Words, phrases, or sketches on stick-on notes or in the notebook.	<ul><li>Place where you made a personal connection</li><li>Predictions</li><li>Place where you found out something about a character</li><li>Wonderings</li><li>Place where you learned new information</li><li>Place that you found confusing</li><li>Place that you found interesting</li><li>Memorable language</li><li>Place that reminded you of another book</li></ul>
Short Writes	A few sentences or paragraphs produced quickly in a notebook or a long stick-on note that is placed in a notebook.	<ul><li>Reaction to the writer's style</li><li>A prediction</li><li>Response to a selected quote</li><li>Response to a peer's thinking</li><li>Reaction to a character</li><li>Thoughts about the writer's craft</li><li>Thoughts about the writer's message</li><li>Comments on the writer's point of view</li><li>Thoughts about how the text reveals life issues</li><li>New understandings or insights</li><li>Using knowledge of the genre to think about character, plot, theme, setting</li><li>Links to other texts</li></ul>

re 28-1. *Writing and Drawing About Reading*

Writing and Drawing About Reading (CONTINUED)

	DESCRIPTION	EXAMPLES
Graphic Organizers	Words, phrases, sketches, or sentences on graphic organizers or drawn in a notebook.	▫ Story map ▫ Web ▫ Time sequence chain ▫ Comparison/contrast chart ▫ Cause/effect chart ▫ Problem/solution chart ▫ Grid for comparing elements or taking notes ▫ Outline
Longer Responses	Longer responses (including sketches) in the notebook elaborating on thinking about one or several texts.	▫ Letter to the teacher with reply (ongoing dialogue about texts) ▫ Double-column entry (2-column responses with material from the text, a category or questions on the left and response or comments on the right) ▫ Expansion of thinking from the notes, sketches, short writes, or graphic organizers
Published Work	More formal responses to texts that are shared publicly.	▫ Letter to author or illustrator ▫ Book recommendation ▫ Book review ▫ Poem related to a text ▫ Picture book on a topic or subject (e.g., biography) ▫ Opinion essay
Literary Essay	Coherent, longer piece of writing that offers analysis of one or more texts.	▫ Report of an author or illustrator study ▫ Examination of a particular theme across texts ▫ A character analysis or comparison ▫ A book critique

Figure 28-1. *Writing and Drawing About Reading (cont.)*

FUNCTIONAL WRITING

Writing may be functional in a number of ways. Students can write letters to communicate their thinking to others. Writing can be used to support one's memory when preparing to give a talk or write an essay. Writing or sketching can also be used to sustain thinking.

Notes

Readers often make notes so that they can return to particular places in the text; for example, see Sam's notes on *Jericho* (Hickman) (see Figure 28-2).

Many of us habitually take quick notes like these while listening or reading, especially if we have a purpose in mind. Researchers also take notes: notice Natalie's notes in preparation for writing a character sketch of Aunt

Alexandra, in *To Kill a Mockingbird* (Lee) (see Figure 28- Also, see how she used her notes to write a character descr tion (see Figure 28-4).

Note-takers like Sam and Natalie develop their o style. It is important, for note-taking can be informative must be very efficient; otherwise, it interrupts the readi and takes too much time. Good note-takers learn just h much they need to write to support memory.

Lists

Another form of functional writing is the list. Many of us compulsive list makers as we plan our busy lives. Throu interactive writing, primary grade students can make lists

▫ Characters in a story.

▫ Words that describe a character.

Grand Min
has altshimers.

p.4 Jericho
changes name
like title

p.5
She loves
her great grandma
like she
used to be.
She cries

This is confused —
she wetpants—p.11
p.19
Min could
be Arminder!

p.25
When it's now
She says "she goes"
the past it is
"she stopped."

Notes for a Character Sketch of Aunt Alexandra from
To Kill a Mockingbird

• Aunt Alexandra

— Seems Stuck-up, but believes that in a time
like the depression the only thing that separates
the classes is family background, very proud to be a Finch.
— Because of this, doesn't approve of the way
Atticus allows his children such freedom.
— Brothers Francis over Scout because he listens to
whatever she says, sees Scout as a rogue.
— Comes to the house to try and change, doesn't
think Culpurnia is a good influence.
— Fits into Maycomb well.
— gets Atticus to talk to scout and Jem but
he resists her in the end when Scout
began to cry.
— Thinks it's an outrage that scout went into
black church and wanted to get to Cal's
house.
— Argues with Atticus about getting rid of her,
that's where Atticus draws the line
even through all, she still cares about
the kids and sees Atticus as her
brother (after the trial) (when Jem and
Scout are attacked).

Figure 28-3. *Notes for a Character Sketch of Aunt Alexandra from* To Kill a
Mockingbird

Events in a story.

Any kind of collection of items, such as ingredients in
Nail Soup (Zemach).

dents may list word phrases to use in a longer piece of
ting or to engage in reflecting on a specific element of
t. Notice how Tessie made a list of phrases that show the
sage of time in *Charlotte's Web* (White) (see Figure 28-
Students can be taught to make lists to support their
nking for many different purposes, such as preparing for
resentation or summarizing information in preparation
writing.

tches

dents enjoy drawing as a means of communicating
's thinking in images. A sketch (a brief visual image
duced very quickly) takes very little time and is a great
l for thinking. It is, in fact, a form of thinking. Drawing
ps readers think, observe, and remember. The resulting

image takes them back to the ideas they were thinking
about while they were making the sketch.

Students can make quick sketches as they prepare to
discuss a text in book club and then share the sketch as part
of the discussion. You can also ask students to make quick
sketches of their impressions of characters or settings during interactive read-aloud before you show them the book's
illustrations. And you can use sketching in guided reading.
As students finish reading the text (or an assigned section),
they can quickly sketch an open response; alternatively, you
may specify the topic. These sketches will help them discuss
the meaning of the text.

Short Writes/Prompted Writing

Short writes are an excellent way to quickly capture a reader's thinking. They often involve writing to a prompt and
are a good way to help students learn how to address a particular topic. It is important that students have many
opportunities for prompted talk (in interactive read-aloud)
to learn how to engage with an idea and talk about it for a

Character Description of Aunt Alexandra from <u>To Kill a Mockingbird</u>

Aunt Alexandra is a character that you want to hate sometimes but you understand her. She seems stuck-up, but really it's just because she believes that when everybody is poor, the only way there's social distinction is a person's good name—or bad name for that matter. She was raised that way, and she's not evil or rude. "When Aunt Alexandra went to school, self-doubt could not be found in any textbook, so she knew not its meaning. She was never bored, and given the slightest chance she would exercise her royal prerogative: she would arrange, advise, caution, and warn." p. 129. Because of all this she does not approve of Atticus's way of raising his children. She sees their "running wild" as slanderish to the Finch name. For the most part she approves of Jem and she has Francis wrapped around her finger. But she sees Scout as a rogue. Aunt Alexandra fully disapproves of Scout's overalls and manners.

But, unfortunately for Scout, Aunt Alexandra didn't just sit back and whine about it. She convinced Atticus to let her move in and give the children a good Finch influence. She even got Atticus to try and tell his children to behave more like finches, but he was not successful.

Aunt Alexandra fit into Maycomb well and immediately became a usual part of the community. Scout said that she did not fit into their lives, though. She tried to get rid of Calpurnia and was outraged when she found out that Scout had gone to a black church. Atticus put his foot down, though. Calpurnia was part of the family.

Through all of it, Aunt Alexandra cares about Scout and Jem and still acknowledges Atticus as her brother. "I'm sorry brother she murmured. Having never heard her call Atticus 'brother' before . . ." (p. 212). "Aunt Alexandra's fingers trembled as she unwound the crushed fabric and wire from around me. 'Are you all right darling?' she asked over and over as she worked me free. (p. 264). And when she was caring for Scout instead of criticizing her, she didn't even bother to remember how much she hated Scout's overalls. "Had I thought about it then, I would have never let her forget it: in her distraction, Aunty had brought me my overalls." (p. 264).

Figure 28-4. *Character Description of Aunt Alexandra from* To Kill a Mockingbird

period of time. As a focused short write, Stella wrote about why the race between turtle and beaver was a trickster's story and gave her suggestion for another animal that would make a good trickster character (see Figure 28-6). Writing to prompts helps readers focus thinking on a variety of high-level topics related to the deeper meaning of texts. The activity opens up the possibilities for spontaneous response and helps students internalize ways of thinking. When students have regular opportunities to organize and present their thinking related to reading, they have powerful test preparation practice. You may want to specify an audience or specific reasons for the prompts you use.

The following are examples of short, focused prompts for writing about reading:

- Write about what you learned about ____.

- Recall detail from the text and write a response. [*Describe what you thought when . . . and why you thought that*

- Make predictions. [*Write what you think will happen next. Write what ____ will do next. Write how ____ feel if ____. What do you think will happen to ____?*

- Describe a character using specific evidence from the text. [*Write what you think of ____ and why. Write about ____. What kind of a person is ____? What made you think that?*]

- Put yourself in the situation. [*If you were ____, how would you feel about this situation? If you were ____ what would you do?*]

Book: Charlotte's Web	Author: E.B. White
Page Number	Words or Phrases that Show Author's Use of Time
p.1	before breakfast
p.1	smelled of springtime
p.3	half an hour later
p.4	the morning light shone
p.5	along in half an hour
p.6	a minute later
p.7	by the time the bus reached school
p.67	the middle of July
p.67	summer was half gone
p.70	an hour past
p.13	in Winter
p.16	afternoon in June
p.24	about four o'clock
p.30	late that afternoon
p.32	during the night
p.42	first of July
p.44	day in early summer
p.52	Sunday morning
p.77	the day was foggy
p.83	long before Sunday
p.84	the days that followed
p.84	on Sunday

Figure 28-5. *Movement Through Time in* Charlotte's Web

Think critically about the text. [*Did ___ make the right choice? Why or why not? Did the writer make the story see real?*]

How did the author get you interested in the book? Use examples to explain.

Connect the text to your own life. [*In what ways does ___ remind you of someone that you know? In what way does ___ remind you of characters in other books?*]

Think about ___'s (author) writing. Show your thinking about what makes it good writing.

Think about the texts you read about ____(topic). Summarize the important issues or content.

Tell about the character who was the bravest (the fairest, wisest, etc.).

Tell about the character who changed the most and explain why.

Tell about how you got to know the main character in your book.

The race of Turtle and Beaver is a trickster story because Turtle outwitted Beaver. He used his brain and he figured out a way to win the race easier. The plan was to bite on Beaver's tail so he would flick Turtle to the ground and Turtle would win. Turtle did't swim at all. All he did was bite on Beaver's tail and stayed there. This trickster story is just a story with a little brain power.

I think another animal that would be a good trickster character would be a fox. A fox is sly. It is very tricky. I chose this animal because in the story "The Gingerbread Man," the fox outsmarterd the gingerbread man. The fox ate the gingerbread man instead of helping it. I think that is tricky. The fox is my choice of a trickster character.

Figure 28-6. *Stella's Short Write About the Race Between Turtle and Beaver*

After using a variety of short writes, students will likely use these ways of thinking to reflect on and interpret their reading as they write on their own in the reader's notebook.

Involve your students in short writes often. A short piece of writing as an open response or to address a specific question is not as daunting as a long piece, and it strengthens the ability to compose, write, and organize a response.

Letters

Letters, discussed in the previous chapter, are an important form of writing about reading and can involve all four kinds of writing mentioned above. Students use letters to communicate ideas, report information, and tell stories. Letters can also include poetic language.

In any case, letters are a basic form of writing about reading. Readers write to a real audience such as an author, illustrator, peer, or their teacher about topics they know and care about. Visualizing a known audience makes it easier to write with voice because the writer is directing her thinking to someone in particular. Once the form of letter writing is learned, it has infinite possibilities.

Letters to Readers/Writers At first, the "other" reader/writer is the teacher. In Chapter 27 we describe dialogue letters and their many benefits and include a number of examples. We recommend using these dialogue letters for quite a long time and continuing them throughout the grades. Students become very comfortable with the authentic dialogue and learn from the response of their teachers. Sharing through letters promotes emotional engagement and enjoyment of texts (see the example in Figure 28-7).

Sometimes you may have students share their letters with each other or even respond to each other, especially if you are working with a large number of students. Peer responses will not lift students' thinking the way your own responses do, but peer letters have benefits. Having students talk and write to one another about books helps create a community of readers. You can also use e-mail for these ongoing conversations. In addition, you can have students write to students in another class, or even across geographic and international boundaries.

Letters to Authors/Illustrators As your students come to know authors and illustrators through their books, they will enjoy writing to them to share their thoughts. Students who have rich reading experiences quickly develop favorite writers or illustrators and will want to express their opinions and experiences. A kindergarten child can express a simple message as Silva did (see Figure 28-8). Even Silva, a young child, can express preferences to Eric Carle. She is learning that reading is communication with a writer. In Sara's letter to Beverly Cleary (Figure 28-9), notice that she speaks to Cleary "writer to writer," saying that she is working on her third book. She also points out influences that encourage her to write; one of your jobs as a teacher is to provide this encouragement. (Beverly Cleary actually responded to Sara's letter!) Notice how Anna questions the author of *Bud, Not Buddy* in her letter to Christopher Paul Curtis (Figure 28-10) and Rebecca demonstrates knowledge of a variety of texts and shows genuine curiosity in her letter to Patricia MacLachlan (Figure 28-11). In the letter to Hilary McKay (Figure 28-12), Anita, a student who has been reading and writing for many years, reveals her understanding of character development. In the last paragraph, she discusses what she has noticed about the writer's style and even provides some suggestions!

Students read, think, and learn about a variety of important topics. They can write letters to others to express their understandings of specific topics, such as baseball, cooking, or war. The expository writing may require further reading. Letters to the editor and informational writing serve to summarize one's thinking. Notice how these writers across the grades are learning to reflect on what they have learned through reading in letter form.

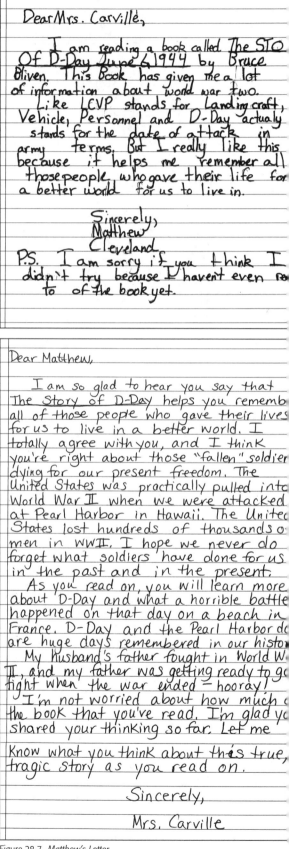

Figure 28-7. *Matthew's Letter*

DearEric carle
My favorite Book
is little cloud.My Favorit
prte is Wen he trns
into A hat wth a flor.
How old are you?
Silva

re 28-8. *Letter to Eric Carle*

ry Entries

en students write an entry in a diary or journal from the
spective of a biographical subject or character, they con-
er the setting, plot, relationships, and issues. This
uires deep consideration of traits and feelings as well as
es and setting.

Some children's books are written in the form of a diary
include diary entries, such as *The True Confessions of
rlotte Doyle* (Avis), or *Spider Boy* (Fletcher). These
dels help readers consider the first person narrative.
ce they understand the genre, your students can assume
role of almost any character or biographical subject as
and did in his diary entries for *Slakes Limbo* (Holman)
e Figure 28-13).

uble-Column Entries

e way to help students notice and think deeply about the
guage of texts is to have them respond to a quotation or
cific language the writer used. Often, you can select the
te yourself from a book you have read aloud and then
your students to write about it and share their respons-
Steven responded to a quote from *Sister Anne's Hands*
rbiecki) (see Figure 28-14). In assigning this task, his
cher first explained why she chose the quote and offered
own responses. At other times, you may want to have
dents respond to language they have selected them-
ves. In her response, Rebeka related a quote from

Dear beverly clery I have
read lots oF your books.
like dear mr. hensaw and I
have all oF your ramona
books in Fact I lust finish
~~the~~ last book in the ramona
series. I love to read your
books. I even startedt•
write some books in my 2h grad
and v~~s~~ grad class. I am in ~~•~~ 2nd
grad. ~~•~~ What was the frist
book you rote? Also how old were
you when you woee it?

I love to read and write!
I am working on my 3rd book. MY
'2nd book is called animals animals
animals. It is a true animal
'Fact story. I don't ~~•~~ no
what the story I am working on
'now is going to be called. MY

perants work with some body
who cupies my story and
stuff and makes storys
and books out of them.

Sunnsherly sara

Figure 28-9. *Letter to Beverly Cleary*

469

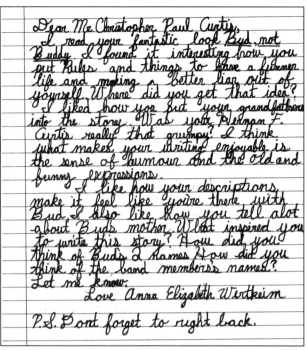

Dear Mr. Christopher Paul Curtis,
I read your fantastic book Bud, not
Buddy. I found it interesting how you
put Rules and things to have a funner
life and making a better lian out of
yourself. Where did you get that idea?
I liked how you put your grandfather
into the story. Was your Herman F.
Curtis really that grumpy? I think
what makes your writing enjoyable is
the sense of humour and the old and
funny expressions.
I like how your descriptions
make it feel like you're there with
Bud. I also like how you tell alot
about Buds mother. What inspired you
to write this story? How did you
think of Buds 2 Names How did you
think of the band members's names?
Let me know.
Love Anna Elizabeth Wertheim

P.S. Dont forget to right back.

Figure 28-10. *Letter to Christopher Paul Curtis*

Dear Patricia MacLachlan,

  I read Sarah, Plain and Tall
and am now reading Caleb's story,
I am also planning on reading
Skylark. I'm not sure what order
they go in though.

  I loved the way you wrote
Sarah, Plain and Tall, My favorite
sentence was "Tell them I sing" When
I read that I thought about Frank
Sinatra, I don't know why but I did

  Caleb's story is so far one of
my favorite books. All the excitment,
Cassie and the grandfather. It all
really grabbed my attetion.

  Cassie is a real chatter box. I
think she should be the host of
a talk show. But shes one of my
favorite characters.

  Are these storys real life, are
they about someone you knew or know?

  I hope I find some more of
your books so I can share them
with my sister.

                    Love,
                    Rebecca

P.S. please try to write back. Thanks!

Figure 28-11. *Letter to Patricia MacLachlan*

Because of Winn-Dixie (DiCamillo) to her own perso
experiences, as explained in column 2 (see Figure 28-1
Lara responded to a quote from *The Rainbow People*
Figure 28-16). Yirin wrote a thoughtful response to *Coy*
Autumn in his entry (see Figure 28-17).

The double-column format for close analysis of a tex
a good way to record these responses. The first column c
tains a phrase, sentence, or paragraph the reader has sel
ed from a text. Their responses are in the column to
right. The response may tell:

- What this quote makes me think about.

- What I like about this quote.

- Why I chose this quote.

Figure 28-18 shows ongoing double-entries from Be
reader's notebook in which he records his thinking ab
Milkweed (Spinelli).

Write Around

You might want groups of students to engage in a wri
conversation about texts. After reading *The Game* (auth
groups of three middle school students responded to ea
other about the text (see Figure 28-19).

Graphic Organizers

Graphic organizers can help students analyze narrative
informative texts in order to understand them better. T
can also be used as a planning tool to organize one's thi
ing about a text. The visual representation of informat
shows the relationships between ideas in the text and he
the reader see the way the text "works." For exam
graphic organizers can be used to:

- Compare and contrast text elements—charact
  topics, settings, events, feelings (see Figure 28-20,
  About Frogs (Arnosky)).

- Illustrate cause and effect.

- Show a time sequence.

- Show traits of a character or setting.

- Illustrate main ideas and supporting information
  subtopics.

- Provide evidence for summary statements.

- Show the parts of a text.

The DVD that accompanies this book contains 100 grap
organizer forms (character grids and T charts, for exa

Ms. Hilary McKay
c/o Margaret K. McElderry Books
Simon & Schuster Children's Publishing Division
1230 Avenue of the Americas
New York, NY
10020

Dear Ms. McKay,

My name is Anita Desai, and I am in 5th grade at Columbus School for Girls, in Columbus OH. I recently finished your book, Indigo's Star. I thought it was really great, and extremely interesting. I was wondering if you had based the characters on people that you know, and if you have any children that you like to base your characters on. Where do you usually get your characters names from? I am always looking for good names for characters. I thought it was a great idea to name all the Casson children after colors.

My family does not relate to the Casson family at all, which, I think, is why I love reading about them. Of all the characters, I think, I relate the most to Rose, even though I don't draw on the kitchen wall! I think the main thing that Rose and I have in common is that if we really want something we will do anything to make it happen. In your book Saffy's Angel I thought that Rose was very smart, and would grow up to be a very kind, yet strong person, and I loved seeing that happen in this book. I think that in Indigo's Star you got to learn a lot more about Rose and what she is really like.

I thought that the relationship between Indigo and Tom was interesting to watch growing over the course of the book. To me their relationship is the perfect example of how you don't have to be alike to be best friends. I think that some of the best matches can be with people who are exact opposites. I loved reading about how Tom starts to take the fear of bullies out of Indigo, and in turn, how Indigo gives Tom a much needed family.

I was wondering if you were going to write more books about the Casson children. I would love to read more of them, and given that the names Saffy's Angel and Indigo's Star both have the name of one of the children and then a symbol of something that turns out to be very important in the book, you may be able to make something like a Casson Children collection. What seems to be another key part to your books are the "informal" members of the Casson family such as Sarah, and Tom. In these two books the main character always meets a friend and they will be in a way adopted as informal members of the family. I think that these two books are perfect together, because neither one needs the other one to be able to understand it, though they seem to be tied together in a way that is almost un-explainable.

I look forward to reading more of your books, and hope to someday read more about the Casson family.

Sincerely,

Anita Desai
Age: 10

re 28-12. *Letter to Hilary McKay*

October 1, 1974

I, Aremis Slake, am an orphan. I sleep on a cot in the kitchen. My glasses are broken and I can not see more than a few feet. My only friend is dead. I have no family.

October 2, 1974

It started with a sweater I found on the subway. They took it away from me and played with it. I was hungry and I ran to the subway.

October 3, 1974

I am far from home, but have no home. I live on the subway now.

Figure 28-13. *Roland's Diary Entries for* Slake's Limbo

Title: Sister Anne's Hands by MaryBeth Lorbiecki;	Thinking from Quote...
Quote from story	When Sister Anne said "And others are tight as a fist," I think she was talking about the person who threw the air plane. It rymin me of some one that was realy mean to me at second gade. And when she said "their hearts wide open." I think she was teaching the students to not be mean to other people. like don't be mean to people who has deferent skin color.
Then she seemed to warm up to us a little, "One thing you're going to learn is that some folks have their hearts wide open, and others are tight as a fist. The tighter they are, the more dangerous,"	

Figure 28-14. *Steven's Response to* Sister Anne's Hands

ple). Start using simple graphic organizers with younger children by doing them together as shared/interactive writing. With older students who have not used graphic organizers before, start by working together at the easel or on a transparency. Try to avoid simply handing out graphic organizers as assignments; you don't want students to think of them as a "fill-in-the-blank" work sheet. The real value of using organizers is the talk and thinking that surround them.

Rebeka
~~Because of Winn-dixie~~
Kate Dicamillo

I know about the Civil war," I told her. That was the war between the south and north over slavery.	That line made me think of pink and say. It made me think of when my grandpa was in the war but not the Civil. It was when my grandpa was in a helacoptair and he was shooting and he got shot in the feet it still hurts now.

Figure 28-15. *Rebeka's Response to* Because of Winn-Dixie

The Rainbow people

Quote or passages from the book	What this made me think of
• The cold mountain water fed fields of rice with grains as big as his fingers and vegetables with leaves as tall as him. But the people who tended them were the thinnest, boniest people he had ever seen.	• That made me think of the beautifully woven stories my mother used to tell me. About hard working farmers who tried desperately to save enough food for winter, but always the landlord takes everything away. They would involve powerful dragons, beautiful ladies and brave heroes, always battling with swords cutting into the brave warriors skin and letting the warm blood drip down. It also reminded me of the childhood my mother had working in the fields letting sweat drip down her forehead and land into the soft, rich soil.

Figure 28-16. *Lara's Response to* The Rainbow People

Grid

The open-framework grid in Figure 28-21 is a comparison of the characters in *Flying Solo* (Fletcher), a story told from the perspective of a sixth grader. A blank copy of this grid can be found on the accompanying DVD. As Michael read the text, he added information. Understanding the meaning of the whole story depends heavily on knowing the characters and their motivations. Keeping an ongoing grid like this helps the reader keep up with and remember them. You can use a grid form to compare any number or type of elements across texts and with students of any age.

Posters/Advertisements

Students also enjoy preparing provocative posters or advertisements for texts. This task requires that they evaluate ideas about elements of the text and select those that are most interesting. Then, without giving away important information that should be surprising to the reader, the

Description of character or something the character does, says, or thinks or that someone says about the character.	What this made me think about the character.
The bicycle was great. The clothes were okay. The new puppy was FANTABULOUS! But the best thing of all was Daddy. It was like the two of us were really together – maybe against the whole world. Just the two of us. I don't really know how to explain it, but it made me feel really special.	I think Brad was like a team with his dad. No matter who tried to argue with them, they would always stick together. This also made me think that Brad's father was really softhearted for Brad when he agreed to let him keep the coyote.
"He's fine," Daddy said. For an instant Adelee almost smiled. Then she let me go, jabbed both fists against her hips, and glared at me. "Where have you been?" she demanded. Before I could say anything, she slugged me on the arm. "You scared us half to death," she sniffed. "I can't believe you'd scare us like that. We thought you fell in	I think that even though Adelee was mean and sometimes annoying to Brad, she really cared for him like brother and sister. "Brat," she'd call him and get him in trouble, but she really was a true sister – I mean, I haven't ever heard of a sibling that was nice their whole life! Continued...
the pond... We thought you–" She broke off, sniffling.	

Figure 28-17. *Yirin's Response to* Coyote Autumn

Samantha

I feel that "The Game" isn't really a game. It probably happened to the author. I don't think that it's toy soldiers. I think it's real people in the war. Why was this war started? Kids should not play with plastic soldiers or toy guns because then they would probably join war on the bad side. They pretend it's funny but it's not.

Samantha

I think the same thing that it is not toys, it is real soilders. I'm thinking it really happened to some soilders but not all of them. Some people that think it is funny, it is not because in wars soilders die and kids are laughing at soilders and kids don't realize that it really happend to actual soilders. I don't agree that it happend to the author.

Denise

I agree with both of you. I think that she wants kids to know what happens with the wars and how it affects other people.

Keisha

Figure 28-19. *Responses to* The Game

Quotes from Milkweed by Jerry Spinelli	
Quote	**Thinking**
"The only thing magnificent about this was his uniform. I saw half a little black moustache – it seemed to be dripping out of his nostril – a scrawny neck, a head that seemed more dumpling than stone. Can this be Himmler? The Number Two Jackboot? He could be. He looked like Uncle Sheps!! I knew how to prove it one way or the other."	In this quote I believe the author is saying that the main character's curiosity can cause great trouble.

Figure 28-18. *Ben's Reader's Notebook Entry about* Milkweed

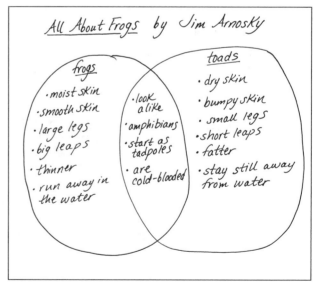

Figure 28-20. *Compare/Contrast Chart for* All about Frogs

transform their ideas into language and visual images. These posters may be the paper-and-ink variety, displayed on the classroom walls, or computer-screen "pop ups."

NARRATIVE WRITING

Narrative writing "tells a story." Many of the texts that students read, both fiction and nonfiction, are narratives, and readers internalize them through a series of summaries. Narrative responses to reading reconstruct the narrative or some part of it in a way that communicates something important about the text to others. They also help the reader remember the stories.

Summaries

Students are often called on to retell and/or summarize a text, skills that are also frequently required on state achievement tests. Retelling and summarizing involve many of the same cognitive actions but have some differences as well. Both require the reader to remember the important information in the text.

A retelling involves producing all the important details in order, from beginning to end, and is a low-level, basic skill. Young children can learn to produce retellings, especially if they have worked as a group using shared or interactive writing. The mural in Figure 28-22 is a retelling of *Gingerbread Baby,* by Jan Brett, completed in interactive writing. Caitlin guided these young students to retell the story by making a map showing where the gingerbread baby started and all the places and people he encountered during his adventures. Individual children drew each episode; then, together, they placed them in order and indicated the trail between them by drawing arrows. Labels, composed in interactive writing, were added to each picture. This kind of very concrete demonstration of retelling will help children internalize the process.

A summary, on the other hand, reconstructs the essence of the text. The important information is there, but the writer is highly selective, including only that which is necessary. Reginald wrote a short summary of *The Report Card* (Clements) that includes the critical information (see Figure 28-23).

A summary can also be included as a piece of another form. A *plot summary* is simply a statement of the essence of the plot in a text. It is the briefest form of telling what was important about a text. For example, writing book reviews for a specified audience is a way to make summarizing an authentic task. Later in this chapter, you will look at a few examples of book recommendations and reviews. You will notice in each example that the students are using an engaging lead, a plot summary, and personal responses to the book.

Scenes for Readers' Theater

Creating a readers' theater script requires close examination of the text and is a good partner or small-group activity. The partners select events from the text and create the roles of the narrator who describes the action, setting, etc., and each of the characters, borrowing language from the dialogue in the text. Once students have created these scripts, they will enjoy performing them in class. (See the DVD that accompanies this book

Character Grid				
Flying Solo by Ralph Fletcher				
Character	Description or Traits	Actions (Does)	Dialogue (Says or Thinks)	Feelings
Rachel White	• 6th grader • silent • Mean to Tommy	• Reads a lot • Wouldn't take the pie.	• "OH MY God". Rachel whispered • Doesn't talk • "The right to remain silent." • "Writing words is like flying"	• Sad about Tommy • Feels guilty • Afraid to talk • Misses her father
Bastian Fauvell	• Moved a lot • A brat	• John is best friend • Has bad names for everybody	• Why don't they call it shedded newspaper • "Kids Rule"	• Sad/worried about his dog • Mad about moving
Jessica Cooke	• Skinny and tall • Different	• Eats a lot • does everything	• I want to be chief justice in the Supreme Court • Because I always get a hundred on spelling tests	• Confident • Doesn't like flying solo • Thinks they are going to get in trouble
Sean O'Day	• Hungry • Slender • pale and sleepy	• Dreams about a dog • Mumbles • Takes food when it's given to him • Writes about Rachel	• Thanks	• Afraid of his father • Hungry all the time
Christopher Ransom	• Big • Rich • Loud and obnoxious	• Writes about Sir Francis Brave Fart	• Opinion • Fact • "Sky and Jessica sitting in a tree K-I-S-S..."	
Karen Ballard	• Good student • Responsible • Class president	• Goes along with "Flying Solo"	• Quiet	• Thinks flying Solo is a challenge

Figure 28-21. *Character Grid* Flying Solo

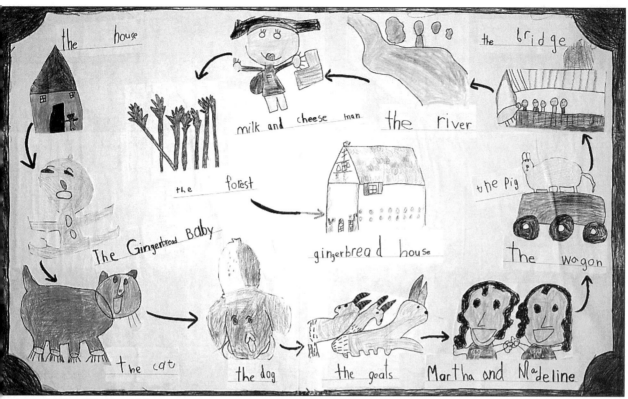

re 28-22. *Retelling of* Gingerbread Baby

The Report Card by Andrew
Clements is about two students who
do not like the way tests and
grades separate the kids into smart,
average, and dumb. The main
character, Nora and her friend Stephen
decide to do something about it. In
fifth grade, Nora is a super soccer
player and an average student. But
Nora has a secret. She has known
since she was two and a half that
she is not just smart. She is a
genius but hides it from everyone, even
her parents, because she wants to be
normal. Nora began by making bad
grades on purpose, and by making a
statement about tests and grades. She
got in trouble, but the kids made
their point and the adults listened.

re 28-23. *Summary of* The Report Card

d Chapter 21 for examples.) You will want to create some
amples for students to perform before asking them to cre-
their own.

rtoons/Storyboards

artoon or storyboard version of a text is built from visu-
images. Notice the detail in Leo's series of cartoons about

The Tortoise and the Hare (see Figure 28-24). He provides
detail and carefully shows sequence.

INFORMATIONAL WRITING

A great deal of required writing is informational; the
demand for this kind of writing increases grade-by-grade.
By using texts as a base, you can help your students learn
about others and their world and also learn how informational texts are organized. Below we single out several kinds
of informational writing.

Short Writes

Students can also share what they have learned in short
writes. Kindergarten students shared their thinking in
images and words to show what they learned about animals
from books they listened to (see Figure 28-25).

Outline

Outlining helps students understand the relationships
among ideas in the text, identifying those that are major
and those that are supporting. Once prepared, an outline
helps the reader remember the text and find information
quickly (see Figure 28-26). Outlining requires the presentation of points, subpoints, and sub-subpoints. In the process,

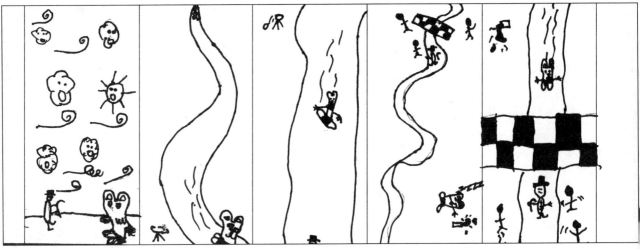

Figure 28-24. *Leo's Storyboard About* The Tortoise and the Hare

I lrdl Thte a Dolphin
are Is not a fish

A The sea
horse has a
tail like a monkey.

Tail

I lrd that a kaiple
esea Lzve.

I learned that a caterpillar eats leaves.

A sea horse uses
its tail for holding
on to seaweed not
for swimming.

Figure 28-25. *Short Writes About Animals*

dents learn how a text "works" and are able to use this
ill when planning their own informational writing.

thor Study

students get to know authors, they enjoy writing about
eir favorites. Think about the rich summary of information
out Eric Carle that was completed in shared writing in
gure 27-6 in the previous chapter. These informational
eces may be straightforward biographies or may involve
mparison, analysis, and critique, as in Anita's profile of
nily Dickinson (see Figure 28-27). Writing about an author
courages analytical and critical thinking about the writer's
aft, prompts close examination of texts, and requires read-
s to use evidence from the text to support their thinking.

A brief version of information from an author study of
dy Blume is presented in Figure 28-28.

ustrator Study

udents may also want to write about illustrators, perhaps
amining several of their works in terms of mood, integra-
on of ideas and visual images, or artistic technique.
oticing the way illustrations and text form a coherent
hole promotes knowledge of the writer's craft. Additionally,
increases artistic appreciation and demands that students
aw evidence from visual images to support their thinking.

Our Natural Resources
I. Introduction
    A. Definition of Natural Resources
    B. Uses of Natural Resources
II. The Types of Natural Resources
    A. Nonrenewable Resources
    B. Renewable Resources
        1. The water cycle
    C. Using Resources wisely.
        1. Recycling
III. Natural Resources of the United States
    A. soil
    B. Our Water and forests
    C. fish
IV. Conservation in the United States
    A. Beginning of the Conservation
    B. Conservation today

ure 28-26. *Example of an Outline*

Literary Essay

A literary essay is a formal piece of writing that involves analytical thinking. The writer is required to organize thoughts,
support that thinking with examples, and revise and edit to
be sure that the argument is clear to the reader. Examples of
literary essays are provided in Figures 28-29 and 28-30, the
first by a fifth grader, the second by a middle school student.

Interview (Author or Expert)

An interview of an author or expert is another way to help
students engage in deeper thinking about a topic or about
texts. Here, the student constructs a series of questions and
then conducts an interview with the subject. Older students
may even construct the interviewee's responses by imagining them from knowledge of the subject's life or work (for
example, historical accounts, letters, etc. the subject has
written). Students also can interview peers or older students
who have published works. The interaction at the heart of
this process, in addition to leading to written texts, lets students experience consulting first-hand sources and using
the question-and-answer format.

"How-To" Articles

Students can present their thinking about a variety of readings on a topic by writing an explanation of how something
can be done. For example, they might read several books on
terrariums and then write an article on creating your own
terrarium.

Photo Essays, Picture Essays, PowerPoint Presentations

Photo essays or picture essays are an engaging form for
sharing information. With the advent of digital photography, students can now easily produce multimedia presentations using PowerPoint or other publishing programs. They
can also scan their own drawings into the computer. This
ability to communicate through visual images is consistent
with the wide variety of Internet research that students do
today, and it will be important for their future. Presenting
information via PowerPoint is a very specific genre.
Students need to learn how to select key statements and
phrases and use graphics to organize and present information that keeps listeners engaged and on track.

Reports

A *report* presents factual material in an organized way, citing sources of information. Years of content-area study pre-

The First Nobody: The Life of Emily Dickinson
by Anita Desai

To outsiders the life of Emily Dickinson was no more then a poof of hair and a bustle of a skirt, for this was all they saw of her. However, her life was anything but boring. Though she never left her house for the last twenty-five years of her life, Emily Dickinson's world was full of adventure. The poems she wrote took her into different worlds where life was the way she liked. To outsiders she was called Myth, because nobody ever saw her, and she always ran from visitors. To her sister Lavinia, the only person who would keep up with her strange ways, Emily was sometimes seen as the person behind the curtain. Emily chose to spend her time writing poems on little slips of paper, which somehow always seemed to disappear right after she was finished writing. The remainder of her time was spent in her garden planting and nurturing her plants and flowers. Nobody, besides the few magazine editors that she showed poems to in hopes that they would be published, ever saw any of her finished work.

Emily Dickinson only published thirteen poems in her lifetime. Most editors thought that her poems were too uncontrolled and lacked continual quality. Emily suffered from Bright's Disease, which is a Kidney Disease, and died at the age of fifty-five. It was not until after her death in 1886, when Lavinia was looking through her dresser, that anybody knew where all of those sheets of paper went. As Lavinia opened the bottom drawer of Emily's dresser, poems jumped out at her. Emily had stuffed 1,789 poems into her dresser. With the help of a family friend, Mabel Loomis Todd, Lavinia was able to crack the code that was Emily's almost illegible handwriting, and realize what a poetic genius her sister really was. Emily's words had such meaning and were so compelling that she was determined to publish her sister's work, and in 1890, four years after Emily died, she did just that.

Today Emily Dickinson's poems are still being published, and her work is considered some of the best that has ever been written. One of her most famous poems is called I am nobody, and to me it shows Emily's reason for hiding in her room and garden,

I'm nobody! Who are you?
Are you — Nobody — too?
Then there's a pair of us!
Don't tell! they'd banish us — you know!
How dreary — to be — somebody!
How public — like a frog —
To give your name — the livelong June —
To an admiring bog!

Figure 28-27. *Anita's Profile of Emily Dickinson*

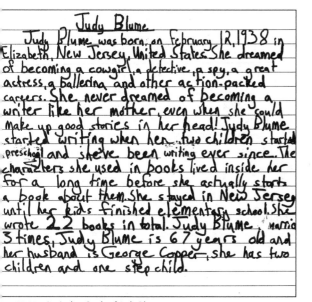

Judy Blume

Judy Blume was born on February 12, 1938 in Elizabeth, New Jersey, United States. She dreamed of becoming a cowgirl, a detective, a spy, a great actress, a Ballerina and other action-packed careers. She never dreamed of becoming a writer like her mother, even when she could make up good stories in her head! Judy Blume started writing when her two children started preschool and she've been writing ever since. The characters she used in books lived inside her for a long time before she actually starts a book about them. She stayed in New Jersey until her kids finished elementary school. She wrote 22 books in total. Judy Blume married 3 times. Judy Blume is 67 years old and her husband is George Copper, she has two children and one step child.

...ure 28-28. *An Author Study of Judy Blume*

...re students for the demanding task of gathering, select-
...g, and organizing information from which to produce
...ports. The roots of reporting begin in kindergarten. For
...ample, Kris read a carefully selected group of nonfiction
...xts about growing to her kindergartners and modeled
...iting for them in a way that supported them as they wrote

their own books (see the example in Figure 28-31). You will notice that she has demonstrated how to approximate the spelling of unfamiliar words so they will take risks in their own writing.

With a high level of support like this, these students are able to produce informative pieces of content writing that include illustrations. With continued good instruction and guidance and experience, students begin to read a variety of material and produce organized and coherent reports. Figure 28-32 is a young child's report on what she learned about animals that come from eggs after listening to several books read aloud. Figure 28-33 is an older student's report on wolves.

It is easy to access a huge amount of information on the Internet, but most teachers still require their students to consult and reference printed texts as well. In any case, selecting and organizing interesting information is the key. Reports do not have to be long! Creating a relatively short but well-written report that includes supporting evidence is a highly sophisticated skill. Notice the care with which Anita presents her report on apothecaries in Colonial America (see Figure 28-34).

LITERARY ESSAY
Animal Farm: *A Comparison of the Book to the Movie* BY A FIFTH GRADER

Many people have read George Orwell's controversial book, *Animal Farm*. Some have tried to recreate his influential satire in the form of a movie. Although there were good intentions, along with inexcusable efforts to sustain Orwell's message, the purpose of *Animal Farm*'s story was not adequately portrayed. Because of the distortions of Orwell's original book, the transition from book to movie has diluted the powerful statement that Orwell originally meant to make by writing *Animal Farm*. The three main structural differences that caused dilution were the changes in characterization, propaganda, and the plot. A main factor that makes the movie differ from the book is the characterization. The biggest change, that affected the entire plot, was that Jessie basically took Clover's place in the story. Jessie was the suspicious one that was good friends with Boxer and Benjamin. Jesse also had added on character traits. She opposed the fact that Napoleon and Snowball had taken her puppies. She was not as subdued as Clover had been of how Jessie was in the book. Another change in character was Napoleon and Snowball's relatives. They did more joint actions and consulted each other more. Benjamin was given a sort of non-conditional, every-steady characterization. The Benjamin in the movie was not very Benjamin-like and he didn't have that same aura. He talked with the rat and planned an escape with Jessie. He never even made his cynical or cryptic remarks. I was very disappointed with Benjamin's portrayal. Boxer, in the beginning, was more on type. He led the animals to raid the food storage, and into the farmhouse after the rebellion. Moses's character was also altered. He had wanted to stay with Tony and even followed him all the way back to the bar. He wasn't as spirited in animalism as he had been in the book. He was also a little more daring, with his sugar candy mountain campaign. He was squawking to Boxer all about it right after he had collapsed. One thing that was understandable about the change in characterization was the people. They needed a little more credit in the movie version since it was people making it instead of animals. Pilkington and Mrs. Jones knew that it was Jones negligence that caused the Rebellion and made sure that he knew it, too. Pilkington even told him to get out of town because he was just a disgrace. There was no sympathy for Jones.

...ures 28-29. *Literary Essay:* Animal Farm: *A Comparison of the Book to the Movie by a Fifth Grader*

LITERARY ESSAY

Animal Farm: *A Comparison of the Book to the Movie* BY A MIDDLE SCHOOL STUDENT

A couple of the changes were understandable, though. For example, dialogue had to be different because things that could be implied from the description in the book needed to be said aloud to be clearly understood in the movie. The one thing that was just plain irritating was the fact that there were so many unnecessary changes and a lot of them were just stupid, for lack of a better word. They were what really weakened the show. A dog was recruited that wasn't even in the book. Old Major died of a gunshot instead of a peaceful death in his sleep. The humans tried to listen in on the animals. Some other guy shot Snowball instead of Jones. Mr. Whymper was the one that gave the pigs whistles and became more of a friend instead of just a business partner. There was never even a Battle of the Windmill, which, in turn, made Boxer's collapse less believable and took away some of his greatness. Napoleon had a statue built of him and he gave himself a leader award first class. The ending was simply atrocious and extremely disappointing. The empowering feeling that the card game watched through the window scene was just tossed aside and replaced with a dismissible meeting between Pilkington, his wife, and Napoleon. Then speeches weren't even given. It was just a nonchalant, "Toast to 'Animal Farm.' On no, I've changed it back to Manor Farm." Jess was the only one that saw it and said to Lorny Little, "I can't tell them apart."

Figures 28-30. *Literary Essay: Animal Farm: A Comparison of the Book and the Movie by a Middle School Student*

News or Feature Articles

Readers can also prepare concise news or feature articles (articles that lead with the most important information and then offer supporting details) about their reading. Writing a news article requires considering the audience, paying attention to the "lead," and presenting the information in an interesting way. Drafting, revising, and editing are important parts of the process. As shown in Figure 28-35, with his teacher's help Ferris has improved his news article considerably.

Editorials/Op-Ed Pieces

An *editorial* is a persuasive opinion about an important, and usually controversial, current issue. Writers of editorials are required to present an organized argument and cite evidence to support the points they are making. They often use "signal words" such as *the evidence is* or *as a result*. (Chapter 13 discusses signal words.) Writing editorials demands analytical and critical thinking.

Biographical Sketches

A *biographical sketch* is a short article summarizing a person's accomplishments. The writer selects the most interesting or important information about the person and may express her own opinion about the subject.

Reviews and Recommendations

Students who have had a great deal of experience writing about reading over the years will be ready to write book talks or short reviews to interest readers in their books. Paul has written a short recommendation that he gave as a quick book talk on *White Star: A Dog on the Titanic* (Crisp) in reading workshop (see Figure 28-36).

Figure 28-31. *Modeled Writing About Chicks*

Tommy has written a quick book talk on *Half-a-Moo Inn* (Fleischman) (Figure 28-37), and Sara and Courtne share their short recommendations on a card that they rea aloud to the class and then clipped to the book (see Figur 28-38 and 28-39).

Figure 28-40 is Anita's book review of *Anne Frank, t Diary of a Young Girl*. Notice that she not only summ rizes the book but also discusses her own response to Writing a review requires thinking about all aspects of a te:

Diamond * corre ia

June 8 2005

Anms   Thot Cam
        fram a Eggs

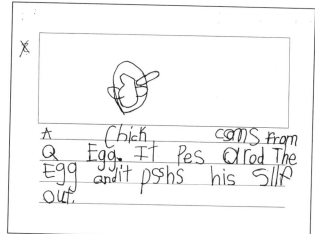

A   Chick   coms from
a Egg. It Pes arod The
Egg andit pshs his Sllf
out.

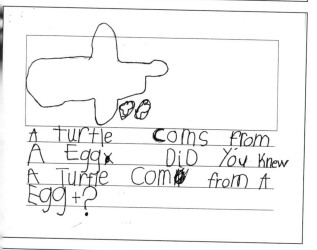

A Turtle   Coms from
A Egg   DiD You Knew
A Turtle Comp from A
Egg +?

A   Duck. Coms from a
E Egg X y   DiD You Know
A   Duck sib oh A Egg
gis like A hen?

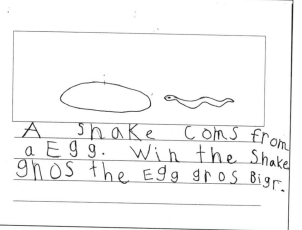

A   snake Coms from
a Egg. Win the Shake
gnos the Egg gros Bigr.

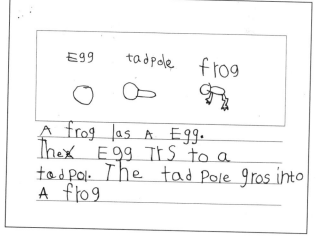

A frog las A Egg.
The Egg Trs to a
tadpol. The tad pole gros into
A frog

Wolves

By: Steven

What are Wolves?

Wolves look like dogs. Wolves eat meat and when some wolves want the meat, the ones that are eating the meat bark and growl. Wolves are often playful and friendly with each other, but just like dogs, they can be fierce. Most wolves live together in families with about six or seven adult wolves. All the wolves nuzzle the leader to show him they will obey him. Three to twelve wolf pups are born in underground dens in early spring. The wolf pups fight each other to decide who is the strongest. When wolves go to the water,

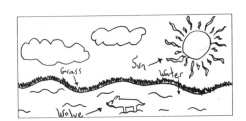

they get wet. When the wolves get out from the water, they shake themselves dry, just as dogs do. When a wolf returns from hunting, the cubs leap up and lick its face. Wolves chase musk and oxen in the autmn. Before wolves go hunting, they stand together, lift their noses, and howl loudly.

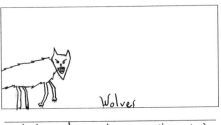

Wolves

Just like dogs, wolves use their tails and ears, and sometimes their whole bodies, to show their feelings. They show anger by curling back their lips and snarling. Wolves whine and growl, bark and howl. Every sound means something different.

Figure 28-33. *Wolves*

The Apothecary in Colonial America
By Anita Desai

 From the time of Galen, the creator of the system of medicine, to the times of pediatricians and nurses, medicine has been a vital practice. The colonial apothecary is a perfect example of that. In the New World the job of the apothecary was not very easy.

Apothecaries had to rely on herbs 75% of the time, and did not have most of the modern medicine that was developing in Europe. Apothecaries used chalk lozenges for heartburn, and made pills out of turpentine and deer dung. They also used leeches for bloodletting and willow bark to treat fevers. Other treatments used oyster shells, dried orange, juniper berries, turmeric, lavender, cloves, as well as native flowers. Apothecaries relied on bloodletting for a lot of things. To take blood from somebody you needed to cut off circulation on one arm and then have the patient flex their hand to increase the swelling. After this they would stretch the fingers of the patient to pop a vein.

Apothecaries needed many tools for their job. Among them were different molds, spatulas, different sized bottles, leech jars, different sized mixing bowls, scoopers, applicators, and pill rollers. Apothecaries may also have had an operating chair to perform minor operations. One of the most important tools for an apothecary was the mortar and pestle, which is a tool for grinding herb, and powders. Some apothecaries used a levigating stone and muller instead of a mortar and pestle.

The apothecary had a twenty-four hour job. If a patient fell ill at one o'clock in the morning, the apothecary would make a house call to drop off the right medicine. To become an apothecary you would need a three to six year apprenticeship. During your time as an apprentice, you would learn how to prepare and sell drugs, and understand the basics of math and science so that you would be able to give out the right dosage.

The job of the apothecary is a lot like the job of a pharmacist today. The apothecary usually owned a small shop that sold medicine, tobacco and cigars. The apothecary was usually a man, and needed to be able to stand the site of blood. Often apothecaries had a college degree in medicine, though this degree was not required.

Apothecaries were very important in the history of Colonial America. Some important names in the history of apothecaries are William Davice, who was the earliest owner of an apothecary shop in Massachusetts, and Kenneth McKenzie who owned an apothecary shop in Williamsburg, Virginia. Apothecaries had to deal with

ure 28-34. *Anita's Report on The Apothecary in Colonial America*

many different diseases that we now have better remedies for such as malaria, yellow fever, diphtheria, cholera, and French pox.

The everyday life of the apothecary was like that of most white people. He would probably have had children and would have owned slaves if he lived in the Southern Colonies. He would usually have had an office at home and at his shop. This way he would be able to work at home, and have an assistant work at the shop. If an apothecary was rich enough, he might have bought some of his drugs from Europe. If not, he would have had to rely on what could be grown in America. The apothecary knew most people in town because of his house calls.

So, the next time you think of an apothecary, don't think of just a druggist, think of somebody who played a vital role in colonial America, or somebody who worked to help the health of others. And next time you are at the doctor's office, say thank you when he or she give you a prescription, and think about how far medicine has come since the time of the colonial apothecary.

Bibliography

Books
- Richardson, Lillian and Charles. The Pill Rollers, Harrisonburg: Old Fort Press, 2003.
- Thompson, Charles. The Mystery and Art of the Apothecary. Philadelphia: J.B. Lippincot Co, 1927.
- Gill, Harold. The Apothecary in Colonial Virginia. Charlottesville: University Press of Virginia, 1972.
- Nixon, Joan. Ann's Story. New York: Yearling Books, 2002.
- Colonial Williamsburg Official Guide Book and Map. Williamsburg: Colonial Williamsburg Inc., 1965.

Internet Articles
- www.mcps.k12.md.us/schools/forestoakms/site%20pages/Academics/scocial%20st
- www.history.org/history/teaching/apoth.cfm
- www.germantownacademy.org/academics/ls/3/Colonial/ColonialDay/market/apothecary01.htm

Figure 28-34. *Anita's Report on The Apothecary in Colonial America* (cont.)

According to the New York Times article on
3/10/05, "Clinton Seeks Uniform Ratings In
Entertainment for Children," by Raymond Hernandez,
Senator Clinton wants industry leaders to create
a uniform rating system that would warn
parents of sex and violence in video games and
other entertainment for children. Clinton
pointed out one particular video game, Grand
Theft Auto, a series that allow players to go
on crimes, shooting and beating people at
random. Mrs. Clinton told the television
industry to give warnings about a video
game's content in every commercial break.
The industry leaders should create a
uniform rating system.
The rating system should be created. Parents
would understand what their kids are watching.
After kids watch violent things, they could also
behave like that, pushing, hitting, or kicking
other people, but if the parent knew what the
rating was, the kids won't do that. The
system should be formed, so parents could
see how violent an entertainment could be
and they would also have more control
over what their kids are watching. Therefore,
the uniform rating system should be created.

Figure 28-35. *Ferris's News Article*

selecting what is most important, and putting words together that will influence the audience's thinking about the text.

Projects

A project is a creative body of work (often a PowerPoint or
multimedia presentation) that discusses a topic in an
organized and coherent way. Many kinds of writing and
visual images are usually included.

POETIC WRITING

Poetic writing includes both responding to the literary language of a text and creating a poem *about* a text (or a
character or subject in it). Students can also write poems in
response to a text. Kal has written a poem inspired by *Owls*
(Gibbons) (see Figure 28-41).

Poem About a Text

Students may retell a story, as Emilio does in his poem
about *Mudball* (Tavares), the true story of Andy Oyler (see
Figure 28-42), or describe the setting. Figure 28-43 is an
impression of the setting of the fantasy *The Dark Hills
Divide* (Carman).

Notice how Alexes created a poem inspired by Yolen's
Mary Celeste (see Figure 28-44) and Anna created a poem
for two voices inspired by *Bunnicula* (Howe) (see Figure
28-45). You can see that the students have learned how to
use the technique of repetition in poetry workshop.

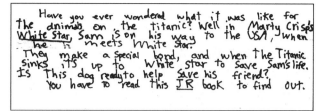

Figure 28-36. *Paul's Recommendation for* White Star

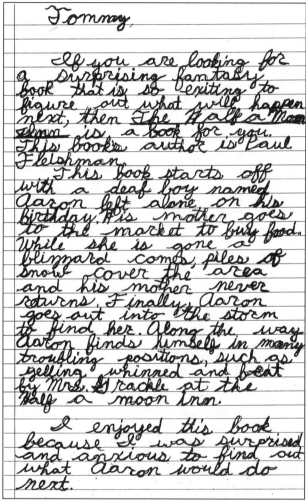

Figure 28-37. *Tommy's Recommendation for* Half-a-Moon Inn

TEACHING STUDENTS TO WRITE ABOUT READING

We have summarized a variety of genres or forms for writing about reading in Figure 28-46. Obviously, there are a
great many forms in which students can share their thinking about reading! The list in Figure 28-46 overlaps the
very wide range of genres for writing that students learn to
produce in a writing workshop but does not include all of
them. Nonetheless, writing about reading will make a
strong contribution to your students' reading and writing

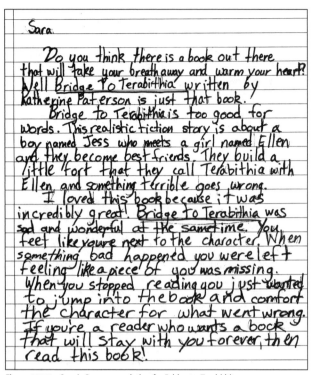

Sara

Do you think there is a book out there that will take your breath away and warm your heart? Well Bridge To Terabithia written by Katherine Paterson is just that book.

Bridge to Terabithia is too good for words. This realistic fiction story is about a boy named Jess who meets a girl named Ellen and they become best friends. They build a little fort that they call Terabithia with Ellen and something terrible goes wrong.

I loved this book because it was incredibly great. Bridge To Terabithia was sad and wonderful at the same time. You feel like youre next to the character. When something bad happened you were left feeling like a piece of you was missing. When you stopped reading you just wanted to jump into the book and comfort the character for what went wrong. If youre a reader who wants a book that will stay with you forever, then read this book!

Figure 28-38. Sara's Recommendation for Bridge to Terabithia

Courtney
Book Recommendation

Do you like a book with a lot of excitement and a little mystery? Well then your going to like the book "After noon of the Elves." by Janet Taylor Lisle! This book is a fantasy.

It's about a nine year old girl named Hillary who's so curious about her friend Sara-Kate. Hillary is determind to find out more about Sara-Kate. You probably thinks it's about two normal little girls right? WRONG! There are many strange and unique things about Hillary and Sara-Kate.

I really enjoyed reading this book because the author used specific details and a lot of luscious language to help you picture whats going on in the story. I really think you'll love this book.

Figure 28-39. Courtney's Recommendation for Afternoon of the Elves

abilities. It is also obvious that not all of these genres will be used during a single year of study.

Types of writing about reading should be *taught first* rather than simply *assigned* after a brief explanation. A new form should generally be demonstrated in a response to read-aloud and worked on cooperatively a number of times before students are expected to produce it independently. The talk that surrounds and supports writing in the genre is important and should not be left to chance. It is important to plan talk as an integral part of the reading and writing process (see Figure 28-47).

We cannot take for granted that a form or genre is easy enough for students to assimilate without explicit instruction. The form may be fairly easy, but understanding the kind of thinking required to produce it is usually much more complex. The general sequence shown in Figure 28-48 works well. These ten steps can be used over and over again as you introduce different genres.

Steps one and two are always to read and talk about texts. You would not want to demonstrate any new genre using a text that has not been discussed. After students are very familiar and comfortable with a genre, you can ask them to write about a new text in the genre independently.

Steps three, four and five are all part of modeling how to write in the genre, and you may need more than one demonstration. Let's think about these steps using letters an example. You might want to write a different letter your class on chart paper every day for a week, Monday through Friday. Use books you read aloud to the class and that the children know well. Each day, have your student talk about the letter, underlining in red the sentences which you reveal your thinking (and also noticing conventions such as greeting, date, and closing). By Friday, your students will have a very good idea of the characteristics the genre and will be ready to try it on their own.

Shared writing comes into play in *step six*. You can read a book aloud and discuss it with the children. Then, together, compose a letter (written on chart paper) to the class next door. After the students reflect on the letter, cite places where they expressed their thinking and check it for conventions.

Steps seven and eight are related. When students first try the genre on their own, it is a good idea to follow the process all the way through. One way to start is to have all students write in the genre on the same day (maybe Friday, so that you can be sure you'll be able to respond them or share them in the group). During the discussion

486

Anne Frank,
The Diary of a Young Girl

During the Holocaust over 11,000,000 people died. Six million of those killed were Jews. Others who were victims of Adolph Hitler's horrid wrath included Catholics, Gypsies, homosexuals, and people of African Origin. Anne Frank, the Diary of a Young Girl is a sad, yet true, account of one Jewish girl's life in hiding from the Nazis and their power.

In the year 1942 Anne's family, which consisted of her, her sister, Margot, her mother, Edith, and her father, Otto, moved into 263 Prisengracht Road, in Amsterdam, Holland, in the hopes that they could stay alive and together during the war. With them was the Van Daan family and a man named Albert Dussel. The eight of them lived in fear of the fact that one day the SS men could push aside the bookshelf that separated their home from the outside world, and send them off to a concentration camp. Sadly, on August 4, 1944 their worst nightmares became a reality. SS Sgt. Karl Silberbauer entered the Annex, and took them to one of the SS headquarters, where they sent the different family members to Auschwitz where all of them besides Otto Frank lost their lives. This book tells the story of their time in hiding from Anne's very own eyes and ears. Anne talks about a side of the war that you hardly ever hear of. It shows a true account of what one girl thought while she was in hiding, and how with each passing day her hope could strengthen, weaken, or possibly die.

In my opinion this book is an extremely sad, but touching story. The feeling that Anne is able to convey through her journal is unbelievable. Anne was a humble girl who was always optimistic, and that alone seemed to be more inspiration than anything else in this book. To me the book showed a side of the Holocaust that could not have been expressed in 1,000,000 museums. The book was real, it was not a vision of what most probably was true, it was the hard core truth. It taught me about what someone would have to give up to try to stay alive, and how in most situations that person's attempts would fail. It also taught me about the bravery of those who risked their lives to save those in danger. I would recommend this book to anybody who wants to learn about the holocaust, and is not afraid of the terror that went on during the six years between the beginning of the war in 1939, and the liberation of the work and concentration camps in 1945. This book has touched many people in this world, and today one of those people is me. We can never take back the millions who were lost during the Holocaust, but we can help prevent such terrors from happening again. It could be as simple as not letting people talk cruelly about others behind their backs, or not assuming that just because you dislike one person you will not like everybody else around them. This book has opened my eyes to a new side of this world's history and I will never forget what I have learned from it.

ure 28-40. *Anita's Book Review of* The Diary of Anne Frank

Owls

Owls
Remarkable species
Owls
swoop through the night sky
Owls
feast on gophers and mice
Owls
glide through the sky
as silent as wind blowing by
waiting for its prey.

Figure 28-41. *Kal's Poem Inspired by* Owls

A Poem From Mudball, by Matt Tavares
by
Emilio

Little Andy Oyler
At bat in pouring rain,
Millers trailing,
Bases loaded.
CRACK!

Little Andy Oyler
Heading for muddy first.
"Where's the ball?
A score 3 to 1.

Little Andy Oyler
Heading for muddy second
"Where's the ball?"
A score 3 to 2.

Little Andy Oyler
Heading to muddy third
"Where's the ball?"
A score 3 to 3.

Little Andy Oyler
Coming home to win.
The shortest home run
In history.

Figure 28-42. *Emilio's Poem about* Mudball

Bridewell

To the north giant mountains.
To the east thick forest.
To the west dark hills.
To the south lonely sea.
Bridewell.
High-walled city,
Hub of the wheel,
Center of this small universe,
A safe prison.

Figure 28-43. *An Impression of the Setting of Bridewell in* The Dark Hills Divide

Unsolved
Inspired by
The Mary
Celeste by Jane
Yolen

The mystery of a floating
boat:
Unsolved.
A missing crew
register too:
Unsolved.
The mystery of no flag
of distress:
Unsolved.
A missing chronometer
sextant too:
The mystery of the Mary Celeste
Unsolved.

Figure 28-44. *Alexes's Poem Inspired by* Mary Celeste

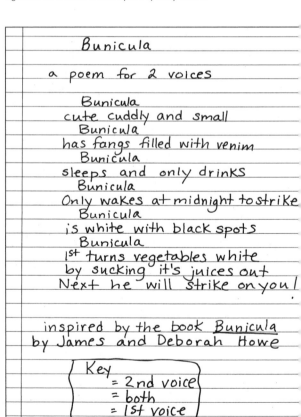

Bunicula

a poem for 2 voices

Bunicula
cute cuddly and small
Bunicula
has fangs filled with venim
Bunicula
sleeps and only drinks
Bunicula
Only wakes at midnight to strike
Bunicula
is white with black spots
Bunicula
1st turns vegetables white
by sucking it's juices out
Next he will strike on you!

inspired by the book Bunicula
by James and Deborah Howe

Key
= 2nd voice
= both
= 1st voice

Figure 28-45. *Anna's Poem for Two Voices Inspired by* Bunnicula

Genres and Forms for Writing About Reading

TYPE	DESCRIPTION	PURPOSE AND VALUE TO THE READER/WRITER
Functional Writing		
Notes	A series of words or phrases recorded on stick-on notes (lined or unlined), index cards, or in a notebook for use in talk or later writing.	▫ Records ideas to aid the reader/writer's memory for later talk and writing. ▫ Helps reader/writer remember a series of ideas ▫ Serves as a resource for writing a longer piece.
Lists	A series of specific words or phrases written one under the other (descriptive characteristics or a series of memorable words or phrases).	▫ Organizes information into a form that the reader/writer can use later for talking or writing about a longer piece. ▫ Helps reader/writer to summarize and categorize information during or after processing a text.
Sketches	A brief visual image, produced quickly to represent thinking.	▫ Allows reader/writer to get a response or major ideas down quickly to use as a reminder in later discussion. ▫ Enables the reader/writer to show thinking in images instead of words.
Short Writes	A group of sentences, produced quickly as immediate response to a particular text; may address any aspect of a text (characters, plot, theme, issues, setting, genre) or compare aspects of texts; can aid in preparing for tests.	▫ Helps readers/writers get ideas down quickly to capture responses that can be used in discussion or writing. ▫ Prompts thinking about a particular aspect of a text. ▫ Serves as a resource for discussion. ▫ Can be prompted or open-ended. ▫ Can be functional or informational.
Letter to Another Reader/ Writer About a Book (audience may be the teacher)	A correspondence between two readers in which they engage in a dialogue, sharing what they are thinking about a text; includes opinions, analyses, questions, personal memories or responses, critiques, evidence to support opinions.	▫ Provides an authentic conversational setting in which to discuss (in writing) any aspect of a text. ▫ Helps a reader/writer get thoughts down in an authentic communication that someone else will read and provide genuine response. ▫ Provides a dialogue that prompts the reader/writer to respond to specific ideas.
Letter to an Author or Illustrator of a Book	A correspondence to an author or illustrator about a text or a group of texts; includes opinions, questions, personal response and connections, and critiques.	▫ Requires the reader/writer to think analytically about a text or across several texts. ▫ Requires the reader/writer to think about the author/illustrator and the information that person might be able to provide. ▫ Enables expression of response and questioning within an authentic dialogue.

Figure 28-46. *Genres and Forms for Writing About Reading*

Genres and Forms for Writing About Reading (CONTINUED)

TYPE	DESCRIPTION	PURPOSE AND VALUE TO THE READER/WRITER
Functional Writing		
Diary Entries	An entry or series of entries in a journal or diary from the perspective of a biographical subject or a character, focusing on the setting, issues, or relationships.	▫ Requires perspective-taking to enter into the subject's or character's role. ▫ Helps the reader/writer summarize and/or extend the description of a character's or subject's traits or the challenges of the setting or the times.
Double-Column Entry	Written response in two columns, with a phrase, sentence, or quote from the text or a question in the left column and room for the reader's thinking on the right.	▫ Provides a specific piece of text to elicit a written response. ▫ Makes it easy for the reader/writer to accumulate responses that can later be used as an inspiration for discussion or longer writing.
Quote and Response	Written response to a memorable sentence or group of sentences (from a text) that are worth a reader's thinking; may be selected by the teacher or the individual reader. Can be set up as a two-column entry.	▫ Provides an accessible, specific piece of text to inspire "close reading" and brief response. ▫ Helps readers to identify places in the text that are meaningful. ▫ Engages readers in considering each other's responses (when circulated to individuals as a "write around" (Rief 1998)).
Graphic Organizer	A visual representation of information that shows the relationship between ideas or their organization; for example, character webs, descriptions, compare/contrast, statement with evidence, T chart, time line or problem/solution, story map.	▫ Helps a reader/writer to see the way the text works or the way ideas are related or information is organized. ▫ Helps a reader/writer to organize information in the reader's mind. ▫ May provide a road map to support the reader/writer in producing a longer piece of writing.
Grid	An open-ended table or chart that provides a framework for analyzing and comparing elements of a text (a form of a graphic organizer).	▫ Helps a reader organize thinking about the text. ▫ Reveals interrelationships among elements of a text. ▫ Supports analytical thinking. ▫ Can be used as a resource for writing an essay or other longer piece.
Poster/Advertisement	A visual image with art and writing that tells about the text in a way that is attention-getting or persuasive.	▫ Helps a reader/writer think of what is most interesting about a text. ▫ Helps reader think about how to use text content to persuade. ▫ Helps a reader/writer think about what might interest others about a text or topic (talking perspective).

Figure 28-46. *Genres and Forms for Writing About Reading (cont.)*

Genres and Forms for Writing About Reading (CONTINUED)

TYPE	DESCRIPTION	PURPOSE AND VALUE TO THE READER/WRITER
Narrative Writing		
Plot Summary	A brief statement of the essence or plot in a text.	<ul><li>Supports the reader/writer's memory of the text.</li><li>Helps a reader/writer determine what is the most important information in the text.</li><li>Provides the basis for sharing thinking.</li><li>Provides a good record to help the reader/writer get back to the meaning even much later.</li></ul>
Summary	A few sentences that tell the most important information from a text.	<ul><li>Enables a reader/writer to evaluate information in a text.</li><li>Requires that a reader/writer select the information that is most important in a text.</li><li>Helps the reader/writer remember what has happened (or the important information in the text) to inform further reading.</li><li>Helps the reader/writer remember what has happened (or the important information in the text) for discussion or writing after reading.</li><li>Helps the reader/writer remember what has happened (or the important information in the text) so that he/she can connect to other texts while reading.</li></ul>
Scene from a Text for Readers' Theater	A script with a narrator and parts designed to enable readers to become the voices of characters; may be prepared by teacher as a model or prepared by experienced students.	<ul><li>Expands the reader's understanding of the narrator in text.</li><li>Requires practice in identifying dialogue.</li><li>Requires thoughtful attention to the important and interesting parts of a text to create script.</li><li>Involves thinking about the characters' feelings, motivations, and ways of expressing themselves.</li><li>Involves perspective-taking.</li><li>Provides much practice in fluent, expressive reading.</li></ul>
Cartoon/ Storyboarding	A succession of graphics or stick figures used to present a story or information. Students quickly draw pictures or sketches representing significant events in a text. These sketches are organized to reflect the structure of the text and can be used as a basis for writing.	<ul><li>Enables the reader to communicate their ideas in images that tell a story or give a sequence.</li><li>Helps students learn to select important information.</li><li>Helps students learn to summarize.</li><li>Can be used as a basis for writing.</li></ul>

ure 28-46. *Genres and Forms for Writing About Reading (cont.)*

Genres and Forms for Writing About Reading (CONTINUED)

TYPE	DESCRIPTION	PURPOSE AND VALUE TO THE READER/WRITER
Informational Writing		
Outline	A list of headings and phrases that identify main points, subpoints, and sub-subpoints presented in an organized way to show their relationship in the visual form.	▫ Helps reader/writer to identify and understand the major ideas and supporting ideas in a text. ▫ Helps the reader/writer to show evidence for conclusions. ▫ Provides a quick way for the reader/writer to look back over the whole text and how it is organized.
Author Study	A piece of writing that provides information about an author and his/her craft as exemplified in several specified works; may involve comparison, analysis, critique.	▫ Engages the reader/writer in analytical and critical thinking about the writer's craft. ▫ Prompts noticing a writer's particular style or how style changes in response to a subject. ▫ Provides the reader/writer with opportunities to express analytical or critical thinking in writing. ▫ Requires using evidence from the text to support thinking.
Illustrator Study	A piece of writing that provides information on an illustrator and his/her craft as exemplified in several specified works; may involve artistic analysis, response to mood, analysis of integration of ideas and visual images; observation of technique.	▫ Provides the opportunity for the reader/writer to think of the text (picture book or illustrated chapter book) as an artistic whole. ▫ Provides opportunities for artistic appreciation. ▫ Requires thinking about the meaning of the text in comparison to the visual images. ▫ Requires drawing evidence from visual images and describing them.
Literary Essay	A formal essay that presents an idea(s) about a text or texts and may include a short retelling of the text.	▫ Requires planning and organizing. ▫ Involves drafting, revising, and editing to be sure the argument is clear to the reader. ▫ Involves developing a new understanding from a well-presented argument. ▫ Requires analytical and critical thinking on the part of the reader. ▫ Requires using evidence from the text to support thinking. ▫ Requires reaching the quality of publication.
Interview (Author or Expert)	A series of questions and responses designed to provide information about an author or expert on a topic.	▫ Requires deeper thinking about a topic or author's work. ▫ Provides an opportunity to use interaction to create a written text. ▫ Provides experiences in using first-hand sources. ▫ Provides experience in using question-and-answer format. ▫ Requires reader to have knowledge on a topic to determine points of inquiry.

Figure 28-46. *Genres and Forms for Writing About Reading (cont.)*

Genres and Forms for Writing About Reading (CONTINUED)

TYPE	DESCRIPTION	PURPOSE AND VALUE TO THE READER/WRITER
Informational Writing		
"How-To" Article	An article that explains to readers how something is made or done and gives specialized knowledge.	□ Requires the reader/writer to be an "expert" on the topic through reading about it. □ Requires careful attention to sequence. □ Requires the reader/writer to think about the audience's understanding.
Photo Essay, Picture Essay, or PowerPoint Presentation	A series of photographs, drawings, or digital photography that explains a topic or event.	□ Provides opportunity for the reader/writer to use visual images in an organized way to communicate thoughts and ideas. □ Provides the opportunity for the reader/writer to connect illustrations and brief pieces of text as an integral whole. □ Requires the organization of visual, written, and digital information. □ Requires the consideration of the audience's understanding of images and text.
Report	Factual information presented in an organized way.	□ Requires the reader/writer to gather, organize, and select information from many different sources (primary and secondary). □ Requires the use of a variety of text features. □ Provides experience in organizing information in a logical way. □ Requires attention to the audience's understanding of information, selecting terms and concepts that must be clearly defined in the text. □ Provides experience in careful documentation of the sources of information. □ Requires citing of evidence to support exposition or argument.
News or Feature Article	Factual information written to inform readers about and share interest in a topic.	□ Requires the reader to select a compelling topic. □ Requires the reader/writer to evaluate, select, and organize important information. □ Requires the reader/writer to organize and present information in a form that will make it accessible and interesting to the audience (e.g., prose, brochure). □ Requires the reader/writer to consider the audience.

Figure 28-46. Genres and Forms for Writing About Reading (cont.)

Genres and Forms for Writing About Reading (CONTINUED)

TYPE	DESCRIPTION	PURPOSE AND VALUE TO THE READER/WRITER
Informational Writing		
Editorial/Op-Eds	Ideas organized and presented in writing to communicate information or a specific opinion on a topic or issue. Written to persuade the reader and improve society or the world.	□ Requires organizing information to support an argument. □ Requires use of structures and signal words that are characteristic of argument (*because of, as a result, the evidence is, we must conclude because . . .*). □ Requires citing of evidence to support argument or opinion. □ Requires documentation of the truth of evidence to support argument or opinion.
Biographical Sketch	A short article written to show appreciation for accomplishments that provides information about a person's life or achievements.	□ Requires the reader/writer to select the most important information about a subject. □ Allows the reader/writer to express appreciation for individuals considered to be important.
Review or Recommendation	An article written to give readers advice on a book, topic, product, or place.	□ Requires the reader/writer to think about how to produce a text that will persuade an audience. □ Requires the reader/writer to carefully consider all aspects of the topic, product, book, or place and select what is most important. □ Requires the reader/writer to think about the kind of information that will be valuable to the audience.
Project	A creative body of work that presents ideas and opinions about texts or topics in an organized way; usually includes visual images along with text (examples–book cover, jackdaw, accordion, PowerPoint).	□ Provides the opportunity for an extended and creative piece of work that incorporates many different kinds of information-gathering. □ Requires the reader/writer to organize and represent different kinds of visual and print information. □ Requires the reader/writer to take perspective of the audience. □ Produces a public piece of work.
Poetic Writing		
Poem About a Text	A poetic text written in response to a prose text; may focus on any aspect of text (character, plot, setting, a story even, an individual's achievement); may be written in first, second, or third person; may be written for one or more voices.	□ Stretches thinking by enabling the reader/writer to express thoughts in another genre. □ Provokes deeper thinking about some aspect of a text. □ Provides a product that has artistic quality that others can appreciate and compare to the original text.

Figure 28-46. *Genres and Forms for Writing About Reading (cont.)*

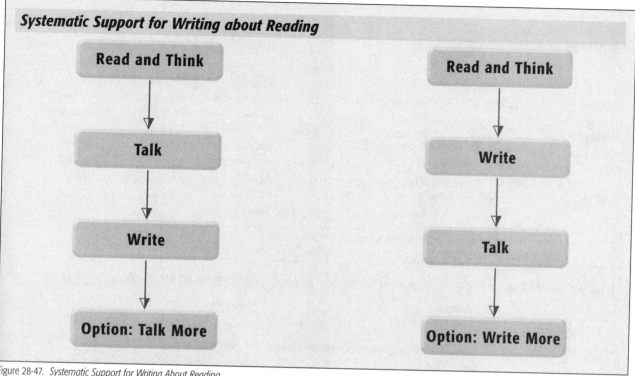

Figure 28-47. *Systematic Support for Writing About Reading*

you can prompt students to say what they think and then mention examples of things that might be included in the piece of writing.

Step nine is more open-ended. If students have learned to use the form or genre, they can then apply it to the books they are reading independently. If you think they need more support, they can first write with a partner. It is usually wise to have the students use the genre quite a few times (step ten), so that they have learned the processes and internalized the characteristics. If you move on to other genres too quickly, they may become confused or forget what they have learned.

Ultimately, you want students to know the genres so well that they can use them independently. They will then have a repertoire of forms or genres with which to represent their thinking about their own reading or to include in longer pieces of writing. The general demonstration-to-independence sequence is shown in Figure 28-49. A more detailed explanation of ways you can move from common text experiences to writing about reading independently is presented in Figure 28-50.

The key to success in teaching these genres or forms is to use interactive read-aloud frequently to engage all students

Learning to Write About Reading

1. Enjoy reading texts together.
2. Think and talk together about the texts.
3. Demonstrate writing about the text in a particular genre or form.
4. Show other examples of writing in the genre or form and make them available for reference.
5. Analyze the characteristics of the writing genre or form.
6. Have students work with you to create a text in the genre or form that you modeled.
7. Have the students try writing in the genre or form with a partner and/or on their own.
8. Have students share their writing and reflections on the process.
9. Have students use the genre or form to reflect on their own reading.
10. Encourage students to write in the genre or form several times to develop fluency and ease, enabling them to select it as a possibility for their writing in the future.

Figure 28-48. *Learning to Write About Reading*

FROM DEMONSTRATION TO INFORMED CHOICE IN LEARNING:
Learning to Write About Reading

Students develop the habit of reading, thinking, and talking about texts.	Teacher demonstrates the process of writing in a genre or form as students observe and contribute.	Students write in a genre or form as a whole group with teacher support (modeled, shared, or interactive writing).	Students write in a genre or form with a partner or independently within the whole-group or small-group setting. (optional)	Students write independently in a genre or form about a common text that has been read aloud to the whole group and then share.	Students use the genre or form to write independently about their own reading.	Students select from a variety of genre or forms to write independently about their own reading.

Figure 28-49. *From Demonstration to Informed Choice in Learning: Learning to Write About Reading*

Using Common Text Experiences as a Basis for Teaching Students to Write About Reading

STEP	DESCRIPTION	EXAMPLES
Establish common text experiences.	▫ Read selected texts aloud to students. ▫ Invite them to discuss texts and talk about their thinking. ▫ Model discussing ideas or information in the text that provides a foundation for writing in a genre.	▫ Watch for favorite read-aloud texts. ▫ Revisit texts for more discussion. ▫ Sometimes reread the entire text or a part of it.
Write *for* students based on common text experiences.	▫ Model writing the genre or form for students so they can observe the process and discuss it. ▫ Repeat the process several times with different texts. ▫ Review some of the pictures in a text to bring back ideas. ▫ Leave the products displayed in the room or in a place where they are easy for students to access.	▫ Make notes after reading aloud. ▫ Demonstrate how to sketch what you are thinking after reading aloud. ▫ Create any kind of graphic organizer and have students contribute to filling it in (for example, a character web). ▫ Have a quote from the text already written in the left column and ask students to contribute to the right column (two-column entry).
Write *with* students based on common text experiences.	▫ Use a chart to create an example of the genre or form for writing about reading. (Students compose the content for the chart and may do some of the writing.) ▫ Take several days to create the chart, returning to it to help students remember the text. ▫ Discuss the process. ▫ Have students create a version of the chart in their reader's notebook. ▫ Go through the process several times. After experience, students may suggest the form the writing will take.	▫ Create a letter to an author from the class. ▫ Create a two-column entry based on a student-chosen quote. ▫ Use a graphic organizer to record something the students have noticed about the text.

Figure 28-50. *Using Common Text Experiences as a Basis for Teaching Students to Write About Reading*

Using Common Text Experiences as a Basis for Teaching Students to Write About Reading
(CONTINUED)

STEP	DESCRIPTION	EXAMPLES
Have students write *with support* about any common text experience (one from interactive read-aloud or guided reading)	□ Invite students to discuss a common text. □ Recall demonstrations and examples of the genre for writing about reading. □ Have students (alone or in pairs) try the genre at the group meeting. (They use clipboards to do their writing.) □ Confer individually with students to assist them. □ Have them share and discuss their writing.	□ Have everyone use the same quote for a two-column entry and then compare responses. □ Have students sketch and then write before sharing responses. □ Have half the group use one graphic organizer and the other half use another. □ Have all of the group do character webs but select different characters authors on a subject of a biography.
Have students write independently in a genre for writing about reading.	□ Assign students a genre or form in which to write about a common text experience. □ After students have learned to use several genre or forms very well, let them choose between two or several. □ Have students work independently but simultaneously and within a defined time period. □ Have students share and discuss their writing. □ Keep a list of genres taught so that it will be easier for you and the students to select. □ Create a scrapbook of examples in each genre to use as references.	□ Have students write letters to different characters. □ Have students choose different ways to present a character—web, letter, sketch and description, dialogue, letter from a character to another. □ Have students search the text to find where the writer has used comparison/contrast. □ Have students select two or three quotes and write about them in two-column entries.

Figure 28-50. *Using Common Text Experiences as a Basis for Teaching Students to Write About Reading (cont.)*

in hearing high-quality texts. As the examples indicate, often students work on the same assigned writing activity simultaneously. Types of writing about reading are added throughout the year and grade-by-grade as appropriate, so there is plenty of time to introduce each one and use it extensively.

USING MINILESSONS TO HELP STUDENTS WRITE ABOUT READING
Through the minilessons that you provide at the beginning of reading or writing workshop, you can actively teach students how to write in a variety of ways about reading. In the minilesson in Figure 28-51, Mr. P. is helping his students become more aware of note-taking as a way to keep a record of their thinking as a resource for discussion and letter writing. His students had already written on stick-on notes and in notebooks during independent and guided reading, but they had not had systematic instruction on why and how to do it.

With the minilesson principle written on a chart as a constant reminder, the teacher helped students recall a text he had previously read to them, then had them discuss it with each other while he made notes. After reading some of his notes aloud to the class and asking them to comment, he demonstrated how these notes helped him extend his thinking about the text. He then turned the task over to the students, who wrote some notes on their own and then shared them with a partner. Mr. P. concluded the lesson by repeating the minilesson principle and asking them to write notes about the book they are reading.

These young students will not learn good note-taking from this single lesson; they will need many more experiences over several years. But the purposes and benefits of writing about reading have been brought to their attention.

"Readers write notes to help them think about their reading and to share their thinking with others."

MR. P.: We read this book together, *When Marian Sang,* by Pam Munoz Ryan, with illustrations by Brian Selznick, then thought about it and talked about our thinking together. Today, I am going to guide you through a quick look at the illustrations to remind you of what we talked about. [SHOWS PICTURES FROM THE BOOK.] "Readers write notes to help them think about their reading and to share their thinking with others." [READS FROM CHART.] That is written on the chart. Turn and talk in partners about your thinking while I write some of my thinking in my reader's notebook." [WRITES WHILE CHILDREN TALK.] Let me read to you some of my notes. [READS SELECTED NOTES FROM THE NOTEBOOK (SEE FIGURE 28-51).] What do you notice about my thinking?

JEN: You were remembering some of the stuff in the book.

KAREN: You wrote things so you could remember them—like she could sing twenty-four notes.

BEN: You wrote why you thought there was church music on every page.

CHARLES: You wrote things you weren't interested in.

NAZ: You were interested in Eleanor Roosevelt, because you wrote a note to remember to get the letter.

MR. P.: I did want to remember some specific facts, but I was also writing some questions. I made a note to myself to get Eleanor's letter because I saw the website in the back. Here it is in my notebook and also the picture of Marion singing at the Lincoln Memorial. I really found that a very inspiring story and I was proud of the first lady. So my writing really helped me think more about the book and about the times Marion lived.

BEN: Like we write notes on stick-on notes so we can remember what to talk about.

MR. P.: Yes, you can write about anything—things to remember, things to talk about, things to think more about. You can write a list of phrases or sentences, whatever works best for you. Writing about your thinking will help you think more about the book and have a record to look back on. Writing is a record of our thinking. We might want to think more, notice more, or change our minds. When we write about our thinking, we also have it to share with others. Take your reader's notebook and write some notes about your thinking about *When Marion Sang.* [STUDENTS WRITE IN THEIR NOTEBOOKS.] Now, turn and talk to a partner about your writing. [STUDENTS TURN AND TALK UNTIL THE TEACHER CALLS THEM TO ATTENTION.] When you are reading today, write some notes in your reader's notebook. Your notes will help you write your letter this week. Remember, **"Readers write notes to help them think about their reading and to share their thinking with others."**

NOTE: This was a minilesson to model note-taking. The next minilesson can help readers take their lists and use them for a longer piece.

Figure 28-51. *Sample Minilesson: "Readers write notes to help them think about their reading and to share their thinking with others."*

SUPPORTING STUDENTS ACROSS CONTEXTS

Students can write about any books they hear or read. Writing about reading does not belong within any one instructional context. In fact, it should be pervasive throughout the entire language/literacy framework. These genres are appropriate anytime students will benefit from writing in support of their thinking and talking. Once they learn to use these genres or forms efficiently, most writing about reading will not take up very much time. Figure 28-53 is a list of ways to support students in writing about reading. These suggestions apply to any of the genres previously discussed.

Once students have learned a variety of ways to use writing to reflect on their reading, they will have powerful tools at their disposal.

SUGGESTIONS FOR PROFESSIONAL DEVELOPMENT

TEACHING A GENRE FOR WRITING ABOUT READING

1 Meet with a group of grade-level colleagues.

2 Have each person bring to the meeting some books the have recently read aloud.

3 After looking through the types of genres for writin about reading in this chapter, have each person sele one type to teach, using the interactive read-aloud boo as a resource.

4 Have each person draw up a simple sequence of lesson for teaching the genre. Consider:

  □ The experience students have had in using the gen or form. (Don't just assume they have.)

Notes:

Marion—

Grew up loving music b/c it was part of her life.

Unusual – she could sing 24 notes

Wanted to sing opera

Words from church music on every page — shows how important music and religion to her?

Words to songs match her feelings –
    e.g. Let My People Go (Jim Crow laws)

Studied in Europe

Couldn't sing in Constitution Hall – Why?

Eleanor Roosevelt – invited to sing at Lincoln Memorial to 75,000 people

Finally sang at Met

Gets letter from Eleanor

Figure 28-52. *Selected Notes from a Reader's Notebook*

WAYS TO SUPPORT STUDENTS IN
Writing About Reading

- Create a list of genres or forms for writing about reading; include examples of each that you can refer to as you teach.
- Display minilesson charts you created when you taught the genre or form.
- Create a scrapbook with sections that show two or three good student examples of each genre or form.
- Re-teach the minilesson using other text examples as needed.
- Pull together a small group of children who need extra support in using a genre or form.
- Use the genre in connection with a text students have read with your support in a guided reading group.
- Support individuals through individual conferences as they work on writing about reading.

Figure 28-53. *Ways to Support Students in Writing About Reading*

- The kinds of demonstrations and models students will need.
- Whole- or small-group experience (such as shared or partner writing) that will make it easy for students to understand the genre.
- The task that can be turned over to the students so that they can use it independently.
- The number of times students should use the genre so that they will know its characteristics.

5 Have participants share their plans. Some may wish to use the same books and plans so that they can compare results.

6 Set another meeting time.

7 Have each person implement the lesson, taking note of students' comments as evidence of thinking.

8 Hold a follow-up meeting to share results.

9 Share lesson plans across the group, and refine them as more people try them.

CHAPTER TWENTY-NINE

MEETING THE DIVERSE NEEDS OF ENGLISH LANGUAGE LEARNERS

Marianthe knew this day would come (her first

day of school in a new country).

"I won't know anyone. I won't understand what they say.

They won't understand. Everything is so different."

"Only on the outside," said Mama. "Inside, people are the same."

—ALIKI (MARIANTHE'S STORY)

The term *English language learner* includes any student for whom standard academic English is not a first language. Since 1992, the percentage of English language learners in American public schools has increased by more than eighty-four percent. And in nearly half the states, English language learners now comprise between five and ten percent of K–12 enrollment, according to the Department of Education *(www.ed.gov/about/offices/list/olea/index.html)*.

With a chapter focusing on English language learners, you might think we assume all students so designated are similar, to be treated the same. As every teacher who works with English language learners knows, nothing could be farther from the truth. English language learners are highly diverse as individuals. Each learner has a different range of experiences with the English language, regardless of age or grade.

In any classroom that includes English language learners (and that's most classrooms today), the majority of students may be from the same language group or there may be a wide variety of language groups. Either way, you have to make decisions about how to accommodate them.

Each option we describe in this chapter is highly flexible and applicable in a variety of ways. Each must be determined by your in-depth knowledge of the students you teach. And almost all the routines you build into your classroom to support English language learners will also support native English speakers who need extra help.

ENGLISH LANGUAGE LEARNER DIVERSITY

English language learners may be of any age and in any grade, from kindergarten through high school. They may be from cultures very different from or similar to your own. The language they speak may have much in common with English, making it easy for you to pronounce names and

learn a few words, or the language's graphic symbols and phonology may be very different from English. Some languages do not have a written version; others, like some Chinese dialects, are not alphabetic. Print conventions in other languages may also be different, with writing proceeding from bottom to top or right to left. In addition, individual English language learners vary greatly. You may find students who:

- Have recently immigrated to an English-speaking country, at whatever age, and are learning oral English for the first time.

- Have recently arrived in an English-speaking country but have learned oral English beforehand.

- Can read and write "academic" English but have difficulty interacting with others conversationally.

- Have been residents of an English-speaking country for some time but live in a homogenous language community and so are learning English for the first time.

- Speak English in everyday conversation but are only beginning to learn to read and write in English.

- Can speak, read, and write in English but have limited vocabulary and knowledge of the syntax.

- Speak several languages, including English, but have limited knowledge of how to read and write English.

- Are learning English as a third, fourth, or fifth language.

This diversity suggests that the way human beings learn language is endlessly fascinating and endlessly varied. Yet all English language learners have many things in common:

- They implicitly know, understand, and use the sounds of at least one language.

- They implicitly know, understand, and use the syntax structure of at least one language.

They are in the process of learning a new language—either from the beginning or at more advanced levels.

They will very likely be bilingual speakers (perhaps speakers of many languages) all their lives—a real advantage in today's society.

They have the opportunity to become bilingual readers and writers.

They are making connections between the known language and the new language and will benefit from those relationships.

They need to engage in real conversation in English every day.

They need to be able to share their strengths.

They need to explore themes central to their lives.

They need to be immersed in and use language purposefully all the time.

They bring a rich background of language and culture into our classrooms that has the potential to benefit all students.

They need to feel safe so that they can take risks in the process of learning.

In other words, English language learners are not starting at square one. A child who speaks a language, even the conversational language of the home, has gone through the *acquisition* phases that researchers have discovered to remarkably consistent for all the languages in the world (Lindfors 1987). They have learned a system of rules (*grammar*), a vocabulary (*lexicon*), a sound system (*phonology*), and a system of meaning (*semantics*). This knowledge is largely held implicitly, or unconsciously, and has been acquired through interaction with others. The wider the opportunities for interaction, the richer the language learning systems children will develop. The child has learned how to learn language, and this process is a resource in learning to speak, read, and write English. Clay (1990) refers to language as an example of a self-extending system—one that fuels its own learning by expanding scope and complexity as it is used.

One of the most important concepts to keep in mind when helping English language learners is that they must perceive their talking, reading, and writing in this new language as meaningful. English may be new, but it must be understood to be language. Becoming literate in a language you are just learning is quite a challenge, and the process is not parallel to a highly literate person in English learning a second language. If you know the process of reading, learning to speak and read in another language is inherently different from learning to read for the first time in another language you do not speak.

An important factor in comprehension is attention—the reader has only so much of it. For example, effortless and automatic word recognition frees one's attention to consider the meaning of a text. Speed in recognizing the word and simultaneously accessing its meaning is important. Getting a word "right," though necessary, is not enough if a large part of one's attention must be devoted to the process of solving it. Unusual or highly complex syntax can also require one's attention and limit comprehension. Even as proficient adult readers we sometimes have to revisit a long sentence with many dependent clauses and complex punctuation simply to sort out the meaning. Here's an example: "Oh, say can you see by the dawn's early light what so proudly we hailed at the twilight's last gleaming, whose broad stripes and bright stars through the perilous fight from the ramparts we watched were so gallantly gleaming, and the rockets red glare, the bombs bursting in air gave proof through the night that our flag was still there?" If we did not know this lyric so well, it might take a second or two to figure out the subject of this interrogative sentence is "you," and "what so proudly we hailed at the twilight's last gleaming" is a noun clause functioning as the direct object. Further, "whose broad stripes and bright stars" refers to "what so proudly we hailed." It's complicated.

THE LITERATURE OF DIVERSITY

When we think about English language learners, we also need to think about literature that includes them. Literature that reflects diversity is sometimes called *multicultural literature*. According to scholars of children's literature, multicultural literature focuses on individuals or groups who vary from the mainstream population of the United States, which is largely European rooted and English speaking (Bishop 1992). But our population is rapidly becoming so diverse that someday there may not be an identifiable mainstream! Corliss (2005) defines the literature of diversity as "literature that reflects the broad range of human experience and a global kaleidoscope of cultures" (p. 5). Literature about people of color has been emphasized simply because it has been neglected in the past.

We must keep vigilant watch on the reading materials we provide students to be sure they reflect our pluralistic society. Multicultural literature is important not just to English language learners or other diverse groups but to all students, who must develop the knowledge they need to be effective citizens of this pluralistic world. Truly great literature of diversity challenges stereotypical views of any group; expands understanding, respect, and empathy; and even changes views of justice and power. The literature of diversity may be fiction or nonfiction and can focus on any area of diversity, including:

◘ Racial.

◘ Cultural.

◘ Geographic.

◘ Religious.

◘ Gender.

◘ Language.

It is important that English language learners see themselves in the books they hear read aloud, read for themselves, and discuss with one another. Interactive read-aloud is a wonderful way to share the literature of diversity with your students. Some excellent stories focusing on language are described here or earlier in this book:

◘ *My Name Is Yoon* (Recorvits) and *The Name Jar* (Choi), both stories about little Korean girls who arrive at English schools.

◘ *Journey Home* (Uchida), the story of a Mexican family who work in the United States but make a journey home to their village for Christmas.

◘ *In the Small, Small Deep Night* (Kurtz), the story of an African girl who comforts her little brother on their first night in a new country by telling traditional tales. (See *www.fountasandpinnellleveledbooks.com)*

◘ *Los Pollitos Dicen: The Baby Chicks Sing* (Syverson-Stork and Hall), a collection of traditional games, nursery rhymes, and songs from Spanish-speaking countries, a wonderful resource that has rhymes in both English and Spanish that primary age children will enjoy.

For guided reading, you will want to include a wide varie of biographies. Here are just a few:

◘ *Meet Yo-Yo Ma* (Leveled Readers), the story of a worl renowned cellist (see Chapter 13).

◘ *Pat Mora: Two Languages One Poet* (Leveled Reader the story of a famous Latina poet who writes in bc Spanish and English (introduced later in this chap and Chapter 10).

◘ *Sitti's Secret* (Bhihab Nye), the story of a child with grandmother in Palestine (see Chapter 15).

For additional suggestions, you may want to visit our dat base at *www.fountasandpinnellleveledbooks.com* whe you can sort biographies as a genre and the particular lev you need.

PRINCIPLES FOR SUPPORTING COMPREHENSION WITH ENGLISH LANGUAGE LEARNERS

Specific instructional techniques for working effective with English language learners are based on a number general principles, each applicable in many differe instructional situations:

1 *Select all texts carefully to be sure that they support* ∕ *readers.* It is always important to select texts carefull but when you are working with English language lear ers, these decisions are even more important. Studer encounter texts throughout the day—in interacti read-aloud, literature discussion, guided reading, ind pendent reading, writing workshop, and all the conte areas. This large quantity of material presents issues f English language learners—related to language, course, but also to concepts, ideas, and informatic Students must bring to this challenge not only what th currently know about language but also their bac ground and experience.

2 *Surround all text experiences with meaningful ta.* To establish conversational ease with English langua learners, you need to develop a shared vocabulary. If y realize what your students already know about langua you can be alert to helping them understand new la guage features. When you read aloud to students, int duce texts to them in guided reading or guide them literature discussion. You can use this shared langua to enhance their understanding. The more meaning

language they hear, the more they can learn. The more language they hear, the more familiar it will be when they encounter similar structures in texts. If a text is very difficult for them in language, structure, and content, it will be incomprehensible. Examine texts carefully to decide the points of access for your students. Language and content should be accessible with your teaching support. Don't choose texts that are too far out of their reach. Easy and familiar content expressed in novel language will help students learn new labels and ways to talk about something they already understand. Easy texts with just a little new content are also good choices.

Provide many opportunities for group support. In many ways, we all rely on group support in order to perform competently. We are inspired to join in singing "The Star Spangled Banner" at a sporting event when we would hesitate to perform it as a solo. Group reading does not take the place of the independent processing you want your students to develop, but it is a highly engaging literacy experience from which they can learn. You can create group reading experiences by inviting students to join in at specific points as you read texts aloud, and you can engage them in shared reading of all kinds of texts (see Chapter 21). The scaffolding offered by others enables them to try out the language without calling attention to themselves.

Use texts with visual images whenever possible. If you have traveled to a country where you do not speak or understand the language, you know how important visual images can be. Pictures instantaneously convey comprehensible information to your students. The large number of picture books available in all genres and appropriate for all ages, kindergarten through grade eight, is a real benefit to English language learners. You and your students can talk about the pictures in any text at any time. You will want to use picture books in interactive read-aloud and in guided reading and have baskets full of them in the classroom library.

Provide several ways to access meaning. You can rephrase or paraphrase complex language using simpler words and sentences. Signs of confusion in your students alert you to the need to paraphrase directions or tricky language that you find in a text. By building on what they already know, students can gradually take on new ways of using language. Paraphrasing is also important because you want your students to become very flexible, accessing meaning in more than one way.

6 *Repeat, repeat, repeat.* We have all had the experience of hearing something several times before truly understanding it. Speak slowly and clearly and repeat directions and/or ask children to repeat them. All students feel more confident and competent if they truly understand what is expected of them and if they are given plenty of time to construct that understanding. In the long run, you will save time because students will become more independent. Also, give the students many opportunities to hear and/or read the same texts. Each time they experience the text, they are able to attend to new elements of language and meaning.

7 *Explain and demonstrate whenever possible.* When in doubt, explain concepts and ideas to students in ways they can understand. Also, provide explicit and visible demonstrations when appropriate. This is especially helpful when you are introducing new texts to students in guided reading. Rather than waiting to see if they "get it," do whatever you need to do to assure accessibility to the language structures and information in the text. Since the language of this new and more challenging text is likely to be difficult, you want to be sure the content is fully accessible. The central goal of guided reading is not acquiring content knowledge, although that usually happens. The goal is expanding and improving strategic processing, which will be difficult if students are also struggling to understand content.

8 *Engage students in repeating English language vocabulary and structures whenever possible.* No one can develop language proficiency simply by listening. We learn through interaction. As students take on the vocabulary and structures of English, they need opportunities to try them out for themselves. At first, you may find that students who have limited English knowledge are reluctant to speak. We even observe a "silent phase" for newly arrived immigrants who enter a bewildering new environment where they understand very little and cannot

communicate their needs. Even students who speak English with fair proficiency may have had previous negative experiences that reduce their willingness to speak. Daily successful interactions can increase children's comfort in speaking English. You can make their language instructions successful by designing highly supported instruction. Provide language models that students can take on and use as their own. Look for ways to provide some form of "rehearsal" so that students can be more confident in speaking. Shared reading, guided reading, and individual reading conferences are all contexts in which English language learners can try out new vocabulary and language structures.

9 *Provide a safe environment for language use.* All students need to participate in a respectful classroom where it is safe to make mistakes. In safe classrooms mistakes are expected and considered part of learning. Throughout the day, you can model for your students respectful listening, paraphrasing, searching for clarification, and responding to a speaker's intended meaning rather than to the form. You can also explicitly teach such behaviors to all students and insist on respectful interactions throughout the day. Soon, active listening and thoughtful responding will become a beneficial habit that will serve all students well throughout their lives.

10 *Make the school and classroom a welcoming place for families.* One of the best ways to make students feel comfortable in your school and classroom is to invite families to participate. Have signs in all of the languages your students speak and be sure that pictures, artwork, and texts on display reflect the various communities. Find out as much as you can about the languages and cultures of the children you teach so that you can bring these cultures into the classroom through a variety of books. Make it possible for parents to bring their younger children with them when they visit the school for conferences or just to observe. Value the knowledge or resources the family can offer. Encourage children to write about their lives and customs. Publicly recognize students' efforts through displays and programs so that parents can see what their children are doing. Validate the student's home life so you can build a student's self-esteem and sense of identity.

PLANNING AND ADJUSTING INSTRUCTION FOR ENGLISH LANGUAGE LEARNERS

There are many ways to plan and adjust instruction to provide more support for English language learners. Below are categorized lists of specific suggestions. At first, they may seem overwhelming, but if you try a few in each category, you will soon find that they will become habits and your instruction will automatically accommodate these learners day-by-day.

PRACTICAL SUGGESTIONS FOR MANAGING LESSONS

One of the first considerations in working with English language learners is to be sure that they understand what you are asking them to do. It will be hard to deliver effective instruction if your students cannot perform the tasks you have designed. These are some suggestions for helping English language learners participate fully and competently in reading lessons:

1 Show children what you mean when you give directions. You may need to act out or demonstrate entire sequence of action and have children do them while you observe and assist the first few times.

2 Have children repeat directions to one another or say them aloud as they engage in an activity.

3 Pair English-speaking and English language learners so that they can check their actions with each other.

4 Paraphrase directions so that you know you are using simple, clear language. Watch for feedback from students to be sure they understand.

5 When possible, use short, simple sentences that are easy to understand.

6 Give English language learners more "wait and think" time. Say, "Let's think about that for a minute," before calling for answers. Demonstrate to students how you think about what you are going to say.

Once your instructional routines are set up and students understand them, you can work intensively in a wide range of instructional contexts to expand their knowledge of spoken and written English.

ORAL LANGUAGE DEVELOPMENT

The most supportive way you can help English language learners is to interact with them in conversation. It is also very beneficial for them to converse with their peers, but your intentional support and periodic direct teaching are even more important. These are some suggestions for helping students develop greater control when speaking and listening to English:

1 Demonstrate new language structures through simple conversational exchanges. Introduce games that require repeating the same language structures, each time inserting different content. For example, make a chart of children's names and siblings. Then have them use sentences like these: "My name is ____." "____ has two brothers." "____ has one sister and one brother." "I like to ____." Have them go through such sequences over and over so that they overlearn the language structures.

2 Use conversational exchanges based on pictures and objects that children understand and that they can connect to their own lives (for example, writing tools, kitchen or eating implements, toys): "I have a spoon. I can use it to eat soup." Again go for overlearning.

Be sure that you know the correct way to pronounce students' first and second names. Work at it and ask for feedback from the students or their parents. Children will appreciate these efforts.

If you possibly can, learn a few words in the students' languages. Involve the whole class in making a simple dictionary with a few words in each language.

Provide "rehearsal" opportunities by modeling the language, having students try it out, and then designing activities that give them a chance to use it meaningfully, making it their own.

Help students prepare for discussion by holding a brief small-group "meeting before the meeting" to let them try out their discussion points and practice sharing their thinking about the text. This process will allow them to speak up more confidently in both small- and large-group settings.

Tell traditional stories and recite poems and songs from the students' own languages and cultures (or invite community members to do so). These cultural symbols will enrich all your students' learning and add to the sense of community. Repeat favorites and have students learn some of them by heart.

Be aware of potential challenges for English language learners in all oral and written contexts. You may need to explain vocabulary, homonyms, idioms and colloqui-

alisms, irony and sarcasm, literary language, complex verb tenses, multiple adjectives in a phrase, prepositional phrases that start a sentence, and complex sentences.

INTERACTIVE READ-ALOUD AND LITERATURE DISCUSSION

Interactive read-aloud will greatly benefit your English language learners. Reading aloud models language use. Picture books provide contextual support. If the text is within students' power to understand, reading it aloud is a demonstration that written English is interesting and pleasurable. Through interactive read-aloud, you can greatly expand students' listening vocabularies. If you invite them to use some of the terms in conversation, you can also increase their speaking vocabularies. Through discussion, your students can extend their understanding of the text, but you can also explain important concepts that they may be finding difficult to understand and help them learn English labels for things. But the most important benefit of interactive read-aloud is the constant exposure it provides to English language syntax. Hearing grammatical structures of English over and over again helps English language learners form an implicit knowledge of the rules. These are some suggestions for adjusting interactive read-aloud sessions for English language learners:

1 Increase the amount of time you read aloud and engage in extended discussion of the texts. This will help all students expand language knowledge.

2 Stick to simple texts that your students will be able to understand. You can explain concepts, but there should not be too much to learn within any one text. Otherwise, a read-aloud will turn into one long vocabulary lesson and children will lose the meaning of the text.

3 Remember that English language learners can usually understand more than they can perform. You can help them give voice to their understandings.

4 Watch for responses that show you which texts English language learners enjoy. Reread those texts several times so that students will have many chances to remember the language. Rereading books will help children acquire and make use of language that goes beyond their current understanding.

5 Choose texts with illustrations that your students will enjoy and that will expand their understanding.

6 Be sure that children's own cultures are reflected in the material you read aloud to them. They should see illustrations with people like themselves in books and have their cultures reflected in the food, celebrations, customs, dress, holidays, and events they encounter in the stories.

7 When you read aloud, be sure that English language learners are not seated in peripheral positions (to the side or in the back). They especially need to see, hear, and participate.

8 Give English language learners a "preview" of the text by holding a brief small-group discussion with them before reading the text to the entire group. You can show pictures, talk about the content, and even read the whole book or sections of it. In this way, English language learners will hear the text twice, understand it better, and be able to participate more actively in the discussion.

9 Have students "turn and talk" before asking them to offer their ideas to the whole group. The various routines described in Chapter 18 (turn and talk, partners, circle talk) will be especially beneficial to English language learners because they will have a chance to "rehearse" some dialogue before speaking in the large group.

SHARED AND PERFORMED READING

From the very simple texts that kindergartners and first graders read in a shared way to the more sophisticated poems and readers' theater texts that upper elementary and middle school students enjoy, shared and performed reading are highly productive for English language learners. These activities provide:

- Group support so that students can produce the language with others.

- An authentic opportunity to reread texts.

- The opportunity to repeat English language words and sentence patterns.

- The opportunity to practice reading a text to understand it.

- The opportunity to practice pronouncing English words.

These are some suggestions for helping English language learners benefit from shared and performed reading:

1 Select texts for shared reading that have simple, easy sentences. Learning a new language is much more than decoding words. English language learners are learning new syntactic structures, and they need to absorb simple sentence patterns before they go on to complex ones.

2 Once a shared reading text is learned, it becomes a language resource for your students. You can use it as an example, revisiting the text to help children remember specific words or phrases. Individuals can refer to it to recall vocabulary or pattern their own writing after the language structures.

3 Rhythmic and repetitive texts are beneficial to English language learners. The repetition will give them maximum experience with the syntax of English and will help them develop an implicit understanding of noun–verb agreement, plurals, and other concepts.

4 Personal poetry books made up of poems used in shared reading are texts older learners can return to again and again to revisit meaning, vocabulary, and language structures. Rereading this material, even overlearning it, will support fluency.

5 If you are able to find some traditional rhymes or songs from students' own languages, you can use these for shared and performed reading. If they are not too complicated, all students will enjoy reading them in a shared way. (A simple traditional rhyme in Spanish is shown in Figure 29-1.)

6 English translations of traditional rhymes or songs in students' native languages are a great resource. (See the translation of "Roses Are Red" in Figure 29-2.) The

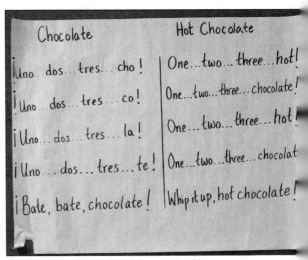

Figure 29-1. *A Simple, Traditional Rhyme in Spanish*

"echo" reading, with one group reading a line in English and the other group echoing the line in the other language. *Los Pollitos Dicen, The Baby Chicks Sing* (Syverson-Stork and Hall) has many rhymes with good potential for shared reading. *Cool Salsa: Bilingual Poems on Growing Up Latino in the United States* (Carlson) is a wonderful collection of poems for older students. Figure 29-3 shows the first few lines of a poem by Pat Mora in English and Spanish.

GUIDED READING

Guided reading is an essential instructional context for helping English language learners take on the independent reading of English. In guided reading, you can:

- Engage students in using language throughout the lesson.
- Match the books to the readers' current abilities, including their knowledge of content and understanding of English syntax and vocabulary.
- Provide introductions that will increase familiarity and reduce confusion.
- Provide opportunities to read with support.
- Provide a rich discussion of the meaning of the text, with the opportunity to untangle confusions.
- Check regularly on students' oral reading to determine accuracy, fluency, and comprehension.

As you plan for guided reading lessons for English language learners, these adjustments will be especially beneficial:

Include English language learners in guided reading groups even if they have limited understanding of English. They can read very simple texts, and it will give them an opportunity to interact with you and others. You can find numerous texts with picture support.

Select texts that have language structures, concepts, or vocabulary that will be within readers' control with your support. Try not to include too many new things to learn in any one text.

In the introduction, include as much "practice" as needed to help students become familiar with the new language structures. Identify language structures that will be challenging and repeat them yourself in conversation, but also have students repeat them several times and talk about their meaning.

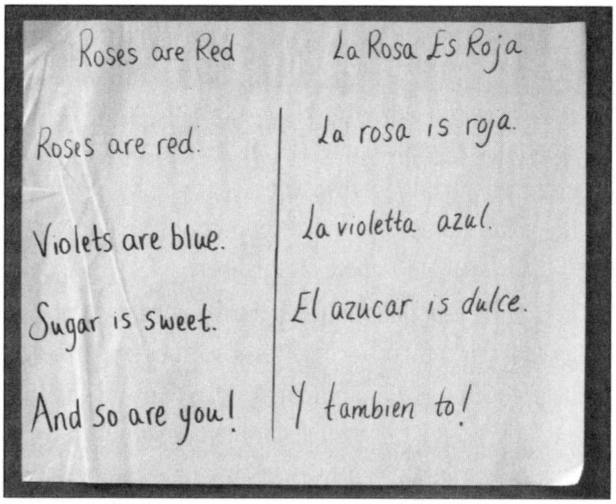

Figure 29-2. *Roses Are Red*

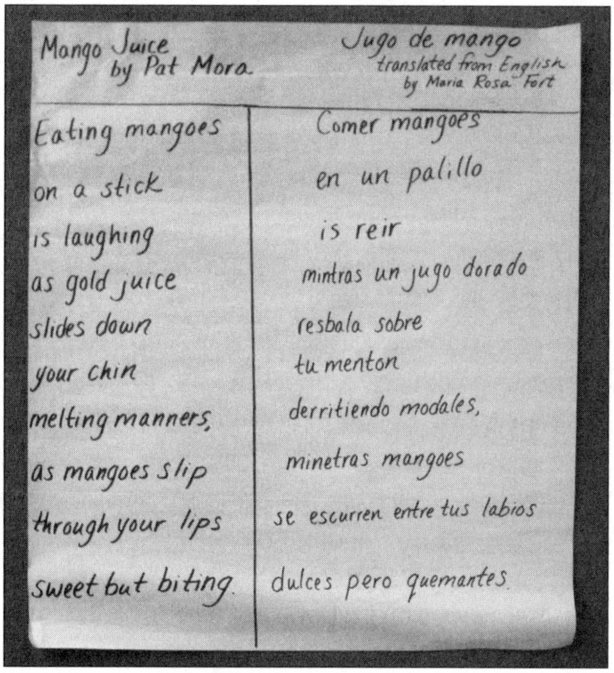

Figure 29-3. *"Mango Juice" by Pat Mora*

4 During the introduction, use pictures, concrete objects, or demonstrations that will help students understand the concepts and ideas in the text. Don't ask students to read any text they will not understand.

5 During the introduction and discussion of the text, help students use words they already know to help them understand new English words.

6 As a regular routine, ask students to identify any words or phrases in the text that they cannot understand. This will help students learn to monitor their own understanding,

provide feedback to you on the appropriateness of the text, and give you an opportunity to clarify concepts.

7 Include word work. One or two minutes of preplanned emphasis on particular words will help students become familiar with how English works, learn many new high-frequency words, and make connections among words (see Chapter 24 for more on this).

8 Rereading is not normally a part of guided reading, but teachers sometimes include it for various reasons—to help students recall information in the text, work on fluency, or revisit a tricky sentence. Including more rereading in your lessons for English language learners gives them more experience with English words and structure.

9 Create readers' theater scripts from some of the texts you use in guided reading (see Chapter 17). After reading the text, students will enjoy revisiting it again in readers' theater as they work on their interpretations.

The following introduction to a guided reading lesson is based on the beginning chapter book *Fox and His Friends* (Marshall) (see Figure 29-4). The teacher actively supports English language learners. Some expressions and particular words are repeated throughout the book in a very natural way. For example, the word *serious* is repeated enough times that the reader can easily derive its meaning, but most English language learners will need more explicit help in doing so. Expressions such as "you're joking" and

---

INTRODUCTION TO
Fox and His Friends

Ms. R.: Yesterday you started reading *Fox and His Friends.*

MARIA: It's really funny.

SAM: Yeah, a funny book.

Ms. R.: It is funny. What do you remember that was funny?

PETER: He thought she would tell her mom.

SAM: They climbed up on a high thing, a . . .

JESSE: Telephone pole.

CAROLINE: A telephone pole and then she didn't tell on him.

Ms. R.: Louise didn't tell on him and he said "You're okay, Louise." Remember that Fox wanted to go out to have fun with the gang? That's something to remember about Fox. He always wants to go and have fun with his friends and sometimes he calls them "the gang." Well, in the story your read yesterday, it was Saturday and Fox wanted to go out to have fun but Mom said he had to take care of Louise, his little sister. He said, "You're joking" to his mom. Have you ever said that?

MAURA: "You're joking" is like you are telling a joke not meaning what you say.

SAM: Yes, you could say "you're joking" when you mean "you don't really mean that!" But Mom was not joking, and Fox had to take Louise. In the next chapter, that is going to happen again. Mom has a surprise for Fox. He has to take care of Louise. What do you think he says?

STUDENTS: "Are you joking?"

Ms. R.: That's exactly what he says, but Mom means it. She is *serious.* Say *serious.*

STUDENTS: Serious.

Ms. R.: Find *serious* on page 28, where Mom gives Fox a serious look like this. [DEMONSTRATES A SERIOUS LOOK.]

PETER: So he has to take her again.

MARIA: I have to take my sister all the time.

Ms. R.: So you have that problem! Look on page 29. Fox takes Louise and they meet his friends Dexter, Carmen, and Junior. And he just tells them "Don't mind her." Do you know what that means?

CAROLINE: Don't tell her?

Figure 29-4. *Introduction to* Fox and His Friends

INTRODUCTION TO
Fox and His Friends (CONTINUED)

Ms. R.: You see that phrase at the bottom of the page. "Don't mind her," said Fox. He means, just don't pay any attention to her. Pretend she isn't even there. Turn the page. They run for the pool, and Dexter says, "Last one in the pool is a monkey's uncle!" A monkey's uncle? That's just something to say to get everyone to race to the pool. And they were having a wild time. But then they start talking about jumping from the high board, and that is really scary. Louise—remember he says "don't mind her" so they aren't paying much attention to her. Think what she did the last time Fox didn't pay attention.

PETER: She climbed up.

SAM: Maybe she's going to go up on the high board.

Ms. R.: Maybe, and she does something and Fox says, "Uh-oh," because it's trouble. Read this next chapter.

Figure 29-4. *Introduction to* Fox and His Friends *(cont.)*

"uh-oh" also appear several times in the text. This text is user-friendly, because most of these expressions appear more than once, giving the reader more opportunities to internalize them. The previous day the children had read the first chapter, "Fox in Trouble," and Ms. R., their teacher, had used many of these expressions in her introduction. In this introduction to "Fox Gets Wet," the second chapter, she helped students recall what happened in the first episode, because some of the language and vocabulary will be helpful in reading the second episode. She then had students repeat some of the language, and she explained some significant vocabulary words.

Ms. R. had also created a readers' theater script (see Figure 29-5) to use after the reading that shows Fox's dilemma in jumping off the high board after his little sister has done so. The script included language taken verbatim from the text. This rereading of *Fox and His Friends* provided the opportunity for students to process the language again, becoming more comfortable with the language structure, getting to know the English expressions, and internalizing the vocabulary.

Let's examine an introduction to a biography, *Pat Mora: Two Languages, One Poet* (Level P) (see Figure 29-6). This text has words in both English and Spanish and includes quite a few abstract words, such as *culture, tradition,* and *heritage.* Notice that the teacher, Mrs. S., provided a very rich introduction, visiting almost every page of the book, pointing out vocabulary words, and explaining concepts to the students. She used almost all of the difficult concept words in conversation so that students would have heard them right before reading the text. She did not spend a long time on the introduction, but she did provide a massive amount of support for meaningful reading. Look at the transcript of the discussion the guided reading group had after reading *Pat Mora: Two Languages, One Poet* (Leveled Readers) (see Figure 29-7). Notice that students were able to share their perspectives on the text and that they felt free to bring up confusions they have experienced.

INDEPENDENT READING

Becoming independent as a reader is essential for all students. English language learners need to use their systems of reading strategies every day, so you will need a wide variety of books in the classroom library. The materials English language learners read should be meaningful and interesting to them, so it is quite a challenge to fill the library. These are some suggestions for helping English language learners in their independent reading:

1 Evaluate the classroom library to be sure that you have a good selection of books on the levels that your students can read independently. Also, be sure to include some books in the first language of your students (even if they cannot read them very well) as well as books with familiar settings and themes. Include a variety of books on tape at the listening center.

2 In book talks, be sure to include below-grade-level texts that are (or are close to) age appropriate and have interesting content. This will facilitate students' independent choices when they need to read easier texts. Value individual reading conferences as they provide a valuable opportunity for the student to do most of the talking.

3 During individual interactions, provide more support for students by clarifying tricky vocabulary.

READERS THEATER SCRIPT:
"Fox Gets Wet," from Fox and His Friends

FOX: Hi.

CARMEN: Who's the kid?

FOX: Don't mind her.

DEXTER: Last one in the pool is a monkey's uncle!

FOX: This is wild!

DEXTER: Who will jump from the high board?

CARMEN: Not I.

JUNIOR: Not I.

FOX: I don't like high places.

CARMEN: Where's that kid?

FOX: Uh-oh.

DEXTER: How did she get up there?

CARMEN: We weren't watching.

FOX: Come down right *now*!

LOUISE: Come and get me.

FOX: You'll be sorry when I do!

NARRATOR: Fox climbed the ladder.

FOX: I don't like this at all.

NARRATOR: Fox felt his knees begin to shake.

DEXTER: Don't look down.

NARRATOR: Fox got to the top. Louise was not there. Fox felt all funny inside.

FOX: Uh-oh.

DEXTER: Go on and jump!

CARMEN: The kid did it.

JUNIOR AND LOUISE: Jump!

FOX: Everyone is watching!

NARRATOR: Fox closed his eyes. He jumped. He hit with a big splash.

DEXTER, CARMEN, JUNIOR, AND LOUISE: Hooray for Fox! What a fine jump!

FOX: Louise, I want to speak with you alone.

LOUISE: Uh-oh!

Figure 29-5. *Readers' Theater Script: "Fox Gets Wet," from* Fox and His Friends

---

4 During individual interactions, help students understand idioms that might be unfamiliar.

5 During individual interactions, help students use new-language structures.

6 During individual interactions, help students prepare—and sometimes rehearse—something that they can share with others about the text.

7 During individual interactions, talk about the meaning of the whole story—how the text "works" to provide a better foundation for understanding.

8 At the end of reading workshop, have students first talk with a partner before sharing something with the entire group.

We have provided transcripts of three reading conferences (see Figures 29-8, 29-9, and 29-10). In the first example, the teacher helps Alli, who is reading *Meet M&M* (Ross), understand the new word *pail*, which is just another label for a word she already knows. She also points out an expression, "take turns," and discusses its meaning. In the second example, the teacher helps Sari, who is reading *Dogs,*

learn a new word and its meaning. In the third example the teacher helps Sam by discussing how a complex text works and letting him know what to expect in terms of vocabulary.

SHARED/INTERACTIVE WRITING

Writing can greatly assist English language learners in taking on new vocabulary and language structures. You can use shared writing or interactive writing as part of your large-group minilesson or add it to a guided reading lesson to extend students' knowledge of English. As described in Chapters 27 and 28, interactive writing is used primarily in kindergarten and grade one because students are still learning the basics of writing and it is interesting and helpful for them to share the pen with the teacher. However, many teachers have found interactive writing helpful in supporting English language learners in later grades. Shared writing is basically the same process but is quicker because the teacher acts as the scribe and the group can produce more writing. Some suggestions for using shared/interactive writing with your English language learners are:

INTRODUCTION TO
Pat Mora: Two Languages, One Poet

[*Pat Mora: Two Languages, One Poet* is a biography of the Latino writer, Pat Mora. The biography begins with Pat's birth in El Paso, Texas, and continues to the present day.]

MRS. S.: Today, you are going to read a biography about a very interesting woman who is a poet. She writes in two languages, English and Spanish. I really like this book because Pat Mora—that's her name—writes wonderful poems and she used to be a teacher.

JAZMINE: I can write in two languages.

BRIANNA: So can I.

MRS. S.: Yes, lots of you can write in two languages and that is really special. You will read about how Pat Mora was born in El Paso, Texas, and that she loved to read when she was a little girl. She lived in a bilingual home. *Bilingual* is a word you have heard many times, but take a look at it on page 4. Find it and say it.

STUDENTS: Bilingual.

MRS. S.: Pat's family encouraged her to read. That means that they wanted her to read and helped her. You know how sometimes someone in your family has a special influence on you? Well, Pat's Aunt Ignacia used to tell her stories in both English and Spanish. Turn to page 6, and you'll see Aunt Ignacia. You know how to say *aunt* in Spanish.

BRIANNA: *Tia.*

MRS. S.: Yes, *Tia* Ignacia. Later, you'll find out that Pat wrote a story about her *Tia* Ignacia. Turn to page 7. There she is, being a teacher, but she did think about other careers, like being a doctor. She never dreamed she could have a writing career. Do you know what career means?

GRACIE: It means what you do—like being a teacher.

JAZMINE: A *career* is what you have when you grow up.

MRS. S.: Find "career" on this page. When Pat grew up, she had a writing career.

ALEX: I'd like to do that!

MRS. S.: Maybe some of you will have a writing career. Look at page 8. Do you see where it says the 1980s and 1990s, sort of like a date? That means the period of time all through the 1980s—1981, 1982, 1983, 1984, and so on. That's a way a writer has of telling you the period of time in Pat's life. You'll also find out that Pat wrote fiction and nonfiction besides poetry. We have been talking about those genres. Another thing you'll find in this book are words in Spanish. For example, you'll see the word *cat*.

STUDENTS: *Gato.*

MRS. S.: That's an easy one, but if you look at page 10, you will see *cancion verde*, which means *green song*. How can you tell from the print *cancion verde* is a Spanish word?

ALEX: It's written differently.

GRACIE: It's in italics.

MRS. S.: Those italics will signal to you to be thinking Spanish and you will also see some pronunciation guides right after the word that will help you know how to pronounce it. In this book, the writer talks about *traditions, culture,* and *heritage*—like a Mexican American heritage. All those things were very important to Pat and they are connected.

BRIANNA: Your culture is like songs, a food, and stuff your family does. It's traditions, too—like what you do at Christmas.

MRS. S.: Pat held Mexican American culture in deep affection. That means she really loved the traditions of her culture, and she wrote about them. She thought they were *unique*. That means they are special and different. You can see on page 15 that she even helped to start the *Dia de los Ninos, Dia de los Libros,* Children's Day, Book Day in English. She wanted to honor her culture and also reading.

e 29-6. *Introduction to* Pat Mora: Two Languages, One Poet

Pat Mora: Two Languages, One Poet (CONTINUED)

JAZMINE: *Dia* is *day* and *libros* is *books.*

MRS. S.: Do you know what *heritage* means?

JAZMINE: It's what you inherit? Like I got some money from my grandpa?

MRS. S.: It's a little like that, but it is really more than money. It's everything—the traditions, the culture—everything you have learned just from being part of your kind of family. Pat's family is Mexican American, so she loved her unique Mexican American heritage. So when you are reading *Pat Mora,* you will learn about her but you will also learn about her traditions and culture and Mexican-American heritage. Read the whole book and come back to talk about what you found most interesting about this bilingual writer.

Figure 29-6. *Introduction to* Pat Mora: Two Languages, One Poet *(cont.)*

DISCUSSION OF
Pat Mora: Two Languages, One Poet

MRS. S.: What did you find most interesting about Pat Mora?

BRIANNA: She's bilingual and she writes in two different languages.

ALEX: She's even published books in Spanish and English.

JAZMINE: There were Spanish words in it.

GRACIE: She liked to read and then she became a writer.

ALEX: I like it that she was bilingual.

MRS. S.: I agree. I really thought it was interesting that she could write and publish books in two languages. It's hard enough to write in one language! And as I said, I like it that she was a teacher, too. Do you remember some of the reasons why Pat became a writer? What do you think was important to her?

GRACIE: Well, she read a lot and that helped her know how to write poems and books.

JAZMINE: She liked to hear stories. I was wondering whatever happened to Aunt Ignacia.

ALEX: Probably she died because she was so old when Pat was a little girl, but Pat wrote a book about her so everybody remembers her.

MRS. S.: Anything else?

GRACIE: Maybe when she was a teacher she still liked to write and see what kids like to read. So when she got a chance, she just stopped and did her writing.

MRS. S.: Is there anything about Pat's biography that reminded you of your own life?

BRIANNA: I can talk and write in both Spanish and English, but probably not as good as she can.

ALEX: She's grown up!

GRACIE: When we wrote the memoir of someone in our family, that was kind of like Pat writing about her Aunt Ignacia.

MRS. S.: Yes, and it might be that someday some of you could publish one of your stories about a very interesting person in your family if you keep writing. Anything else?

JAZMINE: I didn't get how to say the words that were all spelled out.

MRS. S.: Did anyone else have trouble with the pronunciation guides on page 13?

ALEX AND GRACIE: Yes.

MRS. S.: Let's go over it quickly. [DEMONSTRATES AND CHILDREN PRACTICE.]

BRIANNA: The pictures are neat, too!

Figure 29-7. *Discussion of* Pat Mora: Two Languages, One Poet

SUPPORTING ENGLISH LANGUAGE LEARNERS DURING
INDEPENDENT READING:
Meet M&M (LEVEL K)

MR. L.: I see you are reading *Meet M&M*. Did you know that it is a series?

ALLI: No.

MR. L.: Are you liking it?

ALLI: Yes.

MR. L.: Read a little bit right where you are.

ALLI: [READS.] *"Rub-* . . . [TOLD: RUB-A-DUB-DUB] *M and M in the bug," they sang at bath time. They took turns piling bubbles in the yellow p-p-* [TOLD: PAIL] *that belong to both of them.*

MR. L.: *Rub-a-dub-dub* is a song that they were singing [SINGS A SNATCH OF THE SONG]. But do you know what a pail is?

ALLI: [SHAKES HEAD.]

MR. L.: It's a bucket like the bucket of markers we have. It holds things and has a handle. Can you see it in the picture?

ALLI: Yes. [POINTS.]

MR. L.: This yellow pail is holding bubbles right now, and it is going to be important later. And they "took turns." That means Mimi would put some bubbles in and then Mandy would take her turn and put bubbles in. They took turns. [TEACHER SETS OUT.] Read that last sentence again.

Figure 29-8. *Supporting English Language Learners During Independent Reading: Meet M&M*

SUPPORTING ENGLISH LANGUAGE LEARNERS DURING
INDEPENDENT READING:
Dogs

MRS. P.: How is your reading?

SARI: I'm reading about dogs.

MRS. P.: I like dogs. Is anything tricky for you?

SARI: This word. [POINTS TO PANTING.] It's like *pants*?

MRS. P.: You probably have not used that word before. Look at the picture. His tongue is out, and he is breathing in and out like you do when you run a lot. Start reading here, and you'll see how it helps the dog.

SARI: [READS.] *Dogs put their t-t-tongues out like this when they want to cool* [HESITATES] *down.* They are hot?

MRS. P.: Yes, when dogs are hot, they pant. This dog is panting and that helps him cool down.

SARI: Why?

MRS. P.: I'm not sure, but maybe it just gets cool air in.

Figure 29-9. *Supporting English Language Learners During Independent Reading: Dogs*

SUPPORTING ENGLISH LANGUAGE LEARNERS DURING
INDEPENDENT READING:
The Eye, the Ear, and the Arm (LEVEL Y)

Ms. K.: Are you enjoying *The Ear, the Eye, and the Arm*?

SAM: It's kind of funny but interesting. I can't figure out some of the things.

Ms. K.: What are you finding hard?

SAM: Well, it has robots and some kinds of words in italics that are hard to say, and I'm not sure about this [points to *microchip bird*]. And there are funny names.

Ms. K.: You have found what makes this book so interesting! Let me show you some things about it. Let's look back at page 2. Do you see where it says *September second, 2194*? This book is about people living far in the future, so there are going to be some scientific words. We know "microchips" because they are in computers. But in this book, the house cleaners and even the birds have microchips—they are robots made like computers. I wonder why?

SAM: Maybe there aren't any birds anymore.

Ms. K.: Could be. Here's another one, on page 8—a *holophone*. That's just what they call a telephone, but it's a robot, too. You are going to find some names from this place in the future, like this one. [POINTS TO MHONDORO.] These might be hard to pronounce. I don't even know how to pronounce it and that doesn't matter when I am reading silently. If I am reading aloud, I just give it a try. And the names might sound quite a bit different from names you know because the writer is trying to create a strange new world.

SAM: What's the "mellow"?

Ms. K.: Some names will tell what people do. The Mellower that you were reading about is a person who says poetry and makes people feel good. *Mellow* means feeling peaceful or good.

SAM: Yeah, he said good stuff about them and sort of put them to sleep.

Ms. K.: That's right, in a trance. He hypnotized them. Let me know when you want to talk some more about it.

Figure 29-10. *Supporting English Language Learners During Independent Reading:* The Eye, the Ear, and the Arm

1 After reading a text in guided reading, help students compose a group summary.

2 When reading a longer text in guided reading, construct a chapter-by-chapter summary to help students keep track of the story.

3 Use interactive or shared writing to make a list of idioms and their meaning.

4 After reading aloud, make a list of interesting language and/or new words with the students.

5 After reading aloud, have students write words or phrases to describe a character.

6 After reading aloud, ask students to construct their own group text on a related topic or with a similar structure.

7 Help students as a whole group or small group compose meaningful texts about themselves, their families, and their experiences, which they can reread to develop knowledge of written English.

8 Use interactive or shared writing to help students generate what they have learned (new information) from a text you have read aloud or one they have read in guided reading.

9 Use interactive or shared writing about characters or about themselves to help students understand comparative structures—for example, big and small or taller and shorter.

DIVERSE LEARNERS

If you are working with English language learners, you are fortunate. You are teaching the future of North America— probably the world. We have much to teach these children, but they also have much to teach us. In teaching English language learners effectively, you are stretching yourself as a professional; you are creating flexibility in your teaching to accommodate a wide range of learners. Many children, even if they are not English language learners, need this kind of flexibility and explicit instruction. The skills you employ in teaching these students will extend to all learners.

SUGGESTIONS FOR PROFESSIONAL DEVELOPMENT

LEARNING ABOUT LANGUAGE GROUPS

1 Convene an informal study group to discover as much as you can about the language and cultural groups to which the students in your school belong.

2 Begin with listing the variety, to create awareness of the richness in your school. If you have many different language groups, divide the assignments.

3 Use the Internet, library, and neighborhood sources to find out as much as you can about the particular language group. Make a list of easy-to-learn terms and/or phonetic representations of common names. If possible find some traditional poetry or other literature.

4 Have a series of lunch sessions in which you take a look at one group (or one set of information) at a time.

5 Discuss the implications for adjusting your instruction for this particular group of students.

6 Have everyone bring one planned lesson—independent reading minilesson, interactive writing session, interactive read-aloud session, or guided reading lesson—to your next meeting.

7 In groups of two or three, use the language and cultural information you have collected to discuss how you would adjust the lesson to support the particular English language learners you are interested in helping.

EACHING FOR FLUENCY ACROSS INSTRUCTIONAL CONTEXTS

Fluency gives language its musical quality, its rhythm and flow, and makes reading sound effortless.

—JO WORTHY AND KAREN BROADDUS

ency is a critical aspect of our students' development as ders, and we cannot assume they will develop it on their . Many children will require careful teaching in whole- up, small-group, and individual contexts.

CHING FOR FLUENCY

cessful teaching for fluent reading depends on using ropriate materials. For any reader at any level, there is inverse relationship between text difficulty and fluency; chances for fluency increase as the difficulty of the text eases.

You will need to analyze texts students are expected to d for themselves in relation to the factors that effect flu- y (see Chapters 6 and 7). You will also want to inten- ally select materials that help you demonstrate and h for fluency.

ECTING MATERIALS

ts are used for different purposes and in different ructional contexts. No one kind of text will support the ge of reading instruction needed at every grade level. ough readers should be able to read any good text with ncy, here are some things to look for when fluency is the l of your instruction.

ts with Memorable Language

guage that appeals to students and "rings in their ds" is likely to be remembered:

"Once upon a time in a deep, deep forest, there lived. . . ."

'I'll huff, and I'll puff, and I'll blow your house down."

'I do not like green eggs and ham."

"What's Christmas without presents!' said Jo."

"Harry Potter—the boy who lived!"

"It is a truth universally acknowledged that a single man in possession of a good fortune must be in want of a wife."

Chances are at least some of the above quotes instantly recall books to mind. When you read aloud texts that have memorable language, you are making larger units of language available to your students and supporting phrasing and fluency. They will remember how you put your words together while reading and hear those phrases in the same way. Once they have noticed and experienced memorable language, students will know to watch out for it. Soon, even younger children will be able to pick out language they like in the texts they read for themselves. Literature discussion will become increasingly enriched by the examples of memorable language students find in the texts they have read or heard.

Texts with Repeating Phrases

Listeners of all ages enjoy hearing texts with repeating phrases. The refrain from "The Gingerbread Man," "Run, run, as fast as you can," is a good example. When you are reading and rereading favorite texts, encourage children to join in on the refrains. They will experience what it feels like to say words in a fluent phrased way. When children read texts for themselves, a repeated phrase offers a kind of "lift": they can read it effortlessly because it is so easy to remember. This is not the same as simply memorizing the text. Cued by the print, they recognize these language patterns and internalize them.

Poetry and Rhyme

For young children, poems, chants, rhymes, and songs have natural qualities that help them become familiar with rhythm and tone. They are easy to remember and fun to repeat.

Text with Natural Language Patterns

It doesn't help to tell children to make their reading "sound like talking" if the text has little relation to what they understand as oral language. Of course, almost no written text conforms exactly to oral language, and readers do not expect that. If most of the language of a text is highly accessible to the reader, then some literary language is not a problem. The example below is a section of *Peaches the Pig* (Leveled Readers), a level D book that makes use of language that will sound natural to readers, as well as some dialogue:

1 Peaches saw some horses.
2 "Can I play with you?" she asked.
3 "Yes," said the horses.
4 "You can gallop with us."
5 But pigs can't gallop.
6 So Peaches went on.

Lines 1 and 5 are very close to oral language, as is the dialogue in lines 2, 3, and 4 (the assignment of dialogue is peculiar to written language). The last line, 6, has a literary quality different from oral language, and this sentence is repeated five times throughout the text. *Peaches the Pig* is a good example of a text that provides the support of natural language and a small amount of more literary language to stretch the reader.

Texts with Dialogue
Dialogue in texts needs to be read with expression that approximates talking. Most fiction texts have dialogue, which helps the reader know the characters. Here's an example:

"And it would be quite nice if you stopped jumping down Ron's and my throats, Harry, because if you haven't noticed, we're on your side."

There was a short pause.

"Sorry," said Harry in a low voice.

"That's quite all right," said Hermione with dignity. Then she shook her head. "Don't you remember what Dumbledore said at the end-of-term feast last year?"

Harry and Ron both looked at her blankly, and Hermione sighed again.

"About You-Know-Who. He said, '*His gift for spreading discord and enmity is very great. We can fight it only by showing an equally strong bond of friendship and trust—*'"

"How do you remember stuff like that?" asked Ron, looking at her in admiration.

"I listen, Ron," said Hermione with a touch of asperity.

"So do I, but I still couldn't tell you exactly what—"

"The point," Hermione pressed on loudly, "is that this sort of thing is exactly what Dumbledore was talking about. You-Know-Who's only been back two months, and we've started fighting among ourselves. And the Sorting Hat's warning was the same—stand together, be united—"

"And Harry said it last night," retorted Ron, "if tha[t] means we're supposed to get matey with the Slytherins, fa[t] chance."

"Well. I think it's a pity we're not trying for a bit of inter[] House unity," said Hermione crossly. (*Harry Potter and th[e] Order of the Phoenix,* J. K. Rowling, p. 223)

It's all there—Harry's anxiety, the rivalry between Ron [and] Hermione, Hermione's academic talent, integrity, and g[ood] sense, and their feeling about the Slytherins, resident[s of] another house at the school. Upper elementary and mi[ddle] school children's ability to recognize these voices and [the] meaning in them depends on their having recognized [dia]logue like "Can I play with you?" when they were youn[g].

Texts at Appropriate Levels of Difficulty
A gradient of text will be the most helpful tool in teach[ing] your students to read with fluency and phrasing. Cha[pter] 12 describes the importance of matching books to rea[ders] so that fluency is possible. If a text is too difficult, the[re's] no point in teaching for fluency. In independent read[ing,] students do not choose books by level, but your knowle[dge] of text difficulty will help you guide their choices. The [gra]dient will be of particular help in working with student[s in] guided reading, where you can provide some very exp[licit] instruction in fluency.

TEACHING FOR FLUENCY IN ALL INSTRUCTIONAL CONTEXT[S]
The lens of fluency can be applied in whole-group, sm[all]group, and individual settings. We have identified a n[um]ber of instructional techniques applicable in each of t[he] settings (see Figure 30-1). Some techniques, such as r[ead]ers' theater, can be used in both whole-group and sm[all] group settings by employing slightly different logis[tics.] Others can be used only when working with individuals, [as] individual interactions can take place in independent r[ead]ing or while children read the text during guided read[ing.] (Chapters 22, 24, 25, and 26 have more detailed discuss[ion] of some of these techniques.)

Whole-Class Instruction
Whole-class instruction includes interactive read-aloud as well as shared and performed reading of many [dif]ferent kinds of texts, including poetry. It also includes r[ead]ers' theater that involves the entire class. Here are s[ome] suggestions for supporting fluent reading through wh[ole-]class instruction:

Teaching for Fluent Phrased Reading

WHOLE-CLASS CONTEXTS	SMALL-GROUP CONTEXTS	INDIVIDUAL CONTEXTS
1 Demonstrations of fluent phrased reading.	1 Appropriate text levels.	1 Reading without finger pointing.
2 Discussion of the meaning of texts.	2 Avoidance of texts that are too difficult.	2 Prompting for fluency and phrasing.
3 Attention to aspects of fluency as demonstrated.	3 Practice of difficult language structures before reading.	3 Prompting for use of punctuation.
4 Demonstration of rereading to gain understanding.	4 Use of dialogue in a text.	4 Prompting for the use of meaning and language structure.
5 Attention to quality of language.	5 Repeated readings of texts.	5 Repeated readings.
6 Listening to books on tape or CD.	6 Shared or choral reading of some sections of a text.	6 Reading easy texts.
7 Shared reading of a common enlarged text.	7 Read-aloud of sections to provide evidence for discussion.	7 Rereading passages to demonstrate fluency and phrasing.
8 Partner reading of texts.	8 Self-evaluation of fluency and phrasing.	8 Using a card to guide the eyes or showing phrases with mask or fingers.
9 Readers' theater.	9 Incorporation of choral reading in guided reading lessons.	9 Attending to text features such as boldface and italics.
10 Choral reading of poems and larger texts.	10 Demonstration of how to read punctuation.	10 Attending to dialogue and refrains.
11 Memorization of poems.	11 Demonstration of fluent expressive reading.	11 Writing with fluency.
12 Voluminous reading of easy materials.	12 Attention to text features such as boldface, all capitals, or italics.	12 Recognizing words effortlessly.

ure 30-1. *Teaching for Fluent Phrased Reading*

Provide consistent, daily demonstrations of fluent phrased reading. During an interactive read-aloud, you place a model of fluent phrased reading before your students every day.

Draw students' attention to aspects of fluency as you have demonstrated them in each interactive read-aloud. Ask students to notice how you read a particular phrase, sentence, or passage and to comment on how you used your voice to show what the writer meant (or how you were thinking about the meaning).

Focus on the meaning of the text, and reflect the meaning with your voice. There can be no true fluency if the reader doesn't understand the author's message. During interactive read-aloud, talk with students about the meaning the author might have intended. Allow for different interpretations and demonstrate with your voice how you might read a sentence or passage to reflect those interpretations.

4 *Demonstrate rereading to gain fuller understanding.* During an interactive read-aloud or in shared reading, you can demonstrate that rereading is a useful tool to help clear up confusions or increase understanding. When questions arise, go back to a section of the text that has important information and reread it aloud one or more times. Ask students to listen carefully and notice your expression and tone; then ask them to talk about their thinking.

5 *Draw attention to language that evokes images or has a poetic quality.* If you genuinely enjoy the language of a text, you can draw students' attention to it during interactive read-aloud or shared reading. After they have learned to notice interesting language, you can elicit examples from them and then go back to reread these phrases or sentences. Sometimes you may even want to record very memorable quotes on a chart as a resource for writer's workshop. Noticing language will help students move away from robotic, word-by-word reading.

6 *Use shared reading of a common enlarged text.* The text can be a "big book," a chart, a story or informational piece created through shared or interactive writing, or an enlarged poem. Having all students look at the same text is helpful in teaching fluency and phrasing. For emergent readers, show children how to point crisply under each word because your goal is to help them learn to match word-by-word while reading (see Figure 30-2). After students have this behavior under control, you can vary instruction to help them understand phrasing and stress as described below:

Figure 30-2. *A Teacher Using a Pointer*

- Slide the pointer under the words, telling students to "read it all at once" or "read it like talking."

- Use a large card to mask part of the sentence and ask them to "read it all together" (for example, *said the pig*).

- Place temporary colored highlighting tape on phrases that you want them to emphasize or to read all at once.

- Underline words or make them boldface to help students learn where to place stress.

7 *Teach students to use partner reading.* Pair two students reading at similar levels and give them texts they can read easily. Stress that the goal is fluent phrased reading. They can read in unison, helping each other with forward momentum; "echo" each other (first one, then the other) reading a page; or alternate every other page.

8 *Use readers' theater to help students find the "voice" in dialogue.* Having students become characters or a narrator is an excellent and enjoyable way to support fluent reading. Biography can "come alive" when students speak as if they are the subject. (See Chapter 21 for a detailed description.)

9 *Engage the whole class in choral reading of poems and longer texts.* Encourage students to use their voices as instruments to convey their interpretation of the text. Often, they will need to discuss the meaning and come to a group decision about which words to stress and how to phrase the reading.

10 *Have students select some poems to memorize.* Memorization can be overdone, but it has a place, especially if there is some choice. Committing a poem to memory means that the student will have read it and said it aloud many times. It is always useful to have some powerful language in your head that you will perhaps remember and call on for the rest of your life.

11 *Provide many easy books in the classroom library that students can "sail through" for pleasure.* None of us would be fluent if we read only at our most challenging levels. For instructional purposes, we do want students to take on harder texts, but speed and fluency are built through effortless reading. Provide materials and time for students to engage in a large amount of easy reading.

12 *Create a listening center with books on tape or CD.* Even older students will enjoy listening to the wide array of audio books available today. Performing audio books has become an art, and many pleasurable hours of listening are to be had at the push of a button. When children listen to a text, they can give full attention to the story or the information. Listening to audio books does not take the place of independent processing or small-group instruction, but it provides an excellent demonstration of fluent, expressive reading. Students can also "read along" using a copy of the text. Younger students can read out loud, keeping up with the recorded voice. Older students can read silently.

Small-Group Instruction

SG Small-group instruction includes guided reading, literature discussion, and any other kind of gathering of students for a particular purpose. Guided reading is an ideal setting in which to teach for fluency because the texts are selected to match the readers and the situation is highly supportive. Literature discussion helps as well because students are prompted to go back to specific sections of the text and reread parts to support their thinking; they use the language of the text in their discussion. Here are fifteen suggestions for supporting fluency through small-group instruction:

Through careful text selection, assure that fluent phrased reading of the guided reading book is possible. If a text is too difficult for students to read smoothly, even with your support, they will not be learning to read with fluency. You will not expect a high level of fluency on the first reading of a more challenging text, because you want some problem solving to take place; however, you should hear some phrasing and stretches of fluent reading.

Be cautious about raising the difficulty level of texts. Be sure students can read a text fluently before moving on to a more challenging level.

In the text introduction for guided reading, have students say some of the difficult or unfamiliar language structures. It is highly beneficial for readers to have some of these phrases in mind, especially if they are difficult idioms or are part of dialogue.

Give the students background or literary knowledge they do not have so they will be familiar with it as they read. Having this prior knowledge will free up attention for fluency and phrasing.

Use dialogue as a way to support phrasing and expression. In guided reading and in revisiting a text for small-group literature discussion, dialogue is an important resource. Teach students to notice the quotation marks that signal dialogue and to see dialogue as a unit. They should always know who is talking even if the dialogue is not assigned (see Chapter 25). They should think about that character's voice and how it would sound. Choose texts that have exciting dialogue so that children can practice making their reading sound like talking. Sometimes texts that have a repeating refrain lend themselves to expressive reading.

6 *Have students notice, mark, and use phrases.* Make a list of phrases. Have your students read each phrase as a word group so they can hear a variety of word groups that go together. Do the same with some sentences, having students think about ways to group words in the sentence. Finally, do the same with a paragraph. Reread these texts a few times so your students can develop ease in concept of phrasing.

7 *In partners with one section of a previously read text, have students practice reading phrases and the other marking phrases on a reproduced or retyped copy.* After both partners have read, they can discuss why they paused in certain places to create phrases. Coming back to the group, students can compare their pausing and its relationship to the meaning of the text, noticing that there is probably more than one way to read a text in phrases. This will be particularly helpful to students who may read fast but slide right over the punctuation and reflect little phrasing.

8 *Include repeated readings as appropriate.* Engage students in repeated oral rereading. On first reading of a moderately challenging text, students will slow down to problem-solve and speed up again at the easy stretches. In repeated readings, the task will become much easier. If possible, find authentic reasons for rereading.

9 *Scaffold fluency through shared or echo reading of some sections of a text.* For students who have difficulty in achieving fluency, even on familiar and easy texts, incorporate some shared or choral reading into the guided reading lesson. After the text has been read and you are sure the students understand it, read the text yourself and have them follow along, reading with you. You will be reading fluently and the students will be reading along just behind you or they may echo your reading of a sentence or two. Reread the text several times. After several readings, you can drop out and let the students continue reading on their own. If they falter, come back in so that fluency is maintained.

10 *During discussion of the text, encourage students to provide evidence for their thinking by referring to and reading aloud sections of the text.* The more stu-

dents can refer back to the text, the more they will notice the language structure and the underlying meaning. After reading a text in guided reading, ask students to share a passage that really interests them, provides some surprises, highlights a writer's style, or contains an idea they found interesting. Let them read these passages aloud, bringing their interpretations to the text. The goal is to make others understand their thinking about the passage. All of this contributes to fluency and provides an authentic reason to read aloud.

11 *Have students evaluate their own fluency and phrasing.* After reading a text in guided reading, ask children to evaluate how the reading sounded. Demonstrate (and have individual children demonstrate) how to read so that it sounds like talking. Then let the children read the text again.

12 *Incorporate choral reading into guided reading.* Have children read in chorus a text or section of a text that lends itself to expressive reading. They can practice it several times and then present it to the class. You may want to divide the material into two parts so that pairs or threesomes alternate.

13 *Demonstrate how to read punctuation.* In the introduction to a text in guided reading or as you teach for processing strategies after reading, demonstrate to students how to "read the punctuation." Show children how to make your voice go down when you see a period, make your voice go up when you see a question mark, take a short breath when you see the comma (or dash), use emphasis when you see the exclamation point, etc.

14 *Model fluent reading when introducing text in guided reading.* Illustrate how to use phrasing and fluency and have students follow the print as you read. Then ask them to read (individually or in unison) the particular sentences that you demonstrated.

15 *Call attention to text features that cue stress and expression.* Authors often use text features such as boldface or italics to help readers access the meaning. In the selection below, the writer uses italics to help readers along:

"You're joking," said Fox.
"I am *not* joking!" said Mom.
And she gave Fox a look.
"Come on, Louise," said Fox. (*Fox and His Friends*, Marshall, p. 5)

The italicized *not* adds emphasis to Mom's comment and helps us interpret her look, which leads to Fox's resigned comment to Louise.

Individual Instruction

You have the opportunity to teach students independently in at least two contexts: independent work and guided reading. When other students are working in centers (primary grades) or reading or writing independently (intermediate grades and middle school), you will primarily be working with small groups of students in guided reading or literature discussion groups. But you can also move around the room at the beginning of the period or between groups having reading conferences with individual students.

In guided reading, when students are reading the text either softly or silently to themselves, you have the chance to interact briefly with individual students. Most teachers just ask students to read aloud at whatever point they are in the text. (All students are reading at their own pace.)

After listening for a few minutes, you can briefly do some individual teaching, which may include demonstrating, prompting, and reinforcing fluency. These individual interactions can be very powerful.

As you work with individuals, you can use almost all of the previous suggestions for teaching fluency in groups. You have the additional advantage of being able to tailor your demonstrations to the individual, holding the student's complete attention. Also, you can listen and prompt the reader in very specific ways. We end this chapter with a list of suggestions for working individually with students to support fluency and phrasing.

1 *Teach students to read without pointing to words with a finger.* Students will not be able to achieve fluent, phrased reading while they are sorting out the complexities of word-by-word matching, pointing to each word; too much slow, halting reading like this will eventually interfere with the development of fluency. Be sure that texts include easy words and concepts, as well as some repetition and predictability, so that students will be able to focus on matching the spoken words to the print. Notice whether in rereadings their speed picks up and they include some phrasing. As their eyes take over the process, encourage children to drop the finger, bringing it back only when needed for problem solving. As

about text level C, strongly encourage reading without following along with the finger. It should not be necessary for children to point when reading aloud for you. We suggest some prompts to support reading without a finger (see Figure 30-3).

2 *Prompt students to use fluent phrased reading.* While conferring individually with students during independent reading, prompt them to make their reading "sound like talking." (See Figure 30-4 for some suggestions.)

3 *Prompt readers to use punctuation.* While conferring with students as they read aloud, prompt them to notice punctuation. For example, they should use a falling tone at a period and a rising tone at a question mark.

4 *Prompt students to read for the author's message and to use language structure.* Consistently talk with students about the meaning of the text read and the sound of the language. Ask them to read aloud and "make your voice show what you think the author meant" or "make it sound like talking."

Encourage students to reread some texts or sections of a text. On first reading of a moderately challenging

text, students will slow down to problem-solve and speed up again at the easy stretches. In repeated readings, the task will become much easier.

6 *Have students read many easy texts in order to develop fluency.* Promote a large amount of easy reading. Provide time each day for students to read and reread texts. Developing fluency requires a lot of practice.

7 *Reread passages to think about the meaning and to practice fluency and phrasing.* As part of guided read-

---

Prompts to Support Reading Without a Finger

- Read it with your eyes.
- Make your eyes move forward or look ahead with your eyes.
- Hold your book on the edges.
- Read these words together. [Show a word group with a card strip or finger.]
- Put your thumb on the left edge and move it down the line to help you keep your place.
- Take your finger off the page and use your eyes to read.

Figure 30-3. *Prompts to Support Reading Without a Finger*

Demonstrating, Reinforcing, and Prompting for Fluent Phrased Reading

ASPECTS OF FLUENCY	FACILITATIVE LANGUAGE FOR TEACHING
Rate	- Listen to me read. Can you read it like that? - I'm going to read this faster. Listen to how I read this. - Read these words quickly. [Indicate.] - Can you read this quickly. [Indicate.] - Read this part again, faster. - Move your eyes forward quickly so that you can read more words together. - You read it faster that time.
Pausing	- Listen to me read this. Can you hear me take a little breath at the comma? - Listen to me read. Can you hear me take a little breath when I see the commas? - Take a little or short breath when you see a comma. - Take a little or short pause when you see the comma or dash. - Make a full stop at the period. - Make your voice go down when you see the period. - The period means your voice makes a full stop. - Make your voice go up when you see the question mark and stop. - Read it again and make a full stop. - Read the punctuation. - Set off the parentheses by stopping before and after them. - You took a little breath. - You made a full stop.

e 30-4. *Demonstrating, Reinforcing, and Prompting for Fluent Phrased Reading*

Demonstrating, Reinforcing, and Prompting for Fluent Phrased Reading (CONTINUED)

ASPECTS OF FLUENCY	FACILITATIVE LANGUAGE FOR TEACHING
Phrasing	□ Listen to me read this part. Now read it just like I did. □ Listen to how I put my words together. □ Can you make it sound like this? [Model.] □ Make it sound like talking. □ Put your words together so it sounds like talking. □ Put your words together so it sounds like the way you talk. □ Read these words together. [Indicate.] □ Read this much all together. [Cover part of print with card or finger.] □ Read it like this. [Model.] □ Now put these words together. □ These words make sense together. Read them together. □ Read this much. [Indicate.] □ Try that again and put your words together. □ You put your words together. Good reading. □ You made it sound like talking.
Stress	□ Listen to how I make my voice louder. □ Listen to how this sounds. [Model.] □ Make your voice louder when you see the big [boldface] print. □ Make your voice louder when you see words in capital letters. □ You made your voice louder when you saw the bold print [capital letters].
Intonation	□ Listen to me read this. Can you hear my voice go down at the end? □ Listen to me read this. Can you hear my voice go up at the question mark? □ Listen to me read this. Can you hear how excited my voice sounds? □ Make your voice go down at the period. Then stop. □ Make your voice show excitement when you see the exclamation point. □ Make your voice go down at the period. Make your voice go up when you see the question mark. □ Use emphasis when you see the exclamation point. □ Make your voice sound like the character is talking when you see the speech marks [talking marks, quotation marks]. □ Make it sound like the characters are talking. □ Make your voice sound like the character is talking. □ You made your voice go down [up]. □ Make your voice show that you understood what the author intended. □ You sounded excited when you read that part.
Integration	□ Listen to how I read this. Can you read it the same way? □ Make your reading sound interesting. □ Read it like the author is telling the story. □ Tell the story with your voice. □ How do you think your reading sounds? □ Make your reading sound smooth like this. [Model.] □ You made your reading sound good that time. □ You are reading it like you are telling a story.

Figure 30-4. *Demonstrating, Reinforcing, and Prompting for Fluent Phrased Reading (cont.)*

ing, ask students to reread texts or part of texts, emphasizing fluency and phrasing.

8 *Use a small card to prompt efficient eye movement.* If a child is having difficulty reading with fluency, using a small card as a temporary prop can prompt a shift in behavior. You can also use your thumb to cover words, revealing only a phrase and tell the reader to "read this much" or "read these words together."

  □ Slide the card over the text to move the reader along and force the eyes to read ahead of the voice. Ms. R. is moving the card from left to right across the text of *Fox and His Friends* so that the student will read the clauses "I don't have a suit" and "said Fox" as units. She keeps using the card for several more lines, dropping out as the reader gets the idea.

  □ Mask all of the sentence except the phrase you want the student to notice. Use this technique only on texts that are easy for students to read. It is probably more useful on lower-level texts where the print is not so dense, but you can use it with older readers by typing out double-spaced portions of a text.

9 *Prompt students to notice words in boldface, all capitals, and italics.* These text features help students understand how to emphasize particular words.

10 *Call attention to dialogue and refrains.* Often, a student will be reading a text that includes dialogue and/or repetitive refrains. These texts provide many opportunities to read with fluency and phrasing. When texts have dialogue or repetitive refrains, you can have the student "echo" you or read in unison with you.

11 *Involve children in writing.* As a child acquires literacy, fluency is important in both reading and writing. It is important for young children to practice writing the sequence of letters in a word and to do it with a minimum of attention. Becoming fluent in writing words helps children learn and remember them in every detail; these words then become resources. Through writing, children learn a lot about the relationships among sounds and letters as well as the patterns in words, all of which can transfer to reading.

Work for rapid, unconscious recognition of high frequency words. Rapid word recognition is essential for fluent reading. As you work with individuals, notice the degree to which they can effortlessly read high frequency words. Even very young children should quickly begin to read words like *the* and *it* without overt problem solving. Have the child write the word quickly several times and in different places, checking it with a finger. Have the child make the word with magnetic letters, take it apart, and remake it as quickly as possible, again, checking the word with a finger.

SUMMARY

You have a concept of fluent phrased reading and will need to assure your students have the same concept. When you allow your students to read dysfluently day after day, they may habituate ineffective reading. You will want to be active and persistent in teaching your students that they are reading language, not individual words. There will be numerous opportunities in the variety of texts you use in a day to teach for fluent phrased reading at all levels.

SUGGESTIONS FOR PROFESSIONAL DEVELOPMENT
ANALYZING THE DIMENSIONS OF FLUENCY

1 Convene colleagues from one grade level (or have several grade-level groups work together).

2 Have each person record one student reading for two or three minutes. (Most laptop computers or cell phones record well enough for this purpose.) Participants should also bring a copy of the text that the student has read.

3 Play each recording and use the Scale for Assessing Fluency in Chapter 8 and on the accompanying DVD to rate the reader and analyze strengths and needs. Rate them individually and then discuss the results.

4 Have the group look at texts from the leveled collection and:

  □ Find a text that matches the reader's current strengths.

  □ Examine the text to find features that will support fluency as well as opportunities to teach and prompt for fluency.

  □ Suggest some individual interactions with this reader that will support more fluent reading.

5 After the exercise, discuss:

  □ The role of the particular text in supporting fluency.

  □ The importance of persistence and consistency in helping children move toward more fluent reading.

CHAPTER THIRTY-ONE

EXPANDING VOCABULARY ACROSS INSTRUCTIONAL CONTEXTS

Learners move from not knowing a word, to being somewhat acquainted with it, to attaining a deeper, richer knowledge that allows them to use new words in many modalities of expression.

—CAMILLE BLACKOWICZ AND PETER FISHER

New words are added to languages every day! Our English lexicon (vocabulary) has been constructed over centuries by borrowing words from other languages and incorporating them into our own linguistic forms of expression. English is truly an example of a *combined* language, built as people from different parts of the world have interacted through trade and economics, agriculture and industry, wars and colonization. Added to that, as technology changes over the years, new words are created to label emerging concepts: *googled, blog, wikis, cyber, Internet.* Once created, these words take on new layers of meaning and are applied in many ways. We can talk about a microscope or a micro-miniskirt. We can describe a Teflon skillet or a Teflon politician. In addition, new cultural ideas and fashions add words or create new meanings for existing words: one generation may think of *heavy metal* as steel beams; the next generation listens to it as a form of music; and the next may form yet another definition.

Then, too, people create words all the time for the pleasure and expressive delight of doing so. Here are some great new words that have not made it into the dictionary yet but are floating around in oral language: *sniglet,* a very little bit; *chillax,* to really relax (even more than *chill out*); *ginormous,* really big; *phonecrastinate,* to wait to see caller ID before answering the phone; *onionate,* to offend someone with bad after-dinner breath.

The general lexicon and our own personal vocabularies are growing constantly. How do we keep up? We learn new words every day—either because we need them or because they are interesting—through talking, listening, and reading. Our language skills—oral and written—expand as we add new vocabulary. And using language effectively is critical to our quality of life. As proficient language users, we have systems for expanding our speaking, listening, reading,

and writing vocabularies. We know how to learn words.

The more we can help our students develop these learning systems, the more independent and proficient they will become as language users: one thing is certain, no one can learn all the vocabulary words they need by memorizing them one at a time. There are over 600,000 words in English (a number that is always growing), and we borrow words all the time from other languages. We must be able to pick up new words through our interactions with others and with texts (whether we listen to them or read them). This means developing a habit of noticing new words, becoming curious about them, and selecting some of them to become part of our own ways of using language.

SYSTEMS FOR LEARNING NEW WORDS

As word learners, we are curious, constantly seeking meaning. It is difficult to describe the many layers of cognition that take place in the sophisticated word learning system we as proficient readers have developed. We rarely meet word with which we are totally unfamiliar. Consider th sentence below:

> The concatenation of events surrounding his accomplishments resulted in the eponymous title, but he eschewed laudatory commentary, choosing, instead, modesty, the homiletic heart of his culture and society.

It has quite a few multisyllable words, and chances are yo know all or most of them. But let's suppose you don't kno any of these words:

- *Concatenation.* You know that this is a noun because the *-tion* ending, and you further know that it is deriv from a verb—probably *concatenate.* That's the w words work: think of *explain* and *explanation.* Yo might connect *concatenation* with *converge, conve tion, connect,* and think that it has something to do wi things coming together. This theory would be reinforc by the prepositional phrase *of events,* which indicates what might be coming together. Reading the rest of the sentence, you would realize that this *concatenation of events* has a result—the *eponymous title.* You would be right, because *concatenation* means a series of things or events regarded as causally or dependently connected.

Eponymous. This one is easier! You know that this is an adjective because it modifies the noun *title* and also because of the ending, *-ous,* as in *tremendous, fabulous, famous.* Further, you can connect the word with *synonym, antonym,* or *homonym,* with *nym* referring to name. Or you can connect it with *epidermal, epidemic, epidural, epilogue, epitaph,* with *epi-* meaning *on, over, upon.* So you would hypothesize that the word has something to do with a person ("his") who has accomplished a lot and as a result a title has been created from his name. You would be right, because *eponymous* means derived from the name of a person, real or mythical, who is associated with a place, period, movement, theory. For example, Pennsylvania was named for William Penn.

Eschewed. If you don't know it, this is harder. But context can still help. You know that something important happened in the first part of the sentence for which the subject probably got awards or praise. The word *but* signals that the subject is doing something unexpected relative to *laudatory* commentary; and if you have some connections to *laud* (possibly built from your experience in church) you know that it means some kind of praise or glory. So, possibly the person is refusing praise or glory for his accomplishments. You would be right because *eschewed* means to shy away from or avoid. It's related to *sciuhan,* to fear, akin to "shy."

Homiletic. This word is still harder, and the sentence gives little help, but you can actually comprehend the sentence without knowing the exact meaning of *homiletic.* Structurally, you know that a word ending in *-ic,* which means "of the nature of," is likely to be an adjective (*aerobic, frantic, angelic*). You would notice that *homiletic* modifies *modesty,* which is a moral value, and attach that to society. Knowing that modesty is valued in the individual's culture is enough to catch the meaning of the sentence. You might also make a

connection with *homo-,* meaning *human,* or *homily,* meaning sermon or a moralizing talk.

We don't encounter sentences like this very often, but it is obvious that our vocabulary systems allow us to deal with them. In figuring out the words in this sentence, we have used:

- Phonics to take the word apart and notice its components.
- Phonics to pronounce the word.
- Language syntax to notice the place and function of the word in the sentence (parts of speech).
- Word structure to notice endings and the way they mark the function of the word in the sentence.
- Meaning of the entire sentence to hypothesize meaning of individual words.
- Word connections to notice the roots of word.

What a complex series of thinking processes!

It should be obvious that we do not learn vocabulary from dictionary definitions alone. The strategic word solver accesses many sources of information simultaneously in a process akin to inquiry. The result is comprehension of text, a rewarding process and outcome. A reader engaged in the process over time will add many words to her or his reading vocabulary (and speaking vocabulary, although many words are seldom used in oral language). But simply seeing a word once and hypothesizing its meaning competently enough to understand a text is not enough. To make a word yours, you need either to read and interpret it many times or to use it yourself, which is the most effective way to acquire new vocabulary.

Proficient readers have acquired this way of learning to the degree that it is automatic and largely unconscious. As highly proficient readers who seldom meet unfamiliar vocabulary, we may even get a little rush of pleasure at learning a new word and telling others about it. That's a great position to be in, because we have plenty of attention to give to this new learning. But our students need our help in developing vocabulary learning systems.

CREATING COMPETENT ACQUIRERS OF VOCABULARY

The ultimate goal of teaching vocabulary is creating competent word learners. Vocabulary is learned through many different avenues, so it is important to keep in mind the kind of teaching that will help students learn and use new words. Competent vocabulary acquirers:

- Learn new words by encountering them in context during conversation and in their reading.

- Connect new words with those they already know, a process that accelerates and becomes more efficient as their vocabularies grow.

- Use word parts and their functions (for example, affixes, base words, and root words) to identify the meaning of new multisyllable words.

- Recognize when words have the same (or about the same) meaning (synonyms).

- Recognize when words have opposite meanings (antonyms).

- Recognize that words may have multiple meanings and use context to determine the precise meaning intended by the speaker or writer.

- Determine the meanings and pronunciations of words using dictionaries and other references.

- Understand figurative uses of words like similes and metaphors.

- Recognize connotation and denotation of new words.

- Use contextual clues and knowledge of language understand new words while listening and reading.

- Use new words in talk and writing.

There are many kinds of vocabulary, receptive and proc tive (see Figure 31-1). *Receptive vocabulary* includes words we understand when we hear or read them; *proc tive vocabulary* includes the words we use to commu cate as a speaker or writer.

It is important that as teachers we understand voca lary to be the words for which we know the meaning. ease and utility of our vocabularies vary by context. Th about the words that you:

- Can understand when you are listening to oral l guage.

- Can use in prepared, formal presentations.

- Can use in informal conversation.

- Do use in informal conversation frequently because t come to mind easily.

- Can recognize and understand in reading.

- Can use in writing.

- Can recognize any ironic, satiric, or figurative wa which they may be used.

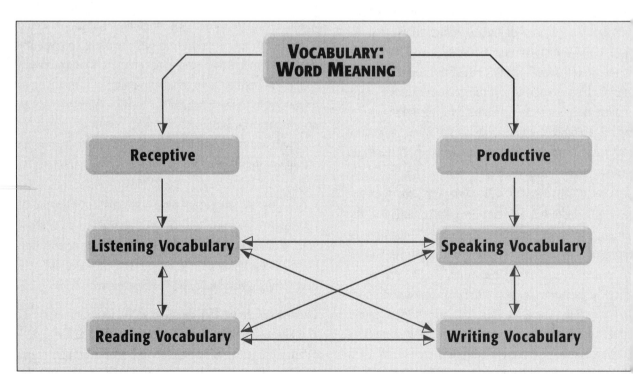

Figure 31-1. *Vocabulary: Word Meaning*

□ *Do* use in writing because they come to mind easily.

□ Can articulate a specific and clear definition for.

Chances are, you will have different but overlapping words in each of these categories. If you think about a word that you truly know, you realize that you can pronounce it, read it, write it, understand it in many different contexts, understand how its meaning may change subtly, use it in a decontextualized way, be explicit and articulate in describing its meaning, understand any figurative or ironic uses the word may have. The list of words you truly know might be quite a bit shorter than your total vocabulary, but it would still be a very long list, containing more words than you could possibly have learned through "vocabulary lessons."

Beck, McKeown, and Kucan (2002) describe a continuum of knowing a word. These "shades of knowing" encompass several dimensions, as indicated in Figure 31-2.

Some words we may never know at the highest level (and don't need to). Other words simply do not lend themselves to a rich understanding. But even many of the simple words we learned in childhood take on new meaning as we have experiences with language. For example, our understanding of the word *school* began when we were toddlers and was at first confined to the preschool or elementary school we attended. Now we might think of *school* in a lot of other ways:

□ He is a gentleman of the old school.

□ He has a schoolboy's sense of humor.

□ She is well schooled in her topic.

□ I learned it in the school of hard knocks.

□ He is a professor in the School of Law.

□ As an artist, she belongs to the school of Impressionism.

□ She schooled herself in patience.

□ We were schoolmates.

□ We'd better go back to the schoolroom until we get it right.

□ I saw a school of whales from the boat.

□ We must go to school on the mistakes of our predecessors.

Language is infinitely fascinating. Our vocabularies have been built over years of encountering, noticing, understanding, and using words in many different contexts. They represent knowledge that we carry with us all our lives. They are the means of unlocking the deep-meaning systems through which we understand the world and communicate with others. Literacy rests on (and adds to) this foundation of oral language knowledge.

THE ROLE OF VOCABULARY IN COMPREHENSION

The important role of vocabulary in reading comprehension has long been recognized (Heimlich and Pittelman 1986; Chall, Jacobs, and Baldwin 1990; Graves 1987, 2000). One's vocabulary level is highly predictive of one's level of reading comprehension. Words are how we label our concepts and ideas. This prior knowledge is key to understanding what we read, so vocabulary is a good predictor of how well the reader will comprehend a text (Nagy 1998, 2000). But comprehension transcends vocabulary; it is about much more than just the words. Meaning is communicated by the way words are presented according to the rules of grammar. It is about the deep and symbolic meaning of a text as a whole.

Effective vocabulary instruction has a positive impact on reading comprehension (Nagy and Herman 1987). It is therefore crucial to ensure that vocabulary instruction is not neglected. Moreover, good vocabulary instruction can help to narrow the gap between children of higher and lower socioeconomic groups (Biemiller 2004). Citing studies that show

Shades of Knowing a Word[1]

□ Understands and can use the word in context or in isolation; knows multiple meanings, connotations, and figurative uses when appropriate.

□ Understands and can use the word in some contexts and knows one or two definitions of it.

□ Knows one definition of the word and can use it in some contexts, but has difficulty applying it with precision and accuracy.

□ Knows the word in one context only and is unable to use it flexibly.

□ Has some familiarity with the word, like knowing whether it has positive or negative connotations.

□ Has a hypothesis as to the meaning of the word based on the context.

□ Remembers hearing the word before.

□ Does not know the word and has not heard it.

[1] Adapted from Beck 2002, p. 10.

Figure 31-2. *Shades of Knowing a Word*

vast differences in vocabulary knowledge among higher- and lower-socioeconomic-status first graders, Beck, McKeown, and Kulcan (2002) makes a strong case for robust vocabulary instruction. High-socioeconomic-status first graders know about twice as many words as lower-socioeconomic-status children. This difference tends to persist throughout schooling; for example, high-performing high school seniors know four times as many words as low-performing seniors. Researchers have identified vocabulary limitations as a major factor in the "achievement gap" between higher-income and disadvantaged students (Biemiller 1999).

RESEARCH ON VOCABULARY INSTRUCTION

Most of us remember vocabulary instruction as learning words and definitions and then being tested either by: (1) writing definitions; (2) matching words and definitions; or (3) matching words and synonyms. It may or may not surprise you that this kind of instruction is largely ineffective.

Nagy (1988) has criticized two kinds of traditional instruction: (1) learning words by studying definitions and (2) learning words primarily through experiencing them in contexts. Although he recognizes that dictionaries are very useful, Nagy identifies several problems related to this traditional method of vocabulary instruction. First, "definitions alone can lead to only a relatively superficial level of word knowledge. By itself, looking up words in a dictionary or memorizing definitions does not reliably improve reading comprehension" (pp. 4–5). Definitions are not always good or helpful, and they may not be appropriate to what the student is trying to read. They are narrow and do not provide enough information (or provide irrelevant information). Reading comprehension depends on wide and rich knowledge rather than just definitional knowledge. While recognizing the value of teaching words in context, Nagy also criticizes contextual approaches as seldom providing enough information to come to a precise definition; in addition, a single context is seldom enough to help a student learn a word. He recommends a combined approach that provides rich definitions, many examples and illustrations, and an array of specific techniques.

Research indicates that reading is an important way to acquire vocabulary incidentally. Nagy & Herman (1987) as well as Stanovich (1986) found that students who read more have larger vocabularies. And steps can be taken to decrease the incidental and random way readers acquire words by helping children learn some efficient vocabulary acquisition strategies that they can apply before, during, and after reading (Baumann, Kame'enui, and Ash 2003). For example, children can learn strategies for deriving the meaning of a word from context or using word structure to identify the base or root word and its function in the sentence.

Ruddell (1994) agrees that a combination of approaches is the most likely way to help students improve their vocabularies. For example, readers do need strategies for deriving the meaning of words from context, but they also need to realize when they do not comprehend and know how to search for meaning (Graves 1997). Finally, readers need some specific knowledge of words to provide a broad base for more learning.

Beck, McKeown, and Kulcan (2002, p. 8) describes three tiers of words, a quite useful concept in planning vocabulary lessons:

1 First-tier words are very simple and basic. They are mostly learned without instruction. Examples are *summer, family, hungry.*

2 Second-tier words appear frequently in the vocabularies of mature language users. They are not connected to a particular domain but are pervasive. Examples are *fascinate, unfortunate, enthralled, mentioned.*

3 Third-tier words are specialized and are often related to scientific domains. They are usually learned through content area study and appear very infrequently in the language. Examples are *ectoplasm or cabriolet.*

Beck's advice is to focus intentional vocabulary instruction on the second-tier words and help children make connections among words so that when learning a word like *unfortunate,* they also have an idea of the meaning of words like *fortune, fortunate, fortunately, misfortune.* This makes sense, as long as the vocabulary instruction is meaningful to students and takes place alongside rich encounters with words in texts through interactive read-aloud, shared reading, guided reading, literature discussion, and independent reading.

After synthesizing scientific research on how vocabulary is learned, the National Reading Panel reported that "(1) most vocabulary is learned indirectly, and (2) some vocabulary must be taught directly" (*Put Reading First* p. 34).

It seems necessary to incorporate both direct lessons on vocabulary and intentional conversation about words into all the contexts in which students encounter words.

Beck also suggests promoting vocabulary development during read-aloud by asking open-ended questions that prompt children to talk about and make connections among the ideas in the story, then following up with direct, interactive vocabulary instruction that gives children a chance to contribute their own experience with words.

SPECIFIC VOCABULARY LESSONS AND INTEGRATED INSTRUCTION

What does all this research on vocabulary instruction mean to us as teachers? We suggest the following:

1 We need a menu of dynamic and effective options for teaching vocabulary directly.

2 Vocabulary instruction needs to include the intentional conversations we have with students about word meanings in all reading and writing contexts.

3 Vocabulary instruction should be highly interactive so that students participate in constructing meanings.

4 Vocabulary instruction should be integrated so that students can make connections across instructional contexts.

WHAT TO TEACH IN VOCABULARY INSTRUCTION

The first decision is what to teach in your vocabulary instruction. Whether you are integrating vocabulary instruction into reading, writing, and word study lessons or planning specific vocabulary lessons, you need to select words and categories of words to teach based on your students' needs and experience.

Beck, McKeown, and Kulcan (2002) estimate there are about seven thousand word families (related words) in their category of second-tier words, or about seven hundred words to learn each year from kindergarten through ninth grade. They suggest that learning as many as 400 words each year will contribute significantly to comprehension of texts. It is obvious that word learning must be strategic and accelerative rather than pure memorization!

You certainly will not be picking 400, or even 100, words out of the air as you plan lessons. Rather, you should think about the types or categories of words you want your students to learn over time. Figure 31-3 is a list of different

types of words that all students should have in their vocabularies by the end of middle school or junior high school.

The shaded portions of the figure show the estimated grade levels at which these words might be taught *in explicit vocabulary lessons*. (Some of these areas are broad; it will take several years to develop an in-depth knowledge of a word category and become familiar with many examples.) Of course, students may well meet examples of all types of words in their reading and writing at any level—and they may bring them to your attention or you to theirs.

You can begin with the easy examples that students encounter often in reading or want to use in writing. Students will already know examples that fit into the category. What they are really doing is connecting words that are alike and learning the characteristics and functions of words in that category. These actions are strategic: once a category is identified and understood, it is easier to learn new words that fit within it. You may want to use sorting activities or lists to help children understand the different categories of words, but it may be more useful to work with words in context. After all, the only reason to recognize these categories is to use them in interpreting oral and written language.

Early Concept Words

This category includes very specific sets of labels that illustrate central concepts: colors, numbers, days of the week, months of the year, and seasons. These words are essential for functioning in society, and they are usually learned before a child enters school or in kindergarten. You may have English language learners who know these concepts very well but do not yet know the English labels for them.

Labels

This category includes the familiar words we use every day. These groups of related words increase over time and can be related to simple content area study. Some examples are:

- Family words: *father, mother, sister, brother, aunt, uncle, grandmother, grandma, grandfather, grandpa, cousin, godmother, godfather.*
- Neighborhood words: *street, sign, shop, houses, sidewalks.*
- Food words: *pizza, carrots, bread, ice cream.* (Food words can be subcategorized: *desserts—ice cream, cake, cookies, fruit, candy.*)
- Animal words: *birds, dogs, cows, horses.*

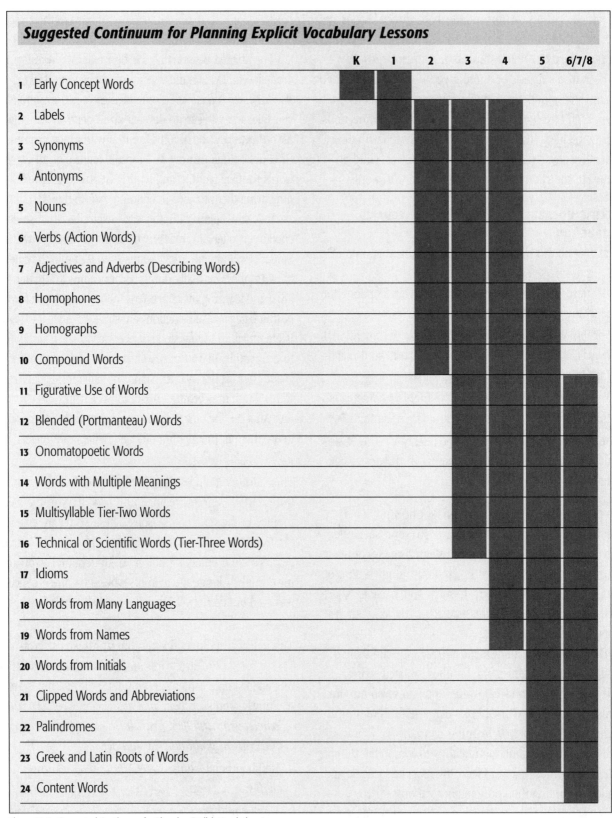

Figure 31-3. *Suggested Continuum for Planning Explicit Vocabulary Lessons*

Synonyms

Synonyms are words that mean the same or almost the same. Have children explore simple synonyms after they have encountered them in reading and writing and discussed them informally. For example, you may have read a selection aloud and explained a word by using a synonym. In interactive writing, you may have asked children to choose between two synonyms as they composed pieces. For beginning lessons, children should be working with words that they understand and can read. A sample lesson on synonyms is presented in Figure 31-4.

You may want to generate lists of words and write them on charts as resources that students can use to make their writing more interesting, for example:

- Words for *good tasting*: *great, delicious, excellent, marvelous, tasty, mouth-watering.*
- Words for *movement*: *walked, ran, crept, strolled, raced, marched, hiked.*
- Words for *said*: *cried, shouted, whispered, answered, replied, called.*

Antonyms

Some words mean about the opposite and are called *antonyms*. Increasing children's awareness of antonyms will help them understand the meaning of words in sentences. They will gradually expand the number of contrasting pairs of words they know. These connections create a richer understanding of the meanings of words and help children expand their vocabularies. Work with antonyms after children have encountered words that have opposite meanings in their reading and writing and discussed them informally. For example, you may have read a selection aloud and explained a word by saying it is the opposite of another word, or in shared reading or interactive writing. You may have used words to indicate opposites, like *wet* and *dry*. It is important that children can read and know the meaning of the words you use. A sample lesson on antonyms is presented in Figure 31-5.

Nouns

Nouns are words that represent a person (which in the abstract may also be an animal), a place, or a thing (which can be something highly abstract, such as hope). We learn nouns all our lives through new experiences. Students

---

Sample Lesson on Synonyms

1 Suggested language: "Today, you are going to be learning about words that mean the same or almost the same." If children have previously learned about antonyms, you might want to remind them that they know words that mean the opposite, like *yes* and *no* or *day* and *night*. The words they will be working with today mean the same.

2 Present ten words on word cards (for example, *begin/start, fix/mend, earth/world, high/tall, shut/close, end/finish, happy/glad, little/small, pick/choose, fast/quick*). Use examples children understand and can read. You can substitute other pairs of words that children know. You may want to make a chart of synonyms to which you can gradually add more pairs.

3 Suggested language: "This word is *begin*. What is this word?" Children respond *start*. "What do you notice about these words?" Children may say that they mean the same. You will always want to use the word in a sentence, or invite the children to use it in a sentence.

4 Suggested language: "Words that mean the same are called *synonyms*. You say that word." Have children say the word *synonym* several times, perhaps clapping on each syllable. Accept approximate pronunciation of the word. You might want to tell them that *synonym* and *same* start with the letter *s*. It will take many examples for children to know and remember this technical word. It is more important for them to internalize the concept.

5 Present and discuss the other pairs of words, matching them in a pocket chart. Use some of them in sentences to test whether they mean about the same or are *synonyms*.

6 Tell children that they will be playing Concentration with synonyms. Unless children are very proficient at reading and already know some synonyms, limit the game at first to the words you have presented in the lesson. (You might want to include duplicates of the words to make the game more complex.) They take a set of cards and lay them all flat on the table. They take turns turning one card over, reading it, then turning over another and seeing if it matches. The player with the most pairs wins. After playing the game, each child writes two pairs of synonyms on a piece of paper.

re 31-4. *Sample Lesson on Synonyms*

Sample Lesson on Antonyms

1 Suggested language: "Today you are going to be learning about words that mean about the opposite."

2 Present ten words on word cards (for example: *big/little, bottom/top, dry/wet, ending/beginning, fat/thin, girl/boy, go/stop, give/take, good/bad, hot/cold, in/out, left/right, love/hate, night/day, noisy/quiet, on/off, rich/poor, sad/glad, slow/fast, stop/start, up/down*). Be sure that children understand and can read the words. You can substitute other pairs of words that children know.

3 Suggested language: "These two words are *big* and *little*. What can you tell me about these words?" Children will respond that the words mean the opposite. Illustrate this simple contrast by asking children to use the words in sentences.

4 Suggested language: "Words that mean the opposite or just about the opposite are called *antonyms*. You say that word." Have children say the word *antonym* several times, perhaps clapping on each syllable. Accept approximate pronunciation of the word. It will take many examples for children to know and remember this technical word. It is more important for them to internalize the concept.

5 Present and discuss the other pairs of words, matching them in a pocket chart. Use some of them in sentences to test whether they are antonyms. You may want to make a chart of antonyms.

6 Tell children that they will be playing Concentration with antonyms in the word study center. Limit the game at first to the words you have presented in the lesson, especially if children lack experience with antonyms. (You may want to include duplicates of the words to make the game more complex.) They take a set of cards and lay them all flat on the table. They take turns turning one card over, reading it, then turning over another and seeing if it matches. The player with the most pairs wins. After playing the game, each child writes two pairs of antonyms on a piece of paper.

Figure 31-5. *Sample Lesson on Antonyms*

---

should recognize nouns as a category by second or third grade. They have been learning simple and concrete nouns since they were babies, but over time they stretch this category to include more abstract concepts.

Verbs

Verbs are sometimes called "action words," because they tell what a noun or pronoun does. As students become more sophisticated, they will develop a more complex understanding of verbs: active and passive verbs or nouns that become verbs and vice versa.

Adjectives and Adverbs (Describing Words)

Adjectives and *adverbs* modify nouns and verbs and are sometimes called "describing words" to make the concept easier to understand. A sample lesson on adjectives is presented in Figure 31-6.

Homophones

Words can *sound* the same but look different and have different meanings. Once children grasp this important principle, they can begin to develop examples and form categories for these *homophones*. When they use a homophone, they have to think carefully about meaning and spelling. Be sure that you use sentences that all children can repeat and understand to help them develop contextual meaning for each of the words.

Work on this concept after children know the conventional spelling of many high frequency words and are independently writing their own texts with many conventional spellings and good attempts at unfamiliar words. Simple charts like the one in Figure 31-7 will help student remember the distinction between homophones. This kind of chart can also be used in an independent activity, with words on cards backed in Velcro or placed in a pocket chart.

Homographs

Words can *look* the same but mean different things in context and sound different. Grasping this important principle and having a large repertoire of examples of *homograph* will help children check their own understanding more carefully. It will also help them be more accurate in pronunciation when reading aloud and will untangle confusions.

Homographs are often confusing to young readers. Although the words are spelled the same, in reading them children must pay close attention to context because they are pronounced differently and have different meanings relative to the words that surround them in continuous text. To understand this concept, children should have a great deal of experience reading words in context. Awareness of the syntax of written language, developed by hearing it read aloud, will help children figure out homographs. Be sure

Sample Lesson on Adjectives

1 Suggested language: "Here is a great page from one of the books you have really liked to hear me read, *The Gruffalo*. The writer, Julia Donaldson, is really good at helping us know that the mouse describes the gruffalo so well that the other animals could imagine what he looked like. She uses a lot of describing words. Let's read it together."

2 Read the excerpt in a shared way.

3 Suggested language: "In the first line the writer talks about a *creature*—that is a noun. It's the gruffalo, and he has *claws*, which is another noun. What word does the writer use to describe the gruffalo's claws?

4 Children respond with *terrible*.

5 Ask children to look for other words in the excerpt that are describing words.

6 End by making a list of describing words and what they are describing.

> *But who is this creature with terrible claws,*
> *and terrible teeth in his terrible jaws?*
> *He has knobbly knees and turned-out toes,*
> *and a poisonous wart at the end of his nose.*
> *His eyes are orange, his tongue is black;*
> *He has purple prickles all over his back.*

DESCRIBING WORD:	WHAT IT TELLS ABOUT:
terrible	claws
terrible	teeth
terrible	jaws
knobbly	knees
turned-out	toes
poisonous	wart
orange	eyes
black	tongue
purple	prickles

Figure 31-6. *Sample Lesson on Adjectives*

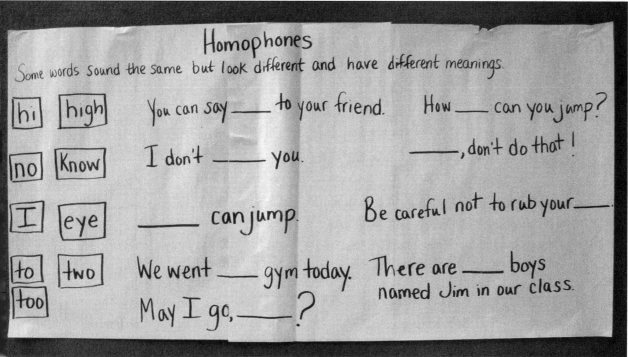

Figure 31-7. *Homophones*

these experiences are in place before working with homographs in isolation. Even adults often mispronounce homographs before they figure out the context, so don't expect immediate accuracy. The important thing is for students to understand the principle and notice homographs in sentences. You can use a chart like the one in Figure 31-8 to remind students of the concept of homographs and help them practice the different pronunciations.

Compound Words

Compound words are a combination of two smaller words. Sometimes the meaning of the whole word is clear from the component parts (*earring, earthquake, campfire, jellyfish, keyboard*). Sometimes the meaning is metaphorical (*brainstorm, skyscraper*). Sometimes the meaning is historical; for example, *turnpike* roads (called *pikes*) had moveable barriers consisting of a horizontal pole or bar that had to be turned in order to gain access to them. Students will enjoy creating families of compound words that have similar components (see Figure 31-9).

Once they understand the concept of what a word is and can identify word boundaries, children can easily identify and read simple compound words such as *into* and *sidewalk*. As they grow more familiar with the concept, they will find the historical origins of words interesting. They can also make a collection of words that are used together so often that they might someday become compound words (*day care*, for example). Also, they can learn to recognize and use hyphenated compound words, for example *jack-in-the-box* or *blue-line*.

Figurative Use of Words

One of the more abstract understandings that students need to develop is the figurative use of words. Writers use figurative language, such as similes (comparisons using *like* or *as*) and metaphors (comparisons without *like* or *as*), to create sensory imagery and make their writing more interesting. Understanding how these comparisons are created and used is basic to helping children comprehend the literary language that they will meet in texts. Figurative language is especially challenging to English language learners as are idioms and colloquialisms. Poems like "December Leaves" (see Figure 31-10) can be an important vehicle for helping them move from the literal to the figurative meaning of words.

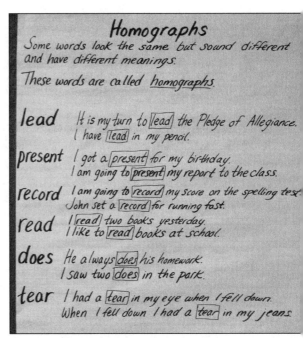

Figure 31-8. *Homographs*

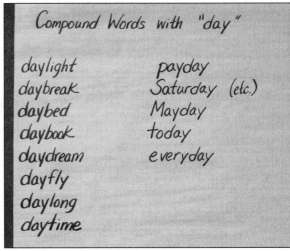

Figure 31-9. *Compound Words with "Day"*

Blended (Portmanteau) Words

Words like *horrific* and *horrendous* have been coined combining existing words (*horrible, terrific, tremendous*). Students can think about why people would have combined words to communicate a more nuanced meaning; in the process, they will begin to understand how words have evolved. *Internet* is a great example. They can collect these neologisms (see the chart in Figure 31-1 they may even enjoy becoming neologists themselves creating new words.

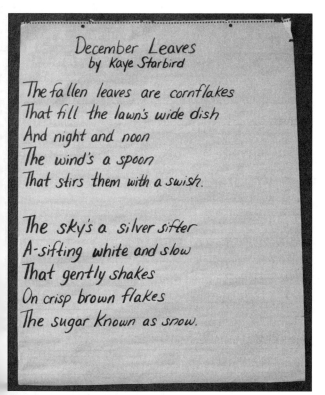

Figure 31-10. *December Leaves*

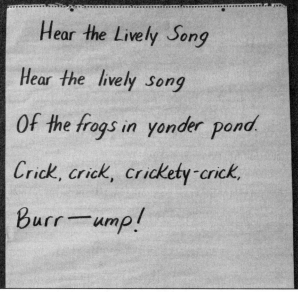

Figure 31-11. *Blended Words*

Onomatopoetic Words

Words that mimic sounds are a very enjoyable part of language, and readers will meet them everywhere in fiction, nonfiction, and poetry. Understanding and using simple onomatopoetic words will help students enjoy reading and make their own writing more interesting. As they encounter complex literature and poetry, understanding this category of words will be important. Children will learn such words very early by way of onomatopoetic verses such as "Hear the Lively Song" (see Figure 31-12). Later, they can formalize their knowledge of this kind of poetic language and recognize it in many different contexts.

Content Words

Children learn content words all the time, in various domains:

- Weather words: *hot, cold, wet, rain, wind, snow, weather, cloud, sun, heat, mild, sleet, fair, drizzle.*
- Transportation words: *airplane, truck, motorcycle, train, ship, jet, flight.*
- Economic words: *stores, shops, buy, sell, sale, price, money.*
- Technical language related to animals: *insects, antennae, coat, fur, life cycle.*

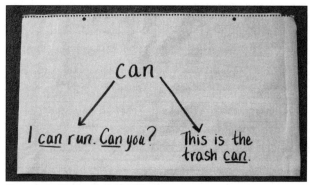

Figure 31-12. *Onomatopoetic Words in "Hear the Lively Song"*

Figure 31-13. *Words with Multiple Meanings*

535

Your state curriculum standards or district guidelines across the grades will provide many different categories of these content words. Students will also meet them in the informational texts they read at every level.

Words with Multiple Meanings

Words can have more than one meaning. Once children learn this concept, they will begin to figure out which meaning is meant in a particular context. For beginning lessons, be sure that children already know two or more meanings for the words you highlight, either because they use them in oral language or have heard them in texts you have read aloud. Charts like the one shown in Figure 31-13 will help you illustrate the various meanings.

Multisyllable Tier-Two Words

Many of the types of words mentioned in this section qualify as Beck's tier-two words. Because these words are likely to appear frequently in a wide variety of texts, they are very useful to students. You can identify tier-two words in texts students are reading and select those related to which they already have some conceptual understanding. For example:

- *Reality* is a word students can access by understanding the word *real*.
- *Detest* is a word for an idea students may understand as *hate* or *dislike*.
- *Mutter* is a word for an idea students may understand as *talking softly* or *talking in a way that is hard to hear*.

Those words become available to students because of what they already know but allow them to describe the concepts with more precision.

Technical or Scientific Words (Tier-Three Words)

Highly technical words appear very infrequently in the language and are connected with specific domains of knowledge (examples of these words include *technocracy, aerate, proboscis, baleen, tautological, transpiration, enzyme*). They are usually encountered during deeper study of the content areas and are not really useful for general vocabulary lessons. Instead, work to help readers use context and readers' tools such as glossary when they read in content areas. Studying Greek and Latin roots will give students better access to many of these words.

Idioms

Idioms are single words or phrases that have taken on meanings peculiar to themselves. The original meaning of some of these phrases, such as "raining cats and dogs" or "my dogs are tired," have been lost; others ("don't bug me," for example) may be easier to interpret. Children will no doubt encounter idioms in the dialogue they read in fiction, and sometimes in nonfiction as well. Understanding what an idiom is will help them be alert to the use of this particular kind of metaphor and look for a meaning that is not obvious.

By the time children enter grade three, they will have encountered many idioms in both conversation and print but may not recognize them as language forms. They will recognize some idioms immediately but may need to be taught others. Notice how easily your students recognize and pick up the meaning of idioms in their reading and/or use idioms in oral language or writing. When they have an implicit knowledge of some good examples, you can teach a formal lesson. You may want to make a class collection of idioms, which will be especially helpful to English Language Learners.

Words from Many Languages

Many English words come from other languages. Young students can easily understand that food names such as *taco* and *spaghetti* come, respectively, from Spanish and Italian. As they grow more sophisticated, they can learn to research the origins of many words; for example, that *triage* comes from the French word *trier*, to sift, and means any system of assigning priorities of medical treatment based on the urgency or chance for survival.

Words from Names

Many words in English are derived from names of people and places. Once that concept is understood, children will enjoy creating lists of words and their name origins. For example, the *sandwich* was named for the English Earl of Sandwich, who created the concept of the portable meal consisting of a slice of meat between two pieces of bread. The *hamburger* was named after Hamburg, Germany, where it was created. *Pasteurized milk* is the result of a process invented by Louis Pasteur.

Words from Initials

Today, acronyms created from the first letters of a compound term are commonplace. Many of these are in such common use that they are known as words, although technically they are not. *Sonar* (*so*und *na*vigation *r*anging) just one example.

Clipped Words and Abbreviations

Clipped words are shortened forms of longer words: *automobile* has become the more efficient *auto,* for example. Students will enjoy discovering these words and learning the longer words from which they came. Also, in English many convenient abbreviations are in everyday use (*Mr., Mrs., St.,* for example). These conventions are easily learned and speed communication.

Palindromes

Palindromes are just plain fun. While not an essential area of vocabulary, they can increase students' enjoyment of and interest in words. A *palindrome* is a word that reads the same backwards or forwards (*madam,* for example). (The word *palindrome* comes from the Greek word for *wheel,* which turns backwards and forwards.)

Greek and Latin Roots of Words

Knowing the Greek and Latin roots of many English words is extremely helpful in understanding multisyllable words. For example, the root *aud* has to do with hearing and helps us understand words like *audible, audiotape, inaudible, auditorium, audiovisual,* etc. A root like *urb*, which means *city,* help us understand words like *urban* and *suburban* (which also contains the root *sub,* meaning *under*). Logic is required to use Greek and Latin roots to derive the meaning of words. Once the process is learned, it is a powerful strategy for accessing words.

PLANNING INTERACTIVE VOCABULARY LESSONS

To capture student interest, you will want to consider a number of approaches to teaching interactive vocabulary lessons in which you explicitly introduce new vocabulary words and strategies. Most of these techniques are appropriate beginning in second or third grade. These lessons can occur anytime during the day, take only a few minutes, and help students become more flexible in connecting words.

Word Webs

Make a schematic diagram of alternatives for specific words. For example, you might place the word *said* in the middle and then branch out with all the words you could use instead—*told, exclaimed, cried, replied, asked, answered.*

Word Analogies

Demonstrate word analogies (*happy* is to *sad* like *big* is to *little*) and help students generate their own. You can make a game out of analogies, with one group proposing a set of words that are related in some way and other groups coming up with pairs of words that are related in the same way (synonyms, antonyms, smaller to larger, subsets, etc.). This activity will become increasingly sophisticated as students learn more, and will be helpful in preparing for tests.

Word Substitution

Put several sentences on a chart and help students think of synonyms of nouns, verbs, adjectives, or adverbs in the sentence. You do not need to use the names for parts of speech. Just ask students, "What other word could we use here?" Change one or two words and invite students to discuss any changes in meaning (large or very subtle) that they notice.

Words in Context

Help students understand how context affects the meaning of words. Look at several sentences that exemplify different meanings of words. (Choose the sentences from children's literature selections you have previously read aloud or other material students have previously encountered.) You don't have to be too restrictive about the difference in meanings. For example, you could have them think about the differences between *running* down the street and a *runny* nose or *running* for election.

Use previously read children's literature selections to help students realize that words can be used figuratively. Write words on a chart and specify in two columns (or more) the various meanings—literal and figurative.

Explore word connotations. For example, what does it mean that "foxes are *sly.*" Here, *sly* means clever but also *sneaky*. What are the differences between *clever* and *sly*? Point out these word connotations while reading aloud to students. Connotations have grown up around the way words have been used over the years—both formally and informally.

Word Sorting

Word sorting helps students form hypotheses about the properties of written words (Henderson 1990; Templeton and Bear 1992; Zutell 1996, 2000). You can demonstrate principles by showing students a collection of words and asking them to discover connections and contrasts. After your demonstration, students can sort words on their own. Older students can write their sorts in categories in a word study notebook. For a more detailed description of using word sorts, see *Guiding Readers and Writers* (Fountas and Pinnell 2000). Categories for sorting can be "open," which means students create their own, or "closed," which means the categories are preidentified.

There are a large number of ways to sort words that have implications for vocabulary development:

- Sorting nouns, verbs, adjectives, and adverbs.
- Sorting words into semantic categories: weather, family, transportation, mammal, reptile.
- Sorting words by base word or root word.

Semantic Mapping

In semantic mapping, children use their prior knowledge (which has been shown to be very important in comprehension; see Heimlich and Pittelman 1986, and Nagy 1988) to create diagrams showing how words are related. The simple forms of semantic mapping shown in Figure 31-14 are appropriate for second or third graders. (A word web is a form of semantic mapping.)

Semantic mapping can be connected to texts that you read aloud to students. (Start the map before reading and extend it afterward.) Place a key word, perhaps one that represents a theme, on a chart and then invite students to brainstorm words they know that are related. For example, the joy of music and its universal healing quality, even in the face of tragedy, is a major theme of *The Harmonica* (Johnston 2004); a semantic map based on this text is shown in Figure 31-15. Students brought their own knowledge to this semantic map, but they also probed the literary work to discover the many ways the writer embroidered the concept by using precise vocabulary. They discovered that the writer was using many concepts related to music as symbols for love and courage.

Semantic Feature Analysis

Semantic feature analysis takes semantic mapping a step further. "Semantic feature analysis is one of the instructional methods that deals most explicitly with relationships among word meanings" (Nagy 1988, p. 14)

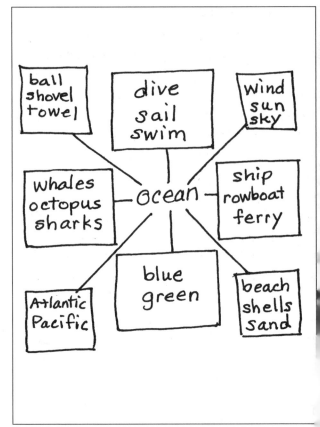

Figure 31-14. *An Example of Semantic Mapping*

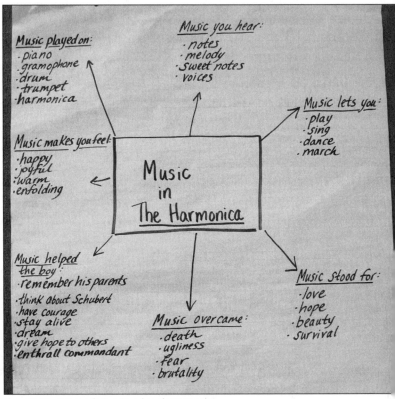

Figure 31-15. *A Semantic Map Based on* The Harmonica

Semantic Feature Analysis

	FOR MANY PEOPLE	FOR ONE OR A FEW PEOPLE	HAS WHEELS	GOES ON LAND	GOES ON WATER	GOES IN THE AIR	BIG
car	–	X	X	X	–	–	–
boat	–	X	–	–	X	–	–
airplane	?	?	X	X	?	X	X
bus	X	–	X	X	–	–	X
motorcycle	–	X	X	X			
helicopter	X	X	X	X	–	X	X
bicycle	–	X	X	X	–	–	–
ship	X	–	–	–	X	–	X
ferry	X	–	–	–	X	–	X
seaplane	?	?	–	–	X	X	X

Figure 31-16. *Semantic Feature Analysis*

In it, students consider what (and whether) certain pertinent features apply to related words and make a grid depicting the results (see Figure 31-16). The activity can be conducted in a very open way, adding words and adding features.

Comparison/Contrast

You can use semantic mapping to connect and compare words. This activity is especially helpful to students in revealing the subtle "shades" of meaning that writers convey in using different words. In *My Rotten Redheaded Older Brother,* Patricia Polacco uses several different words to describe how characters talk. By teasing out the subtle differences between these verbs (see Figure 31-17), students were able to consider the writer's craft.

Hierarchies

Many word meanings are categorical. You start with a higher-level concept, such as *feelings,* and then move to subcategories. You can help students think of these vocabulary words in relation to each other (see Figure 31-18).

Linear Relationships

Sometimes it is instructive to organize words along a continuum so that students can see the precision with which they communicate meaning. Figure 31-19 arranges words related feelings in increments from very negative to very positive.

STRESSING THE IMPORTANCE OF CONCEPTS

Whatever techniques or approaches you use in direct vocabulary instruction, they will not be effective if students do not understand the concepts the words represent. Learning new words means learning new concepts, sometimes very subtle. For example, *predator* means something subtly different from *hunter,* and it is important to help readers understand these subtle differences. Whenever possible, bring the underlying concepts to light through discussion and examples, and draw students' attention to words during meaningful reading and writing experiences.

INTEGRATING VOCABULARY INSTRUCTION

In addition to specific lessons, you will want to integrate vocabulary instruction into all your students' reading and writing experiences. It is especially important to make sure that younger children attend to the meaning of words when they hear stories and engage in shared reading. We provide suggestions for thirty-five ways to integrate vocabulary instruction, explained briefly in Figure 31-20.

Interactive Read-Aloud and Literature Discussion

Reading aloud does not take the place of explicit vocabulary instruction, but it is essential for word learning. If your students have limited vocabularies, you need to increase the

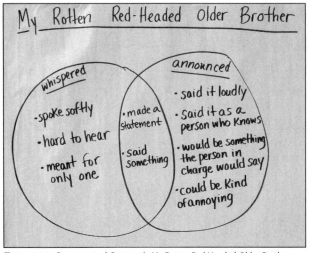

Figure 31-17. *Compare and Contrast in* My Rotten Red-Headed Older Brother

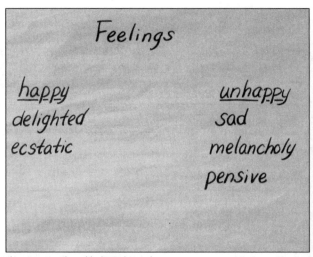

Figure 31-18. *Hierarchical Word Meanings*

Figure 31-19. *Relationships Among Words*

amount of reading aloud you do, as well as your intentional conversation that highlights word meanings. From kindergarten throughout elementary school, reading aloud to children and discussing the meaning of what they have heard are critically important ways to expand their oral vocabularies (which strongly impacts their reading and writing vocabularies). Read aloud every day and provide time for discussion. During an interactive read-aloud, you can stop at an interesting word and explain the meaning or go back to certain words that you sense students are having difficulty understanding.

In literature discussions, you can call special attention to several words from the text, inviting the children to talk about them and make connections to what they know. You can also introduce intentional conversation that includes words students will be reading or have read. Ask students to bring up words that they find tricky so you can clear up confusions. As a follow-up activity, you can use any of the techniques listed previously in this chapter.

Shared Reading

Shared reading (see Chapter 21) is an excellent opportunity to help students expand vocabulary, because you are working with a text that will be very familiar to them. With the high level of support you provide in shared reading, even young children can become familiar with sophisticated vocabulary. For example, a teacher using *The Promise* (Hughes) for shared reading helped students understand the word *commanded* (see Figure 31-21). Notice that the teacher not only explained the word but also modeled using it and invited students to use it.

Another interesting way to develop vocabulary through shared reading is to have students try to substitute synonyms or antonyms for words in a familiar text. In *The Promise,* suppose you asked students to substitute a word for *little* in this text:

Princess Ana heard a little voice.
"I'll help."

You might discuss with students the implications—for the personality of the possessor of that voice and for the story— of substituting words such as *tiny, quiet, loud,* and *noisy* for the word *little.*

You might also use a highlighter (marker or tape) to draw children's attention to words that you then discuss with them. Use any approach described in this chapter to

Thirty-Five Ways to Integrate Vocabulary Instruction

Interactive Read-Aloud and Literature Discussion	▫ Increase the amount of text that students encounter through read-aloud. ▫ Draw attention to the meaning of words before, during, and after reading aloud to students. ▫ Use intentional conversation that includes words students will be reading or have heard you read. ▫ Use interactive vocabulary lessons to deepen understanding of how a writer has used a word to create meaning in a specific text. ▫ Have students discuss words that they found interesting or didn't understand.
Shared Reading	▫ While rereading a familiar text, mask a word and have students predict it, talking about its meaning in the sentence. ▫ Select words from a familiar text and have students locate and discuss their meaning. ▫ Mask words and substitute alternative words (synonyms or antonyms) within a text and discuss the way the substitution changes the meaning, even if only slightly. ▫ For a text produced through interactive or shared writing, have students illustrate pages, thinking about the meaning of the words. ▫ Highlight words within a text and help students connect them with other words that have a similar meaning.
Guided Reading	▫ Use new words in conversation during the introduction to the text. ▫ Discuss and locate new words during the introduction to a text. ▫ Help students connect new words to concepts they already know. ▫ For difficult and new ideas that are central to understanding the text, teach *both* the concept and the word. ▫ Teach students specific strategies for deriving the meaning of words from context. ▫ Teach and then prompt students to monitor their own understandings as they read. ▫ Use word webs or similar interactive vocabulary techniques after students have read new words in a text. ▫ Use semantic feature analysis to compare the words in the text and their relationships. ▫ Have students revisit the text to discover hierarchical relationships among concepts. ▫ Have students keep lists of new and interesting words in their reader's notebooks.
Independent Reading	▫ Ensure a large variety of texts for independent reading. ▫ Encourage students to use new words as they write about their reading in their reader's notebooks. ▫ During sharing, have students give examples of interesting new words they have noticed.
Word Study	▫ Teach students to make connections among words by meaning. ▫ Teach students to make connections in flexible ways—word part, part of speech (noun, verb, etc.), affixes, sounds, meaning. ▫ Have students play Lotto, Concentration, and other games using synonyms, antonyms, homophones, and homographs. ▫ Use poems to help students learn about synonyms, antonyms, onomatopoetic words, nouns, verbs, adjectives, adverbs, and metaphors. ▫ Teach many different kinds of words. ▫ Help students sort words by meaning. ▫ Help students understand the structure of a word and its relation to meaning. ▫ Have children make "sentence pictures" to illustrate the meaning of words.
Writing Workshop	▫ Draw attention to the writer's selection of words in mentor texts used for minilessons. ▫ Encourage students to use new and interesting words as they revise their own writing. ▫ In minilessons, create charts that help students make connections to words they want to use in their writing. ▫ While conferring with students about their writing, help them substitute synonyms to convey the precise meaning they intend.

Figure 31-20. *Thirty-Five Ways to Integrate Vocabulary Instruction*

The Promise—*Third Reading*

TEACHER: You did a great reading of *The Promise!* Let's look at a word from this book. On page 4 it says,

"Oh, no!" said Princess Ana. "My ball!" "Help me! Now!" she commanded. But no one came.

Think about the word *commanded.* What do you think that means?

SARI: She wanted them to do it.

LISA: She told them to do it.

JAKOB: It means that she was the boss.

TEACHER: That's right. The princess was the kind of person who really wanted other people to do what she said. She *commanded* them. That means when she said it, they better do what she said. She was the boss. She was the *commander*.

Figure 31-21. *Vocabulary Focus–Shared Reading of* The Promise–*Third Reading*

elaborate on the meaning of words. Take every opportunity to connect words in a text by meaning.

Guided Reading

In guided reading, it is important to explain new words during the introduction to the text, but don't overdo it. Preteaching words can take up a lot of time and interfere with reading the text. You will want to have students locate, visually examine, and think about the meaning of a few essential words before reading the text and to revisit others in the discussion afterward as appropriate. Help students connect new words to their current understanding of concepts. If a new idea is key to understanding the text, teach *both* the concept and the new word. If a text has a very large number of words that you need to bring to student's attention, it is probably too hard.

Guided reading is an excellent setting in which to help students develop word-solving strategies from context. You might select a word that students might not know but could figure out from context (*terrible,* for example). Ask students to talk about what the word means within the context and help them learn how to use context to discover meaning. Show students how to monitor their own understanding, and prompt them to realize when they do not understand. Have students revisit the text to discover word relationships. After reading, you can do some explicit teaching

for vocabulary as part of the extension if you feel more is needed, using any technique listed in this chapter, such as word webs or semantic feature analysis. Students can use reader's notebooks (see Chapter 27) to record their word exploration.

Independent Reading

Bottom line—it is extremely important to provide a large variety of texts for students to read independently. In your minilessons you can draw attention to interesting words, and you can also invite children to offer examples of new words when they share their reactions to their reading. In conferences, probe students' understanding of the words in texts they are reading and take the opportunity to explain and discuss word meanings. Build interest in noticing and thinking about the meaning of words in all reading.

Word Study Lessons

Word study is a highly productive area in which to boost students' vocabulary knowledge. Here you can provide specific instruction on various aspects of words, many of which will impact students' ability to grasp the meaning. You can teach students to make connections among words in many ways, including word parts, word function (noun, verb, adjective, adverb), word structure (for example, words that end in *-ed* or *-ing*), affixes, sounds, meaning, and compound words. As an extension of word study lessons, students may play a variety of games (Concentration, Lotto, word searches) that focus on word meanings.

Through the "buddy study" spelling system (Pinnell and Fountas 1998), you can help students make connections between words by meaning. When students are working on their spelling words over several days, have them spend some time connecting their spelling words with other words that mean the same or opposite or are related in other ways (categories, word roots, etc.). This will help students become more flexible in their understandings about words.

Writing Workshop

In writing workshop you are helping students express their own thinking in writing. That means they should be able to use words effectively, and to do that they must understand their meaning. Even though a writing workshop does not include direct vocabulary instruction, you can draw attention to words in a way that helps students learn more about them. Writers must think deeply about the precise meaning conveyed by words. In minilessons using mentor texts and in writing conferences, you can draw attention to the writer's choice of words as one important characteristic of effective writing, encourage students to use new and interesting words in their own writing; and create charts that illustrate synonyms and other connections that will help students bring to mind a greater variety of words to use in writing.

EVIDENCE OF VOCABULARY LEARNING

A key to effective vocabulary instruction is discovering evidence that your students are learning new words. To learn 400 new words each year, they must add to their vocabularies every day. Vocabulary building is not a linear process. We constantly enrich our vocabularies by discovering richer meanings for words we know and by making connections among words. Do your students:

1 Show interest in words?

2 Notice and comment on new words that they meet in texts?

3 Actively search for meaning when they meet a new word?

4 Understand and search for new meanings for words that they meet in context?

5 Demonstrate strategies for solving unfamiliar words when they meet them for the first time in oral or written language?

Consider alternative definitions of words in the search for meaning while reading?

Use new words in discussion?

Use new words in writing?

Try to use more interesting words in their writing even if they are unsure of their spelling?

Show evidence of a growing body of known words?

SUMMARY

On average, students need to learn about three thousand words per year, if not more. An extensive vocabulary will serve students well, as it is an important contributor to reading comprehension. You have numerous opportunities to teach for vocabulary knowledge implicitly and explicitly throughout the day. As we discussed, most of it can be acquired through extensive reading, because the texts will be richer than oral language. Specific teaching within each reading context will help your readers learn how to learn word meanings and build a rich bank of known words. You will also want to spend time using the specific teaching approaches we described in this chapter. In addition, you may find the variety of graphic organizers provided on the DVD that accompanies this book useful in your vocabulary instruction.

SUGGESTIONS FOR PROFESSIONAL DEVELOPMENT

ANALYZING OPPORTUNITIES TO BUILD VOCABULARY KNOWLEDGE

1 Bring colleagues together to examine a group of texts with the lens of vocabulary development. Just about any group of high-quality texts will work.

2 Have colleagues work in groups to identify opportunities in these texts to help students expand vocabulary.

3 Have each group select several interesting words and then brainstorm how they would guide conversations to help students understand them.

4 Then have them select one of the activities in this chapter that will help students learn about the *category* of words.

FINAL THOUGHTS

This book covers a wider age and grade range than any of the other volumes we have produced. Writing it enabled us to read and reread hundreds of books in a variety of genres. We thought deeply about what these texts demand of children along a continuum of learning. We found that all texts, from simple to complex, require readers to think beyond literal meaning. It has been a pleasure for us to explore these texts and to think, talk, and write about them. The process has reinforced the idea that as teachers we must also be readers who enjoy the full benefits of being literate people.

It was also helpful and enlightening to consider how children grow over the years in their ability to understand and think about texts. The idea of thinking *within, beyond,* and *about* texts from very early through highly sophisticated reading has helped us see learning as a lengthy developmental process supported by good instruction. Teaching for comprehending and fluency must be integral to all literacy teaching. When we believe that reading is a process of making meaning using all available sources of information, we keep readers connected to the meaning of texts all the time. If every year, in all instructional contexts, *we teach through the lens of comprehending,* students will have spent many thousands of hours seeing and hearing powerful demonstrations, engaging in effective whole-group lessons and small-group instruction, processing texts independently with understanding and fluency, and talking about books with others. Every child, every single day, should have the opportunity to read many texts with understanding and fluency. Within a community of readers and writers, that can happen.

We hope that you, too, enjoy your own life as a literate person. We believe that is the foundation for teaching others. Find time to read the books that your students enjoy. You'll find that many of them are better than adult books! Continue to read in ways that enhance your life, and share that process with your students. The more you can share your own thinking and literary experiences with your students, the more they will value the reading and writing in their lives as essential.

Teacher Resources: Description of Print Materials on the DVD

GRAPHIC ORGANIZERS

"A graphic organizer is a visual diagram that shows the relationships among a number of ideas. Use graphic organizers to help students see the important interrelationships in the information they are reading or to become aware of the way authors have structured a text. These insights help students with their own writing as well as reading." (*Fountas & Pinnell, Guiding Readers and Writers, Grades 3-6: Teaching for Comprehension, Genre, and Content Literacy,* Heinemann, 2001, p. 441.

For every type of graphic organizer you use:

- Select it carefully to serve your goals for comprehending.
- Use the form first with the whole group or a small group—demonstrating it on a chart or projected image.
- Demonstrate the form several times before expecting students to use it independently.
- Have students work as partners before expecting them to fill out a type of organizer independently.
- Be sure that there is discussion using the graphic organizer so that students can see how it helps them (rather than simply as an assignment).

In this collection you will find graphic organizers that will support your students' thinking in the following ways.

Graphic organizers can help readers record, remember, and reflect on their thinking about reading. For example:

- Record their responses to particular aspects of a text (language, character, story problem, etc.) for later discussion or writing.
- Record interesting information and thinking over the reading of a text to support memory of details that serve as evidence for thinking.

Graphic organizers can help readers make connections across texts. For example:

- Notice elements (topics, language, themes) that are similar across texts.

- Use information from one text to help in understanding another text.
- Connect characters by trait across texts.

Graphic organizers can help readers analyze texts to notice structure. For example:

- Understand the organization of a fiction text—beginning, middle, and end.
- Understand the rising and falling action of a fiction text.
- Represent the way events and information are presented.
- Notice, use for understanding, and learn from the underlying structures in nonfiction texts: compare/contrast, temporal sequence, problem/solution, description, cause/effect.

Graphic organizers can help readers think analytically about literary elements in fiction. For example:

- Notice and use character traits. Infer characters' motives, feelings, and reasons for actions.
- Understand the setting, its characteristics and influence on the story.
- Understand the development of the plot.
- Understand the problem and solution.

Graphic organizers can help readers learn to analyze texts to notice the writer's craft. For example:

- Notice the language that writers use and record responses to it.
- Notice how writers begin and end their stories.
- Notice language that evokes sensory images.
- Notice how writers show movement through time.
- Notice and record how writers reveal characters.

Graphic organizers can help readers notice and learn new vocabulary from reading texts. For example:

- Notice and record new and interesting words during or after reading.
- Notice and record new meanings for known words during or after reading.
- Notice and record evidence within the text that helps define them.

TOOLS TO SUPPORT THINKING–GENERAL

These graphic organizers can be used to support thinking in many different ways, including the full range of strategic actions.

General: Relating Ideas (Web 1)
General: Relating Ideas (Web 2)
General: Thinking and Evidence (Personal Knowledge and the Text)
General: Supporting Thinking (Evidence from the Text)
General: Distinguishing Fact and Opinion
General: Thinking Over Time
General: Recording Questions ("I Wonder")
General: Quick Sketch
General: Making Predictions (Fiction)
General: Making Connections Between Texts
General: Recording Thinking
General: Recording, Thinking, Providing Evidence
General: Recording, Thinking, Relating to Writing
General: Making Predictions with Supporting Evidence
General: Recording Thinking with Supporting Evidence (Personal and Text)
General: Identifying and Assessing Language in Texts
General: Topic and Details (1)
General: Topic and Details (2)
General: Main Ideas and Details
General: Predicting and Confirming
General: Chapter Notes
General: Summarizing
General: Relationship of Topic and Details (1)
General: Relationship of Topic and Details (2–Multiple)
General: Relationship of Ideas and Details

TOOLS TO SUPPORT THINKING ABOUT GENRE

Writing: Looking Across Writers and Titles
Writing: Author Study
Writing: Noticing Effective Writing
Writing: Foreshadowing

TOOLS TO SUPPORT THINKING ABOUT GENRE

These graphic organizers can be used to support readers' understanding of the features of different genres, both fiction and nonfiction.

Genre: Comparisons, Fiction/Nonfiction
Genre: Historical Fiction, Evidence from the Text
Genre: Historical Fiction, Noticing Details

Genre: Fiction/Nonfiction, Feature Analysis
Genre: Science Fiction, Use of Description
Genre: Fiction, Description and Details
Genre: Comparing Versions of Folk Tales

TOOLS TO SUPPORT THINKING ABOUT CHARACTERS (OFTEN APPLICABLE TO BIOGRAPHICAL SUBJECTS)

These graphic organizers can be used to support readers' analytical thinking about characters in fiction or the subjects of biography.

Characters: Noticing Character Traits
Characters: Noticing Language and What It Reveals about Characters
Characters: Inferring Characters' Feelings (Main Character or Subject)
Characters: Exploring Relationships Between Characters
Characters: Examining How Events Influence Characters
Characters: Inferring Characters' Feelings (Multiple Characters)
Characters: Examining Characters' Decisions
Characters: Relating Behavior to Character Traits
Characters: Traits and Evidence
Characters; Searching for and Noticing Information that Reveals Characters
Characters: Analyzing Characters' Traits or Feelings
Characters: External and Internal Traits
Characters: Searching for Evidence of Characters' Traits
Characters: Providing Text Evidence for Characters' Traits (1)
Characters: Providing Text Evidence for Characters' Traits (2)
Characters: Relating Character Traits and Goals (also for Biography)
Characters: Analyzing Characters (also for Biography)
Characters: Analyzing Characters—What They Say, Look, Do (also for Biography)
Characters: Noticing Information Across a Text
Characters: Comments and Evidence (also for Biography)

TOOLS TO SUPPORT UNDERSTANDING INFORMATIONAL TEXTS

These graphic organizers can be used to help readers understand and use the specific features of informational texts.

Informational Texts: Book and Print Features
Informational Texts: Analysis
Informational Texts: Noticing and Using Readers' Tools
Informational Texts: Understanding Persuasive Writing

Informational Texts: Analyzing Persuasive Writing

Informational Texts: Analyzing Elements

Informational Texts: Evaluating Accuracy

Informational Texts: Underlying Structures, Timeline

Informational Texts: Underlying Structures, Sequence

Informational Texts: Underlying Structures, Problem and Solution (1)

Informational Texts: Underlying Structures, Problem and Solution (2)

Informational Texts: Underlying Structures, Problem and Solution (3)

Informational Texts: Underlying Structures, Cause and Effect (1)

Informational Texts: Underlying Structures, Cause and Effect (2)

Informational Texts: Underlying Structures, Compare and Contrast (1)

Informational Texts: Underlying Structures, Compare and Contrast (2)

TOOLS TO SUPPORT THINKING ABOUT TEXT STRUCTURE

These graphic organizers can be used to help readers understand and use the organizational structure of texts.

Text Structure: Flashback

Text Structure: Identifying Multiple Stories

Text Structure: Identifying Two Plots

Text Structure: Identifying Multiple Plots

Text Structure: Story Map

Text Structure: Identifying Elements (with Problem/Solution)

Text Structure: Identifying Elements (with Outcomes)

Text Structure: Beginning, Middle, and End

Text Structure: Identifying Problem and Solution (Fiction)

Text Structure: Examining Plot Structure (Fiction)

Text Structure: Looking at Sequence (1)

Text Structure: Looking at Sequence (2)

Text Structure: Looking at Sequence (3)

Text Structure: Looking at Sequence (4)

Text Structure: Timeline of Events (1)

Text. Structure: Timeline of Events (2)

Text Structure: Selecting Important Events (and Reporting in Sequence)

Text Structure: Timeline and Events (also for Nonfiction)

Text Structure; Noticing Stories within Stories (Fiction)

TOOLS TO SUPPORT SYNTHESIS OF NEW CONTENT

These graphic organizers help readers identify new information while reading and integrate it into their existing knowledge.

Content: Thinking about Content Across Texts

Content: Identifying New Information and Further Searchin

Content: Identifying New Information (with Search Strategies)

Content: Synthesizing New Information

Content: Identifying What Is Known, What We Want to Learn, and What Was Learned

Content: Identifying What Is Known, What We Want to Learn (with Possible Solutions)

TOOLS TO SUPPORT THE GROWTH OF VOCABULARY

These graphic organizers help readers acquire new words and their meanings as well as develop strategies for acquiring new vocabulary words.

Vocabulary: Figuring Out What Words Mean

Vocabulary: Using History to Derive Meaning

Vocabulary: Figure of Speech

Vocabulary: Predicting and Confirming Word Meaning (Dictionary)

DESCRIPTION OF OTHER PRINT MATERIALS ON THE DV

ANALYZING READING BEHAVIORS TO EXPAND THINKING
ANALYZING READING BEHAVIORS TO SUSTAIN PROCESSING

Use these two forms to help you keep the systems of strat gic actions in mind when you are observing individuals small groups of students read and talk about texts, whe you confer with them, and when you are examining the writing about reading.

ANALYZING TEXT FACTORS

The ten factors to consider when analyzing texts are preser ed on this form, with space for notes as you examine texts

ASSESSMENT OF LETTERS IN READERS' NOTEBOOKS

You can consider five different aspects of the letters a either make open-ended notes on them or assign poin Older students can use the form for self-assessment. Yc can also modify this form to meet your district's criteria.

AUTHORS' WEBSITES

Use these sites to provide information for "writer talks" a to support author study.

CHECKLIST FOR EVALUATING LITERATURE DISCUSSION

You can use this checklist to evaluate a meeting of a book club (discussion group). Work on one aspect at a time so that they build a sense of the characteristics of a productive book club meeting.

EVALUATING THE QUALITY OF THE CLASSROOM LIBRARY

Use this form to tally the numbers of texts in each category. You can also list content areas and literacy content, as well as cultures/races represented in your collections. Special types include any reading materials you have that are in unusual formats or do not fit into a category. You will then know where to invest any funds that come your way.

GUIDED READING OBSERVATION SHEET

Use this form to record observations of students' reading and talking during guided reading lessons. Write students names above each box. You can write directly on the form or place a stick-on note in the square for recording. You can later move it to the student's file.

PLANNING FOR INTERACTIVE READ-ALOUD: TEXT SETS ACROSS THE YEAR

On these lists you will find suggested text sets for each month of the school year, grades K through 7/8. There are more text sets on the list than you probably can acquire or use during one year. This list will provide suggestions from which you can select. Many books can be used at several grade levels.

SCALE FOR ASSESSING FLUENCY

This scale provides a way of looking at the elements of fluency. You may want to use it as part of your individual assessment of students. Noticing where students need more support can help to make your teaching more precise.

SYSTEMS OF STRATEGIC ACTIONS FOR PROCESSING WRITTEN TEXTS: OBSERVATIONAL NOTES

This form lists all twelve systems of strategic actions with space on either side to make notes as you observe students.

TALKING ABOUT READING: OBSERVING FOR EVIDENCE OF THINKING—FOUR STUDENTS AND SIX STUDENTS

These forms are designed to help you be more specific in your observations of students during interactive read aloud, literature discussion, guided reading, or any other context.

Write the names of individual students at the top of each of the next four columns. You can make a check or write a quick note as you categorize students' responses.

TALKING ABOUT READING: OBSERVING FOR EVIDENCE OF THINKING—OBSERVING A GROUP

This form is designed to help you be more specific in your observations of students during interactive read aloud, literature discussion, guided reading, or any other context. Write the names of individual students at the top of each of the next four columns. You can make a check or write a quick note as you categorize students' responses.

SAMPLE OPENINGS FOR INTERACTIVE READ-ALOUD

Here you will find sample "openings" to specific texts for interactive read aloud at (1) K/Grade One; (2) Grade Two and Grade Three; (3) Grades Four, Five, and Six; and (4) Grades Six, Seven, and Eight. The first column provides some sample language for the opening. In the second column you will see an analysis of how the opening influences children's thinking.

THINKING ABOUT OUR BOOK CLUB DISCUSSION

You and your students can use this list to guide their self-evaluation of each book club discussion. A good idea is to enlarge it and place it on a chart so that they can readily refer to it. You may also want to give students a copy to glue in their Readers' Notebooks.

TODAY IN BOOK CLUB, I . . .

Students can use this list to evaluate their own participation in book club discussions.

THINKING ACROSS GENRES: WITHIN, BEYOND, AND ABOUT THE TEXT

Use this form to gather evidence of different kinds of thinking over time as your students explore different genres. You can make brief notes on individuals or on groups.

TITLES FOR TEXT TALK (K-1), (2-3), (4-5), (6-8)

Use this list of books to guide in the selection on books that are rich for discussion on interactive read aloud, pair talk, triad talk or in book clubs.

QUESTIONS TO ASK ABOUT FACTUAL TEXTS

Use this form as a guide for examining the features of information texts.

BIBLIOGRAPHY OF CHILDREN'S BOOKS

Ackerman, Karen. 1995. *The Night Crossing*. NY: Yearling.

Ada, Alma Flor. 1997. *Dear Peter Rabbit*. NY: Aladdin Books.

Adams, Richard. 1976. *Watership Down*. NY: Avon Books.

Adler, David. 1990. *A Picture Book of Martin Luther King Jr*. NY: Holiday House.

Adler, David. 2004. *Cam Jansen and the Mystery of the Circus Clown*. NY: Puffin.

Arnosky, Jim. 2002. *All About Frogs*. NY: Scholastic, Inc.

Arnosky, Jim. 1996. *All About Deer*. NY: Scholastic, Inc.

Avi. 1997. *The True Confessions of Charlotte Doyle*. NY: HarperTrophy.

Berger, Gilda & Melvin. 1999. *Why Don't Haircuts Hurt?* NY: Scholastic, Inc.

Bernard, Waber. 2001. *Ira Sleeps Over*. NY: Novel Units

Bitton-Jackson, Livia. 1999. *I Have Lived a Thousand Years: Growing Up in the Holocaust*. NY: Simon Pulse.

Borden, Louise. 2004. *The Day Eddie Met the Author*. NY: Aladdin Books.

Bradby, Marie. 2000. *Momma, Where Are You From?* NY: Orchard Books.

Brenner, Barbara. 1996. *Thinking About Ants*. NY: Mondo Publishing.

Brett, Jan. 1999. *Gingerbread Baby*. NY: Putnam Juvenile.

Bridges, Ruby. 1999. *Through My Eyes*. NY: Scholastic, Inc.

Brown, Margaret Wise. 1947. *Good Night Moon*. NY: HarperCollins.

Bruchac, Joseph. 2004. *Rachel Carson: Preserving a Sense of Wonder*. Golden, CO: Fulcrum Publishing.

Bulla, Clyde Robert. 1990. *A Lion to Guard Us*. NY: Houghton Mifflin Company.

Bunting, Eve. 1998. *So Far From the Sea*. NY: Clarion Books.

Burnett, Frances Hodgson. 1998. *The Secret Garden*. NY: HarperTrophy.

Cameron, Ann. 1989. *The Stories Julian Tells*. Des Plains, IL: Yearling.

Card, Orson Scott. 1994. *Ender's Game*. NY: Tor Science Fiction.

Carle, Eric. 1990. *A Very Quiet Cricket*. NY: Philomel Books.

Carlson, Lori. 2005. *Cool Salsa: Bilingual Poems on Growing Up Hispanic in the United States*. NY: Ballantine Books.

Carman, Patrick. 2005. *The Dark Hills Divide*. Waterville, ME: Thorndike Press.

Choi, Yangsook. 2001. *The Name Jar*. NY: Dragonfly Books.

Cleary, Beverly. 2001. *The Mouse and the Motorcycle*. NY: HarperCollins.

Clements, Andrew. 2005. *The Report Card*. NY: Aladdin Books.

Coerr, Eleanor. 1997. *Sadako*. NY: Putnam Juvenile.

Cole, Joanne. 1996. *On the Bus with Joanna Cole: A Creative Autobiography*. Katonah, NY: Richard C. Owens, Publishers.

Cooper, Susan. 1999. *The Dark Is Rising*. NY: Aladdin Books.

Creech, Sharon. 2003. *Love That Dog*. London: Bloomsburg Publishing.

Creech, Sharon. 2005. *Walk Two Moons*. NY: HarperCollins.

Crisp, Marty. 2004. *White Star: A Dog on the Titanic*. NY: Holiday House.

Crocker, Carter. 2003. *The Tale of the Swamp Rat*. NY: Philomel Books.

Davies, Nicola. 2001. *Bats Love the Night*. Cambridge, MA: Candlewick Press.

Day, Alexandra. 1991. *Good Dog, Carl*. NY: Simon & Schuster.

de Paola, Tomie. 1990. *Pancakes for Breakfast*. NY: Voyager Books.

DeLuise, Dom. 1994. *Charlie the Caterpillar*. NY: Simon & Schuster.

DiCamillo, Kate. 2001. *Because of Winn Dixie*. Cambridge, MA: Candlewick Press.

Felton, Harold. 1976. *Deborah Sampson: Soldier of the Revolution*. NY: Dodd, Mead and Company.

Filipvoic, Zlata. 1995. *Zlata's Diary*. NY: Viking, Penguin.

Fleischman, Paul. 1991. *The Half-a-Moon Inn*. NY: HarperTrophy.

Fleischman, Paul. 1999. *Seedfolks*. NY: HarperTrophy.

Fletcher, Ralph. 1998. *Spider Boy*. NY: Yearling.

Fletcher, Ralph. 2000. *Flying Solo*. NY: Yearling .

Fontes, Ron. 2005. *Rachel Carson*. NY: Scholastic, Inc.

Frank, Anne. 1953. *Anne Frank: The Diary of a Young Girl*. NY: Bantam, Doubleday, Dell.

Freedman, Russell. 1994. *The Wright Brothers*. NY: Holiday House.

Gaiman, Neil. 2005. *The Wolves in the Walls*. NY: HarperCollins.

Galdone, Paul. 1985. *The Little Red Hen*. NY: Clarion Books.

Gibbons, Gail. 2002. *Tell Me, Tree: All About Trees for Kids*. NY: Little Brown and Company.

Giblin, James Cross. 1994. *Thomas Jefferson: A Picture Book Biography*. NY: Scholastic, Inc.

Giles, Jenny. 1996. *Sally and the Sparrows*. New Haven, CT: Nelson Price Milburn.

Gleman, Evelyn. 1999. *White Socks Only*. Morton Grove. IL: Albert Whitman & Co.

Gray, Libba Moore. 2000. *Dear Willie Rudd*. NY: Aladdin Paperbacks.

Grimes, Nikki. 2002. *Talking About Bessie*. NY: Orchard Books.

Haddix, Margaret Peterson. 2000. *Among the Hidden*. NY: Aladdin Books.

Hall, Nancy Abraham. 1999. *Los Pollitos Dicen: The Baby Chicks Sing*. NY Little Brown & Company

Hamanaka, Sheila. 1990. *The Journey: Japanese Americans, Racism, and Renewal*. NY: Orchard Books.

Hesse, Karen. 1994. *Lester's Dog*. NY: Random House.

Hesse, Karen. 1999. *Out of the Dust*. NY: Scholastic, Inc.

Hickman, Janet. 1996. *Jericho*. NY: Morrow/Avon.

Holman, Felice. 1986. *Slake's Limbo*. NY: Aladdin Books.

Hopkinson, Deborah. 2002. *Under the Quilt of the Night*. NY: Atheneum/Anne Schwartz Books.

Hotze, Sollace. 1988. *A Circle Unbroken*. NY: Clarion Books.

Howe, James. 2004. *Bunnicula*. NY: Simon & Schuster.

Howe, James. 2006. *Pinky and Rex.*. NY: Simon & Schuster.

Hughes, Monica. 2004. *The Promise*. Allston, MA: Fitzhenry & Whiteside.

Hurwitz, Johanna. 1999. *Anne Frank: Life in Hiding*. NY: HarperTrophy.

Jackson, Donna M. 1996. *Bone Detectives*. NY: Little Brown and Compan

Johnston, Tony. 2004. *The Harmonia*. Watertown, MA: Charlesbridge Publishing

Jordan, Helene J. 1992. *How Seeds Grow*. NY: HarperTrophy.

Knudson, Rozanne. 1985. *Babe Didrikson: Athlete of the Century*. NY: Viking Kestrel.

Koja, Kathe. 2004. *Buddha Boy*. NY: Penguin Group.

Konigsburg, E.L. 1998. *A View From Saturday*. NY: Aladdin Books.

Krauss, Ruth. 2002. *The Carrot Seed*. NY: HarperCollins.

Kurtz, Jane. 2005. *In the Small, Small Deep Night*. NY: HarperCollins.

Le Guin, Ursula K. 1984. *A Wizard of Earthsea*. NY: Spectra.

Lee, Harper. 1960. *To Kill a Mockingbird*. NY: Warner Books.

Leveled Readers. 2004. *Butterflies*. Boston: Houghton Mifflin Company.

Leveled Readers. 2004. *Clothes*. Boston: Houghton Mifflin Company.

Leveled Readers. 2004. *Getting Dressed*. Boston: Houghton Mifflin Company.

Leveled Readers. 2004. *The Diary of Anne Frank*. Boston: Houghton Mifflin Company.

Leveled Readers. 2004. *The Game*. Boston: Houghton Mifflin Company.

Leveled Readers. 2004 *Lands of the Rain Forest*. Boston: Houghton Mifflin Company.

Leveled Readers. 2004 *Orson Welles and the War of the World*. Boston: Houghton Mifflin Company.

Leveled Readers. 2004. *Hannah Brown, Union Army Spy*. Boston: Houghton Mifflin Company.

Leveled Readers. 2004. *Meet Yo-Yo Ma*. Boston: Houghton Mifflin Company.

Leveled Readers. 2004. *Nikki Giovanni*. Boston: Houghton Mifflin Company.

Leveled Readers. 2004. *Pat Mora: Two Languages One Poet*. Boston: Houghton Mifflin Company.

Leveled Readers. 2004. *Peaches the Pig*. Boston: Houghton Mifflin Company.

Leveled Readers. 2005. *My Cat*. NY: Houghton Mifflin Company.

Levine, Gail Carson. 1998. *Ella Enchanted*. NY: HarperTrophy.

Lionni, Leo. 1974. *Alexander and the Wind-up Mouse*. NY: Dragonfly Books.

Lorbiecki, Mary Beth. 1998. *Sister Anne's Hands*. NY: Puffins Books.

Lowry, Lois. 2005. *Number the Stars*. NY: Bantam Doubleday Dell Publishing Group.

Marshall, Edward. 2002. *Fox and his Friends*. NY: Scholastic, Inc.

Martin Jr., Bill. 1996. *Brown Bear, Brown Bear, What do you see?* NY: Henry Holt & Co.

Master, Edgar Lee. 1992. *Spoon River Anthology*. NY: Signet Classics.

Nguyen, Kien. 2002. *The Tapestries*. NY: Little Brown and Company.

Nye, Naomi. 1997. *Sitti's Secret*. NY: Simon & Schuster

O'Brien, Robert. 1986. *Mrs. Frisby and the Rats of NIMH*. NY: Aladdin Books.

Older, Jules. 2002. *Ice Cream: Great Moments in Ice Cream History*. Cambridge, MA: Charlesbridge Publishing.

Oxenbury, Helen. 1997. *We're Going on a Bear Hunt*. NY: Little Simon.

Park, Linda Sue. 2003. *A Single Shard*. NY: Dell Yearling.

Patz, Nancy 2003. *Who Was the Woman Who Wore the Hat?*. NY: Dutton Juvenile.

Paul, Christopher . 2002. *Bud, Not Buddy*. NY: Yearling.

Paulson, Gary. 1993. *The River*. NY: Yearling.

Paulson, Gary. 1998. *Brian's Winter*. NY: Laurel-Leaf.

Paulson, Gary. 1999. *Hatchet*. NY: Random House.

Paulson, Gary. 2001. *Brian's Return*. NY: Laurel-Leaf.

Paulson, Gary. 2003. *Brian's Hunt*. NY: Random House.

Peck, Richard 2002. *A Year Down Yonder*. Puffin Books.

Peters, Katherine. 1995. *Willy the Helper*. Boston: Houghton Mifflin Company.

PM Animal Facts. 1994. *Owls*. Barrington, Rigby PM.

PM Story. 1994. *Baby Bear's Present*. Crystal Lake, IL: Rigby.

Polacco, Patricia. 1992. *Chicken Sunday*. NY: Putnam Juvenile.

Polacco, Patricia. 1998. *My Rotten Redheaded Older Brother*. NY: Simon & Schuster.

Polacco, Patricia. 1998. *Thank You, Mr. Falker*. NY: Philomel Books.

Polacco, Patricia. 2001. *Mr. Lincoln's Way*. NY: Penguin Group.

Randell, Beverly. 1969. *Baby Bear's Present*. Crystal Lake: Rigby.

Randell, Beverly. 1969. *Father Bear's Surprise*. Crystal Lake, IL: Rigby.

Randell, Beverly. 1994. *The Lazy Pig*. Crystal Lake, IL: Rigby.

Randell, Beverly. 1996. *Baby Bear Goes Fishing*. Crystal Lake, IL: Rigby.

Raven, Margot Theis. 2004. *Circle Unbroken*. NY: Farrar, Straus, & Giroux.

Recorvitis, Helen. 2003. *My Name is Yoon*. NY: Farrar, Straus, & Giroux

Riley, Kana. 1995. *Peaches the Pig*. Lexington, MA: D.C. Heath.

Riley, Kana. 1997. *Rosie's Pool*. NY: Houghton Mifflin Company.

Ringgold, Faith. 1999. *If a Bus Could Talk*. NY: Simon & Schuster Children Publishing.

Romanek, Trudee. 2002. *ZZZ: The Most Interesting Book You'll Ever Read About Sleep*. Tonawanda, NY: Kids Can Press.

Ross, Pat. 1997. *Meet M & M*. NY: Penguin Books.

Rotner, Shelley & Cheo Garcia. 1999. *Pick a Pet*. NY: Scholastic, Inc.

Rylant, Cynthia. 1988. *Every Living Thing*. NY: Aladdin Books.

Rylant, Cynthia. 1997. *Poppleton*. NY: Blue Sky Press.

Rylant, Cynthia. 2006. *Henry and Mudge the First Book*. NY: Aladdin Books.

Selden, Bernice. 1989. *The Story of Walt Disney, Maker of Magical Worlds*. NY: Bantam Doubleday Dell Books.

Sendak, Maurice. 1988. *Where the Wild Things Are*. NY: HarperCollins.

Shreve, Anita. 1997. *Resistance*. Boston: Back Bay Books.

Siebert, Diane. 2000. *Cave*. NY: HarperCollins.

Silverstein, Shel. 1964. *The Giving Tree*. NY: HarperCollins.

Smith, Betty. 1998. *A Tree Grows in Brooklyn*. NY: Perennial Classics.

Snicket, Lemony. 2004. *A Series of Unfortunate Events: The Reptile Room*. NY: HarperCollins.

Spinelli, Jerry. 2003. *Milkweed*. NY: Alfred A. Knopf.

Spinelli, Jerry. 2005. *Maniac Magee*. NY: Little Brown and Company.

Spufford, Francis. 2002. *The Child That Books Built*. NY: Metropolitan Books.

Stevens, Janet. 1995. *Tops and Bottoms*. NY: Harcourt.

Tan, Amy. 1992. *The Kitchen God's Wife*. NY: Ivy Books.

Tavares, Matt. 2005. *Mudball*. Cambridge, MA: Candlewick Press.

Tolkien, J.R.R. 1951. *The Lord of the Rings*. Boston: Houghton Mifflin Company.

Tunnell, Michael. 1997. *Mailing May*. NY: HarperTrophy.

Uchida, Yoshiko. 1978. *Journey Home*. NY: Simon & Schuster.

Udry, Janice May. 1987. *A Tree is Nice*. NY: HarperTrophy.

Uhlberg, Myron 2005. *Dad, Jackie, and Me*. Atlanta: Peachtree.

Wallace, Bill. 2002. *Coyote Autumn*. NY: Aladdin Books.

White, E.B. 1952. *Charlotte's Web*. NY: HarperCollins.

Williams, Vera B. 1984. *A Chair for My Mother*. NY: HarperTrophy.

Winter, Jonah 2005. *Roberto Clemente*. NY: Atheneum/Anne Schwartz Books.

Woodson, Jacqueline. 2001. *The Other Side*. NY: Putnam Juvenile.

Yep, Lawrence. 1992. *The Rainbow People*. NY: HarperTrophy.

Yin. 2003. *Coolies*. NY: Puffin Books.

Yolan, Jane. 2002. *Mary Celeste*. NY: Simon & Schuster

Yolen, Jane. 1990. *The Devils Arithmetic*. NY: Puffin Books.

Yolen, Jane. 1992. *A Letter from Phoenix Farm*. Katonah, NY: Richard C. Owen Publishers.

Yolen, Jane. 2005. *The Devil's Arithmetic*. NY: Penguin Books.

Zemach, Harve. 1964. *Nail Soup*. Chicago: Follett Pub Co.

PROFESSIONAL REFERENCES

Allen, J. 1999. *Words, Words, Words: Teaching Vocabulary in Grades 4-12*. York, ME: Stenhouse Publishers.

Allington, R.L. 1983. "The Reading Instruction Provided Readers of Differing Reading Ability," *Elementary School Journal, 83*: 548-559.

Alvermann, D.E. 2000. "Classroom Talk About Texts: Is It Dear, Cheap, or a Bargain at Any Price?" In B. M. Taylor, M. G. Graves, and P. Van Den Broek (Eds.). 2000. *Reading for Meaning: Fostering Comprehension in the Middle Grades*. New York: Teachers College Press and Newark, DE: International Reading Association. pp. 136-151.

Angelillo, J. 2003. *Writing about Reading: From Book Talk to Literary Essays, Grades 3-8*. Portsmouth, NH: Heinemann.

Armbruster, B.B., and J. O. Armstrong. 1993. "Locating Information in Text: A Focus on Children in the Elementary "Grades." *Contemporary Educational Psychology, 18*(2), 139-161.

Armbruster, B.B., and T. H. Anderson. 1984. "Structures of Explanations in History Textbooks, or so What if Governor Stanford Missed the Spike and Hit the Rail?" *Journal of Curriculum Studies, 16* (2), 181-194.

Baumann, J.F., E. J. Kame'enui, and G. Ash. 2003. Research on Vocabulary Instruction: Voltaire Redux. In J. Flood, D. Lapp, J. Jensen, and J.R. Squire, Eds. *Handbook of Research on Teaching the English Language Arts* (2nd edition): 752-787. New York: Macmillan.

Beck, I.L, and M.G. McKeown. 2001. "Text Talk: Capturing the Benefits of Read-aloud Experiences for Young Children." *The Reading Teacher* (55): 10-20.

Beck, I.L. M. G. McKeown, and L. Kucan, L. 2002. *Bringing Words to Life: Robust Vocabulary Instruction*. New York: The Guildford Press.

Biemiller, A. 2004. Teaching Vocabulary Instruction Needed. In J. Baumann & E. Kame'enui, Eds., *Vocabulary Instruction: Research to Practice*. New York: The Guilford Press.

Biemiller, A. 1999. *Language and Reading Success*. Cambridge, MA: Brookline Books.

Bishop, R.S. 1992. "Multicultural Literature for Children: Making Informed Choices." In V.J. Harris (Ed.), *Teaching Multicultural Literature in Grades K-8* (pp. 37-53). Norwood, MA: Christopher-Gordon Publishers.

Block, C.C., L.B. Gambrell, and M. Pressley (Eds.). 2002. *Improving Comprehension Instruction: Rethinking Research;, Theory, and Classroom Practice*. Jossey-Bass and Newark, DE: International Reading Association.

Bomer, R. 1994. *Time for Meaning: Crafting Literate Lives in Middle & High School*. Portsmouth, NH: Heinemann.

Bomer, R., and K. Bomer. 2001. *Reading and Writing for Social Action*. Portsmouth, NH: Heinemann.

Carver, Ronald. 2000. *The Cause of High and Low Reading Achievement*. Mahwah, NJ: Laurence Erlbaum.

Cazden, C. 1988. *Classroom Discourse: The Language of Teaching and Learning*. Portsmouth, NH: Heinemann.

Chall, J.S., V.A. Jacobs, and L.E. Baldwin. 1990. *The Reading Crisis: Why Poor Children Fall Behind*. Cambridge, MA: Harvard University Press.

Clay, M. M. 2002. *An Observation Survey Of Early Literacy Achievement* (2nd edition), Portsmouth, NH: Heinemann.

Clay, M.M. 1975. *What Did I Write?* Auckland, NZ: Heinemann Educational.

Clay, M.M. 1991. *Becoming Literate: The Construction of Inner Control*. Portsmouth, NH: Heinemann.

Clay, M.M. 2001. *Change Over Time in Literacy Learning*. Auckland, New Zealand: Heinemann Educational.

Clay, M.M. 2004. "Talking, Reading, Writing." *Journal of Reading Recovery*, (3): 1-16.

Corliss, J.C. 1998. *Crossing Borders with Literature of Diversity*. Norwood, MA: Christopher-Gordon.

Dole, J.A. 2000. "Explicit and Implicit Instruction in Comprehension." In B. M. Taylor, M. G. Graves, and P. Van Den Broek (Eds.). 2000. *Reading for Meaning: Fostering Comprehension in the Middle Grades*. New York: Teachers College Press and Newark, DE: International Reading Association. pp. 52-69.

Duke, N. K. 2003. "Informational Text? The Research Says, "Yes!" In L Hoyt, M. Mooney, and B, Parkes (Eds.). 2003. *Exploring Informational Texts: From Theory to Practice*. Portsmouth, NH Heinemann. pp. 2-25.

Duke, N.K. 1999. *The Scarcity of Informational Texts in First Grade* Ann Arbor: Center for the Improvement of Early Reading Achievement.

Ebbing, Linda. January 3, 2005. Teenagers Are Intense Users of Instant Messaging. *Journalnow.com: Your guide to life in Northwes North Carolina, Online partner of the Winston-Salem Journal*. Cox News Service. P. 1.

Eeds, M., & Peterson, R. 1991. Teacher as curator: learning to ta about literature. *The Reading Teacher, 45*, 118-126.

Elley, W.B. 1991. "Acquiring Literacy in a Second Language: The Effe of Book-based Programs." *Language Learning, 41*(3), 375-411.

Fountas, I. C., and G.S. Pinnell. 2001. *Guiding Readers and Writer Teaching Comprehension, Genre, and Content Literac* Portsmouth, NH: Heinemann.

Fountas, I.C., and G.S. Pinnell. (2008). *A Benchmark System f Assessing Children's Reading*. Portsmouth, NH: Heinemann.

Fountas, I.C., and G.S. Pinnell. 1996. *Guided Reading: Good Fi Teaching for All Children*. Portsmouth, NH: Heinemann.

Fountas, I.C., and G.S. Pinnell. 1999. *Matching Books to Reade Using Leveled Books in Guided Reading, K-3*. Portsmouth, N Heinemann.

untas, I.C., and G.S. Pinnell. 2006. *Leveled Book List, K-8: 2006-2008 Edition*. Portsmouth, NH: Heinemann. Also available at www.FountasandPinnellLeveledBooks.com.

untas, I.C., and G.S. Pinnell. 2006. *Leveled Books, K-8: Matching Texts to Readers for Effective Teaching*. Portsmouth, NH: Heinemann.

ebody, P., and R.C. Anderson. 1983. "Effects of Vocabulary Difficulty, Text Cohesion, and Schema Availability on Reading Comprehension." *Reading Research Quarterly, 18,* 277-294.

eman, E. and B. Lehman. 2001. *Global Perspective in Children's Literature.*

eman, E.B., and Diane Goetz Person. 1998. *Connecting Informational Children's Books with Content Area learning*. Boston: Allyn and Bacon.

ldenberg, C. 1992. Instructional conversations: Promoting comprehension through discussion. *The Reading Teacher, 46,* 4, 316-326.

od, R. H., D. C. Simmons, and E. J. Kame'enui. 2001. "The Importance and Decision-Making Utility of a Continuum of Fluency-Based Indicators of Foundational Reading Skills for Third-Grade High-Stakes Outcomes." *Scientific Studies of Reading* 5: 257–88.

aves, M.F. 1987. The Roles of Instruction in Fostering Vocabulary Development. M. McKeown and M. Curtis, Eds. *The Nature of Vocabulary Acquisition*: 165-184. Mahway., NJ: Lawrence Erlbaum Associates.

aves, M.F. 2000. "A Vocabulary Program to Complement and Bolster a Middle-Grade Comprehension Program." In B. M. Taylor, M. G. Graves, and P. Van Den Broek (Eds.). 2000. *Reading for Meaning: Fostering Comprehension in the Middle Grades*. New York: Teachers College Press and Newark, DE: International Reading Association. pp. 116-135.

eenwood, S. 2004. *Words Count: Effective Vocabulary Instruction in Action*. Portsmouth, NH: Heinemann.

rste, J., K.G. Short, and C. Burke. 1995. *Creating Classrooms for Authors*. Portsmouth, NH: Heinemann.

sbrouk, J. E., and G. Tindal. 1992. "Curriculum-Based Oral Reading Fluency Norms for Students in Grades 2 Through 5." *Teaching Exceptional Children* 24 (3): 41–44.

imlich, J.E., and S.D. Pittelman. 1986. *Semantic Mapping: Classroom Applications*. Newark, DE: International Reading Association.

nderson, E. 1990. *Teaching Spelling, 2nd Ed.* Boston: Houghton Mifflin.

nry, Marcia K. 2003. *Unlocking Literacy: Effective Decoding and Spelling Instruction*. Baltimore, MD: Paul H. Brookes Publishing Co.

ldaway, D. 1979. *The Foundations of Literacy*. Sydney: Ashton Scholastic, also Portsmouth, NH: Heinemann.

yt, Linda, M. Mooney, and B. Parkes (Eds.). 2003. *Exploring Informational Texts: From Theory to Practice*. Portsmouth, NH: Heinemann.

dson, R. F., H. B. Lane, and P. C. Pullen. 2005. "Reading Fluency Assessment and Instruction: What, Why, and How?" *The Reading Teacher* 58 (8): 702–14.

nston, P. 1997. *Knowing Literacy: Constructive Literacy Assessment*. York, ME: Stenhouse Publishers.

Krosto, J.V., and Bamford, R.A. (2004). *Nonfiction in Focus: A Comprehensive Framework for Helping Students Become Independent Readers and Writers of Nonfiction, K-6*. New York: Scholastic.

Langer, J.A. (1984). "Examining Background Knowledge and Text Comprehension." *Reading Research Quarterly, 19,* 468-481.

Lindfors, J. W. 1999. *Children's Inquiry*. New York: Teachers' College Press.

Lubliner, S. 2005. *Getting into Words: Vocabulary Instruction that Strengthens Comprehension*. Baltimore: Paul H. Brookes.

McCarrier, A., G.S. Pinnell, and I.C. Fountas. 2000. *Interactive Writing: How Language and Literacy Come Together*. Portsmouth, NH: Heinemann.

McKenna, M.C., and R.D. Robinson. 1997. *Teaching through Text: A Content Literacy Approach to Content Area Reading*. 2nd Edition. New York: Longman.

Moll, Luis. 1992. "Funds of Knowledge for Teaching: Using a Qualitative Approach to Connect Homes and Classrooms". *Theory into Practice, 31* (2), 132–4.

Mooney, M. 2003. "The *Why* of Some of the Features of Informational Texts. In L. Hoyt, M. Mooney, and B, Parkes (Eds.). 2003. *Exploring Informational Texts: From Theory to Practice*. Portsmouth, NH: Heinemann. pp. 37-51.

Nagy, W.E. 1988. *Teaching Vocabulary to Improve Reading Comprehension*. Urbana, IL, and Newark, DE: National Council of Teachers of English and the International Reading Association (ERIC clearinghouse on Reading and Communication Skills).

Nagy, W.E. and P. Herman. 1987. Breadth and Depth of Vocabulary Knowledge: Implications for Acquisition and Instruction. In M. McKeown and M. Curtis. Eds. *The Nature of Vocabulary Acquisition*. Mahwah, NJ: Lawrence Erlbaum Associates. pp. 19-36.

Nagy, W.E., and J. Scott. 2000. Vocabulary. In M.L. Kamil, P.B. Mosenthal, P.D. Pearson, and R. Barr, Eds. *Handbook of Reading Research* (Vol. III): 269-284. Mahwah, NJ: Lawrence Erlbaum Associates.

National Institute of Child Health and Human Development. 2000. *Report of the National Reading Panel: teaching children to Read: An Evidence-Based Assessment of the Scientific Research Literature on Reading and Its Implications for Reading Instruction: Reports of the Subgroups*. Washington, D.C.: U.S. Department of health and Human Services, NIH Pub. No 00-4754.

Owocki, Gretchen. 2003. *Comprehension: Strategic Instruction for K-3 Students*. Portsmouth, NH: Heinemann.

Palinscar, A.S., and A.L. Brown. 1984. "Reciprocal Teaching of Comprehension-Fostering and Monitoring Activities." *Cognition and Instruction* (1): 117-175.

Pilgreen, J. L. 2000. *The SSR Handbook: How to Organize and Manage a Sustained Silent Reading Program*. Portsmouth, NH: Boynton/Cook Publishers.

Pinnell, G.S., and I.C. Fountas. 1999. *Matching Books to Readers: Using Leveled Books in Guided Reading, K-3*. Portsmouth, NH: Heinemann.

Pinnell, G.S., and I.C. Fountas. 1998. *Word Matters: Teaching Phonics and Spelling in the Reading/Writing Classroom*. Portsmouth, NH: Heinemann.

Pinnell, G.S., and I.C. Fountas. 1998. *Word Matters: Teaching Phonics and Spelling in the Reading/Writing Classroom.* Portsmouth, NH: Heinemann.

Pinnell, G.S., and I.C. Fountas. 2002. *Leveled Books for Readers, Grades 3-6.* Portsmouth, NH: Heinemann.

Pinnell, G.S., and I.C. Fountas. (in press). *A Continuum of Literacy Learning, K–8: A Guide for Teaching.* Portsmouth, NH: Heinemann.

Pinnell, G.S., J. J. Pikulski, K. K. Wixson, J. R. Campbell, P. B. Gough, and A.S. Beatty. 1995. *Listening To Children Read Aloud. Data From NAEP's Integrated Reading Performance Record (IRPR) At Grade 4.* Report No. 23-FR-04. Prepared by Educational Testing Service. Washington, DC: Office of Educational Research and Improvement, U.S. Department of Education.

Pressley, M. 2000. "Comprehension Instruction in Elementary School: A Quarter-Century of Research Progress." In B. M. Taylor, M. G. Graves, and P. Van Den Broek (Eds.). 2000. *Reading for Meaning: Fostering Comprehension in the Middle Grades.* New York: Teachers College Press and Newark, DE: International Reading Association. pp. 32-51.

Put Reading First: the Research Building Blocks for Teaching Children to Read: Kindergarten through Grade I. Armbruster, B., Lehr, F, and Osborn, 2001. Center for the Improvement of Early reading Achievement.

Raphael, T. 1986. "Teaching Question Answer Relationships, Revisited." *The Reading Teacher* (39) 6, 516–522.

Raphael, T. E. 2000. "Balancing Literature and Instruction: Lessons from the Book Club Project." In B. M. Taylor, M. G. Graves, and P. Van Den Broek (Eds.). 2000. *Reading for Meaning: Fostering Comprehension in the Middle Grades.* New York: Teachers College Press and Newark, DE: International Reading Association. pp. 70-94.

Rasinski, T. 2005. *The Fluent Reader: Oral Reading Strategies for Building Word Recognition, Fluency, and Comprehension.* NY: Scholastic.

Rief, Linda. 1991. *Seeking Diversity: Language Arts with Adolescents.* Portsmouth, NH: Heinemann.

Rosenblatt, L. M. 1938. *Literature as Exploration.* New York: Noble and Noble Publishers.

Rosenblatt, L. M. 1978. *The Reader the Text the Poem.* Southern Illinois University Press.

. Ruddell, M.R. 1994. Vocabulary Knowledge and Comprehension: A Comprehension-Process view of Complex Literacy Relationships. In R. Ruddell, M.R. Ruddell, and H. Singer, Eds. *Theoretical Models and Processes of Reading* (4th ed.): 414-437. Newark, DE: International Reading Association.

Sadler, C.R. 2001. *Comprehension Strategies for Middle Grade Learners: A Handbook for Content Area Teachers.* Newark, DE: International Reading Association.

School Board of Alachua County. 1997. *Curriculum-Based Assessment in Alachua County, Florida: Vital Signs of Student Progress.* Gainesville, FL.

Sipe, Lawrence. (1998). Learning the Language of Picture Books. *Journal of Children's Literature, 24,* 2, 66-75.

Sipe, Lawrence. (1998). Learning the Language of Picture Books. *Journal of Children's Literature, 24,* 2, 66-75.

Snow, C.E., M.S. Burns, and P. Griffin, Eds. 1998. *Preventing Read Difficulties in Young Children.* Washington, D.C.: Natio Academy Press.

Spufford, F. 2002. *The Child that Books Built: A Life in Reading.* Picador, Henry Holt..

Stahl, S.A., and M.M. Fairbanks, M.M. 1986. The Effects of Vocabu Instruction: A Model-based Meta-analysis. *Review of Educatio Research, 56,* 72-110.

Stanovich, K.E. 1986. Matthew Effects in Reading: Some Consequen of Individual Differences in the Acquisition of Literacy. *Read Research Quarterly, 21,* 360-406.

Stanovich, K.E., and A.E. Cunningham. 1992. "Studying Consequences of Literacy Within a Literate Society: The Cogni Correlates of Print Exposure." *Memory and Cognition, 20,* 51-

Sweet, A.P., and C. Snow. "Reconceptualizing Reading Comprehensio In Block, C.C., L.B. Gambrell, and M. Pressley (Eds.). 20 *Improving Comprehension Instruction: Rethinking Resear Theory, and Classroom Practice.* Jossey-Bass and Newark, International Reading Association. pp. 17-53.

Taylor, B.M., M. G. Graves, and P. Van Den Broek (Eds.). 2000. *Read for Meaning: Fostering Comprehension in the Middle Grad* New York: Teachers College Press and Newark, DE: Internatio Reading Association.

Templeton, S., and D.R. Bear. 1992. *Development of Orthograp Knowledge and the Foundation of Literacy: A Memor Festschrift for Edmund H. Henderson.* Hillsdale, NJ: Lawre Erlbaum.

Tierney, R.J., and D.P. Pearson. 1993. Learning to Learn from Tex Framework for Improving Classroom Practice. In R.B. Ruddell, M Ruddell, and H. Singer, H., Eds. *Theoretical Models and Processe Reading,* Fourth Edition: 496-513.

Tovani, C. 2000. *I Read It, but I Don't Get It: Comprehens Strategies for Adolescent Readers.* Portland, ME: Stenhouse.

Trilling, Lionel, and Harold Bloom., (eds.) 1973. *Prose and Poe New York, Oxford, and Toronto: Oxford University Press.

Van Den Broek, P., and K. E. Kremer. 2000. "The Mind in Action: W It Means to Comprehend During Reading." In B. M. Taylor, M. Graves, and P. Van Den Broek (Eds.). 2000. *Reading for Meani Fostering Comprehension in the Middle Grades.* New Y Teachers College Press and Newark, DE: International Read Association. pp. 1-31.

Vygotsky, L.S. 1978. *Mind in Society: The Development of Hig Psychological Processes.* Cambridge, MA: Harvard University Pre

Vygotsky, LS. 1986. *Thought and Language.* Cambridge, MA: N Press.

Wilhelm, J.D. 2001. *Improving Comprehension with Think-Alo Strategies: Modeling What Good Readers Do.* New York: Schola Professional Books.

Zutell, J. 1996. "The Directed Spelling Thinking Activity (DS Providing an Effective Balance in Word Study Instruction." *Reading Teacher, 50:* 98-108.

Zutell, J. 1999. "Sorting It Out through Word Sorts." *Voices on W Matters: Learning about Phonics and Spelling in the Liter Classroom.* Portsmouth, NH: Heinemann.